Comparative Politics of Southeast Asia

Aurel Croissant • Philip Lorenz

Comparative Politics of Southeast Asia

An Introduction to Governments and Political Regimes

 Springer

Aurel Croissant
Institute of Political Science
Heidelberg University
Heidelberg, Germany

Philip Lorenz
Institute of Political Science
Heidelberg University
Heidelberg, Germany

ISBN 978-3-319-68181-8   ISBN 978-3-319-68182-5   (eBook)
https://doi.org/10.1007/978-3-319-68182-5

Library of Congress Control Number: 2017955823

This Springer imprint is published by Springer Nature
The registered company is Springer International Publishing AG
The registered company address is: Gewerbestrasse 11, 6330 Cham, Switzerland

To our students.

Acknowledgments

During our courses on different aspects of Southeast Asian politics, we often wished we could recommend a single chapter to our students to prepare for their presentations and papers on a given country. The fact that such chapters did not exist is the ultimate reason for this textbook. It is a considerably revised and updated version of a German book published by Aurel Croissant in 2015, and we hope it will now be useful to political scientists, journalists, area experts, and others everywhere.

Preparing this manuscript for publication we benefitted from the help of Stephan Giersdorf, who contributed to the original draft of the Malaysia chapter; Thomas Wencker, who drew the maps; Rebecca Abu Sharkh, who served as the native English language editor; and Susanne Schneider and Janika Lohse, who helped prepare the bibliography. We are grateful for their help.

While we did our best to avoid any formal and factual errors and inaccuracies, some will inevitably remain in the text. We encourage the reader, to help us find and correct them.

Since this book is ultimately the result of teaching Southeast Asian politics, a part of our jobs we both thoroughly enjoy, we dedicate this book to our students.

Contents

List of Abbreviations

ABS	Asian Barometer Survey
AFP	Armed Forces of the Philippines
AFPFL	Anti-Fascist People's Freedom League (Myanmar)
APM	Parliamentary Majority Alliance (Timor-Leste)
APODETI	Timorese Popular Democratic Association
ARMM	Autonomous Region of Muslim Mindanao (Philippines)
ASEAN	Association of Southeast Asian Nations
BERSIH	Commission for Free and Fair Elections (Malaysia)
BI	Bank Indonesia
BIA	Brunei Investment Agency
BJT	Proud Thai Party (Thailand)
BLDP	Buddhist Liberal Democratic Party
BMA	Bangkok Metropolitan Area
BN	National Front (Malaysia)
BNDP	Brunei National Democratic Party
BPK	Audit Board (Indonesia)
BS	Socialist Front (Malaysia)
BSPP	Burmese Socialist Program Party
BTI	Bertelsmann Transformation Index
CDA	Constitutional Draft Assembly (Thailand)
CDC	Community Development Councils (Singapore)
CDF	Chief of Defence Force (Singapore)
CEC	Chief Executive Committee
CGDK	Coalition Government of Democratic Kampuchea
CNE	National Election Commission (Timor-Leste)
CNRP	Cambodian National Rescue Party
CNRT	National Resistance Council (Timor-Leste)
COMECON	Council for Mutual Economic Assistance
COMELEC	Election Commission (Philippines)
CPA	Council for Presidential Advisors (Singapore)
CPF	Central Provident Fund (Singapore)
CPM	Communist Party of Malaya

CPP	Cambodian People's Party
	Communist Party of the Philippines
	Chartthaipartana Party (Thailand)
CPSU	Communist Party of the Soviet Union
CPV	Communist Party of Vietnam
CSO	Civil Society Organizations
CTP	Chart Thai Party
DAP	Democratic Action Party (Malaysia)
DDR	Disarmament, Demobilization, and Reintegration
DDSI	Directorate of Defence Services Intelligence (Myanmar)
DIM	Problem Inventory List (Indonesia)
DP	Democrat Party (Thailand)
DPD	Regional Representative Council
DPR	People's Representative Council
DPRD	Regional People's Representative Council
DRV	Democratic Republic of Vietnam
ECCC	Extraordinary Chambers in the Courts of Cambodia
EDSA	Epifanio de los Santos Avenue (main Metro Manila Highway)
ENEP	Effective Number of Electoral Parties
EPU	Economic Planning Unit (Malaysia)
F-FDTL	Falintil-Defense Forces of Timor-Leste
FALINTIL	Liberation Armed Forces of Timor-Leste
FDI	Foreign Direct Investment
FNL	National Liberation Front (Vietnam)
FRETILIN	Revolutionary Front for an Independent Timor-Leste
FUNCINPEC	United Front for an Independent, Neutral, Peaceful and Cooperative Cambodia
GAD	General Administrative Department (Myanmar)
GAM	Movement Free Aceh (Indonesia)
GDP	Gross Domestic Product
GDSI	General Department of Strategic Intelligence (Vietnam)
GLC	Government-linked Companies (Singapore)
GRC	Group Representation Constituencies (Singapore)
GRU	Gurkha Reserve Unit (Brunei)
HCMC	Ho Chi Minh City
HDB	Housing and Development Board (Singapore)
HDI	Human Development Index
HRP	Human Rights Party (Cambodia)
ICP	Indochina Communist Party
IMF	International Monetary Fund
INGO	International Non-Governmental Organization
INTERFET	International Force in East Timor
ISA	Internal Security Act
ISF	International Stabilization Force
ISP	Internet Service Provider

JBC	Judicial and Bar Council (Philippines)
KBL	New Society Movement (Philippines)
KKN	Corruption, Collusion and Nepotism (Indonesia)
KNP	Coalition for National Unity (Philippines)
KomnasHAM	National Human Rights Commission (Indonesia)
KOTA	Association of Timorese Heroes
KPI	Indonesian Broadcasting Commission
KPK	Corruption Eradication Commission (Indonesia)
KPNLF	Khmer People National Liberation Front (Cambodia)
KPU	General Election Commission (Indonesia)
KRIS	Constitution or the Federal Republic of Indonesia
KY	Judicial Commission (Indonesia)
LDP	Liberal Democratic Party (Malaysia)
	Liberal Democratic Party (Philippines)
LEDAC	Legislative-Executive Development Council (Philippines)
LGBT	Lesbian-Gay-Bisexual-Transgender
LGC	Local Government Code (Philippines)
LGU	Local Government Units (Philippines)
LP	Liberal Party (Cambodia)
	Liberal Party (Philippines)
LPAF	Lao People's Armed Forces
LPRP	Lao People's Revolutionary Party
LSM	Self-reliant Community Institutions (Indonesia)
LWU	Lao Women's Union
MA	Supreme Court (Indonesia)
MACC	Malaysian Anti-Corruption Commission
MAF	Malaysian Armed Forces
MCA	Malaysian Chinese Association
MDB	1Malaysia Development Berhad (Malaysian Sovereign Wealth Fund)
MIB	Malay Islamic Monarchy
MIC	Malaysian Indian Congress
MILF	Moro Islamic Liberation Front
MINDEF	Ministry of Defence (Singapore)
MK	Constitutional Court (Indonesia)
MMP	Multi-Member Plurality
MNLF	Moro National Liberation Front
MOD	Ministry of Defense
MOE	Military-Owned Enterprise
MOHA	Ministry of Home Affairs (Myanmar)
MP	Member of Parliament
MPLA	Malayan People's Liberation Army
MPR	People's Consultative Assembly (Indonesia)
MRHA	Maintenance of Religious Harmony Act (Malaysia)
NAP	New Aspiration Party (Thailand)

NASC	National Assembly Standing Committee (Laos)
NCCC	National Counter Corruption Commission (Thailand)
NCMP	Non-Constituency Member of Parliament (Singapore)
NCPO	National Council for Peace and Order (Thailand)
NDF	National Democratic Force (Myanmar)
NDSC	National Defense and Security Council (Myanmar)
NEC	National Election Commission (Cambodia)
NEP	New Economic Policy (Malaysia)
NGO	Non-Governmental Organization
NLD	National League of Democracy (Myanmar)
NMP	Nominated Members of Parliament (Singapore)
NP	Nationalist Party (Philippines)
NPA	New People's Army (Philippines)
NPC	National People's Coalition (Philippines)
NRP	Norodom Ranariddh Party (Cambodia)
NTUC	National Trade Union Congress (Singapore)
NU	Nahdlatul Ulama (Indonesia)
NUP	National Unity Party (Myanmar)
	Nationalist Unity Party (Philippines)
OB	"out of bounds"
ODA	Official Development Assistance
OECD	Organization of Economic Co-operation and Development
OFW	Overseas Filipino Workers
OIC	Organisation for Islamic Cooperation
OPM	Organization for a Free Papua (Indonesia)
	Office of the Prime Minister (Malaysia)
PAD	People's Alliance for Democracy (Thailand)
PAKAR	People's Awareness Party (Brunei)
PAN	National Mandate Party (Indonesia)
PAO	Provincial Administrative Organization (Thailand)
PAP	People's Action Party (Singapore)
PAS	Pan-Malaysian Islamic Party
PBB	Moon and Star Party (Indonesia)
PBS	Sabah United Party (Malaysia)
PD	Democratic Party (Indonesia)
PDI	Democratic Party of Indonesia
PDI-P	Democratic Party of Indonesia Struggle
PDK	Party of Democratic Kampuchea (Cambodia)
PDP-Laban	Philippine Democratic Party-Power of the Nation
PDR	People's Democratic Republic
PDRC	People's Democratic Reform Committee (Thailand)
PKB	National Awakening Party (Indonesia)
PKI	Communist Party of Indonesia
PKP	Communist Party of the Philippines (Huk)
PKR	People's Justice Party (Malaysia)

PKS	Prosperous Justice Party (Indonesia)
PM	Prime Minister
PMBU	Prime Minister Bodyguard Unit (Cambodia)
PMO	Prime Minister's Office
PMP	Force of the Filipino Masses
PNI	National Party of Indonesia
PNTL	National Police of Timor-Leste
POLRI	Police of the Republic of Indonesia
PPP	People's Prosperity Party (Indonesia)
PPT	People's Party of Timor
PR	Proportional Representation
PRB	People's Party of Brunei
PRS	Sarawak People's Party (Malaysia)
PSD	Social Democratic Party (Timor-Leste)
RAM	Reform the Armed Forces Movement (Philippines)
RBAF	Royal Bruneian Armed Forces
RCAF	Royal Cambodian Armed Forces
RI	Republic of Indonesia
RIS	Federal Republic of Indonesia
RMR	Royal Malay Regiment
RTAF	Royal Thai Armed Forces
RTM	Radio Television Malaysia
SA	Singapore Alliance
SAF	Singapore Armed Forces
SAP	Social Action Party (Thailand)
SCM	Supreme Council of the Magistracy (Cambodia)
SDA	Singapore Democratic Alliance
SDP	Singapore Democratic Party
SEA	Southeast Asia
SLORC	State Law and Order Restoration Council (Myanmar)
SMC	Single-Member Constituency
SMP	Single-Member Plurality
SNI	National Intelligence Service (Timor-Leste)
SNTV	Single Non-Transferable Vote
SOE	State-Owned Enterprise
SPDC	State Peace and Development Council (Myanmar)
SPP	Singapore People's Party
SRP	Sam Rainsy Party (Cambodia)
SRV	Socialist Republic of Vietnam
STAE	Secretariat for Electoral Administration (Timor-Leste)
TAO	Tambon Administrative Organization (Thailand)
TNI	Indonesian National Armed Forces
TRT	Thais love Thais
TVRI	Television of the Republic of Indonesia
UDT	Timorese Democratic Union

UEC	Union Election Commission (Myanmar)
UMNO	United Malay National Organization
UN	United Nations
UNA	United Nationalist Alliance (Philippines)
UNMISET	United Nations Mission to Support East Timor
UNMIT	United Nations Integrated Mission in East Timor
UNTAC	United Nations Transitional Authority in Cambodia
UNTAET	United Nations Transitional Authority in East Timor
USDA	Union Solidarity and Development Association (Myanmar)
USDP	Union Solidarity and Development Party (Myanmar)
UUD	Basic Law (Indonesia)
VFF	Vietnamese Fatherland Front
VGCL	Vietnam General Confederation of Labour
VOC	United East India Company (Netherlands)
VPA	Vietnamese People's Army
WGI	World Governance Indicators
WVS	World Value Survey

Government and Political Regimes in Southeast Asia: An Introduction

1.1   Countries and Cultures of Southeast Asia

The term "Southeast Asia"[1] is a neologism. It was used occasionally in academic texts in the 1920s but only entered more general use after the Allied Forces established the "South East Asia Command" (SEAC) in December 1943 to coordinate their campaign against the Japanese Imperial Army in the region north of Australia, south of China, and east of India. Southeast Asia as a region is an extraordinarily diverse collection of states, which vary widely in history, demographics, culture, economy, political systems, and the political challenges they face. From precolonial through colonial times and to the present day, the region has been marked more by contrasts and differences than by commonalities. Geographically, Southeast Asia is divided into an insular or maritime region, comprising Brunei, Indonesia, parts of Malaysia,[2] the Philippines, and Timor-Leste,[3] and a mainland or continental part, including Burma,[4] Cambodia, Laos, the Malay Peninsula, and Vietnam. Malay-Polynesian cultural and linguistic influences have shaped Maritime Southeast Asia, and with the exception of the predominantly Catholic Philippines, Islam is the dominant religion of this part of

---

[1]There is no generally accepted convention on spelling the term. In the United Kingdom, the term "South East Asia" or "south east Asia" are generally preferred, while in the United States, Southeast Asia is more commonly used. This textbook employs the spelling "Southeast Asia," as it is the spelling countries in the region have adopted through the Association of Southeast Asian Nations (ASEAN).

[2]The Federation of Malaya was renamed Malaysia after Singapore, Sarawak, and Sabah (British Northern Borneo) joined the Federation in 1963.

[3]The name East Timor is still commonly used and was employed by Indonesia during its occupation. Since independence in 2002, Timor-Leste is the country's adopted and internationally recognized name.

[4]The country was known as Burma from 1948 until 1989, when the ruling military junta changed its name from Burma to Myanmar. Myanmar is the transliteration of the official state name from the original Birman. This book employs both names interchangeably.

© Springer International Publishing AG 2018
A. Croissant, P. Lorenz, *Comparative Politics of Southeast Asia*,
https://doi.org/10.1007/978-3-319-68182-5_1

the region. Chinese-Tibetan (Tibeto-Burman, Shan, Thai, Lao, and Vietnamese) and Mon-Khmer languages as well as the religious influence of Buddhism historically shaped mainland Southeast Asia. Cultural differences further subdivide both maritime and continental Southeast Asia into highland and lowland regions. While the lowlands have historically been the economic, political, and cultural centers, the highlands have been home to most ethnic minorities. Until now, most highland areas are sparsely populated and economically less developed than the central lowlands. Highland areas have also been more resistant to state penetration than the lowlands (Scott 2009).

The precolonial kingdoms and empires of Southeast Asia were not "modern" territorial states in the Western, Weberian sense, with unitary and centralized administrations, and the state's monopoly on the legitimate use of force over a clearly demarcated territory. Instead, local rulers were in tributary relationships with more powerful overlords within loosely defined and constantly shifting political geographical spaces. Relationship networks between more and less powerful rulers rather than territories were the constituent parts of these "mandala states." The extent to which the supreme ruler could control his subordinates waxed and waned over time, yet it was always greater closer to the center and would peter out towards the periphery (Wolters 1999, p. 17). Beginning in the sixteenth century, Western imperial interest in the region grew steadily and the colonial experience—initially under Iberian, later under northwestern European powers, and from the late nineteenth century on including the United States—became a dominant influence on the political order and living conditions for most of the region's inhabitants. Today, colonial legacies remain essential to understanding national politics in Southeast Asian countries.

1.2   Southeast Asia in Colonial Times

With the exception of Siam, the whole region came under Western colonial rule at some point between 1511, when the Portuguese conquered the Sultanate of Malacca, and the 1920s. Pinpointing the onset of colonial rule is often impossible, as authority was imposed sequentially. In the Dutch East Indies, today's Indonesia, the establishment of the colonial capital Batavia (Jakarta) in 1619 to the subjection of Aceh in 1912 took almost three centuries (Andaya 1999; Tarling 1999). In the Philippines, Spanish colonial rule began in 1565, but the Spanish crown failed to conquer much of the south, including Muslim Mindanao and the Sulu archipelago. After taking over the colony from the Spanish, it took the United States almost two decades to consolidate control over its new dominion. Even after that, Muslim Mindanao was administered separately (Abinales and Amoroso 2005). For the sake of clarity, Table 1.1 provides the year of the onset of colonial rule based on a significant early event.

Even though the organization and practice of colonial rule differed widely, it has become standard practice to categorize colonial rule as either direct or indirect (Trocki 1999, pp. 90–97). First proposed by Furnivall (1960), this analytical

Table 1.1 Colonial rule over Southeast Asia

	Colonial power	Onset of colonial rule	Year of independence
Brunei	Great Britain	1888	1984
Burma	Great Britain	1826	1948
Cambodia	France	1863	1954
Indonesia	Netherlands	1619	1949
Laos	France	1893	1954
Malaysia	Great Britain	1786	1957
Philippines	Spain	1565	–
	USA	1898	1946
Singapore	Great Britain	1819	1965
Thailand	–	–	–
Timor-Leste	Portugal	1586	1975
	(Indonesia)	(1975)	(2002)
Vietnam	France	1859	1954

Notes: The year of independence given denotes the country's accession to the United Nations. Vietnam, Cambodia, and Laos gained full sovereignty from France in 1954, following the Geneva Conference. The Dutch recognized Indonesian independence in 1949, but West-Papua remained under colonial administration until 1967. The country chapters provide more detail on the timing and process of colonization and decolonization

differentiation is useful, but also misrepresents the reality in the individual colonies, where different institutional models often coexisted. All colonies underwent incremental change, caused more by ad hoc adjustments to local conditions than a sophisticated preexisting strategy of institutional design.

Direct rule, under which the administrative structure of the colonial power supplanted existing political structures, was the exception (Houben 2003, p. 149). Examples include French Cochin China, i.e., parts of southern Vietnam and eastern Cambodia as well as the British Straits Settlements on the Malayan Peninsula and "Ministerial Burma." The more common indirect rule, marked by collaboration with and through traditional rulers, was practiced in large parts of British Malaya, Brunei, most of Cambodia, and Laos. Here, the imperial powers co-opted traditional rulers and indigenous elites into a dual administrative and government structure. A Western resident or district administrator at the regional level cooperated with traditional rulers who commanded power and legitimacy at the local level (Houben 2003, p. 149).

Dutch rule in Java is an example of indirect rule (Kuitenbrouwer 1991). In theory, Javanese rulers governed their territories autonomously and were merely influenced by the Dutch. In truth, however, the Dutch held ultimate control at the local level. In a similar vein, French protectorates in Tonking, Annam, Cambodia, and Laos remained under nominal authority of the Vietnamese Emperor or the Kings of Cambodia and Laos, respectively. However, it was the French Governor General who exercised actual control over these territories (cf. Woodside 1976).

Western colonialism reached its apex between 1870 and 1914 (Osborne 1990), when territorial demarcation was completed and had created clearly defined political and administrative units that aspired to emulate Western models of statehood. In practice, the clash of European aspirations and local conditions instead resulted in hybrid models that combined traditional and Western state institutions in both form and function (Schlichte 2005).

The process of economic, political, cultural, and demographic change that began in the nineteenth century was accelerated by the vertical and horizontal expansion of colonial rule at the beginning of the twentieth century. Military expansion, infrastructural development, economic dominance, and the imposition of new legal systems by the colonial powers supplanted traditional governing arrangements and weakened the authority of local rulers. Uncertain about the loyalty and authority structures among the general population, the colonial powers looked to politically loyal minorities for support. These included Chinese and Indians for the administration of British Malaya and Burma, Vietnamese in the French protectorates, Ambonese in the Dutch colonial army, and Karen, Chin, and Kachin in the British military in Burma (Hack and Rettig 2009).

Linking local markets to the international capitalist system of the colonial powers often resulted in segmented regional economic conditions, a trend aggravated by the immigration of Chinese and Indian labor to Southeast Asia, mostly to the Malayan Peninsula, Thailand, and Indonesia. Together, this influx of new populations and the expanding reach of political-economic centers into the colonial peripheries (Brown 1994) changed the ethnic composition in much of Southeast Asia and created new lines of conflict, many of which remain virulent until today. In reaction to the changes brought about by colonialism, reform movements emerged all over the region following the World War I (Kratoska and Batson 1999). Unlike previous rebellions or insurgencies, these movements were neither a reaction to acute social or economic crises nor attempts to return to precolonial conditions (Berger 2009). Instead, their goal was to create sovereign nation states based on Western notions of statehood.

The reasons for the emergence of these movements differed as widely as the background of their members. Still, some trends can be identified: First, improved education opportunities for the colonial population, the adoption of Western administrative models, and the expansion of travel opportunities and communication channels had created an indigenous middle class and intelligentsia. Second, tensions between the local population and Asiatic and European migrants had increased. Third, the collapse of European and world markets in the aftermath of World War I and the Great Depression had strained most colonial economies. Finally, many reformers were motivated by the spread of anti-colonial ideologies, communism foremost among these, and wanted to emulate the model of the Japanese Meiji reforms or the Chinese (1911) or Russian (1917) revolutions (Trocki 1999; Owen 2005).

In countries like Burma or Indonesia, the struggle for independence pitted representatives of the cultural majority, striving for territorial nationalism based on recognition of the political and territorial unity created by colonizers, against members of ethnic minorities, who favored ethnic nationalism that would give them their own state (Kratoska and Batson 1999, pp. 253–255, 286–288). Other groups were neither interested in nationalism nor independence but demanded limited social and religious reforms (ibid.).

The political turmoil of the Great War and the economic downturn of the Great Depression ultimately ended Western predominance in the Asia Pacific region (Berger 2009). During the Second World War, Japanese military victories in Southeast Asia further energized national movements: After Japanese troops conquered Dutch, British, and American colonies in Southeast Asia in 1942, the occupation force fostered anti-Western sentiment by promoting nationalist groups and promising them independent statehood (Christie 2000, pp. 11–13). Even though the Japanese occupation continued, nationalist leaders in Burma and the Philippines declared independence in 1943 and the Indonesian nationalists Sukarno and Hatta proclaimed independence in August 1945, mere days after the Japanese surrender. While the Netherlands tried to restore its control over Indonesia militarily, the Dutch government ultimately recognized Indonesia's independence in 1949.

The process of decolonization in the Philippines and British Malaya took a different course. The Philippine national movement had emerged during the latter years of Spanish colonial rule and during the 1880s, and many intellectuals demanded the colony should receive equal treatment as a Spanish province within the kingdom. When the demand was ignored, the secret society "Kapitunan" began a military resistance against Spanish troops in 1896, but the group proved politically and militarily unprepared to gain independence (Abinales and Amoroso 2005, pp. 102–105). Following the Spanish-American War of 1898, control over the Philippines passed to the United States. After breaking down the opposition of Philippine nationalists militarily, the new colonial administration managed to co-opt the indigenous elite by granting them a limited level of administrative autonomy (Abinales and Amoroso 2005, p. 134). With the creation of the Commonwealth of the Philippines in 1935, the United States promised to grant full independence after a 10-year interim period. Even though the Japanese occupation delayed the plan for an orderly transition of power, the Philippines finally became an independent republic in 1946.

British Malaya also gained independence through negotiations rather than national revolution. The British practice of integrating the traditional elite into the colonial administration meant that a Malayan national movement only emerged relatively late (Stockwell 1977). Moreover, the Chinese, Indians, and Malays of its segmented population were not easily unified into an anti-British position. Ultimately, the struggle against the Communist Party of Malaya (CPM), supported mainly by the Chinese population, brought the British colonizers and the Malay elite together when the party began a guerilla war in 1946 (Loh 2005, p. 22). In order to overcome segmentation and prepare the country for independence in 1957, the British mediated "the Bargain" in 1955, a social contract among the country's three main ethnic groups that granted Chinese and Indians citizenship in exchange for accepting the constitutionally guaranteed political predominance of the Malay population.

1.3   Southeast Asia Since the End of Western Colonialism

Most Southeast Asian states achieved independence between 1946 and 1965. Brunei, however, only became independent in 1984, while Indonesian troops occupied Timor-Leste after the Portuguese left the island in 1975. While few states recognized the occupation, Timor-Leste only attained independence in 2002. Irrespective of the differing modes of decolonization—through violent struggle in Vietnam and Indonesia, bargaining in Malaysia, Singapore, the Philippines, Laos, and Cambodia, or through political pressure in Burma—colonial rule often segmented the subject population along ethnic, religious, or linguistic lines (Table 1.2). The emerging states lacked a universally accepted vision of the nation, and national minorities in many countries made their own territorial or national claims against the nascent central governments.

In Southeast Asian postcolonial societies, nation-building was the project of political and intellectual elites in the almost complete absence of a common sense of nation and culture. The resulting "invention of traditions" (Hobsbawm 2005) was almost inevitably based on the historical experiences, political mythology, and cultural symbols of particular groups within the segmented societies. Such was the case for Thai, Malay, and Indonesian nationalism (Berger 2009, pp. 32–41). During this process, elites often made use of colonial constructs of identity: The concept of Malay-ness adopted by the new Malaysian state, for example, derived

Table 1.2 Population, territory, and social heterogeneity in Southeast Asia around 2015

	Population (in Mio)	Area (sq. km)	Index of linguistic fragmentation[a]	Index of religious fragementation[b]
Brunei	0.414	5765	0.456	0.555
Cambodia	15.458	181,035	0.157	0.277
Indonesia	242.968	1,904,569	0.846	0.405
Laos	7.019	236,800	0.678	0.584
Malaysia	30.949	329,847	0.758	0.584
Myanmar	56.890	676,578	0.521	0.447
Philippines	102.624	300,000	0.849	0.333
Singapore	5.312	719	0.748	0.744
Thailand	68.2	513,120	0.753	0.266
Timor-Leste	1.201	14,874	0.897	0.238
Vietnam	95.261	331,210	0.234	0.690

Source: CIA (2017) and Croissant et al. (2009)

[a]The Index of Linguistic Fragmentation is a measure of linguistic heterogeneity in the country based on the index of diversity developed by Joseph Greenberg. It gives the probability by which two randomly picked inhabitants have a different first language. It ranges from 0 to 1, where 0 denotes a country with only one native language and 1 denotes a country where every inhabitant speaks a different language (Simons and Fennig 2017). Mathematically, it is equivalent to Douglas Rae and Michael Taylor's Index of Fractionalization, calculated as $1 - \sum (p_i)^2$, where p_i is the share of language i among the total population

[b]The Index of Religious Fragmentation is calculated along the same lines

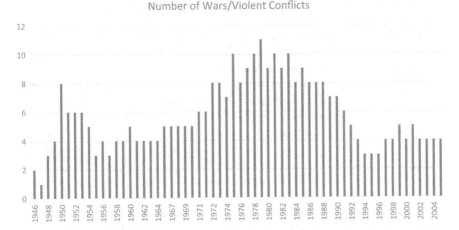

Fig. 1.1 Number of violent conflicts in Southeast Asia, 1945–2005. Source: Data compiled from CONIS (Conflict Information System) based at Heidelberg University. The graphic includes all intra- and interstate violent conflicts and wars involving any of the 11 countries covered in this book, see also Croissant et al. (2009)

from the British "Malay Reservation Act" of 1913. It defined ethnic identity as the combination of a common descent or race, the use of the Malay language, and the practice of Islam.

The lack of integration within the emerging social order and the latent tensions between political units and national identities created the tinder for several violent conflicts that flared up after independence. Some of these secessionist conflicts, as in Burma, the Southern Philippines, Southern Thailand, and West Papua, persist until today. Whether social conflict could quickly be contained within institutional channels or resulted in military violence had profound effects on the process of state-building (Slater 2010; Vu 2010). The first decades following the Second World War have been characterized as an era of elite-driven and often violent nation-building in Southeast Asia: During these years, the region was plagued by an above-average incidence of armed conflict (Brown 1994, 2008). Ethno-nationalist and ideological lines of conflict often overlapped, as in Malaysia, Thailand, and Laos. The region only grew more peaceful after the Cold War era proxy conflicts in Laos (1960–1973), Vietnam (1958–1975), and Cambodia (1970–1991) had ended (Fig. 1.1). Even though the turn of the century engendered an upsurge of ethno-nationalist violence—partly caused by the political upheavals of the Indonesian transition in 1998/99—this has not reversed the underlying trend (Trinn and Croissant 2012).

Several factors account for the ebb in violent conflict since the 1980s. First, the number of great power interventions in the region and tensions among ASEAN countries significantly decreased (Dosch 1997). Second, parts of Southeast Asia became centers of economic growth, which helped reduce internal socioeconomic tensions and strengthened intraregional ties. Especially Singapore, but also

Indonesia, Thailand, Malaysia, and more recently Vietnam, have sustained high growth rates (Table 1.3). Even the Asian Financial Crisis of 1997/98 could not reverse this trend. Economic growth has fueled more effective poverty reduction campaigns, increased per capita income, and expanded education opportunities, urbanization, the middle class, and cultural change.

These socioeconomic changes were not without political consequences. While authoritarian regimes ruled the region in the mid-1980s, the following decade saw several regime transitions from dictatorship to democracy. Following the downfall of Philippine President Ferdinand Marcos in 1986, authoritarian regimes in Thailand (1992) and Indonesia (1998–1999) collapsed under popular demands for democratization. In Cambodia (1993) and Timor-Leste (2002), democracy was instituted under the aegis of the United Nations (Case 2002; Croissant 2004; Shin and Tusalem 2009).

Despite the optimism caused by these developments in the 1990s, democracy could not uphold its triumphant entry into the region. The failure of democracy in Cambodia in the late 1990s, the erosion of democratic standards in the Philippines, the collapse of civilian rule in Thailand in 2006 and 2014, and the absence of additional cases of democratization seem to indicate that at the beginning of the twenty-first century, the state of democracy in Southeast Asia has stagnated. Additional democratic transitions seem unlikely, and the future of current processes of transformation such as in Myanmar is uncertain at best (Case 2015; Croissant 2015; Bünte 2015).

There are three groups of political regimes in the region.[5] The first group of countries falling under "electoral authoritarianism" (Schedler 2006) includes Cambodia, Malaysia, Singapore, and—following the election of 2012—Myanmar. Formal democratic institutions in these countries coexist with authoritarian political practices (Schedler 2006; Howard and Roessler 2006, p. 367). In these regimes, elections are "widely viewed as [the] primary route to power" (Levitsky and Way 2010, p. 13). However, governments systematically abuse their powers and insulate their position against political challengers by imposing disadvantages on opposition parties, curtailing the development of civil society and the media, and suppressing political dissent. While opposition parties in Malaysia are in a position to challenge the ruling Barisan Nasional (National Front) government, no opposition force in Singapore is able to threaten the hegemonic position of the People's Action Party (PAP). The level of competition between government and opposition condoned by Hun Sen's Cambodian People's Party (CPP) places Cambodia somewhere between Singapore and Malaysia. While he has tolerated some competition, recent events suggest a more hegemonic turn (Case 2009; Karbaum 2008; Strangio 2014). Recent

---

[5]The concept of the political regime denotes that part of the political system that determines who is granted access to political power, under which conditions and within which limits this power is exercised (Lawson 1993, p. 187). Comparative politics most commonly distinguishes authoritarian and democratic regimes. Liberal democratic regimes provide open, pluralistic access to political power, rule within constitutional limits, and respect for the rule of law and political authority is based on popular sovereignty (Merkel 2004).

Table 1.3 Indicators of modernization and human development in Southeast Asia

	Brunei	Cambodia	Indonesia	Laos	Malaysia	Myanmar	Philippines	Singapore	Timor-Leste	Thailand	Vietnam
GDP per capita, PPP (current international $)											
1990	55,119	707 (1993)	1793	1045	6755	464	2591	22,167	–	4298	3705
2015	78,369	3490	5675	5691	26,950	5249	7387	85,382	2399	16,340	6034
Human Development Index (HDI)											
1975		0.533	0.468	0.423	0.615			0.725		0.614	
2012	0.855	0.543	0.629	0.543	0.769	0.498	0.654	0.895	0.561	0.690	0.617
Medical doctors per 10,000 inhabitants (2008)	11	2	1	3	7	4	12	15	1	3	6
Land lines and mobile phones per 100 inhabitants (2008)	115	29	75	35	118	2	80	170	–	102	116
Internet users per 100 inhabitants (2008)	55.3	0.5	7.9	8.5	55.8	0.2	6.2	69.6	–	23.9	24.2
Percentage of economically active population in the agricultural sector (2008)	2	71	41	–	18	–	44	2	–	43	56
Literacy (percent, above age 15) (2008)	95	77.6	92	72.7	92.1	91.9	93.6	93	–	94	90
Primary School Enrollment Rate (2008)	107	116	119	112	97	117	110	–	113	93	104
Secondary School Enrollment Rate (2008)	97	40	74	44	68	53	82	–	51	74	67
Tertiary Education Enrollment Rate (2008)	16	7	21	13	32	11	29	–	15	45	10
Percentage of urban population (2008)	75	22	53	31	71	33	66	100	28	34	28

Source: Authors' compilation based on UNDP (2011, 2015), UNESCO (2017), and World Bank (2017)

developments in Myanmar point in the opposite direction. Following the deeply flawed elections of 2010, the military junta seems to be transitioning the regime towards more competitive electoral authoritarianism. The National League for Democracy, the party of opposition icon Aung San Suu Kyi, managed to win 43 out of 46 seats in the by-elections held in 2012 and secured a landslide victory with a two-thirds majority during the regular parliamentary elections of 2015 (Bünte 2016). Yet, the 25% reservation quota for members of the military in the legislature and the wide military prerogatives that limit the civilian government's effective power to govern in very significant ways demonstrate the persistence of authoritarian structures in the country.

The second group of "closed autocracies" that lack multiparty elections includes Brunei, Laos, Vietnam, and Thailand since the coup of May 2014. These regimes do not tolerate even limited political competition. Laos and Vietnam are among only five self-proclaimed communist single party states that survived the end of the Cold War in 1989/90 and the dissolution of the Soviet Union in 1991.[6] The authoritarian sultanate in Brunei is one of only five countries that hold no national parliamentary elections.[7]

The third group of "defective democracies" (Merkel 2004) includes the Philippines, Indonesia, and Timor-Leste.[8] The stability and quality of these defective democracies differ widely (Bünte and Croissant 2011, p. 4). In the Philippines, political violence is common, civilian control over the military is limited, civil liberties are not guaranteed, and the rule of law is weak (Abinales and Amoroso 2005). In Thailand, the political controversies surrounding Prime Minister Thaksin Shinawatra culminated in a military coup d'état in 2006. After the return to civilian democratic rule between 2008 and 2014, the military staged another coup against the pro-Thaksin government in May 2014 (Ferrara 2015), switching its regime type from a defective democracy to military rule. In Timor-Leste, the democratic process and the effectiveness of democratic institutions are fragile, but democratic elections and political rights have remained relatively robust and functional (Croissant and Abu Sharkh 2016). Even though clientelism, neo-patrimonialism, and untamed politicking are rampant in Timorese politics, democracy as an abstract ideal and democratic turnover of power are accepted among both the political elite as well as the wider population. In the region, Indonesia remains the only country that has somewhat stabilized its democratic system, even though it has not yet become a consolidated liberal democracy (Mietzner 2015).

Thanks to its variety of regime types and the large variance of theoretically relevant explanatory factors, Southeast Asia presents political scientists with a

---

[6]The others are China, North Korea, and Cuba (Dimitrov 2013).

[7]The others are China, Saudi Arabia, United Arab Emirates, and Qatar (Groemping 2015).

[8]Defective democracies are "diminished subtypes" of democracy. While elections in defective democracies are sufficiently free and fair, other institutional prerequisites of liberal democracy are constrained. Constitutional limits and checks on the democratically legitimized leadership can be missing—namely civil rights, the rule of law, and horizontal accountability—or the effective power of democratically elected authorities to govern is limited (Merkel 2004).

"natural laboratory" (Abrami and Doner 2008, p. 229) to test competing theories of political change. Levels of socioeconomic modernization, paths to state and nation-building, ethnic heterogeneity, colonial heritage, the structure of governing coalitions and elite formations, the shape and extent of interest and civil society organizations, as well as institutional factors like type of government or electoral system all differ widely. There are federal as well as unitary states, numerous different types of parties and party systems, vastly different levels of cohesion and professionalism in the national armed forces, and different levels of coercion employed by the governments to uphold their rule (Slater 2010). Finally, regimes vary in their claims to legitimacy, religious traditions span a wide spectrum, and national ideologies as well as individual value patterns are highly diverse (Slater 2010; Case 2009). Carving out these details and analyzing their causes and effects is among the goals of this textbook.

1.4   The Structure of This Book

The developments addressed above have raised interest in the region and the need for concise information about its political structures, processes, and actors in the past decades. Until now, however, the political economy of Southeast Asian developmental states has dominated the research agenda. The lack of concise current monographs that focus on the national political and social systems in the region from a comparative perspective stands in stark contrast to this. In order to fill this lacuna, this textbook provides a systematic introduction to the political systems of Brunei Darussalam (Brunei), Cambodia, Indonesia, Laos, Malaysia, Myanmar, the Philippines, Singapore, Thailand, Timor-Leste, and Vietnam. It combines detailed studies of single cases with comparative accounts. It focuses on the structures, processes, and actors of the political system as well as the current political situation. Compiled by comparative political scientists, its intended audience includes students of political science without regional expertise and students of area studies. In addition, it is meant as a resource for other political and social scientists in research and teaching, as well as journalists and other professionals. We hope it will provide its readership with a well-founded introduction to Southeast Asia as an area of study.

The descriptions and analyses in this textbook are based on past and current research of both authors on democracy and democratization, autocratic regimes, political parties, civil society, civil–military relations, and the political institutions in the region based on their own field research as well as comprehensive surveys of international research literature. In most cases, the authors relegate primary sources to an auxiliary position and focus on relatively accessible secondary material. Most sources will, therefore, be accessible to the average reader looking for more in-depth information without command of one of the regional languages. Asian names from non-Latinized languages have been transcribed in their most commonly used Latin form.

Two considerations have influenced the structure of this textbook. On the one hand, each political system is presented and analyzed individually and in great depth in the form of country chapters to foster a deeper understanding of the whole system and the interaction of its components. On the other hand, this country-based approach is complemented by an explicit and systematic comparative perspective. All country chapters follow a similar structure, and while all chapters focus on current politics, they also discuss the historical origins and context of national politics and current challenges. The textbook concludes with a comparative summary and an outlook into possible future political developments in the region.

References

Abinales, P. N., & Amoroso, D. J. (2005). *State and society in the Philippines (State and society in East Asia series)*. Lanham: Rowman & Littlefield.

Abrami, R., & Doner, R. F. (2008). Southeast Asia and the political economy of development. In E. M. Kuhonta, D. Slater, & T. Vu (Eds.), *Southeast Asia in political science: Theory, region, and qualitative analysis* (pp. 227–251). Stanford: Stanford University Press.

Andaya, B. W. (1999). Political development between the sixteenth and eighteenth centuries. In N. Tarling (Ed.), *Cambridge history of Southeast Asia: Volume I, Part 2: From c. 1500 to c. 1800* (pp. 341–401). Cambridge: Cambridge University Press.

Berger, M. T. (2009). The end of empire and the cold war. In M. Beeson (Ed.), *Contemporary Southeast Asia* (2nd ed., pp. 29–46). Basingstoke: Palgrave Macmillan.

Brown, D. (1994). *The state and ethnic politics in Southeast Asia*. London: Routledge.

Brown, G. K. (2008). Horizontal inequalities and separatism in Southeast Asia: A comparative perspective. In F. Stewart (Ed.), *Horizontal inequalities and conflict: Understanding group violence in multiethnic societies* (pp. 252–284). New York: Palgrave Macmillan.

Bünte, M. (2015). *The end of Myanmar's military-guided electoral authoritarianism: The 2015 elections* (Southeast Asia Research Centre Working Paper No. 176). Hong Kong: City University Hong Kong.

Bünte, M. (2016). Myanmar's protracted transition: Arenas, actors, and outcomes. *Asian Survey, 56*, 369–391. https://doi.org/10.1525/as.2016.56.2.369

Bünte, M., & Croissant, A. (2011). Introduction. In A. Croissant & M. Bünte (Eds.), *The crisis of democratic governance in Southeast Asia* (pp. 1–15). Houndmills: Palgrave Macmillan.

Case, W. (2002). *Politics in Southeast Asia: Democracy or less*. Richmond: Curzon.

Case, W. (2009). Low-quality democracy and varied authoritarianism: Elites and regimes in Southeast Asia today. *Pacific Review, 22*, 255–269. https://doi.org/10.1080/09512740903068214

Case, W. (2015). Democracy's mixed fortunes in Southeast Asia: Topor, change, and trade-offs. In W. Case (Ed.), *Routledge handbook of Southeast Asian democratization* (pp. 3–23). London: Routledge.

Christie, C. J. (2000). *A modern history of Southeast Asia: Decolonization nationalism and separatism* (2nd ed.). London: I.B. Tauris.

CIA. (2017). *The world factbook*. Langley: Central Intelligence Agency.

Croissant, A. (2004). From transition to defective democracy: Mapping Asian democratization. *Democratization, 11*, 156–178. https://doi.org/10.1080/13510340412331304633

Croissant, A. (2015). Southeast Asian militaries in the age of democratization: From ruler to servant? In W. Case (Ed.), *Routledge handbook of Southeast Asian democratization* (pp. 314–332). London: Routledge.

Croissant, A., & Abu Sharkh, R. (2016). *As good as it gets?: Stateness and democracy in East Timor*. Unpublished Manuscript, Heidelberg.

Croissant, A., Wagschal, U., Schwank, N., & Trinn, C. (2009). *Kulturelle Konflikte seit 1945: Die kulturellen Dimensionen des globalen Konfliktgeschehens*. Baden-Baden: Nomos.

Dimitrov, M. K. (2013). Understanding communist collapse and resilience. In M. K. Dimitrov (Ed.), *Why communism did not collapse: Understanding authoritarian regime resilience in Asia and Europe* (pp. 3–39). New York: Cambridge University Press.

Dosch, J. (1997). *Die ASEAN: Bilanz eines Erfolges. Akteure, Interessenlagen, Kooperationsbeziehungen*. Hamburg: Abera.

Ferrara, F. (2015). Democracy in Thailand: Theory and practice. In W. Case (Ed.), *Routledge handbook of Southeast Asian democratization* (pp. 351–370). London: Routledge.

Furnival, J. S. (1960). *The governance of modern Burma*. New York: Institute of Pacific Relations.

Groemping, M. (2015). *Southeast Asian elections worst in the world*. http://www.newmandala. org/southeast-asian-elections-worst-in-the-world/

Hack, K., & Rettig, T. (Eds.). (2009). *Colonial armies in Southeast Asia*. London: Routledge.

Hobsbawm, E. J. (2005). Introduction: Inventing traditions. In E. J. Hobsbawm & T. Ranger (Eds.), *The invention of tradition* (10th ed., pp. 1–15). Cambridge: Cambridge University Press.

Houben, V. J. H. (2003). Southeast Asia and Islam. *The Annals of the American Academy of Political and Social Science, 588*, 149–170. https://doi.org/10.1177/0002716203588001010

Howard, M. M., & Roessler, P. G. (2006). Liberalizing electoral outcomes in competitive authoritarian regimes. *American Journal of Political Science, 50*, 365–381. https://doi.org/ 10.1111/j.1540-5907.2006.00189.x

Karbaum, M. (2008). *Kambodscha unter Hun Sen: Informelle Institutionen, politische Kultur und Herrschaftslegitimität*. Münster: LIT Verlag.

Kratoska, P., & Batson, B. (1999). Nationalism and modernist reform. In N. Tarling (Ed.), *Cambridge history of Southeast Asia: Volume II, Part 1: From c. 1800 to the 1930s* (pp. 253–320). Cambridge: Cambridge University Press.

Kuitenbrouwer, M. (1991). *The Netherlands and the rise of modern imperialism: Colonies and foreign policy 1870–1902*. New York: Berg.

Lawson, S. (1993). Conceptual issues in the comparative study of regime change and democratization. *Comparative Politics, 25*, 183. https://doi.org/10.2307/422351

Levitsky, S., & Way, L. (2010). *Competitive authoritarianism: Hybrid regimes after the Cold War*. New York: Cambridge University Press.

Loh, F. K. W. (2005). Globalization, development and democratization in Southeast Asia. In F. K. W. Loh & J. Öjendal (Eds.), *Southeast Asian responses to globalization: Restructuring governance and deepening democracy* (pp. 17–57). Copenhagen: NIAS Press.

Merkel, W. (2004). Embedded and defective democracies. *Democratization, 11*(5), 33–58.

Mietzner, M. (2015). Indonesia: Democratic consolidation and stagnation under Yudhoyono, 2004–2014. In W. Case (Ed.), *Routledge handbook of Southeast Asian democratization* (pp. 370–384). London: Routledge.

Osborne, M. E. (1990). *Southeast Asia: An illustrated history*. Ithaca: Cornell University Press.

Owen, N. G. (Ed.). (2005). *The emergence of modern Southeast Asia: A new history*. Honolulu: University of Hawai'i Press.

Schedler, A. (2006). The logic of electoral authortarianism. In A. Schedler (Ed.), *Electoral authoritarianism* (pp. 2–35). Boulder, CO: Lynne Rienner.

Schlichte, K. (2005). *Der Staat in der Weltgesellschaft: Politische Herrschaft in Asien, Afrika und Lateinamerika*. Campus: Frankfurt am Main.

Scott, J. C. (2009). *The art of not being governed: An anarchist history of upland Southeast Asia*. New Haven: Yale University Press.

Shin, D. C., & Tusalem, R. F. (2009). East Asia. In C. W. Haerpfer, P. Bernhagen, R. F. Inglehart, & C. Welzel (Eds.), *Democratization* (pp. 356–376). Oxford: Oxford University Press.

Simons, G. F., & Fennig, C. D. (Eds.). (2017). *Ethnologue: Languages of the world* (20th ed.). Dallas: SIL International.

Slater, D. (2010). *Ordering power: Contentious politics and authoritarian leviathans in Southeast Asia*. Cambridge: Cambridge University Press.

Stockwell, A. J. (1977). The formation and first years of the United Malays National Organization (U.M.N.O.) 1946–1948. *Modern Asian Studies, 11*(4), 481–513.

Strangio, S. (2014). *Hun Sen's Cambodia*. New Haven: Yale University Press.

Tarling, N. (Ed.). (1999). *Cambridge history of Southeast Asia: Volume II, Part 1: From c. 1800 to the 1930s*. Cambridge: Cambridge University Press.

Trinn, C., & Croissant, A. (2012). Democratic and semi-democratic conflict management in Southeast Asia. In J. J. Schwarzmantel & H. J. Kraetzschmar (Eds.), *Democracy and violence: Global debates and local challenges* (pp. 188–217). London: Routledge.

Trocki, C. (1999). Political structures of the nineteenth and early twentieth centuries. In N. Tarling (Ed.), *Cambridge history of Southeast Asia: Volume II, Part 1: From c. 1800 to the 1930s* (pp. 75–126). Cambridge: Cambridge University Press.

UNDP. (2011). *Human development report 2011: Sustainability and equity: A better future for all*. Houndmills: Palgrave Macmillan.

UNDP. (2015). *Human development report 2015: Work for human development*. Houndmills: Palgrave Macmillan.

UNESCO. (2017). UNESCO Institute for Statistics Data Center. Accessed June 12, 2017 from http://data.un.org/Browse.aspx?d=UNESCO

Vu, T. (2010). *Paths to development in Asia: South Korea, Vietnam, China, and Indonesia*. Cambridge: Cambridge University Press.

Wolters, O. W. (1999). *History, culture, and region in Southeast Asian perspectives* (2nd ed.). Ithaca, NY: Southeast Asia Program Publications.

Woodside, A. B. (1976). *Community and revolution in modern Vietnam*. Boston: Houghton Mifflin Company.

World Bank. (2017). *World development indicators*. http://data.worldbank.org/products/wdi

Brunei Darussalam: Malay Islamic Monarchy and Rentier State

2

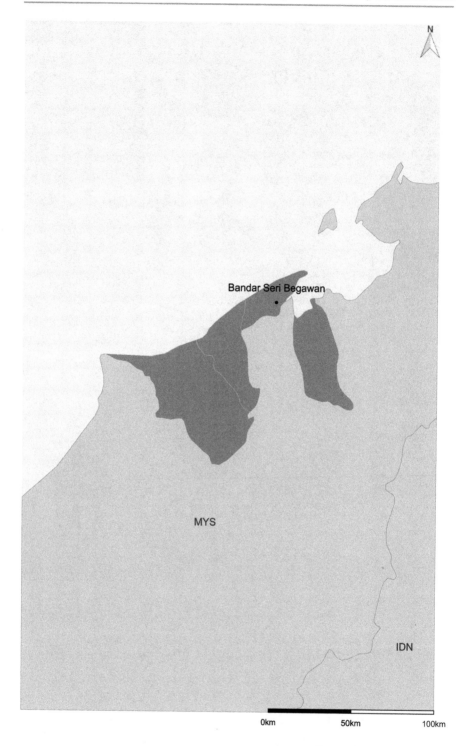

2.1 Historical Background

The Sultanate Brunei Darussalam (*Negara Brunei Darussalam*, "Nation of Brunei, Abode of Peace") is situated in the northwestern part of the island of Borneo. The Limbang valley, part of the Malaysian state of Sarawak, separates the eastern and western territories of the sultanate. With a population of 414,000, Brunei is a microstate (see Table 2.1). Only about 65% of the total population has citizenship. Most citizens are of Malayan descent; an estimated fifth belongs to indigenous groups (Saunders 1994, p. 175). The remainder of the population consists of "permanent" (8%) and "temporary" residents (27%). Most permanent residents are ethnic Chinese who were not granted citizenship when Brunei declared its independence but received Bruneian travel documents. The majority of temporary residents are foreign workers from various South Asian and Southeast Asian countries employed in the construction and service sectors. Islam is the official state religion and Muslims (mostly followers of the *Shafi'i* school) make up 75% of the population, whereas Christians and Buddhists represent 9.4 and 8.5%, respectively (DEPD 2010). The head of state is the Sultan (*Yang Di-Pertuan*, He, who is Lord) who represents the country's highest religious and political authority (Art. 3 [2004], Constitution of Brunei Darussalam), making it the only absolute monarchy in Southeast Asia. The constitution, first drafted in 1959, provides no separation of powers: The Sultan's principal authority is not diminished by parliament and he remains head of judiciary.

According to the national founding myth, the Sultanate's political history began when Sultan Awang Alak Betatar converted to Islam in 1363 and established today's ruling dynasty (Talib 2002, p. 143). The current Sultan Hassan al Bolkiah

Table 2.1 Country profile Brunei Darussalam

Population	Year of full national sovereignty	Form of government
443,593	1984	Monarchy
Total area	**Current constitution promulgated**	**Head of state**
5765 km^2	1959	Sultan Hassanal Bolkiah (since 1967)
GDP p.c. (2005 PPP, 2012)	**Official language**	**Head of government**
54,100	Malay	Sultan Hassanal Bolkiah (since 1967)
Ethnic groups	**Democracy score (BTI 2016)**	**System of government**
Malay 66.7%, Chinese 11.1%, Indigenous 6%, Others 12.1%	–	Parliamentary
Religions	**Regime type**	**Cabinet type**
Muslims 75%, Christians 9.4%, Buddhists 8.5%, Others 7.9%	Royal autocracy	No-party cabinet

Sources: CIA (2017) and DEPD (2010, 2011)

ascended the throne in 1967 as the 29th member of the house Bolkiah (Saunders 1994, p. 43). At the height of its power between the fifteenth and seventeenth century, the Sultan ruled over all of Borneo, the Sulu Archipelago, and Palawan. Following the arrival of European colonial powers in the sixteenth century, the Sultanate slowly lost much of its influence over maritime trade. In the nineteenth century, the Sultan had to forgo control over much of Borneo, finally ceding external sovereignty to the British in the Anglo-Bruneian Treaty of 1847. Threatened by complete collapse after internal strife, Brunei was only saved when the British offered the Sultan a "Treaty of Protection" in 1888 and installed a Resident in 1905. Under the terms of the 1906 Supplementary Protectorate agreement, recommendations of the British Resident were binding on every matter except for religious affairs (Saunders 1994, pp. 47, 107).

The residency system remained in place until 1959 and—paradoxically—enabled the ruling dynasty to consolidate its political power and strip competing nobles of their influence. When the Royal Dutch Shell discovered large petroleum reserves in Brunei in 1929, the country quickly became the third largest source of petroleum in the British Commonwealth. This gave the Sultanate a steady stream of revenue, especially after the off-shore production of oil and natural gas began in the 1950s. Fueled by oil revenues, Brunei transformed from a mainly agrarian-based to a "rentier state" economy. With abundant natural resources and a small population, Brunei Darussalam has one of the highest levels of GDP per capita in Southeast Asia (cf. World Bank 2017b).[1]

The 1950s and 1960s marked a turning point in Brunei's political development. The birth of the sovereign Federation of Malaya (1957) and the approaching end of British control over Sarawak and Sabah triggered the emergence of a pan-Bornean movement led by the Brunei People's Party (*Partai Rakyat Brunei*, PRB). Founded in 1956, PRB demanded the formation of the sovereign Federated States of Borneo under the nominal leadership of the Sultan of Brunei. Sultan Omar Ali Saifuddin III and the aristocratic elite, however, favored a closer association with Malaysia and opposed the expansion of popular participation and democratic rights (Lindsey and Steiner 2012, p. 498; Singh 1984, p. 125), especially after a new Treaty of Protection (1959) granted Brunei almost complete political and administrative autonomy, leaving the British High Commissioner only control over foreign policy, internal security, and defense. Consequently, the first Bruneian constitution, proclaimed that same year at the insistence of the British government, instituted a consultative

---

[1]Rentier states are states that regularly receive most or all of their revenues from rents, such as oil revenues or income derived from the exploitation of other natural resources (Beck 2007). Rents can be accumulated from economic and political resources (i.e., development aid or military assistance) or migrant remittances. Rentier states are characterized by the relative absence of revenue from domestic taxation and can freely allocate resources to service political interests (Beblawi and Luciani 1987; Herb 2005). Since rentier states often are governed by autocratic leaders and lack democratic institutions (Ross 2001), resources are used to stabilize authoritarian rule. Depending on the percentage of government revenue made up of rents, countries can be categorized as weak (20–30%), intermediate (30–40%), or strong (more than 40%) rentier states (Beck 2007).

assembly with a handful of indirectly elected members, called the Legislative Council. The PRB managed to win all 16 elected seats of the council's 33 total seats in the first popular vote in August 1962 (Saunders 1994, p. 147). When the Sultan proved unwilling to include the PRB in the decision-making process, the national movement radicalized (Lindsey and Steiner 2012, p. 501). In December 1962, PRB cadres and the pro-Indonesian National Army of North Kalimantan (*Tentara Nasional Kalimantan Utara*, TNKU) started an uprising that was easily crushed by British troops but provided the Sultan with the opportunity to establish emergency rule, dissolve the legislative council, and ban all political parties.

Negotiations between Brunei and the Malayan government over the Sultanate's accession to the Federation failed over the allocation of oil and gas revenue and the constitutional status of the Sultan relative to the other traditional Malay rulers.[2] In not joining Malaysia, the Sultan remained in full control of oil revenues and was under no pressure to introduce more representative and participatory political institutions (Tey 2007, pp. 268–269). In 1967, Omar Ali Saifuddin III abdicated in favor of his son Hassanal Bolkiah, dodging British pressure for the return to a constitutional regime. A renewed Brunei-British Treaty in 1979 opened the way to full national sovereignty, which was realized on January 1, 1984.

Since independence, the stability of the political regime rests on four pillars. The first is the legitimation of the absolute monarchy through the concept of *Melayu Islam Beraja* or the Malay Islamic Monarchy (MIB). The second pillar is "soft repression" to prevent public criticism and opposition. Third, the Sultanate secures its national sovereignty and independence through membership in the Association of Southeast Asian Nations (ASEAN), the United Nations (UN), and the Organization for Islamic Cooperation (OIC) as well as its bilateral defense and security cooperation with the United Kingdom and Singapore. Fourth, resource abundance and oil revenues provide the means to co-opt Malay elites and middle classes in a rentier-based "authoritarian bargain" (Desai et al. 2009), in which citizens relinquish political rights for economic security and exchange political loyalty for economic benefits and social welfare.

Brunei is the fourth largest producer of liquid gas worldwide; oil and gas deposits are exploited in a joint venture between the state, multinational corporations, and a new Chinese-Malay business elite largely organized around the Brunei Shell Petroleum conglomerate (Gunn 1993). The revenue is administered by the Brunei Investment Agency (BIA), Brunei's sovereign petroleum fund under the auspice of the ministry of finance. However, any private business conducted by the ruling family is kept strictly separate from the state budget and remains inscrutable for outsiders (Gunn 2008, p. 6).

The rentier state literature identifies various mechanisms by which rents can exert a stabilizing effect on authoritarian rule (Ross 2001). Since the 1980s, 70–93% of Brunei's state revenue comes from the oil and gas sector (cf. Fig. 2.1).

---

[2]For more details on the constitutional status of the traditional Malay rulers on the Malayan Peninsula, see Chap. 6.

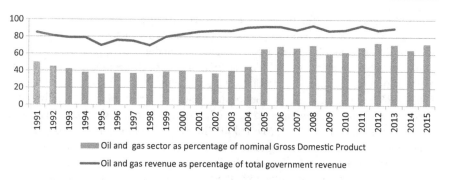

Fig. 2.1 Oil and gas sector's contribution to GDP and government revenue in Brunei (1991–2015). Source: Authors' calculation based on DEPD (2010, 2011) and IMF (2006, 2012)

This allows the government to forgo an income tax for individual citizens and precludes demands for greater political participation ("taxation effect"). The so-called spending effect also contributes to the depolitization of the public: The government uses oil and gas revenues to finance a generous welfare system, also known as "shellfare" (Gunn 2008), that includes subsidies for fuel, housing, and staple foods as well as free education, university stipends for citizens to study abroad, and access to affordable quality health care (Saim 2009; Gunn 1993). Rents have also allowed the government to create a sizeable public sector that provides more generous health benefits, old age pensions, and higher income than the private sector. This fosters the development of patron–client relationships and rent-seeking among the Malay middle class and mostly Chinese-speaking entrepreneurs and ensures their loyalty to the continued existence of the ruling monarchy (Kershaw 2001, p. 29; Gunn 2008, p. 1; Lindsey and Steiner 2012, p. 509). Material benefits are awarded based on socioeconomic status groups, which has precluded the creation of modern political or social associations ("modernization effect"). Finally, oil and gas revenues have been used to finance a very sizeable security sector that provides regime security ("repression effect"). In the region, Brunei's per capita military spending is only surpassed by Singapore, and the Global Militarization Index puts the Sultanate at rank 14 among the 150 countries surveyed by the Bonn Center for International Conversion (BICC 2013; IISS 2014).

2.2   Constitutional Development

Brunei's constitutional order rests on two documents: the Constitution of 1959 (with major revisions enacted in 2004 and 2006) and the Succession and Regency Proclamation of the same year (Cheong 2001; Tey 2008). Even though Brunei has had a written constitution since 1959, its pseudo-constitutionalism merely formalizes the Sultan's absolute sovereignty. The document was drawn up under pressure from the British and the PRB, but without the participation of social groups. Moreover, instead of constituting a parliamentary regime, the Sultan remains Brunei's center of political gravity and possesses exclusive government authority. Hence, the absolute sovereignty of the Sultanate itself is Brunei's "Grundnorm" (basic norm): all positive laws derive their validity from his person (Tey 2007).

The constitutional text consists of a preamble and eleven sections with a total of 87 articles. In addition, the document contains several preliminaries concerning basic concepts as well as appendices that are not part of the constitution proper. The text considers the Sultan's power absolute and not limited or bound by basic or human rights. A series of constitutional reforms between 2004 and 2006 introduced the free exercise of religious beliefs as the only basic right (Art. 3, I). Beyond that, constitutional reforms in the mid-2000s confirmed the Sultan's prerogative to wield all executive and legislative powers and amended the section concerning the Legislative Council (*Majlis Mesyuarat Negara*). Under the revised 2004 Constitution, the Sultan is now free to adopt or reject any amendment to the constitution, and the Legislative Council is further proscribed from discussing any matters that might reduce the rights and powers of the Sultan and his family or matters relating to the national doctrine of the Malay Islamic Monarchy (Ng 2011, p. 39). Furthermore, while already suspended under emergency rule since 1962, the constitutional review of laws and royal decrees is now explicitly banned (Art. 84c). Finally, the constitution now extends complete legal immunity to the Sultan and any government official acting on behalf or under the authority of the Sultan (Art. 84b). The amendments also clarified that Brunei's official religion is Islam according to the interpretation of the *Shafi'i* school, one of the four schools of legal thought in Sunni Islam. Changes to the appendix constitutions now also clarify that a number of influential government offices can only be held by Malay Muslims, including that of the Auditor General, the Chairman of the Public Service Commission, and cabinet ministers (Art. 3, V).

2.3   System of Government

According to the constitution, Brunei is a hereditary constitutional monarchy. In practice, however, the country has to be considered an absolute monarchy: The position of the monarch is not functionally separate from the legislature and the government, and an elected parliament does not share power with the Sultan (Friske 2008, p. 17). In addition, the Sultan possesses absolute sovereignty in religious and political matters and presents the highest judicial authority. The current Sultan and Official Head of State (*Yang-Di Pertuan*) of Brunei is Hassanal Bolkiah,[3] who succeeded to the throne in 1967.

Succession to the throne, legal age requirements, and regency periods are regulated in the Succession and Regency Proclamation of 1959. Usually, the Sultan

---

[3]The Sultan's full name, including his patronymic, is Sultan Haji Hassanal Bolkiah Mu'izzaddin Waddaulah ibni Al-Marhum Sultan Haji Omar Ali Saifuddien Sa'adul Khairi Waddien.

appoints a crown prince as his heir during his life time. In case the Sultan has not provided for an heir, an heir is designated by a Council of Succession. If necessary, a Council of Regency appointed by the Sultan conducts all government affairs until the designated heir comes of age. Both the Council of Succession and the Council of Regency are formed from Brunei's hereditary nobility (Sidhu 2010, p. 68). In addition to his duties as head of state, the constitution assigns three key roles to the Sultan: head of religion, prime minister, and commander-in-chief of the armed forces (Art. 3). The Sultan is assisted by five constitutionally mandated government bodies. The Sultan presides over the Council of Ministers (Art. 20–22) in his role as prime minister and acts as his own minister of defence since 1986 and minister of finance since 1998 (Damit 2002, p. 86). He can appoint and dismiss other ministers at will, and the constitution does not detail the number or portfolio of the different ministries. Brunei currently has 16 ministers, including the state-appointed Mufti and the attorney general. To be eligible for a ministerial post, a candidate has to be a Bruneian citizen, but the Sultan is free to make exceptions. Traditionally, several important cabinet posts are held by members of the royal family. Currently, the Sultan's brother serves as minister of foreign affairs and minister of trade and the crown prince serves as senior minister in the office of the prime minister. After independence, however, some ministerial posts were given to technocrats, and state-level and under-secretary positions in the cabinet were used to co-opt ethnic Chinese into the government apparatus (Talib 2002, p. 137). The Privy Council (*Majlis Mesyuarat Di-Raja*, Art. 5–8) advises the Sultan on constitutional amendments, on matters of honorary titles and ceremonial offices, as well as on questions regarding succession and regency. While the Council has no formal political authority, it is an important instrument for the Sultan to integrate the traditional nobility into the political system and foster individual loyalty among nobles (Braighlinn 1992). The Religious Council (*Majlis Ugama Islam*, Art. 3) advises the Sultan in matters relating to Islam and assists in drafting religious laws whereas the *Adat Istiadat Council* (Majlis Mesyuarat Adat Istiadat, Art. 3a) assists the Sultan in matters of Malay traditional rights and customs.

Finally, the Sultanate's autocratic character also determines the organization and role of the Legislative Council (Majlis Mesyuarat Negara, Art. 23–38 and Art. 39–55). The Sultan alone has right of initiative. While the Council is to be consulted before bills are enacted into law and can debate annual budget proposals in closed session, its decisions and recommendations are not binding. The Sultan can enact laws and the national budget without the Council's consent. In addition, the Sultan also has unlimited power to issue emergency decrees, which are immediately legally binding (Tey 2007, p. 271). Even in its internal affairs, the *Majlis Mesyuarat Negara* is not an independent body since the Sultan determines its size, term of office, and mode of creation by proclamation. The Sultan can suspend or dismiss any councilor at any time (Art. 31). Originally, the Legislative Council consisted of 33 members, 16 of which were determined through indirect elections. The remaining members were either appointed directly by the Sultan or became members ex officio as heads of other government bodies. From 1970 to 1984, the Sultan appointed councillors, and between 1984 and 2004 it was suspended before the Sultan re-established the Council in 2004 as a fully appointed body. After the recent constitutional reforms, the Legislative Council can have no more than 51 members. The prime minister, the minister for foreign affairs, and the Crown Prince are among the six ex officio members. Up to 30 members can be appointed by the Sultan and no more than 15 members can be determined in elections. The first such election since 1965 was held in 2011. Village elders and the heads of the country's four districts formed an electoral college that elected nine members for the current Council. Altogether, the Council currently has 35 members, all of whom have to be Bruneian citizens and at least 20 years of age (Thambipillai 2012; Case 2012).

2.4 Legal and Judicial System

Brunei's legal system mixes British common law and the *Shafi'i* Islamic school, the latter of which is the major source of law in the country. The court system is bifurcated into Islamic courts that deal with matters like matrimonial or inheritance law and Sharia-regulated criminal cases and secular courts modeled after the British system. The state courts are organized in three tiers: lower magistrate courts, intermediate courts, and the Supreme Court as the court of last resort and appellate court of the country. The judicial reforms in 1998 and 2000 abolished the traditional *kadi* court system and introduced a three-tiered system of Sharia courts (Lindsey and Steiner 2012, p. 445). These courts have exclusive jurisdiction over all matters under Islamic law including criminal proceedings, if Sharia law applies. All national citizens and permanent residents are subject to these courts, irrespective of their individual religious faith. In the case of jurisdictional conflict between state and religious courts, decisions of the Sharia courts take precedent over their secular counterparts (Lindsey and Steiner 2012, p. 460).

Brunei has no constitutional court as judicial review is irreconcilable with the Sultan's position as the sole source and center of executive, legislative, and juridical power. Similarly, the legal immunity granted to the Sultan and those who act on his behalf or under his authority rules out any legal redress in administrative disputes. Government officials are only subject to judicial procedure in their private and never in their official capacity (Cheong 2001).

The Sultan appoints all judges. Their tenure ends when they turn 65, although the Sultan can grant extensions. The Ministry of Justice was dissolved as an autonomous body in the late 1990s. Instead of a separate ministry, the State Judicial Department, subordinate to the Prime Minister's office, now audits and monitors the administrative conduct of both secular and religious courts. As head of religion, the Sultan formally presides over the Islamic courts, but in practice the Ministry of Religious Affairs and the Office of the State Mufti monitor the court's adjudication. The state has a monopoly on Islamic legal opinions (*fatwa*). These can only be issued by the Religious Council appointed by the Sultan (Lindsey and Steiner 2012, p. 390).

Bruneian courts are known for their professionalism, especially compared to other countries in the region, dating back to its times as a British protectorate.[4] While most court positions today are held by Bruneian citizens, British influence persists because most judges study law in Great Britain or Malaysia.

The World Bank's Rule of Law Index ranks Brunei second in the region, surpassed only by Singapore. This is a counterintuitive finding considering the latent tension between parts of the Islamic legal code and basic civil liberties and principles of the rule of law, such as (gender) equality before the law as well as the complete lack of judicial independence and the legal accountability of government officials. Despite the opaque nature of the ruling family's business interests and the prevalent rent-seeking behavior among the elite,[5] the perceived level of corruption in the country is relatively low compared to other Southeast Asian countries (Transparency International 2015; World Bank 2017b).

2.5   Political Parties and Elections

Brunei is one of only five states in the world that does not hold any kind of representative national elections for the legislature (Groemping 2015).[6] Although the constitution, as noted, provides for a limited number of elected legislative councilors, no popular election has taken place since 1962.

Brunei's first political party, the Pan-Bornean PRB, was founded in 1956, making Brunei a latecomer in terms of political party development in the region. The PRB so far is the only political party to develop a party ideology and preside over an organized membership base (Sidhu 2010, p. 185). The PRB is also the only party ever to have participated in elections with its own chosen candidates, but it was quickly banned after the election following its participation in the 1962 antiroyal uprising.

Political parties were legalized again in 1985 but need authorization from the Ministry of Interior and are obliged to submit yearly reports on their activities to renew their registration. There is no formal party law, but political parties are regulated under the Societies Order of 2005, which applies to most kinds of social associations. Only full citizens are allowed to be members of a political party, and members of the public service or the armed forces are prohibited from joining parties altogether. This precludes a large number of citizens from becoming active in party politics and remains the most important obstacle for the development of a genuine party system (Saunders 1994, p. 185). Furthermore, since 1962, political

---

[4]Until 1988, Brunei's highest judicial authority also served as the presiding judge in the Supreme Court of the British Hong Kong Crown Colony.

[5]One example is the collapse of the Amedeo conglomerate in 1998 that was led by Prince Muda Haji Jefri Bolkiah, the country's then Minister of Finance and Head of BIA. The prince supposedly embezzled 14.8 billion USD and transferred them to foreign accounts (Gunn 2008).

[6]The others are PR China, Saudi Arabia, the United Arab Emirates, and Qatar.

parties are not allowed to nominate their own candidates in national or local elections. Members for the Legislative Council, village elders, and district heads are elected as individuals. It, therefore, comes as no surprise that political parties have failed to establish themselves as meaningful political organizations (Sidhu 2010, pp. 185–187).

Currently, the National Development Party (PP) is the only party that has partially overcome these difficulties and avoided complete collapse. The National Democratic Party of Brunei (BNDP), founded in 1985, quickly lost its permit after several members publicly criticized the government. Royalist parties like the National Solidarity Party of Brunei (PPKB) and the Brunei People's Awareness Party (PAKAR) remained largely inactive and were deleted from the registry of associations in 2005 and 2008, respectively. With the major exception of the PRB, all Bruneian parties to date contain only several dozen to a few hundred individuals, and none serve any governmental or electoral function. Yet the autocratic government benefits from their existence because the semblance of political reform and legal opposition they create deflects some foreign criticism of the regime (Horton 2005, p. 181; Roberts and Onn 2009, p. 64).

2.6   State Administration

The territory of Brunei is administratively divided into districts and municipalities (*daerah*), subdistricts (*mukim*), and villages (*kampong*) or long house communities, which is the traditional form of settlement of several of Brunei's indigenous groups. About 70% of the country is covered by tropical rainforests, and 70% of the population is concentrated in Brunei's main district of Brunei-Muara and its 18 subdistricts, which includes the national capital Banda Seri Begawan. The remaining population is divided between the southwestern Belait district (eight subdistricts, 16.5% of the population), the southern Tutong district (eight subdistricts, 11%), and Temburong district (five subdistricts, 2.5%), which are physically separate from the rest of Brunei by the Limbang corridor that is part of the Malaysian state Sarawak (DEPD 2011). Most of the country's Chinese minority lives in the urban areas of the Brunei-Muara and Belait districts. Belait is also the center of Brunei's oil and natural gas sector, and a permanent British military contingent and the Gurkha Reserve Unit are garrisoned there to protect the Seria oil fields.

There are no formal regulations regarding local government bodies. The district governments and municipalities are subordinate to the Ministry of Home Affairs and the Prime Minister's Office. Village elders and district heads are elected by the local population after the candidates—often former bureaucrats or military officers—are cleared by the government (Heiduk 2008, p. 55). As government officials, they receive a salary and are bound by government instructions. Their official role is mostly limited to mediating local conflict and acting as an intermediary between the local population and the state administration (Case 1996, p. 131; Damit 2004, 2007, p. 104). The quality of infrastructure and government services is relatively even across districts because of Brunei's small size and compares favorably to the rest of the region. Consequently, and because of the relatively homogenous population, there is little vertical conflict among different ethnic groups. Lingering tensions with Malaysia about contested border territories were resolved peacefully in 2009.

2.7   Civil–Military Relations and the Security Sector

The impressive oil and gas revenues allow the government to provide for a large security apparatus. The government spent an average of around 15% of its total budget for security and military defense during the last decade. In the region, it was outspent only by Singapore (BICC 2016; IISS 2017). The seeming decline in military expenditure relative to GDP from an average of more than 6% down to about 2.5% in recent years (see Fig. 2.2) does not reflect an absolute decline. Instead, this is caused by an expansion of the overall GDP after oil revenue increased since the late 1990s. Considering this expenditure, the security sector containing 11,400 military and police personnel, and the welfare benefits they enjoy, can be considered part of Brunei's "shellfare" system.

Brunei's security sector consists of three main services: The Royal Brunei Armed Forces (RBAF), the Gurkha Reserve Unit (GRU), and the Royal Brunei Police (RBP), which also includes paramilitary units. Roughly 80% of Brunei's defense and security spending goes to the Armed Forces and the Gurkha Reserve Unit. The RBAF are an all-voluntary force that only accepts citizens with a Malay ethnic background into its ranks. In 2013, about 7000 soldiers and officers were on active duty, most of them in the army. While about 60% of the defense budget covers

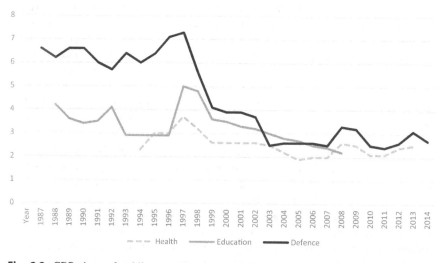

Fig. 2.2 GDP share of public expenditure for defense, health, and education in percentage (1988–2015). Source: World Bank (2017a)

personnel cost, Brunei has also invested in a range of modern equipment. The focus on technology—rather than manpower—meant that a lack of qualified personnel occasionally delayed the commissioning of new weapon systems (Kershaw 2011, p. 113). The RBAF are the embodiment of the Bruneian nation and symbolize the country's sovereignty. While essentially an external defense force with limited responsibilities in domestic security, Bruneian troops have also participated in multinational peace operations, including Cambodia (1993/1998), Aceh (2005), Mindanao (2004), and Lebanon (2011). In addition, the military provides support for the civilian government in disaster management and in counterterrorism as well as for counterinsurgency operations (Ministry of Defence 2015). In addition, a British Army Gurkha Battalion has been stationed in Brunei since 1962 under the terms of a mutual defense agreement. Furthermore, Singapore has established two military training camps in Brunei, and there is a close military cooperation between the two countries (Huxley 2000). The RBAF is under the authority of the Ministry of Defense, but the Sultan remains commander-in-chief.

The remaining two security services guarantee the country's domestic security and provide repressive means to protect the authoritarian regime in case of internal unrest. The Royal Bruneian Police is controlled by the Sultan in his role as prime minister and commands about 4400 men, 1700 members of them with paramilitary training and equipment. Key priorities for the police force in Brunei include maintaining public order, crime prevention, but also border policing, counterterrorism, and monitoring of opposition activities. With a ratio of slightly more than 1000 police officers per 100,000 people, Brunei is one of the best-policed nations in Asia (authors' calculations based on Interpol 2014; Small Arms Survey 2013). Police violence and repression against the population are relatively rare, not least because the crime rate and the level of political activities are low. Still, like Singapore, Brunei can rely on the Internal Security Act (ISA), a legacy of colonial rule. The ISA allows the Ministry of Home Affairs and the police to arrest anybody suspected of having acted or being likely to act in a way that would threaten security without evidence or a warrant, hold suspects incommunicado for investigation, and detain them indefinitely, though in recent decades it has been rarely used. Finally, the Gurkha Reserve Unit, a paramilitary force, is under the authority of the Sultan in his role as minister of defence. It was recruited in 1974 from former soldiers of British Gurkha Regiments, British officers, and retired members of the Singaporean Police. The overall strength of the GRU varies between 400 and 2000 troops and officers (Sidhu 2010; IISS 2017), and its key tasks are protecting the Seria oil fields, public facilities, and government offices. In the framework of Brunei's civil–military relations, the unit also serves as an organizational counterweight to the military and provides the Sultan's personal security detail.

2.8 Civil Society and Media System

Civil society, conceptualized as an intermediary realm between the differentiated spheres of the private, the economy, and the state, in which public actors articulate and organize social interests, values, and demands (Croissant 2000), is extremely weak in Brunei. Legal and political constraints, the exclusion of the Chinese minority, the vertical structure of society, and the group formation effect of the rentier state (cf. Ross 2001) make nonhierarchical interaction across ethnic, religious, or socioeconomic cleavages very difficult and have precluded the creation of civic associations, especially among the state dependent middle class and the rank of entrepreneurs (Gunn 1999, p. 228; King 2008, p. 78). The Societies Order of 2005 restricts freedom of association and organized political activities by requiring organizations of more than ten people to register with the government, and the government enjoys full discretion to register or dissolve such groups. Only registered parties and associations may engage in organized political activity, and political speeches are tightly regulated. Similarly, unionism is largely moribund after the PRB-dominated Brunei United Labor Front was banned in 1963 (Leake 1990, p. 123). Additional factors preclude the formation of stronger unions, including the ban on government employees joining unions and the fact that most workers in the petroleum and gas industry and the construction sector are foreign overseas workers who are on temporary visas and come from Asian countries with weak traditions of unionism. In conjunction with strict regulations of religious activities by the Ministry of Religion, the absence of legal guarantees for the freedom of opinion and the freedom of assembly and speech, and constant surveillance by the government and police, this allows the state to effectively curtail associational life (Roberts and Onn 2009, p. 63).

Brunei's media also remain tightly constrained. Nationwide access to TV and radio and the internet is widely accessible, but authorities monitor online material, and all domestic newspapers, radio stations, and television channels are linked to the government; for example, two of the three daily newspapers are owned by a brother of the Sultan.[7] Newspapers and magazines, including foreign editions, need a permit that is issued and renewed by the Ministry of Home Affairs on an annual basis. Self-censorship is common among journalists. This is reflected in Brunei's position in the Press Freedom Index, where it is consistently ranked in the last third of the sampled countries, but still well ahead of most of its regional neighbors (156th of 180 countries; Reporters Without Borders 2017).

There is a lack of systematic research and valid data on the political attitudes and political culture of Brunei's population.[8] Restrictions on international and local researchers alike have rendered systematic attempts to gather survey data difficult, and the empirical base for analyses and conclusions is thereby narrow (King 2008, pp. 25, 31). However, at least in rural Brunei, conservative attitudes colored by Islam, which are prevalent in rural areas across maritime Southeast Asia, the lack of opportunities for political participation, and the internal cohesion of society have so far inhibited the politicization of the population (Kershaw 2011, p. 110).

---

[7]In Brunei, 71.4% of the population has access to the internet—behind Singapore with 81.2 and slightly ahead of Malaysia with its 69.6% (Internet World Stats 2017).

[8]Brunei, East Timor, and Laos are the only countries in the region for which the Asian Barometer Survey does not provide any data.

Despite the absence of any significant challenge to royal supremacy since independence in 1984, the Sultanate has attempted to create new techniques of legitimation. One such instrument is the concept of the Malay Islamic Monarchy. The MIB doctrine was developed by the former Director for Information, Ustaz Badaruddin (an Islamic scholar); was first mentioned by Sultan Hassanal Bolkiah in his independence proclamation on January 1, 1984; and was officially proclaimed on the Sultan's 44th birthday in 1990 (Braighlinn 1992, p. 19). As a means of "self-legitimization" for the monarchy, it rests on three key elements (Talib 2002, p. 143): (1) The monarchy as custodian of Malay language, culture, and tradition; (2) the monarchy as custodian of Islam and Islamic law; and (3) the Malay Sultanate as a form of absolute monarchy ordained by god, cutting across socioeconomic cleavages, albeit not across ethnic or religious lines (Saunders 1994, p. 187; Lindsey and Steiner 2012, p. 507). The MIB, therefore, constitutes an attempt to legitimate the absolute monarchy by the sanctity of (invented) tradition and stands in stark contrast to the Sultan's subordination to British authority before the 1960s (Braighlinn 1992; Talib 2002, p. 143).

The adoption of the title "Head of Religion" in 2004 and the religious emphasis it signifies is another expression of this attempted traditionalization of personal rule and has been flanked by an ongoing Islamization of public life (Saunders 1994, p. 188, 170). The national doctrine is now part of the school and university curriculum (Lindsey and Steiner 2012, p. 431), and the government has become an active patron of religious boarding schools, the Mecca pilgrimage, and the development of an Islamic banking system. The introduction of Sharia courts and the Sultan's announcement in October 2012 that corporal punishment for heinous crimes (*hudud*) would henceforth be applied in Brunei are likely further attempts to stress the regime's Islamic credentials. In essence, the MIB concept has proclaimed the ideal of a pious and benevolent dictator working for the social and economic well-being of his subjects (Braighlinn 1992, p. 29; Kershaw 2001, p. 21).

2.9 Outlook

As the only ruling monarchy in Southeast Asia, the Sultanate of Brunei is often seen as a political anachronism in the region. Yet it is also a beacon of political stability in Southeast Asia. Following recent studies on the stability of authoritarian regimes, which emphasize the importance of legitimation, co-optation, and repression for the reproduction of authoritarian rule, it could be argued that the royalist regime has managed to strike a balance between legitimation, co-optation, and repression as the three pillars of authoritarian rule.[9] Regarding their relative importance for

---

[9]Co-optation describes any attempt to buy fealty or compliance, whereas repression is meant to coerce it. Finally, legitimation attempts to induce voluntary compliance through tradition, charisma, or reference to public welfare, popular sovereignty, or utopian ideology (Gerschewski et al. 2013) or instruments (Backes 2016).

regime stability and political control in Brunei, these three "pillars" or "strategies" of authoritarian rule can be arranged in the following order: As in all authoritarian regimes, repression plays a role in Brunei. This is reflected not least by the reports of international organizations, such as Freedom House, Amnesty International, and Reporters without Borders. However, if and when repression takes place, it occurs mainly in its softer forms of social control and surveillance, while hard repression such as torture, political murder, or even terror has little to do with the political reality in Brunei. More important for regime resilience, compared to repression, is the co-optation of Malay elites and the population. Yet contrary to the current conventional wisdom of authoritarianism studies (Gandhi 2008; Schedler 2009; Pepinsky 2014), representative institutions like elections, parliaments, and parties are irrelevant for the inner workings of the absolute monarchy. Instead, the government uses oil and gas revenue to provide material incentives in exchange for political loyalty. Finally, the concept of *"Melayu Islam Beraja"* is meant to bolster the royalist regime's legitimacy, even though it remains unclear how strongly the MIB actually resonates with the beliefs and attitudes of its citizens. Whether the concept of MIB will be sustainable in the long run remains an open question. Of lesser importance is another stabilizing factor identified by Oliver Schlumberger in his work on rentier states in the Middle East. Schlumberger (2006) argues that the international buyers of oil and natural gas are reluctant to jeopardize their established business relationships with autocratic rulers in the Arab world and therefore forgo active democracy promotion in oil exporting countries. However, Brunei's most important export markets are Japan, South Korea, the ASEAN countries, and China, none of which have a history of active democracy promotion anyway. Nevertheless, the primacy of economic linkages to autocratic regimes and Brunei's position in the global periphery further contribute to the stability of the absolute monarchy. There are no signs that the royalist social contract may break down or that the cohesion of the ruling coalition could collapse.

However, there are a number of challenges that could undermine its paternalistic social contract and threaten political stability in the future. First, rentier economies generally have little incentive to modernize and diversify their economic bases (Beck and Schlumberger 1999; Ross 2001; Beck 2007). For the foreseeable future, Brunei's economic growth will be closely intertwined with the international oil and gas market prices. At its height in 1985, the petro-sector made up 76.1% of GDP (Saunders 1994, p. 165). Even though this share was reduced to around 40% in 2000, it has increased again since 2005, largely due to the rise in oil and gas prices (cf. Fig. 2.1). In addition, the opportunities for the implementation of a viable strategy of economic diversification is limited by a lack of skilled workers, capital and management skills, the conservative and rigorous character of the political system, and the vested interests of the dominant elite coalition (Cleary 2014, p. 123; Odano and Islam 2013). Another challenge concerns the weak integration of the Chinese minority into Brunei politics and society. The Islamization of society in recent decades, which has been promoted under the concept of *"Melayu Islam Beraja"* as a means of political legitimation, is accompanied by the further cultural marginalization of the Chinese, indigenous, and Christian minorities and illustrates the exclusive nature of royalist nation-building in Brunei. Finally, the monarchy needs to continually legitimate the absence of democratic institutions and more meaningful opportunities for political participation. While the national doctrine of MIB has become the most important legitimation of the Sultan's claim to absolute power (Lindsey and Steiner 2012, pp. 323–324, 506), it is a double-edged sword, as the public could expect a higher standard of ethical conduct from the Sultan himself and members of the ruling dynasty. Moreover, this legitimation strategy is vulnerable to challenges by religious actors who might propose their own radical and transnational notion of Islam and politics.

References

Backes, U. (2016). 'Ideocracy': A sketch on the history of a concept. In U. Backes & S. Kailitz (Eds.), *Ideocracies in comparison: Legitimation – co-optation – repression* (pp. 13–39). London: Routledge.

Beblawi, H., & Luciani, G. (1987). *The Rentier state: Nation, state and integration in the Arab world*. London: Croom Helm.

Beck, M. (2007). Der Rentierstaats-Ansatz und das Problem abweichender Fälle. *Zeitschrift für Internationale Beziehungen, 14*, 43–70. https://doi.org/10.5771/0946-7165-2007-1-43

Beck, M., & Schlumberger, O. (1999). Der Vordere Orient: ein entwicklungspolitischer Sonderfall?: Rentenökonomie, Markt und Liberalisierung. In P. Pawelka & H.-G. Wehling (Eds.), *Der Vordere Orient an der Schwelle zum 21. Jahrhundert* (pp. 57–79). Wiesbaden: Westdeutscher Verlag.

BICC. (2013). *Global militarization index 2012*. Bonn: Bonn International Center for Conversion.

BICC. (2016). *Global militarization index 2015*. Bonn: Bonn International Center for Conversion.

Braighlinn, G. (1992). *Ideological innovation under monarchy: Aspects of legitimation activity in contemporary Brunei*. Amsterdam: VU University Press.

Case, W. (1996). Brunei Darussalam in 1995: New party politics and diplomatic presence. *Asian Survey, 36*, 130–134. https://doi.org/10.2307/2645809

Case, W. (2012). Brunei in 2011: Early electoralism and social progress. *Asian Survey, 52*, 233–237. https://doi.org/10.1525/as.2012.52.1.233

CIA. (2017). *The World Factbook*. Retrieved June 23, 2017, from https://www.cia.gov/library/publications/the-world-factbook/

Cheong, D. (2001). *Administrative accountability and the law in Brunei Darussalam*. Bandar Seri Begawan: Center for Strategic and Policy Studies.

Cleary, M. (2014). *Oil, economic development and diversification in Brunei Darussalam*. London: Macmillan.

Croissant, A. (2000). Zivilgesellschaft und Transformation: Ein internationaler Vergleich. In W. Merkel (Ed.), *Systemwechsel 5: Zivilgesellschaft und Transformation* (pp. 9–49). Opladen: Leske & Budrich.

Damit, M. Y. b. A. (2002). Negara Brunei Darussalam: Light at the end of the tunnel. *Southeast Asian Affairs*, 81–91. https://doi.org/10.1355/SEAA02E

Damit, M. Y. b. A. (2004). Brunei Darussalam: Steady ahead. *Southeast. Southeast Asian Affairs*, 63–70.

Damit, M. Y. b. A. (2007). Brunei Darussalam: Towards a new era. *Southeast Asian Affairs*, 103–113.

DEPD. (2010). *Brunei Darussalam statistical yearbook 2010*. Bandar Seri Begawan: Department of Economic Planning and Development.

DEPD. (2011). *Brunei Darussalam statistical yearbook 2011*. Bandar Seri Begawan: Department of Economic Planning and Development.

Desai, R. M., Olofsgard, A., & Yousef, T. M. (2009). The logic of authoritarian bargains. *Economics & Politics, 21*, 93–125. https://doi.org/10.1111/j.1468-0343.2008.00337.x

Friske, T. (2008). Monarchien—Überblick und Systematik. In G. Riescher & A. Thumfahrt (Eds.), *Monarchien* (pp. 14–24). Baden-Baden: Nomos.

Gandhi, J. (2008). *Political institutions under dictatorship.* Cambridge: Cambridge University Press.

Gerschewski, J., Merkel, W., Schmotz, A., Stefes, C., & Tanneberg, D. (2013). Warum überleben Diktaturen? In S. Kailitz & P. Köllner (Eds.), *Autokratien im Vergleich* (pp. 111–136). Baden-Baden: Nomos.

Groemping, M. (2015). *Southeast Asian elections worst in the world.* Accessed June 22, 2015, from http://www.newmandala.org/southeast-asian-elections-worst-in-the-world/

Gunn, G. C. (1993). Rentier capitalism in Negara Brunei Darussalam. In K. Hewison, R. Robison, & G. Rodan (Eds.), *Southeast Asia in the 1990s* (pp. 109–132). St. Leonards: Allen & Unwin.

Gunn, G. C. (1999). *Language, power and ideology in Brunei Darussalam.* Athens: Ohio University Center for International Studies.

Gunn, G. C. (2008). Brunei Darussalam: Dynastic fallout, economic crisis and recovery? Accessed June 1, 2017, from http://naosite.lb.nagasaki-u.ac.jp/dspace/bitstream/10069/20942/5/toasia_49_01.pdf

Heiduk, F. (2008). Brunei. In G. Riescher & A. Thumfahrt (Eds.), *Monarchien.* Baden-Baden: Nomos.

Herb, M. (2005). No representation without taxation?: Rents, development, and democracy. *Comparative Politics, 37*, 297. https://doi.org/10.2307/20072891

Horton, A. V. M. (2005). Brunei in 2004: Window-dressing an Islamizing Sultanate. *Asian Survey, 45*, 180–185. https://doi.org/10.1525/as.2005.45.1.180

Huxley, T. (2000). *Defending the Lion City: The armed forces of Singapore.* St Leonards: Allen & Unwin.

IISS. (2014). *The military balance 2014: International Institute for Strategic Studies.* London: Oxford University Press.

IISS. (2017). *The military balance 2017: International Institute for Strategic Studies.* London: Oxford University Press.

IMF. (2006). *Brunei Darussalam: Statistical Appendix.* IMF Country Report No. 06/428.

IMF. (2012). *Brunei Darussalam: Statistical Appendix.* IMF Country Report No. 12/193.

Internet World Stats. (2017). *Internet usage statistics: World internet users and 2017 population stats.* https://www.internetworldstats.com/stats.htm

Interpol. (2014). Brunei. Accessed June 1, 2017, from https://www.interpol.int/Member-countries/Asia-South-Pacific/Brunei

Kershaw, R. (2001). *Monarchy in South-East Asia: The faces of tradition in transition.* London: Routledge.

Kershaw, R. (2011). The Last Brunei revolt?: A case study of microstate (in-)security. *Internationales Asienforum, 42*(1-2), 107–134.

King, V. (2008). The middle class in Southeast Asia: Diversities, identities, comparisions and the Vietnamese case. *International Journal of Asia Pacific Studies, 4*(2), 73–109.

Leake, D. (1990). *Brunei: The modern Southeast Asian Islamic Sultanate.* Kuala Lumpur: Forum.

Lindsey, T., & Steiner, K. (2012). *Islam, law and the State in Southeast Asia.* New York: I.B. Tauris.

Ministry of Defence. (2015). *RBAF introduction.* Accessed June 1, 2017, from http://www.mindef.gov.bn/SitePages/RBAF%20Introduction.aspx

Ng, J. (2011). The State of Brunei Darussalam: Rule of law for Human Rights. In Human Rights Resource Center (Ed.), *The ASEAN region: A baseline study* (pp. 33–51). Depok: University of Indonesia.

Odano, S., & Islam, S. (2013). Economic development in a small open economy with a rich resource endowment: The case of Brunei. *The Hikone Ronso, 398*, 84–96.

Pepinsky, T. B. (2014). The institutional turn in comparative authoritarianism. *British Journal of Political Science, 44*(3), 631–653. https://doi.org/10.1017/S0007123413000021.

Reporters Without Borders. (2017). 2017 World Press Freedom Index: Dashed hopes after Spring. RSF. Accessed June 22, 2017, from https://rsf.org/en/ranking

Roberts, C., & Onn, L. P. (*2009*). Brunei Darussalam: Cautious on political reform, comfortable in ASEAN, pushing for economic diversification. *Southeast Asian Affairs, 2009*, 63–74.

Ross, M. (2001). Does oil hinder democracy? *World Politics, 53*(3), 325–361.

Saim, H. (2009). Social protection in Brunei Darussalam: Current state and challenges. In M. G. Asher, S. Oum, & F. Parulian (Eds.), *Social protection in East Asia: Current state and challenges. ERIA research project report* (pp. 124–156). ERIA: Jakarta.

Saunders, G. (1994). *A history of Brunei*. Kuala Lumpur: Oxford University Press.

Schedler, A. (2009). The new institutionalism in the study of authoritarian regimes. *Totalitarianism and Democracy, 6*(2), 323–340.

Schlumberger, O. (2006). Rents, reform, and authoritarianism in the Middle East. *Internationale Politik und Gesellschaft, 2*, 43–57.

Sidhu, J. S. (2010). *Historical dictionary of Brunei Darussalam* (2nd ed.). Lanham, MD: Rowman & Littlefield.

Singh, R. (1984). *Brunei, 1839-1983: The problems of political survival*. Singapore: Oxford University Press.

Small Arms Survey. (2013). *Small Arms Survey* 2013. Accessed June 1, 2017, from http://www.smallarmssurvey.org/publications/by-type/yearbook/small-arms-survey-2013.html

Talib, N. (2002). A resilient monarchy: The sultanate of Brunei and regime legitimacy in an era of democratic nation-states. *New Zealand Journal of Asian Studies, 4*(2), 134–147.

Tey, T. (2007). Brunei's revamped constitution: The sultan as the Grundnorm? *Australian Journal of Asian Law, 9*(2), 264–288.

Tey, T. (2008). Brunei: Entrenching an absolute monarchy. *Constitutionalism in Southeast Asia, 2*, 7–37.

Thambipillai, P. (*2012*). Brunei: Making progress slowly. *Southeast Asian Affairs, 2012*, 89–100.

Transparency International. (2015). *Corruption perception index*. Accessed June 1, 2017, from https://www.transparency.org/news/feature/corruption_perceptions_index_2016

World Bank. (2017a). *World development indicators*. http://data.worldbank.org/products/wdi

World Bank. (2017b). *Worldwide governance indicators*. http://data.worldbank.org/data-catalog/worldwide-governance-indicators

Cambodia: From UN-Led Peace-Building to Post-Genocidal Authoritarianism

3

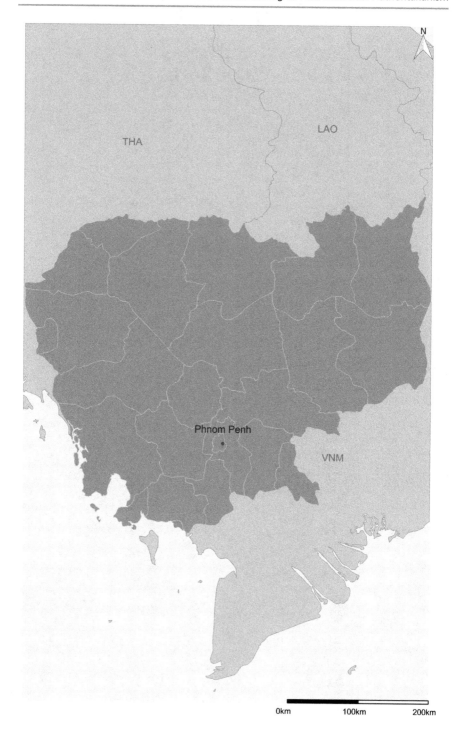

3.1 Historical Background

In the past 25 years, the Kingdom of Cambodia has experienced a threefold transformation: from civil war to postwar reconstruction, from a socialist one-party state to a multiparty electoral system, and from a centrally planned economy to a market economy (see Table 3.1 for the Country Profile). Following the 1991 Paris Peace Accords, the United Nations Transitional Authority in Cambodia (UNTAC) cleared the way for the country's transition from civil war to a postwar order. The end of the UNTAC period in 1993 was the onset of significant reform attempts in Cambodia's government, politics, economy, and society. Most importantly, the one-party state of the Cambodian People's Party (CPP) was replaced by a multiparty system, which included regular elections, multiparty competition, and an emerging civil society. However, most political scientists seem to agree that regular multiparty competitive elections coexist with tenuous civil and political rights and weak horizontal and vertical accountability. Furthermore, the dominant party is in control of the electoral process. Therefore, scholars disagree whether the political regime should be classified as an "unconsolidated democracy" (Un 2004), a "dominant party illiberal democracy" (Peou 2006), "electoral authoritarianism" (Diamond et al. 2013), "competitive authoritarianism" (Levitsky and Way 2010), or a "semi-democracy" (Case 2015).

The history of the Khmer Empire of Angkor, the historical predecessor of what is today the Kingdom of Cambodia, can be traced back to the ninth century CE. At the height of its power in the thirteenth century, the Angkor Empire stretched from the southern parts of Laos across the Mekong Delta to southern parts of Thailand

Table 3.1 Country profile Cambodia

Population	Year of full national sovereignty	Form of government
16,204,486 Mio	1953	Monarchy
Total area	**Current constitution promulgated**	**Head of State**
181,035 km^2	1993	King Norodom Sihamoni (since 2004)
GDP p.c. (2005 PPP, 2012)	**Official language**	**Head of government**
2149	Khmer	Hun Sen (since 1985)
Ethnic groups	**Democracy Score (BTI 2016)**	**System of government**
Khmer 90%, Vietnamese 5%, Chinese 1%, others 4%	3.73 (range from 1 to 10, higher scores indicate higher levels of democracy)	Cabinet system
Religions	**Regime type**	**Cabinet type**
Buddhists 96.9%, Muslims 1.9%, Other 1.2%	Autocracy	Single-party cabinet

Sources: CIA (2017), BTI (2016) and Pew Research Center (2016)

(Ricklefs 2010, pp. 44–45, 148–149). The Empire of Angkor survived until 1431, when it fell to Siam. Compared to the "Golden Age" of the Khmer Empire, the Khmer Kingdom lost much of its regional power and territory, a result of continued external threats by Siam and Champa (present-day Vietnam) as well as domestic succession disputes. By the early nineteenth century, the Vietnamese even directly administered Cambodia, "placing puppets on the throne and striving to assimilate the Khmers, whom they regarded as 'barbarians', into Vietnamese culture" (Tully 2005, p. 10). Squeezed between Siam and Vietnam, only the French arrival in 1860 precluded Cambodia's complete annexation. Seeking assistance in fending off Siam and Vietnam, the Cambodian King signed a protectorate agreement with France in August 1863. In 1887, the French proclaimed the establishment of the *Union Indochinoise*, or the Indochina Union, comprising Cambodia and the three constituent regions of Vietnam: Tonkin, Annam, and Cochin-China.[1] From 1897 on, Cambodia's chief colonial official, responsible to the French Governor General and appointed by the Ministry of Marine and Colonies in Paris, was a resident general (résident supérieur) who governed under the nominal authority of the Cambodian king (Tully 2002).

Although debt slavery and feudal landholding patterns were abolished by the French in 1884, and in 1913 a consultative council was created, the old Khmer elites still controlled the countryside (Tully 2002). Aside from collecting taxes more efficiently, the French did little to transform Cambodia's village-based economy, and infrastructure and industry remained rudimentary. Nevertheless, there was considerable immigration from other regions of French Indochina, which created a plural society similar to those of British Burma and Malaya (cf. Chaps. 6 and 7). While foreigners dominated the more developed sectors of the economy (i.e., rubber plantations) and the colonial bureaucracy expanded rapidly, French nationals held the highest positions, and even in the lower positions of the bureaucracy Cambodians found few opportunities as the colonial rulers preferred to fill these administrative posts with Vietnamese (Peou 2000).

In stark contrast to the Vietnamese-populated territories of Indochina, Cambodia remained relatively quiescent politically, although national consciousness was emerging among the handful of educated Khmer who composed the urban-based elite in the 1930s (Brocheux and Hémery 2011, Chap. 7). This began to change during World War II, when the French government in Vichy was forced to allow Japanese troops into the country. The Japanese encouraged King Norodom Sihanouk (1922–2012) to declare independence in March 1945, but momentum towards independence collapsed after the Japanese surrendered (Ricklefs 2010, pp. 311–312). In 1946, Cambodia was granted self-rule within the newly created French Union, and following the adoption of a new constitution in 1947, it had its protectorate status abolished in 1949. The Kingdom obtained full national sovereignty in November 1953.

---

[1]Laos was forced to join the Indochina Union in 1893 (cf. Chap. 5).

In 1955, King Sihanouk resigned and started to rule as prime minister in the new personalistic authoritarian regime. Sihanouk repressed both bourgeois and communist opposition to his personal regiment, the latter of which he termed the "Khmer Rouge." Following a policy of international neutrality, Sihanouk condoned the use of Cambodian territory as a refuge and supply route for South Vietnamese Communists (Peou 2000, pp. 40–41). In 1970, a US-sponsored coup d'état organized by General Lon Nol and a coalition of military officers and civilian elites against Sihanouk while he was abroad ushered in a period of military rule. In response, Sihanouk allied himself with the Khmer Rouge to enlist support from peasants and villagers (Heder 2004). In the ensuing civil war, republican troops under President Lon Nol quickly lost control over much of Cambodia to the Communists. The fall of Phnom Penh in April 1975 was followed by a 4-year reign of Khmer Rouge terror under the leadership of Pol Pot, during which approximately one-fifth of the population was murdered or died as a result of misrule (Kiernan 2003). Violence and terror was directed against ethnic minorities like the Vietnamese, Chinese, and the Muslim Cham as well as against bureaucrats and soldiers of the Republic, intellectuals, teachers, the middle class and landowners, as well as members of the regime (Kiernan 1998). Finally, the Khmer Rouge regime turned on itself, enacting a series of extensive purges that triggered the defection of many military and party cadres to Vietnam. When the xenophobic regime finally turned against Vietnam, Vietnamese troops invaded eastern Cambodia and ousted the Khmer Rouge in December 1978 (Peou 2000, pp. 101–102).

The pro-Vietnamese government of the People's Republic of Kampuchea (from 1989 on: State of Cambodia, SoC) immediately got involved in a low intensity war with the so-called Coalition Government of Democratic Kampuchea (CGDK), a three-party coalition of the Khmer Rouge, the royalist FUNCINPEC (Front uni national pour un Cambodge indépendant, neutre, pacifique, et coopératif), and the Khmer People's National Liberation Front (former pro-Lon Nol forces) formally led by Norodom Sihanouk. By the mid-1980s, neither Vietnam, the People's Revolutionary Party of Kampuchea (since 1991: Cambodian People's Party, CPP) under Prime Minister Hun Sen, nor the CGDK forces (with support from Thailand, China, and the United States) were in a position to win the confrontation.

Faced with military stalemate and domestic economic problems, the Vietnamese government withdrew its troops in 1989. The government in Phnom Penh could now no longer hope for victory, despite its continued numerical military advantage. Informal negotiations between the CGDK and SoC led to official peace talks in Paris in 1991. Under the guidance of the UN Security Council's Permanent Five and supported by the governments of Australia, Indonesia, Japan, and other concerned states, the warring parties signed the Paris Accords in 1991, which mandated the establishment of an interim government, the United Nations Transitional Authority in Cambodia (UNTAC).

While UNTAC was to supervise the Cambodian authorities in five areas of sovereign activity—defense, finance, foreign affairs, information, and public security—it exercised executive power only indirectly. The previously established bureaucratic structures, which were riddled with cadres of the ruling CPP, remained responsible for the execution of UNTAC's directives. In addition, the Paris Accords stipulated the creation of a Supreme National Council (SNC), a semi-sovereign power-sharing coalition of all four warring parties with Norodom Sihanouk as its titular head. Unlike the UN government in East Timor (cf. Chap. 11), UNTAC only possessed supreme government authority, while the CPP-controlled bureaucracy remained in charge of implementing its decisions. Most importantly, UNTAC failed to guarantee the neutrality of powerful ministries like Defense, Security, Home Affairs, and Finances (Findlay 1995, p. 155). Disarmament and demobilization measures affected about a quarter of all combatants, mostly FUNCINPEC and KPNLF and a few CPP troops but not the Khmer Rouge, who withdrew from the peace process in 1992 (Hendrickson 2001).

The election of a Constituent Assembly in May 1993, even though boycotted by the Khmer Rouge, turned out to be UNTAC's biggest success. Voter turnout was 89.5%, despite (empty) Khmer Rouge threats to disrupt the poll. The elections brought about a surprising victory for the FUNCINPEC led by Prince Ranariddh. FUNCINPEC and the Buddhist Liberal Democratic Party together won 68 of 120 total seats, whereas the CPP led by Hun Sen gained 51 seats. When the CPP refused to accept the election results, FUNCINPEC and the CPP formed a grand coalition led by Ranariddh and Hun Sen. Subsequently, the assembly adopted a constitution that envisaged a parliamentary monarchy with King Norodom Sihanouk as head of state. This ended the UNTAC mission in September 1993.

However, power-sharing proved to be fragile. In 1997, conflicts between the two major parties escalated into bloody fights, viewed by many as a coup d'etat by Hun Sen (CPP) against Ranariddh (FUNCINPEC). The reasons for this escalation remain a matter of dispute among observers (Roberts 2001). Notwithstanding its cause, in the aftermath of the 1997 "coup," an increasingly authoritarian regime emerged and persists until today. Due to objections from the international community, Hun Sen was forced to reinstate some standards of multiparty competition in the 1998 elections. Since then, the stability of Prime Minister Hun Sen's "personalist dictatorship" (Morgenbesser 2017) rests on four pillars. The first is the CPP's firm control over the electoral process, from the preparation of the polls to the postelection phase, which effectively prevents a level playing field and renders the electoral defeat of the CPP unthinkable. Second, the government uses its control over state institutions to co-opt strategic groups like the business sector, bureaucrats, CPP cadres, and security sector elites into the regime coalition by allocating posts as well as material and immaterial rewards in exchange for loyalty (Cock 2010, p. 529; Bader 2015). While the opposition has no access to material rewards or protection from state repression, those opposition politicians willing to switch sides can participate in the distribution of state resources and the exploitation of the national economy, like FUNCINPEC did after it became CPP's junior coalition partner between 1998 and 2013 (Hughes 2009, pp. 54–55). Secondly, Hun Sen's personal control over the security apparatus, decision-making processes within the CPP, the management of government affairs, and his access to state resources have created a form of "institutionalized nepotism" (Karbaum 2008, p. 276) in which power and authority are highly personalized and concentrated in his hands and help him maximize the likelihood of his political survival (Strangio 2014; Morgenbesser 2017).

Third, co-optation and personalization are flanked by repression against opposition politicians, journalists, and civil society activists. In addition to politically motivated violence, the government tolerates basic human rights violations committed by members of the regime coalition, such as land grabbing, illegal logging, and real estate speculation. While hard repression—i.e., political killings during election campaigns—has declined since the late 1990s (Hughes 2006; Un 2011), this does not signal increased political liberalization, but instead authoritarian consolidation, as the Hun Sen government no longer feels the need to rely on high-intensity repression to secure its political survival.

Fourth, the regime strives to legitimate its claim to power against its citizens and the international community. On the one hand, Hun Sen stylizes himself as the only person able to guarantee economic development and social peace (Karbaum 2008, pp. 332–333). Regular elections at the national and local level also serve regime legitimation functions, as the polls demonstrate the political strength of the ruling party and the electoral weakness of the other parties (Hughes 2009, p. 34). On the other hand, combining democratic forms with autocratic substance and playing the game of free but unfair multiparty elections also serve the purpose of legitimating the regime vis-à-vis international donors and Western governments who still have leverage over the Cambodian government (Hill and Menon 2013), even though new donors such as the People's Republic of China and South Korea have emerged as additional sources of developmental aid (Ear 2009, p. 153; Un 2013, pp. 147–148). Official Development Assistance—mostly from Western governments and international organizations such as the World Bank, IMF, and Asian Development Bank— has declined from 16.4% of GDP in 1995 and 120.7% of government expenditure in 2002 but still stood at 6.5% of GDP and 57.3% of government expenditure in 2011.

While the regime has seemingly struck an equilibrium with a combination of calibrated repression, legitimation, and co-optation, latent challenges to Hun Sen's rule remain. First, the existence of competitive elections gives the opposition a chance to challenge and weaken the regime within its institutional boundaries. The existence of nominally democratic institutions secures the persistence of arenas of political contestation, in which opposition parties or civil society organizations can challenge the autocratic incumbents (Levitsky and Way 2002, p. 54). Among these, the electoral arena is the most important. Though elections in Cambodia are not entirely free and fair, they are more than just a "facade," and the opposition does have a chance to achieve an electoral upset. This was the case in 2013, when a unified opposition won 55 out of 123 seats in the National Assembly.

Second, despite challenging legacies of genocide, civil war, poverty, and underdevelopment, post-UNTAC Cambodia has undergone a process of structural transformation and cultural change. Today, democratic values and ideals are much more prevalent than during the UNTAC period, and a rudimentary civil society and urban middle class have emerged (Un 2011, p. 546; Öjendal and Lilja 2009, p. 7). Even though Cambodian civil society is still fragile, under constant pressure from the government, and its NGOs are heavily dependent on external funding, civic associations can be extremely helpful to opposition parties, with civil society groups playing the role of "watchdogs." In addition, independent media coverage does exist as civil society organizations or opposition parties often produce their own publications. Hence, opposition groups and social movements have the chance to articulate protest and dissent. Furthermore, journalists and bloggers can also play the role of "watchdogs." While the government tries to minimize the exposure of citizens to alternative information and views by placing restrictions on autonomous means of communication, media content, and media consumption, the logic of co-optation and legitimation in Cambodian politics constrains the "menu of manipulation" (Schedler 2006) from which the Hun Sen government can choose specific strategies of containment vis-à-vis dissenting voices in civil society and the media.

Finally, the political loyalty of regime elites to the existing political order depends to a large extent on the ability of the government to buy their support by granting access to private goods for the members of its "winning coalition" (Bueno de Mesquita et al. 2003). These include direct monetary benefits, indirect monetary benefits (e.g., tax relief or exemptions), selective tolerance against corrupt officials and business practices, and impunity from criminal prosecution. So far, the Hun Sen government has been able to offer access to development funds, rents from the exploitation of natural resources like timber, as well as windfall profits from economic growth to buy loyalty from its supporters. However, economic growth is mainly driven by the expansion of the textile and tourism sectors, and liberalization of the national economy has increased its vulnerability to external shocks, demonstrated by the growth slump in 2009 in the aftermath of the global financial crisis. Hence, it remains to be seen if or how an increasingly diversified, integrated, and globalized economy will negatively affect the ability of the regime to guarantee an ongoing and sufficient flow of economic spoils.

3.2 Constitutional Development

Cambodia's 1993 Constitution[2] is a result of the implementation of the 1991 Paris Agreement, which required the election of a Constituent Assembly that was then to draft a constitution. After the 1993 election, the Constituent Assembly appointed a Drafting Committee with six members from FUNCINPEC, five from the Cambodian People's Party (CPP), and one from the Buddhist Liberal Democratic Party (BLDP), that is, roughly equal to each party's share of seats in the assembly (Marks 2010; Brandt 2005, p. 11). FUNCINPEC and the CPP effectively controlled the process, and there was little participation from either NGOs or members of the Assembly in the formulation of the constitution (Marks 2010). Tellingly, the deliberations of the committee were confidential and committee members were not allowed to talk about the drafting process in public (Menzel 2008). When the committee finally presented the UNTAC a draft, it

---

[2]Prior constitutions were promulgated in 1947, 1972, 1976, and 1981; the last one was amended in 1989 (Croissant 2014).

received harsh criticism due to the lack of provisions for an independent judiciary and protections of human and civil rights as well as the far transversal prerogatives it gave the Head of State (Shawcross 1994, p. 32). As a result, CPP leader Hun Sen and FUNCINPEC chairman, Prince Norodom Ranariddh, presented their own drafts to Prince Norodom Sihanouk, the titular head of the Supreme National Council, for his approval. On that basis, Sihanouk mediated a compromise and sidelined the Constituent Assembly's own drafting committee. After only five days of consultation, the assembly adopted the text on September 21, 1993 by a vote of 113 in favor of ratification, five against, and two abstentions (Findlay 1995, p. 9).

The 1993 constitution combines elements of the 1947 constitution—itself inspired by the French Fourth Republic—and the reformed socialist constitution of 1989 and is influenced by foreign constitutions, the UN Charta, and the Universal Declaration of Human Rights (Menzel 2008, p. 67). According to Article 1, Cambodia is an elective parliamentary monarchy and a constitutional democracy. The kings role is ceremonial and integrative; he reigns but shall not govern (Art. 7). Cambodia is the only country in Southeast Asia whose Constitutional Court follows the model of the French *Conseil constitutionnel*. After several amendments, the constitution has 16 sections, 158 articles, and an appendix with seven additional articles concerning the amendment process and the national assembly (Hill 2008). Most of the constitutional amendments were enacted in response to political crises and conflicts between the government and the king or between government and opposition. Major amendments concerned the establishment of a Senate, the succession to the royal throne, the election of the prime minister, and the special procedure for the amendment of the constitution itself. Originally, the election of the prime minister and constitutional amendments each required a two-thirds majority in the National Assembly. Following two amendments in 2004 and 2006, however, a newly constituted National Assembly can amend the constitution by majority, and the prime minister is elected by a majority of the members of parliament. Obviously, these amendments have reinforced the position of the parliamentary majority and served to formalize the factual distribution of power to the benefit of the ruling CPP and its leader, Prime Minister Hun Sen.

3.3 System of Government

Cambodia is an elective constitutional monarchy. The executive power of the government lies with the king and the Council of Ministers, led by the prime minister. Judicial power rests with the Constitutional Council and Supreme Council of the Magistracy as well as the lower courts. The legislative branch consists of a popularly elected National Assembly and an indirectly elected Senate (Upper House), established in 1999. Other elected bodies at the local level are the commune Councils, which, in turn, elect 57 of the 61 senators.

Since the restoration of the monarchy in 1993, the king serves as head of state (see Fig. 3.1). The late Norodom Sihanouk, who reigned from 1942 until 1955 and again from 1993 to 2004, abdicated in 2004. His son, Norodom Sihamoni, was

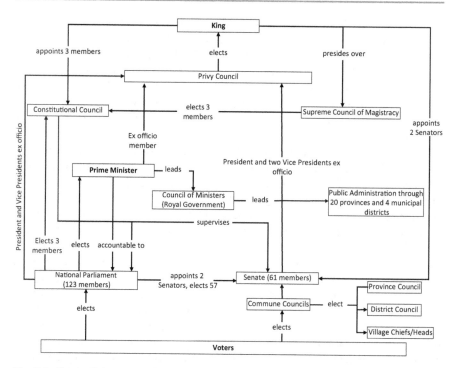

Fig. 3.1 Cambodia's system of government. Source: Authors' adaptation from Karbaum (2008, p. 117)

named king for life by the nine members of the Royal Privy Council on October 14, 2004. The prime minister, presidents, and vice-presidents of the National Assembly and Senate as well as the supreme patriarchs of the two largest fraternities of Theravada Buddhism, Mana Nikaya and Dhammayutika Nikaya, are ex officio members of the Privy Council.

The constitution defines the king as a sovereign who reigns but does not rule (Art. 7). He cannot dissolve the cabinet or dismiss the prime minister and is confined to a representative, ceremonial, and integrative role. The king is the formal Commander-in-Chief of the armed forces; chairs the National Defense Council; signs bills into laws; signs international treaties; appoints the government, ambassadors, judges and high civilian officials, and military officers; and—on behalf of the national government—declares states of war and emergency. In the execution of these duties, the king has no political discretion. Even though the formal political role of Cambodia's monarchy has been limited, King Sihanouk was an important stabilizing force in Cambodian political life and was regularly called upon by both Cambodia's politicians and international leaders to resolve crises. Since his corononation, King Sihamoni has shown little eagerness to get involved in politics. In contrast to King Sihanouk, the current king has carried out his duties without using royal authority—for example, the power to persuade by communicating with the parliament through royal messages that cannot be subject to debate

(Art. 18)—or personal authority to openly criticize government or opposition leaders. While the late King Sihanouk once refused to preside over the opening of the National Assembly in 2003 until the three political parties sorted out that year's disputed election, King Sihamoni has even convened the CPP-only Assembly amid the opposition's claims of election fraud in 2013 (McCargo 2014).

In Cambodia, the government comprises of the prime minister (the head of government) and the cabinet (the Council of Ministers). The installation of the government requires a formal investiture vote by the National Assembly on both the prime minister and the ministers he or she chooses to form the Cabinet, followed by formal confirmation by the King (Art. 118). A motion of no confidence can dismiss individual members of the government, including the Prime Minister, but so far there have been no such instances. The prime minister leads the Cabinet and can change its organization at will, following the 1994 law on the Organization of the Council of Ministers (Royal Government of Cambodia 1994). Between 1993 and 2013, CPP and FUNCINPEC formed a coalition government, initially led by two co-prime ministers of equal status and since 1998 led by a single Prime Minister (Hun Sen) alone. After FUNCINPEC failed to win any seats in the 2013 election, CPP formed a single-party government.

The power-sharing formula of 1993 that created the CPP-FUNCINPEC coalition government brought together political combatants for whom the election was a continuation of the war, rather than the basis for sharing power agreeably (Ashley 1998, p. 55). Bringing in all relevant parties into the government and giving them their share of posts in the cabinet and bureaucracy created the foundation for the CPP's network of patronage relationships. In this regard, the Cabinet mainly serves as a spoils system for the Prime Minister. He is able to grant the major sociopolitical, economic, and administrative members of the regime coalition access to the spoils of the state in return for their complacency concerning the existing order. As a result, Cambodia has one of the largest cabinets in the world: in 2007, it comprised the prime minister, eight deputy prime ministers, 28 senior ministers, 135 state secretaries, 146 undersecretaries, and about 1000 government advisors in the rank of a minister or state secretary (Karbaum 2008, pp. 118–120). This proliferation of cabinet posts and the organizational fragmentation of the administration primarily serve the prime minister's political survival. In contrast, the political functions of the ministries have been downgraded: While they often merely tackle routine operations, the Prime Minister's Office and the Office of the Council of Ministers serve as the administrative nerve center of the government (Karbaum 2008).

Following Arend Lijphart's conceptualization of different types of bicameral parliaments (Lijphart 2012), Cambodia's legislature branch, consisting of the National Assembly and Senate, is a case of weak bicameralism. The first chamber (the National Assembly) is directly elected by voters, but the 61 members of the second chamber (the Senate, *Protsaphea*) are elected indirectly by the Commune Councilors (57), appointed by the king (two), and elected by the National Assembly (two), all for a term of 6 years. Membership in the Senate is incompatible with a government office or National Assembly mandate. The procedure of formation of the Upper House ensures that the party that holds the majority in the National Assembly and the Commune Council (i.e., the CPP) also controls the Senate. In political reality, therefore, the Upper House is the extended arm of the ruling party. In fact, the major reason for the creation of the Senate in 1999 was to expand the prime minister's ability to grant patronage to political loyalists. Serving as a senator not only guarantees a sizeable financial allowance, but is also associated with significant social prestige and access to additional rents and other financial rewards.

In terms of formal constitutional power, the Senate is clearly subordinate to the National Assembly. According to the Constitution, the powers of the National Assembly (*Rodsasphea*) include leading legislation, creating the government and other state bodies, and holding the government accountable. The 123 members of the National Assembly are elected for 5-year terms under a proportional representation system (closed party list in multimember districts, see below). The National Assembly elects the prime minister and the Council of Ministers by an absolute majority of its members (until 2006: two-thirds majority), and 30 of its members can initiate a vote of no confidence against the prime minister or individual cabinet ministers (Art. 98). The National Assembly has a right of petition and interpellation, ratifies international treaties, and confirms the declaration of a state of war or emergency and the appointment of high-ranking civilian officials and military officers. Finally, a tenth of the members of the Assembly, a quarter of the members of the Senate, or the presidents of both houses can initiate a preventive or retroactive judicial review of legislation by the Constitutional Council (Art. 140 and 141).

Although both houses of parliament participate in the legislative process, the actual political importance of the second chamber is negligible. The constitution distinguishes between laws amending the constitution that require a two-thirds majority in the National Assembly and other laws that require an absolute majority. Draft laws may be initiated by members of both houses of parliament or the prime minister, but almost all bills and items for discussion are drawn up by the government. As a rule, the National Assembly debates bills in three readings before they are put to a vote. When a majority of the Assembly votes in favor of a bill, it moves up to the Senate, where it is debated for a maximum of 30 days and five days for urgent matters. If the senators do not object to the bill, the king has to sign it into law. In case the Senate amends or objects to the bill, it is returned to the National Assembly. Any changes or objections by the Senate can be sustained or defeated by a majority vote in the Assembly, after which the king signs the bill into law.

In political reality, executive–legislative relationships in Cambodia are characterized by the subordination of the parliament vis-à-vis the government (Case 2011, p. 53). So far, no committees of inquiry have been formed, the government often ignores parliament, and most of the time, opposition parties are excluded from participating in the various parliamentary committees. Members of the Council of Ministers have rarely issued the mandatory accountability reports to parliament, and members of parliament almost never make use of their right of initiative (Peou 2007, p. 91; Un 2011, p. 554). The government often uses its constitutional prerogative to pass government decrees after parliament issues a token authorization (Menzel 2008, p. 53). For most of the post-1993 period, parliament has, therefore, been regarded as relatively docile, and most criticism has focused around its inability to act as an adequate check on the executive (Case 2011; Un 2011).

Several factors contribute to this weakness of parliament (Case 2011, p. 53). First, the electoral system in Cambodia give party bosses a great deal of power over parliamentarians, encouraging a relatively high degree of roll-call discipline and discouraging defections from parliamentary groups. According to electoral law, members of parliament who change party affiliations or are expelled from their party will lose their seat and can be replaced without election by the respective party leaders (Menzel 2008, p. 54; Un 2011). A second reason is the partisan leadership style of parliamentary leaders such as the speaker of the Nation Assembly, who consistently denied the opposition any of their parliamentary rights (Peou 2007, p. 92). Third, several constitutional amendments have limited the legislative immunity of MPs from prosecution for their actions in parliament. Fear of prosecution has thus become a potent motivator for members of parliament to change their vote (Karbaum 2008). However, the opposition has also contributed to the weakening of parliament. To counter the CPP's hegemony, the opposition repeatedly gridlocked parliamentary procedures or blocked the opening of parliamentary sessions. This gave the government the pretext to pass several constitutional amendments lowering the necessary quorum for parliamentary votes, for example, for the election of the prime minister or constitutional amendments in the first session of a newly elected parliament (Peou 2007, p. 94). Even though opposition parties have time and time again tried to turn parliament into an area of political contestation and to challenge the ruling party through boycotts and public protest, the existence of an elected multiparty legislature has so far mainly served the regime in sustaining a network of patronage relationships with the major sociopolitical, economic, and administrative actors of the country. Moreover, with large majorities in parliament, the government has been able to sustain its political hegemony of the ruling elite in parliament and government.

3.4 Legal and Judicial System

The current legal system of Cambodia is a synthesis of diverse historic, legal, and ideological concepts and multiple interventions. Before French colonization (1863), Cambodia followed a system of customary law that was influenced by Buddhist and Khmer traditions and rituals. During the colonial period, the Cambodian legal and judicial systems were based almost entirely on the French civil law system (Kong 2012). Following independence in 1954, Cambodia's legal system was also modeled after the French system, and a comprehensive legal framework governing commercial, civil, and family relationships regulated day-to-day life (Peng 2012). The civil war and Khmer Rouge policies from 1975 to 1979 completely destroyed all legal institutions and laws of Cambodia's previous regimes. Unlike other self-declared communist parties in the region, the Khmer Rouge abolished any semblance of legality; party cadres exercised absolute power and dispensed (in)justice arbitrarily (Un 2009, p. 74). Following the Vietnamese invasion of December 1978, Cambodia had to rebuild a legal system from scratch, as nearly all legal professionals had been killed by the Khmer Rouge. Between 1979 and 1989, the Communists established a Marxist–Leninist legal system influenced by the Vietnamese Model.

The current legal system, which emerged from the Paris Peace Accords and the UNTAC period (1991–1993), is an amalgamation of Cambodian customs, the French-based legal system, and the common law system, as well as legacies of the former socialist law system heavily influenced by the Vietnamese model (Kong 2012). The various sources of law include the constitution, a French-inspired criminal law, a civil law system influenced by the Japanese model, royal decrees and proclamations, as well as ministerial decrees that provide the core of existing legislation (Peng et al. 2012). In rural areas, customary laws and forms of informal mediation remain widespread (Kong 2012, p. 12). Over the last two decades, there have been many initiatives by developmental organizations and Western donors in the area of law and judicial reform. Yet reforms towards a better rule of law and a well-functioning judicial system have made only little progress, partly because the government consistently refuses to undertake fundamental reforms or commit adequate funding for the grossly underfunded and understaffed judiciary (Un 2011, p. 550).

Full judicial power in Cambodia is vested in the courts by the 1993 Constitution (Art. 51). The judiciary comprises the Supreme Court, the Appellate Court, 24 Provincial/Municipal Courts, a court of appeal, and the military courts, which have jurisdiction only over military offenses (Peou 2006, p. 50). In addition, there is a Constitutional Council and a new hybrid court, the Extraordinary Chambers in the Courts of Cambodia (ECCC). According to the constitution, the Supreme Council of the Magistracy (SCM) used to be the authority responsible for the appointment of judges and public prosecutors as well as enact disciplinary measures, etc. The SCM is also responsible for the election of the Cambodian and international judges to the ECCC. It functions under the authority of the king and consists of the minister of justice, the president of the Supreme Court and the Appellate court, the attorney general, and three additional judges (Kong 2012, p. 12). In 2005, a decree by the prime minister stripped the SCM of most of its functions and transferred them to the ministry of justice (Peou 2007, p. 98). The 1993 Constitution also established the Constitutional Council as the highest constitutional authority in Cambodia, vested with the authority to ensure that the principles and rules of the constitution are upheld. It has nine members, of which the National Assembly, king, and SCM each select three (Art. 137). Candidates need a university degree in law, administration, or economics and "significant" experience in these fields, but no training or practical experience as legal experts. The main task of the court is judicial review. It can conduct abstract review, that is, rule on whether proposed statutes conform with the constitution, both a priori and a posteriori, following an appeal by king, prime minister, president, or one-tenth of the members of the National Assembly and Senate.[3] Its competences also comprise concrete review, which can be initiated by courts against a provision to be applied in a concrete case. Furthermore, disputes

---

[3] A quarter of senators are necessary to appeal for a posteriori review.

between the two houses of parliament over competencies and procedure can be brought before the court. Finally, the Council has the power to review the ministry of interior's decision to deny political parties registration and it may arbitrate disputes on general election results (Menzel 2008). However, in practice, there is neither a functional system of judicial review nor a working separation of judicial and political powers. Like other public institutions, the courts are essential elements of Hun Sen's neo-patrimonial spoils system, and a majority of Councilors in the Constitutional Council are members of the ruling CPP (Peou 2007, p. 99). It comes as no surprise, therefore, that judicial independence and impartiality are compromised and judicial review remains weak (Menzel 2008, p. 59).

In 2003, after protracted negotiations, the international community and the Cambodian government agreed to set up the Extraordinary Chambers in the Courts of Cambodia. It was meant to try "senior leaders of Democratic Kampuchea and those who were most responsible for the crimes and serious violations of Cambodian penal law, international humanitarian law and custom, and international conventions recognized by Cambodia, that were committed during the period from 17 April 1975 to 6 January 1979."[4] The ECCC is a genuinely hybrid court—the first of its kind—in which domestic and international actors and procedures coexist (Manning 2012; Dosch 2012). As several critics argue, however the ECCC "represents less a victory for victims or for advocates of transitional justice than it is a reflection of the interests of the Cambodian government and those international actors who collaborated with a series of repressive regimes in Cambodia, including the current Hun Sen regime" (Ainley 2014, p. 125).

Overall, the Cambodian judiciary suffers from a combination of incompetence, corruption, and political interference, which makes it difficult to achieve effective reform. Compared to other countries in the region, the gap between law and reality is particularly wide in Cambodia. According to the World Bank Governance Indicators, the rule of law is weaker in Cambodia than in most other Southeast Asian countries and has further deteriorated in recent years (World Bank 2017). Unsurprisingly, the general public puts little trust in a judicial system that is widely perceived as unable to provide justice or the protection of human rights. Moreover, the government has not hesitated to use the courts to punish opposition parties and to silence its critics in the past (Un 2009, p. 77, 2012, p. 202; Karbaum 2008, p. 152). The combination of ineffective arrangements, endemic rent-seeking behavior, weak institutional capacity, a lack of transparency and accountability, and frequent political interferences render effective prosecution of office abuse and corruption illusory. Consequently, Transparency International's Corruption Perception Index ranked Cambodia as the most corrupt country in Southeast Asia in 2015 (Transparency International 2015).

---

[4]Law on the Establishment of the Extraordinary Chambers, with inclusion of amendments as promulgated on October 27, 2004 (NS/RKM/1004/006).

3.5   Electoral System and Elections

Elections are nothing new in Cambodia, but genuinely competitive ones have been a rarity. Universal male and female suffrage was introduced in 1946 and 1956, respectively. From 1946 to 1992, there were ten parliamentary elections, one presidential election, as well as five national referenda (Hartmann 2001, p. 57). However, only the elections of 1946, 1947, and 1951 can be considered somewhat competitive. One of the most important legacies of the UNTAC-initiated reform process is the institutionalization of regular multiparty elections. Since 1993, there have been five general elections for the National Assembly, three commune-level elections, and two indirect elections for the Senate. Table 3.2 presents the results for National Assembly and Senatorial elections.

At the same time, however, elections have frequently been mired in controversy. Local civil society organizations, opposition parties, regional election watchdogs, and Cambodian and Western academics criticize the lack of integrity of the electoral process, the sloped playing field, and a political milieu that prizes partisanship above neutrality and impartiality.

The core of the current electoral arrangements for the National Assembly were established by the United Nations, which introduced a proportional representation system with mostly multi-member districts in the early 1990s. The Senate was established in 1998. Under the 2005 Senate Election Law, the chamber is indirectly elected by members of the Commune Councils. The local councils are elected under proportional representation every 5 years.

For the National Assembly elections, each of the 24 provinces or municipalities constitutes an electoral district. Under the 1993 UNTAC Election Law, the number of legislative seats allocated to each district was proportional to its estimated population. The seats in every province were to be assigned to individual candidates according to closed lists submitted by political parties to the election authorities. The candidate nomination procedures were left up to the parties. The UN election law selected the "greatest remainder" formula (LR-Hare). According to this system, the initial seat allocation gave each party a whole number of seats based on its proportion of the vote. If there were additional seats to be filled, the party whose fractional remainder was the largest received the first unassigned seat in the district (Gallup 2002; Croissant 2016). These arrangements were mostly retained in the revised election law passed in 1997 with the exception of a switch from the "greatest remainder" to the "highest average" (d'Hondt) formula. Electoral formulae for the Senate and for the more than 1600 Commune Councils largely resemble the one used for National Assembly elections: They are elected through a proportional representation system in which only nationally registered political parties can compete. Cambodia's current electoral rules are, therefore, a result of the peculiarities of the early stages of the transition process.

The most important feature of the electoral arrangements for the National Assembly is the choice of the province as the electoral constituency. Cambodia's 24 provinces display a very wide variation in population (Croissant 2016, pp. 16–18). The minimum of one seat for each province and the small size of

Table 3.2 Parliamentary elections in Cambodia, 1993–2013[a]

Party		National assembly					Senate		
		1993[b]	1998	2003	2008	2013	1999	2006	2012
Cambodian	Votes (%)	38.2	41.4	47.3	58.1	48.7	n/a	n/a	77.8
People's Party	Seats (n)	51	64	73	90	68	31	45	46
FUNCINPEC	Votes (%)	45.5	31.7	20.7	5	3.6	n/a	n/a	–
	Seats (n)	58	43	26	2	–	21	10	–
Buddhist	Votes (%)	3.8	–	–	–	–	–	–	–
Liberal Democratic Party	Seats (n)	10	–	–	–	–	–	–	–
Sam Rainsy	Votes (%)	–	14.3	21.8	21.9	–	n/a	n/a	–
Party	Seats (n)	–	15	24	26	–	7	2	–
Human Rights	Votes (%)	–	–	–	6.6	–	–	–	–
Party	Seats (n)	–	–	–	3	–	–	–	–
Norodom	Votes (%)	–	–	–	5.6	–	–	–	–
Ranariddh Party	Seats (n)	–	–	–	2	–	–	–	–
Cambodian	Votes (%)	–	–	–	–	44.4	–	–	22.2
National Rescue Party[c]	Seats (n)	–	–	–	–	55	–	–	11
Others and	Votes (%)	12.5	12.6	10.1	2.7	6.9	–	–	–
Independents	Seats (n)	1	–	–	–	–	–	–	–
Total	Votes (%)	100	100	100	100	100	n/a	n/a	n/a
	Seats (n)	120	122	123	123	123	59[f]	61[f]	61[f]
Voter turnout	%	89.6	93.7	83.22	75.21	68	n/a	n/a	n/a
Effective	Votes	2.8	3.4	3.1	2.5	2.2	n/a	n/a	1.5
Number of Parties[d]	Seats	2.3	2.4	2.2	1.7	1.9	2.4	1.5	1.4
LSq-Index[e]		9.2	10.3	11.2	12.8	7.2	n/a	n/a	n/a

Source: Authors' calculations with data from IPU (2014), COMFREL (2013), and Wüpper (2006)
[a]Includes only political parties with votes/seats share of 3% or more
[b]Constitutive Assembly
[c]SRP and HRP merged in 2012 to become CNRP
[d]The effective number of parties is a measure of party system fragmentation developed by Laakso and Taagepera (1979). It is calculated as $\frac{1}{\sum_{i=1}^{n} p_i^2}$, where p_i is the share of votes (ENEP) or seats (ENEP) of party i
[e]The Least Squares Index (LSq), a measure of voting system disproportionality proposed by Gallagher (1991). It is calculated as $\sqrt{\frac{1}{2} \sum_{i=1}^{n} (V_i - S_i)^2}$, where V_i is the share of votes of party i and S_i is its share of seats
[f]Includes appointed Senators

the National Assembly (123 members) produces a high degree of malapportion-ment (ibid.). Furthermore, the d'Hondt system that is used to allocate seats in each electoral district tends to over-represent larger parties, and in the relatively small constituencies of Cambodia's electoral system, this effect can be very strong. However, the system does not necessarily benefit only the ruling party: In 2013, the oppositional CNRP benefited from the d'Hondt formula (Croissant 2016, p. 19).

The electoral system has had a significant impact on the development of Cambodia's party system. On the one hand, it has been very successful in preventing fragmentation at the statewide level. The difference between the "effec-tive number of parties" (votes) and "the effective number of parties" (seats; cf. Table 3.2) was very high in the second to fourth election, but declined to a much lower level in 2013, as smaller parties penalized by the electoral system disappeared (FUNCINPEC) or converged into other formations (SRP and HRP). The D'Hondt system's bias against small parties when applied to small districts is reflected in the relatively high levels of disproportionality shown in Table 3.2. Although the index of disproportionality (Least Squares Index, or "Gallagher Index," LSq) fell in the most recent election, suggesting some degree of adaptation by party elites, electoral rules encourage the concentration of votes around the two largest parties. In fact, the unification of the opposition Sam Rainsy Party (SRP) and the Human Rights Party (HRP) into the Cambodia National Rescue Party (CNRP) was a major step towards defragmenting the opposition in Cambodia. On the other hand, the existing closed party-list system strengthens the position of party leaders relative to their candidates, as troublesome deputies can be pushed into unelectable positions on the list or even excluded altogether.

Since 1993, elections in Cambodia have assumed an empowering role in defin-ing the country's political outlook. Unlike in Vietnam, Laos, Singapore, and—until recently—Myanmar, elections in Cambodia are competitive and provide voters with the opportunity to express their support for or displeasure with the ruling party's policies and performance. Opposition parties are given some political space within the system and can use elections to seriously contest for power. While the electoral system is characterized by malapportionment and disproportionality, such characteristics are not exceptionally strong and do not threaten the meaning of competitive elections as the primary means of gaining power in Cambodia. While the method by which votes are cast and how these votes are converted into seats in an assembly are no cause for concern, the regulations that govern the appropriate conduct of elections and the implementation of these rules are. One of the main concerns regarding the integrity of the electoral process includes problems with the voter list and the registration process. Another electoral integrity problem is the misuse of state resources, especially in terms of access to and use of coercive power, and a flawed media environment. Finally, many national and international observers have raised doubts about the impartiality, professionalism, and effective-ness of the National Election Commission (NEC), which is in charge of all aspects of the elections.

3.6 Political Parties and Party System

The history of political parties in Cambodia dates back to the early post-WWII period. Between 1946 and 1951, with establishment of the Democratic Party and the Liberal Party, the Communist Kampuchean People's Revolutionary Party (KPRP), and the royalist *Sangkum Reastr Niyum* (commonly known as *Sangkum*), three ideological currents emerged that would dominate the party system for the next four decades (Karbaum 2008; de Zeeuw 2010; Peou 2015). In the post-UNTAC period, the Cambodian party system experienced several transformations. The three noncommunist parties that were once part of the CGDK have disappeared, just like the remnants of the Khmer Rouge PDK after it merged with CPP in 1998 (Roberts 2001).

From 1993 until 2013, the royalist FUNCINPEC was the junior partner in a coalition government with the CPP, except for a short interregnum in 1997/98 and 2003/04. While many domestic and international observers initially viewed FUNCINPEC as a credible alternative to the CPP and a force of political change, the party more or less degenerated into a satellite of the CPP's comprehensive patronage network and has suffered from factionalism and frequent internal conflicts (de Zeeuw 2010, p. 1191). The steady decline of the party culminated in the 2013 general elections, when the party failed to win a single seat in the National Assembly. The decline of the FUNCINPEC and its replacement as a major oppositional force by the liberal Sam Rainsy Party (SRP), itself a FUNCINPEC breakaway faction, despite perpetual intimidation and violence, is evidence of a substantial, growing, and resilient popular support for opposition parties. After its merger with the Human Rights Party in 2013, the resulting CNRP has become the main opposition party. Although the SRP—and, since 2013, the CNRP—is often described as the only alternative to CPP dominance, the party is highly personalistic and clientelistic in character, exhibits strong anti-Vietnamese nationalism, harbors weakly institutionalized party structures, and has a rather limited membership. Moreover, it conducts opposition for the sake of opposition but at times has difficulties providing substantial alternatives to government policies (Peou 2015). As Table 3.2 demonstrates, Cambodia's party system has stabilized as an asymmetric two-party system with the ruling CPP in power and the CNRP dominating the opposition, leaving only limited chances for other political parties to win seats in elections. In November 2017, the government ordered the dissolution of the CNPR for collusion with foreign powers (i.e. the United States), threatening to end to the post-1993 multiparty system (Croissant 2018).

The CPP is the successor of the pro-Vietnamese People's Revolutionary Party of Kampuchea (PRPK), which ruled Cambodia from 1979 until 1991. Although the party has renounced the principles of Marxism–Leninism, it still exhibits many features of a socialist state party. For example, the military, police, and civilian bureaucracy are co-opted into the party apparatus to such a degree that makes it almost impossible to differentiate between state and party. For instance, many high-ranking judges, police officers, and generals are members of the party's Central Committee. The President of the Supreme Court is a member of the CPP's Central Committee and the President of the Appellation Court as well as the President of the

Table 3.3 Commune council elections, 2002–2017

			2002	2007	2012	2017
CPP		Seats (%)	68.4	70.4	72.3	55.9
		Votes (%)	60.8	60.8	61.8	50.7
FUN	FUNCINPEC	Seats (%)	19.6	6.1	1.7	0
NRP		Votes (%)	21.8	13.4	6.7	1.9
SRP	CNRP	Seats (%)	11.9	23.4	25.7	43.0
HRP		Votes (%)	16.9	25.2	30.7	43.8
Others		Seats (%)	0	0	0	1.1
		Votes (%)	0.2	0.5	0.7	5.5

Sources: COMFREL (2012); Croissant (2018)

Human Rights Commission are also members of the Central Committee. The National Party Congress meets every 5 years and elects the Central Committee of the CPP. The latter determines the Political Bureau (Politburo), the party's supreme decision-making body. Until the early 2000s, there were rivalries between the top cadres, many of whom had served as Khmer Rouge party functionaries or military commanders and fled to Vietnam to evade the series of purges in the 1970s. Today, Hun Sen has consolidated his leadership position by suppressing or co-opting internal opponents. In the process, a relatively large group of regime supporters emerged who have gained access to spoils but who are also easily replaceable: Between 1992 and 2008, the CPP's Central Committee increased from 60 to 268 members, while the size of the Politburo increased from 17 to 30 people (Karbaum 2008, pp. 101–103). The electoral strength of the party rests on its control over local political arenas (Slocomb 2004, p. 462, cf. Table 3.3). Even though party structures outside of Phnom Penh are weak, the communes have been under firm CPP control since the 1980s, and the party has not only usurped many of the functions of the state, but has also enmeshed the entire political and social system of Cambodia under its "benevolent" strongman, Prime Minister Hun Sen (Strangio 2014). In particular, CPP cadres use state infrastructure during election campaigns to mobilize voters or oblige officials such as the police or teachers to engage publicly for the CPP (Peou 2007, p. 105; Un 2008, p. 1; Karbaum 2008, p. 97).

3.7   State Administration and Decentralization

Precolonial Cambodia was not a state in the modern European or Weberian sense, but a mandala system: the king and royal court only had direct politico-military and administrative-economic control over areas close to the center of the realm. Other local power holders were bound to the center by tributary relations and oaths of loyalty. The French created municipalities (*khum*) as the basis of their administrative structure and extended the center's power projection through appointed heads of local administration, a practice independent Cambodia continued (Slocomb 2004, p. 453; Sedara and Öjendal 2009, p. 126). This basic administrative structure is still in place today. The territory of the Kingdom of Cambodia is administratively divided into 21 provinces (*khet*), the Special Capital Region of Phnom Penh, and the three municipalities (*krung*) of Sihanoukville, Pailin, and Kep. Provinces are divided into districts (*srok*) and municipalities; provincial districts are divided into communes (*khum*) and villages (*phum*), whereas municipalities are divided into *khans* and the *khans* into *sangkats*. All 1633 communes and *sangkats*, 197 districts and boroughs, provinces, and independent cities have a uniform administration established by law (Niazi 2011). Provincial governors and the governor of the capital city and the three *krung* as well as the district heads and their deputies are appointed by the government and are subordinate to the Ministry of Interior. Frequent rotations in office and a large number of deputy positions have fragmented subnational executives and have prevented officeholders from establishing political strongholds. Local executives have little influence on public administration, making these posts attractive mostly for their patronage potential (Karbaum 2008, p. 123).

Local councils are elected under a proportional representation system every 5 years. So far, there have been three rounds of local elections (2002, 2007, and 2012; cf. Table 3.3). As Table 3.3 exhibits, council elections confirm the political dominance of the CPP, which has nearly monopolized the commune seats since the first local council elections in 2002. The control of the commune councils, which are responsible for selecting village chiefs, forms the backbone of the ruling party's electoral strength at the national level (Sedara and Öjendal 2009, p. 126).

Similar to many other Southeast Asian countries over the last 25 years, Cambodia has experimented with decentralization reforms. However, unlike Indonesia or the Philippines, it lacks a domestic reform coalition that could have realized a comprehensive decentralization agenda. Instead, the initiatives for decentralization in Cambodia have come from international donors and development agencies. The rationale for decentralization has been to strengthen the presence and legitimacy of the state at the local level after decades of conflict and turmoil. However, since the rural areas have always been the political backbone of the CPP, the party has supported the direct election of Commune Councils after 2001 (Blunt and Turner 2005, p. 85). As a result of the reforms, the introduction of local elections provided an opportunity for the CPP to further strengthen its political control over local politics (Turner 2006, p. 269; Hughes 2009; Bünte 2011). So far, the transfer of policy authority or fiscal powers to subnational units has been quite limited in Cambodia, and the central government operates under deconcentrated structures that bypass the subnational units (Blunt and Turner 2005, p. 81). This leaves local administrations, whose executive administrators are subordinate to the interior ministry, with the job of merely implementing national directives (Karbaum 2008, p. 125). Moreover, the current legal framework still has notable gaps. While provincial and district councils are meant to monitor the activities of governors and district heads originally appointed by the Interior Ministry, these bodies are subordinate to the interior ministries themselves and the law has no provisions on how accountability works in practice (Hughes 2010, p. 87). The Ministry of Economy and Finances monitors the finances of provinces and districts. While provinces and large municipalities draw about 75% of their revenue from taxes and other local sources, about 80% of revenues at the district level and beneath are transfer payments or other handouts from the central government: about 16.7% have a foreign source and only 2.5% are generated locally (2002–2007; see Niazi 2011, p. 45). The quality of government services in general suffers from a narrow financial basis of subnational units, a lack of coordination among sectoral ministries, rudimentary monitoring capabilities, low salaries, and non-existent accountability mechanisms for officials. Government employees are often underqualified and lack a professional attitude; moreover, there is no incentive-based recruitment or promotion system (Turner 2006; Karbaum 2008).

3.8   Civil–Military Relations and the Security Sector

Partly reflecting the legacy of the civil war and the UN's only partially successful disarmament, demobilization, and reintegration (DDR) operation, but also as a consequence of the trajectories of post-UNTAC civil–military relations, Cambodia has a bloated security sector. According to data collected by the International Institute for Security Studies (IISS), in 2014, Cambodia had a civil–military balance of 8.2 active military personnel per 1000 people, higher than, for example, Thailand (5.3) and Vietnam (5.2; IISS 2014). According to the constitution, the king is Supreme commander-in-chief of the Royal Cambodian Armed Forces (RCAF) and chairs the Supreme Council for National Defense (Art. 23-24). Actual military command authority rests with the military Commander-in-chief and civilian leadership with the Minister of Defense. The National Police is controlled by the Interior Ministry and commanded by the General Commissioner, a police general. The military police is part of the RCAF, but it also serves civilian purposes similar to the Gendarmerie. The latter was created in 1995 to guarantee regime security but also as a counterterrorism and counterinsurgency force; it enforces court orders and supports the penal system (Peou 2006; Un 2009; Phnom Penh Post 2013). The Gendarmerie is technically subordinate to the Army General Staff but reports directly to the Prime Minister (Danish Centre for Human Rights 2001, p. 62). While it is technically part of the armed forces, the Prime Minister Bodyguard Unit (PMBU) is also under Hun Sen's personal control. It is equipped with heavy weapons and, to counterweight the armed forces, was separated from the RCAF in 2009. It has been used to monitor demonstrations and is widely suspected of human rights violations (HRW 2010; The Cambodia Daily 2013). Until 2009, PMBU was part of Army Brigade 70, which played an important role during Hun Sen's coup d'état against Co-Prime Minister Norodom Ranariddh in July 1997 (Un 2011, p. 553). An elaborate network of intelligence services complements the repressive apparatus. These include the military intelligence service, the General Information Department, anti-terror units, a bureau on organized crime, and the Central Security Forces. All intelligence activities are controlled by the Central Security Department, a section of the Interior Ministry (Karbaum 2008, pp. 202, 199). In addition to the official government forces, the government can rely on the services of the "Pagoda Boys" thugs, a violent youth organization loyal to Hun Sen (Chambers 2015).

Police and Gendarmerie together can muster about 67,000 troops, 7000 of which are part of the Gendarmerie. With a ratio of 400 police officers per 100,000 inhabitants, Cambodia is the best-policed territorial state in the region (authors' calculation based on IISS 2014). The armed forces, including the army, navy, air force, and PMBU, have a total strength of 124,000 soldiers and officers, most of them in the army (IISS 2014, p. 229). Unlike in other countries in the region, the armed forces are not primarily meant to counter internal security threats or guarantee regime security, as this task is left for the police, intelligence services, and the PMBU. Rather, the CPP used the RCAF as a means to bind violent actors to the regime. Shunning demobilization after 1993, most civil war combatants have been absorbed into the armed forces or police (Hendrickson 2001; Peou 2007). This includes the Khmer Rouge, who had withdrawn from the peace process in 1993 and only ended their war against the government in 1998. Absorbing this wide array of combatants has bloated the officer corps, and today RCAF has 2200 generals, i.e., one general per 58 regulars (The Cambodia Daily 2014).

The military also serves as a huge spoils network (Chambers 2015; Morgenbesser 2017). In absolute numbers, Cambodia has one of the lowest defense budgets in ASEAN. However, the defense budget is augmented by spending for internal security, and according to data from the renowned Stockholm International Peace Research Institute (SIPRI 2015), Cambodia's military spending rose more than 56% between 2010 and 2014 alone. For 2016, the National Assembly approved a defense budget of USD383 million, a 17% increase against spending in 2015. The defense allocation amounts to around 9% of total government expenditure for the year and about 2% of GDP (Parameswaran 2015). Moreover, the budget is augmented by spending for internal security: The average combined expenditure on military and internal security amounted to 15.4% of total government expenditure in the period from 2002 to 2014 (authors' calculation based on World Bank 2017). Because of the lack of public disclosure of the defense budget, little is known beyond the aggregate sum. Yet several national and international observers note that corruption is endemic and institutionalized in the security sector. Transparency International's 2015 report gave Cambodia an "F" (the lowest possible rating) in its Government Defense Anti-Corruption Index (Transparency International 2015). Because the ruling CPP has near total control of the country's defense and security policy, parliament has little to no ability to oversee the defense budget, monitor procurement, or scrutinize the military's commercial activities. Furthermore, evidence suggests that little separation exists between the chains of command and the chains of payment in Cambodia's military, further contributing to the proliferation of ghost soldiers, bribery, and unpredictability in promotions (Chambers 2015). According to various reports, senior army, military police, and police officers are all heavily involved in illegal activities, including illegal logging and land grabbing, whereas the lower ranks try to bolster their pay by engaging in the private security sector, drug or small arms trade, prostitution, and racketeering (Hendrickson 2001; Peou 2007; Karbaum 2008; Global Witness 2009; Heder 2012). Unsurprisingly, military commanders and CPP cadres, including key leaders, have no interest in institutionalizing democratic civilian control and good governance in the security sector. The miltary's own economic interests in arms sales, timber, gems, and other illegal or illicit economic activities are too widespread, and civilian members of the regime have to rely on the coercive capacity of the security apparatus for day-to-day repression of the political opposition.

3.9   Political Culture and Civil Society

The authoritarian nature of CPP rule also affects the development of civil society in Cambodia. Similar to other electoral autocracies in Southeast Asia, there is limited space for a pluralistic media and civil society in Cambodia. At first glance, quantitative indicators such as the number of national and international NGOs in the country seem to indicate a remarkable deepening of the structures and organizations of Cambodian civil society since the early 1990s. However, Cambodia's NGO sector as part of a "modern" civil society did not emerge out of spontaneous grassroots energies. Rather, it is the product of international intervention and continued support. More conducive political conditions during the UNTAC mission and ongoing international support after 1993 have created an external demand for cooperation partners, to which Cambodian NGOs have reacted. Nonetheless, NGOs have had only limited impact in terms of creating conducive conditions for the development and consolidation of a vibrant civil society. The Cambodian government has tolerated the internationally sponsored growth of the NGO sector and the rise of an externally financed aid and development economy (Dosch 2012) because, first of all, it did not want to risk its access to development aid and, secondly, because some of these organizations fulfill basic state functions and so relieve societal pressure on the government apparatus. Unlike Cambodia's legal framework, which is less restrictive than, for instance, those in Laos, Vietnam, Malaysia, and Singapore, the country's political conditions are increasingly difficult (Curly 2004). In fact, according to Freedom House, Cambodia has experienced a steady erosion of core rights such as the extent of freedom of assembly and associational rights over the past 10 years (see Table 3.4). Even for "apolitical" NGOs active in areas such as environmental protection, forest and land rights, and natural resource management, it has become more difficult to remain active. While the political space for civil society actions is less restrictive in large cities such as Phnom Penh, constraints are particularly tough in the countryside. The safeguarding of rural areas from human rights and democracy NGOs derives from political and strategic calculations on the part of the ruling party (Hughes 2009). As argued above, rural residents are the backbone of the CPP's electorate, and since 1993, the CPP has fiercely defended the rural heartland from competing political and ideological rivals. Furthermore, particular organizations that are active "on the ground" face a real threat potential since their activities pose a possible threat to the economic interests of members of the armed forces, the police, the government, and the ruling party as well as corrupt bureaucrats who engage in illegal economic activities (Hughes 2003; Peou 2007).

Table 3.4 Freedom House ratings for Freedom of Assembly and Association, 2006–2014

	2006	2007	2008	2009	2010	2011	2012	2013	2014
Brunei	3	3	3	3	3	3	3	3	3
Cambodia	6	6	6	5	5	4	4	3	3
Indonesia	8	9	9	9	9	10	9	9	8
Laos	1	1	1	1	1	1	1	0	0
Malaysia	6	6	5	6	6	6	5	5	6
Myanmar	0	0	0	0	0	0	2	4	4
Philippines	9	5	8	8	8	8	8	8	8
Singapore	4	3	3	3	3	3	4	4	4
Timor-Leste	8	7	7	7	7	7	7	7	7
Thailand	8	5	5	6	6	5	6	6	6
Vietnam	2	2	2	2	1	1	1	1	1

Source: Freedom House (2014)
Notes: Freedom House measures the degree of actual freedom of association and organization based on three indicators and 16 questionnaire items on a scale of 0 to 12. Higher values indicate more freedom. Disaggregated scores are only available since 2006

Civil society activities in Cambodia fall into five broad categories: (1) democracy and human rights organizations; (2) development organizations involved in education, health, credit, income-generating, and other activities; (3) support organizations focusing on human resources and organizational development training activities; (4) community-based organizations (CBOs); and (5) research and other analytical work and advocacy activities covering various development issues. Some of the more "political" and internationally well-connected organizations have a professional structure and are internationally networked, giving them some protection from government repression (Hughes 2005, p. 80; Un 2011, p. 557). Development organizations that offer parallel service delivery, informally seconding ineffective government agencies, and CBOs can work relatively unmolested by the government as long as their activities do not clash with the vested interests and rent-seeking behavior of regime elites (Un 2011, p. 557). In contrast, the NGO advocacy sector suffers from a perception of being overly critical of the government, particularly in the area of human rights.

Traditionally, the dominant form of social organization was Pagoda-based associations, which encouraged volunteerism and social service in Cambodia and had strong participation at the village level. Pagoda associations existed before the war, survived the Khmer Rouge terror reign, and are now again present in a number of rural areas, but they do not seem to be linked systematically into development programs or decentralized government structures and are considered quite separate from the NGO sector in Cambodia (Mutz 2003; UNDP 2012). In contrast, for example, to Myanmar, the monastic orders have been successfully co-opted by the authoritarian regime (Karbaum 2008, p. 151; Harris 2005, pp. 191, 211).

In addition to regulatory constraints, several other factors hinder the development of a more vibrant civil society in Cambodia. The first is the lack of social resources necessary for sustainable civil society development, particularly the dramatic deficits of human and social capital (Colletta and Cullen 2000, pp. 17–33). Decades of communist dictatorship, civil war, and genocide have prevented the emergence of any meaningful form of public sphere and civic culture (Colletta and Cullen 2000; Sen 2012; Inada 2013; Hill and Menon 2013, p. 4).

Secondly, government officials tend to equate critique by social organizations regarding specific government policies with political opposition and "treason." In fact, many leaders of human rights and democracy NGOs are overseas Khmers or former political prisoners who are strongly anti-authoritarian and sometimes anti-CPP and anti-Vietnamese (Un 2006, p. 240). Furthermore, some of the issues these NGOs advocate such as the rule of law, anti-corruption, accountability, judicial reform, and protection of human rights are also part of the opposition agenda. Third, more political NGOs often receive funding from Western democracy aid agencies. Thus, in the eyes of the government, human rights organizations are political organizations. The government can accuse these organizations of being opposition.

Furthermore, repression and the use of violence by the government to "tame" civil society are anticipated by social organizations in such a way that many groups attempt to be "apolitical." However, NGOs' cautious efforts not to transcend the informal limits of what is acceptable and what is not impose even greater limitations on their activities. Self-restraint prevents human rights and democracy NGOs from taking a firm stance on political issues and from mobilizing the public behind those issues.

Finally, attributes such as accountability, transparency, equal participation, and mass participation—part of an idealized concept of NGO work—may have been lost during the process of importation and transplantation of the concept of NGOs and civil society in Cambodia. In fact, the organizational structures, operations, and internal governance of many NGOs do not exemplify democracy. Rather, such NGOs are comparable to state institutions that are hierarchical, centralized, and nondemocratic in their decision-making. While the lack of democratic practices within the NGO community is influenced by the wider Cambodian society, in which patronage, autocracy, and hierarchy are prevalent, especially those NGOs run by founder-directors are prone to autocratic, hierarchical, and centralized management, with patron–client relationships constituting a dominant feature. Most NGOs are not well-institutionalized but instead highly personalized and dependent on the "leadership" qualities of persons. The personalization of internal structures and processes, however, may contradict the progressive ideas of NGOs regarding democracy and individual "empowerment" (Richardson 2001, p. 7; Un 2006, p. 243, 2004).

The trajectory of democracy and authoritarianism in Cambodia since 1991 clearly demonstrates that a vibrant civil society and a political culture that supports democracy are not prerequisites for establishing democracy. Yet, most scholars view both as necessary ingredients for a consolidated democracy. The failure of post-UNTAC democracy to consolidate—and its eventual transgression into a new form of electoral authoritarianism—might therefore also reflect the incongruence of democratic institutions and mass political culture in Cambodia. In this regard, the data of the Asian Barometer Survey project show that perceptions of democracy are more ambivalent: On the one hand, support for democracy as an abstract system of government is higher than the Southeast Asian average. However, the number of respondents who believe democracy is appropriate for Cambodia is considerably lower. Only about half the respondents believe democracy to be preferable to any other system of government, the second lowest number in all of Southeast Asia (it is lowest in the Philippines). Furthermore, support for the current political system is much stronger than in the Philippines, Thailand, or Indonesia (Chang et al. 2013, p. 157).

This seems to indicate that the government has successfully transformed the provision of public goods (economic development, societal peace, and political stability) into political support and "performance-based legitimacy" (Schmidt 2016) to legitimize its rule. In another study, more than three-quarters of respondents believed their country was on the right track in 2009 (Un 2011, p. 559; Chang et al. 2013, pp. 158–160). But using performance as an alternative mode of legitimation may not only strengthen the political regime but could also turn out to be a major weakness. First of all, the rhetoric of the regime obviously contrasts with the political reality of corruption, nepotism, and repression. Second, reliance on performance-based legitimation might lead the authoritarian regime into what Samuel Huntington (1991, p. 50) terms the "performance dilemma": If the regime bases its efforts to legitimize its power on (political or economic) performance, a future performance crisis might very well trigger a legitimacy crisis. However, the legitimacy of the Hun Sen regime might be undermined not only if it fails to deliver on its promises, but also if it succeeds in achieving its purpose: Economic development presumably increases the capacity of a society to place demands on a government. Individuals are more likely to desire participation in government and have greater expectations for their government and its institutional framework (see also Inglehart and Welzel 2005). In this regard, the poor showing of the CPP in the 2013 election—the worst since 1998 when it won only 64 of 122 seats—and the magnitude of opposition gains put pressure on the Hun Sen government. It needs to address growing socioeconomic tensions and the deepening anger of many voters over rural land conflicts, corruption, as well as urban disenchantment with high youth unemployment and decades of one-party rule. Finally, the regime's claim to be the sole guarantor of post-genocidal peace is somewhat undercut by demographic change: Nowadays, half of the Cambodian population was born after 1990, and 70% of Cambodians are 29 years or younger (UNDP 2012). The young generations grown up in the post-UNTAC period did not genocide or civil war and may be less willing to relinquish political rights in exchange for economic and physical security.

3.10 Media System

Until the UNTAC period, there had been no independent media in Cambodia for almost a quarter of a century. The UNTAC administration promoted and supported a free and pluralist media landscape as a central component of the postwar reconstruction process. After exiled resistance members returned to Cambodia following the peace accords, the number of newspapers exploded from seven in 1991 to more than 80 around 2000, and the number of registered news organizations jumped from around 20 at the time of the 1993 elections to 50 one year later and to 200 by the 1998 elections (Clarke 2000, pp. 248–249). Whereas state television and the radio had previously been dominated by propaganda, UNTAC also initiated the creation of Radio UNTAC, a national news station. Today, there are more than 10 television stations, a mix of state and privately owned broadcasters, and over 80 radio stations, which reach most of the country's overwhelmingly rural population (Ritter 2008). While the Cambodian press used to be relatively free, only few people outside of the large cities use newspapers as a prime source of information, whereas electronic media such as television and radio—much more relevant sources of information for the majority of the populace—are strictly controlled by the government. Moreover, in the last decade, freedom of the press and media pluralism have come under pressure, as the government issued new legal restrictions and stepped-up informal constraints. Especially the broadcast media environment is tilted heavily in favor of the CPP. The absence of equal access to and use of media, specifically television and radio, favors the ruling CPP but disadvantages other contesting political parties. Government control is either exercised directly through state-owned media or indirectly through private media businesses closely associated with the regime party (Un 2011, p. 548).[5]

As a result, the electoral process is biased by the fact that opposition voices have very limited space to showcase their platforms to voters. Newspaper coverage is more balanced than broadcast media, but broadcast and (increasingly social) media are more widely used to provide political parties with better opportunities to spread their messages. Furthermore, journalists and media activists suffer from politically motivated intimidation and there have been acts of violence against editors and journalists, including 13 murders and disappearances between 1994 and 2014 (CCHR 2014). This downward trend is reflected in the scores reported by Reporters without Borders, where Cambodia is ranked 132nd of 180 countries (Reporters without Borders 2017) and Freedom House's Freedom of the Press Index, where Cambodia is ranked close to Singapore and Malaysia (Freedom House 2017).

Of course, social media and other internet services have become more important in recent years, and internet-based communication has quickly created new sources of information and channels for free communication. As of 2017, 25.5% of the population had internet access—lagging behind Indonesia (50.4%) and at around the same level as Timor-Leste (27.5%) but ahead of Laos (19.9%) or Myanmar (22.4%; Internet World Stats 2017). In addition to political parties, numerous non-governmental organizations, including election observers and human rights organizations, have increased their online presence and used social media to

---

[5]Cambodians get their news primarily from TV or radio—83 and 79%, respectively (IRI 2013)—which are either controlled by Hun Sen's family or close associates of the regime. The only state television station, Television of Kampuchea (TVK), is run by the armed forces, monitored by the Ministry of Information and known for its government-friendly reporting (Karbaum 2008, pp. 149, 174).

disseminate information. In this regard, the passing of a new Telecommunication Law (2014) and the ongoing debate about a "Cybercrime Law" provide additional reasons for concern, and media experts warn that the sweeping, broad, and overreaching regulations could easily be used to infringe basic freedoms and to target civil society activists (Gerry and Moore 2015, p. 639).

3.11 Outlook

Given the circumstances, it is not surprising that Cambodia's UN-guided experiment with democracy has failed. As Un explains, Cambodia democratized not because but in spite of the existing social conditions (Un 2006, p. 243) and democracy quickly failed after the power-sharing arrangements of the UNTAC era were put to the test (Croissant 2008). The UN-led international interim governments helped to mitigate problems of civil strife, insecurity, and political instability and helped to establish the formal institutions of democracy. However, the case of Cambodia demonstrates that, "immediately satisfactory elections do not necessarily mean that a democratic government or any of the essential elements of democracy (the rule of law, and independent judiciary and a professional non-partisan civil service including the police and military, and another "free and fair" election) will be guaranteed" (Austin 2003, p. 189). Even in the absence of civil war and large-scale political violence, the "politics-as-war" (Sartori 1987, p. 224) in Cambodia never transformed into "restrained partisanship" (Higley and Burton 2006, p. 11). Furthermore, the country neither had expansive experience with democracy and the rule of law nor an active civil society that external proponents of democratization could have built upon.

Cambodia's political regime combines formal democratic institutions and authoritarian political practices. It brings together elements of democracy, party rule, and personal authoritarianism. Increasingly, strong neo-patrimonial tendencies dominate representative institutions, like parliament, parties, and elections (Morgenbesser 2017). So far, the regime successfully combines repression, legitimation, and co-optation, but in its logic of political survival, emphasizes the co-optation of potential spoilers into the regime's patronage pyramid and spoils network. This system of carrot and sticks—a combination of restrictive, targeted measures of repression on the one hand and the distribution of economic rents on the other hand—is strength and weakness at once (Burgos and Ear 2010, p. 623; Hughes 2008, p. 73; Cock 2010; Strangio 2014; Morgenbesser 2017). Moreover, the government can keep repression to a minimum as long as supporters can be bought off, reducing the regime's dependency on the repressive apparatus. On the other hand, however, Cambodia lacks both the reserves of legitimacy still apparent in the ideological dictatorships of Laos or Vietnam as well as the strong economic track record of Malaysia or Singapore. Its future survival will depend on the availability of short-term economic handouts. From this perspective, the elections of 2013 have been an important stress test for the regime because they signaled a loss of support for the ruling party and the need for even more patronage spending.

Signs of growing cooperation between the CPP and CNRP in what was termed a "culture of dialogue" in 2014 evaporated quickly. After members of the opposition publicly criticized the regime leadership, the government reacted with a crackdown, including the expulsion of opposition MPs from parliament and a series of arrests and warrants against many senior opposition politicians (O'Neill 2016). Following the 2017 commune election, Cambodia saw the further decline of political and civil liberties. Although the escalation crackdown is said to be part of a campaign of intimidation, violence, and misuse of courts and law intended to weaken or neutralize political opposition ahead of the 2018 national election, it is a sign that authoritarianism in Cambodia is hardening and that Prime Minister Hun Sen might finally attempt to abolish the multiparty system that has been in place since the UNTAC mission in favor of single-party dictatorship under his personal control. Even though China has become an important partner of the Cambodian government, the country still depends on Western donors for financial assistance (Ear 2009; Bader 2015). This limits the government's ability to increase repression during a regime crisis to compensate for a momentary loss of control. However, with Western influence waning and China stepping up, questions concerning the overall long-term political development of Cambodia are emerging.

References

Ainley, K. (2014). Transitional justice in Cambodia: The coincidence of power and principle. In R. Jeffery & H. J. Kim (Eds.), *Transitional justice in the Asia-Pacific* (pp. 125–156). New York: Cambridge University Press.

Ashley, D. (1998). The failure of conflict resolution in cambodia: Causes and lessons. In F. Z. Brown & D. G. Timberman (Eds.), *Cambodia and the international community: The quest for peace, development, and democracy* (pp. 49–78). Singapore: ISEAS.

Austin, D. (2003). Democracy and democratization. In C. J. G. Sampford, R. C. Thakur, & W. Maley (Eds.), *From civil strife to civil society: Civil and military responsibilities in disrupted states* (pp. 180–204). Tokyo: United Nations University Press.

Bader, J. (2015). *China's foreign relations and the survival of autocracies*. London: Routledge.

Blunt, P., & Turner, M. (2005). Decentralisation, democracy and development in a post-conflict society: Commune councils in Cambodia. *Public Administration and Development, 25*, 75–87. https://doi.org/10.1002/pad.349

Brandt, M. (2005). *Constitutional assistance in post-conflict countries: The UN experience: Cambodia, East Timor & Afghanistan*. New York: United Nations Development Program.

Brocheux, P., & Hémery, D. (2011). *Indochina: An ambiguous colonization 1858-1954*. Berkeley: University of California Press.

BTI. (2016). *Bertelsmann transformation index 2016*. Gütersloh: Bertelsmann Foundation.

Bueno de Mesquita, B., Smith, A., Siverson, R., & Morrow, J. (2003). *The logic of political survival*. Cambridge: MIT Press.

Bünte, M. (2011). Decentralization and democratic governance in Southeast Asia. In A. Croissant & M. Bünte (Eds.), *The crisis of democratic governance in Southeast Asia* (pp. 131–150). Houndmills: Palgrave Macmillan.

Burgos, S., & Ear, S. (2010). China's strategic interests in Cambodia: Influence and resources. *Asian Survey, 50*, 615–639. https://doi.org/10.1525/as.2010.50.3.615

Case, W. (2011). *Executive accountability in Southeast Asia: The role of legislatures in new democracies and under electoral authoritarianism* (East West Center Policy Studies 57). Honolulu: East-West Center.

Case, W. (2015). Democracy's mixed fortunes in Southeast Asia: Topor, change, and trade-offs. In W. Case (Ed.), *Routledge handbook of Southeast Asian democratization* (pp. 3–23). London: Routledge.

CCHR. (2014). *Journalists killed in Cambodia: Harrassment of Media 2008–2012 map*. Phnom Penh: Cambodian Centre for Human Rights.

Chambers, P. W. (2015). 'Neo-Sultanistic tendencies': The trajectory of civil-military relations in Cambodia. *Asian Security, 11*, 179–205. https://doi.org/10.1080/14799855.2015.1108965

Chang, A., Chu, Y.-h., & Welsh, B. (2013). Southeast Asia: Sources of regime support. *Journal of Democracy, 24*, 150–164. https://doi.org/10.1353/jod.2013.0025

CIA. (2017). *The world factbook*. Langley: Central Intelligence Agency.

Clarke, J. (2000). Cambodia. In S. A. Gunaratne (Ed.), *Handbook of the media in Asia* (pp. 242–262). New Delhi: SAGE.

Cock, A. (2010). Anticipating an oil boom: The "Resource Curse" thesis in the play of Cambodian politics. *Pacific Affairs, 83*, 525–546. https://doi.org/10.5509/2010833525

Colletta, N. J., & Cullen, M. (2000). *The nexus between violent conflict, social capital and social cohesion: Case studies from Cambodia and Rwanda*. Accessed July 15, 2015, from http://documents.worldbank.org/curated/en/2000/09/1574622/nexus-between-violent-conflict-social-capital-social-cohesion-case-studies-cambodia-rwanda

COMFREL. (2012). *Final assessment and report on 2012 commune council elections*. Phnom Penh: Committee for Free and Fair Elections in Cambodia.

COMFREL. (2013). *2013 National assembly elections final assessment and report*. Phnom Penh: Committee for Free and Fair Elections in Cambodia.

Croissant, A. (2008). The perils and promises of democratization through United Nations transitional authority: Lessons from Cambodia and East Timor. *Democratization, 15*, 649–668. https://doi.org/10.1080/13510340801972403

Croissant, A. (2014). Ways of constitution-making in Southeast Asia: Actors, interests, dynamics. *Contemporary Southeast Asia, 36*, 23–51. https://doi.org/10.1355/cs36-1b

Croissant, A. (2016). *Electoral politics in Cambodia: Historical trajectories and current challenges*. Singapore: ISEAS.

Croissant, A. (2018). Cambodia in 2017. Descending into Dictatorship? *Asian Survey, 58*, 1.

Curly, M. (2004). *The role of the non-profit sector in transitional Asian economies: Cambodia ten years after UNTAC*. Conference paper presented at the 15th Biennial Conference presented at the Asian Studies Association of Australia, Canberra, 29 June–2 July 2004.

Danish Centre for Human Rights. (2001). *The police in Cambodia. Project Assessment Report Cambodia*. Copenhagen: Danish Centre for Human Rights.

de Zeeuw, J. (2010). 'Sons of war': Parties and party systems in post-war El Salvador and Cambodia. *Democratization, 17*, 1176–1201. https://doi.org/10.1080/13510347.2010.520549

Diamond, L. J., Plattner, M. F., & Chu, Y.-H. (Eds.). (2013). *Democracy in East Asia: A new century (A journal of democracy book)*. Baltimore, MD: Johns Hopkins University Press.

Dosch, J. (2012). The role of civil society in Cambodia's peace-building process. *Asian Survey, 52*, 1067–1088. https://doi.org/10.1525/as.2012.52.6.1067

Ear, S. (2009). The political economy of aid and regime legitimacy in Cambodia. In J. Öjendal & M. Lilja (Eds.), *Beyond democracy in Cambodia* (Democracy in Asia Series, Vol. 12, pp. 151–189). Copenhagen: NIAS Press.

Findlay, T. (1995). *Cambodia: The legacy and lessons of UNTAC*. Oxford: Oxford University Press.

Freedom House. (2014). *Freedom in the World 2014*. Retrieved July 15, 2015, from https://freedomhouse.org/

Freedom House. (2017). *Freedom of the press index 2017: Press freedom's dark horizon*. Accessed June 2, 2017, from https://freedomhouse.org/report/freedom-press/freedom-press-2017

Gallagher, M. (1991). Proportionality, disproportionality and electoral systems. *Electoral Studies, 10*, 33–51. https://doi.org/10.1016/0261-3794(91)90004-C

Gallup, J. (2002). Cambodia's electoral system: A window of opportunity for reform. In A. Croissant, G. Bruns, & M. John (Eds.), *Electoral politics in Southeast & East Asia* (pp. 25–75). Singapore: Friedrich Ebert Foundation.

Gerry, F., & Moore, C. (2015). A slippery and inconsistent slope: How Cambodia's draft cybercrime law exposed the dangerous drift away from International Human Rights Standards. *Computer Law & Security Review, 31*, 628–650.

Global Witness. (2009). Welcome to Cambodia: How Cambodia's elite has captured the country's extractive industries .

Harris, I. C. (2005). *Cambodian Buddhism: History and practice*. Honolulu: University of Hawai'i Press.

Hartmann, C. (2001). Cambodia. In D. Nohlen, F. Grotz, & C. Hartmann (Eds.), *Elections in Asia and the Pacific: A data handbook, Volume II: South East Asia, East Asia, and the South Pacific* (pp. 53–83). Oxford: Oxford University Press.

Heder, S. R. (2004). *Cambodian communism and the Vietnamese model*. Bangkok: White Lotus Press.

Heder, S. (2012). Cambodia: Capitalist transformation by neither Liberal Democracy nor Dictatorship. *Southeast Asian Affairs, 2012*(1), 103–115.

Hendrickson, D. (2001). Globalisation, insecurity and post-war reconstruction Cambodia's precarious transition. *IDS Bulletin, 32*, 98–106. https://doi.org/10.1111/j.1759-5436.2001.mp32002009.x

Higley, J., & Burton, M. G. (2006). *Elite foundations of liberal democracy (Elite transformations)*. Lanham: Rowman & Littlefield.

Hill, C. (2008). Vietnam: Constitutional development in a re-united Country. In C. Hill & J. Menzel (Eds.), *Constitutionalism in Southeast Asia: Volume 1: National Constitutions/ ASEAN charter* (pp. 327–355). Singapore: Konrad Adenauer Foundation.

Hill, H., & Menon, J. (2013). *Cambodia: Rapid growth with institutional constraints* (ADB Economics Working Paper Series, Vol. 331). Manila: Asian Development Bank.

HRW. (2010). Cambodia: Halt US Aid to Abusive Military Units. *Human Rights Watch*. Retrieved July 16, 2015, from http://www.hrw.org/news/2010/07/08/cambodia-halt-us-aid-abusive-military-units

Hughes, C. (2003). *The political economy of Cambodia's transition, 1991-2001*. London: Routledge.

Hughes, C. (2005). Candidate debates and equity news: International support for democratic deliberation in Cambodia. *Pacific Affairs, 78*, 77–93. https://doi.org/10.5509/200578177

Hughes, C. (2006). Violence and voting in post-1993 Cambodia. In A. Croissant, S. Kneip, & B. Martin (Eds.), *The politics of death: Political violence in Southeast Asia* (pp. 319–342). Münster: LIT Verlag.

Hughes, C. (2008). Cambodia in 2007: Development and dispossession. *Asian Survey, 48*, 69–74. https://doi.org/10.1525/as.2008.48.1.69

Hughes, C. (2009). Reconstructing legitimate political authority through elections? In J. Öjendal & M. Lilja (Eds.), *Beyond democracy in Cambodia* (Democracy in Asia Series, Vol. 12, pp. 31–70). Copenhagen: NIAS Press.

Hughes, C. (2010). Cambodia in 2009: The party's not over yet. *Southeast Asian Affairs, 2010*(1), 84–99.

Huntington, S. P. (1991). *The third wave: Democratization in the late twentieth century*. Norman: University of Oklahoma Press.

IISS. (2014). *The military balance 2014: International Institute for Strategic Studies*. London: Oxford University Press.

Inada, J. (2013). *Analysis of the survey on social capital in Cambodia*. Retrieved July 16, 2015, from http://www.senshu-u.ac.jp/scapital/pdf/08inada,sscr4.pdf

Inglehart, R. F., & Welzel, C. (2005). *Modernization, cultural change, and democracy: The human development sequence*. Cambridge: Cambridge University Press.

Internet World Stats. (2017). *Internet usage statistics: World internet users and 2017 population stats*. https://www.internetworldstats.com/stats.htm

IPU. (2014). *Interparliamentary Union Parline Database Cambodia*. Accessed June 20, 2017, from http://www.ipu.org/parline-e/reports/2051_arc.htm

IRI. (2013). *International Republican Institute Survey of Cambodian Public Opinion: October 28—November 10, 2013*. Washington: International Republican Institute.

Karbaum, M. (2008). *Kambodscha unter Hun Sen: Informelle Institutionen, politische Kultur und Herrschaftslegitimität*. Münster: LIT Verlag.

Kiernan, B. (1998). *The Pol Pot regime: Race, power, and genocide in Cambodia under the Khmer Rouge, 1975–79*. New Haven: Yale University Press.

Kiernan, B. (2003). *How Pol Pot came to power: Colonialism, nationalism, and communism in Cambodia, 1930–1975*. New Haven: Yale University Press.

Kong, P. (2012). Overview of the Cambodian legal and judicial system. In H. Peng, K. Phallack, & J. Menzel (Eds.), *Introduction to Cambodian law* (pp. 5–23). Phnom Penh: Konrad Adenauer Foundation.

Laakso, M., & Taagepera, R. (1979). 'Effective' number of parties: A measure with application to West Europe. *Comparative Political Studies, 12*(1), 3–27.

Levitsky, S., & Way, L. (2002). The rise of competitive authoritarianism. *Journal of Democracy, 13*, 51–65. https://doi.org/10.1353/jod.2002.0026

Levitsky, S., & Way, L. (2010). *Competitive authoritarianism: Hybrid regimes after the Cold War*. New York: Cambridge University Press.

Lijphart, A. (2012). *Patterns of democracy: Government forms and performance in thirty-six countries* (2nd ed.). New Haven: Yale University Press.

Manning, P. (2012). Governing memory: Justice, reconciliation and outreach at the extraordinary chambers in the Courts of Cambodia. *Memory Studies, 5*, 165–181. https://doi.org/10.1177/1750698011405183

Marks, S. P. (2010). The process of creating a new constitution in Cambodia. In L. E. Miller & L. Aucoin (Eds.), *Framing the state in times of transition: Case studies in constitution making* (pp. 207–244). Washington: United States Institute of Peace Press.

McCargo, D. (2014). Cambodia in 2013: (No)country for old men? *Asian Survey, 54*, 71–77. https://doi.org/10.1525/as.2014.54.1.71

Menzel, J. (2008). Cambodia—From civil war to a constitution to constitutionalism? In C. Hill & J. Menzel (Eds.), *Constitutionalism in Southeast Asia 2: Reports on National constitutions* (pp. 37–69). Singapore: Konrad Adenauer Foundation.

Morgenbesser, L. (2017). Misclassification on the Mekong: The origins of Hun Sen's personalist dictatorship. *Democratization, 29*, 1–18. https://doi.org/10.1080/13510347.2017.1289178

Mutz, G. (2003). Zivilgesellschaftliche Entwicklung in Südostasien. *Aus Politik und Zeitgeschichte*, (35–36), 32–38.

Niazi, T. (2011). *Deconcentration and decentralization reforms in Cambodia recommendations for an institutional framework*. Manila: Asian Development Bank.

O'Neill, D. C. (2016). Cambodia in 2015: From cooperation to conflict. *Asian Survey, 56*, 155–161. https://doi.org/10.1525/as.2016.56.1.155

Öjendal, J., & Lilja, M. (2009). Beyond democracy in Cambodia. Political reconstruction in a post-conflict society? In J. Öjendal & M. Lilja (Eds.), *Beyond democracy in Cambodia* (Democracy in Asia Series, Vol. 12, pp. 1–30). Copenhagen: NIAS Press.

Parameswaran, P. (2015). Cambodia boosts defense budget for 2016. The Diplomat. Accessed June 15, 2017, from http://thediplomat.com/2015/12/cambodia-boosts-defense-budget-for-2016/

Peng, H. (2012). In K. Phallack & J. Menzel (Eds.), *Introduction to Cambodian law*. Phnom Penh: Konrad Adenauer Foundation.

Peng, H., Phallack, K., & Menzel, J. (Eds.). (2012). *Introduction to Cambodian law*. Phnom Penh: Konrad Adenauer Foundation.

Peou, S. (2000). *Intervention and change in Cambodia: Towards democracy?* Chiang Mai: Silkworm Press.

Peou, S. (2006). Consolidation or crisis of democracy? Cambodia's parliamentary elections in 2003 and beyond. In A. Croissant & B. Martin (Eds.), *Between consolidation and crisis: Elections and democracy in five nations in Southeast Asia* (pp. 41–83). Münster: LIT Verlag.

Peou, S. (2007). *International democracy assistance for peacebuilding: Cambodia and beyond*. Basingstoke: Palgrave Macmillan.

Peou, S. (2015). Party and Party system institutionalization in Cambodia. In A. Hicken & E. M. Kuhonta (Eds.), *Party system institutionalization in Asia: Democracies autocracies and the shadows of the past* (pp. 212–236). New York: Cambridge University Press.

Pew Research Center. (2016). *Religious composition by country 2010–2050*. Pew Research Center. Accessed June 15, 2017, from http://www.pewforum.org/2015/04/02/religious-projection-table/

Phnom Penh Post. (2013). *Many hues of Cambodia's might*. Retrieved July 16, 2015, from http://www.phnompenhpost.com/7days/many-hues-cambodia%E2%80%99s-might

Reporters without Borders. (2017). *2017 World Press Freedom index*. RSF. Accessed June 22, 2017, from https://rsf.org/en/ranking

Richardson, M. (2001). *NGO sector report*. Phnom Penh: Cambodia NGO Support Network.

Ricklefs, M. C. (2010). *A new history of Southeast Asia*. Basingstoke: Palgrave Macmillan.

Ritter, M. (2008). *Medien und Demokratisierung in Kambodscha*. Berlin: Frank & Timme.

Roberts, D. (2001). *Political transition in Cambodia 1991-1999: Power, elitism and democracy*. London: Curzon.

Royal Government of Cambodia. (1994). *Law on the organization and functioning of the council of ministers*. Retrieved July 16, 2015, from http://www.bigpond.com.kh/council_of_jurists/constit/cons002g.htm

Sartori, G. (1987). *The theory of democracy revisited*. Chatham: Chatham House.

Schedler, A. (2006). The logic of electoral authortarianism. In A. Schedler (Ed.), *Electoral authoritarianism* (pp. 2–35). Boulder, CO: Lynne Rienner.

Schmidt, M. G. (2016). Legitimation through performance?: Output legitimacy in authoritarian regimes. In U. Backes & S. Kailitz (Eds.), *Ideocracies in comparison: Legitimation—co-optation—repression* (pp. 289–304). London: Routledge.

Sedara, K., & Öjendal, J. (2009). Decentralization as a strategy for state reconstruction. In J. Öjendal & M. Lilja (Eds.), *Beyond democracy in Cambodia* (Democracy in Asia Series, Vol. 12, pp. 101–136). Copenhagen: NIAS Press.

Sen, V. (2012). Social capital in an urban and a rural community in Cambodia. *Cambodia Development Review, 16*, 6–10.

Shawcross, W. (1994). *Cambodia's new deal: A report*. Washington: Carnegie Endowment for International Peace.

SIPRI. (2015). *SIPRI yearbook: Armaments, disarmament and international security*. Oxford: Oxford University Press.

Slocomb, M. (2004). Commune elections in Cambodia: 1981 foundations and 2002 reformulations. *Modern Asian Studies, 38*, 447–467. https://doi.org/10.1017/S0026749X03001215

Strangio, S. (2014). *Hun Sen's Cambodia*. New Haven: Yale University Press.

The Cambodia Daily. (2013). *More four-star generals added to RCAF's top-heavy ranks*. Retrieved July 16, 2015, from http://www.cambodiadaily.com/archives/more-four-star-generals-added-to-rcafs-top-heavy-ranks-52240/

The Cambodia Daily. (2014). *Armed security doubled for human rights day rallies*. Retrieved July 16, 2015, from http://www.opendevelopmentcambodia.net/tag/prime-minister-hun-sens-personal-bodyguard-unit/

Transparency International. (2015). *Corruption perception index.* Accessed June 1, 2017, from https://www.transparency.org/news/feature/corruption_perceptions_index_2016

Tully, J. A. (2002). *France on the Mekong: A history of the protectorate in Cambodia, 1863–1953.* Lanham: University Press of America.

Tully, J. (2005). *Short history of Cambodia: From empire to survival.* Sydney: Allen & Unwin.

Turner, M. (2006). From commitment to consequences. *Public Management Review, 8,* 253–272. https://doi.org/10.1080/14719030600587471

Un, K. (2004). *Democratization without consolidation, 1993-2004.* Unpublished dissertation. De Kalb: Northern Illinois State University.

Un, K. (2006). State, society and democratic consolidation: The case of Cambodia. *Pacific Affairs, 79,* 225–245. https://doi.org/10.5509/2006792225

Un, K. (2008). *Cambodia's 2008 parliamentary elections: Prospects for opposition politics* (Asia Pacific Bulletin, Vol. 22). Honululu: East-West Center.

Un, K. (2009). The judicial system and democratization in post-conflict Cambodia. In J. Öjendal & M. Lilja (Eds.), *Beyond democracy in Cambodia* (Democracy in Asia Series, Vol. 12, pp. 70–1001). Copenhagen: NIAS Press.

Un, K. (2011). Cambodia: Moving away from democracy? *International Political Science Review, 32,* 546–562. https://doi.org/10.1177/0192512111417120

Un, K. (2012). Cambodia in 2011: A thin veneer of change. *Asian Survey, 52,* 202–209. https://doi.org/10.1525/as.2012.52.1.202

Un, K. (2013). Cambodia in 2012: Beyond the crossroads? *Asian Survey, 53,* 142–149. https://doi.org/10.1525/as.2013.53.1.142

UNDP. (2012). *World population prospects: The 2012 revision.* New York: United Nations Development Program.

World Bank. (2017). *Worldwide governance indicators.* http://data.worldbank.org/data-catalog/worldwide-governance-indicators

Wüpper, A. (2006). Senatswahlen in Kambodscha. *KAS-Auslandsinformationen, 3,* 99–117.

Indonesia: Challenges of Conflict and Consensus in the Era of Reformasi

4

© Springer International Publishing AG 2018
A. Croissant, P. Lorenz, *Comparative Politics of Southeast Asia*,
https://doi.org/10.1007/978-3-319-68182-5_4

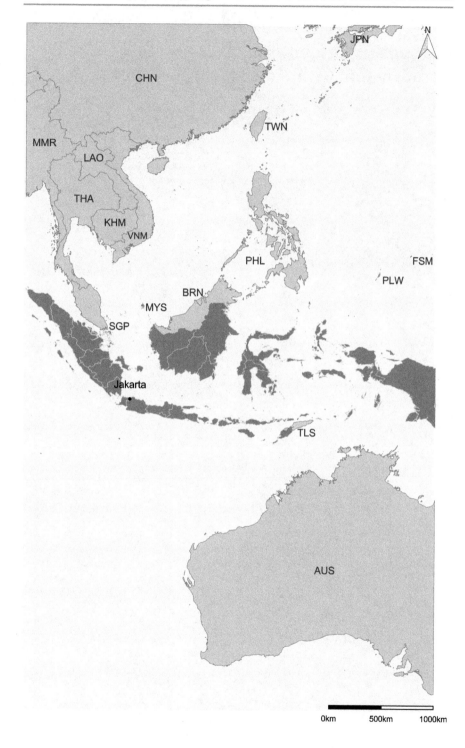

4.1 Historical Background

The Republic of Indonesia is the world's largest archipelagic state with more than 13,000 islands. It is the most populous Muslim-majority country in the world and one of Southeast Asia's ethnically most heterogeneous societies. It is also the largest economy in the region and is regarded one of only a few relatively stable and well-functioning democracies in this part of the world (see Table 4.1).

Like in Timor-Leste and the Philippines, the Portuguese and Spanish were the first Europeans to arrive at the Indonesian archipelago in the sixteenth century. The Dutch United East India Company (*Vereenigde Oostindische Compagnie*, VOC) followed in 1595 and established its headquarters in Batavia (Jakarta) in 1619. Through a series of military campaigns and agreements with local rulers, the VOC was able to gain access and eventually control over the Eastern Indonesian Spice Islands and the sea lanes passing through western Indonesia. Initially, the Dutch rarely ventured into the hinterland and exercised political control mainly through agreements with local rulers rather than through direct rule (Taylor 2004, p. 198). After the dissolution of the VOC, the British-Dutch Treaty of 1824 established an area of control for the Dutch government that closely resembled the shape of modern Indonesia, even though Dutch control over vast parts of the archipelago remained patchy and incomplete (Ricklefs 2008, p. 179). In the 1830s, a new

Table 4.1 Country profile Indonesia

Population (2017)	Year of full national sovereignty	Form of government
260,580,739	1949	Republic
Total area	**Current constitution enacted**	**Head of state**
1,904,569 km^2	1945	Joko Widodo (since 2014)
GDP per capita, PPP (constant 2011 international $) 2015	**Official language**	**Head of government**
10,385	Bahasa Indonesia	Joko Widodo (since 2014)
Ethnic groups	**Democracy score (BTI 2016)**	**System of government**
Javanese 40.1%, Sundanese 15.5%, Malay 3.7%, Batak 3.6%, Madurese 3%, Betawi 2.9%, Minangkabau 2.7%, Buginese 2.7%, Bantenese 2%, Banjarese 1.7%, Balinese 1.7%, Acehnese 1.4%, Dayak 1.4%, Sasak 1.3%, Chinese 1.2%, other 15%	6.90 (range from 1 to 10, higher scores indicate higher levels of democracy)	Presidential
Religions	**Regime type**	**Cabinet type**
Muslim 87.2%, Christian 7%, Roman Catholic 2.9%, Hindu 1.7%, other 0.9%	Democracy	Multiparty coalition

Source: CIA (2017), BTI (2016), and World Bank (2017b)

agricultural policy, the so-called Cultivation System (*cultuurstelsel*), was introduced. This system forced villages to set aside a fifth of their arable land for the production of export crops that were to be delivered to the colonial authorities as land rent. This approach was a great economic success for the colonial authorities and made local possessions much more lucrative, leading the Dutch to expand their area of control. Nonetheless, the process of effectively converting the East Indies into a unified colonial dependency took several decades before areas such as Kalimantan (Borneo), the South Eastern Islands (Nusa Tenggara), Bali, and—in 1908—Aceh were brought under Dutch control.

A new liberal colonial program, decreed by Queen Wilhelmina in 1901, was the impetus for the further expansion and intensification of Dutch rule. Under the so-called Ethical Policy, the Netherlands provided financial assistance for the extension of health and education services and to stimulate the growth of the rural economy (Vickers 2005, pp. 17–19). In addition, access to education created a new local elite looking for "Western" employment opportunities but often still tied into traditional society. This elite formed the spearhead of organized nationalism, spread Bahasa Indonesia as a *lingua franca* throughout the archipelago, and became the nucleus of an emerging independence movement (Ricklefs 2008, pp. 193–195). It was during this time that the first mass organizations, including Islamic organizations[1] such as the modernist *Muhammadiyah* (1912), the traditionalist *Nahdlatul Ulama* (NU, 1926), and political parties like the Indies Social Democratic Association (1914), which became the *Partei Komunis Indonesia* (PKI) in 1924, were created. Similar to the French in Indochina, the Dutch colonial power tried to repress political nationalism and anticolonial activism, but to no avail. When the Japanese invaded Indonesia in January 1942, the colonial government was quickly swept away (Ricklefs 2008, p. 227).

The collapse of Dutch rule in the East Indies provided a fertile environment for Indonesian nationalists. Despite increasingly repressive and exploitative Japanese rule, nationalist leaders such as Sukarno and Mohammad Hatta were able to trade support for political concessions. Two days after Japan's official surrender on August 15, 1945, Sukarno and Hatta proclaimed the sovereign Republic of

---

[1]Islam in Indonesia is not a monolithic phenomenon. Anthropologists traditionally differentiate a strict, relatively scriptural practice of Islam (*santri*) and one that is more syncretistic in nature and integrates Sunni and Sufi practice with indigenous rituals and ancestral worship (*abangan*). Today, the parallel distinction between a modernist and traditionalist interpretation is more common (Bush 2009, p. 29). Religious scholars trained in the Middle East brought modernism to Indonesia in the 1920s and 1930s. It stresses the individual study of Islam's scriptural sources in the Sunna and Koran. In contrast, traditionalist Islam places more trust in the magisterium of religious teachers, the *ulema*. Consequently, the two religious mass organizations associated with modernist and traditionalist Islam are called "Followers of Mohammed" (*Muhammadiyah*) and "Awakening of the Religious Scholars" (*Nahdlatul Ulama*). Modernism is more prevalent in the urban centers of Indonesia, in West Java, and Aceh, whereas traditionalism is stronger in rural areas and especially East Java. Within each school there are more liberal and radical members as well as different attitudes towards the relationship of Islam and politics. However, there are more radical Islamists among modernist Muslims in Indonesia (van Bruinessen 2002).

Indonesia, ushering in one of the most confusing periods in modern Indonesian history. On Java and Sumatra, a motley collection of Indonesian fighters took up a guerilla-style campaign against returning Dutch troops trying to retake their colonial possessions. After international criticism of the ruthless Dutch counterinsurgency campaign, the Netherlands finally accepted Indonesian independence on December 27, 1949.

The struggle for independence left Indonesia with a wide array of political forces, including the secular National Party of Indonesia (PNI) under Sukarno, the communist PKI, the traditionalist NU, the modernist *Masyumi*, and the military (TNI/ABRI). After a series of short-lived parliamentary governments, Indonesia's first president Sukarno established himself as a charismatic leader (Feith 1962) and established the authoritarian "Guided Democracy" based on the doctrines of corporatist "functional groups" (*golongan karya*, Golkar) and *Pancasila* (see Sect. 4.2) in 1957. His support coalition included almost all relevant political groupings, including the military and—after 1962—the PKI (Sundhaussen 1982, p. 156). Despite the army's hostility, Sukarno strengthened his ties with the Communists and followed an increasingly erratic economic and foreign policy. In 1965, the social, political, and economic structures of the new nation were near to collapse (Ricklefs 2008, p. 338). On the night of September 30 to October 1, 1965, tensions culminated when a group of left-leaning air force officers killed several members of the military leadership in a botched coup attempt (Roosa 2006, pp. 62–81). In retaliation, Major General Suharto and several anticommunist groups orchestrated a violent campaign against PKI and real or suspected Communists, which quickly escalated. Between October 1965 and March 1966, more than 500,000 people were killed. Once the PKI was eliminated as a political force, Sukarno was made to first transfer executive control to the new strongman, Suharto, and finally, on March 27, 1968, the presidency as well.

President Suharto transformed elements of Sukarno's "Guided Democracy" into his "New Order" government (Slater 2010). Next to the president and the bureaucracy, the military became part of the "New Order Pyramid" (Liddle 1985, p. 71), providing regime security and helping control society through surveillance and coercion. While this initially made the military-as-institution very influential, Suharto slowly shifted this influence towards individual military officers loyal to himself over the next three decades, transforming his "New Order" regime from military domination to personalistic authoritarian rule (Slater 2010). In order to circumscribe the remaining military political influence on the national level and include it into his patronage system, the President successfully balanced the military factions in parliament and Golkar, the regime party. Golkar was created as a joint vehicle for military and bureaucratic political domination. However, because Suharto fostered the gradual civilianization of Golkar, by the 1990s, the military-as-institution was no longer able to influence politics without Suharto's backing (Tomsa 2008, p. 39).

Suharto also managed to restore the fledgling economy and created stable growth through a combination of liberal reforms and nationalist development planning (Pepinsky 2009, pp. 43–45). A boom in the production of oil and natural gas in the 1970s meant the regime could expand its administrative reach and capacity (Smith 2007), and Suharto increasingly relied on this revenue to stabilize his regime coalition with patronage payments (Slater 2010). The resulting system of Corruption, Collusion, and Nepotism (*Korrupsi, Kollusi, Nepotisme*, KKN) proved flawed when Indonesia's economy collapsed following the Asian Financial Crisis and a severe drought in 1997, as Suharto was unwilling to alienate his patronage network by implementing the necessary reforms. When mass protests against the regime erupted across the country, soft-liners in the military and Golkar leadership pushed Suharto to step down in favor of his vice president, Bahruddin Yusuf Habibie, on May 21, 1998 (Honna 2003, pp. 160–165). Under Habibie and his democratically elected successor Abdurrahman Wahid, Indonesia entered into *reformasi*, the era of democratization.

In the first years after the transition from dictatorship to democracy, Indonesia experienced several political crises. The country was rocked by a series of violent communal conflicts and challenged by an outburst of Islamic terrorism. However, today most ethnic conflicts have calmed down and religiously motivated terrorism never endangered the survival of democracy. The new democracy survived the impeachment of President Wahid in 2001, and free and fair elections are widely accepted as the only legitimate means of gaining government power. The country successfully passed the "two turnover test," meaning that an incumbent party was voted out of office twice, leading to peaceful transfers of power in 2004 and 2014. Despite its resilience in the face of political and economic crises, however, democracy in Indonesia is not fully consolidated yet. Four major challenges remain.

The first one relates to the unintended consequences of elite settlement and elite cooperation as the main mode of integrating potential spoilers of the old autocratic regime coalition into the new democratic system (Aspinall 2010). On the one hand, these old elites now have a stake in the democratic process (Horowitz 2013). On the other hand, the ruling oligarchy of the ancient regime quickly reestablished itself in the new democratic order (Robison and Hadiz 2004), with potentially negative consequences for transitional justice, better rule of law, and less KKN. A second challenge, related to the first, concerns the anemic quality of the rule of law, endemic corruption in politics and the state, and the still low capacity of the Indonesian state, which block comprehensive structural reforms, undermine regulatory efforts of the state, and weaken democratic accountability. Third, Indonesia's democracy has not yet overcome the nation's manifold problems relating to social and economic justice. While democratization and party competition have contributed to greater government spending on social security, health, education, housing, and personal social services, which, among other things, contributed to a reduction of absolute poverty in Indonesia (Aspinall 2014; see Table 4.2), vertical inequalities and horizontal regional disparities persist (McCulloch and Sjahrir 2008). Perceptions of socioeconomic injustice, in turn, contribute to political dissatisfaction with the workings and political performance of democracy.

Fourth, although Indonesia's achievements with regard to press freedoms, political rights, labor rights, and women's rights have been far-reaching and impressive, it still suffers serious shortcomings when it comes to the protection of religious

Table 4.2 Poverty and income inequality in Indonesia, 1996–2011

	1996	1999	2005	2011
% of population with less than USD2/day	30.7	33.3	17.3	13.0
Relative income of top and bottom decile	6.7	5.8	7.7	9.6
Gini-index[a]	31.3	29.0	34.0	38.1

Source: World Bank (2017a)

[a]Measure for income inequality, 1 denotes equal distribution, 100 perfectly unequal distribution

freedoms (Crouch 2013; Hefner 2016). Several domestic and foreign scholars have voiced concerns about a deepening climate of religious intolerance, contributing to sectarian violence against apostates from Islam and religious minorities (Alfitri 2008; Mietzner 2009a, p. 109).

4.2 Constitutional History

Indonesia's constitutional history is complex (cf. Table 4.3). In anticipation of the Japanese defeat, the nation's first constitution was drafted as a very short "Basic Law" in April 1945 (*Undang-undang dasar* 1945, UUD 1945). Its preamble stressed the need for a unitary republic and established the *Pancasila* doctrine as a normative principle for all government action: belief in one god,[2] a just and civilized humanity, the unity of Indonesia, democracy guided by wisdom and deliberation by representatives of the people, and the achievement of social justice for all the people of Indonesia.

A Dutch-Indonesian Round Table Conference in December 1949 ended the 4-year conflict between the Netherlands and the Republic over the control of Indonesia, but the Dutch government formally transferred sovereignty to the Republic of the United States of Indonesia (*Republik Indonesia Serikat*, RIS), instead of the existing Republic of Indonesia. This meant the existing constitution was abandoned in favor of a new federal constitution (KRIS; Indrayana 2008a, p. 96). The Indonesian side suspected that the Dutch had proposed a federal solution to weaken the new state, and KRIS was, therefore, quickly replaced with a new Provisional Basic Law (*Undang-undang Dasar Sementara* 1950, UUDS 1950). Although this constitution abolished federalism in favor of a unitary republic, it also adopted a list of basic rights from the KRIS (Supomo 1964; Indrayana 2008a).

A Constituent Assembly elected in 1955 to draft a permanent constitution failed primarily over the role of Islam in the constitution (Nasution 1992). Sukarno used this as a pretext to decree a return to the original constitution of 1945, which stipulated a strong president indirectly elected by the People's Consultative

---

[2]Officially recognized "religions" (*agama*) include Islam, Catholicism, Protestantism, Buddhism, and Judaism. Even Hinduism, the dominant religion on Bali, is legally considered a monotheistic religion. Other "beliefs" (*kepercayaan*) like ancestral worship or animism, prevalent in eastern Indonesia, are not considered religions.

Table 4.3 Indonesia's constitutions, 1945–2016

Constitution in force	Name	Days in effect	Length (words BI)	Reason for replacement
18/08/1945–31/01/1950	Basic Law of 1945 (UUD 1945)	1627	1334	Transfer of sovereignty to RIS
31/01/1950–17/08/1950	Constitution of the United States of Indonesia (KRIS)	198	11,571	Dissolution of RIS
17/08/1950–05/07/1959	Provisional Basic Law of 1950 (UUDS 1950)	3244	7003	Proclamation of Guided Democracy
05/07/1959-	Basic Law of 1945 (UUD 1945)		1334 (4708 after amendments)	In force (with amendments)

Source: Authors' compilation with dates taken from Ricklefs (2008)

Assembly (*Majelis Permusyawaratan Rakyat*, MPR). The vague nature of the UUD 1945 allowed Sukarno, and later Suharto, to rule largely on the basis of presidential and MPR decrees (Liddle 1985, p. 70).

After Suharto resigned in May 1998, constitution builders chose to revise the 1945 Constitution that had been in force from 1945 to 1949 and again from 1959 to 1998. The decision to revise the existing constitution rather than redraft a new constitution altogether was based on a compromise between political parties, who wanted to avoid the deadlock that arose in the 1955 Constituent Assembly over religious issues. Over the course of 3 years, the MPR prepared and adopted four amendments to the 1945 Constitution. However, as Indrayana notes, the amendments between 1999 and 2002 affected "95% of the chapters, 89% of the Articles, and 85% of the paragraphs" of the constitutional text and "are either new or were alterations of the originals" (Indrayana 2008a, p. 101). Consequently, the substance of every chapter in the constitution except the chapter on religion was amended (Indrayana 2008a, pp. 101, 105).

The constitution is preceded by a preamble, which incorporates the *Pancasila* philosophy and the idea of a unitary state. Both the principles of *Pancasila* and the unitary nature of the republic, but also the presidential system of government, remained more or less uncontroversial (Ellis 2005, p. 6). However, many of the elucidations previously listed in the constitution's annex were now included in the constitutional text itself. Furthermore, as a response to the repressive policies of the Suharto regime, the constitution now has a bill of rights and extensive provisions for the rule of law. Yet it still lacks certain basic rights such as the right not to confess a faith (negative freedom of religion) and a reference to the principle of equality between men and women. In addition, basic rights can be suspended or curtailed for security reasons or to protect religious sensitivities (Stockmann 2007, p. 22; Alfitri 2008). Other major amendments introduced direct popular elections for the presidency (Art. 6A) and more detailed regulations on presidential legislative powers. As a response to public criticism of the ambiguous role of the MPR in the impeachment of President Wahid in 2001, the impeachment procedure was also revised. In addition, the legislative and budgetary authority of parliament was strengthened and a constitutional court and other watchdog agencies were established for the first time. Finally, the MPR has the authority to amend and enact the constitution: amendments may be initiated by a third of the members of the MPR and can be enacted by a majority of the House. However, Art. 37 of the constitution stipulates that the unitary character of the state must not be changed. Once the MPR ratified the sum of all constitutional amendments in 2003, the constitutional reform process was considered complete (Horowitz 2013).

4.3   System of Government

Indonesia is a "unitary state in the form of a republic" (Art. 1,1 UUD45) with a presidential system of government. The legislature is comprised of two houses, the People's Representative Council (*Dewan Perwakilan Rakyat*, DPR) and the Regional Representative Council (*Dewan Perwakilan Daerah*, DPD), but legislative power mainly rests with the DPR. The president holds main executive power and fulfils an important legislative role. The judiciary is organized as a separate branch of government and is headed by the Supreme Court and Constitutional Court (Art. 24C). In addition, the constitution lists the central bank (Bank Indonesia, BI; Art. 23D) and the Audit Board (*Badan Pemeriksa Keuangan*, BPK; Art. 23E) as additional independent government bodies. The Corruption Eradication Commission (KPK), the General Election Commission (KPU), the Election Monitoring Body (*Bawaslu*), the Judicial Commission (KY), and the Human Rights Commission (*Komnas HAM*) are additional watchdog agencies established by law.

4.3.1   Head of State and Government

In Indonesia, the president is the head of state and the head of the government (see Fig. 4.1). Prior to 2004, president and vice president were indirectly elected by the MPR. Since 2004, both are popularly elected for a 5-year term that is renewable once. In general elections, presidential candidates run together with vice presidential candidates on a "party ticket." That is, voters only vote for one ticket; in contrast to the Philippines, they cannot choose a presidential candidate from one ticket and a vice presidential candidate from another ticket. Any party or coalition of parties that gained a total of 20% of seats or 25% of votes in the previous DPR election can nominate a presidential ticket (UU 42/2008, Art. 9). Should no ticket gain over half of the total valid votes as well as at least 20% of votes in at least half of Indonesia's provinces after the first ballot, a runoff is held. The introduction of direct presidential elections and the runoff system with limited opportunities for political parties to nominate candidates creates strong institutional incentives for

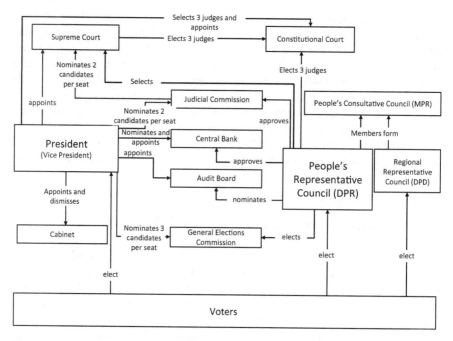

Fig. 4.1 Indonesia's system of government. Source: Authors' compilation

coalition politics. In fact, two of the three popularly elected presidents since Suharto's ousting in 1998 already won a majority of the popular vote in the first round (see Table 4.4).

Until 1999, the president was politically accountable only to the MPR (Ellis 2005). There was no term limit, which made it possible for Suharto to rule for 32 years. Fears of another strongman rule led to the introduction of popular elections for the presidency, the imposition of a two-term limit on presidential candidates, and the amendment of impeachment rules. Today, impeachment is an enumerated power of the DPR that allows formal charges to be brought against the president for alleged crimes. Impeachment proceedings may be commenced by the DPR on its own initiative. If a two-thirds majority of the DPR adopts a resolution of impeachment, the Constitutional Court debates the resolution's legality before it is forwarded to the MPR, which then can remove the president from office if three-fourths of its members support the impeachment (Indrayana 2008b, p. 174).

The vice president is officially no more than the first person in the presidential line of succession upon death, resignation, or removal of the president. However, a vice president with strong parliamentary backing can have considerable influence and may preside over tasks such as drafting and communicating the administration's policies, serving as advisor to the president or facilitator of dialogue between president and parliament. The vice presidential candidate is often chosen to "balance a ticket" that combines a religious candidate with a secular nationalist or a Javanese candidate with a candidate from one of the outer islands

Table 4.4 Presidential elections in Indonesia, 2004–2014[a]

	Candidate	Votes (%, first round)	Votes (%, runoff)
2004	Susilo Bambang Yudhoyono	33.6	60.6
	Wiranto	22.2	
	Megawati Sukarnoputri	26.2	39.1
	Amien Rais	14.7	
	Hamzah Haz	3.0	
2008	Susilo Bambang Yudhoyono	60.8	
	Jusuf Kalla	12.4	
	Megawati Sukarnoputri	26.8	
2014	Joko Widodo ("Jokowi")	53.2	
	Prabowo Subianto	46.8	

Source: KPU (2014)

[a]Until 2004, the president was indirectly elected by the MPR

(King 2004, p. 181). Since democratization, the presidential ticket has also foreshadowed the core of a later government coalition.

The president is assisted by a cabinet. Ministers are selected by the president and are directly responsible to the president alone, but parliament has to approve major changes to the responsibilities of different ministries (King 2004, p. 86). The cabinet is called Council of Ministers and includes resort ministers, coordinating ministers, and cabinet-level officials such as the attorney general and the chief of the State Intelligence Agency.

Indonesian cabinets have always tended to be large, as positions are used to establish patronage or to reward political allies. While in office, ministers representing political parties often focus on maximizing the patronage potential of their office rather than their contribution to government work (Sherlock 2009, p. 342). Anticipating future problems of cabinet discipline and the need for broad legislative majorities, Indonesian presidents often create oversized "rainbow coalitions" and entrust technocrats unaffiliated with political parties with key portfolios (Diamond 2009; Slater and Simmons 2012).

The constitutional amendments after the downfall of Suharto strengthened the system of horizontal accountability (Ellis 2005, p. 15) but hardly reduced the constitutional powers of the presidency. The president is commander-in-chief of the National Armed Forces, can invoke a state of emergency, and has broad authority over government policies, including foreign policy. However, the DPR has a role in ratifying international treaties if these necessitate changes to existing legislation as well as in the presidential nominations of ambassadors. Military and police chiefs also require parliamentary confirmation. While presidential executive orders are now regulated in greater detail and have to be confirmed by parliament (King 2004, p. 26), "government decrees in lieu of law" (*Perpu*) can only be adopted or rejected by the DPR unanimously, giving them some potential to dissolve legislative deadlocks (Lindsey 2002). The president's most important legislative power, however, is Art 20.2, which mandates the "mutual agreement" of parliament and government before any bill can be enacted into law. Even without

Table 4.5 Presidential powers in Indonesia, 1998 and 2002

	1998	2002		1998	2002
Legislative Powers (total)	8	8	Nonlegislative Powers (total)	12	11
Package Veto/Override	4	4	Cabinet Formation	4	3
Line Item Veto/Override	0	0	Cabinet Dismissal	4	4
Decree Powers	2	2	Censure	4	4
Exclusive Introduction of Legislation	1	1	Dissolution of Assembly	0	0
Budgetary Powers	1	1			
Proposal of Referenda	0	0			

Source: King (2004, pp. 231–234)
Notes: Scores based on index proposed by Shugart and Carey (1992, p. 150)

a formal veto, the president only signs bills into law he or she or a cabinet member bound by presidential instruction has already approved (King 2004, p. 232). Furthermore, the government introduces the national budget after each ministry has consulted the parliamentary commissions in its area of responsibility (Juwono and Eckardt 2008, p. 299). During the actual budget negotiations, parliament can determine the size and appropriation of the overall budget as well as individual budget items. In recent years, members of parliament have often used this to benefit their electoral districts or trade provisions for financial kickbacks (Juwono and Eckardt 2008, p. 302). Like any regular law, the budget can only be passed if government and parliament reach mutual agreement. Without such agreement, the previous annual budget remains in effect.

Table 4.5 compares the scores of presidential power in the two basic dimensions of presidential power (legislative/nonlegislative) identified by Shugart and Carey (1992, p. 150) before and after the constitutional amendments of 1999–2002. Shugart and Carey rate the relative authority of president and parliament according to 10 items. All the ten legislative and four other powers are rated on a scale of 0–4 points. With a score of 8 in the first dimension, and 11 (2002) in the second, the Indonesian president is more powerful than any other popularly elected president in Southeast Asia and—in regard to his or her legislative powers—than the U.S. president. Yet, it is important to note that Indonesia's president is much weaker in terms of appointing authority than the president of the Philippines (see Chap. 8).

4.3.2 Parliament and Legislative Process

Until 2004, the People's Consultative Assembly (*Majelis Permusyawaratan Rakyat*, MPR) was the highest constitutional body in Indonesia. It consisted of all members of the DPR and representatives of various "functional groups" such as the military, the civil service, and regional administrative units, who were mainly appointed by the president. Suharto used his appointments to control the MPR politically (Kawamura 2010, pp. 5–6). Until 2001, the sheer extent of formal political powers wielded by the MPR (which included the DPR) made it a "super parliament" (Braun 2008, p. 84). Following the constitutional amendments from 1999 to 2002, the MPR lost its legislative and electoral functions completely. As it does not play any role in either legislation or the creation of government, it can no longer be considered a second chamber or "upper house."

Since 2003, the legislative branch of government comprises the People's Representative Council (*Dewan Perwakilan Rakyat*, DPR) with 560 members and the Regional Representative Council (*Dewan Perwakilan Daerah*, DPD). Elections for both houses of parliament are held simultaneously 3 months prior to the first round of presidential elections. Membership in either house is incompatible with any other government office, and members of the armed forces or the national police must retire before running for parliamentary office.

DPD "represents the odd combination of limited powers and high legitimacy" (Sherlock 2006, p. 7). It has 136 representatives, four from each of the 34 provinces. Nonpartisan candidates from the respective provinces are elected through a single-non-transferable-vote system (SNTV). That is, each voter has a single vote, and the four candidates with the highest vote totals in each province are elected. Its functions are mainly deliberative: The DPD can initiate bills concerning regional affairs, which, however, are channeled through DPR, and it must be consulted on parliamentary bills regarding provincial or regional matters (Ziegenhain 2015, p. 196).

The constitution entrusts the DPR with the authority to pass legislation and the national budget as well as to hold the government accountable (Art. 20A.1). Compared to other legislatures worldwide, the DPR has strong budgetary powers (Wehner 2006) and in the region stands out for the strength of its monitoring powers (Rüland et al. 2005). Groups of at least 13 members can form party caucuses, and the DPR chair is usually a member of the largest caucus in parliament. As a "working parliament," the DPR conducts most of its work in 11 standing committees (*komisi*). Additionally, there is a budget committee with delegates from all other committees and two influential parliamentary steering committees (*badan permusywaran*, Bamus and *badan legislatif*, Baleg). Parliament can also create special committees for investigative purposes or for legislative processes cutting across the normal committee structure (Juwono and Eckardt 2008, p. 298; Braun 2008, p. 220). The *komisi* have an average of 50 members and reflect parliamentary majorities (Schneier 2008, p. 203). Since each DPR member is on only one committee and DPR's standing orders are vague on committee procedures, each committee develops very distinct procedures and patterns of authority. This "balkanization" of parliamentary work (Sherlock 2010, p. 166) makes it difficult for external observers to follow the legislative process, let alone influence it successfully (Rüland et al. 2005, p. 230; Sherlock 2010, p. 172). During negotiations cutting across different committees, committee membership is often more indicative of individual policy positions than party affiliation (Sherlock 2010, p. 166). The committees also oversee the examination, selection, or confirmation of candidates for other government bodies, including military and police commanders.

While it is not uncommon for celebrities without political experience to be elected to parliament, most MPs are former government officials or businessmen (Datta et al. 2011). In recent years, military retirees (*purnawirawan*) have also increasingly played important roles in the DPR and subnational parliaments (Aminuddin 2016; Gunawan 2017). Overall, DPR is a relatively inefficient parliament: between 2005 and 2009, only half of the prioritized legislative processes could be concluded (DPR 2010).

The annual National Legislative Program (*program legislasi nasional*, Prolegnas), developed jointly by government and DPR leadership, identifies priority bills for the upcoming sitting periods. The initial drafts of most bills part of the Prolegnas are developed by government ministries. Parliamentary initiatives can be developed by individual parliamentarians, one or several committees, and need at least ten signatures from members of parliament before the Baleg steering committee can appoint one of the standing committees or a special committee for its deliberation (cf. Fig. 4.2). Draft laws originating from DPD also have to be adopted as a DPR initiative. Once a bill is assigned to a committee, the government appoints an official representative for the first stage of the legislative process. This gives the government a first chance to delay deliberations (Schneier 2008). From this point on, parliamentary and government initiatives follow the same procedure. Each parliamentary faction as well as the government develop "Problem Inventory Lists" (*daftar inventarisasi masalah*, DIM) that identify points of contention in the bill and propose alternative formulations. Once these problems have been resolved and members of the committee no longer raise concerns about the bill, it is considered passed, usually without a formal vote. The Bamus steering committee then schedules the bill for a plenary vote. This "deliberation until consensus" (*musyawarah untuk mufakat*) is a basic norm of Indonesian parliamentary procedures. Because it gives every parliamentary group an effective veto over legislation, deliberations are often protracted. Even if a clear majority is in favor of a draft, committee members often rather scrap a bill than force a formal vote and violate the consensus principle (Febrian 2009). Even though consensus and voting are equally valid ways of passing a law, "they are not equally valued" (Braun 2008, p. 127).

The main reason why DPR has consistently fallen short of its legislative agenda is that the government, as mentioned, has an effective veto over any piece of legislation. Because the government is usually represented by a ministry, special interests have sometimes used the need for "mutual agreement" to protect the status quo. The military, for example, has so far derailed any attempt to reform the military justice system through its influence over the Department of Defense (Braun 2008, pp. 192–193).

At the second stage of the legislative process, the plenary is informed about the results of the first stage and government and parliamentary party groups issue their final statements on the bill. As during the first stage, formal votes are rare. When they do happen, party discipline is usually low (Sherlock 2008, p. 13). If government and parliament cannot agree on the content of the bill, it fails and cannot be reintroduced to parliament during that term. If the bill is passed, the president signs it into law or it becomes valid after 30 days without a signature.

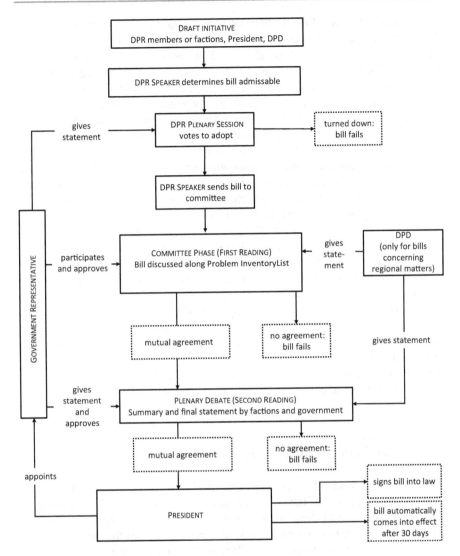

Fig. 4.2 The legislative process in Indonesia's DPR. Source: Authors' compilation

4.3.3 Other Agencies of Horizontal Accountability

Another important feature of the institutional reforms since 1999 is the emergence of a complex system of horizontal accountability mechanisms (Morlino et al. 2011; Ziegenhain 2015), including the Audit Board (BPK), the Judicial Commission (KY), and the Corruption Eradication Commission (KPK). In addition, there are also agencies monitoring elections and observing the protection of political rights and civil liberties. Such "vertical accountability mechanisms" include the General

Election Commission (KPU), the Election Monitoring Body (*Bawaslu*), the National Ombudsman, and the National Human Rights Commission (*Komnas HAM*).[3] Finally, the Constitutional Court (MK) and the Supreme Court (MA) are at the interface of horizontal and vertical accountability. Among the different horizontal accountability bodies, the KPK has garnered the most public attention (Crouch 2008). Originally established in 2002 to integrate all existing anticorruption initiatives, the KPK quickly became a relatively autonomous law enforcement agency with the power to investigate corrupt officials and to circumvent the existing problems in the criminal justice system (Fenwick 2008b, pp. 408, 416–418). The commission initially focused on investigating mid-ranking state officials, but has also initiated investigations against high-ranking officials and politicians since 2009 (Butt 2011, pp. 183–186, 383–386). The KPK cooperates closely with designated national and regional Anticorruption Courts (Tipikor). Thanks to their use of more independent lay judges (Tahyar 2010, p. 286) and a loose reading of criminal legislation, these courts reached a conviction rate of 100% for the almost 250 cases KPK deliberated until 2009 (Butt 2009b). Because of its investigations, the KPK repeatedly fell afoul of other political actors. The DPR recently reduced the Commission's leeway in deciding which cases to pursue and increased the maximum number of professional Tipikor judges. In addition, a legal loophole provides an opportunity for police and public prosecutors to undermine the independence of the KPK: Once they are under police investigation, KPK members are automatically suspended and lose their position, no matter if they are officially charged with a crime. In at least two cases, the police exploited this loophole to fabricate allegations that led to the removal of commissioners (Butt 2009b).

4.4   Legal and Judicial System

Indonesia's legal system is a "complex amalgam" of traditional, customary or *adat*, Islamic, and state law. The latter is based on the Roman Dutch civil law system and enacted and enforced by the government (Lindsey and Santosa 2008, p. 3; Nurjaya 2015). Legal pluralism is a means to integrate plural communities into the Indonesian nation, but is also a source of conflict, as different common law traditions of different indigenous communities can contradict each other or collide with state laws (Pompe 2008; Bowen 2003; Lukito 2013). For example, certain criminal offences cannot be prosecuted effectively because the civil law legal principle of *ne bis in idem* (not twice in the same) implies that comparatively light *adat* sentences for crimes like rape preempt harsher sentences in state courts. State judges also reference *adat* to prosecute offenses that merely violate their personal sense of justice instead of positive criminal laws (Pompe 2008, p. 111).

---

[3]Suharto established *Komnas HAM* in 1993 to deflect international criticism of his human rights record.

The Islamic legal principles adopted into the codified state law during Suharto's "New Order" were mostly restricted to family, inheritance, or banking law. Following the process of administrative decentralization since 1999, Indonesian provinces, municipalities, and districts are permitted to pass Sharia-based local regulations, *peraturan daerah*, or "perda," focusing on moral enhancement ("morality regulations"; cf. Bush 2008). Like state courts, religious courts (*pengadilan agama*) authorized to apply these regulations are subject to judicial review by the Supreme Court. The state court system, which possesses jurisdiction over criminal and civil law cases, has two additional tiers, starting with state courts (*pengadilan negara*) at the district level and a court of appeals at the provincial level.

Under the New Order government, courts were essentially "instruments of power" and were deeply integrated into Suharto's authoritarian style of governance (Bourchier 2008, p. 103). This has had lasting effects on the professionalism and capacity of the court system as a whole, and numerous corruption scandals after 1999 have further tarnished the reputation of the "judicial mafia" (Butt and Lindsey 2011). More recently, individual courts for administrative, tax, human rights, and labor disputes have been established so judges can specialize in a single field of law, but this innovation has also created institutional friction and jurisdictional disputes (Bedner 2010, pp. 209–211). The problems relating to weak capacity and corruption in the judiciary are also apparent in Indonesia's position in international rankings: According to the World Bank's Rule of Law indicator, Indonesia ranks seventh among the eleven countries considered, trailing even Vietnam and the Philippines (World Bank 2017c). In the Corruption Perception Index of Transparency International, Indonesia has experienced a more positive trend and was ranked fourth in the region in 2015 (Transparency International 2015).

The Constitutional Court (*Mahkamah Konstitusi*, MK) established in 2003 quickly acquired a reputation as an independent, incorruptible, and efficient institution. Modeled after the South Korean Constitutional Court in structure and jurisdiction and after the German tradition of specialized judicial review, the court has nine judges (Hendrianto 2010). The Supreme Court, the DPR's Committee III for Judicial Affairs, and a presidential commission each select three justices for a 5-year term that is renewable once (UUD45, Art. 24C.3). The Constitutional Court then elects a chief justice from their ranks. After their appointment by the president, the justices cannot be recalled and hold their office until the end of their term or until they reach the pension age of 65. The court has full administrative and budgetary autonomy. Together, these regulations are supposed to secure the court's independence (Croissant 2010; Mietzner 2010b).

The Constitutional Court is responsible for the judicial review of parliamentary laws, the resolution of constitutional disputes among constitutionally mandated political institutions, election disputes and decisions over party bans, and the admissibility of the presidential impeachment process (Art. 34C.1). Most of the cases heard by the court are election complaints, followed by cases for judicial review and institutional disputes (see Table 4.6). Constitutional complaints grant individuals, traditional communities, legal persons, and government institutions access to judicial review if they feel an act of parliament violates their

Table 4.6 Forms of action and verdicts at the Indonesian Constitutional Court, 2003–2015

	Judicial review			Institutional disputes		Electoral disputes (regional)	
	Claims	Decided	Successful	Claims	Decided	Claims	Decided
2003	24	4	0	0	0	–	–
2004	27	35	11	1	1	–	–
2005	25	28	10	1	0	–	–
2006	27	29	8	6	3	–	–
2007	30	27	4	3	2	–	–
2008	36	34	10	5	4	30	18
2009	78	32	15	1	1	4	12
2010	81	61	17	1	0	275	224
2011	86	94	21	10	4	161	131
2012	118	97	30	6	6	132	104
2013	109	74	22	4	1	136	112
2014	140	67	26	1	0	9	6
2015	140	75	25	1	1	147	146
Total	921	657	199	40	23	894	753

Source: Authors' calculation, based on MK (2013, 2014, 2016)
Note: Cases filed includes granted, rejected, not accepted, and withdrawn. No cases filed for impeachment or party bans

constitutional rights (Stockmann 2007, pp. 26–27). While, formally, there is no abstract judicial review and claimants have to demonstrate that the act affects them personally and immediately, the court has developed a broad interpretation of affectedness (Hendrianto 2010, pp. 162–163, 170).

In its first years, the Constitutional Court developed a strong reputation as a guardian of the constitutional order. For example, the court's very first judicial review decision struck down a clause that would have restricted its jurisdiction to review laws passed after 1999 (Stockmann 2007, pp. 31–33) and has since annulled several criminal law provisions used as instruments of political repression under Suharto (Mietzner 2010b, pp. 408–409). In October 2011, the judges granted an appeal against a revision of the Law on the Constitutional Court that would have restricted the Court's authority to review clauses concerning the Constitutional Court itself and those not explicitly mentioned by an applicant (*ultra petita*). On several occasions, the Court has ruled against the government when it invalidated, in part or *in toto*, laws deregulating the nation's oil and natural gas, energy, and water supply sectors and has declared parts of the national budget unconstitutional (Stockmann 2007, pp. 53–61; Butt 2009a, p. 2). Finally, in one of its most controversial decisions, the Court in 2008 invalidated the closed-party list system, a decision that led the Election Commission to adopt an open-list PR system. This had far-reaching consequences, as it moved the existing party-centered electoral system to a more candidate-centric system (Butt 2015, pp. 205–211; Fox 2016).

Despite its positive track record, there are also some limitations to be mentioned that might constrain the role of the Constitutional Court as a guardian of a constitutional order based on the principles of the rule of law. First, court decisions have no effect on ongoing judicial proceedings or past verdicts based on the respective piece of legislation and present no legal grounds for appealing a verdict (Clarke 2008, p. 449; Stockmann 2007, p. 38). Similarly, even if the Constitutional Court voids a law, the decision has no effect on the government regulation implementing the law (Stockmann 2007, pp. 34–37). Secondly, the Supreme Court (*Mahkamah Agung*, MA) reviews all administrative regulations, executive orders, and court proceedings not under the review authority of the Constitutional Court. However, the Supreme Court rarely accepts cases concerning the constitutionality of administrative regulations or presidential decrees (Butt and Lindsey 2008, p. 256) and has refused to consider Constitutional Court decisions in its own decisions in several cases. Consequently, the government can easily circumvent the Constitutional Court by reintroducing invalidated laws as government regulations (Butt and Lindsey 2008, p. 241).

Nevertheless, the creation of the Constitutional Court was an overall success. Civil society organizations (CSOs) have used the court's lenient criteria for admissibility to hold the government and parliament accountable for their legislative activity (Fenwick 2008a). Unlike in Thailand (cf. Chap. 10), the court has established itself as a respected mediator in elite disputes and has helped depolarize political competition (Mietzner 2010b, pp. 406–407, 2010a).

4.5 Electoral System and Elections

While the Dutch introduced an indirectly elected People's Council (*Volksraad*) with limited advisory powers in 1918, the first general election to the legislature was held in 1955. From 1971 onwards, the New Order regime had regular representative national elections for the DPR heavily manipulated in favor of Suharto's Golkar party. Revisions to electoral and party laws as well as constitutional reforms in the period 1999 to 2003 introduced generally free and fair direct elections for president as well as for both chambers of parliament. Since 1999, there have been four rounds of elections for the DPR, three elections to the DPD, and three direct presidential elections.[4] Table 4.7 shows the results of all DPR elections in the *reformasi* era.

The minimum voting age is 17 years; married persons can vote regardless of age, whereas members of the military and the police do not have the right to vote in elections. Candidates for the presidency, DPR, DPD, and the regional parliaments have to be at least 21 years of age, profess a religious belief, and possess a high school degree. For presidential elections, presidential and vice president candidates, as noted, are elected on one ticket in a two-round system. Only parties or coalitions of parties that win at least 25% of the national vote or comprise 20% of the seats in the national parliament can officially nominate candidates. The electoral system

---

[4]In 1999, the president was indirectly elected by the MPR.

Table 4.7 DPR elections in Indonesia since 1999[a]

	1999		2004		2009		2014	
	Votes (%)	# of Seats	Votes (%)	# of Seats	Votes (%)	# of Seats	Votes (%)	# of Seats
Crescent Star Party (PBB)	1.8	14	2.6	11	–	–	–	–
Democrat Party (PD)	–	–	7.5	56	20.9	148	10.2	61
Functional Groups Party (Golkar)	20.9	120	21.6	127	14.5	108	14.75	91
Great Indonesia Movement (Gerindra)	–	–	–	–	4.5	30	11.8	73
Indonesian Democratic Party—Struggle (PDI-P)	37.4	154	18.5	109	14.0	93	19.0	109
National Awakening Party (PKB)	17.4	51	10.6	52	4.9	26	9.0	47
National Mandate Party (PAN)	7.3	35	6.4	53	6.0	42	7.6	49
People's Conscience Party (Hanura)	–	–	–	–	3.8	15	5.3	16
Prosperous Justice Party (PKS)	–	–	7.3	45	7.9	59	6.8	40
United Development Party (PPP)	10.7	58	8.1	58	5.3	39	5.5	39
National Democratic Party (Nasdem)	–	–	–	–	–	–	6.7	35
Other parties	4.5	30	17.4	39	18.2	0	3.4	0
Total	100	462	100	550	100	560	100	560
Turnout	93.0		84.1		71.0		75.1	
Effective number of parties[b]	5.0	4.7	8.6	7.1	9.7	6.1	9.0	8.2

Source: Carr (2017), IPU (2014) and KPU (2014)
[a]Only parties with at least 3% of votes or seats are shown ("relevant parties")
[b]Without appointed TNI/Polri faction. See Table 3.2 for details on calculation

used for the DPR is proportional representation (PR) with closed party lists (1999), restricted open lists (2004) and, since 2009, open party lists in multi-member districts.[5]

---

[5]The restricted open-list system required voters to vote for one party and, if they wish, one candidate from that party. However, this would only have resulted in the election of a particular candidate out of the order in which names appear on the party list if that candidate gained more than a full Hare Quota of individual votes.

The election law requires that political parties must have established party offices in at least three-fourths of all provinces and in half of the districts to nominate candidates for the DPR. Moreover, to prevent excessive fragmentation and thereby make it easier to form stable governments, political parties must surpass a threshold of 3.5% of the total national vote. The Election Commission allocates seats among those parties that have obtained at least 3.5% of the national vote using the Hare quota method, while the allocation of remaining seats to political parties is based on the largest remainder (LR Hare). For the DPD, candidates stand on an individual basis. Each province returns four members through a single non-transferable vote (SNTV) system in which each voter has one vote and the four candidates with the highest number of votes in each district are elected (cf. Table 4.8).

Since 2001, the General Election Commission (KPU) is responsible for organizing elections at the national, provincial, municipal, and district level. Since national and subnational elections are "synchronized," altogether, approximately 15,000 seats are filled on a single election day, with the number of candidates easily exceeding 300,000 (Ufen 2010; Thalang 2005). Naturally, this poses tremendous logistical challenges for the KPU, which have been exacerbated by budget cuts in recent years and the revision of election law at short notice, such as the change from restricted to open party lists in 2009 (Mietzner 2012, p. 212). Despite these and other problems such as illegal political financing and vote buying (Groemping 2015), expert surveys such as the Election Integrity Project evaluate electoral integrity in Indonesia favorably compared to the region and even globally (see Fig. 4.3).

4.6 Political Parties and Party System

The electoral system is one of several factors that shaped the development of Indonesia's post-authoritarian party system. Although most political parties were founded after 1998 (Tomsa 2008, p. 173) and despite longer-term evolutions in Indonesian religious life that resulted in a "de-aliranization" (Ufen 2008) of party politics, the origins of some political parties can be traced to the political streams (*politik aliran*) that shaped the party system in the pre-Suharto period (Mietzner 2008).[6] In this regard, Herbert Feith's categorization differentiates five *aliran* that were represented by a political party, namely: nationalists (Sukarno's National Party of Indonesia, PNI); Islam (NU and Masyumi); Javanese traditionalists (Partindo); social democrats (PSI); and Communists (PKI; Feith and Castles 2007). Suharto's New Order regime eliminated the PKI and forced the remaining Islamic parties to

---

[6]Originally, *aliran* characterized different cultural streams in Javanese society (Geertz 1960). However, to explain party system origins and changes, some party researchers (Ufen 2008, 2012) use it similarly to the concept of political cleavages in Lipset and Rokkan's "cleavage model" (Lipset and Rokkan 1967).

Table 4.8 Indonesia's Post-Suharto election system

	Presidency	DPR				DPD		
	2004–2014	1999	2004	2009	2014	2004	2009	2014
Electoral system	Two-round	PR	PR	PR	PR	SNTV	SNTV	SNTV
# Seats		500	550	560	560	128	132	136[a]
# Appointed seats		38	0	0	0	0	0	0
# Of districts	1	26	69	77	77	32	33	34
District magnitude		4–82	3–12	3–10	3–10	4	4	4
Choice of candidature	Individual	Closed list	Semi-open list	Open list	Open list	Individual	Individual	Individual
# Of votes	1	1	1	1	1	1	1	1
Tier	National	District	District	District	District	Province[b]	Province[b]	Province[b]
Seat allocation formula		LR Hare	LR Hare	LR Hare	LR Hare	Highest vote	Highest vote	Highest vote
Legal threshold		0	0	2.5%	3.5%	0	0	0
Length of term	5	5	5	5	5	5	5	5
Term limit	2	–	–	–	–	–	–	–

Source: Hicken and Kasuya (2003), Rüland (2001), Schmidt (2010), extended by the authors

[a]Four seats are vacant

[b]Indonesian provinces comprise several districts. For DPD elections, each province constitutes one electoral district

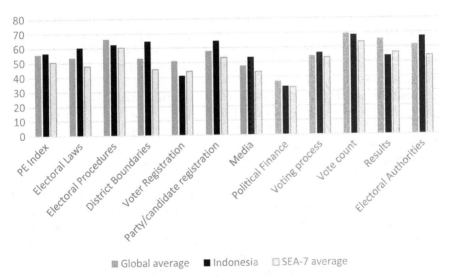

Fig. 4.3 Perceived Electoral Integrity Index, Indonesia 2014. Note: The PEI Index, standardized along a 100-point score, collects views from over 2000 experts and covers a total of 180 elections in 139 countries held between July 1, 2012, and December 31, 2015. SEA-7 presents the average for seven elections in seven Southeast Asian countries (Cambodia, Malaysia, Myanmar, Philippines, Thailand, Singapore, and Indonesia) in the period 2013 to 2015. Source: PEI (2016)

merge into the United Development Party (PPP), whereas the PNI was merged with non-Islamic and nationalist parties into a new party called the *Partai Demokrasi Indonesia* (Indonesian Democratic Party, PDI). In addition to these two parties, Suharto's Golkar was the only other political party allowed to register. A 1973 ban on all party activities at the local level gave Golkar an edge over the PNI and PPP as the regime party was represented locally through government officials and Golkar's ostensibly nonpolitical member associations. In 1986, *Pancasila* was established as the "single basis" (*azas tunggal*) for all parties and societal associations, further compressing the ideological spectrum (Mietzner 2013, p. 37).

With the end of the New Order regime, the party system has again expanded. In addition to the PPP and a number of other traditionalist (National Awakening Party, PKB), modernist (National Mandate Party, PAN), and moderate Islamist (Prosperous Justice Party, PKS) parties, there is the Indonesian Democratic Party of Struggle (PDI-P) of Megawati Sukarnoputri—the daughter of Indonesia's first president, Sukarno—which replaced the PDI. In addition, there are several other parties, including three nationalist parties established or led by former military officers, such as the Democratic Party of former President Lt. Gen. Yudhoyono (SBY), the Great Indonesia Movement Party (Gerindra) of retired Lt. Gen. Prabowo, and the Hanura Party (People's Conscience Party) of former Gen. Wiranto. Even though Golkar is still the second largest party in parliament, it has lost its hegemonic position, and with each successive election, voters have spread their support across a wider array of parties. Looking at the election data displayed in Table 4.7, the most important features of political competition in the post-Suharto era are the very high levels of fractionalization of the party system and the increasing competitiveness of the electoral contest. The effective number of political parties increased from an average of 1.9 under Suharto to 5.0 in 1999 and 8.2 in 2014. In addition, the degree of competitiveness—measured as the difference between the strongest and second strongest party in terms of the percent of votes—is very high. This means Indonesia has transitioned from a hegemonic and noncompetitive party system in the late Suharto era to an extremely fragmented multiparty system with two dominant parties to an extreme multiparty system with a balance of power among parties (Croissant and Völkel 2012).

Observers disagree about the consequences of the evolution of political parties and the party system for the deepening and consolidation of democracy in Indonesia. Some scholars stress that political parties in Indonesia are well institutionalized relative to other Southeast Asian countries (Croissant and Völkel 2012; Mietzner 2013). Although some political parties have regional strongholds, party-centric electoral rules coupled with the de facto prohibition of local or regional parties have fostered incentives for candidates to campaign on broad national platforms of reform and development rather than on ethnicity (Fox 2016). This has contributed to a higher degree of party system nationalization than for example in Thailand or the Philippines—with positive consequences for the political performance of the democratic system (Croissant and Schächter 2008). Likewise, Mietzner uncovers a convergence of party competition to the political center (Mietzner 2013). Consequently, overly broad multiparty coalitions are the norm (Sherlock 2009).

In contrast, more skeptical observers stress that Indonesian parties have become more personalistic, as the move from a party-centered to a more candidate-centric electoral system in 2009 freed candidates from their party platforms and offered them incentives to campaign on their personal attributes and local connections (Tan 2012; Fox 2016). Additionally, the introduction of direct executive elections has shifted voters' attention to the presidential race and has generated incentives for the creation of new parties, whereas decentralization has empowered branch-level actors and increased electoral localism (Allen 2014). Finally, Slater's account of coalition politics reveals the existence of an inclusive party "cartel," formed to minimize the risk of elections by ensuring access to power and state resources for all parties (Slater and Simmons 2012; Slater 2014; but see Mietzner 2013 for a contrasting assessment).

4.7   State Administration and Decentralization

Due to difficult background conditions, Indonesia's nascent democracy has faced considerable challenges to its stateness.[7] While Indonesia built up relatively high levels of state capacity under the New Order regime, the collapse of Suharto rule in

---

[7]For more details on the concept of stateness, see Chap. 11 on Timor-Leste.

1998 and the devastating economic crisis of 1998/99 seemed to have rapidly eroded this capacity (Mietzner 2017a, b). Even though fears that the nation itself might disintegrate and that Indonesia would turn into a failing state (Rotberg 2002) may have been exaggerated (Mietzner 2017b), the downfall of the New Order regime was beset by a number of violent conflicts, both of a communal and separatist nature. Horizontal violent conflicts between different local communities were fought along ethnic or religious lines and persisted until 2001, and since then resurfaced occasionally as "small town wars" (van Klinken 2007). Several factors contributed to this wave of intercommunal violence. Most importantly, the Suharto government had promoted emigration from over-populated Java to the outer islands through a policy of positive discrimination that favored migrants over indigenous communities. This created conflicts over settlement, land for cultivation, and income opportunities. When the existing mechanisms of control and coercion lost strength during the transition and security forces were overwhelmed or unwilling to contain discontent (Tajima 2009), open conflict erupted along these lines as "local politics by other means" (van Klinken 2007, p. 138). In some places, vested interests and security forces even seem to have fanned the violence to further their own interests (Gledhill 2012).

Similarly, the origins and root causes of vertical conflicts between the state and ethnic movements in the periphery of the nation state (i.e., Aceh and Irian Jaya) had more to do with the legacies of colonial rule and Suharto's repressive policies of nation-building, political centralization, and economic exploitation of the periphery than with democratization. In fact, in the cases of Aceh and Irian Jaya, the western half of the island of Papua, separatist movements such as the *Gerakan Aceh Merdeka* (Free Aceh Movement, GAM) and the Organization for a Free Papua (*Organisasi Papua Merdeka*, OPM) had fought the security forces for decades (Missbach 2011; Chauvel 2004). However, these conflicts intensified in the early years of *reformasi* (Bertrand 2004).

Yet, Indonesia has successfully overcome most challenges to its political order and its monopoly of force and reorganized and rebuilt its administrative state capacity to some extent. Furthermore, the rapid introduction of major structural, institutional, and fiscal reforms in response to the increased articulation of demands from subnational groups for autonomy ("big bang decentralization," cf. World Bank 2003) helped consolidate more democratic center–periphery relations and established new, noncoercive forms of conflict mediation and political participation at the district and provincial levels. However, as several critics observe, Indonesian democracy paid a high price for preventing national disintegration and re-accessing state capacity. First of all, as Mietzner (2017a) writes, "Indonesian democracy only endured by making concessions to conservative forces nesting in key areas of state capacity whose continued influence keeps the quality of democracy low." For example, many observers notice that much of the abuse of power and systematic corruption that focused on Jakarta during the Suharto era has now shifted to the local level (Bünte 2011). Furthermore, as Tim Campbell mentions in the 2007 GOLD report, "Indonesia's sudden 'Big Bang' of reform is notable for the scope of change, but not for the integrated, long term solution needed" (Campbell 2008, p. 286).

Even though Indonesia had already experimented with some degree of regional autonomy during the 1950s, the New Order quickly reestablished tight central control all the way to the village level (Antlöv 2003, p. 195). Since 1979, Indonesia has had a deconcentrated administrative structure consisting of provinces (*provinsi*), rural and urban districts (*kabupaten* and *kota*), subdistricts (*kecamatan*), and villages (*desa*). The decentralization of political, administrative, and financial authority following the transition favored the district level and was implemented very quickly (World Bank 2003, p. 3). As a consequence of the reform, 2.9 of the 3.9 million civil service employees, 239 national agencies in the provinces and 3933 in the districts, and 16,000 additional service providers were transferred to regional governments (World Bank 2003). Local parliaments at the provincial (DPRD I) and district level (DPRD II) are now popularly elected and have real legislative authority. Until 2004, district heads, mayors, and governors were elected indirectly and since then are elected directly with a qualified majority of at least 30% of the vote (*pilkada*). A law returning Indonesia to indirect elections passed by the lame duck DPR following the 2014 election was quickly reversed after the new DPR came into office (Hamayotsu and Nataatmadja 2016).

Fiscal decentralization increased the share of expenditure by subnational units from 15.8% during the last budget under Suharto to 39% in 2011. At the same time, the local share of state revenue only increased from 5 to 7.2% (see Harjowiryono 2012, p. 126). Consequently, districts and provinces still depend on Jakarta for the appropriation of sufficient funds. These grants consist of a fixed base amount and do not take into account regional differences and preclude a system of equalization transfers between rich and poor districts (World Bank 2003). Even though the share of revenue controlled by the districts has increased since, the new national allocation formula earmarks the funds for use in education, thus reducing subnational autonomy.

Decentralization was not only meant to reduce regional tensions in Indonesia, but also to increase Indonesia's administrative capacity, the second major challenge to its stateness. Today, the administration at both the national and subnational level still suffers from a mechanistic allocation of underqualified personnel (Turner et al. 2009). One of the main reasons is a process called "blossoming" (*pemekaran*), that is, the proliferation of provinces and districts, which has precluded the development of economies of scale in the subnational units. The number of provinces increased from 26 in 1999 to 34 in 2012 and the number of districts from 292 to 495 (Kimura 2010). The partition of existing units is largely motivated by the bureaucratic and financial rents generated from the fixed base allocation of funds and civil service jobs for every new subnational unit, irrespective of size (Fitrani et al. 2005). Since the national government still essentially pays for wage increases and has fully funded the transfer of underqualified subnational personnel into the civil service, there are no incentives to reduce administrative staff to sustainable levels (Kaiser et al. 2006). Only occasionally have local executives and private actors managed to establish a "heterodox reform symbiosis" and improved administrative efficiency (von Luebke 2009). Finally, decentralization has not contributed to a homogenization of the socioeconomic landscape in Indonesia: While the economic performance of different provinces has somewhat converged, growth has usually been focused in a few districts (McCulloch and Sjahrir 2008, p. 10).

4.8   Civil–Military Relations

The origins of the National Armed Forces of Indonesia (*Tentara Nasional Indonesia*, TNI) reach back to the Dutch colonial era and the ensuing struggle for independence (1945–1949) and predate the creation of independent civilian state structures.[8] Confronted with dysfunctional political institutions, violent insurgencies, and economic crises, the military played an exceptional role under Sukarno's Guided Democracy and became the predominant political force within the New Order regime, second only to President Suharto (Slater 2010). This was reflected, first of all, in the so-called territorial structure, under which the military command structure ran parallel to the civilian administrative structure down to the village level. This structure was meant to improve the military's ability to conduct guerilla warfare against a superior opponent, but was used primarily to suppress regional rebellions and political opposition (Sebastian 2006, p. 179; Aspinall 2005). Consequently, the commanders of key territorial commands at the highest echelon, especially on Java, wielded significant political influence during the New Order. Second, the military's Dual Function (*dwifungsi*) doctrine, under which the military performed sociopolitical as well as traditional defense and security roles, was institutionalized during the New Order. The military became entwined with political institutions, most evident in its dominant position in Golkar, its reserved seats in parliament, and the occupation of many civilian administrative positions, minister posts, and governorships by active soldiers (Rinakit 2005). Finally, the Indonesian military became an important economic actor, leading observers to consider this the third role in an expanded "*trifungsi*" (McCulloch 2003). Initially meant to improve the local supply chain needed for guerilla warfare (Crouch 1988, pp. 275–277), starting in the 1960s, the military also took over state enterprises, and the different service branches and special forces established foundations as holding companies for their business interests (Mietzner and Misol 2012). Yet from the late 1970s onward, the military's position as the most powerful political institution deteriorated as Suharto's rule grew increasingly personalist. When the president began civilianizing Golkar during the late 1980s, the military was no longer able to influence politics without Suharto's backing (Tomsa 2008, p. 39). Consequently, "what started as a system of oligarchic military rule evolved into a highly personalized regime, backed in nearly equal measure by military and civilian organizations" (Slater 2010, p. 133). Meanwhile, Suharto could rely on the army

---

[8]TNI was the original name of the Indonesian Armed Forces. It was changed to *Angkatan Bersenjata Republik Indonesia* (Republic of Indonesia Armed Forces/ABRI) when Suharto incorporated the national police (POLRI) into the military's ranks. In 2000, the name was changed back to TNI.

to control and, if necessary, repress political parties, trade unions, student movements, religious leaders, and newspapers (Aspinall 2005). Yet Suharto's misuse of the military promotion system and patronage politics generated internal divisions. By the mid-1990s, the military was deeply factionalized into "losers" and "winners" of Suharto's "franchise system" (McLeod 2008, p. 200; Lee 2015).

Suharto's personalized system proved flawed when the Asian Financial Crisis hit Indonesia in late 1997. Faced with widespread popular unrest and challenges to the regime, the Golkar leadership and military commander General Wiranto asked Suharto to step down in order to subdue economic and social upheaval (Mietzner 2009b, p. 126; Lee 2015). Suharto yielded on May 21, 1998, and transferred power to his vice president, Bacharuddin Jusuf Habibie (1998–1999), ushering in the *reformasi* period. Habibie, whose role was to serve as an interim president until new elections could be held and who had little popular support, was faced with two major problems after taking office: First, he had to convince the Indonesian public and the international community that he was willing to implement painful economic reforms and to prepare Indonesia for democracy by disempowering the old regime elite, including the military. Second, he had to keep the military from challenging these reforms while at the same time bringing the deteriorating security situation under control (Mietzner 2006, pp. 10–11). Nevertheless, the early years of the transition saw significant reforms: The military and police (POLRI) were formally separated in April 1999; the military gave up its *dwifungsi* doctrine; active officers had to leave most posts in the civilian administration; and the military cut its ties with Golkar (Hafidz 2006, p. 119). Under Presidents Wahid (1999–2001) and Megawati (2001–2004), the military also lost its reserved seats in DPR, MPR, and the subnational legislatures. The passage of the State Defense Law in 2002 and the Law on the Armed Forces of Indonesia (2004, generally referred to as TNI Law) mandated the military's complete departure from its political activities, implementing long-standing demands by civil society activists (Gunawan 2017; Lorenz 2015).

Although the military has undergone major changes since 1998 and there are no signs that it would seek a return to its New Order role, the impetus for further military reform has weakened in recent years, with important bills on the military justice system and revisions to national security legislation stuck in parliament (Lowry 2016; Gunawan 2017). The existing defense and security legislation limits the scope of parliamentary oversight, and the Ministry of Defense cannot yet be considered an effective civilian policy-making agency. The effectiveness of democratic control over the TNI still very much depends on the individual relationship between civilian politicians—especially the president—and the military leadership. Furthermore, internal security operations are not fully civilianized because vague and unclear regulations still give the military relatively large leeway to influence its mission profile and create jurisdictional conflicts with the civilian police (HRW 2006; Sebastian and Iisgindarsah 2012). In addition, many laws still await full implementation, including the regulation of military businesses and their conversion into civilian businesses and the ban on individual business activities (Mietzner and Misol 2012). Finally, there has been little progress in the past 15 years on improving military accountability, and efforts to end the prevailing military "culture of impunity" have failed (Aspinall 2010, p. 23; Lowry 2016, p. 20). There are still reports of violence against civilians in crisis regions, and local protests against (illegal) military business activities are sometimes suppressed by local units. Even in the rare cases where officers are indicted for their involvement in these activities, they receive lenient punishments from military courts or judges drop charges in exchange for bribes (Croissant et al. 2013, pp. 114–116; Lowry 2016).

4.9 Civil Society and Patterns of Political Orientations

Events in Indonesia since 1997 demonstrate that a democratic political culture and a strong civil society are not necessary conditions for the onset of democratic transitions. However, the question is how much progress Indonesia has made towards a democratic political culture and a flourishing civil society in the 15 years or so since democratization.

Public opinion research on Indonesia's political culture prior to 1998 is sparse. However, in regard to the post-*reformasi* era, Asian Barometer Survey (ABS 2017) data shows that popular support for democracy is relatively high in Indonesia. In 2011, 58.6% of respondents indicated that democracy was preferable to any other political regime type—trailing Japan, South Korea, and Thailand, but well ahead of Taiwan, Mongolia, and the Philippines. On the other hand, many Indonesians lack a coherent understanding or hold authoritarian notions of democracy: In 2009, 41% of respondents did not have a clear understanding of democracy (IFES 2010, p. 33). Furthermore, the percentage of respondents who believe that democracy can solve Indonesia's problems has dropped from 76.2% in 2006 to 68% in 2011. In 2011, only 9.8% of respondents perceived democracy as important or more important than economic development. This is the lowest value for any of the 11 countries surveyed in the ABS (Chang et al. 2013). In addition to those who still view *reformasi* with skepticism, there are many Indonesians who believe they are worse off today than they were under Suharto. Finally, compared to their counterparts in Southeast Asia, democratic institutions in Indonesia suffer from rather low—and decreasing—levels of public trust. For instance, only 73.7% of respondents in 2014 reported some or a great deal of trust in the Chief executive, and 61.1% in the national government, whereas 52.9% trusted the national parliament and 46% the political parties. The averages for seven Southeast Asian countries were 76.7%, 73.3%, 69.6%, and 58.6%, respectively (ABS 2017).

These responses are an oft-noted symptom of the revival of authoritarian nostalgia in Indonesia in recent years—commonly referred to as "SARS."[9] However, this does not suggest that Indonesian democracy is experiencing an acute legitimacy crisis that is threatening political stability or the survival of the democratic system. Considerable dissatisfaction with democracy is not necessarily a sign of crisis.

---

[9]*Sindrom Aku Rindu Suharto* or "I Miss Suharto Syndrome".

Rather, it could contribute to the further deepening of democracy if democratically legitimated authorities and institutions become more responsive to new and rising social demands.

Despite all this, Indonesia has seen the emergence of a vital civil society since the transition to democracy (Lussier and Fish 2012; Mietzner 2012). The burgeoning number of CSOs includes independent labor unions, a myriad of community-oriented and rights-oriented groups, advocacy and single-issue groups, and many other NGOs.[10] The most important social associations in Indonesia are Islamic organizations, such as *Muhammadiyah* and *Nahdlatul Ulama* claiming 30 and 40 million members, respectively (Mujani and Liddle 2009). These organizations are often considered the nucleus of modern civil society in Indonesia (Nyman 2009, p. 259).

While the New Order did tolerate a degree of organizational pluralism as long as associations and NGOs did not criticize or openly challenge the government (Weiss 2006, p. 222), and a degree of freedom in academic and press comments was allowed, civil society activists seeking political visibility and assertiveness faced state repression. In order to avoid confrontation with the Suharto regime, whose policy did not give room for any genuine opposition, the concept of "self-reliant community institutions" (*lembaga swadaya masyarakat*, LSM, cf. Eldridge 1996) emerged. While it is impossible to give exact numbers, observers estimated the total number of NGOs and CSOs in 1990 to have been 600–800,000, around half of which are considered LSMs (Weiss 2006, p. 222).

Together with the regime's efforts to co-opt or incorporate all manners of functional groups into Golkar's network of about 270 associations (Beittinger-Lee 2009, p. 113), this precluded the resurgence of civil society as a meaningful political force or the emergence of a diverse and durable alliance of extra-parliamentary opposition groups challenging the authoritarian status quo. Of course, during the anti-regime protests of 1997/98, cooperation between different groups resurged but quickly faltered after Suharto stepped down and the political struggle moved from the streets to the institutional arena of the political system (Lane 2009).

In fact, the authoritarian legacy of a tamed civil society is still strong in Indonesia, despite the new civic associationalism after 1999 (Beittinger-Lee 2009, p. 118). While most groups remain moderate in their means and goals, civil society remains fragmented into urban, secular, and liberal segments and more conservative, often religious groups in more rural areas (Nyman 2009, p. 260). Many NGOs have established working relationships with political decision-makers despite the lack of institutional access channels. These groups successfully pushed for constitutional reforms, the reform of election and party laws, as well as the reordering of civil–military relations (Lorenz 2015) and combatting corruption.

---

[10]Of course, the historical origins of contemporary civil society are much older. For example, more traditional forms of mutual help (*gotong royong*) and rotating credit associations (*arisan*) have existed in Java and other places for centuries (Hadiwinata 2009, p. 280; Geertz 1960).

While student groups have criticized them for their reliance on foreign funding and for cooperation with government and political parties, civil society activists helped to deepen democracy and prevent the retrenchment of democratic reforms (Mietzner 2012). Even the more conservative groups stress peaceful means of interest articulation and at least NU promotes a very moderate interpretation of the Quran (Fachruddin 2005) in the tradition of a "Civil Islam" (Hefner 2000). In areas affected by communal and religious violence, Islamic and Christian organizations have contributed to the peaceful resolution of conflict by establishing local concordance democracies (Henley et al. 2007; Bräuchler 2011). Nevertheless, there is also the "dark" side of Indonesia's uncivil society (Beittinger-Lee 2009): Voluntary means and processes developed within non-state organizations or associations and informal groups can strengthen the collective identity of their members, but they can also have negative social effects by insulating groups from "outsiders," reinforcing exclusive identities and homogenous groups, and creating intercommunal tensions (Hadiwinata 2009). Moreover, some of the self-proclaimed defenders of Islam, who promote vigilantism and violence against religious minorities or "Un-Islamic" elements—such as the Islamic Defender Front—are uncivil society organizations (Wilson 2011).

4.9.1   Media System

During Suharto's rule, the media was controlled by the Department of Information and literature was screened by the Department of Education and Culture. The political liberalization following 1998 saw the lifting of many restrictions on newspapers and other media and the enactment of constitutional guarantees for freedom of expression and opinion, freedom of information, and freedom of the press. Today, Indonesia's media environment is ranked among the most vibrant and open in the region. The pluralistic print media landscape—there are several hundred newspapers, magazines, and tabloids in the country today (Irawanto 2011)—has been freed from licensing requirements, and media disputes have been adjudicated by an independent Press Council (*Dewan Pers*) since 1999. President Abdurrahman Wahid dissolved the Department of Information in 1999. The Ministry for Communication and Information Technology and the national Broadcasting Commission (KPI) grant licenses for broadcast media. The latter also observes compliance with broadcasting legislation and guarantees pluralism of ownership and content in the media sector. KPI can impose penalties for transgressions like the violation of religious values, the dissemination of obscene content, or biased political reporting (Jurriëns 2009, pp. 35–37). However, certain restrictions on the right to freedom of information still apply because of the flawed implementation of the 2008 Law on Public Information Transparency and the 2010 State Intelligence Law, which civil society groups have criticized as a threat to journalistic freedom. In addition, the prohibition of blasphemy under Article 156 of the Indonesian criminal code has negative implications for media freedom, and authorities continue to challenge the Press Council's mandate by bringing defamation charges against journalists to court

(Freedom House 2017). Although organizations like Reporters Without Borders and Freedom House rank the political and legal environment for a pluralist media system in Indonesia favorably in comparison to the rest of the region, they also note a decline of press freedom in recent years and in global comparison: Indonesia ranked only 124 of 180 countries in the 2017 World Press Freedom Index (Reporters without Borders 2017) and 97 of 199 countries in the 2015 Freedom of the Press report (Freedom House 2015). This is no longer primarily the result of illicit government influence but reflects increasing concerns about the ability of media tycoons to distort political news through their control of major media outlets. There have also been numerous incidences of violence against journalists reporting from crisis regions like Papua or the Moluccas or on the military's shady businesses at the local level. In addition, finding the right balance between religious sensitivities and press freedom is getting increasingly difficult for journalists (Pintak and Setiyono 2010).

About 90% of Indonesians refer primarily to television for information on political issues, whereas only 10% of the population regularly reads newspapers (IFES 2010, p. 19). After the rapid expansion of web access, about 50.4% of the population today have a working internet connection, trailing the Philippines (52), Vietnam (52.1), Thailand (60%), Malaysia (69.6), and Singapore (81.2; Internet World Stats 2017). Contemporary commercial television is well established, and ten media conglomerates compete with the former state monopolist Television of the Republic of Indonesia (TVRI) for viewers, including two 24-hour news networks with large market shares (Mietzner 2013, pp. 108–109). TVRI provides politically balanced coverage but struggles with low ratings (Nugroho et al. 2012, p. 103). Even though most private media conglomerates have links to political parties, reporting is relatively balanced (Hill 2007). The fact that 12 corporations control the lion's share of the national media sector market has raised concerns that concentration in ownership structure could undermine media pluralism and democracy (Ida 2011; Haryanto 2011) but still place Indonesia far ahead of more authoritarian media markets like Malaysia, Cambodia, or Singapore. Despite some anecdotal evidence about journalistic self-censorship (Tapsell 2012), there are numerous examples of investigative and critical reporting about politically sensitive issues. This includes presidential corruption in the so-called Bulog-gate and Brunei-gate scandals that contributed to President Wahid's downfall, the environmental consequences of illegal oil drilling, and the parliamentary investigation of the government bailout of the state-owned Bank Century (Tomsa 2007, pp. 83–84; Kimura 2011; Tapsell 2012). The mass media have also become an important tool for voter education and political campaigning after 1999 (Liddle and Mujani 2007; Mietzner 2013, p. 109).

4.10   Outlook

Since the fall of Suharto, Indonesia has overcome a number of challenges, including the impeachment of President Abdurrahman Wahid in 2001, the aftermath of the tsunami of 2004, the fallout of the global financial crisis of 2008/09, and a highly divisive election campaign in 2014, without suffering any lasting damage. Considering its difficult background conditions, few observers expected Indonesia to become what is considered "Southeast Asia's strongest and most stable democracy" (Mietzner 2012). Although there is, as noted, a certain authoritarian nostalgia prevalent today and widespread dissatisfaction with the way the electoral process, party politics, and the democratic institutions in general work, Indonesia's democracy has—so far—been able to defend itself against the destructive impact of populism that is haunting democracies in the rest of Southeast Asia (Mietzner 2015b). First, the combination of declining but still relatively well-institutionalized political parties and centripetal institutions of democratic governance inhibit the rise of polarizing political outsiders of a caliber like Rodrigo Duterte in the Philippines (cf. Chap. 8). Second, in contrast to Thailand, the Indonesian military has come to terms with democracy. As long as the civilian government is not faced with destabilizing mass contention or attempts by civilian elites to pull the military back into politics, it is highly unlikely that TNI will have the motive or the opportunity to intervene in politics again, either as arbitrator or as actual ruler. Third, Indonesia's inclusive and incremental process of elite settlement and democratization have helped establish a strong democratic elite consensus. Today, all politically relevant groups, with the exception of some extremist organizations, have found access to the political process through democratic institutions and have, hence, little reason to undermine them (Horowitz 2013).

Still, the consensus-driven political process also means that reforms are rarely swift, encompassing, and thorough. Institutional obstacles and the fragmented party system often result in diluted initiatives that are unlikely to solve the country's many remaining problems. Paradoxically, the Indonesian public has very high expectations for the political efficacy of its government and in the long term, this and the slow pace of reform could erode popular support for democracy. It is still unclear if the hopes democratic reformers have put into the election of Joko "Jokowi" Widodo—Indonesia's first president without a military background or roots in the political class and who was inaugurated in October 2014—are fully justified. So far, many of his political decisions seem to indicate that he will follow the example set by his predecessors and respect the interests of the established elite, especially within his own party (Hamayotsu and Nataatmadja 2016; Mietzner 2015a).

References

ABS. (2017). *Asian barometer survey: Electronic data release for Wave 4, 2014-2016.* http://www.asianbarometer.org/data/data-release

Alfitri. (2008). Religious liberty in Indonesia and the rights of "deviant" sects. *Asian Journal of Comparative Law, 3*(January), 1–27.

Allen, N. W. (2014). From patronage machine to Partisan Melee: Subnational corruption and the evolution of the Indonesian party system. *Pacific Affairs, 87*, 221–245. https://doi.org/10.5509/2014872221

Aminuddin, M. F. (2016). *Dataset 'Military retirees in Indonesian politics, 1998-2014'.* Heidelberg: Springer.

Antlöv, H. (2003). Village government and rural development in Indonesia: The new democratic framework. *Bulletin of Indonesian Economic Studies, 39*, 193–214. https://doi.org/10.1080/00074910302013

Aspinall, E. (2005). *Opposing Suharto: Compromise, resistance, and regime change in Indonesia.* Stanford: Stanford University Press.

Aspinall, E. (2010). The irony of success. *Journal of Democracy, 21*, 20–34. https://doi.org/10.1353/jod.0.0157

Aspinall, E. (2014). Health care and democratization in Indonesia. *Democratization, 21*, 803–823. https://doi.org/10.1080/13510347.2013.873791

Bedner, A. (2010). 'Shopping forums': Indonesia's administrative courts. In A. J. Harding & P. Nicholson (Eds.), *New courts in Asia* (pp. 209–230). Routledge: London.

Beittinger-Lee, V. (2009). *(Un)civil society and political change in Indonesia: A contested arena.* London: Routledge.

Bertrand, J. (2004). *Nationalism and ethnic conflict in Indonesia.* Cambridge: Cambridge University Press.

Bourchier, D. (2008). Positivism and romanticism in Indonesian legal thought. In T. Lindsey (Ed.), *Indonesia: Law and society* (2nd ed., pp. 94–104). Annandale: Federation Press.

Bowen, J. R. (2003). *Islam, law, and equality in Indonesia: An anthropology of public reasoning.* Cambridge: Cambridge University Press.

Bräuchler, B. (2011). The transformation of the media scene: From war to peace in the Moluccas, Eastern Indonesia. In K. Sen & D. T. Hill (Eds.), *Politics and the media in twenty-first century Indonesia* (pp. 119–140). London: Routledge.

Braun, S. (2008). *Indonesia's presidential democracy.* Berlin: dissertation.de.

BTI. (2016). *Bertelsmann transformation index 2016.* Gütersloh: Bertelsmann Foundation.

Bünte, M. (2011). Decentralization and democratic governance in Southeast Asia. In A. Croissant & M. Bünte (Eds.), *The crisis of democratic governance in Southeast Asia* (pp. 131–150). Houndmills: Palgrave Macmillan.

Bush, R. (2008). Regional Sharia regulations in Indonesia: Anomaly or symptom? In G. Fealy & S. White (Eds.), *Expressing Islam: Religious life and politics in Indonesia* (pp. 174–191). Singapore: ISEAS.

Bush, R. (2009). *Nahdlatul Ulama and the struggle for power within Islam and politics in Indonesia.* Singapore: ISEAS.

Butt, S. (2009a). Conditional constitutionality, pragmatism and the rule of law. *Legal Studies Research Paper, 28*(9).

Butt, S. (2009b). 'Unlawfulness' and corruption under Indonesian law. *Bulletin of Indonesian Economic Studies, 45*, 179–198. https://doi.org/10.1080/00074910903040328

Butt, S. (2011). Anti-corruption reform in indonesia: An obituary? *Bulletin of Indonesian Economic Studies, 47*, 381–394. https://doi.org/10.1080/00074918.2011.619051

Butt, S. (2015). *The constitutional court and democracy in Indonesia.* Leiden: Koninklijke Brill.

Butt, S., & Lindsey, T. (2008). Economic reform when the constitution matters: Indonesia's constitutional court and article 33. *Bulletin of Indonesian Economic Studies, 44*, 239–262. https://doi.org/10.1080/00074910802169004

Butt, S., & Lindsey, T. (2011). Judicial mafia: The courts and state illegality in Indonesia. In E. Aspinall & G. van Klinken (Eds.), *The state and illegality in Indonesia* (pp. 189–215). Leiden: KITLV Press.

Campbell, T. (2008). Conclusion. Decentralization and democracy: A global perspective in 2007. In World Bank (Ed.), *Decentralization and local democracy in the world: First global report 2008* (pp. 282–306). New York.

Carr, A. (2017). *Psephos: Adam Carr's election archive.* Accessed June, 10, 2017, from http://psephos.adam-carr.net/

Chang, A., Chu, Y.-h., & Welsh, B. (2013). Southeast Asia: Sources of regime support. *Journal of Democracy, 24*, 150–164. https://doi.org/10.1353/jod.2013.0025

Chauvel, R. (2004). *The Papua conflict: Constructing Papuan nationalism. History, ethnicity, and adaptation* (Policy studies, Vol. 14). Washington, DC: East-West Center.

CIA. (2017). *The World Factbook.* Langley: Central Intelligence Agency.

Clarke, R. (2008). The Bali Bombing, East Timor trials and the Aceh Human Rights Court: Retrospectivity, impunity and constitutionalism. In T. Lindsey (Ed.), *Indonesia: Law and society* (2nd ed., pp. 430–454). Annandale: Federation Press.

Croissant, A. (2010). Provisions, practices and performances of constitutional review in democratizing East Asia. *The Pacific Review, 23*, 549–578. https://doi.org/10.1080/09512748.2010.521851

Croissant, A., Kuehn, D., Lorenz, P., & Chambers, P. W. (2013). *Democratization and civilian control in Asia.* Houndmills: Palgrave Macmillan.

Croissant, A., & Schächter, T. (2008). Die Nationalisierung politischer Parteiensysteme in Ostasien. *Politische Vierteljahresschrift, 49*(4), 618–640.

Croissant, A., & Völkel, P. (2012). Party system types and party system institutionalization: Comparing new democracies in East and Southeast Asia. *Party Politics, 18*, 235–265. https://doi.org/10.1177/1354068810380096

Crouch, H. A. (1988). *The army and politics in Indonesia.* Ithaca: Cornell University Press.

Crouch, M. (2008). Indonesia's national ombudsman reforms: Salvaging a failed experiment. In T. Lindsey (Ed.), *Indonesia: Law and society* (2nd ed., pp. 382–405). Annandale: Federation Press.

Crouch, M. (2013). *Law and religion in Indonesia: Conflict and the courts in West Java.* London: Taylor & Francis.

Datta, A., Jones, H., Febriany, V., Harris, D., Kumala Dwi, R., Wild, L., et al. (2011). *The political economy of policy-making in Indonesia: Opportunities for improving the demand for and use of knowledge.* London: Overseas Development Institute.

Diamond, L. J. (2009). Is a 'rainbow coalition' a good way to govern? *Bulletin of Indonesian Economic Studies, 45*, 337–340. https://doi.org/10.1080/00074910903424035

DPR. (2010). *Serving the mandate and aspirations of the people: Five-year report for 2004-2009.* Jakarta: General Secretariat Republic of the Indonesia House of Representatives.

Eldridge, P. (1996). Development, democracy and non-government organizations in Indonesia. *Asian Journal of Political Science, 4*, 17–35. https://doi.org/10.1080/02185379608434070

Ellis, A. (2005). *Constitutional reform in Indonesia: A retrospective.* Stockholm: International IDEA.

Fachruddin, F. (2005). *Educating for democracy: Ideas and practices of Islamic civil society associations in Indonesia.* Unpublished Doctoral Dissertation, University of Pittsburgh, Pittsburgh.

Febrian. (2009). *Handbook on the legislative process.* Jakarta: UNDP Indonesia.

Feith, H. (1962). *The decline of constitutional democracy in Indonesia.* Ithaca, NY: Cornell University Press

Feith, H., & Castles, L. (2007). *Indonesian political thinking: 1945-1965* (1st ed.). Jakarta: Equinox Pub.

Fenwick, S. (2008a). Administrative law and judicial review in Indonesia: The search for accountability. In T. Ginsburg & A. H. Y. Chen (Eds.), *Administrative law and governance in Asia: Comparative perspectives* (Vol. 4, pp. 329–358). Abingdon, Oxon: Routledge.

Fenwick, S. (2008b). Measuring up?: Indonesia's anti-corruption commission and the new corruption agenda. In T. Lindsey (Ed.), *Indonesia: Law and society* (2nd ed., pp. 406–429). Annandale: Federation Press.

Fitrani, F., Hofman, B., & Kaiser, K. (2005). Unity in diversity? The creation of new local governments in a decentralising Indonesia. *Bulletin of Indonesian Economic Studies, 41*, 57–79. https://doi.org/10.1080/00074910500072690

Fox, C. (2016). *Personal votes & ethnic politics: Democracy and ethnic campaigning in Indonesia.* Poland: IPSA World Congress Poznan.

Freedom House. (2015). *Freedom of the Press Index 2014: Harsh laws and violence drive global decline.* Accessed June 2, 2017, from https://freedomhouse.org/report/freedom-press/freedom-press-2015

Freedom House. (2017). *Freedom of the Press Index 2017: Press freedom's dark horizon.* Accessed June 2, 2017, from https://freedomhouse.org/report/freedom-press/freedom-press-2017

Geertz, C. (1960). *The religion of Java.* Glencoe: The Free Press.

Gledhill, J. (2012). Competing for change: Regime transition, intrastate competition, and violence. *Security Studies, 21,* 43–82. https://doi.org/10.1080/09636412.2012.650592

Groemping, M. (2015). *Southeast Asian elections worst in the world.* Accessed June 22, 2015, from http://www.newmandala.org/southeast-asian-elections-worst-in-the-world/

Gunawan, A. B. (2017). Civilian control and defense policy in Indonesia's Nascent democracy. In A. Croissant & D. Kuehn (Eds.), *Reforming civil-military relations in new democracies* (pp. 129–150). Heidelberg: Springer VS.

Hadiwinata, B. S. (2009). From "heroes" to "troublemakers"?: Civil society and democratization in Indonesia. In M. Bünte & A. Ufen (Eds.), *Democratization in Post-Suharto Indonesia* (pp. 276–294). London: Routledge.

Hafidz, T. S. (2006). *Fading away?: The political role of the army in Indonesia's transition to democracy, 1998-2001* (IDSS Monograph, No. 8). Singapore: ISEAS.

Hamayotsu, K., & Nataatmadja, R. (2016). Indonesia in 2015: The peoples presidents rocky road and hazy outlooks in democratic consolidation. *Asian Survey, 56,* 129–137. https://doi.org/10.1525/as.2016.56.1.129

Harjowiryono, M. (2012). Pengembangan Sistem Pembiayaan antar Pemerintah die Indonesia. In Direktorat Jenderal Perimangan Keuangan—Kementerian Keuangan (Ed.), *Desentralisasi Fiskal di Indonesia: Satu Dekade setelah Ledakan Besar* (pp. 123–146). DJPK: Jakarta.

Haryanto, I. (2011). Media ownership and its implications for journalists and journalism in Indonesia. In K. Sen & D. T. Hill (Eds.), *Politics and the media in twenty-first century Indonesia* (pp. 104–118). London: Routledge.

Hefner, R. W. (2000). *Civil Islam: Muslims and democratization in Indonesia (Princeton studies in Muslim politics).* Princeton, NJ: Princeton University Press.

Hefner, R. W. (2016). Indonesia, Islam, and the new U.S. administration. *The Review of Faith and International Affairs, 14,* 59–66. https://doi.org/10.1080/15570274.2016.1184444

Hendrianto. (2010). Institutional choice and the new Indonesian Constitutional Court. In A. J. Harding & P. Nicholson (Eds.), *New courts in Asia* (pp. 158–177). London: Routledge.

Henley, D., Schouten, M. J., & Ulaen, A. J. (2007). Preserving the peace in post-New Order Minahasa. In H. Schulte Nordholt & v. G. Klinken (Eds.), *Renegotiating boundaries: Local politics in post-Suharto Indonesia* (pp. 307–326). Leiden: KITLV Press.

Hicken, A., & Kasuya, Y. (2003). A guide to the constitutional structures and electoral systems of east, south and southeast Asia. *Electoral Studies, 22,* 121–151. https://doi.org/10.1016/S0261-3794(01)00053-1

Hill, D. T. (2007). Maneuvers in Manado: Media and politics in regional Indonesia. *South East Asia Research, 15*(1), 5–28.

Honna, J. (2003). *Military politics and democratization in Indonesia.* London: Routledge.

Horowitz, D. L. (2013). *Constitutional change and democracy in Indonesia.* Cambridge: Cambridge University Press.

HRW. (2006). *Too high a price: The human rights cost of the Indonesian military's economic activities.* New York: Human Rights Watch.

Ida, R. (2011). Reorganisation of media power in post-authoritarian Indonesia: Ownership, power and influence of local media entrepreneurs. In K. Sen & D. T. Hill (Eds.), *Politics and the media in twenty-first century Indonesia* (pp. 13–25). London: Routledge.

IFES. (2010). *Electoral survey 2010.* Washington, DC: International Federation for Electoral Systems.

Indrayana, D. (2008a). Indonesia: In search for a democratic constitution (1945-2008). In C. Hill & J. Menzel (Eds.), *Constitutionalism in Southeast Asia 2: Reports on national constitutions* (pp. 95–121). Singapore: Konrad Adenauer Foundation.

Indrayana, D. (2008b). *Indonesian constitutional reform, 1999–2002: An evaluation of constitution-making in transition*. Jakarta: Kompas Book.

Internet World Stats. (2017). *Internet usage statistics: World internet users and 2017 population stats*. https://www.internetworldstats.com/stats.htm

IPU. (2014). *Interparliamentary union parline database Indonesia*. Accessed June 20, 2017, from http://www.ipu.org/parline-e/reports/2147_A.htm

Irawanto, B. (2011). Riding waves of change: Islamic press in post-authoritarian Indonesia. In K. Sen & D. T. Hill (Eds.), *Politics and the media in twenty-first century Indonesia* (pp. 67–84). London: Routledge.

Jurriëns, E. (2009). *From monologue to dialogue: Radio and reform in Indonesia*. Leiden: KITLV Press.

Juwono, V., & Eckardt, S. (2008). Budget accountability and legislative oversight in transition: The case of post-Suharto Indonesia. In R. Stapenhurst, R. Pelizzo, D. M. Olson, & L. von Trapp (Eds.), *Legislative oversight and budgeting: A world perspective, WBI development studies* (pp. 293–309). Washington, DC: World Bank.

Kaiser, K., Hofman, B., World Bank, Kadjatmiko, & Suharnoko Sjahrir, B. (2006). *Evaluating fiscal equalization in Indonesia*. Jakarta: World Bank Publications.

Kawamura, K. (2010). *Is the Indonesian President or strong or weak?* (IDE Discussion Paper 235).

Kimura, E. (2010). Changing the rules: Historical conjuncture and transition in Indonesia. *Asia Pacific Viewpoint, 51*, 248–261. https://doi.org/10.1111/j.1467-8373.2010.01429.x

Kimura, E. (2011). Indonesia in 2010. *Asian Survey, 51*, 186–195. https://doi.org/10.1525/as.2011.51.1.186

King, B. A. (2004). *Empowering the presidency: Interests and perceptions in Indonesia's constitutional reforms, 1999-2002*. Doctoral dissertation, Ohio State University, Columbus.

KPU. (2014). *Nasional Rekapitulasi final 2014*. Jakarta: Komisi Pemilihan Umum.

Lane, M. (2009). *Mass mobilisation in Indonesian politics 1960-2001: Towards a class analysis*. PhD Dissertation, University of Wollongong, Wollongong.

Lee, T. (2015). *Defect or defend: Military responses to popular protests in authoritarian Asia*. Baltimore: Johns Hopkins University Press.

Liddle, R. W. (1985). Soeharto's Indonesia: Personal rule and political institutions. *Pacific Affairs, 58*(1), 68–90.

Liddle, R. W., & Mujani, S. (2007). Leadership, party, and religion: Explaining voting behavior in Indonesia. *Comparative Political Studies, 40*(7), 832–857.

Lindsey, T. (2002). Indonesian constitutional reform: Muddling towards democracy. *Singapore Journal of International and Comparative Law, 6*, 244.

Lindsey, T., & Santosa, M. A. (2008). The trajectory of law reform in Indonesia: A short overview of legal systems and change in Indonesia. In T. Lindsey (Ed.), *Indonesia: Law and society* (2nd ed., pp. 2–22). Annandale: Federation Press.

Lipset, S. M., & Rokkan, S. (Eds.). (1967). *Party systems and voter alignments: Cross-national perspectives*. New York: The Free Press.

Lorenz, P. (2015). *Principals, partners and pawns: Indonesian civil society organizations and civilian control of the military*. http://www.ub.uni-heidelberg.de/archiv/18730

Lowry, B. (2016). *The puzzle of security sector reforms in Indonesia*. Barton: The Strategist.

Lukito, R. (2013). *Legal pluralism in Indonesia: Bridging the unbridgeable*. Abingdon: Routledge.

Lussier, D. N., & Fish, M. S. (2012). Indonesia: The benefits of civic engagement. *Journal of Democracy, 23*, 70–84. https://doi.org/10.1353/jod.2012.0017

McCulloch, L. (2003). Trifungsi: The role of the Indonesian military in business. In J. Brömmelhörster & W.-C. Paes (Eds.), *The military as an economic actor* (pp. 94–123). Houndsmill: Palgrave Macmillan.

McCulloch, N., & Sjahrir, B. S. (2008). *Endowments, location or luck? Evaluating the determinants of sub-national growth in decentralized*. Indonesia: World Bank.

McLeod, R. H. (2008). Inadequate budgets and salaries as instruments for institutionalizing public sector corruption in Indonesia. *South East Asia Research, 16*, 199–223. https://doi.org/10.5367/000000008785260464

Mietzner, M. (2006). *The politics of military reform in post-Suharto Indonesia: Elite conflict, nationalism, and institutional resistance.* East-West Center: Washington, DC.

Mietzner, M. (2008). Comparing Indonesia's party systems of the 1950s and the post-Suharto era: From centrifugal to centripetal inter-party competition. *Journal of Southeast Asian Studies, 39* (3), 431–453.

Mietzner, M. (2009a). Indonesia in 2008: Democratic consolidation in Soeharto's shadow. *Southeast Asian Affairs, 2009*(1), 105–123.

Mietzner, M. (2009b). *Military politics, Islam and the state in Indonesia. From turbulent transition to democratic consolidation.* Singapore: ISEAS.

Mietzner, M. (2010a). Indonesia's direct elections: Empowering the electorate or entrenching the New Order oligarchy? In E. Aspinall & G. Fealy (Eds.), *Suharto's new order and its legacies: Essays in honour of Harold Crouch* (pp. 173–190). Canberra: ANU Press.

Mietzner, M. (2010b). Political conflict resolution and democratic consolidation in Indonesia: The role of the constitutional court. *Journal of East Asian Studies, 10*, 397–424. https://doi.org/10.5555/jeas.2010.10.3.397

Mietzner, M. (2012). Indonesia's democratic stagnation: Anti-reformist elites and resilient civil society. *Democratization, 19*, 209–229. https://doi.org/10.1080/13510347.2011.572620

Mietzner, M. (2013). *Money, power and ideology: Political parties in post-authoritarian Indonesia.* Honolulu: University of Hawai'i Press.

Mietzner, M. (2015a). Indonesia: Democratic consolidation and stagnation under Yudhoyono, 2004-2014. In W. Case (Ed.), *Routledge handbook of Southeast Asian democratization* (pp. 370–384). London: Routledge.

Mietzner, M. (2015b). *Reinventing Asian populism: Jokowi's rise, democracy, and political contestation in Indonesia.* Honolulu: East-West Center.

Mietzner, M. (2017a). Authoritarian elections, state capacity, and performance legitimacy: Phases of regime consolidation and decline in Suharto's Indonesia. *International Political Science Review, 65*, 1–14. https://doi.org/10.1177/0192512116687139

Mietzner, M. (2017b). *State capacity in post-authoritarian Indonesia: Securing democracy's survival, Entrenching its low quality.* Unpublished manuscript.

Mietzner, M., & Misol, L. (2012). Military businesses in post-Soeharto Indonesia: Decline, reform and persistence. In J. Rüland, M.-G. Manea, & H. Born (Eds.), *The politics of military reform: Lessons from Indonesia and Nigeria.* Berlin: Springer VS.

Missbach, A. (2011). *Politics and conflict in Indonesia: The role of the Acehnese Diaspora.* New York: Routledge.

MK. (2013). *Laporan Tahunan 2012.* Jakarta: Mahkamah Konstitusi.

MK. (2014). *Laporan Tahunan 2013.* Jakarta: Mahkamah Konstitusi.

MK. (2016). *Laporan Tahunan 2015.* Jakarta: Mahkamah Konstitusi.

Morlino, L., Dressel, B., & Pelizzo, R. (2011). The quality of democracy in Asia-Pacific: Issues and findings. *International Political Science Review, 32*, 491–511. https://doi.org/10.1177/0192512111418334

Mujani, S., & Liddle, R. W. (2009). Muslim Indonesia's secular democracy. *Asian Survey, 49*(4), 575–590.

Nasution, A. B. (1992). *The aspiration for constitutional government in Indonesia: A socio-legal study of the Indonesian Konstituante, 1956-1959.* Jakarta: Pustaka Sinar Harapan.

Nugroho, Y., Putri, D. A., & Laksmi, S. (2012). *Mapping the landscape of the media industry in contemporary Indonesia.* Jakarta: Centre for Innovation Policy and Governance and HIVOS Regional Office Southeast Asia.

Nurjaya, I. N. (2015). Is the constitutional and legal recognition of traditional community laws within the multicultural country of Indonesia a genuine or pseudo recognition? *Constitutional Review, 1*(2), 50–68.

Nyman, M. (2009). Civil society and the challenges of the post-Suharto era. In M. Bünte & A. Ufen (Eds.), *Democratization in Post-Suharto Indonesia* (pp. 251–275). London: Routledge.

PEI. (2016). *The perceptions of electoral integrity dataset: Version 4.5*. Accessed June 22, 2017, from https://sites.google.com/site/electoralintegrityproject4/projects/expert-survey-2

Pepinsky, T. B. (2009). *Economic crises and the breakdown of authoritarian regimes: Indonesia and Malaysia in comparative perspective*. Cambridge: Cambridge University Press.

Pintak, L., & Setiyono, B. (2010). The mission of Indonesian journalism: Balancing democracy, development, and Islamic values. *The International Journal of Press/Politics*. https://doi.org/10.1177/1940161210391784

Pompe, S. (2008). Between crime and custom: Extra-marital sex in modern Indonesian law. In T. Lindsey (Ed.), *Indonesia: Law and society* (2nd ed., pp. 105–114). Annandale: Federation Press.

Reporters Without Borders. (2017). *2017 World press freedom index*. RSF. Accessed June 22, 2017, from https://rsf.org/en/ranking

Ricklefs, M. C. (2008). *A history of modern Indonesia since c. 1200* (4th ed.). Houndmills: Palgrave Macmillan.

Rinakit, S. (2005). *The Indonesian military after the new order*. Singapore: NIAS Press.

Robison, R., & Hadiz, V. R. (2004). *Reorganising power in Indonesia: The politics of oligarchy in an age of markets*. New York: RoutledgeCurzon.

Roosa, J. (2006). *Pretext for mass murder: The September 30th movement and Suharto's coup d'Etat in Indonesia*. Madison: University of Wisconsin Press.

Rotberg, I. R. (2002). *Failed states in a world of terror*. Accessed June 22, 2017, from https://www.foreignaffairs.com/articles/2002-07-01/failed-states-world-terror

Rüland, J. (2001). Indonesia. In D. Nohlen, F. Grotz, & C. Hartmann (Eds.), *Elections in Asia and the Pacific: A data handbook, volume II: South East Asia, East Asia, and the South Pacific* (pp. 83–128). Oxford: Oxford University Press.

Rüland, J., Jürgenmeyer, C., Nelson, M. H., & Ziegenhain, P. (2005). *Parliaments and political change in Asia*. Singapore: ISEAS.

Schmidt, A. (2010). Indonesia's 2009 elections: Performance challenges and negative precedents. In E. Aspinall & M. Mietzner (Eds.), *Problems of democratisation in Indonesia: Elections, institutions and society* (pp. 100–121). Singapore: ISEAS.

Schneier, E. V. (2008). Evolving patterns of legislative oversight in Indonesia. In R. Stapenhurst, R. Pelizzo, D. M. Olson, & L. von Trapp (Eds.), *Legislative oversight and budgeting: A world perspective, WBI development studies* (pp. 201–215). Washington DC: World Bank.

Sebastian, L. C. (2006). *Realpolitik ideology: Indonesia's use of military force*. Singapore: ISEAS.

Sebastian, L. C., & Iisgindarsah. (2012). Taking stock of military reform in Indonesia. In J. Rüland, M.-G. Manea, & H. Born (Eds.), *The politics of military reform: Lessons from Indonesia and Nigeria* (pp. 29–56). Berlin: Springer VS.

Sherlock, S. (2006). Indonesia's regional representative assembly: Democracy, representation and the regions. A report on the Dewan Perwakilan Daerah. *CDI Policy Papers on Political Governance, (1)*, 1–47.

Sherlock, S. (2008). Indonesia's anti-pornography bill: A case study of decision making in the Indonesian parliament (DPR). *Friedrich-Naumann Stiftung Hintergrundpapier, (10)*, 1–17.

Sherlock, S. (2009). SBY's consensus cabinet—lanjutkan? *Bulletin of Indonesian Economic Studies, 45*, 341–343. https://doi.org/10.1080/00074910903424043

Sherlock, S. (2010). Parliament in Indonesia's decade of democracy: People's forum or chamber of cronies? In E. Aspinall & M. Mietzner (Eds.), *Problems of democratisation in Indonesia: Elections, institutions and society* (pp. 160–178). Singapore: ISEAS.

Shugart, M. S., & Carey, J. M. (1992). *Presidents and assemblies: Constitutional design and electoral dynamics*. Cambridge: Cambridge University Press.

Slater, D. (2010). Altering authoritarianism: Institutional complexity and autocratic agency in Indonesia. In J. Mahoney & K. Thelen (Eds.), *Explaining institutional change: Ambiguity, agency, and power* (pp. 132–167). New York: Cambridge University Press.

Slater, D. (2014). Unbuilding-blocs: Indonesia's accountability deficit in historical perspective. *Critical Asian Studies, 46*, 287–315. https://doi.org/10.1080/14672715.2014.898456

Slater, D., & Simmons, E. (2012). Coping by colluding: Political uncertainty and promiscuous powersharing in Indonesia and Bolivia. *Comparative Political Studies.* doi:https://doi.org/10.1177/0010414012453447

Smith, B. B. (2007). *Hard times in the lands of plenty: Oil politics in Iran and Indonesia.* Ithaca: Cornell University Press.

Stockmann, P. (2007). *The new Indonesian constitutional court: A study into its beginnings and forst years of work.* Jakarta: Hanss Seidel Foundation Indonesia.

Sundhaussen, U. (1982). *The road to power: Indonesian military politics , 1945-1967.* New York: Oxford University Press.

Supomo, R. (1964). *The provisional constitution of the republic of Indonesia, with annotations and explanations on each article.* Ithaca, NY: Cornell University.

Tahyar, B. H. (2010). The politics of Indonesia's anti-corruption court. In A. J. Harding & P. Nicholson (Eds.), *New courts in Asia* (pp. 279–298). New York: Routledge.

Tajima, Y. J. (2009). *Order and violence in authoritarian breakdowns: How institutions explain communal violence in Indonesia.* PhD Dissertation, Harvard University, Cambridge.

Tan, E. K. (2012). Singapore: Transitioning to a "new normal" in a post-Lee Kuan Yew era. *Southeast Asian Affairs, 2012*(1), 265–282.

Tapsell, R. (2012). Old tricks in a new era: Self-censorship in Indonesian journalism. *Asian Studies Review, 36*, 227–245. https://doi.org/10.1080/10357823.2012.685926

Taylor, J. G. (2004). *Indonesia: Peoples and histories.* London: Yale University Press.

Thalang, C. (2005). The legislative elections in Indonesia, April 2004. *Electoral Studies, 24*(2), 326–332.

Tomsa, D. (2007). Party politics and the media in Indonesia: Creating a new dual identity for Golkar. *Contemporary Southeast Asia, 29*(1), 77–96.

Tomsa, D. (2008). *Party politics and democratization in Indonesia: Golkar in the post-Suharto era.* New York: Routledge.

Transparency International. (2015). *Corruption perception index.* Accessed June 1, 2017, from https://www.transparency.org/news/feature/corruption_perceptions_index_2016

Turner, M., Imbaruddin, A., & Sutiyono, W. (2009). Human resource management: The forgotten dimension of decentralisation in Indonesia. *Bulletin of Indonesian Economic Studies, 45*, 231–249. https://doi.org/10.1080/00074910903040336

Ufen, A. (2008). From Aliran to dealignment: Political parties in post-Suharto Indonesia. *South East Asia Research, 16*(1), 5–41.

Ufen, A. (2010). The legislative and presidential elections in Indonesia in 2009. *Electoral Studies, 29*, 281–285. https://doi.org/10.1016/j.electstud.2010.02.003

Ufen, A. (2012). Party systems, critical junctures, and cleavages in Southeast Asia. *Asian Survey, 52*, 441–464. https://doi.org/10.1525/as.2012.52.3.441

van Bruinessen, M. (2002). Genealogies of Islamic radicalism in post-Suharto Indonesia. *South East Asia Research, 10*(2), 117–154.

van Klinken, G. A. (2007). *Communal violence and democratization in Indonesia: Small town wars.* London: Routledge.

Vickers, A. (2005). *A history of modern Indonesia.* Cambridge: Cambridge University Press.

von Luebke, C. (2009). The political economy of local governance: Findings from an Indonesian field study. *Bulletin of Indonesian Economic Studies, 45*, 201–230. https://doi.org/10.1080/00074910903040310

Wehner, J. (2006). Assessing the power of the purse: An index of legislative budget institutions. *Political Studies, 54*, 767–785. https://doi.org/10.1111/j.1467-9248.2006.00628.x

Weiss, M. L. (2006). *Protest and possibilities: Civil society and coalitions for political change in Malaysia*. Stanford, CA: Stanford University Press.

Wilson, I. (2011). Reconfiguring rackets: Racket regimes, protection and the state in post-New Order Jakarta. In E. Aspinall & G. van Klinken (Eds.), *The state and illegality in Indonesia* (pp. 239–260). Leiden: KITLV Press.

World Bank. (2003). *Decentralizing Indonesia: A regional public expenditure review overview report*. Jakarta: World Bank Indonesia.

World Bank. (2017a). *Poverty and equity database*. Washington: World Bank.

World Bank. (2017b). *World development indicators*. http://data.worldbank.org/products/wdi

World Bank. (2017c). *Worldwide governance indicators*. http://data.worldbank.org/data-catalog/worldwide-governance-indicators

Ziegenhain, P. (2015). *Institutional engineering and political accountability in Indonesia, Thailand, and the Philippines*. Singapore: ISEAS.

Laos: The Transformation of Periphery Socialism

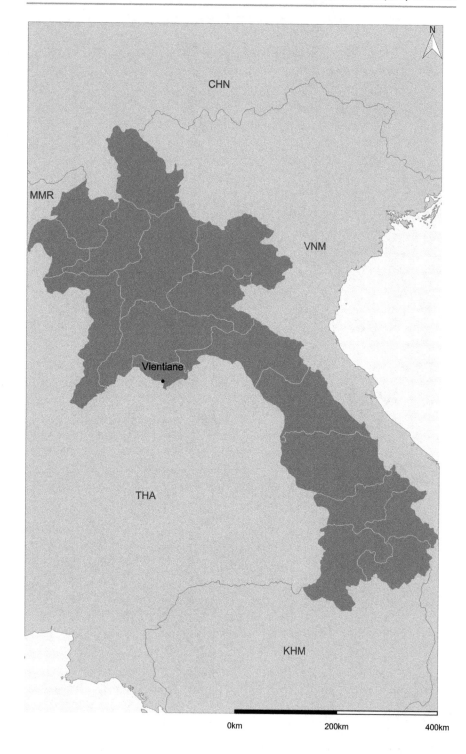

5.1 Historical Background

The Democratic People's Republic of Lao is one of only five communist single-party regimes in the world today (Dimitrov 2013, p. 5).[1] When the Lao People's Revolutionary Party (*Phak Paxaxôn Pativat Lao*, LPRP) took power in 1975, more than 80% of the population was engaged in subsistence farming (Soukamneuth 2006, p. 48), making Laos a case of peripheral socialism in an economically underdeveloped society (Fitzgerald 1985). As a landlocked country with a sparsely populated hinterland, politicized ethnic identities, and a history of a weak central power, Laos struggles with unfavorable circumstances for economic development. Wedged in by more powerful neighbors, the country was frequently threatened both politically and military (see Table 5.1 for the Country Profile).

The Kingdom of Lan Xang, founded in 1354, was the precursor of modern Laos. It covered the territory of today's Laos, parts of Myanmar, and parts of contemporary northern Thailand (Stuart-Fox 1997, p. 6). Historical memories of the ancient kingdom still play a key role in postcolonial nation-building and Laos's socialist politics of legitimacy (Tappe 2008). After Lan Xang was divided into the kingdoms of Luang Prabang, Vientiane, and Champasak in 1707/13, all three eventually became vassal states of Siam and Vietnam (Schneider 2001, p. 11), delaying the emergence of Lao nationalism until the era of French colonialism between 1893 and 1946 (Evans 2002, pp. 70–83).[2] While Luang Prabang as the royal seat initially became a French protectorate in 1893, in 1898, all of modern Laos was fully integrated into the French Indochina Union and unified with French colonial possessions in Vietnam and Cambodia. The royal court remained in Luang Prabang, but authority was de facto exercised by France and the rest of Laos was reorganized into provinces directly ruled by the French government in Vientiane, represented by a resident governor (Evans 2002, p. 45; Brocheux and Hémery 2011). In the "hybrid" colonial bureaucracy, all senior posts were reserved for French bureaucrats. Mid-level positions open to "Asians" were mostly held by Vietnamese civil servants, whereas the protected royal dynasty, the local aristocracy, and former ruling classes remained sidelined (Brocheux and Hémery 2011). Ethnic Lao were also shunned for auxiliary tasks in the colonial army, as the French relied on members of the Tai Dam or Hmong ethnic groups for support (Schneider 2001, p. 21).

During World War II, the compromise between the French government of Marshall Petain in Vichy and Tokyo "recognized French sovereignty over Indochina" (Brocheux and Hémery 2011, p. 338), including Laos, but Japanese military units could be freely stationed in all of French Indochina and the colonial economy was tightly tied to Japan's. In March 1945, however, all French civilian and military personnel were interned and the Japanese Imperial Army took direct

---

[1] The others are Vietnam, Cuba, North Korea, and the People's Republic of China. Throughout this chapter, "communism" and "socialism" are used interchangeably.

[2] Lao are members of the country's majority ethnic group, whereas Laotian encompasses all citizens of Laos (Schneider 2001).

Table 5.1 Country profile

Population (2016)	Year of full national sovereignty	Form of government
7,126,706	1949	Republic
Total area	**Current constitution enacted**	**Head of state**
236,800 km^2	1991	Bounnyang Vorachit (since 2016)
GDP p.c. (2005 PPP, 2012)	**Official language**	**Head of government**
$2925	Lao	Thongloun sisoulit (since 2016)
Ethnic groups	**Democracy score (BTI 2016)**	**System of government**
Lao 53.2%, Khmou 11%, Hmong 9.2%, Others 26.6%	2.95 (range from 1 to 10, higher scores indicate higher levels of democracy)	Parliamentary
Religions	**Regime type**	**Cabinet type**
64.7% Buddhists, 1.7% Christians, 33.5% Others	Autocracy	Single-party government

Source: CIA (2017), BTI (2016)

control over Laos, together with the rest of French Indochina. In the final months of the war, the Japanese supported the formation of a non-communist nationalist movement called Lao Issara ("Free Laos"). In October 1945, the Lao Issara declared the sovereign "Lao Nation" (*Pathet Lao*) and formed a provisional government. While French troops regained control of the country in 1946, France agreed to proclaim Laos as a self-governing constitutional monarchy within the French Union in 1949 (Evans 2002, p. 89). In November 1953, however, Laos gained full sovereignty.

During the Vietnam War or Second Indochina War, the Royal Lao Government pursued a policy of neutrality, but the country quickly became another front in the rapidly escalating conflict. Together with a US-funded "Secret Army" of irregular units, government troops fought a civil war against the *Pathet Lao*, the military branch of the Laotian People's Party founded in 1955 (renamed Lao People's Revolutionary Party in 1972, LPRP), and regular North Vietnamese troops (Evans 2002). The conflict was exacerbated by the massive American bombing campaign to disrupt the Ho Chi Minh Trail, the main North Vietnamese supply line that passed through Laos. During this phase of the conflict, more bombs were dropped on Laos than on Germany during World War II (Soukamneuth 2006, p. 14).

Under the 1973 Paris Peace Accords, all foreign troops were withdrawn from Laos and a ceasefire between the royal government and *Pathet Lao* resulted in a government of national unity. However, the Communists took power in Laos in 1975 after the anti-communist regimes in South Vietnam and Cambodia collapsed. The so-called "Red Prince" Souphanouvong, who had been the figurehead leader of the LPRP during the war, became president of the Lao PDR, while Kaysone

Phomvihane, general secretary of the LPRP since 1955, became prime minister and strongman of the regime.

Since 1975, the single-party regime of the LPRP has gone through various stages of development. In the initial phase of establishing party rule, the LPRP took complete control of the government and state apparatus. Inspired by the Soviet Union and Vietnam, the party also initiated a socialist transformation of the economy and society, implemented a campaign of repression against "counterrevolutionaries" and the ruling classes of the *ancien régime*, organized mobilization campaigns, and tried to indoctrinate the population in its Marxist–Leninist ideology. Still, the totalitarian control of the population and the use of violence remained less intense than in Vietnam and Cambodia (Stuart-Fox 1997). Despite the nationalization of banking, industries, and commerce and the collectivization of agriculture, the low level of economic development and the negligible role of foreign capital in a predominantly rural economy (Soukamneuth 2006, p. 48) meant that central economic planning only began with the first 5-year plan in 1981. Even though the LPRP faced only sporadic resistance from loyalists of the old regime, ethnic minorities, and disillusioned *Pathet Lao* cadres (Stuart-Fox 1997, p. 176), an estimated one-tenth of the Laotian population fled the country within the first 5 years of communist rule, mostly better-educated Lao and members of ethnic minorities like the Hmong (Soukamneuth 2006, p. 50). The collectivization of agriculture resulted in food shortages and again swelled the stream of refugees until the program was stopped in late 1979 with the so-called "seventh resolution" in which Kaysone Phomvihane suggested the party would tolerate private property (Freeman 2006, p. 125).

The second stage of economic corrections and political institutionalization took place from 1979/80 to 1991. The regime came to terms with the realities on the ground and cancelled further measures towards a centrally planned economy. In addition, the LPRP, which had ruled without a constitutional basis since 1975, also formally institutionalized its reign by promulgating a constitution in 1991. Both economic reforms and institutionalization were a reaction to the failure of previous economic policies and the emergence of centrifugal tendencies among local party cadres in the provinces. Furthermore, from the mid-1980s on, the LPRP faced the looming end of economic and military aid from the Soviet Union and other communist Council for Mutual Economic Assistance (COMECON) member states, which had made up 60% of the country's overall foreign aid in 1979 (Evans 2002, p. 189). Similarly, the Vietnamese government signaled its intention to cut back financial and military assistance for the Vientiane government, whereas Western donors and international financial institutions and development agencies demanded political reforms in exchange for economic aid and development assistance. Economic problems caused by the inefficiencies of the centrally planned economy, geopolitical changes, and the need to find new sources of external aid finally led to the announcement of a "New Economic Mechanism" (NEM) in 1986 (Stuart-Fox 1997, p. 182). The aim of the NEM was the transition from a socialist economy to a market economy through the introduction of open market policies and market economic principles, including the liberalization of domestic and foreign trade and investments, the abolition of price controls and the privatization of state enterprises, tax and monetary reforms, as well as the modernization of the legal and administrative system (Stuart-Fox 2009c, p. 38). The economic reforms were flanked by the adoption of a new constitution in 1991 (Leather 2008, p. 126) as well as several changes to party bylaws. Oversight over the state administration was transferred from the prime minister to the LPRP Central Committee to reduce the autonomy of provincial party chairs (Freeman 2006, p. 138).

The 1991 Constitution marks the *passage from revolutionary to consolidated party rule*, under which the party and government strove for a model of authoritarian modernization of the economy and society without political liberalization. Laos remains a closed single-party regime in which the LPRP monopolizes access to political office. Other parties are banned and all political decisions are made within the LPRP-controlled party state. However, the policies of LPRP have become less ideological over the past two decades to favor pragmatic goals over communist ideals. Today, LPRP is no longer a revolutionary party and has become primarily an instrument for the political elite to control and exercise political power. It serves as a patronage machine for members of the first and second generation of party and military cadres and their families as well as newly co-opted sections of society. Performance-based legitimation from economic growth and improving the livelihoods of the population have become important new sources of legitimacy for the party. In recent years, nationalist-oriented (instead of ideology-based) claims of legitimacy by the LPRP—who stresses its role as custodian of Lao culture and history and has facilitated a process of nation-building that includes both Lao and national minorities—have become key ingredients of the party's legitimation strategy (Evans 2002; Soukamneuth 2006, p. 50).

In view of these adaptive changes of party rule, some observers argue that the regime can no longer be meaningfully characterized as communist, but has become a "post-socialist" political order (Evans 1998, p. 2; Soukamneuth 2006, p. 44; Stuart-Fox 2009c, p. 11). Yet the socialist ideology still serves as a disciplinary instrument to control party cadres and society (Lintner 2008, p. 173) and while the party's commitment to the economic and social program of socialism remains suspect, adherence to the political structure of the communist party state signifies the enduring importance of Marxist–Leninism.

Even though the absence of any significant political opposition within Laos reflects the strength of single-party rule in the country, the LPRP still faces some challenges that could potentially endanger regime stability in the long term. First, the economic transformation has resulted in rising horizontal socioeconomic inequalities, both between urban and rural areas as well as between the lowland Lao and highland minorities (Stuart-Fox 2009a, p. 157). Second, opaque decision-making procedures and weak government revenues due to inefficient institutions, widespread tax evasion, and persistent corruption have resulted in weak administrative capacity and a low quality of public services. This has limited the government's ability to provide the wider population with public goods like universal access to education and health and social security, amplifying problems of socioeconomic inequality. Third, even though the economy grew an average of 4% annually between 1986 and 2011, this trend is unlikely to continue without major institutional reforms. The privatization of state enterprises owned by the military, party cadres, or their family members, legal reforms in order to strengthen government accountability and rule of law, and a conclusive anti-corruption policy are all badly needed, but reforms in these areas would threaten opportunities for self-enrichment by those elites whose political loyalty is essential for regime survival—especially cadre capitalists, military officers, and co-opted businessmen—and are therefore unlikely to succeed (Stuart-Fox 2009a; BTI 2014). Inefficient institutions will likely persist, which would stabilize party rule in the short- to medium-term, but which threaten the legitimacy and survival of the communist party state in the long run.

5.2 Constitutional Development and Principles

Laos has had three constitutions. The first provisional constitution was promulgated by various nationalist groups led by Lao Issara in 1945. In contrast to this anti-colonial document, the 1947 Constitution for the Kingdom of Laos was drafted in collaboration with French officials and contained several regulations meant to guarantee French influence over the Kingdom of Laos as a unified "autonomous" state within the French Union (Leather 2008, p. 129). The constitution was abrogated in 1975, leaving Laos without a written constitution for the next 16 years. The LPRP governed on the basis of government decrees and decisions made by the Party's Central Committee and Politburo.

Even though parliament was charged with drafting a constitution in the early 1980s, it was only in 1989 that the LPRP Politburo decided to pursue the issue with more urgency and established a high-level constitutional committee (Stuart-Fox 2002, pp. 295–297). A first draft was published in the party newspaper in April 1990, and party organs, ministries, mass organizations, and provincial governments were encouraged to discuss the proposal. This consultative procedure developed an unintended momentum when a small network of intellectuals publicly criticized the draft and demanded the establishment of a multiparty system. Following a series of arrests of critics of one-party rule in Vietnam and Cambodia, the Laotian regime arrested the network's key figures in October 1990 and sentenced them to long prison terms (Johnson 1992). The final draft of the constitution promulgated in August 1991 differed from the original draft in several smaller points, but it remained unchanged in spirit (Leather 2008, pp. 134–136). The 1991 Constitution was amended extensively in 2003 and, again, in 2015. Even though the amended constitution declares the state's commitment to the rule of law and provides for the separation of power, it affirms that the LPRP is a "leading nucleus" (Art. 3) and that all other state organizations function through a process of "democratic centralism" (Art. 5).

With a total length of less than 5000 words, the Lao constitution is a short and often vaguely worded text that in many cases leaves substantive matters open to regulation by government and parliament (Croissant 2014). Rather than being binding for all state organs, it mainly serves as a manual that eases coordination within the party state and as a blueprint that provides guidance for officials and subjects with respect to the kind of actions they are required or allowed to take (cf. Ginsburg and Simpser 2014).

The text consists of 11 chapters and 98 articles. Only the National Assembly has the right to amend the constitution. The first two chapters (Art. 1–12, 13–30) provide the basis of the political system and the socioeconomic order. The two following chapters deal with national defense and security (Art. 31–33) and the fundamental rights and obligations of citizens (Art. 34–51). Chapter 5 through 9 address the legislature (Art. 52–64), the president and the government (Art. 65–74), local government (Art. 75–78), and the judiciary (Art. 79–86). The remaining chapters cover issues like the national language, currency, national flag, anthem, and capital and includes some final provisions.

While the constitution invokes revolutionary achievements like national liberation and the establishment of a socialist regime in the preamble, it is not a typical socialist constitution: There is no mention of a utopian communist society, the dictatorship of the proletariat, or the worker and peasant class. Instead, the text amalgamates elements from other communist constitutions such as the 1977 Soviet Constitution, post-socialist reform constitutions, and innovations from more recent constitutions drafted since the late 1980s (cf. Tan 2002; Elkins et al. 2009). It also retains elements from earlier Laotian constitutions, including the importance of Buddhism as a tradition that deserves special attention and protection and patronage by the state (Art. 9[new]). The articles on the "socioeconomic regime" in Chapter II of the constitution emphasize the constitution's reformist post-socialist character but at the same time emphasize the state's commitment to develop a "sustainable multi-sectoral economy" (Art. 13[new]) rather than a market economy. New universalist elements of the constitution include relatively recent innovations like the principle of gender equality (Art. 37).

Two articles are essential for the actual structure and operation of the system of government. Following the example of the 1977 Soviet Constitution, Article 3 defines the LPRP as the "leading nucleus" of the political system, while Article 5 subordinates all state organizations to the principle of "democratic centralism." The Leninist principle of "democratic centralism" is the ultimate organizational and leadership principle of party, state, and mass organization in all communist states. It is characterized by six elements (cf. Schmidt 2010): (1) a centralist and hierarchical party- and state structure; (2) the supremacy of the party over the state apparatus; (3) a system of hierarchical control from higher to lower echelons of party and state organizations; (4) firm party discipline and a ban on party factions; (5) party control over the selection of state officials; and (6) the principle of collective leadership in the party and state.[3]

Like other authoritarian constitutions, the Lao constitution bears resemblance with democratic constitutions but serves a different purpose (cf. Finer 1979;

---

[3]Of course, in reality, the collective leadership principle has often been superseded by the dominance of personalist leaders like Josef Stalin in the Soviet Union or Mao Zedong in the People's Republic of China.

Ginsburg and Simpser 2014). The constitution is primarily a legal tool to consolidate the party's claim on sociopolitical leadership. Still, its specific content gives some indication about the actual distribution of authority in the political system and serves as an "operating manual" (cf. Przeworski 2014) for the actual functioning of the state and political regime. However, its formal regulations concerning the system of government and the relationship of the legislature, executive, and judiciary remain of secondary importance. De facto, politics in Laos follows the model of the socialist party state, which supersedes all other political, legal, or administrative structures, institutions, and organizations.

5.3 System of Government and the Socialist Party State

Laos is a single-party regime. After taking power in 1975, the LPRP adopted the Soviet system of government with a dual structure of party and state that is still the institutional blueprint for today's political system (see Fig. 5.1). Through its network of party organizations in all administrative units and the dual function of party cadres as party representatives and state officials, the LPRP has complete control and authority over politics. Even though provincial governors enjoy a certain degree of autonomy and state institutions are relatively weak, this allows the party to assert its claim to power nationwide.

Nominally, the National Assembly (*Sapha Heng Xat*, before 1991: Supreme People's Assembly) is the highest state body. Its current 132 members are elected every 5 years. The Assembly has legislative power and by two-thirds majority elects the state president and—on his proposal—the prime minister and the Council of Ministers. Finally, it also selects the judges for the People's Supreme Court and the attorney general. Parliament is in session twice a year for a few weeks and its Standing Committee (NASC) is supposed to oversee the implementation of its decisions, interpret the constitution, and propose candidates for several important state offices, including the president and before 2003, judges of the civil and military courts. It consists of the president of the National Assembly, his deputy, and eight additional members of parliament. The NASC oversees the six parliamentary standing committees and is widely considered to be the key decision-making body within the parliament.

Unlike the Vietnamese National Assembly (see Chap. 12), the Lao National Assembly has not experienced an expansion of its political authority in recent years. It remains a rubber stamp for the Politburo and the Central Committee of the LPRP, and there is no indication that the parliament has ever attempted to exercise some of its constitutional prerogatives to control other organs of the party state or to set an agenda for government policies.

President and prime minister wield executive authority, and the Council of Ministers serves as a cabinet. The government's term of office is tied to the National Assembly's election period. While the prime minister leads the government, he or she usually merely confirms the party leadership's preliminary decision. Outside the authority granted by the president, the prime minister has no formal political

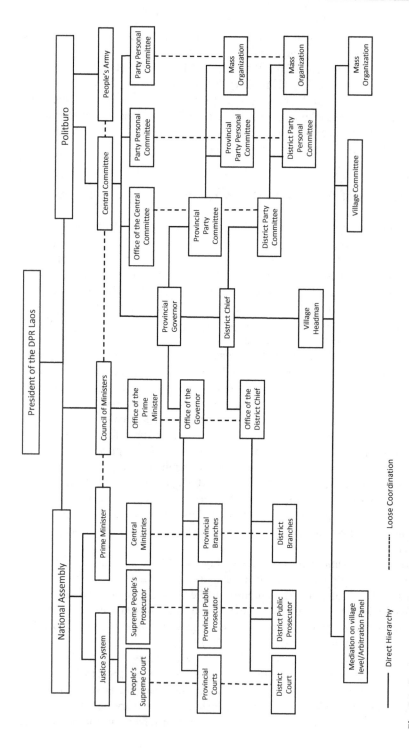

Fig. 5.1 Dual structure of the party state in Laos. Source: Authors' compilation based on UNDP (2005), Soukamneuth (2006, p. 84)

latitude. The prime minister chairs the Council of Ministers, which in March 2016 consisted of 21 cabinet ministers, four deputy prime ministers, the chairs of the National Committees for Planning and Cooperation and the Central Bank, as well as two Ministers for the Government's Office. The Council of Ministers reports directly to the prime minister. Nominally, the ministers and the prime minister are accountable to parliament, while in practice they are accountable to the party's Politburo. The Office of the Prime Minister, which also oversees the implementation of government policies, coordinates the Council of Ministers.

The Office of the President used to be largely symbolic, but the 1991 Constitution and especially the 2003 constitutional amendments have shifted power from the prime minister and the NASC to the president (Leather 2008, p. 141). The president appoints and dismisses the prime minister on the recommendation of the National Assembly and the president of the People's Supreme Court. The president is commander-in-chief of the armed forces, appoints all provincial governors, and presides government meetings. Since the 1990s, the president has also held the office of the Chairman and General Secretary of the Central Committee of the LPRP, which has further strengthened the president's position vis-à-vis the prime minister and other high-ranking party officials.

5.4   Political Parties

With the exception of the Communist Party, modern political parties emerged in Laos only in the 1950s. These political parties did not possess a permanent organizational structure, membership base, or policy platform. Their main purpose was to serve as patronage machines for influential individuals and families (*phu nyai*; Stuart-Fox 2002). Since 1975, the LPRP is the only legal party in Laos.

The LPRP emerged from the Indochina Communist Party (ICP) founded in 1930, but it was not until 1955 that the Lao People's Party was formally established (Schneider 2001, p. 39). The party name was changed to Lao People's Revolutionary Party (*Phak Paxaôn Pativat Lao*) during the second party congress in 1972. It is organized as a Leninist cadre party, was modeled after the communist parties of the Soviet Union and Vietnam, and adheres to the principle of democratic centralism. As in other ruling communist parties, the Politburo and Central Committee are the party's key decision-making bodies. Since 1972, the party is structured along territorial and sectoral lines, meaning that the party is present in provinces and districts as well as in mass organizations, the armed forces, and state organizations. Party membership is necessary to gain access to most government positions and is mandatory for officers in the Lao People's Army (Stuart-Fox 2009c, p. 12). There is a parallel party structure in each ministry, led by a deputy minister who coordinates party activities and ensures that the administration follows the party line (Soukamneuth 2006, p. 58). Until the early 1990s, a significant degree of provincial autonomy emphasized the party's role as the sole centralized state organization. While governors retain significant influence nowadays, their authority results from their position in the LPRP, not their state office (Stuart-Fox 2002, p. 241).

Membership is by personal invitation only, and member selection is subject to prior screening of aspirants by party organs. However, the degree to which candidates have to demonstrate their ideological aptitude is unclear, and there is no reliable data about the actual number of party members. Estimates put the party's membership at about 25,000 in 1975 and 78,000 in 1996 (Stuart-Fox 1997). Until 2011, however, the party is estimated to have increased its membership to 191,780 members (Jönsson 2011; BTI 2014, p. 10). During the 10th party congress in January 2016, the Vientiane Times, the country's only English language newspaper under the Ministry of Information and Culture, reported that 685 delegates represented 252,879 party members [approx. 3.6% of the population (Vaenkeo 2016)]. Some foreign observers suggest that this—to some extent—reflects the successful co-optation of emerging new elites like private businesses, technocrats, and returning wealthy or well-educated emigres, but also the inclusion of members of ethnic minorities into the party (Stuart-Fox 2005, p. 8, 2009b).

The national party congress is held every 5 years, and according to party bylaws, serves as the party's highest decision-making body. Its 685 delegates (2016) elect the Central Committee's currently 69 members and formally decide important party matters. The Central Committee forms sub-committees for party organization, propaganda and training, party administration, the dissemination of party policies, an audit committee for the state and party, and the State School for Political Theory. The 11 members of the Politburo (2016) and the general secretary of the Central Committee are elected by the Central Committee at the party congress and together form the party's power center. Similar to the Central Committee, positions in the Politburo are ranked hierarchically. Changes to the composition and ranking of members in both the Central Committee and Politburo are usually considered to reflect the power relations among different ideological or programmatic wings within the party (Creak 2011; Jönsson 2011). Little is known about how decisions are made inside the Politburo, but the continuity and homogenous character of the composition of this inner circle before and since 1975 seems to have contributed to the emergence of a collective leadership instead of a personalist dictatorship (Stuart-Fox 2009c, pp. 10–12).

Until 1975, the party leadership consisted mainly of two groups of ethnic Lao (Lao Loum): The first group consisted of men who belonged to the old aristocratic elite of the country or were connected to prominent family clans by extensive family ties, representing the party to the outside world. The second group that formed the key leadership, however, consisted of party cadres and military commanders who remained in the political underground until 1975, who were in close contact with the Vietnamese communists, and only became known to the public after the overthrow of the royal government (Stuart-Fox 1997). Although ethnic minorities represented a disproportionally high share of party cadres and guerrilla fighters (cf. Zasloff 1973), Lao Loum predominated the leadership positions in the party and army before and after 1975 (Stuart-Fox 1997, p. 171). Although there has been a gradual change in the composition of party leadership over the last decades, anecdotal evidence suggests that family members of the "old revolutionary elite" (Stuart-Fox 2005, pp. 8–12) still possess considerable influence within the LPRP (ibid.; Gunn 2007).

One of the striking features of the party elite in Laos is their continuity and homogeneity: Those 25 Lao members of the ICP who established the Lao People's Party in 1955 dominated the Politburo and Central Committee into the 1990s before their advancing age forced a generational change.

Another unique feature of the LPRP, compared to other socialist countries, is the overrepresentation of military forces in the party's *loci* of political decision-making. In recent years, however, the composition of the Politburo and the Central Committee has changed: While the number of members of the old revolutionary guard as well as military officers declined in the Central Committee and the Politburo, a new generation of technocratically minded officials has stepped up to replace the armed struggle veterans. Connections with big entrepreneurs in other Asian countries allow non-military figures to build patronage networks quickly, creating new avenues for successful party careers. However, ideological reliability, training in the Soviet Union or Vietnam, decade-long party membership, and good political connections are still the most important conditions for gaining access to the party's enlarged leadership circle (St John 2006; Lintner 2008; Pholsena 2012, p. 60).

5.5 Legal and Judicial System

After 1975, the LPRP replaced the country's legal system with socialist law similar to those in other socialist states. Following Marxist–Leninist legal theory the judiciary was no longer a governing body of state and private action, but a means of enforcing the will of the ruling party. The judiciary was reorganized accordingly, and the corresponding norms (laws and regulations) were introduced. The party created a system of so-called people's tribunals with ad hoc "revolutionary judges" (Stuart-Fox 2009c, p. 23). These courts, usually consisting of local party officials, interpreted party directives as they saw fit (Leather 2008, p. 151). In order to ensure a more uniform application of justice across the country, the Supreme People's Court and the People's Courts at the provincial and city levels were created in 1983. The 1991 Constitution recognized the Supreme People's Court as the "highest judicial organ of the State" (Art. 53) and established a system of people's district courts and military courts. Since 2003, the president of the Supreme People's Court is appointed and can be removed by the National Assembly on the recommendation of the president of the state. A 2003 amendment to the Law on the Supreme People's Court dictates that judicial positions at all subordinate courts are to be determined by the Supreme People's Court instead of the Ministry of Justice or the provincial governors as before. Most likely, this will not strengthen judicial independence, since the highest judicial organ of the state is itself controlled by the party (Stuart-Fox 2009c, p. 27). At all levels of the court system, judges are usually members of the LPRP and judges in important cases are required to consult local coordination committees—which may include the local prosecutor, local government officials, the police, the local office of the National Assembly, and state and party organizations—before making their decisions (Leather 2008, p. 156; BTI 2014). Under the 2015 Constitution, the appointment and removal of members of the judiciary involve the National Assembly, the president, and the NASC. Consequently, Laos has not developed an independent judiciary.

Laos is not a constitutional system. The ruling party in Laos is above the law. The constitution is not binding on the LPRP, and it is subject to interpretation by the National Assembly's Standing Committee, which is again subordinate to the party. There are no administrative courts, and although a government registry of decrees and laws was established in 1993, local government officials are often unfamiliar with or unaware of existing laws (Stuart-Fox 2009c, p. 25). Alarmed by escalating levels of corruption in the civil service and local administration, coupled with mounting popular resentment and public discussion (Stuart-Fox 2009a, p. 158), the Politburo created an Anti-Corruption Commission subordinate to the president, passed an anti-corruption law in 2005, and put forth a law to expand the authority of the State Audit Agency in 2007. So far, these measures have had little effect, and high-ranking party and state functionaries are not prosecuted for corrupt behavior and abuse of office (BTI 2014). Even though the National Assembly amended the anti-corruption law in 2012, corruption and abuse of office remain widespread. The weakness of the judicial system and the rule of law is reflected in the country's low scores in the World Bank's Rule of Law Index (World Bank 2017b) and in the Corruption Perception Index reported by Transparency International (2015). Although the latter reports a certain degree of improvement in recent years, Laos was listed at rank 139 out of 175 countries worldwide in 2015.

5.6   Electoral System and Elections

Laos' first representative national election to the legislature was held in 1951. Altogether there were seven multiparty elections for the National Assembly before 1975, although the Royal Lao Government continually manipulated the electoral system to prevent the political wing of the *Pathet Lao* from competing in elections (Hartmann 2001, p. 133). Under the current political regime, popular elections for district, provincial, and local assemblies were held in 1988, and since 1989, elections for the National Assembly are held every 5 years. The sixth national-level legislative elections took place on March 20, 2016. The public also participates in the election of village heads.

The constitution and the Law on National and Provincial Elections, adopted by the National Assembly in December 2015, provide the legal framework for the election process. Parliamentary elections are organized by a National Election Committee appointed by the president and are executed by the Ministry of the Interior. Under the constitution, all citizens aged 18 or older are eligible to vote, and citizens aged 21 or older have the right to stand in elections, but the LPRP is the only party permitted to contest the elections. All party, state, and mass organizations can propose candidates to the National Election Committee through local election committees (Art. 9, 1997 Election Law). Although there are a few

Table 5.2 Parliamentary election in Laos, 1989–2016

		1989	1992	1997	2002	2006	2011	2016
LPRP	%	n/a	n/a	n/a	n/a	n/a	n/a	n/a
	Seats	65	85	98	108	113	128	144
Non-LPRP	%	n/a	n/a	n/a	n/a	n/a	n/a	n/a
	Seats	14	0	1	1	2	4	5
Total	Candidates	121	154	159	166	175	190	211
	Seats	79	85	99	109	115	132	149
Voter turnout	%	n/a	99.3	99.3	99.9	99.7	99.7	97.9

Source: IPU (2014), Thayer (2003)

"independent" candidates, all candidates have to undergo a strict selection process by the LPRP's own Lao Front for National Construction (*Neo Lao Sang Sat*) and most "independents" are also party members (St John 2006, p. 187; BTI 2014). According to election law, candidates need sufficient knowledge about the policy position of LPRP and endorse it to be eligible for elections (Art. 7). In local-level elections, only candidates approved by the district administration can run and, following the election, the winner has to be confirmed by the district head, who is always a party representative (Art. 27, Law on Local Administration).

The National Assembly elections use a system of plurality rule in 18 multi-member constituencies in which voters cross out the names of candidates they dislike. The official statistics only report the number of votes cast and the lists of "elected" candidates. Like in past legislative elections, there were more candidates than seats to be filled in the 2016 election (cf. Table 5.2).

Even though elections in the Lao PDR are often dismissed as mere charades, they may actually support the stability of party rule in several ways. For example, even without inter-party competition, elections may help the LPRP to bolster its legitimacy. Limited intra-party competition between party members—although opaque and delineated along intra-party faction lines—provides a modest degree of choice for voters, which may help the party to determine the popularity of its personnel and to gain valuable information about the actual levels of regime support among local constituencies (cf. Magaloni 2006; Gandhi and Lust-Okar 2009). Elections can also provide a venue for the co-optation of new elites and potential critics, and give local officials and party cadres an incentive to improve their performance (cf. Malesky et al. 2011). However, as long as the Election Commission does not publish a more detailed breakdown of the election results, it is impossible to determine whether voters express dissent by handing in empty or invalid ballots or use their ability to cross out unpopular candidates from the ballot to express their political preferences. Furthermore, due to the secretive character of the LPRP, it is unknown if the party has reacted to disappointing or unexpected results at the constituency-level by punishing local officials or rewarding successful candidates.

5.7   State and Decentralization

The Lao PDR is a decentralized unitary state. Administratively, the country is divided into 16 provinces (*khoueng*) and one prefecture (*kampheng nakhon*), which includes the capital city of Vientiane, 139 districts (*meuang*), and about 11,000 villages (*ban*). The subdistrict level (*tasseng*) was abolished in 1991, but district administrations still routinely group together villages into zones (*khet*) for planning purposes. Although not designated as official administrative units, the categories of north, central, and southern region are frequently used in government documents.

Provincial governors are appointed by the president and in turn select the district chiefs. One of the striking features of Lao authoritarianism is the high degree of decentralization and the de facto autonomy of the provinces. Unlike "decentralized authoritarianism" in China (Landry 2008), political decentralization predates economic reforms and was not implemented to improve the efficiency of local government services or create creative competition among the country's subnational units (Landry 2008; Heberer n.d.). Instead, it was the result of the precarious conditions under which the party state was established and had to survive after 1975.

Prior to French colonialism, Laos did not have a strong central power. When the three Lao Kingdoms were incorporated into French Indochina, traditional power structures were marginalized but not destroyed and continued in one way or the other at the local level (Zasloff 1973). The fragmentation of political authority under the constitutional monarchy and political instability during the civil war perpetuated the weakness of the state and the national government, dividing the country into different zones controlled by government forces, pro-government irregulars, and the *Pathet Lao*. In addition, the *Pathet Lao* itself was forced to adopt a flexible form of regional and decentralized organization to safeguard its lines of communication and supply, which prevented the party from centralizing political power (Zasloff 1973, p. 1; Stuart-Fox 2009a, p. 169). When the LPRP took power in 1975, the strength of regional party leaders and military commanders and the weak infrastructure linking the provinces to the capital allowed provincial governors to determine party policies at their own discretion. As the economy collapsed in the late 1970s, the central government in Vientiane demanded self-sufficiency among the provinces. Consequently, the provincial governors gained a high degree of political and economic autonomy (Soukamneuth 2006, p. 81; Stuart-Fox 2009a, p. 169). During this period, the governors acted as quasi-feudal lords, monitoring the movement of people, finances, and goods in their territories (Soukamneuth 2006, p. 81).

Yet this particular mode of center–periphery relations created friction between the national priorities of the central government and the regional interests of governors. Following the proclamation of the NEM, the central government gradually formalized the existing devolution of powers to the provinces but also moved to regain economic and administrative initiative by unifying and expanding administrative control (Soukamneuth 2006, pp. 67–69). In addition to abolishing the subdistricts, the central government dissolved local administrative committees as well as provincial and district councils. Furthermore, the central government reasserted its authority over policy planning and budgeting from the subnational authorities (Sida 2004, p. 27). However, the degree of fiscal decentralization is still extensive: In 2006, the provinces accounted for 45% of total government expenditure and 56% of all government revenue (Soukamneuth 2006, p. 269; World Bank 2007, pp. 24–25). This suggests that Laos is one of the most decentralized authoritarian regimes in the world.[4] In addition, about 82% of all civil servants are appointed by the provinces and districts, whereas the party and central government only appoint 7 and 11%, respectively (Soukamneuth 2006, p. 232). While civil servants remain accountable to their government ministry, the provincial governors appoint, supervise, and remove them. Under this system, lack of coordination between ministries and local administrations, overlapping responsibilities, and vaguely formulated regulations engender manifold tensions in central-local relations, organizational dysfunctions, and operational inefficiencies (Soukamneuth 2006, pp. 98–105). However, the administrative capacity of the Laotian state and the quality of its bureaucracy also suffer from a low level of tax revenue, which used to be less than 10% of GDP (Soukamneuth 2006, pp. 145–155), although it increased from 12 to 16% between 2008 and 2014 (World Bank 2017a).

Yet for a long time, the weakness of state structures strengthened the LPRP's unique role as the only truly effective political structure with a nationwide presence. In this regard, it is important to note that even in the late 1970s and early 1980s, when de facto devolution and subnational autonomy was especially strong, the political authority and power of provincial elites, including governors, did not result from their position as state officials but from their rank in the ruling party, and all governors sat on the LPRP's Central Committee (Stuart-Fox 2002, pp. 241–242). However, the 1991 LPRP Constitution strengthened the political center vis-à-vis the periphery by putting forth that all local administrative committees were to be supervised by the party's provincial committees and making all governors accountable to the party's Central Committee. Since 2006, governors are no longer automatically members of the Central Committee, which has further reduced their autonomy.

Despite its relatively small size and population, Laos has always been one of the most ethnically heterogeneous societies in Southeast Asia. According to the 2005 census, there are 49 different ethnic groups in Laos. Ethnic Lao are the largest group at 54.6% of the population, followed by the Khmou with 10.9 and the Hmong with 8%. Several smaller groups with sometimes only a few hundred members make up the remaining 26.5% of the population. Religious diversity is also pronounced: Buddhist's make up 66.8% of the population and 1.5% are Christians. The remaining 30.9% comprise a plethora of animistic beliefs (Lao Statistics Bureau 2005, pp. 14–15). This diversity is often conflated into three groups. First, there are the Lao-Tai speaking, mostly Buddhist Lao Loum, or lowland Lao (roughly 55% of the population). Second, there are the Lao Theung or upland Lao (about 22% of the

---

[4]The average subnational share of government expenditure in autocracies is 17.76% in the period 1972–2000; for government revenue it is 14.05% (Landry 2008, p. 6).

Table 5.3 Discrepancies between geographical areas in Laos

	Population share in percent, 2005	Share of ethnic Lao in percent, 1995	Average monthly household expenditure, 2007/2008	Share of the population below national poverty line, 2007/2008	Adult literacy rate in percent, 2005	Infant mortality rate in percent, 2011
National	100	54.6	100	27.6	70.4	6.8
North						
Phongsaly	3	<20	57.9	46%	43.1	12.0
Luangnamtha	2.6	<16	67.2	30.5	50.6	5.4
Oudomxay	4.7	<12	79.9	33.7	55.9	8.7
Bokeo	2.6	13.4	58.9	32.6	58.1	9.2
Luangprabang	7.2	28.6	100.3	27.2	67.2	8.4
Huaphanh	5	30	67.7	50.5	64.7	10.0
Xayaboury	6	63.4	139.8	15.7	80.4	5.9
Central region						
Xiengkhuang	4.1	44.3	100.9	42	72.7	5.3
Vientiane Capital	12.4	92.6	146.6	15.2	91.7	2.7
Vientiane	6.9	63.8	85.5	28	79.7	3.1
Borikhamxay	4	40.2	93	21.5	77.2	4.5
Khammuane	6	59.4	86.2	31.4	69.9	12.1
Savannakhet	14.7	57.5	108.9	28.5	68.5	8.1
Xaysomboon SR[a]	0.7	19.4	–	–	72.6	–
South						
Saravane	5.8	60	67	36.3	61.6	9.8
Sekong	1.5	<15	69.9	51.8	61.7	7.1
Champasack	10.8	84.8	105.9	10	81.8	8.9
Attapeu	2	36.9	81	24.6	63.9	5.8

Source: Yokoyama (2010), Lao Statistics Bureau (2005), Government of Lao PDR and United Nations (2013), MPI (2011)
[a]Xaysomboun special region was merged into Vientiane province in 2007

population), who typically reside in the slopes of the mountain areas in northern and southern Laos. Third, there are the Lao Sung or highland Lao (about 13% of the Lao population), who speak Sino-Tibetan and Tibetan-Burman languages and reside in the highest altitude areas of the country (Schneider 2001, p. 96).

Although the GDP annual growth rate of Laos averaged 7% from 1989 until 2015 (World Bank 2017a), and despite significant reductions in the overall poverty rate, Laos remains one of the poorest nations in Southeast Asia. Furthermore, inequality appears to be on the rise, following similar patterns as, for instance, in Vietnam and China, and the fruits of economic development have largely bypassed rural Laotians (some 70% of the population), who remain trapped in poverty. Moreover, there remain considerable discrepancies between geographical areas and between ethnic groups.[5] Generally, provinces with a larger share of ethnic minorities and rural provinces in northern and southern Laos tend to have lower household incomes and rates of school enrollment as well as higher poverty rates. Incidences of child mortality are also higher compared to urban areas and provinces with smaller minority populations in the central region (see Table 5.3).

Since the 1950s, Laos had suffered from various armed conflicts between the central government and ethnic minorities. The end of the civil war in 1975 was followed by a long-running low-intensity conflict between government and ethnic Hmong forces, the latter of whom played a major role in the civil war as U.S.-funded irregular troops fighting against *Pathet Lao* forces (Stuart-Fox 1997, p. 176). Yet in contrast to the Kingdom of Laos, the Lao PDR is defined as a multiethnic nation-state (Pholsena 2006) and the LPRP has made some effort to co-opt ethnic minorities into the wider party leadership as members of the Central Committee or Politburo or ministers or appointed governors (BTI 2014).

5.8   Civil–Military Relations

As in other communist regimes in Asia, the Lao People's Armed Forces (LPAF) are a key political and economic actor but are formally under the supremacy of the ruling party. The constitution charges the LPAF with defending the party's revolutionary accomplishments and contributing to national development (Art. 11). It contains no regulations on the character of civil–military relations, including the political control over the armed forces. The party's political leadership and its direct, united, and full control over the armed forces and other security forces is enshrined in the party constitution (Stuart-Fox 2002, p. 309).

Like all communist countries, Laos has instituted compulsory military service. The LPAF command 29,000 troops, 90% of which serve in the army. The military also controls the National Police Agency, but the border police and the political police are subordinated to the Ministry for Public Security. In addition to the regular

---

[5]Overall, poverty rates are twice as high among minorities compared to ethnic Lao (Government of Lao PDR and United Nations 2013, p. 202).

military of about 100,000 militia, troops are organized at the village level and commanded by the provincial governors (Carpenter 2005; Freeman 2006, p. 139; IISS 2014, p. 316).

The president of the state—who is simultaneously general secretary of the Central Committee of the LPRP—is commander-in-chief of the armed forces. While the minister of defence is an active general, the party rather than the ministry controls the LPAF through the Central Committee's Central National Defence and Security Committee. Monitored by the Politburo, it is the most important oversight and decision-making body in all matters of security and defense policy. The Politburo also oversees the General Political Department of the Army and the party committee of the Ministry for Public Security. Additional Committees for National Defense and Security at the provincial level are led by the secretaries of local party committees and are appointed by the Politburo (Stuart-Fox 2002, p. 310).

Originally, the LPRP established the Soviet model of a dual chain of military and political command throughout the armed forces by appointing a political "deputy" commander for each military commander. These political commanders exercised official and unofficial control functions over their military command counterparts and also served to further party interests by indoctrinating soldiers in Marxism–Leninism. However, this system was abolished in 1985, and commanding military officers took over the responsibility of the ideological instruction of their troops. Extensive political training and party membership are mandatory for all officers (Stuart-Fox 2002, p. 310).

The traditional understanding of Lao civil–military relations is that the relationship between the party and the LPAF was historically symbiotic, without functional differentiation or institutional boundaries based on technical specialization. Similar to communist China and Vietnam, this kind of symbiosis can be attributed to the legacy of the Communists' guerrilla war in Laos. Under its form of politico-military combat the fusion of political and military elites was inevitable and the governance of liberated territories was performed largely by the guerrilla army itself (cf. Perlmutter and LeoGrande 1982; Zasloff 1973, pp. 40–63). This party-army symbiosis, however, does not necessarily imply a high degree of congruence or consensus among civilian and military leaders. But rather than taking place along civil–military institutional boundaries, political competition and rivalries are characterized by personalized leadership factions or cliques cutting across party-army boundaries. Consequently, LPAF leaders are well-represented in the LPRP's top decision-making bodies. Especially the Sixth Party Congress of 1996 saw the militarization of the Central Committee and Politburo (see Fig. 5.2).

At the height of military representation in party and state organs, the state president and general secretary of the Central Committee of the LPRP, the chairman of the National Assembly, the prime minister, and up to six government ministers were active or former military officers (Stuart-Fox 2002, p. 243, 2009c, p. 15). However, the professionalization of party organization and changes among leadership generations have caused the military's sharply declining representation in the party's main bodies since the eight congress in 2001. In the ninth and tenth congress in 2011 and 2016, respectively, only three out of the 11 members of the Politburo

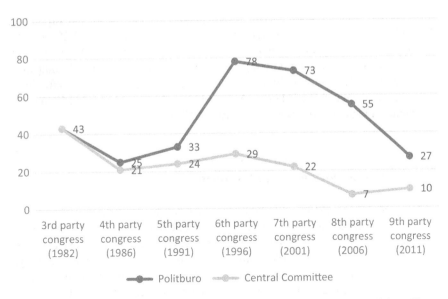

Fig. 5.2 Percentage of military officers in the LPRP Central Committee and Politburo. Notes: Without alternating members. Source: authors' compilation based on Stuart-Fox (1997, p. 203, 208, 2002, p. 238, 2008, 2009c, pp. 14–15), Bourdet (1997), Pholsena (2012, p. 60)

were appointed from among the military ranks. The share of (former) military officers on the Central Committee also declined considerably. Nevertheless, the LPAF continues to play an important role in shaping the political, economic, and social order because the armed forces have become "socialist entrepreneurs" since the introduction of market-oriented policies in the 1980s, i.e., they have linked their communist identity with both national economic development in general and military-owned businesses in particular (Stuart-Fox 2009a, p. 162).

In addition to its national defense and internal security roles, Art. 33 of the 1991 Constitution instructs the LPAF to contribute to the nation's goal of economic autonomy and national reconstruction. There are many facets to this role, including assisting with administrative matters, socioeconomic development, and national disaster response. However, the most prominent role of the LPAF in national reconstruction is in the form of direct ownership of commercial enterprises. Indeed, their involvement in commercial activities has intensified since 1986 with the adoption of the NEM policy. During the second 5-year plan (1986–1991), the LPAF became strongly involved in infrastructure and construction projects, expanding the military's business share in construction, mining, and agriculture (Stuart-Fox 2002, p. 243). While there is no reliable information on the concrete size and economic value of the military-business complex in Laos, most observers agree that commercial activities and military-owned enterprises are actually the main source of income for the LPAF and most military officers. The military also profits from plundering the country's natural resources, often in close connection with the Vietnamese military, local businessmen, and corrupt party officials. For example, military companies like the Mountainous Area Development Corporation (MADC), the Agriculture, Forestry and Development Company (AFD), and the Development of Agriculture, Forestry and Industry Company (DAFI) are key players in the Laotian economy. They—sometimes in collaboration with companies owned by the Vietnamese military—control vast parts of the logging and mining industries and conduct illicit border trade between Laos and Vietnam, China, and Myanmar (Hodgdon 2008; Baird 2010; EU FLEGT Facility 2011).

5.9   Civil Society and Media System

In Laos, access for foreign scholars is limited and local researchers are denied freedom of science. Field work is largely prohibited and data is often interpreted and released through political lenses. It is also one of four Southeast Asian countries not included in either the World Values Survey or the Asian Barometer Survey.[6] Nonetheless, there are a few overviews of contemporary Lao culture and society that shed some light on how cultural elements synthesize with globalization and economic change and on existing patterns of political values, norms, and attitudes (cf. Stuart-Fox 2005, 2008; Rehbein 2010). But writing on contemporary political culture in Laos requires a large degree of faith, and the actual extent to which the population accepts the LPRP's rule as legitimate is extremely difficult to assess.

The legitimacy of the LPRP's regime seems to rest on three pillars. First, the LPRP strives for normative legitimacy within the ideological framework of Marxism–Leninism. While allegiance to official ideology is still relevant, the transformation of revolutionary to established party rule suggests a gradual dilution in its ideological stance ("ideological legitimation", Evans 1998, 2002; Pholsena 2006; Lintner 2008). Second, the Communist Party has increasingly emphasized its nationalist-oriented claims of legitimacy in recent decades. The Lao PDR's official historiography and iconography are manifest attempts to create a connection between the Kingdom of Lan Xang and the LPDR. The regime presents itself as the legitimate successor to the legendary kings of Laos and the protector of Buddhism ("nationalist-traditional legitimation," Tappe 2008; Evans 2002, p. 203). The leadership cult surrounding the revolutionary leader Kaysone Phomvihane, who died in 1992, follows along the same lines (Evans 1998, p. 31; Creak 2011, p. 110). The third pillar of regime legitimacy stems not only from economic growth and the regime's ability to satisfy the social and economic needs of broad segments of the Lao populace ("performance-based legitimation"), but also from the party's 'historical achievements' in the struggle for national sovereignty against French colonialism and American imperialism, providing political stability, and including ethnic minorities into the nation (Pholsena 2006; Stuart-Fox 1997).

---

[6]The others are Brunei, Myanmar, and Timor-Leste.

The absence of any form of organized political opposition within Laos seems to indicate that the LPRP has been successful in its attempts to legitimize its rule. Yet societal peace and regime stability are also—to some extent at least—a result of political repression. Public criticism of the government and party is not tolerated, and there is no space for a critical intelligentsia, political participation, or organized civil society outside of the LPRP (Stuart-Fox 2009c, p. 29). Although the infamous *samana* reeducation camps established after 1975 are no longer in operation, there are still political prisoners in custody and all the media and press remain under the full control of the Ministry for Information and Culture (Jönsson 2011). However, the country's relatively porous borders and the lack of technological means to control social media limit the regime's control of information flows. Yet only 19.9% of the population has access to the internet, tailing even Myanmar (22.4%) and Cambodia (25.5%) and lagging far behind Vietnam (52.1%; Internet World Stats 2017). Laos regularly scores at the bottom of the Press Freedom Index of Reporters without Borders, reaching rank 170 of 180 in 2017 (Reporters without Borders 2017) and 183 of 199 countries in the 2015 Freedom of the Press ranking (Freedom House 2015).

All existing social organizations are legally required to contribute to the development of the country under the leadership of the LPRP. Apart from the Lao Front for National Construction (LFNC), originally founded in 1950s under a different name, there are three additional mass organizations: The Lao Federation of Trade Unions (LFTU), the Lao Women's Union (LWU), and the Lao People's Revolutionary Youth Union (LPRYU). They all serve as a transition belt for the LPRP party line into society and are meant to unify all "patriotic forces," create "national solidarity," and mobilize the masses (Art. 7 of the constitution). At the same time, these organizations serve as a recruiting instrument for the party. Front organizations of the party are subordinate to the LPRP's Central Committee and operate at the national, provincial, district, and village or factory level. Even though all of these organizations have a significant membership base (cf. Fig. 5.3), only the LWU retains a visible presence in Laotian society (Stuart-Fox 2009c, p. 13).

Even though the government has recently issued a decree that legalizes (but also tightly regulates) certain kinds of nonprofit organizations in the country, the legal and political environment remains hostile to the emergence of a genuine, "modern" civil society in Laos (Kunze 2012). While the government has come to accept the Buddhist faith as the national religion, only one officially approved sect of Theravada Buddhism is permitted to operate; the *sangha* remains under the watchful eye of the Religious Affairs Department and is co-opted within the Lao United Buddhist Association (LUBA; Evans 1998, p. 57).

5.10 Outlook

The Lao PDR is a communist party state in transition. Since the mid-1980s, the LPRP has abandoned—at least de facto if not officially—its socialist experiment and is searching for new sources of legitimacy. It is no longer a revolutionary party striving

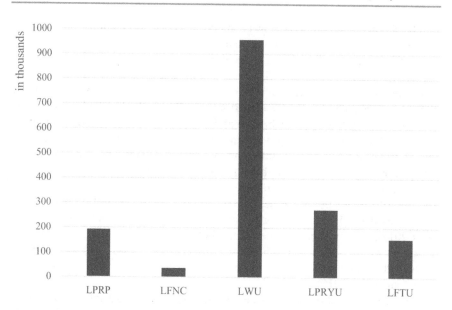

Fig. 5.3 LPRP and mass organization membership, 2007–2011. Notes: Most recent data available for all organizations. Source: authors' compilation based on LWU (2011), Thammavong (2005), Fry (2012), Jönsson (2011)

to realize a utopian communist society but has become a ruling party looking to perpetuate its rule and stabilize the political status quo. In the past, elite cohesion and collective leadership have proved to contribute to political stability: The LPRP succeeded thrice (1992, 2006, 2016) in accomplishing peaceful leadership succession at the top of the party and state without provoking a political crisis or instability. As shown, the persistence and stability of the regime essentially rest on the combination of the three dominant strategies of political survival: co-optation, normative and "output"-based legitimation, as well as selective and institutionalized repression (cf. Gerschewski et al. 2013; Backes 2016).

Despite the collapse of communist rule in other parts of the world, the LPRP has been able to continue its rule well into the early twenty-first century by adjusting its pillars of stability to the changing international and social context. These adjustments include (1) the introduction of a market-based economic system, (2) the selective integration and co-optation of elite groups and parts of the population through access to private goods, (3) the creation of new political institutions like parliament and elections to combine a limited level of elite participation with political and social control, and finally, (4) a "re-traditionalization" of its ideological base, including an increasing reliance on nationalism that has established the party as the guardian of Laotian culture, history, and sovereignty. Of course, the LPRP had always treated Marxism–Leninism and socialist propaganda mostly as a means to mobilize its military and society for Laos' "national liberation" (Soukamneuth 2006, p. 48; Stuart-Fox 2005, p. 11).

While these processes of adaptation are regular features among communist regimes, the LPRP implemented them very successfully thanks to a set of beneficial factors. The LPRP has always been a genuinely indigenous party, even though it depended on military support from Vietnam to take power in 1975 (Evans 1998, 2002). This differs from many Eastern European countries, in which the Soviet Union forced the transition towards communism after the Second World War (Dimitrov 2013). In addition, the party was tightly organized but still flexible because of its "decentralized authoritarianism." Finally, the Laotian government managed to receive not only economic and military assistance from Vietnam, the USSR, and other COMECON countries, but also development aid from Western countries. Currently, foreign assistance (ODA) makes up 8.5% of the Laotian GDP (World Bank 2017b). Moreover, Laos is surrounded by authoritarian regimes in neighboring countries who are all looking for political stability in the region rather than regime change, making any kind of democratic diffusion highly unlikely.

References

Backes, U. (2016). 'Ideocracy': A sketch on the history of a concept. In U. Backes & S. Kailitz (Eds.), *Ideocracies in comparison: Legitimation - co-optation - repression* (pp. 13–39). London: Routledge.

Baird, I. (2010). *Quotas, powers, patronage and illegal rent seeking: The political economy of logging and the timber trade in Southern Laos.* Washington: Forest Trends.

Bourdet, Y. (1997). Laos in 1996: Please don't rush! *Asian Survey, 37,* 72–78. https://doi.org/10.2307/2645776

Brocheux, P., & Hémery, D. (2011). *Indochina: An ambiguous colonization 1858–1954.* Berkeley: University of California Press.

BTI. (2014). *Laos country report.* Gütersloh: Bertelsmann Foundation.

BTI. (2016). *Bertelsmann transformation index 2016.* Gütersloh: Bertelsmann Foundation.

Carpenter, W. M. (2005). Laos: Learning to live with the outside world. In W. M. Carpenter & D. G. Wiencek (Eds.), *Asian security handbook: Terrorism and the new security environment* (3rd ed., pp. 160–166). Armonk: M.E. Sharpe.

CIA. (2017). *The world factbook.* Langley: Central Intelligence Agency.

Creak, S. (2011). *Party congress and national assembly elections in Laos.*

Croissant, A. (2014). Ways of constitution-making in Southeast Asia: Actors, interests, dynamics. *Contemporary Southeast Asia, 36,* 23–51. https://doi.org/10.1355/cs36-1b

Dimitrov, M. K. (2013). Understanding communist collapse and resilience. In M. K. Dimitrov (Ed.), *Why communism did not collapse: Understanding authoritarian regime resilience in Asia and Europe* (pp. 3–39). New York: Cambridge University Press.

Elkins, Z., Melton, J., & Ginsburg, T. (2009). *The endurance of national constitutions.* Cambridge: Cambridge University Press.

EU FLEGT Facility. (2011). *Baseline study 2, LAO PDR: Overview of forest governance, markets and trade.* Kuala Lumpur: EU FLEGT.

Evans, G. (1998). *The politics of ritual and remembrance: Laos since 1975.* Honolulu: University of Hawai'i Press.

Evans, G. (2002). *A short history of Laos: The land in between (Short histories of Asia).* Crows Nest: Allen & Unwin.

Finer, S. E. (Ed.). (1979). *Five constitutions: Contrasts and comparisons.* Harmondsworth: Penguin Books.

Fitzgerald, E. (1985). The problem of balance in the peripheral socialist economy: A conceptual note. *World Development, 13*, 5–14. https://doi.org/10.1016/0305-750X(85)90063-4

Freedom House. (2015). Freedom of the press index 2014: Harsh laws and violence drive global decline. Accessed June 2, 2017, from https://freedomhouse.org/report/freedom-press/freedom-press-2015

Freeman, N. (2006). Laos: Timid transition. In N. J. Funston (Ed.), *Government and politics in Southeast Asia* (2nd ed.). Singapore: ISEAS.

Fry, S. (2012). The Lao federation of trade unions: A classic dualist union. *International Journal of Employment Studies, 20*(2), 32–55.

Gandhi, J., & Lust-Okar, E. (2009). Elections under authoritarianism. *Annual Review of Political Science, 12*, 403–422. https://doi.org/10.1146/annurev.polisci.11.060106.095434

Gerschewski, J., Merkel, W., Schmotz, A., Stefes, C., & Tanneberg, D. (2013). Warum überleben Diktaturen? In S. Kailitz & P. Köllner (Eds.), *Autokratien im Vergleich (Politische Vierteljahresschrift : Sonderheft, Vol. 47)*. Baden-Baden: Nomos.

Ginsburg, T., & Simpser, A. (2014). Introduction: Constitution in authoritarian regimes. In T. Ginsburg & A. Simpser (Eds.), *Constitutions in authoritarian regimes, Comparative constitutional law and policy* (1st ed., pp. 1–21). New York: Cambridge University Press.

Government of Lao PDR, & United Nations. (2013). *The millennium development goals progress report for the Lao PDR 2013*. New York: United Nations Development Program.

Gunn, G. C. (2007). Laos in 2006: Changing of the guard. *Asian Survey, 47*, 183–188. https://doi.org/10.1525/as.2007.47.1.183

Hartmann, C. (2001). Laos. In D. Nohlen, F. Grotz, & C. Hartmann (Eds.), *Elections in Asia and the pacific: A data handbook, Volume II: South East Asia, East Asia, and the South Pacific* (pp. 129–143). Oxford: Oxford University Press.

Heberer, T. (n.d.) *Das politische System der VR China im Prozess des Wandels* (pp. 39–233).

Hodgdon, B. (2008). Frontier country: The political culture of logging and development on the periphery in Laos. *Kyoto Journal, 69*, 58–65.

IISS. (2014). *The military balance 2014: International Institute for Strategic Studies*. London: Oxford University Press.

Internet World Stats. (2017). *Internet usage statistics: World internet users and 2017 population stats*. https://www.internetworldstats.com/stats.htm

IPU. (2014). *Interparliamentary union parline database Lao People's Republic*. Accessed June 20, 2017, from http://www.ipu.org/parline-e/reports/arc/2175_06.htm

Johnson, S. T. (1992). Laos in 1991: Year of the constitution. *Asian Survey, 32*, 82–87. https://doi.org/10.2307/2645202

Jönsson, K. (2011). *Elections but no 'flower revolution' in Laos*. Lund: Asia Portal.

Kunze, G. (2012). Nascent civil society in Lao PDR in the shadow of China's economic presence. In H. Moksnes & M. Melin (Eds.), *Global civil society: Shifting powers in a shifting world* (pp. 154–157). Uppsala: Uppsala University.

Landry, P. F. (2008). *Decentralized authoritarianism in China: The Communist Party's control of local elites in the post-Mao era*. Cambridge: Cambridge University Press.

Lao Statistics Bureau. (2005). *Population census 2005*.

Leather, G. (2008). Laos – A constitution in search of Constitutionalism. In C. Hill & J. Menzel (Eds.), *Constitutionalism in Southeast Asia 2: Reports on national constitutions* (pp. 123–160). Singapore: Konrad Adenauer Foundation.

Lintner, B. (2008). Laos: At the crossroads. *Southeast Asian Affairs, 2008*(1), 171–183.

LWU. (2011). *Lao women's union*. Accessed July 21, 2015, from http://laowomenunion.org.la/index.php?option=com_jdownloads&Itemid=0&view=finish&cid=5&catid=7&m=0&lang=en

Magaloni, B. (2006). *Voting for autocracy: Hegemonic party survival and its demise in Mexico*. Cambridge: Cambridge University Press.

Malesky, E., Schuler, P., & Tran, A. (2011). Vietnam: Familiar patterns and new developments ahead of the 11th party congress. *Southeast Asian Affairs*, 337–363.

MPI. (2011). *The seventh five-year national socio-economic development plan (2011–2015)*. Vientiane: Ministry of Planning and Investment.

Perlmutter, A., & LeoGrande, W. M. (1982). The party in uniform: Toward a theory of civil-military relations in communist political systems. *American Political Science Review, 76*, 778–789. https://doi.org/10.1017/S0003055400189609

Pholsena, V. (2006). *Post-war Laos: The politics of culture, history, and identity*. Singapore: ISEAS.

Pholsena, V. (2012). Laos. In M. J. Montesano & L. P. Onn (Eds.), *Regional outlook: Southeast Asia 2012–2013* (pp. 59–63). Singapore: ISEAS.

Przeworski, A. (2014). Ruling against rules. In T. Ginsburg & A. Simpser (Eds.), *Constitutions in authoritarian regimes, Comparative constitutional law and policy* (1st ed., pp. 21–35). New York: Cambridge University Press.

Rehbein, B. (2010). *Globalization, culture and society in Laos*. London: Routledge.

Reporters without Borders. (2017). 2017 World press freedom index. *RSF*. Accessed June 22, 2017, from https://rsf.org/en/ranking

Schmidt, M. G. (2010). *Demokratietheorien: Eine Einführung* (5th ed.). Wiesbaden: VS Verlag.

Schneider, A. (2001). *Laos im 20. Jahrhundert: Kolonie und Königreich, Befreite Zone und Volksrepublik*. Humboldt Universität zu Berlin Südostasien Working Papers Nr. 21. Berlin: Humboldt Universität.

Sida. (2004). *Governance and participation in Laos*.

Soukamneuth, B. (2006). *The political economy of transition in Laos: From peripheral socialism to the margins of global capital*. PhD Dissertation, Cornell University, Ithaca.

St John, R. B. (2006). The political economy of Laos: Poor state or poor policy? *Asian Affairs, 37*, 175–191. https://doi.org/10.1080/03068370600661466

Stuart-Fox, M. (1997). *A history of Laos*. Cambridge: Cambridge University Press.

Stuart-Fox, M. (2002). *Buddhist kingdom, Marxist state: The making of modern Laos* (2nd ed.). Bangkok: White Lotus Press.

Stuart-Fox, M. (2005). *Politics and reform in the Lao people's democratic republic: Asia research centre working paper 126*. Perth: Murdoch University.

Stuart-Fox, M. (2008). *Historical dictionary of Laos* (3rd ed.). Lanham: Scarecrow Press.

Stuart-Fox, M. (2009a). Laos: The Chinese connection. *Southeast Asian Affairs, 2009*(1), 141–169.

Stuart-Fox, M. (2009b). Political culture and power in the Lao People's Democratic Republic. *Lao Study Review, 3*, 222–267.

Stuart-Fox, M. (2009c). *Politics and reform in the Lao People's Democratic Republic: Asia research centre working paper 126*. Perth: Murdoch University.

Tan, K. Y. L. (2002). The making and remaking of constitutions in Southeast Asia: An overview. *Singapore Journal of International & Comparative Law, 2002*(6), 1–41.

Tappe, O. (2008). *Geschichte, Nationsbildung und Legitimationspolitik in Laos: Untersuchungen zur laotischen nationalen Historiographie und Ikonographie*. Münster: LIT Verlag.

Thammavong, V. (2005). *Role of the Lao people's revolutionary youth union*.

Thayer, C. (2003). Laos in 2002: Regime maintenance through political stability. *Asian Survey, 43*, 120–126. https://doi.org/10.1525/as.2003.43.1.120

Transparency International. (2015). *Corruption perception index*. Accessed June 1, 2017, from https://www.transparency.org/news/feature/corruption_perceptions_index_2016

UNDP. (2005). *Lao People's Democratic Republic: Public administration country profile. Division for Public Administration and Development Management (DPADM) Department of Economic and Social Affairs (DESA) United Nations*. New York: United Nations Development Program.

Vaenkeo, S. (2016). *Laos's 10th Congress elects new party leadership: Vientiane times through Asia News Network*. http://annx.asianews.network/content/laos%E2%80%99-10th-congress-elects-new-party-leadership-8075

World Bank. (2007). *Lao PDR public expenditure review: Integrated fiduciary assessment. Report No. 39791-LA*. Washington: World Bank.

World Bank. (2017a). *World development indicators*. http://data.worldbank.org/products/wdi

World Bank. (2017b). *Worldwide governance indicators*. http://data.worldbank.org/data-catalog/worldwide-governance-indicators

Yokoyama, S. (2010). *Lao health master planning study progress report 1*.

Zasloff, J. (1973). *The pathet leo: Leadership and organization*. Toronto: Lexington Books.

Malaysia: Competitive Authoritarianism in a Plural Society

© Springer International Publishing AG 2018
A. Croissant, P. Lorenz, *Comparative Politics of Southeast Asia*,
https://doi.org/10.1007/978-3-319-68182-5_6

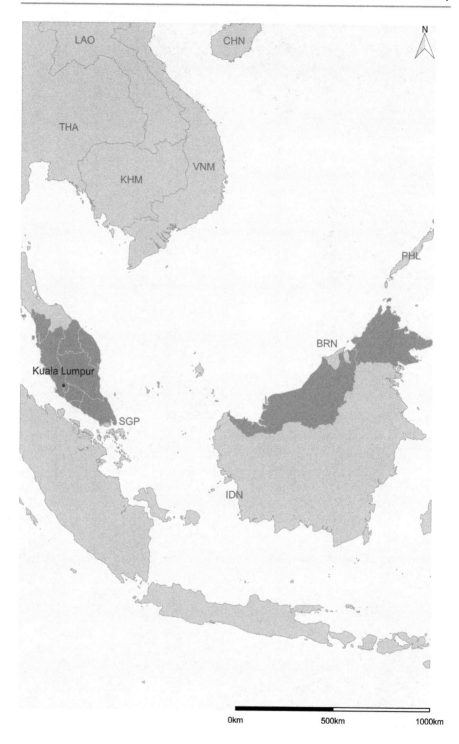

6.1   Historical Background

Strategically situated at the Strait of Malacca, the shortest sea route between East Africa, the Persian Gulf, and China, the Sultanate of Malacca was one of the region's dominant trading powers, a center for spreading Islam, and a profound political power in peninsular Malaysia and throughout the northern Malay Archipelago in the fifteenth century (see Table 6.1 for the Country Profile). However, in 1511, Malacca fell to the Portuguese. Despite several attempts to remove the Europeans from the city by Malay-Muslim rulers and—especially—the neighboring Sultanate of Johor, it was the Dutch East India Company (*Vereenigde Oostindische Compagnie*, VOC) with its local allies who finally wrested Malacca from the Portuguese in 1641. British influence began to expand over peninsular Malaysia from the late eighteenth century onwards, initially through trade and then with the takeover of Penang (1786) and Singapore (1819). The British-Dutch Treaty of 1824 gave control over Malacca to Britain, who merged it with Penang and Singapore to become the "Straits Settlements," governed directly by the British Crown until 1946. With the Treaty of Pangkor (1874), Britain progressively extended its rule over all of peninsular Malaysia as well as North Borneo. The heterogeneous mix of direct colonial rule in the so-called Strait Settlements and indirect rule in the form of Malay royal sovereignty was reflected in the administrative patchwork of "Federated Malay States," the "Unfederated Malay States," the "Straits Settlements," and the British protectorates of Sabah and Sarawak in Northern Borneo. In the Federated States of Perak, Selangor, Negeri Sembilan, and Pahang, the British established a resident system

Table 6.1 Country profile

Population	Year of full national sovereignty	Form of government
31,381,992	1957	Monarchy
Total area	**Current constitution enacted**	**Head of state**
328,657 km^2	1957	King Muhammad V (since 2016)
GDP p.c. (2005 PPP, 2012)	**Official language**	**Head of government**
14,774	Bahasa Malaysia	Mahamed Najib bin Abdul Najib Razak (since 2009)
Ethnic groups	**Democracy score (BTI 2016)**	**System of government**
50.1% Malays, 22.6% Chinese, 11.8% Indigenous, 6.7% Indian, 8.2% noncitizens, 0.7% others	5.23 (range from 1 to 10, higher scores indicate higher levels of democracy)	Parliamentary
Religions	**Regime type**	**Cabinet type**
Muslim 61.3%, Buddhist 19.8%, Christian 9.2%, Hindu 6.3%, Other/ none 3.5%	Autocracy	Multiparty coalition

Source: CIA (2017), BTI (2016)

under which the local Malay rulers—although formally sovereign—had to follow the "advice" of a British resident who possessed de facto authority over all political matters except where local customs or religious matters were concerned. In 1895, however, the Federated States were put under a centralized administrative system. In contrast, the "Unfederated Malay States"—Johor, Kelantan, Terengganu, Kedah, and Perlis—kept their traditional political order dominated by Malays, and it was only in the early twentieth century that the resident system was installed in these states (Ryan 1976, p. 176; Andaya and Andaya 2001, p. 201).

In the Federated States and the Straits Settlements, British investments in public infrastructure, the introduction of a Western legal system, and an emerging modern economy contributed to significantly higher levels of socioeconomic development at independence than in the rest of Malaysia (Kennedy 1962, p. 187; Lange 2009, pp. 184–185). In contrast, indirect rule in other parts of the peninsula reinforced the principle of Malay dominance, both by maintaining the Sultanates and by providing a privileged status for Malays in areas such as the civil service, land ownership, and the educational system. The most profound changes triggered by British colonial rule, however, concerned Malaya's demography. At the early nineteenth century, the population of the Malay Peninsula was 90% Malay. However, following the migration of Chinese and Indian laborers, who were hired as cheap labor for the tin and rubber industries, the share of the Malay population dropped to 50.1% in 1931 (Hirschman 1975). The result was a "plural society" comprised of distinct social orders, living in parallel within one political entity without much intermingling (Furnival 1960, p. 186). While the Chinese mostly acted as intermediary merchants, industrial workers, and entrepreneurs (Snodgrass 1975, p. 263), many Indians were employed in the rubber industry, whereas Malays remained in traditional agriculture or manned local and middle ranks in the public administration, police, and colonial troops (Funston 2006, p. 161). The ethnic division of labor was reinforced by cultural differences and economic inequalities so that when British Malaya became independent in 1957, the average Chinese household income was more than double that of the average Malay household (Hashim 1998, p. 6).

British Malaya was under Japanese occupation during World War II between 1942 and 1945. During this time, local rulers lost influence (Andaya and Andaya 2001, p. 258) and the collapse of Malaysia's export economy escalated ethnic tensions as Chinese and Indian workers now forced into subsistence farming laid claims on arable land previously reserved for Malays. The Japanese tried to curry favor with the Malay by fostering ethnic nationalist groups (Osborne 1979, p. 126). The Chinese population was subject to repression and resisted the occupation by creating the "Malayan Peoples' Anti-Japanese Army" under the leadership of the Communist Party of Malaya (Harper 1999, p. 37; Andaya and Andaya 2001, pp. 260–261). Even after the Japanese surrender, communist guerillas remained in control of parts of the country, exacerbating Malay fears of a Chinese takeover until the British suppressed the insurgency between 1948 and 1955 (Stubbs 1979).

Faced with Malay nationalism and a communist insurgency, the British tried to find a way to reconcile ethnic tensions and begin preparations for an eventual transfer or power (Berger 2009, p. 33). The Malay elite opposed the resulting creation of a Malayan Union from the Federated and Unfederated States including Penang and Malacca in 1946, fearing the loss of their traditional privileges (ibid.). Following this, 41 Malay organizations merged to become the United Malays National Organization (UMNO) in May 1946. The Malayan Indian Congress (MIC), the political vehicle of the Indian community that was founded in the same year, also criticized the proposal but demanded better political participation for the non-Malay population.

The British dissolved the Union in 1948 and instead created the Federation of Malaya that left the sovereignty of Malay Sultans untouched and gave the constituent states more authority. The Malays kept preferential access to administrative positions and only 10% of the Chinese population was granted citizenship (Andaya and Andaya 2001, p. 268). This provoked resistance from the newly established Malayan Chinese Association (MCA). The conflict was resolved in the run-up to the first general election for the Federal Legislative Council in 1955, when UMNO, MCA, and MIC agreed to form a political coalition (the "Alliance"). The political agreement leading to the formation of that alliance—today known as the "Bargain"—enshrined Islam as the official state religion and Malay as the national language and constitutionally guaranteed the authority of the traditional Malay rulers as well as the selection of a Malay prime minister (Mauzy 2006, p. 53). In turn, all Chinese and Indian inhabitants gained citizenship and secured property rights under a market economic system (Crouch 1996). While this elite settlement ensured cultural autonomy, power-sharing, as well as elite cooperation in a multi-ethnic context, the "Bargain" also de facto guaranteed Malay political supremacy over the Chinese and Indian communities.

The Federation of Malaya became a sovereign state in August 1957, and in 1963 Singapore, Sarawak, and Sabah were accepted into the Federation that was renamed Malaysia. However, Singapore's ruling party, the People's Action Party (see Chap. 9), endangered the "Bargain" when it demanded the creation of a "Malaysian Malaysia" with equal rights and privileges for all ethnic groups. Yet the expulsion of Singapore in 1965 could not defuse rising communal tensions. Following the parliamentary election of 1969, clashes between Malays and Chinese in Kuala Lumpur—known as "May 13th Incident"—left 196 people dead (Vorys 1975).

The government imposed a state of emergency, suspended parliament, and completely abolished local elections. It then employed the British Internal Security Act (ISA) to shift Malaysia's political regime towards autocracy (Pepinsky 2007, p. 117). Almost all opposition parties and the former component parties of the Alliance were co-opted into a multiparty coalition under UMNO leadership, the so-called National Front (*Barisan Nasional*, BN; Means 1991). In addition, the government introduced a "New Economic Policy" (NEP) to reduce economic inequality between Indians and Chinese on the one hand and *bumiputera*[1] (Malay

---

[1]This term includes the indigenous peoples of Sabah and Sarawak in addition to the Malay majority.

Table 6.2 Income and property inequality in Malaysia, 1970–1995

	Malay	Chinese	Indians
Average household income (in Ringgit)			
1970	172	394	304
1979	492	938	–
1990	940	1631	–
1995	1600	2896	–
Ownership of share capital %			
1970	2.4	27.2	–
1985	19.1	33.4	–
1990	20.3	44.9	–
1995	20.6	40.9	–
Poverty rate %			
1970	64.8	26.0	39.2
1984	25.8	7.8	10.1
1990	20.8	5.7	8.0

Source: Crouch (2001), Haque (2003), Yusoff et al. (2000)

for "sons of the soil") on the other hand. The *Rukunegara* (National Principles) became the national leitmotif for a culturally heterogeneous society.

In the following decades, Malaysia became a competitive authoritarian regime in which multiparty elections are the main route to power (see Levitsky and Way 2010, p. 13) but the political playing field is tilted in favor of the ruling coalition (Case 2011; Hwang 2003; Slater 2003). Strong economic growth helped bolster the regime's legitimacy and allowed the government to co-opt important elites and groups into the regime coalition. At the same time, the close relationships between BN politicians and economic elites led to extensive "money politics" (Teh 2002).

While the NEP has improved the socioeconomic well-being of *bumiputera*, income inequality persists (Table 6.2). The number of Malays working in agriculture sank from 73 to 21.5% between 1957 and 2000, but this created a new poverty gap between the urban and rural population as well as between the middle class and entrepreneurs on the one hand and workers and peasants on the other hand (Means 1986, p. 113).

Similar to Indonesia and Thailand, the Asian Financial Crisis of 1997/98 hit Malaysia hard and created an oppositional *reformasi* reform movement. However, unlike the authoritarian Suharto government in Indonesia, *Barisan Nasional* remains in power. So far, the ruling elite remains cohesive thanks to its common political and economic interests (Case 2011, p. 453).

After the government declined to implement political reforms, the population seemed increasingly discontented by the extent of money politics and the lack of political participation in Malaysia. In 2008, *Barisan Nasional* and its 14 component parties lost its two-thirds majority in the lower house. In 2013, the opposition *Pakatan Rakyat* (People's Alliance, PR), a loose coalition of three political parties, namely the *Parti Islam Se-Malaysia* (PAS), the Democratic Action Party (DAP), and the People Justice Party (PKR), won a narrow plurality of the popular vote, even though the BN under Prime Minister Najib Razak managed to hold on to a majority of the seats.

6.2 Constitutional History

British rule has influenced the constituional history of Malaysia to a large extent. In 1956, the British authorities and a Malayan delegation, consisting of representatives of the elected Malay government and the traditional rulers, agreed to establish the so-called Reid Commission responsible for drafting the constitution of the Federation of Malaya (Means 1970, p. 171; Hussain 1986, p. 19). The Commission's draft was revised by the traditional rulers and the leaders of the Alliance parties before parliament unanimously approved the text as the *Merdeka* (Freedom) Federal Constitution on August 15, 1957 (Andaya and Andaya 2001, p. 277; Bari 2003, p. 28).

The constitution comprises 14 parts, 183 articles, and 13 "schedules." It grants precedent to the fundamental rights that make up the second section of the constitution (Means 1970, p. 186). However, according to Section 11, the right to life and physical integrity, the right to freedom of movement, and the freedom of expression, assembly, and association contained in Articles 5, 9, 10, and 13 can be restricted (Bari 2003, p. 30). While the constitution establishes Islam as the religion of the Federation (Art. 3), it also grants freedom of religion (Art. 11) and guarantees a secular state (Art. 4). Part III of the constitution contains detailed regulations regarding the once contentious matter of acquisition and termination of citizenship, whereas Article 153 grants Malays and the indigenous people of Sabah and Sarawak special privileges, including reserved positions in civil service, public employment, and the education system, and special provisions concerning the status and prerogatives of Malay traditional rulers. It also provides the basis for the current affirmative action programs and positive discrimination of *bumiputera* in the economy under the so-called New Economic Policy.

Although Malaysia is a federal state (Art. 1), the constitution vests most powers in the national government—including foreign policy, national defense, education, social welfare, finance, and internal security. Under a system of highly centralized federalism, the only areas of substantial importance under control of the states are agriculture, mining, forestry, land, water, and Islamic law (Funston 2006, p. 171).

The constitution stipulates four different procedures of constitutional amendment (Art. 159). The first procedure, concerning the election of senators or elucidations on citizenship regulations, requires a plurality in the Lower and Upper House, the People's Council (*Dewan Rakyat*), and the Council of State (*Dewan Negara*). All other procedures require a two-thirds majority in both houses. In addition, all amendments concerning the status of the nine traditional Malaysian rulers, the constitution of the states, the role of Islam, the privileged position of the *bumiputera*, or Malay as the national language require the consent of the Conference of Rulers (*Majlis Raja-Raja*), which consists of the traditional rulers and the state governors of Penang, Malacca, Sabah, and Sarawak. Should the *Majlis Raja-Raja* veto a proposal concerning the authority of the traditional rulers, both houses of parliament can overturn the veto with a two-thirds majority (Lee 1995, pp. 33–34). Similarly, all changes affecting the Court of Appeals in Borneo, state legislation in Sabah and Sarawak, or the rights of indigenous people in the two states also require the consent of state governors (Art. 161E).

Other constitutional amendments follow the fourth procedure, which requires a two-thirds majority in both chambers of parliament. However, because the government coalition controlled such a majority between 1957 and 2008, a total of 51 so-called Amendment Acts had been adopted by 2007, which concerned more than 675 individual provisions (The Malaysian Bar 2007). A third of these amendments concerned the national territory and became necessary after the expulsion of Singapore in 1965. The first substantive changes to the constitution were enacted in 1971. In response to the 1969 communal riots, these amendments curtailed the freedom of speech by prohibiting the public discussion of citizenship, *bumiputera* privileges, the national language, and the prerogatives of the traditional Malay rulers. In 1988, a series of amendments gave the *syariah* (the Malay spelling of "Sharia") a constitutional basis and established *syariah* courts parallel to the existing court system. Several attempts by members of the Chinese and Indian communities to amend the privileged status of the *bumiputera* were unsuccessful and were suppressed under Part 11 of the constitution.

6.3 System of Government

Malaysia is a constitutional elective monarchy with a federal state parliamentary system of government. Legislative authority rests with parliament and the legislative assemblies of the constituent states while executive authority lies in the head of state and the cabinet led by the prime minister. Malaysia's system of government is executive-heavy and concentrates power in the Office of the Prime Minister, who dominates the legislative process through his parliamentary majority.

6.3.1 Head of State

Malaysia's head of state is the king (*Yang-di Pertuan Agong*). He is elected among the nine traditional Malaysian rulers for a term of 5 years (Appendix V, Section 7 of the Malaysian Constitution). The election follows a rotational system under which each of the nine rulers consecutively serves as head of state. The traditional state sultans of Negeri Sembilan, Selangor, Perlis, Terengganu, Kedah, Kelantan, Pahang, Johor, and Perak and the governors of the four remaining states of Penang, Malacca, Sabah, and Sarawak make up the Conference of Rulers. However, except for its role in constitutional amendments, the Conference only has the right to grant pardons and monitor the application of religious law and must be consulted in the appointment of federal judges. Its role is, hence, mostly symbolic with little genuine political power.

The king serves mostly a representative and ceremonial role; the political directives of the cabinet (Art. 40) bind him, and the rotational system has precluded individual rulers from establishing a permanent base of individual political power.[2] Among his duties, the king appoints the prime minister, who is usually a member of parliament that commands a majority in the lower house. The king can also request the prime minister to dissolve parliament, but the constitution is unclear as to whether the prime minister has to comply with this request (Jones 1995, p. 17). Since 1994, the king no longer has to sign bills to enact them into law (Jones 1995, p. 15). Upon recommendation by the prime minister, the king appoints the cabinet ministers, their deputies, the attorney general, the president, the judges of the Federal Court of Malaysia, the supreme commander of the armed forces, and—on request of the chief minister of each state—the governors for all constituent states without a traditional ruler. Finally, the king is supreme commander of the armed forces, but operational command and control of the Malaysian military rests with the Ministry of Defence. The king is also symbol and custodian of Malay traditions, protector of the *bumiputera* population, and the highest Islamic authority in federal states without a traditional ruler (Ziegenhain 2008, p. 168).

In the past, the king clashed repeatedly with Prime Minister Mahatir bin Mohamad (1981–2003) and, among other things, lost his immunity from criminal prosecution. In 2015, the Conference of Rulers unanimously demanded the government to complete the investigation of a corruption scandal supposedly involving Prime Minister Najib Razak and to punish those involved in the scandal (Lee 2016). In recent decades, the role of the monarch as an integrative force in a plural society is under pressure from two sides. On the one hand, the process of modernization weakened the position of the traditional rulers within the Malay community while on the other hand, members of the Indian and Chinese communities perceive the traditional rulers and the king as an expression of *bumiputera* privilege and discrimination against other communal groups (Singh 1995).

6.3.2 The Legislature

Malaysia has a bicameral parliament, consisting of a 222-member *Dewan Rakyat* (House of Representatives) and a 70-member *Dewan Negara* (Senate). The members of the lower house are directly elected in single-member constituencies for a 5-year term and by-elections are held in case a member of parliament cannot fulfill his or her term and there are still more than 2 years until the next scheduled general

---

[2]At the level of the constituent states, traditional rulers can act more independently. In 2009, the Chief Minister of Perak and chair of the opposition party PAS asked the Sultan of Perak to dissolve the state assembly; he turned down this request and instead appointed an UMNO politician as chief minister (The Star 2010).

election (Art. 54). In the Senate, the 13 state assemblies each elect two senators, whereas the prime minister nominates the remaining 44 senators who are then appointed by the king for a 3-year term. Membership in the lower house is incompatible with a seat in the Senate. The constitution mandates that candidates for appointed positions are either individuals with proven professional experience, a good track record, special skills, or represent important societal groups. Generally, prime ministers mostly nominated members of the Barisan Nasional and its component parties who failed to win a seat in the lower house (Wu 1997, p. 170).

The Senate is intended as a chamber of reflection and review and to protect state interests. From the constitution, it appears that the upper house has the same rights as the lower house, except for financial bills, but the Senate has never used its right to initiate or veto legislation (Funston 2006, p. 180). Overall, the Senate's role in the legislative process is marginal because bills are usually submitted on short notice and the short annual sitting period (2011: 23 days) leaves little room for debate. Furthermore, the Senate can only apply a suspensive veto on bills passed by the lower house, which can easily be repealed.

The ability of the lower house to monitor the government and to influence policy-making is also limited. In the Malaysian political system, almost all legislation is proposed by the government, although legislation has to be approved by both houses of parliament (Heufers 2002, p. 50). Usually, a piece of legislation enters the House of Representatives and goes through the following stages: After the first reading, bills are examined in detail by the respective parliamentary committee. In general, the committees lack staff support and basic information technology capabilities. Moreover, the ruling parties who dominate most cabinets prevent an open-ended or overly critical debate at this stage. Even the budget committee, usually one of the most powerful bodies in parliament and intended to hold the government accountable, has neither a dedicated budget nor scientific or administrative personnel (Abdullah 2008, p. 48). The changes made to a bill in the committee are reported to and debated by the House, which is invited to consider the bill as a whole, approve the changes by the committee, and consider any further proposed revisions. The final version of a bill is then sent to the House for a short final debate without the chance for further amendments.

As in other authoritarian regimes, the House of Representatives is weak in comparison to the executive branch. Furthermore, similar to most other parliamentary systems of government, political confrontation does not take place between the government and the parliament but between ruling coalition parties and the opposition, where the latter can hardly play a dominant role in making parliament work. Nevertheless, opposition members have contributed to the process of checks and balances in the government by asking questions to relevant ministries and by initiating adjournment motions, but also by suggesting alternative policies, some of which were implement by the ruling coalition (Omar 2008). Yet, although the opposition has tried to hold the government accountable through parliamentary inquiries, it usually failed due to a combination of restrictive parliamentary procedures, partisan behavior by the speaker of the House, and the unwillingness of the government to answer questions properly (Case 2011, pp. 443–446).

6.3.3 Government

The prime minister is appointed by the king and is responsible to parliament. The prime minister has to be a naturalized Malaysian citizen,[3] a member of the lower house, and usually belongs to the largest party. Until today, the prime minister has always been an ethnic Malay. The king appoints members of cabinet on recommendation by the prime minister (Art. 43(2b)). Ministers have to be members of either the lower or upper house and are collectively responsible to parliament. In addition to the Prime Minister's Department, the Malaysian cabinet has 24 ministries, whose portfolio can be revised at any time, with the exception of the Ministry of Finance. Since 1957, all prime ministers have come from the UMNO party and have led a multiparty coalition called either "The Alliance" (until 1969) or *Barisan Nasional* (since 1971; see Table 6.3).

In the past, the allocation of the 35 cabinet positions (as of 2015)[4] among the members of the BN aimed to ensure the representation of all ethnic groups present in the ruling coalition. Following the 2013 election, the UMNO took over 21 ministries, the MIC received two ministries, and the remaining cabinet ministries went to six smaller parties and independent candidates (Office of the Prime Minister 2013). For the first time since 1957, the MCA was not allocated any ministry due to the poor results the party obtained in the general elections.

In practice, the prime minister dominates the cabinet and hence the government. During the long reign of Prime Minister Mahatir (1981–2003), the Prime Minister's Department (or Office of the Prime Minister, OPM) became the main power center and coordinating agency inside the government. Since the Asian Financial Crisis in 1997/98, all prime ministers have also held the key post of Minister of Finance. The OPM is assisted by eight cabinet-rank ministers, with oversight over the Economic Planning Unit (EPU) and the Performance Management and Delivery Unit and with oversight over the implementation of government policies. Besides controlling the EPU, the OPM also controls the development budget for five economic Development Corridors. Finally, since 2009, the prime minister-cum-minister of finance is in charge of Malaysia's Sovereign Wealth Fund "1MDB." This gives the prime minister extensive opportunities to control and distribute patronage among politicians, businessmen, and government officials (Slater 2003, p. 91; Lopez 2010). The OPM also oversees the Office of the Attorney General, the Judicial Commission, the Anti-Corruption Commission, and the Public Service Department.

---

[3]This regulation ensured that members of the Indian and Chinese community were de facto excluded from the post at the time of independence.

[4]In addition to ministers with a portfolio, the cabinet also includes several ministers without portfolio, like heads of government agencies or the chairman of the Office of the Prime Minister.

Table 6.3 Governments of Malaysia, 1957–2016

Term of office[a]	Prime Minister	Type of cabinet
31/08/1957–27/06/1959	Tunku Abdul Rahman	Coalition (Alliance)[a]
19/08/1959–01/03/1964	Tunku Abdul Rahman	Coalition (Alliance)
21/03/1964–20/03/1969	Tunku Abdul Rahman	Coalition (Alliance)
10/05/1969–22/09/1970	Tunku Abdul Rahman	Coalition (Alliance)
22/09/1970–31/07/1974	Abdul Razak Hussein	Coalition (Alliance)
24/08/1974–14/01/1976	Abdul Razak Hussein	Coalition (*Barisan Nasional*)[b]
14/01/1976–12/06/1978	Hussein Onn	Coalition (*Barisan Nasional*)
08/07/1978–16/07/1981	Hussein Onn	Coalition (*Barisan Nasional*)
16/07/1981–29/03/1982	Mahathir Mohamad	Coalition (*Barisan Nasional*)
22/04/1982–19/07/1986	Mahathir Mohamad	Coalition (*Barisan Nasional*)
03/08/1986–04/10/1990	Mahathir Mohamad	Coalition (*Barisan Nasional*)
21/10/1990–06/04/1995	Mahathir Mohamad	Coalition (*Barisan Nasional*)
25/04/1995–10/11/1999	Mahathir Mohamad	Coalition (*Barisan Nasional*)
29/11/1999–31/10/2003	Mahathir Mohamad	Coalition (*Barisan Nasional*)
31/10/2003–02/03/2004	Abdullah Ahmad Badawi	Coalition (*Barisan Nasional*)
21/03/2004–13/02/2008	Abdullah Ahmad Badawi	Coalition (*Barisan Nasional*)
08/03/2008–03/04/2009	Abdullah Ahmad Badawi	Coalition (*Barisan Nasional*)
03/04/2009–03/04/2013	Najib Razak	Coalition (*Barisan Nasional*)
06/05/2013–???	Najib Razak	Coalition (*Barisan Nasional*)

Sources: Tan (2001), Office of the Prime Minister (2013)
[a]UMNO, MIC, MCA
[b]*Barisan Nasional* currently consists of 14 parties. The actual number of parties has fluctuated over the years

6.4   Legal and Judicial System

Part IX of the Malaysian constitution concerns the organization of the judicial branch. The judiciary is heavily centralized and based on the English common law system and—to a lesser extent—Islamic law. Generally, there are two types of trials, namely civil and criminal. In civil trials, customary law (*adat*) can be applied, while only Muslims are subject to Islamic law (*syariah*) in these cases. Criminal trials follow the principle of due process, supposedly guaranteeing a fair and public trial with independent judges.

The multilevel hierarchy of courts starts with the Magistrates Courts as the lowest level, followed by the Sessions Courts, the High Courts for Malaya and Borneo (Sabah and Sarawak), the Court of Appeal, and the Federal Court of Malaysia (*Mahkamah Persekutuan Malaysia*), the highest court of the land.[5] There are also various courts outside of this hierarchy of subordinate and superior courts. This includes the *Penghulu* Courts and the *Syariah* Courts on the Malaysian

---

[5]Prior to 1994 the Federal Court was referred to as the Supreme Court.

peninsula and the Native Courts on Borneo, which together form the lowest echelon. Malaysia follows a system of centralized judicial review, meaning the Federal Court also serves as a constitutional court. However, only lower courts can initiate concrete review, and the Federal Court cannot review legislation in abstract. There is also no constitutional complaint. Finally, the Federal Court hears disputes about the jurisdiction of the federal government and the states or between different states (Art. 128).

The court consists of a chief justice, the president of the Court of Appeals, the two presiding judges of Malaysia's High Courts, and at least 11 federal judges (Art. 122). All judges for the higher courts are required to have 10 years of experience practicing law in Malaysia (Art. 123). Federal judges are nominated by the prime minister after consulting with the Conference of Rulers and are appointed by the king.

Since 2009, the prime minister is supported by a Judicial Appointments Commission that is intended to help secure the selection of independent judges but whose members are appointed by the prime minister (Beh 2008; The Malaysian Bar 2008). All judges of the superior courts and the Federal Court retire at the age of 65, but can be dismissed earlier by the king on the prime minister's recommendation if they are found to be unfit for health reasons or a special tribunal finds signs of misbehavior (Art. 125). Since the constitution provides no further details, this allows the government to remove judges it finds disagreeable. Consequently, the Federal Court has failed to act as a guardian of the constitution in recent years. Since the 1994 constitutional amendment, the government can appoint "judicial commissioners," who have the same authority as regular judges and who can become full judges after 2 years (Hector 2003). In addition, all judges at the subordinate courts are members of the civil service and are accountable to the prime minister through the attorney general. Finally, the courts lack budget autonomy.

During the early years of the Federation, the courts, led by the Federal Court, were able to protect the independence of the Malaysian judiciary from government interference (Harding 1990, p. 71). The first three prime ministers had all received legal training in the British tradition and accepted the judiciary's professional ethos (Hector 2003). In the 1980s, however, Prime Minister Mahatir began curtailing judicial independence and in 1988 pushed through a constitutional amendment that gave parliament the authority to regulate the Federal Court's jurisdiction for cases concerning constitutional review (Wu 1999, p. 125). When the chief justice complained about this in a letter to the king, he was removed from office. Two justices who issued concerns about this dismissal also lost their positions (Crouch 1996, pp. 140–141, 202–205). Finally, in the 2000s, the dubious trial of opposition leader and former UMNO Minister of Finance, Anwar Ibrahim, further eroded public trust in the impartiality of the courts. This is also reflected in the decline of the country's rule of law score in the World Bank's Governance Indicators in the mid-2000s (World Bank 2017).

Officeholders who break the law and engage in corruption are not adequately prosecuted. The government's influence on the Malaysian Anti-Corruption

Commission (MACC) became evident when the commission issued a statement in August 2015 in which the prime minister was cleared of any allegations in the 1MDB scandal. In its statement, the MACC said that the money in the prime minister's bank account came from Saudi-Arabian donors. In August 2016, MACC Chief Abu Kassim stepped down from his post 2 years ahead of his contract completion date. Two of his deputies also left the commission. The change at the top was seen as strong evidence of the MACC being a toothless tiger when it comes to fighting corruption within the government's ranks (Beh 2011; Gomez 2012).

6.5   Electoral System and Elections

In the comparative politics literature, Malaysia is often described as a competitive authoritarian regime (Levitsky and Way 2010, p. 318; Giersdorf and Croissant 2011). Competitive authoritarian regimes feature some democratic institutions and regular competitive elections, which distinguish these regimes from other authoritarian regimes (Brooker 2009, p. 224). As a result, even though democratic institutions may be heavily flawed, autocratic incumbents must take them seriously, in contrast to hegemonic authoritarian regimes, where no meaningful contestation of power exists (Howard and Roessler 2006). Even though elections are accepted as the primary means of gaining power, incumbents' abuse of the state places them at a significant advantage vis-à-vis their opponents. The persistence of some democratic institutions in competitive authoritarian regimes secures the existence of various arenas of political contestation (Levitsky and Way 2002, p. 54), among which the electoral arena is the most important. Though elections in competitive authoritarian regimes are not entirely free and fair, they are more than just a "facade" and are generally free of massive fraud. Therefore, the opposition does have a chance to achieve an electoral upset (Levitsky and Way 2002, p. 55). Due to the competitive character of elections in these regimes, these regimes, the manipulation of the manipulation of election results, may be very costly and can even bring down the autocratic order.

The political reality of elections and power in Malaysia after 1957 and until today fits nicely into this description. Since independence, there have been 13 general elections for the House of Representatives (see Table 6.4) and the unicameral State Legislative Assembly in each of Malaysia's states. Sometimes, the opposition won a majority of seats in state legislatures, and in 2008, the opposition even won the plurality of votes at the national level, although the ruling coalition received enough seats to form a government. At the same time, the ruling BN parties methodically and continuously abuse incumbency to ensure a sloped playing field. Elections are the most important tool to confer legitimacy and authenticate authority, make the government somewhat responsive to the electorate, and provide information about policy preferences. While elections are designed to make governments, in the Malaysian context, elections are not intended to break them.

The basic rules of the electoral system were formulated prior to independence for the first federal election in the Federation of Malaya in 1955. These rules,

Table 6.4 Elections for the *Dewan Rakyat* (House of Representatives) in Malaysia, 1959–2013

Party[a]		1959	1964	1969	1974	1978	1982	1986	1990	1995	1999	2004	2008	2013
Alliance	%	51.8	58.5	44.8	–	–	–	–	–	–	–	–	–	–
	Seats	74	89	77	–	–	–	–	–	–	–	–	–	–
Barisan Nasional (BN)	%	–	–	–	60.8	57.2	60.5	57.3	53.4	65.2	56.6	63.9	50.3	47.4
	Seats	–	–	–	135	131	132	148	127	162	148	198	140	133
Democratic Action Party (DAP)	%	4.8	–	12.1	18.3	19.1	19.6	21.0	17.6	12.0	12.7	9.9	13.8	15.7
	Seats	–	–	13	9	16	9	24	20	9	10	12	28	38
Parti Islam Se-Malaysia (PAS)	%	21.3	14.6	20.9	–	15.5	14.5	15.6	7.0	7.2	15.0	15.2	14.3	14.8
	Seats	13	9	12	–	5	5	1	7	7	27	7	23	21
Malaysian People's Movement Party	%	–	–	7.5	–	–	–	–	–	–	–	–	–	–
	Seats	–	–	8	–	–	–	–	–	–	–	–	–	–
People's Justice Party (PKR)	%	–	–	–	–	–	–	–	–	–	11.5	8.9	18.6	20.4
	Seats	–	–	–	–	–	–	–	–	–	5	1	31	30
People's Progressive Party	%	6.3	3.4	3.4	–	–	–	–	–	–	–	–	–	–
	Seats	4	2	4	–	–	–	–	–	–	–	–	–	–
United Sabah Party	%	–	–	–	–	–	–	–	2.3	3.3	2.2	–	–	–
	Seats	–	–	–	–	–	–	–	14	8	3	–	–	–
Sarawak National Party	%	–	–	2.7	5.6	–	–	–	–	–	–	–	–	–
	Seats	–	–	9	9	–	–	–	–	–	–	–	–	–
Sarawak United Peoples' Party	%	–	–	3.0	–	–	–	–	–	–	–	–	–	–
	Seats	–	–	5	–	–	–	–	–	–	–	–	–	–
Social Justice Party of Malaysia	%	–	–	–	5.0	–	–	–	–	–	–	–	–	–
	Seats	–	–	–	1	–	–	–	–	–	–	–	–	–
Socialist Front	%	12.9	16.1	–	–	–	–	–	–	–	–	–	–	–
	Seats	8	2	–	–	–	–	–	–	–	–	–	–	–
Spirit of 46 Malay Party	%	–	–	–	–	–	–	–	14.8	10.4	–	–	–	–
	Seats	–	–	–	–	–	–	–	8	6	–	–	–	–

(continued)

Table 6.4 (continued)

Party[a]		1959	1964	1969	1974	1978	1982	1986	1990	1995	1999	2004	2008	2013
United Democratic Party	%	–	4.3	–	–	–	–	–	–	–	–	–	–	–
	Seats	–	1	–	–	–	–	–	–	–	–	–	–	–
United Sabah National Organization	%	–	–	1.3	–	–	–	–	–	–	–	–	–	–
	Seats	–	–	13	–	–	–	–	–	–	–	–	–	–
Others and Independents	%	2.9	3.1	5.3	10.3	7.2	5.4	6.1	4.9	1.9	2.0	2.1	3.0	1.7
	Seats	5	1	3	0	2	8	4	4	0	0	1	0	0
Total	%	100	100	100	100	100	100	100	100	100	100	100	100	100
	Seats	104	104	144	154	154	154	177	180	192	193	219	222	222
Turnout	%	73.3	78.9	73.6	75.1	75.3	72.1	74.4	70.0	71.8	68.6	73.9	75.9	84.8
Effective Number of Political Parties[b]	%	2.96	2.54	5.05	2.38	2.54	2.33	2.49	2.89	2.18	2.68	2.22	3.04	3.19
	Seats	1.88	1.36	3.15	1.29	1.36	1.34	1.39	1.92	1.39	1.64	1.21	2.14	2.4

Sources: IPU (2013), Carr (2017), Tan (2001, pp. 155–157, 174–175), Election Commission of Malaysia (2015)
[a]This overview lists only parties who attained at least 3% of votes or seats ("relevant parties"). Since Alliance and BN participate in elections as one party, only aggregate results are provided
[b]BN is counted as one party. See Table 3.2 for details on calculation

together with important additions and changes, were incorporated into the constitution adopted in 1957. The electoral system was amended both before and after the 1963 formation of the expanded Federation of Malaysia.[6]

All Malaysian citizens aged 21 or older hold suffrage. Voter registration is voluntary and takes place at the district level. Candidates for parliament can be nominated by political parties or party lists; nonparty candidatures are also permitted. However, since candidates have to provide one of the highest security deposits worldwide (15,000 Malaysian Ringgit or about 3700 EUR), independents and some smaller parties cannot afford the registration fee and are de facto excluded from candidacy (Lee 2007, p. 48).

The original proposal by the Reid Commission in 1957 for an electoral system intended to establish a system that could avoid the political exclusion of the Chinese and Indian communities but still guarantee the dominant position of the Malay community (Lim 2002). The Reid Commission therefore proposed a system that was to be based on three institutional pillars (Crouch 1996; Funston 2006; Lim 2002): First, the introduction of a system of plurality rule in single-member constituencies that privileged the Malay communities and the UMNO in particular. Second, the acceptance of "weightage for area" for rural constituencies ("rural weightage"). In Malaya, Malays were (and are) largely concentrated in rural areas, whereas non-Malays were (and are) concentrated in the urban areas, and therefore, malapportionment in favor of rural areas compared to urban areas increased the electoral power of the Malays (Brown 2005, p. 432; Lim 2002, p. 106). Third, the Reid Commission wanted to establish an independent Electoral Commission appointed by the king that would monitor voter registration, the conduct of elections, and be responsible for the reapportionment of electoral districts every 8–10 years (Lim 2002, p. 106).

Even though the UMNO-dominated Alliance won a vast majority of the seats in the election of 1959, it immediately initiated a series of constitutional amendments to guarantee its electoral hegemony (Brown 2005, p. 433). As a first step, the government majority transferred the authority to reapportion electoral districts to the lower house (Lim 2002, p. 109). The amendments also gave parliament the ability to change the terms of office for the Election Commission, which increased the government's powers over the Election Commission (Lim 2002; Lim and Ming 2006).

From independence until 2013, the number of electoral districts grew from 104 to 222. At the same time, electoral gerrymandering has eroded the principle of "one person, one vote." Districts that have traditionally demonstrated strong support for opposition parties often have disproportionately large electorates compared to districts that have traditionally supported the BN. Sabah and Sarawak, for example, provide 15.5% of the total electorate but receive 25.2% of the seats in the lower

---

[6]Since 1964, state elections (except in Sarawak) are held simultaneously with the general elections. In 1976, the national government abolished electoral local governments (Funston 2006, p. 181).

Table 6.5 Differences in district size on the Malayan Peninsula

Election year	Smallest district (A)[a]	Largest district (B)	Average district size	B/A
1959	10,986	35,549	20,940	3.23
1974	9190	51,534	26,019	5.61
1986	12,171	81,005	39,350	6.66
2004	5079	98,527	46,995	19.39
2013	15,798	144,369	67,882	9.14

Source: Lee (2013, p. 7)
[a]Number of registered voters

house (Borneo Post 2013). The ruling coalition also introduced a stronger rural weighting and between 1974 and 1986 even removed any legal limits to it, leading to a situation where the electorate in urban districts was sometimes five times the size of that in rural districts (Funston 2006, pp. 181–182). In 2004, the smallest district (Putrajaya) held 5079 voters, whereas the largest district (Kapar) held almost 100,000 (see Table 6.5). As a result, the percentage of districts in which Malays represent a majority of voters grew from 56.7% in 1964 to 75.2% in 2008 (Lee 2013, pp. 7–8).

The growing disproportionality of the electoral system has favored *Barisan Nasional*. However, areas in which Malay opposition parties like the *Parti Islam Se-Malaysia* (PAS) enjoyed particularly strong electoral support, as in Kedah, electoral gerrymandering was applied to give more seats to the non-Malay BN parties (Lim and Ming 2006, p. 158). While the BN parties usually won 98% of seats in these "mixed districts," this number sank to 42.4% in 2013 (Lee 2013, pp. 9–10), indicating that Indian and Chinese voters were increasingly willing to vote for a Malay opposition party after it had entered into a multi-ethnic opposition alliance. The creation of this opposition alliance also drained popular support from the Indian and Chinese members of BN. The vote share of MCA plummeted from 19.4% in 1982 (Hoong 1991, p. 27) to 7.8% in 2013 and the party lost most of its seats in parliament. The MIC suffered a similar decline (Hing and Pong 2014).

6.6   Political Parties and Party System

The origin of political parties in Malaysia is bound up closely with the social and economic changes and upheavals that shaped the Malay Peninsula in the first half of the twentieth century. The first "modern" political party was the Communist Party of Malay (CPM), founded in 1930. The CPM operated as an illiberal organization under the British colonial rule, staged an armed insurgency against the Japanese occupation during World War II, and fought a guerilla war against the British authorities and, later, against the Malay government between 1948 and 1960. Following its military and political defeat in the so-called Malayan Emergency, the party and its guerilla force (the Malayan People's Liberation Army, MPLA) continued to subsist on either side of the Thai-Malaysian border before it officially laid down its arms and dissolved in 1989 (Hack 2009). Except for the Communist Party, political parties in Malaya (or Borneo)—by any comparative standard with Western political systems—did not exist until the end of World War II. Yet the period between 1946 and 1955 saw the emergence of quite a substantial number of political party organizations, many of which still exist today. In comparative perspective with the rest of the region, the Malaysian party system stands out due to four dominant features.

First, the emergence of multiparty politics in Malaysia occurred along existing social cleavages, which had a strong and lasting effect on the formation and organization of the party system and patterns of political competition among parties. Despite some obvious differences in the nature of political parties and its dimensions of conflict and competition, the process of establishing new parties and party competition can be explained by the dominant cleavages that existed in the Malay peninsula at the time of the emergence of the party system, i.e., the 1940s and 1950s (Ufen 2012).

Second, compared to most other national party systems in Southeast Asia, Malaysia's party system is relatively well institutionalized, and patterns of competition between parties as well as party-voter alignments are relatively stable. The major political parties such as the UMNO, the (oppositional) Democratic Action Party (DAP), and the Pan-Malaysian Islamic Party (PAS) have developed permanent organizational structures and voter identification with these parties is stable (Hicken and Kuhonta 2015).

Third, contemporary Malaysia actually has a dual-party system: one for the Malay Peninsula (West Malaysia) and another one that emerged in Sarawak and Sabah (East Malaysia). This reflects different cleavage structures, historical legacies, and path-dependent development of political organizations since the early years of Malaysian politics. Overall, the Eastern party system has weaker party organizations and patterns of political competition and more volatile alliance building.

Fourth, there has been a remarkable increase in the degree of party competition in Malaysia since the late 1990s. The country used to have a stable hegemonic party system in which the UMNO as the main ruling party and the lead organization of the *Barisan Nasional* controlled the electoral arena together with its component parties. Today, Malaysia has developed a two-block system with *Barisan Nasional* on one side and the oppositional *Pakatan Rakyat* (People's Alliance, PR), a loose coalition of three political parties, namely the Pan-Islamic Party (PAS), the Democratic Action Party (DAP), and the People Justice Party (PKR), on the other.

With the exception of the conflict between communist and anti-communist parties until the end of the "Emergency" in 1960, the party system was not driven by the cleavage between owners and employers versus workers (Ufen 2012). However, unlike other Southeast Asian party systems like Thailand or the Philippines, cleavages have shaped the party system on the Malay Peninsula (Ufen 2012; Slater 2010). Communal identities and ethnicity are the most important and enduring dimensions of competition. In the formative years of the party system, political elites co-opted their politicized ethnic communities into parties like

UMNO, MIC, and MCA. In the following decades, such originally loose associations developed into more stable party organizations.

The second still relevant cleavage dimension is the conflict between nonreligious or secular and Islamic parties. While UMNO had always been an advocate of Malay interests and privileges, there was a segment of Malay society that demanded a stronger emphasis on the Islamic nature of Malaysian society and identity (Ufen 2012, p. 113). Consequently, in 1951, Muslim clerics founded the *Parti Islam Se-Malaysia* (PAS). The party's electoral base is in the rural and conservative north of the Malay Peninsula, where it has governed the state of Kelantan (1959–1977 and since 1990) and formed coalition governments in Terengganu (1959–1962 and 1999–2004) and Kedah (2008–2013). In recent years, PAS itself split into a more religiously orthodox and a moderate wing, the latter of which has established contacts with secular parties and other opposition groups. The electoral base of more secular opposition parties lies in more urban and economically advanced areas, creating an overlapping rural–urban and religious–secular cleavage. The Democratic Action Party (DAP), formed in 1965 as the Malaysian offshoot of Singapore's People's Action Party, is the urban-secular counterpart to PAS. The party used to represent especially the Chinese middle and working classes (Chin 1996). Prior to 1969 and after PAS left *Barisan Nasional* in 1978, PAS and DAP formed the opposition, although there was little cooperation between the two parties.

However, the emergence of a third cleavage has driven a process of cooperation between the two parties in recent years and has led to the formation of a multiethnic opposition alliance. In the wake of the Asian Financial Crisis of 1997/98, DAP and PAS joined civil society organizations to organize nationwide protests against BN and Prime Minister Mahatir's authoritarian style of government. While, unlike in Indonesia, these protests did not lead to the downfall of the government, the BN and UMNO failed to suppress the formation of a political alternative to their rule. However, in the run-up to the 1999 general elections, civil society activists and supporters and relatives of the former Finance Minister Anwar Ibrahim, who had split from the government in the wake of the economic crisis, created a political platform together with other opposition political parties such as DAP and PAS to build an informal Alternative Front (*Barisan Alternatif*). For the 2008 general elections, Anwar Ibrahim's newly founded Party of Popular Justice (*Partai Keadilan Rakyat*, PKR) and other oppositional political parties created the *Pakatan Rakyat* (People's Alliance), which also contested the 2013 elections. In the 2013 general elections, Pakatan Rakyat won the majority of votes nationwide and 89 seats in the national parliament, whereas the *Barisan Nasional* won 133 of the 222 seats in the House of Representatives (see Table 6.4). However, in 2015, the conservative faction managed to take control of PAS, the main Islamic component of *Pakatan Rakyat*, driving out many moderates. Existing ideological and programmatic differences between the various component parties of the *Pakatan Rakyat* came to light when PAS subsequently advocated for the introduction of Islamic *hudud* penal legislation. This puts the opposition's ability to keep up its pressure on the BN ruling coalition into question (Lee 2016).

In contrast to most other party systems in Southeast Asia, political parties in West Malaysia have also achieved organizational stability, durability, and autonomy; are more or less well linked with society; and have reasonably strong organizational roots among their respective electorates. Voters identify with political parties and 43% of survey respondents in Malaysia report membership in a political party, more than in any other country in the region (Park 2011, p. 43). To organize voters and create this level of identification, the BN parties rely on connections to their ethnic constituencies, and especially UMNO benefits from its network of party bureaus in every electoral district (Gomez and Jomo 1999, p. 255). While other coalition parties depend on UMNO for funding, they have strong roots and voter networks in their respective stronghold districts (Weiss 2009b, p. 16).

On the other hand, most political parties in (West) Malaysia exhibit a lower degree of internal democracy in terms of the participation of the parties' rank-and-file, particularly with regard to candidate selection, policy selection, or intra-party decision-making concerning coalition formation. Decision-making processes tend to be centralized, opaque, and based on personalist networks. All parties, including UMNO, suffer from factional disputes (Singh 1991; Brownlee 2007, pp. 137–139). Even though *Barisan Nasional* is a coalition of parties, it is registered with the Malaysian Registrar of Societies (ROS) as a party, and all component parties compete in elections under a single party logo. The same is not true for *Pakatan Rakyat*, which remains an informal coalition. At the coalition level, informal decision-making procedures are even more important than within its constituent parties. For example, the BN council, nominally the highest party organ as it includes the party leaders of all constituent parties, meets only sporadically and has little political influence (Gomez and Jomo 1999, p. 254). Instead, decisions are made on an informal basis among party leaders with UMNO usually determining the agenda (Weiss 2009b, p. 13).

The party systems of Sabah and Sarawak in Eastern Malaysia differ from West Malaysia in important ways. First of all, political party organizations did not arise until the early 1960s. Second, in contrast to West Malaysia, where the UMNO dominates the BN, the United Traditional Bumiputera Party (PBB), the Sarawak United People's Party (SUPP), and the Sarawak People's Party (PRS) are the dominant members of the Sarawak *Barisan Nasional* coalition. Third, religious and ethnic cleavages do not overlap to the same extent as on the Peninsula, although parties still have an ethnic flavor (Ufen 2012, p. 88). PBB is the party of the Muslim Malay and the indigenous Melanau people, SUPP represents the Chinese minority, and PRS represents the non-Muslim *bumiputera*. In line with an unofficial accord with the PBB, the UMNO does not compete in elections in Sarawak but all governing parties are part of the BN, granting UMNO indirect influence over the government of that state (Ufen 2012, p. 91; Gomez and Jomo 1999, p. 236).

The party system in Sabah also exhibits some unique features. The Chinese community is represented by the Sabah Chinese Association (SCA) and since 1989 by the Liberal Democratic Party (LDP). The non-Malay Muslim population—mostly Tausug (also called Suluk), Sama-Bajau, and some Kadazandusun—is organized in the United Sabah National Organization. In 1985, the Sabah United Party (PBS) formed the state government. It was supported mostly by non-Muslim members of the Kadazandusun ethnic group and opposed what the party and its voters perceived as the Islamization of Sabah and stood for a new ethno-nationalism in opposition to West Malaysian dominance (Ufen 2012, p. 94). After the PBS left the *Sabah Barisan Nasional*, UMNO began campaigning in Sabah, where it does not act as a primarily Malay party but seeks support from Christians, Kadazandusun, and Chinese voters as well (Ufen 2012, p. 98). Party competition again stabilized after UMNO gained power in 1994 and PBS rejoined the government, giving it a strong majority (Ufen 2012, p. 93). In contrast to political parties on the Peninsula, political parties in Sabah and Sarawak are less well rooted in social milieus, are less institutionalized, and are often dominated and financed by local strongmen (Ufen 2012, p. 97). The cleavage between pro- and anti-BN parties has also reached Borneo, but the reform movement is less successful than the parties representing the political status quo (Saravanamuttu and Rusaslina 2011). The fact that UMNO is part of the governing coalition in Sabah has made it extremely difficult for opposition parties to mobilize supporters. In the 2013 state elections, the People's Alliance won only nine of the states' 56 seats, its worst result nationwide.

6.7   Federalism

Malaysia is the only federal state in Southeast Asia. The origins of federalism in Malaysia date back to the colonial era, but the constitutional principle of the vertical separation of powers between the federal government and the states has been contested in practice. Since Sarawak and Sabah joined the Federation in 1963 and the expulsion of Singapore in 1965, the Federation comprises 13 states, 11 states in West Malaysia, and two states in East Malaysia. In addition, the federal government directly governs the Federal Territories, consisting of Kuala Lumpur, Putrajaya, and Labuan. In contrast to the 13 states, the federal territories lack an elected state legislature. Administratively, the country is divided into states and federal territories and districts (called "divisions" in the states of Sabah and Sarawak). The district governments are appointed by state parliaments (Tennant 1973, p. 355). Among the 154 districts, there are 12 city councils, 39 municipal councils, 96 district councils, and seven special local governments. Their regulatory authority is limited to issues enumerated in national legislation and include health care, environmental protection, infrastructure development, and social services (Ibrahim and Abdul Karim 2004).

Malaysia's federalism exhibits two basic features. The first is the asymmetric distribution of powers between the constituent states. The states of Sabah and Sarawak have considerably more autonomy than the other states in areas such as taxation, immigration and citizenship, trade, transportation and communication, fisheries, and several aspects of social affairs, although they have the same constitutional status. The aim of this approach is to protect the distinctive character and interests of these Bornean states and reflect the different historical developments of East and West Borneo under colonial rule. The second feature is the highly centralized system of distribution of powers between the federal government and the states. Malaysia's "centralized" (Huat and Chin 2011) or "minimalist" (Case 2007, p. 141) federalism revolves around the idea that the federal government sets national policies while the state and district governments carry out these policies. As Huat and Chin (2011, p. 208) explain, *Barisan Nasional's* dominance at both the federal and state level means that "the federal-state inter-governmental relation is much characterized by intra- or inter-party relations. Through intra-party control, BN state governments behave more like branches than partners of the federal government. [...] Meanwhile, seen as anomaly, state governments controlled by federal opposition parties are often discriminated, penalized or ignored."

The highly centralized nature of federal-state relations is most clearly reflected in the fiscal structure of the Federation. Between 1963 and 2000, the share of the federal government in total government revenue varied between 77 and 91% (Jomo and Wee 2002, p. 28; Watts 1999, p. 52) and in 2000, the national government's share of total tax revenue was 97.4% (Fjeldstad 2001, p. 8). In general, only the national legislature can pass legislation on taxation and all revenue from direct taxes and tariffs is reserved for the national government. The states only have control over revenues from logging and land concessions, natural resource exploitation, and selected agricultural products. However, even those revenues can be appropriated by the government, as in the case of the "National Petroleum Act 1974," in which the national government took control over the oil and natural gas production in Terengganu, Sabah, and Sarawak and in exchange provided the three states with a 5% compensation for their profit loss (Case 2007, p. 132). To ease budget constraints and balance their budgets, several states have returned some of their regulatory authority to the national government, further centralizing Malaysian federalism (Wee 1996, p. 285).

Lacking autonomous revenue, the states depend on transfers from the federal government, which include (see Jomo and Hui 2003): (1) 10% of all export duties from tin and iron production for the states mining these minerals; (2) general subsidies, like a capitation grant or contingency funds granted for unforeseen needs of the states; and (3) special grants either for specific projects like road maintenance or based on agreements with individual states like Sabah and Sarawak in exchange for joining the Federation in 1963. The national government decides on the volume of federal subsidies after consulting with the National Finance Council, which consists of representatives from the national and federal governments, giving the central government a chance to influence state policies, conduct patronage politics, and punish oppositional state governments by withholding subsidies (Case 2007, pp. 135–137). In the past, states controlled by the government coalition like Selangor, Johor, or Negri Sembilan have received general subsidies, whereas Kelantan did not receive any subsidies between the 1960s and mid-1970s while the governing PAS was part of the national opposition. Payments resumed only after PAS entered the BN coalition in 1974 (Jomo and Wee 2002, pp. 29, 40) and stopped again after PAS left BN and took control of the government in 1990 (Case 2007, p. 140). Similarly, the government ordered the state-owned petroleum company Petronas to withhold payments to Terengganu after PAS took over its government in 1999 (Jomo and Hui 2003, p. 451). Sabah was hit with a ban on lumber exports after the governing PBS left *Barisan Nasional*, supposedly for environmental reasons (Jomo and Wee 2002, p. 37). However, in recent years, the abuse of the power of the purse and federal transfer payments by the federal government to reward or punish states and to ensure the cohesiveness of the *Barisan Nasional* coalition at state and local levels has been increasingly criticized in the online media and public discourse.

6.8   Civil–Military Relations and the Security Sector

Civil–military relations in Malaysia are based on the principles of centralized government control of the armed forces, the recognition of civilian supremacy by the armed forces, military professionalism, and strong informal and historical linkages between the *Barisan Nasional* and the Malaysian Armed Forces (MAF) that have made the MAF a loyal and trustworthy servant of civilian politicians and authorities.

Ethnicity plays a crucial part in shaping civil–military interactions in the plural society of Malaysia. The historical origins of the current model of civil–military relations can be traced back to British rule, when traditional Malay rulers requested the establishment of the Experimental Company of the Royal Malay Regiment (RMR) in 1933 (Blackburn 2006, p. 286; Crouch 1991, p. 122). The RMR was meant to represent Malay "martial traditions" (Enloe 1978), but its first generation of officers were trained by the British and fought the Japanese during World War II (Beeson et al. 2006, p. 459). Traditionally, ethnic Malays are heavily overrepresented in the MAF, and they hold all important command positions. The king is supreme commander of the MAF, and traditionally the Chief of Defence Forces (CDF) is a Malay (Beeson and Bellamy 2008, p. 83). In addition to the three military services of Navy, Army, and Air Force, there is a parallel civilian setup, which runs the Ministry of Defence headed by a secretary-general, whose position is equivalent to that of the CDF.

Even though the MAF's functional focus is mainly on internal and regime security, there has been no military intervention in politics, even when the MAF was involved in internal security roles, particularly during the so-called Emergency (1948–1960) and after 1969. There are several reasons why the internal security experience has apparently not destabilized civil–military relations in Malaysia (Crouch 1991; Nathan and Govindasamy 2001; Beeson and Bellamy 2008).

First, the military had no role in the nationalist movement or the process of gaining sovereignty from the United Kingdom and lacks the legitimacy to govern enjoyed by militaries in Burma and Indonesia, for instance, after their roles in their respective independence struggles.

Secondly, during the height of the communist insurgency in the late 1940s and 1950s, Malaya was still under colonial rule, meaning Malay troops were under British command. The main responsibility for fighting the MPLA was borne by troops of the Commonwealth and the Malay police. Following independence in 1957, counterinsurgency was primarily the task of the police.

Thirdly, British troops were deployed in Malaysia until the 1970s, and the country has not faced any external security threats since the conflict with Indonesia over the integration of Sabah and Sarawak into the Federation (known as *konfrontasi*) stopped in 1966 (Beeson and Bellamy 2008, p. 86). Therefore, the federal government favored spending fiscal resources on economic development over the establishment of a large and costly military, leaving few resources for the armed forces (Nathan and Govindasamy 2001, p. 262).

Fourth, beyond underfunding, the Alliance and the BN governments pursued a series of other measures designed to provide formal channels for MAF officers to participate in policy-making on security issues, such as through the National Security Council (NSC) and various so-called State and District Security Committees that were set up in 1971 as a reaction to the "May 13th Incident." Through these councils, the military has been active in providing basic amenities to rural communities as well as other social services. At the national level, the chief of defence forces and the inspector general of the police sit on the NSC, which also includes the prime minister, the minister of home affairs, as well as other cabinet members (Crouch 1991, p. 124).

Fifth, within the framework of the Alliance and the *Barisan Nasional* government, especially the UMNO established close personal and economic relations between civilian and military elites (Crouch 1991, pp. 127–129). Loyalists of the prime minister hold most of the leadership positions in the armed forces (Ahmad and Crouch 1985, p. 119) and after completing their service, officers often take influential positions in UMNO-controlled businesses (Searle 1999, p. 83). Together, these incentives, the inclusion of former members of the MAF into the BN patronage network, and the common interests of MAF, UMNO, and traditional elites to preserve Malay predominance provide strong incentives for the military to stay loyal to the regime.

Finally, unlike in any other Southeast Asian state, the Malaysian military is second to the police in power and influence. In fact, the police is one of the most important instruments of the state in dealing with internal security and political dissent (Beeson and Bellamy 2008, p. 82). Its equipment, troop strength, and organizational structure are far superior to the military, and apart from routine police duties, the police force also maintains a paramilitary police Field Force, also known as the General Operations Police Force (Beeson and Bellamy 2008, p. 82). The paramilitary police forces receive training in jungle warfare and have heavy combat equipment to deal with internal security issues (Nathan and Govindasamy 2001, p. 263). Reflecting this special importance, the Interior Ministry was often led by the prime minister or one of his deputies (Beeson and Bellamy 2008, pp. 88–89). Unsurprisingly, the police are perceived as highly politicized and willing to use violence against the opposition. Already in 2005, a royal commission criticized police brutality against detainees (Tikamdas 2005). This resulted in the creation of a commission meant to encourage respect for human rights in the police (Shan and Moon 2009), but human rights activists have expressed doubts about its effectiveness. And indeed, several demonstrations for free and clean elections by the Coalition for Free and Clean Elections (BERSIH) were disbanded by the police in 2011 and 2012, resulting in numerous injuries and arrests (New York Times 2012).

6.9   Political Culture and Civil Society

Similar to other competitive authoritarian regimes, Malaysia grants civil society only limited space to organize and articulate dissent. In Malaysia, the government regulates associational activities heavily and tries to either co-opt or even curb the mushrooming of secondary associations. However, Malaysia differs from competitive authoritarian regimes such as Singapore and Cambodia because its civil society organizations "come in a confusing array of manifestations—from academic and professional groups to grassroots groups, business-oriented groups, charity organizations, and most of all, ethnic and religious groups" (Farouk 2011, p. 105; Giersdorf 2017). Yet as Farouk (2011, p. 105) notes, many of these groups have avoided political activities, choosing to concentrate on running specific activities for their members or delivering social welfare services. Moreover, according to Weiss and Hassan (2003, p. 43), few organizations are truly independent from the state.

The origins of Malaysia's contemporary civil society can be traced to the nineteenth century under the British colonial government. At that time, cultural and religious associations, the Chinese education movement, and Malay welfare organizations and rural associations emerged. These groups later paved the way for today's nongovernmental organizations (NGOs; Kaneko 2002, p. 180). Since 1957, three distinct periods of civil society development can be identified (Giersdorf and Croissant 2011).

In the first phase from 1957 to 1969, religious associations and cultural groups formed the core of civil society, with each of the three dominant ethnic communities (Chinese, Indians, and Malays) forming their own associations (Tham 1977). Muslim organizations were a key component of the first period of civil society development; during this period, their numbers increased from 72 to 200 officially registered groups (Tham 1977, p. 34). However, having close ties to the government or been established on the government's initiative, it remains unclear how many of these organizations could actually be classified as part of an autonomous civil society. With 252 organizations registered in 1975, ethnic Indian associations also played an important role (Tham 1977, p. 108). The Chinese education movement led by the *Dong Jiao Zong*[7] was especially active in fostering the maintenance of Chinese schools and the Chinese language in the education system (Weiss 2004, p. 265; Tan 1992; Kua 2005). Furthermore, welfare associations and organizations aiming to represent the interests of the Malayan rural population and which were closely affiliated with the state administration gave

---

[7]*Dong Jiao Zong* consists of the United Chinese School Committees' Association (UCSCA) and the United Chinese School Teachers' Association (UCSTA).

a voice and provided services to rural Malays (Kaneko 2002, p. 180). In contrast to these groups, the Malaysian Trade Union Congress (MTUC) did not play much of a role for the development of civil society in this period (Jesudason 1996, p. 143).

Nevertheless, civil society began to mature from the early 1970s onwards. The growth in this second phase was largely related to the establishment of numerous NGOs, with the number of "old" forms of associations such as agriculture, welfare, and cultural organizations decreasing. The NGOs and social movements fostered a critical debate relating to the environment, consumer protection, women's issues, human rights, labor rights, and education (Kaneko 2002, p. 182). In addition, the "*dakwah*"-movement, referring to the broad Islamic revival in the 1970s, turned into a significant component of civil society, with the Malaysian Islamic Youth Movement (*Angkatan Belia Islam Malaysia*, ABIM) developing into the largest NGO in Malaysia (Jomo and Cheek 1992, p. 79). The Islamic NGOs mobilized large parts of the Malay middle class and students and advocated on behalf of beleaguered peasants (Funston 1985, p. 171). Moreover, human rights activists began to organize in associations such as *Aliran*, and later *Suara Rakyat Malaysia* (SUARAM) and the National Human Rights Society (HAKAM), demanding the government's adherence to human rights (Hassan 2002). Activism around the issue of violence against women rose in the 1980s and was fostered through the Women's Aid Organisation (WAO) and the All Women's Action Society of Malaysia (AWAM; Lai Suat Yan 2003).

In the third phase, from the late 1990s until today, a civil society movement has emerged, which for the first time crossed social and ethnic cleavages (Weiss 2006). Civil society leaders as well as opposition party activists worked together in the *reformasi* movement and demanded the implementation of substantial social and political reforms. The *reformasi* movement marked the apex of civil society activism and symbolized the increasing oppositional capability to articulate dissent. Furthermore, the number of civil society groups grew significantly at that time. The "Coalition of Free and Fair Elections" (BERSIH)—initiated by numerous civil society activists and members of opposition political parties in 2006—stood in the tradition of the *reformasi* movement and organized large streets protests in November 2007 (Weiss 2009a, pp. 754–756). More recently, the collaboration among ideologically diverse elements within BERSIH and PR, its political arm, seems to suffer from centrifugal tendencies (see Sect. 6.7). However, the public reaction to the 1MDB corruption scandal seems to indicate that there is still significant protest potential among civil society.

The comparative civil society literature often assumes that civil society organizations promote civic engagement as "schools of democracy," and by building up civic networks, voluntary associations produce social capital and social trust. The 2007 data of the Asian Barometer Survey (ABS) (2007) indicate that almost one-third of all participants (31.6%) are members of at least one (20.5%) or even two (11.1%) societal associations. However, eight out of ten memberships are in ethnic-based groups that are either not part of civil society, like political parties, or groups whose effects for civil society are questionable, like sports and other recreational clubs, neighborhood associations, and religious groups (see Park 2011). In fact, most of Malaysia's NGOs have around or less than 100 members (Weiss 2006, p. 110). More importantly, ethnic-based political parties and their attendant effects have impeded the development of inter-ethnic civil society organizations that transcend ethnic issues. The narrow membership base of civic associations and the ethnically segmented landscape of civil society negatively affect the (re)production of "bridging social capital" (Putnam 1995) and interpersonal trust: Only 12.9% of respondents trust their fellow citizens (ABS 2012), one of the lowest numbers in all of Asia. About 65% deny trusting members of other religions (WVS 2014).

6.10   Media System

Malaysia has a variety of media outlets. These include 200 TV channels (Abdul Wahab 2006, p. 5), encompassing five national and 13 regional public ones, as well as about 2000 private radio stations. The state TV station *Radio Televisyen Malaysia* (RTM) runs two terrestrial channels. Print media include more than 80 dailies and weekly periodicals in Malay, English, Chinese, Tamil, and Jawi, reaching a total circulation of about 4.5 million, according to government sources (ABC 2010). Chinese newspapers have the highest circulation rates with about 1 million issues daily (George 2007, p. 897). Media coverage varies. About 95% of the population has access to television, radio, and newspapers, and TV is the most important source of information for the population (Weiss 2012, p. 15). Digital media are, however, on the rise. In 2015, 69.6% of the Malaysian population had access to the internet, placing Malaysia in third place in the region, trailing only Singapore and Brunei (Internet World Stats 2017).

The government regularly infringes upon the freedom of the press. All media outlets have to be registered, and legislation like the Press and Publication Act, the Broadcasting Law of 1988, the Official Secrets Act, and the Sedition and Internal Security Act is frequently invoked to limit freedom of expression and press freedom (Rodan 2004). Publishing any form of print media requires a license that has to be renewed annually and can be denied or repealed by the government without justification or legal redress (George 2007). TV programs are subject to similar controls (Nain 2002, p. 129).

In addition to legal controls and political interventions, the co-optation of the media sector by the *Barisan Nasional* has also precluded the development of a pluralistic media landscape. In 1961, UMNO became the majority shareholder of *Utusan Melayu*, a newspaper formerly known for its critical reporting (Anuar 2002, pp. 145–146). The party also owns majority shares in *Utusan Melayu Berhad*, the publisher of several influential Malay newspapers (Gomez and Jomo 1999, p. 232). UMNO also holds shares in the government-friendly media conglomerate "Media Prima Berhad" that owns four national TV stations, three radio stations, and half of Malaysia's English and Malay language newspapers (George 2007, pp. 896–897; ABC 2010). All of these, today, act as mouthpieces of the government. Most Chinese newspapers are controlled by the conglomerate Huaren Management, which in turn is closely associated with the MCA. The MCA owns

The Star, the largest fee-based English newspaper in terms of circulation in Malaysia. These restrictions on the freedom of the press have led to a low ranking of Malaysia in the Press Freedom Index, where it ranks only 144 of 180 countries (Reporters without Borders 2017). The Freedom of the Press Index rates the Malaysian press as not free and ranks it 142nd among 199 countries (Freedom House 2015).

In contrast to the traditional media, digital media are subject to more lenient government control (Liu 2011, p. 41). Attempting to create an "Asian Silicon Valley" in Malaysia, Prime Minister Mahatir created a special economic zone for information and communications technology in 1996 (George 2005, p. 909). To attract foreign investors, the government declared it would abstain from internet censorship in the Multimedia Bill of Guarantee. While the government has indeed acted with restraint and has only blocked pornographic material so far, political bloggers have often come into conflict with law enforcement authorities (Giersdorf and Croissant 2011, p. 12; Reporters without Borders 2012; Weiss 2012, pp. 22–23). Still, the internet remains a source of alternative information and an arena for political debate and discourse. Traffic to news websites made up an estimated third of all Malaysian internet activity in 2008 (Liow and Afif 2010, p. 46). Upcoming elections often intensify the search for alternative information: The website of *Malaysiakini*, a critical online newspaper, collapsed under heavy traffic on election day 2008 (Azizuddin 2009, p. 154), and Twitter reported a total of 300 election-related tweets per minute on election day 2013 (Digital News Asia 2013).

While the political impact of social media is difficult to gauge, opposition parties relied on open communication channels like Facebook, Twitter, or SMS to mobilize voters (Liow and Afif 2010, pp. 44–46). In 2008, then-Prime Minister Badawi said his party had neglected the influence of alternative media to explain government losses (Asian Pacific Post 2008). Obviously, social media is an increasingly important tool for internet-connected urban and middle class voters, and journalists, civil society activists, and opposition parties can more easily avoid censorship and mobilize supporters through it. Therefore, controlling public opinion has become more difficult for *Barisan Nasional* and, as the 2013 general elections seem to confirm, the government still has not found an effective response.

6.11   Outlook

Compared to most other political systems in Southeast Asia, Malaysian politics since 1957 has exhibited an unusually high degree of political and social stability. The elite pact ("Bargain") between political, economic, and communal elites resulted in a political and economic order that protected the interests of both elites and their ethnic constituencies, and following the "May 13th Incident" of 1969, the ruling coalition was able to recalibrate the political order in a more authoritarian form, ultimately resulting in a competitive authoritarian regime. In the following decades, this competitive authoritarian regime guaranteed efficient and peaceful conflict resolution within the ethnically segmented society, as the control of coercive, symbolic, and economic power enabled *Barisan Nasional* to manage existing conflicts peacefully, to co-opt relevant elites, and to survive political crises like the Asian Financial Crisis of 1997/98 (Pepinsky 2009; Slater 2010, pp. 6–16). Yet, the declining electoral prowess of *Barisan Nasional*, reflected in the outcome of the 2008 and 2013 general elections, raise serious doubts about the resilience of the very foundations of authoritarian rule in Malaysia. Especially the dramatic weakening of minority component parties such as MIC and MCA and the formation of a broad, interethnic opposition coalition, as well as the emancipation of civil society indicate that the authoritarian bargain of the 1950s may have become obsolete. About 75% of the national electorate today is younger than 40 and has no personal experience with the 1969 riots; moreover, more than 60% of all Malaysians younger than 35 years do not identify with a particular political party and have no stable party preference (Weiss 2012, p. 47). Increasing electoral volatility, eroding social milieus, political party de-alignment, and a rising number of public protests have forced the government to rely more on coercive measures of control, whereas its traditional tools of co-optation and legitimation have become dull. However, it remains to be seen whether these challenges will eventually trigger political liberalization and a transition of the political system towards a more democratic regime, or if the ruling coalition will react to these increasing pressures by stepping up repression and closing the existing space for political engagement. In fact, there is widespread fear among Malaysians that fundamental changes to the existing political–social order would inevitably result in the loss of long existing privileges. So far, however, UMNO can still rely on the majority of Malay voters as well as the loyalty of bureaucrats, the police, and the military, and there is no indication that it is willing to give up on either the concept of Malay supremacy or its own status as the "natural born" ruling party.

Acknowledgment   The authors are grateful to Stephan Giersdorf for his work on the original draft of this chapter.

References

ABC. (2010). *The ABC report circulation figures for the period ending 30 June 2010*. Kuala Lumpur: Audit Bureau of Circulation.

Abdul Wahab, J. (2006). *Communication technology and the television industry in Malaysia*. Paper submitted for the ARC Asia Pacific Future Network International Conference: Media, policies, cultures and futures in the Asia Pacific Region. Organized by Curtin University of Technology, Perth (27–29 November 2006). http://mediaasiaconference.humanities.curtin.edu.au/pdf/Juliana%20Abdul%20Wahab.pdf

Abdullah, N. R. W. (2008). Eradicating corruption: The Malaysian experience. *Journal of Administration and Governance, 3*(1).

ABS. (2012). *Asian barometer survey: Electronic data release for Wave 3, 2010–2012*. http://www.asianbarometer.org/data/data-release

Ahmad, Z. H., & Crouch, H. A. (Eds.). (1985). *Military-civil relations in South-East Asia*. Oxford: Oxford University Press.

Andaya, B. W., & Andaya, L. Y. (2001). *A history of Malaysia* (2nd ed.). Basingstoke: Palgrave.

Anuar, M. (2002). Defining democratic discourses. The mainstream press. In F. K. W. Loh & B. T. Khoo (Eds.), *Democracy in Malaysia: Discourses and practices* (pp. 138–164). Richmond/Surrey: Curzon.

Asian Pacific Post. (2008). *Malaysian PM admits his "biggest mistake"*. Accessed July 21, 2015, from http://www.asianpacificpost.com/article/2240-malaysian-pm-admits-his-%E2%80%9Cbiggest-mistake%E2%80%9D.html

Azizuddin, M. S. (2009). *The public sphere and media politics in Malaysia*. Newcastle: Cambridge Scholars.

Bari, A. A. (2003). *Malaysian constitution: A critical introduction*. Kuala Lumpur: Other Press.

Beeson, M., & Bellamy, A. J. (2008). *Securing Southeast Asia: The politics of security sector reform*. London: Routledge.

Beeson, M., Bellamy, A. J., & Hughes, B. (2006). Taming the tigers?: Reforming the security sector in Southeast Asia. *The Pacific Review, 19*, 449–472. https://doi.org/10.1080/09512740600984804

Beh, L. Y. (2008). *Parliament passes JAC Bill.*

Beh, L. S. (2011). Public ethics and corruption in Malaysia. In E. M. Berman (Ed.), *Public administration in Southeast Asia: Thailand, Philippines, Malaysia, Hong Kong and Macau* (pp. 171–191). Boca Raton: Springer VS.

Berger, M. T. (2009). The end of empire and the cold war. In M. Beeson (Ed.), *Contemporary Southeast Asia* (2nd ed., pp. 29–46). Basingstoke: Palgrave Macmillan.

Blackburn, K. (2006). Colonial forces as postcolonial memories: The commemoration and memory of the Malay Regiment in modern Malaysia and Singapore. In K. Hack & T. Rettig (Eds.), *Colonial armies in Southeast Asia* (pp. 286–309). London: Routledge.

Borneo Post. (2013). *UPKO Komulakan proposes 18 extra seats for Sabah, Sarawak.*

Brooker, P. (2009). *Non-democratic regimes* (2nd ed.). Houndmills, Basingstoke: Palgrave Macmillan.

Brown, G. K. (2005). Playing the (non)ethnic card: The electoral system and ethnic voting patterns in Malaysia. *Ethnopolitics, 4*, 429–445. https://doi.org/10.1080/17449050500348675

Brownlee, J. (2007). *Authoritarianism in an age of democratization*. New York: Cambridge University Press.

BTI. (2016). *Bertelsmann transformation index 2016*. Gütersloh: Bertelsmann Foundation.

Carr, A. (2017). *Psephos: Adam Carr's election archive*. Accessed June 10, 2017, from http://psephos.adam-carr.net/

Case, W. (2007). Semi-democracy and minimalist federalism in Malaysia. In B. He, B. Galligan, & T. Inoguchi (Eds.), *Federalism in Asia* (pp. 124–143). Cheltenham: Edward Elgar.

Case, W. (2011). Electoral authoritarianism and backlash: Hardening Malaysia, oscillating Thailand. *International Political Science Review, 32*, 438–457. https://doi.org/10.1177/0192512110385296

Chin, J. (1996). The 1995 Malaysian general election: Mahathir's last triumph? *Asian Survey, 36*, 393–409. https://doi.org/10.1525/as.1996.36.4.01p0126j

CIA. (2017). *The world factbook*. Langley: Central Intelligence Agency.

Crouch, H. A. (1991). The military in Malaysia. In V. Selochan (Ed.), *The military, the state, and development in Asia and the Pacific* (pp. 121–137). Boulder: Westview Press.

Crouch, H. A. (1996). *Government and society in Malaysia*. Ithaca: Cornell University Press.

Crouch, H. A. (2001). Managing ethnic tensions through affirmative action: The Malaysian experience. In N. J. Colletta, T. G. Lim, & A. Kelles-Viitanen (Eds.), *Social cohesion and conflict prevention in Asia: Managing diversity through development* (pp. 225–262). Washington: World Bank.

Digital News Asia. (2013). *GE13: A 'social media election' after all.*

Election Commission of Malaysia. (2015). *Election commission of Malaysia.*

Enloe, C. H. (1978). The issue saliency of the military-ethnic connection: Some thoughts on Malaysia. *Comparative Politics, 10*, 267. https://doi.org/10.2307/421649

Farouk, A. F. A. (2011). The limits of civil society in democratising the state: The Malaysian case. *Kajian Malaysia, 29*(1), 91–109.

Fjeldstad, O.-H. (2001). *Intergovernmental fiscal relations in developing countries – A review of issues*: CMI Working Papers 11/2001. Accessed July 21, 2015, from http://bora.cmi.no/dspace/bitstream/10202/214/1/WP2001-11.PDF

Freedom House. (2015). *Freedom of the press index 2014: Harsh laws and violence drive global decline*. Accessed June 2, 2017, from https://freedomhouse.org/report/freedom-press/freedom-press-2015

Funston, N. J. (1985). The politics of Islamic reassertion: Malaysia. In A. Ibrahim, S. Siddique, & Y. Hussain (Eds.), *Readings on Islam in Southeast Asia* (pp. 171–179). Singapore: ISEAS.

Funston, N. J. (2006). Malaysia. In N. J. Funston (Ed.), *Government and politics in Southeast Asia* (2nd ed., pp. 160–202). Singapore: ISEAS.

Furnival, J. S. (1960). *The governance of modern Burma*. New York: Institute of Pacific Relations.

George, C. (2005). The internet's political impact and the penetration/participation paradox in Malaysia and Singapore. *Media, Culture & Society, 27*, 903–920. https://doi.org/10.1177/0163443705057678

George, C. (2007). Media in Malaysia: Zone of contention. *Democratization, 14*, 893–910. https://doi.org/10.1080/13510340701635712

Giersdorf, S. (2017). *Zivilgesellschaft und elektoraler Autoritarismus in Südostasien: Singapur und Malaysia in vergleichender Perspektive*. Wiesbaden: Springer VS.

Giersdorf, S., & Croissant, A. (2011). Civil society and competitive authoritarianism in Malaysia. *Journal of Civil Society, 7*, 1–21. https://doi.org/10.1080/17448689.2011.553401

Gomez, E. (2012). Monetizing politics: Financing parties and elections in Malaysia. *Modern Asian Studies, 46*, 1370–1397. https://doi.org/10.1017/S0026749X12000200

Gomez, E., & Jomo, K. S. (1999). Malaysia. In I. Marsh, J. Blondel, & T. Inoguchi (Eds.), *Democracy, governance, and economic performance: East and Southeast Asia* (pp. 230–260). New York: United Nations University Press.

Hack, K. (2009). The Malayan emergency as counter-insurgency paradigm. *Journal of Strategic Studies, 32*, 383–414. https://doi.org/10.1080/01402390902928180

Haque, M. S. (2003). The role of the state in managing ethnic tensions in Malaysia: A critical discourse. *American Behavioral Scientist, 47*, 240–266. https://doi.org/10.1177/0002764203256186

Harding, A. J. (1990). The 1988 constitutional crisis in Malaysia. *International and Comparative Law Quarterly, 39*, 57–81. https://doi.org/10.1093/iclqaj/39.1.57

Harper, T. N. (1999). *The end of empire and the making of Malaya*. Cambridge: Cambridge University Press.

Hashim, S. M. (1998). *Income inequality and poverty in Malaysia*. Lanham: Rowman & Littlefield.

Hassan, S. (2002). Political non-governmental organizations: Ideals and realities. In F. K. W. Loh & B. T. Khoo (Eds.), *Democracy in Malaysia: Discourses and practices* (pp. 198–215). Richmond/Surrey: Curzon.

Hector, C. (2003). Mahathir and the judges: The judiciary during the Mahathir era. *Aliran Monthly, 23*(8).

Heufers, R. (2002). The politics of democracy in Malaysia. *Asien, 85*(Oktober 2002), 39–60.

Hicken, A., & Kuhonta, E. M. (2015). Introduction: Rethinking party system institutionalization in Asia. In A. Hicken & E. M. Kuhonta (Eds.), *Party system institutionalization in Asia: Democracies autocracies and the shadows of the past* (pp. 1–24). New York: Cambridge University Press.

Hing, L. K., & Pong, T. K. (2014). Thirteenth General Elections (GE13): Chinese votes and implications on Malaysian politics. *Kajian Malaysia, 32*(2), 25–53.

Hirschman, C. (1975). *Ethnic and social stratification in Peninsular Malaysia*. Washington: American Sociological Society.

Hoong, K. (1991). *Malaysia's General Election 1990. Continuity, change, and ethnic politics.* Singapore: ISEAS.

Howard, M. M., & Roessler, P. G. (2006). Liberalizing electoral outcomes in competitive authoritarian regimes. *American Journal of Political Science, 50,* 365–381. https://doi.org/10.1111/j.1540-5907.2006.00189.x

Huat, W. C., & Chin, J. (2011). Malaysia: Centralized federalism in an electoral one-party state. In R. Saxena (Ed.), *Varieties of federal governance: Major contemporary models* (pp. 208–231). New Delhi: Foundation Books.

Hussain, S. b. (1986). *A history of Malaysia – 1945 to 1981.* Penang: Malaysian German Society.

Hwang, I.-w. (2003). *Personalized politics: The Malaysian state under Mahathir.* Singapore: ISEAS.

Ibrahim, F., & Abdul Karim, M. (2004). Efficiency of local governments in Malaysia and its correlates. *International Journal of Management Studies, 11*(1), 57–70.

Internet World Stats. (2017). *Internet usage statistics: World internet users and 2017 population stats.* https://www.internetworldstats.com/stats.htm

IPU. (2013). *Inter-parliamentary union parline database Malaysia.* Accessed June 2, 2017, from http://www.ipu.org/parline-e/reports/2197_arc.htm

Jesudason, J. (1996). The syncretic state and the structuring of opposition in Malaysia. In G. Rodan (Ed.), *Political oppositions in industrialising Asia* (pp. 128–160). London: Routledge.

Jomo, K. S., & Cheek, A. (1992). Malaysia's Islamic movements. In J. S. Kahn & F. K. W. Loh (Eds.), *Fragmented vision: Culture and politics in contemporary Malaysia* (pp. 79–106). Sydney: Allen & Unwin.

Jomo, K. S., & Hui, W. C. (2003). The political economy of Malaysian federalism: Economic development, public policy and conflict containment. *Journal of International Development, 15,* 441–456. https://doi.org/10.1002/jid.995

Jomo, K. S., & Wee, C. H. (2002). *The political economy of Malaysian federalism: Economic development, public policy and conflict containment.* No. 2002/113. Helsinki: United Nations University Press.

Jones, D. (1995). Resolving the constitutional question of the Malaysian king and rulers. *Asian Journal of Political Science, 3*(1), 13–31.

Kaneko, Y. (2002). Malaysia: Dual structure in the state-NGO relationship. In S. Shigetomi (Ed.), *The state and NGOs: Perspective from Asia* (pp. 178–199). Singapore: ISEAS.

Kennedy, J. (1962). *A history of Malaya, A.D. 1400–1959.* London: Macmillan.

Kua, K. S. (2005). *The Malaysian civil rights movement.* Petaling Jaya: SIRD.

Lai, S. Y. (2003). The women's movement in peninsular Malaysia, 1900–99. In M. L. Weiss & S. Hassan (Eds.), *Social movements in Malaysia: From moral communities to NGOs* (pp. 45–74). New York: RoutledgeCurzon.

Lange, M. (2009). *Lineages of despotism and development: British colonialism and state power.* Chicago: University of Chicago Press.

Lee, H. P. (1995). *Constitutional conflicts in contemporary Malaysia.* New York: Oxford University Press.

Lee, J. (2007). Barisan Nasional – Political dominance and the general elections of 2004 in Malaysia. *Südostasien aktuell, 2,* 38–65.

Lee, H. G. (2013). Steadily amplified rural votes decide Malaysian elections. *ISEAS Perspective, 34,* 1–11.

Lee, R. (2016). The dark side of liberalization: How Myanmar's political and media freedoms are being used to limit Muslim rights. *Islam and Christian-Muslim Relations, 27,* 195–211. https://doi.org/10.1080/09596410.2016.1159045

Levitsky, S., & Way, L. (2002). The rise of competitive authoritarianism. *Journal of Democracy, 13,* 51–65. https://doi.org/10.1353/jod.2002.0026

Levitsky, S., & Way, L. (2010). *Competitive authoritarianism: Hybrid regimes after the Cold War.* New York: Cambridge University Press.

Lim, H. H. (2002). Electoral politics in Malaysia. 'Managing' elections in a plural society. In A. Croissant, G. Bruns, & M. John (Eds.), *Electoral politics in Southeast & East Asia* (pp. 101–148). Singapore: Friedrich Ebert Foundation.

Lim, H. H., & Ming, O. (2006). The 2004 general election and the electoral process in Malaysia. In A. Croissant & B. Martin (Eds.), *Between consolidation and crisis: Elections and democracy in five nations in Southeast Asia* (pp. 147–214). Münster: LIT Verlag.

Liow, J., & Afif, P. b. (2010). Debating the conduct and nature of Malaysian politics: Communalism and new media post-March 2008. *Journal of Current Southeast Asian Affairs, 29*(4), 39–65.

Liu, Y. (2011). Crafting a democratic enclave on the cyberspace: Case studies of Malaysia, Indonesia, and Singapore. *Journal of Current Southeast Asian Affairs, 30*(4), 33–55.

Lopez, G. (2010). *Najib's defence against UMNO: Centralising Power.*

Mauzy, D. K. (2006). From Malay nationalism to a Malaysian nation? In L. W. Barrington (Ed.), *After independence: Making and protecting the nation in postcolonial & postcommunist states* (pp. 45–70). Ann Arbor: University of Michigan Press.

Means, G. P. (1970). *Malaysian politics.* London: University of London Press.

Means, G. P. (1986). Ethnic preference policies in Malaysia. In N. Nevitte & C. Kennedy (Eds.), *Ethnic preference and public policy in developing countries* (pp. 95–118). Boulder: Lynne Rienner.

Means, G. P. (1991). *Malaysian politics: The second generation.* Singapore: Oxford University Press.

Nain, Z. (2002). The structure of the media industry. Implications for democracy. In F. K. W. Loh & B. T. Khoo (Eds.), *Democracy in Malaysia: Discourses and practices* (pp. 111–137). Richmond/Surrey: Curzon.

Nathan, K., & Govindasamy, G. (2001). Malaysia: A congruence of interests. In M. Alagappa (Ed.), *Coercion and governance: The declining political role of the military in Asia* (pp. 259–275). Stanford: Stanford University Press.

New York Times. (2012). *Police clash with Malaysia protesters seeking electoral reforms.*

Office of the Prime Minister. (2013). *Former Prime Ministers.*

Omar, M. F. (2008). Parliamentary behaviour of the members of opposition political parties in Malaysia. *Intellectual Discourse, 16*(1), 21–48.

Osborne, M. E. (1979). *Southeast Asia. An introductory history.* Sydney: Allen & Unwin.

Park, C.-m. (2011). Associations and social networks in Southeast Asia: Schools of democracy? In A. Croissant & M. Bünte (Eds.), *The crisis of democratic governance in Southeast Asia* (pp. 39–56). Houndmills: Palgrave Macmillan.

Pepinsky, T. B. (2007). Malaysia: Turnover without change. *Journal of Democracy, 18*, 113–127. https://doi.org/10.1353/jod.2007.0013

Pepinsky, T. B. (2009). *Economic crises and the breakdown of authoritarian regimes: Indonesia and Malaysia in comparative perspective.* Cambridge: Cambridge University Press.

Putnam, R. D. (1995). Bowling alone: America's declining social capital. *Journal of Democracy, 6*, 65–78. https://doi.org/10.1353/jod.1995.0002

Reporters without Borders. (2012). *Blogger held under draconian Official Secrets Act.*

Reporters without Borders. (2017). *2017 World Press freedom index. RSF.* Accessed June 22, 2017, from https://rsf.org/en/ranking

Rodan, G. (2004). *Transparency and authoritarian rule in Southeast Asia: Singapore and Malaysia.* London: RoutledgeCurzon.

Ryan, N. (1976). *A history of Malaysia and Singapore.* Kuala Lumpur: Oxford University Press.

Saravanamuttu, J., & Rusaslina, I. (2011). *The Sarawak Polls 2011: Implications for coalition politics in Malaysia.*

Searle, P. (1999). *The riddle of Malaysian capitalism: Rent-seekers or real capitalists?* Honolulu: University of Hawai'i Press.

Shan, K., & Moon, H. (2009). *EAIC cannot replace IPCMC.* http://www.malaysiakini.com/letters/107626

Singh, H. (1991). Political change in Malaysia: The role of semangat 46. *Asian Survey, 31*, 712–728. https://doi.org/10.2307/2645225

Singh, H. (1995). UMNO leaders and Malay rulers: The erosion of a special relationship. *Pacific Affairs, 68*, 187. https://doi.org/10.2307/2761367

Slater, D. (2003). Iron cage in an iron fist: Authoritarian institutions and the personalization of power in Malaysia. *Comparative Politics, 36*, 81. https://doi.org/10.2307/4150161

Slater, D. (2010). *Ordering power: Contentious politics and authoritarian leviathans in Southeast Asia.* Cambridge: Cambridge University Press.

Snodgrass, D. (1975). Trends and patterns in Malaysian income distribution, 1957–70. In D. Lim (Ed.), *Readings on Malaysian economic development* (pp. 251–269). Kuala Lumpur: Oxford University Press.

Stubbs, R. (1979). The United Malays National Organization, the Malayan Chinese Association, and the early years of the Malayan Emergency, 1948–1955. *Journal of Southeast Asian Studies, 10*, 77–88. https://doi.org/10.1017/S002246340001184X

Tan, L. E. (1992). Dongjiaozong and the challenge to cultural hegemony 1951–1987. In J. S. Kahn & F. L. K. Wah (Eds.), *Fragmented vision: Culture and politics in contemporary Malaysia.* Honolulu: University of Hawai'i Press.

Tan, K. (2001). Malaysia. In D. Nohlen, F. Grotz, & C. Hartmann (Eds.), *Elections in Asia and the Pacific: A data handbook, Volume II: South East Asia, East Asia, and the South Pacific.* Oxford: Oxford University Press.

Teh, Y. K. (2002). Money politics in Malaysia. *Journal of Contemporary Asia, 32*, 338–345. https://doi.org/10.1080/00472330280000231

Tennant, P. (1973). The decline of elective local government in Malaysia. *Asian Survey, 13*, 347–365. https://doi.org/10.1525/as.1973.13.4.01p0320x

Tham, S. (1977). *The role and impact of formal associations on the development of Malaysia.* Bangkok: Friedrich Ebert Foundation.

The Malaysian Bar. (2007). *Major changes to the constitution.*

The Malaysian Bar. (2008). *Bar Council's comments on the judicial appointments commission bill 2008.*

The Star. (2010). *Perkasa: Arrest Ka Siong under ISA.*

Tikamdas, R. (2005). The real test. Challenges and recommendations arising from the Royal Commission report for police reform. *Aliran Monthly, 25*(5).

Ufen, A. (2012). *Ethnizität, Islam, Reformasi: Die Evolution der Konfliktlinien im Parteiensystem Malaysias.* Wiesbaden: Springer VS.

Vorys, K. (1975). *Democracy without consensus.* Princeton: Princeton University Press.

Watts, R. (1999). *The spending power in federal systems: A comparative study.* Kingston: Institute of Intergovernmental Relations.

Wee, C. H. (1996). Fiscal Federalism. In K. S. Jomo & S. K. Ng (Eds.), *Malaysia's economic development: Policy & reform* (pp. 277–316). Kuala Lumpur: Pelanduk Publications.

Weiss, M. L. (2004). Malaysia: Construction of counterhegemonic narratives and agendas. In M. Alagappa (Ed.), *Civil society and political change in Asia: Expanding and contracting democratic space* (pp. 259–291). Stanford: Stanford University Press.

Weiss, M. L. (2006). *Protest and possibilities: Civil society and coalitions for political change in Malaysia.* Stanford, CA: Stanford University Press.

Weiss, M. L. (2009a). Edging toward a new politics in Malaysia: Civil society at the gate? *Asian Survey, 49*, 741–758. https://doi.org/10.1525/as.2009.49.5.741

Weiss, M. L. (2009b). *The antidemocratic potential of party system institutionalization: Malaysia as morality tale?* Accessed July 21, 2015, from http://www.mcgill.ca/files/isid/Weiss.Malaysia.pdf

Weiss, M. L. (2012). *Politics in cyberspace: New media in Malaysia.* Singapore: Friedrich Ebert Foundation.

Weiss, M. L., & Hassan, S. (Eds.). (2003). *Social movements in Malaysia: From moral communities to NGOs.* New York: RoutledgeCurzon.

World Bank. (2017). *Worldwide governance indicators*. http://data.worldbank.org/data-catalog/worldwide-governance-indicators

Wu, M. (1997). *The Malaysian legal system*. Petaling Jaya: Longman.

Wu, M. (1999). The Malaysian judiciary: Erosion of confidence. *Australian Journal of Law, 1*(2), 124–153.

WVS. (2014). *World values survey online data analysis*. Accessed June 20, 2017, from http://www.worldvaluessurvey.org/WVSOnline.jsp

Yusoff, M., Hasan, F., & Jalil, S. (2000). *Globalisation, econoimc policy, and equity: The case of Malaysia*. Paris: OECD.

Ziegenhain, P. (2008). Malaysia. In G. Riescher (Ed.), *Monarchien* (pp. 163–172). Baden-Baden: Nomos.

Myanmar: The Challenging Transition from Military to Democratic Government

7

© Springer International Publishing AG 2018
A. Croissant, P. Lorenz, *Comparative Politics of Southeast Asia*,
https://doi.org/10.1007/978-3-319-68182-5_7

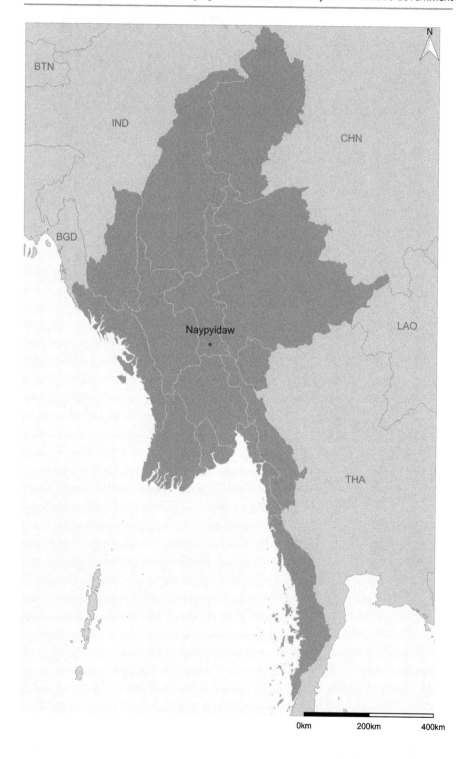

7.1 Historical Background and Current Political Challenges

The Republic of the Union of Myanmar, known as Burma prior to 1989, is one of the ethnically most heterogeneous societies in Southeast Asia with 135 officially recognized ethnic groups (see Table 7.1). Myanmar's ethnic minorities such as the Kachin, Kayah (Karenni), Karen, Chin, Mon, Rohingya, and Shan make up an estimated 30–40% of the population and live primarily in the peripheral states, whereas ethnic Bamars, often called Burmans, settle primarily along the Irrawaddy valley and in Upper Burma (also known as "Burma proper").[1] Since its independence in 1948, the multiethnic society has seen a high number of armed conflicts between the central government and a rich tapestry of different insurgent groups driven by nationalist, ideological, or economic motives. Ethnic conflicts contributed to the rise and persistence of a "praetorian state," in which the Burmese military (*Tatmadaw*) has dominated politics, the economy, and society for more than five decades. In 2011, the military initiated a process of gradual disengagement from day-to-day politics. The ratification of a new constitution followed by disbanding the Burmese junta and reasonably free legislative elections in November 2015 constitute remarkable achievements in the transition from overt military rule towards "something else" (Croissant 2015; Egreteau 2015b). Many scholars have explored possible reasons behind this military-controlled liberalization, although the *Tatmadaw* remains a pivotal political actor and a powerful veto player (Callahan 2012; Huang 2013; Croissant and Kamerling 2013; Dressel and Bünte 2014).

The first Burmese Empire of the Bagan Dynasty, founded in 1044 AD, is often considered the "Golden Age" of Burma. During its 250-year rule, Burman language, culture, and Theravada Buddhism spread along the Irrawaddy valley and into Upper Burma. After internal unrest and the Mongol invasion in the late thirteenth century, the Kingdom finally collapsed around 1300. In the mid-sixteenth century, King Bayinnaung of the Taungoo Dynasty created a second, short-lived Burman Empire. It was followed by the third Burman Empire of the Konbaung Dynasty (1752–1885; Bellwood 1999, p. 116). The Konbaung Dynasty unified Upper and Lower Burma with the Kingdom of Arakan, Manipur, and Assam (Ricklefs 2010, pp. 135–136). After three Anglo-Burmese Wars between 1824 and 1885, the British annexed Upper Burma, and in 1886, Burma became the province of Burma in British India. In 1923, a dual governance structure was established, a so-called diarchy, which left certain issues up to an administration of Burman ministers accountable to a legislature elected under census suffrage. The British governor held executive authority over policy and controlled certain resorts like the police directly. From 1937 until the Japanese invasion in early 1942, Burma

---

[1]There are 135 officially recognized nationality groups, divided into eight national ethnic races (Minahan 2015). In Bamar language, "Burma" is used as a colloquial term for the country and its citizens, whereas "Myanmar" is the more formal version of this name (Zöllner 2000, p. 30). Members of the largest ethnic group are referred to as "Bamar" or "Burmans," while "Burmese" or "Myanmarese" refers to all of the citizens of Burma/Myanmar.

Table 7.1 Country profile

Population	Year of full national sovereignty	Form of government
55,123,814	1948	Republic
Total area	**Current constitution enacted**	**Head of state**
676,578 km^2	2008	Htin Kyaw (since 2016)
GDP p.c. (PPP, 2015)	**Official language**	**Head of government**
1161	Burmese	Htin Kyaw (since 2016)
Ethnic groups	**Democracy score (BTI 2016)**	**System of government**
Burman 68%, Shan 9%, Karen 7%, Rakhine 4%, Chinese 3%, Indian 2%, Mon 2%, other 5%	3.0 (range from 1 to 10, higher scores indicate higher levels of democracy)	Presidential
Religious groups	**Regime type**	**Cabinet type**
Buddhists 87.9%, Christians 6.2%, Muslims 4.3%, others or none 1.6%	Autocracy	Single party (plus military-reserved cabinet posts)

Sources: CIA (2017), World Bank (2017a)

enjoyed limited autonomy under a Burman chief minister and the Burma Office, a British government department (Owen 2005, pp. 86–88).

However, direct British rule was established only in the country's heartland, the so-called Ministerial Burma, and the number of British officials remained remarkably low, leaving most subaltern positions to "Asiatic" officials from different regions of the British Empire. The Chin and Kachin "Frontier Areas" and the Federated Shan States remained under the formal rule of semi-sovereign local rulers. As in Malaysia, British rule over culturally and politically diverse areas and populations and their integration into a single economy created a segmented "plural society" (Furnival 1960, p. 186).[2] Because Burma could not supply sufficient labor during the rice planting and harvesting seasons or in the emerging modern industries, the colonial authorities encouraged labor migration during the late nineteenth and early twentieth centuries. While there was some Chinese immigration after 1852, most immigrants came from Bengal and the Madras state of India. Society in colonial Burma assumed a "three tiered" structure, in which Europeans occupied the top managerial, administrative, and professional positions. On the second tier, Indians and, to a lesser extent, Chinese operated retail shops and held skilled and unskilled jobs in the modern sectors of the economy; Indians also

---

[2]Furnivall's concept of the "plural society" refers to the fragile nature of societies that emerged under European colonial rule. In a plural society, people are bound not by "custom" but by "law" imposed by outsiders. Furnivall argued that plural societies were fragile precisely because they were held together only by economic self-interest and were mediated by the market and the coercive apparatus of European colonial power (Jory 2013).

held more than 50% of all government jobs in Lower Burma in 1931, whereas the British recruited primarily ethnic minorities to serve in the colonial army (Steinberg 2010, p. 29). On the lowest tier were the Bamars, who lived in the villages and worked in the traditional sectors of the economy.

Before the first decade of the twentieth century, the Burmese used to be independent cultivators, possessing a relatively high standard of living. They shunned the low-paying migrant labor jobs, and Indian control of capital was not seen as oppressive as long as the market for rice was good and loans could be easily repaid. However, in the early 1900s, uncultivated land became scarce, population growth began to outstrip economic growth, and fluctuations in the price of rice created new and unstable conditions. Burmese cultivators, dependent on credit loans, faced foreclosure with increasing frequency. This created a class of Indian absentee landlords whose farms were often operated by Indian tenants: Whereas in 1901 only 17% of the cropland had been owned by absentee landlords in the Irrawady delta region, by 1940 this figure had increased to 67%. The resulting social grievances led to local uprisings (Charney 2009, pp. 10–12) and fueled the emergence of a Burman national movement in the 1920s and 1930s led by low level civil servants, university students, and Buddhist monks (Osborne 1990). The *Dobama Asiayone* ("We Burmans-Association") became the core of the Burman Independence Army, created by Aung San with Japanese support in 1940 (Kratoska and Batson 1999).

During World War II, Japanese troops occupied Burma and fostered both the Burman nationalist movement as well as nationalist sentiments among the ethnic minorities (Sidel 2013). The increasingly oppressive nature of Japanese military occupation turned Burman nationals against the Japanese. In early 1945, Aung San and the newly formed Anti-Fascist People's Freedom League (AFPFL) declared war on Japan. In 1946, the British authorities agreed to start negotiations regarding Burma's independence and invited Aung San to become Burma's de facto head of government (Zöllner 2000). During the Panglong Conference in February 1947, the Burmese government under Aung San and representatives of the Kachin, Chin, and Shan agreed on the basic principles for a federal and democratic constitution (Sakhong 2012, p. 3). However, representatives of the other ethnic minorities did not participate in these negotiations and boycotted the 1947 elections for a constitutional assembly that gave AFPFL broad parliamentary control.

In July 1947, Aung San was assassinated by a member of his own party. The new government under Prime Minister U Nu abandoned Aung San's conciliatory approach in favor of a Burman-dominated unitary state (Gravers 1999, pp. 41–43). Shortly after the Union of Burma became independent on January 4, 1948, several insurgencies broke out (Lintner 1999). At the time, the central government had little military means to counter these threats: When General Ne Win took command of the Burmese Armed Forces (*Tatmadaw*), they totaled only around 2000 troops (Callahan 2001, pp. 414–416). Ne Win quickly reorganized the *Tatmadaw* under a centralized command, expanded troop strength, and modernized its military equipment (Selth 2002, pp. 10–11). This allowed the government to regain control over most of the Union's territories. The strength of the new military contrasted sharply with the weakness of civilian institutions. Following factional conflicts within the AFPFL, the *Tatmadaw* forced Premier U Nu to appoint Ne Win as interim prime minister in 1958 (Selth 2002, p. 12). The military handed back control to an elected government in 1960, but U Nu's decision to declare Buddhism the state religion triggered a new wave of ethnic rebellions. Finally, the *Tatmadaw* under General Ne Win staged a coup d'état in 1962.

The military governed until 1974 through a ruling council and then through its Buddhist Socialist Program Party (BSPP; Callahan 2001; Steinberg 2001). Despite institutionalizing a nominally civilian regime, the military remained in full control of the state bureaucracy, the government, and the BSPP, whereas civilians occupied subordinate positions (Taylor 1996; Myoe 2007). Under the official motto of a "Burmese Way to Socialism," industries and trade were nationalized, about 300,000 South Asians were forced to leave the country, and domestic businesses were relegated into the shadow economy (Jones 2013, p. 148). The regime cut most of its existing international links and implemented a strict program of import substitution with the ultimate goal of creating an autarkic domestic economy (Taylor 2009, pp. 342–344). As a result, the contribution of imports and exports to the GDP plummeted from 36% in 1962 to less than 10% in 1987, and the share of the manufacturing sector fell from 37.1 to 23% in 1985 (Myat Thein 2004, pp. 75, 87).

Spiraling inflation, a fuel and rice shortage, and the complete demonetization of small banknotes in September 1987, a decision that in one sweep rendered some 60–80% of the money in the cash-based economy worthless (Guyot 1989), triggered a popular uprising in 1988. In the face of this unrest, Ne Win formally resigned from his post as BSPP leader, although most observers still regarded him as the *éminence grise* behind the government (Steinberg 2001, p. 14). Protests reached a first peak on August 8 ("8-8-88 Uprising"), when coordinated protests occurred in most Burmese towns and cities and particularly in the capital city of Rangoon (today's Yangon). Until then, the regime had relied on the repression of the internal security forces, but now, elite counterinsurgency troops of the *Tatmadaw* were ordered to assist the overwhelmed police in suppressing the protests. In the following crackdown, about 3000 protestors and bystanders were killed (Ferrara 2003). However, the protests did not stop. Following the BSPP's announcement to hold elections within 3 months, the country was swept by another massive wave of protests. Finally, on September 18, the Chief of Staff of the Armed Forces and Defence Minister, Gen. Saw Maung, installed the State Law and Order Restoration Council (SLORC). Army troops began a four-day long massacre during which several thousands of people were killed, injured, or arrested. Nevertheless, the SLORC allowed the National League for Democracy (NLD) under the leadership of Aung San Suu Kyi, the daughter of Aung San, to participate in the elections for a constitutional assembly in 1990. The NLD won 392 out of 485 seats. While the opposition argued that the election provided the NLD with a popular mandate to form the government, military leaders insisted otherwise, put Aung San Suu Kyi under house arrest, and used hard repression to suppress the opposition.

In the following decade, the junta engaged in a massive expansion of the *Tatmadaw*, whose troop size doubled to more than 400,000. Regional army commanders took over all important state functions at the subnational level (Kühn and Croissant 2011, pp. 141–142). The junta—renamed the State Peace and Development Council (SPDC) in 1997—abandoned the experiment with a socialist planned economy in favor of military-dominated rentier capitalism and managed to sign ceasefire agreements with a large number of ethnic rebel groups that guaranteed both parties a share of the earnings from local resources in the territories under rebel control (Nilsen 2013). The resulting mélange of military, rebel, and civilian businesses further weakened state institutions and strengthened the exploitative nature of the military-dominated economic system (Jones 2014).

In 2003, the SPDC announced its roadmap to a civilian government. A handpicked constitutional assembly presented a new constitution in 2008 that was adopted in a rigged referendum the same year. Manipulated elections in November 2010 and the formation of a government under President Thein Sein, a former general, in 2011 completed Myanmar's transition to electoral authoritarianism (Huang 2013; Dressel and Bünte 2014).

Several political reforms followed, including a national dialogue with opposition leader Aung San Suu Kyi, the legalization of political parties, and the release of political prisoners. The regime also eased its limitations on the freedom of speech, association, and assembly. In the general election of November 2015, the NLD won 255 out of the 330 contested seats in the Lower House and 135 of the 168 contested seats in the Upper House. Since Aung San remains barred from ascending to the presidency herself, the parliament elected her close confidant Htin Kyaw Union president on March 15, 2016 (McCarthy 2016).

7.2 Constitutional History

The current constitution came into force on January 31, 2011, and officially replaced the socialist constitution of 1974 that had been suspended by SLORC in 1988. The constitutional process lacked democratic legitimacy along three dimensions (cf. Croissant 2016). First, it lacked "upstream legitimacy" because the constituent assembly that wrote the document did not come into being in a legitimate way. The national convent assembled by SLORC in 1993 originally had 703 members, including 107 representatives who had been elected in 1990. After the NLD withdrew from the convent in 1996, the whole process was suspended and only reestablished in 2004 (Myoe 2007, p. 4). The constitutional convent now included 1088 delegates, only 13 of them elected and none of them from the NLD (Myoe 2007, p. 21). Second, it lacked "process legitimacy" because the military dominated the internal decision-making procedures of the constitution-making body. The Junta had decreed a list of 104 principles that had to be respected and penalized any form of public criticism of the constitutional process (Williams 2009, p. 1668). In most essential points the draft constitution presented in 2008 was identical to the SLORC draft of 1993 (Jones 2014). Third, the process lacked "downstream legitimacy": even though it had been submitted to the people in a referendum in May 2008, many local and international observers attributed the official turnout of 98% and the approval rate of 92% to massive manipulation (Seekins 2009, p. 169; Than 2009, pp. 202–204).

The 2008 Constitution primarily establishes institutions and distributes government power. Only towards the end of the 448 provisions does it mention citizens' rights and responsibilities. Chapter 1 (Art. 1-48) of the constitutional text defines the union as a system of "genuine, disciplined multiparty democracy" (Art. 6d). This chapter decrees the administrative division of the Union into seven regions and states, reserved parliamentary representation and institutional autonomy for the *Tatmadaw*, and special prerogatives for the military commander-in-chief. In addition, Article 20(f) establishes the military as the guardian of the constitution and puts forth the national integrity and sovereignty of the Union. This chapter also guarantees a market economy and rules out the nationalization of businesses and the demonetarization of the national currency. Chapter 2 of the constitution (Art. 49-56) concerns the administrative organization of the state. Chapters 3–6 deal with the basic principles and functioning of state bodies, including the national executive consisting of the president, two vice presidents, the cabinet, and the National Defence and Security Council (NDSC, Art. 57-73), a bicameral national parliament and the regional parliaments (Art. 74-198), and the court system, including the Constitutional Tribunal (Art. 199-292). Chapter 7 enshrines the position of the *Tatmadaw* in the political system (Art. 337-344) and Chap. 8 deals with citizenship and provides a list of civil liberties and duties as well as economic and social rights (Art. 345-390). At first glance, the constitution contains a wide range of substantive rights, but most provisions find their limits in existing legislation, which means that the realization of these rights appears to be almost entirely dependent on the whim of the parliament (Nardi 2014, p. 650). The constitution guarantees the special status of Buddhism but also recognizes Christianity, Islam, Hinduism, and animism as other established religions (Art. 361-2) and rules out the "abuse of religion for political means" and the spreading of religious hatred (Art. 364). Chapters 9 and 10 regulate national and regional parliamentary elections (Art. 391-403) and the status of political parties (Art. 404-409). Chapters 11 and 12 provide regulations for imposing a state of emergency by the president and the authority of the military commander-in-chief (Art. 410-432) and the constitutional amendment process (Art. 433-436). Finally, Chapters 13 through 15 contain regulations on state symbols as well as temporary and closing arrangements (Art. 437-457).

Although the 2008 Constitution includes several innovative elements, it is also firmly rooted in the tradition of the 1947 and 1974 constitutional texts. This includes the lack of a privileged status for constitutional rights provisions and the privileged status of Buddhism. The return to a bicameral legislature, the indirect election of the president by the Union parliament, and the appointment of regional governments by the central government are also inspired by the 1947 Constitution, whereas the division of Burma into seven regions and states is the same as in the 1974 Constitution (Zhu 2009, p. 46). The most important innovations include the constitutional acknowledgment of a market economy and a multiparty system and the equal representation of all 14 states and regions in the Upper House, regardless of their population (Art. 9a, 141). Unlike in the first constitution of 1947, states can no longer legally secede from the Union (Art. 201-202, Constitution of 1947). For the first time in Burma's history, regions and states have elected legislatures and the constitution institutes a Constitutional Tribunal as a separate institution to hear cases for constitutional review (Art. 40).

Amendments to the constitution require the vote of more than 75% of the members of both houses of the Assembly of the Union, which gives the military that controls 25% of the seats a de facto veto. Substantial changes to the constitution such as the status of the presidency, the National and Defence Security Council, and the rules for amending the constitution require additional approval by referendum.

Overall, the constitution reflects the self-interests of the military. It is a "military constitution" drafted in order to demand obedience in the name of the law, to win legal recognition from the international community, and to regulate access to power within the ruling elite (Croissant 2016). It imposes severe constraints on the functioning of the political regime, "something which military rulers typically intend to do to preserve their reforms and protect their personal and corporate interests after leaving power" (Negretto 2013, p. 83). In fact, under the constitution, the *Tatmadaw* is a fourth branch of government. It sets its own budget independently of the president and parliament and has the right to administer and adjudicate all military affairs itself. It appoints the defense, home, and border affairs ministers both in the national cabinet and in the regional governments. It also has the right to veto decisions of the executive, legislative, and judicial branches of the government as far as national security, defense, or military policy are concerned. Members of the *Tatmadaw* enjoy full impunity for any actions taken prior to 2011 (Art. 445), and members of the armed forces can only be tried by the military court system. Furthermore, the armed forces have constitutionally secured a quarter of all seats in the Union parliament and in the 14 state and regional legislative assemblies. Amending the constitution requires military approval. The *Tatmadaw*'s commander-in-chief appoints and removes the military members of parliament and the ministers of defense, home, and border affairs as well as the ministers for border security in the subnational governments (Art. 232). He commands all military units, paramilitary forces, and border troops; has to confirm the appointment of any additional military cabinet member; and can reverse any decision by the military courts (Art. 343). In case the president declares a state of emergency, all legislative and executive powers are transferred to the military commander-in-chief (Art. 40, 149). Finally, the NDSC, an 11-member group of which five are active duty officers, must approve the declaration of a state of emergency and appoints the commander-in-chief, providing the *Tatmadaw* a veto over these decisions (Art. 201).

7.3 System of Government

The Republic of the Union of Myanmar is a unitary state with a presidential system of government. All executive power is vested in the president, who is also head of state. Legislative power is vested in the Assembly of the Union (*Pyidaungsu*

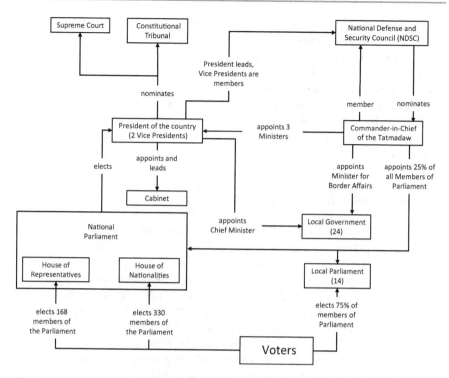

Fig. 7.1 Myanmar's system of government, as of March 2016. Source: Authors' compilation

Hluttaw), which consists of the Upper and Lower House. The 14 ethnic states and regions have unicameral state legislatures and appointed chief ministers. The judiciary is a separate branch of government (see Fig. 7.1). In April 2016, the Union Parliament appointed former opposition leader Aung San Suu Kyi to the official government role of state councilor, allowing her to contact ministries, departments, and other organizations and individuals in an official fashion. It is too early to tell how this position will fit into the broader system of government.

7.3.1 Head of State and Government

The president is head of state and government. The 2008 Constitution abolished the position of the prime minister, although some observers compare the position of a state counsellor that the parliament established in 2016 to the position of a prime minister. The president is not politically accountable to parliament, but unlike in other presidential systems, is indirectly elected by the Assembly of the Union. The elected members of the House of Representatives and of the House of Nationalities and the military representatives in both Houses each form an electoral college that elects one vice president, who then automatically becomes a candidate for the presidency. The joint session of the elected and appointed members of parliament elects the president by plurality rule for a 5-year term that is renewable once. The other two candidates serve as vice presidents (Art. 60). Eligibility criteria for the office are restrictive: Only members of the Union Parliament, who are at least 46 years of age, have lived in Myanmar for the last 20 years, and who are familiar with the political, administrative, economic, and military affairs of the Union can stand for election. Any person who holds a foreign citizenship or whose parents, spouse, children, or children's spouses hold a foreign citizenship are ineligible for the office (Art. 59F). The president and the vice presidents are barred from taking part in the affairs of political parties while in office. The *Pyidaungsu Hluttaw* can impeach the president upon request by a quarter of the members of the Upper or Lower House. If the motion passes with a two-thirds majority of one house, the other house conducts the trial hearings and can impeach the president by a two-thirds majority (Art. 71).

The president represents the Union internationally, has the right of pardon, can impose a state of emergency, and governs the administrative district of the capital Naypyidaw. The president appoints the union ministers who together with the two vice presidents and the attorney general constitute the Union Government. The president also appoints the chief ministers of the 14 regions and ethnic states and the justices of the Supreme Court, the higher courts, as well as for the Constitutional Tribunal. The national parliament and—in case of the heads of the regional governments—the regional parliaments can only turn down these appointments if they violate formal procedures. The president can initiate bills, issue decrees and presidential orders, and has a suspensive veto over parliamentary legislation. Finally, he can request constitutional interpretations and abstract judicial review by the Constitutional Tribunal. He or she also appoints diplomatic personnel and senior bureaucrats, but not high-ranking military officers, who are appointed by the commander-in-chief of the armed forces. Neither does the president have any other authority over the armed forces. The president leads and organizes the cabinet. In the first NLD-led government of March 2016, there were 20 ministers with a portfolio and the minister in the presidential office. Only the ministers of defense, border, and home affairs, appointed by the NDSC, remain active military officers. The cabinet consists largely of NLD politicians but also includes members of the Union Solidarity and Development Party (USDP) and ethnic minority parties (The Guardian 2016).

The constitution also imposes some limitations on presidential authority. Presidential decrees need confirmation by parliament, which can also overturn a presidential veto by plurality vote (Art. 106). More importantly, both the NDSC and the commander-in-chief of the *Tatmadaw* participate in the government. Control over the interior and border protection ministries comes with oversight of the police, the prison system, and the General Administration Department, which oversees all administrative personnel, giving the military de facto control over the whole civilian bureaucracy (Nixon et al. 2013, pp. 14–15). Moreover, under a state of emergency, all executive authority is transferred to the commander-in-chief based on what can be described as a "two-step coup d'état clause" (Nyein 2009, p. 639).

7.3.2 Legislature

Myanmar's Assembly of the Union (*Pyidaungsu Hluttaw*) consists of an Upper House, the House of Nationalities (*Amyotha Hluttaw*) representing the interests of states and regions, and a Lower House, the House of Representatives (*Pyithu Hluttaw*). Together with the regional and state legislatures, the two chambers are elected for 5-year terms. Members of parliament cannot serve in other elected or other government positions. Each of the 14 states and regions elects 12 members to the Upper House; the remaining 56 of the 224 seats are reserved for the military. The House of Representatives has 440 members, of which 330 are popularly elected and 110 are appointed by the military. All 166 military MPs are appointed by the commander-in-chief of the *Tatmadaw*. The duration of their mandate is not delineated and since the opening of the new parliament in 2011, military MPs have been replaced by the army commander on a regular basis (Egreteau 2015c, p. 339). The size of the regional parliaments depends on population numbers and varies between 20 and 143 (Nixon et al. 2013, p. 57), of which one-third of the total elected seats, i.e., 25% of total seats, belong to members of the military.

In Myanmar's symmetrical bicameralism, the Lower and Upper Houses have equal legislative powers: Bills can be initiated by either of the houses and the consent of both houses is needed for the enactment of laws, and the Lower House cannot unilaterally override vetoes or amendments adopted by the Upper House. If there is disagreement between the two houses, a joint session determines the content of the final bill (Butenschøn et al. 2015). With the exception of amendments to the constitution, all decisions are made by simple majority vote. Once a bill has passed in both chambers, it goes to the president for enactment. If the head of state does not veto the bill or parliament overrides his veto, the bill becomes law. Both houses of parliament elect a speaker by simple majority. The speaker allocates seats in the committees, determines the legislative agenda, and presides during plenary sessions. Both the Upper and Lower House can form committees, with the constitution only requiring four standing committees necessary for parliamentary procedure, like the "Government Guarantees, Pledges and Undertakings Committee." The Security and Defence Committee is reserved for military members of the assembly. Elected representatives can be included if "necessary" and "suitable" (Art. 115b). Currently (April 2016), there are 18 standing committees.

Contrary to initial expectations, Myanmar's legislature has proven to be a powerful institution that does not shy away from conflicts with the president or other state organs. In a particularly visible example, the Upper House moved to impeach the Constitutional Tribunal in August 2012 and the motion was supported by civilian legislators from both USDP and NLD, who objected to a decision of the tribunal (see below). Especially since the by-elections held in April 2012, in which the NLD won all 37 contested seats for the House of Representatives, the parliament has developed into a thriving force of political and economic reforms. Opposition MPs and representatives of the USDP, founded by the military in advance of the 2010 election, have used their authority to monitor the government (ICG 2013, p. 1; Holliday 2013, p. 94), although most NLD parliamentarians are inexperienced in lawmaking and other parliamentary affairs. Whether for normative or merely strategic reasons, members of USDP in the first elected Union parliament (2010–2015) sometimes took joint opposition policy positions and cooperated with their opponents. For example, USDP representatives supported NLD's demands to eliminate the *Tatmadaw*'s blocking minority for constitutional amendments provided for in Article 436 (Poling et al. 2014; Soe 2014). Whereas the national parliament acted as an agent of change under President Thein Shein, regional parliaments were far less influential (Lwin 2014).

A number of studies have provided preliminary insights into Myanmar's legislative processes and the behavior of civilian and military members of parliament (ICG 2013; Kean 2014; Egreteau 2015a, b, c). Available circumstantial evidence suggests that in the period 2012–2015, legislative coalitions frequently cut across party lines, strengthening the position of parliament vis-à-vis the government. At the same time, civilian legislators have few regular interactions with their military colleagues. Most MPs in khaki seem to have been drawn from the younger age group of the *Tatmadaw*; two-thirds were ethnic Bamar; and about 40% of the military officers seconded to parliament belong to the group of majors and captains, with only very few senior officers above the rank of lieutenant-colonel (Egreteau 2015c, pp. 347, 350, 361). Yet until now, little is known about the bases on which officers are appointed and removed from the legislature or the actual legislative behavior of military MPs not only in the Union parliament but also in the provincial assemblies. Available studies suggest that the military appointees have not appeared to favor obstructionist tactics systematically. Rather, thus far, the level of their legislative involvement has remained low (Egreteau 2015a, p. 9). However, it is worth noting that military MPs do not always vote as a bloc and have only consistently objected to draft bills that would have interfered with the army's own corporatist interests, or more generally with the three main "national causes" of national integrity, solidarity, and sovereignty (Egreteau 2015a).

7.4 Legal and Judicial System

Myanmar's law system is a combination of customary law, codified English common law, and legislation passed after 1947. The principles of English common and statutory law were implemented by British legal codes of the pre-independence India statutes (Crouch and Lindsey 2014, pp. 5–7). Since independence, the judicial system has evolved through several phases. Under the parliamentary democracy from 1947 to 1962, there was a professional and independent judiciary trained in the Anglo-Indian legal tradition, with the Supreme Court as the highest court of the land, a High Court, and regional courts. Following the 1962 coup, the military dissolved the Supreme Court and abolished the regular court system in favor of so-called Special Courts. The ruling council saw no need to feign adherence to the rule of law and state actions were not bound by law in any predictable manner (Cheesman 2009, pp. 598–599). Under the 1974 Constitution, the judicial system was transformed into a socialist system. The BSPP Socialist State introduced so-called People's Tribunals presided by military officers, BSPP cadres, and loyal bureaucrats who served as enforcers of state power (Cheesman 2011, p. 822; Nardi 2014, pp. 642–644). When the SLORC abandoned socialism in 1988, it returned to the pre-1974 civil court system (Crouch and Lindsey 2014, pp. 5–7; Cheesman 2011, p. 802). Notwithstanding these reforms, the judicial branch of government remained subservient to the executive branch and access to justice in Myanmar remained elusive.

For the past six decades, corruption in the judicial system and abuse of office have been endemic (Steinberg 2010, p. 130). Accordingly, the weakness of the rule of law and high levels of public corruption—affecting all branches of government and all levels of state administration—are reflected in the low rankings of Myanmar in the World Bank's Rule of Law Indicator and Transparency International's Corruption Perception Index. In both indices, the country frequently finishes last or second to last in the region (World Bank 2017b; Transparency International 2015).

Myanmar's history of a politicized judiciary and dysfunctional rule of law means that it would be unrealistic to expect an overnight transformation in this regard. Nevertheless, many observers have noted slow but significant improvements. Even though courts have so far exercised only limited influence on the executive and legislative branches of government, the new constitution at least creates the institutional machinery for judicial review of both branches and authorizes the Supreme Court to enforce fundamental rights. Political activists are now more likely to be charged in court rather than simply incarcerated or assassinated as before. Still, they cannot expect a fair trial, and the poor state of the judicial infrastructure, outdated legal codes, and judicial corruption mean it is difficult for most citizens to gain access to justice (Holliday 2013, p. 95).

Under the 2008 Constitution, the country's civilian courts were reorganized into four levels with the Supreme Court at the apex. As highest judicial body in the land, it presides over 14 state and regional High Courts, 67 District and Self-Administered Area Courts, and 324 Township Courts. Village chiefs ("headmen") also wield certain quasi-judicial powers and there is a parallel system of marital courts. In addition, the constitution introduced a bifurcated system of judicial review steeped in common law: The Supreme Court has jurisdiction over concrete administrative review cases involving constitutional rights, whereas the Constitutional Tribunal serves as a constitutional court with the authority of constitutional review (IBA 2012, p. 56).

The 2008 Constitution guarantees the independence and impartiality of the judiciary, and it mandates public courtroom hearings, a right of defense, and a right of appeal. The formal safeguards for judicial independence are, however, somewhat undermined by the extent of executive control over the judiciary (IBA 2012, p. 57). The president nominates the chief justice and seven to 11 justices of the Supreme Court, and parliament may only withhold its approval if "it can clearly be proved" that the prospective appointee lacks the qualifications prescribed for the post (Art. 301). The chief justice of the High Courts is also appointed by the president; the remaining up to six judges are appointed by the chief minister of the territorial unit (Nardi 2014, p. 650). Judges of the Supreme Court and High Court ordinarily "shall hold office" up to the age of 70 and 65, respectively. The president's powers of appointment are augmented by his or her control over the financing of the court system. Although the Supreme Court is responsible for assessing the judiciary's annual budget in advance, it is the executive's task to present that budget to the legislature (Nardi 2014, p. 650).

For the first time in Myanmar's history, the 2008 Constitution instituted a centralized constitutional court. The nine-member Constitutional Tribunal is empowered to interpret constitutional provisions, to review the constitutionality of enacted legislation, and to resolve constitutional disputes between the Union government, states, regions, and self-administered areas. Its decisions are final and conclusive in all such cases (Art. 324). In contrast to Indonesia, there is no provision for constitutional complaints, and individual citizens do not have direct access to the court. The Union president, the two parliamentary speakers, the chief justice of the Supreme Court, the head of the national election commission, and groups of legislators of at least 10% of the total members of either the Lower or Upper House are entitled to appeal to the Constitutional Tribunal. In case of constitutional disputes between the Union and subnational governments, the chief ministers and speakers of the state or regional parliaments can appeal to the tribunal. All of these actors are also entitled to file a request for constitutional interpretation. Finally, if any ordinary court finds itself having to address a matter within the Tribunal's jurisdiction, it "shall stay the trial and submit its opinion to the Constitutional Court of the Union [for] resolution" (Art. 59b).

The Union president and the two parliamentary speakers each nominate a third of the Tribunal's justices to parliament, and legislators may only withhold approval from persons who are demonstrably unqualified. The justices of the Constitutional Tribunal serve a 5-year term. The first bench (2011–2012) was elected by a parliament that consisted of the military-backed USDP, military representatives, and ethnic minority parties. Following the resignation of the nine justices in 2012, a second bench completed the term until the NLD-dominated parliament in early 2016 elected a third bench.

Members of the Tribunal can be impeached by a motion of either government or parliament (Art. 320-1). The details vary depending on the way the process is initiated, but a legislative chamber can act if two-thirds of representatives vote in favor of charges related to high treason, breach of any constitutional provision, misconduct, the loss of a required qualification for office, or the inefficient discharge of duties assigned by law (Art. 302, 311, 334).

The primary role of the Tribunal is to hear cases concerning the constitutional review of laws issued at either the national, state/regional, or self-administered area level. From 2011 to 2015, the court heard and decided 13 cases. So far, the Tribunal has demonstrated considerable political autonomy from the executive branch of government and repeatedly revoked presidential acts and decrees (Nardi 2014). In contrast, it has been highly dependent on the political will of parliament. In early 2012, the government requested a constitutional assessment on whether parliament could demand the presence of government ministers in all committee meetings, and the court supported the government's position and ruled against such a parliamentary right (Nardi 2014). In reaction to the Tribunal's decision, representatives of the NLD and the USDP argued the decision was "not correct" and that the judges had violated the constitution. After the Upper House voted for impeachment on August 28, all nine judges chose to resign on September 6, 2012 (ICG 2012, pp. 9–11). Even though the impeachment was formally permissible under the constitution (International Bar Association 2012: 38), legislators ignored the fact that decisions by the Constitutional Tribunal cannot be overruled by parliament. Parliament has since amended the law on the Constitutional Tribunal to make the Tribunal report to the president and the speakers of both houses of parliament and appropriated the authority to select the chief justice (Nardi 2014, p. 670).

7.5   Electoral System and Elections

The first elections to the newly created Legislative Council were held across "Ministerial Burma" in November 1922 under census suffrage. Universal suffrage was introduced in 1947. Multiparty elections for the Chamber of Deputies (Lower House) were held regularly between 1951 and 1960. One-party dominance by the AFPFL characterized elections during this period (cf. Table 7.2). Even though there were administrative shortcomings and security issues in some regions, elections were regarded as free and fair (Steinberg 2010). Whereas there were no elections from 1962 until 1974, under the 1974 Constitution, only candidates from the military's Buddhist Socialist Program Party could run in elections. In 1990, the military junta permitted open elections in which the NLD won 80% of seats but SLORC did not allow the newly elected parliament to convene. The 2008 Constitution introduced multiparty elections for the Union parliament and the regional and state assemblies. The last elections to the *Pyithu Hluttaw* were held in November 2015, and despite problems—especially with voter registration and unregulated party finances—the integrity of the elections compared favorably in the region and even globally. According to the Perceptions of Electoral Integrity (PEI) index, the 2015 elections achieved the second-highest quality score among the seven Southeast Asian countries in the project (54.07 compared to an average of 50.59). In January 2016, elections of village tracts and urban ward administrators took place across the country.

The current electoral system was established by the 2008 Constitution. Suffrage is guaranteed for all natural-born citizens who are at least 18 years old, but Article 392 specifies important exceptions to voting rights, for example for members of the Buddhist *sangha*. Natural-born citizens aged 25 (30 for the Upper House) or older are eligible to stand in elections if Myanmar was their general residence for the past 10 years. A passage in the election law that would have banned any convicted criminal from becoming a member of a political party and which would have forced the NLD to exclude numerous members was dropped before the by-election of 2012 (Taylor 2012, p. 227). Candidates can run under a party banner or as independents (Kudo 2011; The Burma Fund 2011). While the Union Election Commission (UEC)

Table 7.2 Parliamentary elections in Myanmar, 1951–2015

Party		1951	1956	1960	1990	2010 (Lower house)	2010 (Upper house)	2015 (Lower house)	2015 (Upper house)
NLD	%	–	–	–	59.8	–	–	57.1	–
	Seats	–	–	–	392	(37[c])	(4[c])	255	135
NUP[b]	%	–	–	–	21.2	19.5	–	–	–
	Seats	–	–	–	10	12	5		
SNLD	%	–	–	–	1.7	–	–		
	Seats	–	–	–	23	–	–	–	3
AFPFL(plus allies)	%	–	–	–	–	–	–	–	–
	Seats	199	148	–	–	–	–	–	–
AFPFL (Stable)	%	–	–	–	–	–	–	–	–
	Seats	–	–	41	–	–	–	–	–
AFPFL (Clean)	%	–	–	–	–	–	–	–	–
	Seats	–	–	158	–	–	–	–	–
UHPC	%	–	–	–	–	–	–	–	–
	Seats	–	14	–	–	–	–	–	–
NUF (u. SUF)	%	–	–	–	–	–	–	–	–
	Seats	–	48	–	–	–	–	–	–
PDF (and allies)	%	19	–	–	–	–	–	–	–
	Seats	–	–	–	–	–	–	–	–
USDP	%	–	–	–	–	56.8	–	28.2	–
	Seats	–	–	–	–	259 (0[c])	129 (1[c])	30	12
SNDP	%	–	–	–	–	0.2	–	–	–
	Seats	–	–	–	–	18	3 (1[c])	–	
RNPP	%	–	–	–	–	2.9	–	–	–
	Seats	–	–	–	–	9	7	–	10

(continued)

Table 7.2 (continued)

Party		1951	1956	1960	1990	2010 (Lower house)	2010 (Upper house)	2015 (Lower house)	2015 (Upper house)
NDF	%	–	–	–	–	7.1	–	–	–
	Seats					8	4		
Others & independents[d]	%	–	–	–	17.2	11.4	–	14.7	–
	Seats	21	33	38	60	19	14	38	11
Tatmadaw (appointed)	Seats	–	–	–	–	110	56	110	56
Total	%	–	–	–	99.9	97.9	–	–	–
	Seats	250	250	250	485	435	224	433	224
	(vacancies)	11	7	13	7	5	0	7	0
Turnout	%	–	–	–	72.6	77.2	76.8	69.7	69.8

[a]Vote shares are only available for 1990 and the Lower House elections of 2010 and 2015
[b]Formerly BSPP
[c]By-elections held on 1 April 2012
[d]"Others" are political parties with less than 2% of total vote/seats
Source: Englehart (2012), Frasch (2001), The Burma Fund (2011), Than (2014), Carr (2017), IFES (2017)

is responsible for voter registration as well as organizing and managing the election of members of the Union parliament and that of the state and regional legislative assemblies, local elections are under the purview of the military-governed General Administrative Department (GAD). The UEC can call by-elections if a member of parliament takes up a government office. Candidates can file an electoral complaint with the commission, but this procedure again requires a considerable fee (Oo 2014, p. 195). All national and subnational legislatures are elected by a system of plurality rule in single-member districts. In September 2014, the USDP proposed to change the system to proportional representation with open or closed party lists, but most ethnic parties and the NLD opposed it.

In 2010, Myanmar held the first elections under the 2008 constitution. Several dozen parties registered, representing a variety of ethnic groups, though the NLD and many other opposition parties boycotted the polls. The military-backed USDP was the only party that filed a full slate of candidates for the Union parliament and the state and regional assemblies. Political space was highly restricted and the political playing field was heavily skewed in favor of the USDP (Kudo 2011, pp. 3–4; Englehart 2012, p. 668) which, unsurprisingly, won a landslide victory (see Table 7.2).

Following the release of Aung San Suu Kyi from house arrest, the NLD decided to participate in by-elections in 2012. Again, the USDP had an unfair advantage, but all parties could campaign freely and were given access to state radio and television (Than 2014). The NLD won 41 seats in the Union parliament, whereas the USDP emerged with a single seat. The fact that NLD managed to defeat USDP even in constituencies with large military and civil service populations indicated strong support for the opposition even among groups close to the government. The general election of November 2015 confirmed the strength of the NLD. On a nationwide basis, the party won 887 of the 1150 contested seats. The ruling USDP came in at a distant second with 117 seats. In both chambers of the Union Parliament, NLD took more than three-fourth of the elected seats and won an absolute majority (taking into account the 25% of seats allocated to the military) in seven regional and three state assemblies. The USDP-led party alliance won an absolute majority only in the Shan State (Dinmore and Guyitt 2015). The election results demonstrate the ambiguous nature of multiparty elections in authoritarian regimes. Rather than stabilizing the military's sway over an electoral authoritarianism, it offered the opposition a chance to challenge the post-2008 regime structures designed to continue military dominance in civilian disguise.

7.6 Parties and Party System

One party—the AFPFL—was at the forefront of Burmese politics after 1945. Founded as a merger of the Burma National Army led by Aung San, the Communist Party of Burma, and the People's Revolutionary Party in March 1945, the AFPFL was victorious in the elections of 1947, 1951, and 1956. The party enjoyed a monopoly on power that reflected its strong support especially among Bamar voters, but it suffered from factional conflicts (Taylor 1996). Before the 1960 elections, the party broke up into two factions, the military-backed "Stable AFPFL" and the "Clean AFPFL" of Prime Minister U Nu, who won the vast majority of parliamentary seats in 1960 (Bigelow 1960; Steinberg 2010). Other political parties and independents had little success, except in those parts of Burma inhabited by ethnic minorities. Following the military coup of 1962, the new rulers dissolved all existing parties and created the Buddhist Socialist Program Party. Following the "8-8-88 Uprising," SLORC replaced the BSPP with the National Unity Party (NUP) and allowed the registration of other political parties. Although 93 political parties contested the 1990 election, only the NLD and a few ethnic or pro-regime parties survived the authoritarian crackdown that followed the elections.

Following the passage of the 2008 Constitution, political parties regained a central role in Myanmar's politics. Art. 39 of the constitution prescribes a multiparty system for the Union, although parties can be banned for "treasonous" activities, abuse of religion for political purposes, or for "directly or indirectly receiving and expending financial, material, and other assistance from a foreign government, a religious association, other association or a person from a foreign country" (Art. 407). Buddhist monks, civil servants and state employees, and members of the *Tatmadaw* cannot join a political party. Political parties who want to contest elections must register with the election commission. Requirements for registration are quite low—political parties must have at least 1000 members, possess 15 executive committee members, and run in at least three constituencies. Consequently, a total of 91 parties registered for the 2015 elections (Myanmar Times 2015). Most parties are small and many focus on their ethnic base; only USDP, NLD, NUP, and the National Democratic Force (NDF) have a national presence.

Two political cleavages have endured in the development of Myanmar's party system since the 1950s. The first one is the center–periphery conflict; the second one is the conflict between pro-military and pro-democracy parties. Accordingly, political parties can be grouped into three blocks, although voting patterns in the Union parliament and party alliances at the state and regional level cut across block lines (Oo 2014).

First, the block of pro-military parties includes the National Unity Party (NUP) and the USDP. SLORC created the NUP as an offshoot of the BSPP but dissolved the party after its poor showing in the 1990 elections. In 2010, former high-ranking members of the pre-1988 regime resurrected the NUP, but following an already weak performance in 2010, it failed to win any seats in 2015. The USDP is an offshoot of the Union Solidarity and Development Association (USDA), formed by the military in 1993 as a mass organization and the civilian arm of the junta. The USDP registered as a party in 2010, its leaders and candidates handpicked by the military junta. Originally, USDP reported more than 20 million members, and its leadership consisted mostly of retired military officers, USDA cadres, and local businessmen (Jones 2013, p. 159). Before 2015, the party dominated parliaments at the national and local level. Compared to other ruling parties in electoral authoritarian regimes in Southeast Asia such as the People's Action Party in Singapore, the Cambodian People's Party, or the UMNO in Malaysia, the USDP is weakly institutionalized and failed to emancipate itself from its perception as a political tool of the *Tatmadaw*. While its MPs had 5 years to build support in their constituencies and benefited from government support, the 2015 elections brought a crushing defeat (cf. Table 7.2).

The majority of political parties belongs to the second, heterogeneous group of ethnic and regional parties. The ethnic parties try to coordinate their activities and position on key issues, for example, through the Nationalist Brotherhood Federation, which is a coalition of 25 minority parties. Even though many of these parties also contest national elections, their focus is primarily on the elections for the legislative assemblies of the ethnic minority states, where the nationally oriented parties are relatively weak. For example, most of the 23 parties achieved representation in at least one of the state or regional parliaments in 2010, but most parties also contested the elections in only one state or region (Yhome 2011; Nixon et al. 2013). Some minority parties align themselves with rebel groups. As with most political parties in Myanmar, their intra-party politics are personalized, informal, and elite-centered (Thawngmung 2012). Most ethnic parties are not clearly aligned along the authoritarianism versus democracy cleavage that separates pro-military parties and the NLD (Oo 2014; Nilsen 2013, pp. 123–124).

The third group of political parties comprises parties, that trace their origins to the 1988 student movement and the 1990 election, and includes several small or tiny parties, the NLD, and the NDF, the latter of which broke away from the NLD in 2010. The parties in this group compete for votes particularly in the Bamar-dominated constituencies (Nilsen 2013, p. 132). Even though all of these parties demand the further democratization of the political regime, their preferred strategies and the details of their preferred democratic institutions differ (Nilsen 2013, p. 131). Whereas the NDF aimed to play a role as a "third force" between the USDP and the NLD, it suffered a defeat in the 2015 election and failed to win any seats. The NLD was established by reform-oriented military officers, politicians, and democracy activists in September 1988 (Yhome 2011, pp. 8–9). Lead by Aung San Suu Kyi, the party won 80% of parliamentary seats in 1990. Soon after the election, however, the party was repressed, its leader placed under house arrest, and many of its members and leaders arrested or driven underground or into exile (Zöllner 2012). In the aftermath, the NLD created alliances with different ethnic parties and participated in a government-in-exile that was initially successful at generating international support. The party boycotted the 2010 election but reregistered for the by-elections in 2012. While the party advocates a nonviolent transition to multiparty democracy and has reopened party offices in most constituencies, its strength lies mostly in the popularity of Aung San Suu Kyi (Zöllner 2012, p. 479; Jones 2013, p. 166).

7.7 State Administration

Myanmar is a centralized unitary state. There are two tiers of government: the central government and the governments of the seven regions and seven states. Whereas the regions have Bamar-majority populations, the populations of the states are composed of mostly ethnic minorities. Despite the terminology distinguishing historically existing ethnic states from Bamar-majority regions, states and regions are constitutionally equivalent. Under the 2008 Constitution, state and regional governments consist of a partially elected unicameral parliament (*hluttaw*), an executive led by a chief minister, a cabinet of state or region ministers, and state or region judicial institutions. The *hluttaw* is composed of two elected members per township, representatives of "national races," and appointed military representatives making up one quarter of the total representatives. The chief minister is selected by the president from among elected or unelected *hluttaw* members and is confirmed by the *hluttaw*. The state or regional minister for border and security affairs is a military officer nominated by the commander-in-chief (Nixon et al. 2013, v).

Below states and regions are the administrative levels of 67 districts and six autonomous regions of the Shan State as well as 325 townships. The latter are the critical building blocks of the national administration (Saw and Arnold 2014). The townships consist of village tracts and village or municipal quarters (see Fig. 7.2).

The General Administration Department (GAD) of the Ministry of Home Affairs (MOHA) supports coordination and communication among the Union government's ministries and connects the capital, Naypyitaw, to approximately 16,000 wards and village tracts. The GAD also provides administrative support to the Union territory of Naypyidaw. However, its primary responsibility is the management of Myanmar's public administrative structures. Governments in the regions and states rely upon the GAD to serve as their civil service. Civil servants are under the supervision of local governments, but their personnel management is directly managed by the MOHA and they are responsible for and accountable to both local governments and the MOHA. Functions and responsibilities of local governments are relatively small compared to the central government. Furthermore, local governments lack human resources and suffer from weak bureaucratic and financial capacities (Saw and Arnold 2014).

Population data is unreliable and contested in Myanmar but does show wide variation in the populations of different states and regions. Levels of socioeconomic development and armed conflict also vary widely (see Table 7.3). Despite their wealth of natural resources, ethnic states are generally poorer and underdeveloped relative to the Bamar regions and some have suffered decades of armed conflict (Smith 2007).

The constitution lists the policy domains over which subnational governments have legislative powers. The specified responsibilities are quite narrow and exclude major areas such as health, education, energy, mining, and forestry (Nixon et al. 2013, pp. 13, 53). The territorial units lack financial resources, and the central government has reserved the authority to tax all major sources of revenue. Together with an insufficient system of national transfer payments, less than 5% of overall government expenditure originates from the subnational level (Nixon et al. 2013, viii). High levels of political, administrative, and fiscal centralization contrast with weak administrative, fiscal, and infrastructural state capacities (Englehart 2005). For example, government revenues have been exceptionally low: Although total revenues (excluding transfers from SOEs) as a percentage of GDP increased from

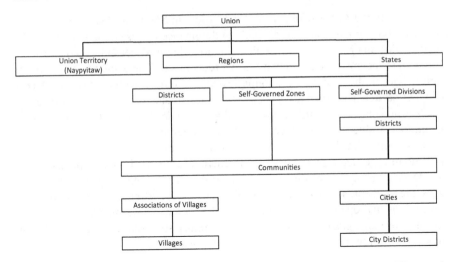

Fig. 7.2 Territorial organization of Myanmar. Source: Authors' compilation based on Nixon et al. (2013)

Table 7.3 Regional asymmetries in Myanmar

	Population (2010, in million)	Intensity of armed conflict (2000–2009)[a]	% of population in poverty (1997)[b]
Regions			
Ayeyawdy (Irawadi)	6.3	8.0	22.7
Bago	4.8	10.0	24.7
Magway	4.1	10.0	37.9
Mandalay	5.8	–	22.2
Sagaing	5.1	12.33	24.9
Taninthayi	1.4	12.33	8.1
Yangon	5.9	9.75	16.7
States			
Chin	0.5	8.0	42.1
Kachin	1.4	10.0	10.1
Kayah	0.3	10.5	35.4
Kayin	1.4	12.18	12.7
Mon	2.1	12.0	19.9
Rakhaing	3.2	12.25	22
Shan	4.5	11.03	12

[a]Average regional intensities from 2000 to 2009. Regional intensity is the sum of five indicators (type and use of armament, number of involved personnel, fatalities and refugees, and destruction) measured on a scale from one to three for each unit, month, and type of armed conflict between state and non-state actors. Higher scores indicate higher levels of violence
[b]National poverty line
Source: Shein and Myint (2001), Nixon et al. (2013, p. 10), Trinn (2015)

5.6 (2009) to 9.3 (2014–15), it is still the lowest in Southeast Asia (OECD 2014, pp. 167–168). Bureaucratic inertia and the dominance of vested interests make the civil service an obstacle for the implementation of policy measures on the ground. In contrast, coercive state capacity is overdeveloped. The *Tatmadaw* claims the lion's share of the country's economic resources as the government spends 4.18% of GDP on defense expenditure and military commanders are in control of many state-owned enterprises (IISS 2014). In addition, under the SLORC/SPDC government, the military fired several thousand government officials suspected of sympathizing with the democracy movement and transferred most administrative tasks to military-led Local Order Reconstruction Councils (LORC, renamed Peace and Development Councils in 1997; Than 2006, p. 221). Political liberalization and ceasefire agreements with many rebel groups have strengthened non-military institutions and opened contested areas to the national government. However, so far there are no signs of a comprehensive administrative reform that could disempower local military commanders and regional warlords.

7.8   Civil-Military Relations

Burma/Myanmar is the paradigmatic case of a "praetorian state" that emerges in countries with low levels of political institutionalization and high levels of political mobilization, fragmented political parties and civilian elites, and a politically self-conscious military. The mismatch between the organizational strength of the *Tatmadaw* and the weak institutionalization of civilian organizations as well as the lack of sustained support for democratic structures was key for political developments after 1948, in which the military played a highly significant role in key political structures and institutions, acting either as the actual ruler (1958–60, 1962–1974, 1988–2011) or controlling politics behind the scenes through a chosen civilian agent (1974–1988 and 2011–2016).

The extraordinary durability of military rule and the fact that the *Tatmadaw* was able to initiate a top-down transition in which it carved out political autonomy, substantial policy prerogatives, and veto powers contrasts with the experiences of other military regimes in Southeast Asia and in other world regions. Generally, military dictatorships are highly unstable and short-lived, as they usually lack the organizational strength to govern and maintain power and are prone to intra-military conflicts (Geddes 1999; Ezrow and Frantz 2011). The enigma of durable military rule in Myanmar lies in the ability of military elites to create a well-organized and cohesive military institution, solving credible commitment problems between military factions and maintaining respect for hierarchy among officers. More specifically, three factors helped the *Tatmadaw* avoid the characteristic instability of military regimes. First, military rule in Myanmar was the result of a "corporative coup" (Brooker 2009): The 1962 coup and the installment of the SLORC in 1988 were supported by key military elites, and the military junta included all services and relevant power groups within the *Tatmadaw*. Moreover, both the Revolutionary Council established after 1962 and the SLORC were composed entirely of military officers loyal to Ne Win (Steinberg 2001; Callahan 2005). The resulting "hierarchical military regimes" (Linz and Stepan 1996) managed to institutionalize power-sharing arrangements between different military partial elites, which made sure no individual faction would be able to undermine the power base of the military government within the military-as-institution (Croissant and Kamerling 2013). This immunized the regime against possible countercoups.

Second, the military government established a buffer of legitimacy after 1962 by creating mass organizations like the BSPP and, after 1988, the USDA/USDP, stressing the military's leadership on the "Burmese way to socialism" and the struggle to defend the nation against separatist insurgencies in the periphery. Following the "8-8-88 Uprising," the *Tatmadaw* successfully recalibrated its own strategy of legitimation. It gave up any socialist claim of transforming society in favor of a limited phase of military transitional rule by the SLORC/SPDC with the official aim of establishing a "disciplined democracy" (Taylor 2005, p. 21). The creation of new military and political institutions also allowed the government to monitor and control society. Immediately after taking power in 1988, SLORC created a new institutional structure that extended direct and complete military control over the political system. While day-to-day governance was conducted by a prime minister and his cabinet, all cabinet posts with the exception of health and education were held by military officers (Taylor 2009, p. 394). The police were reorganized and put under the direct control of the *Tatmadaw* (Than 2006, p. 225). Following the 1990 elections, the military tried to improve its relations with the wider population through the Union Solidarity and Development Association, which played an important role for the political indoctrination of the population, the creation of paramilitary units, and the repression of political dissidents (Hlaing 2004, p. 406; Taylor 2006; see below). The regime also expanded its propaganda activities to portray the military as the only reliable and functioning national institution (Than 2006, p. 245; Steinberg 2007, p. 126).

Third, the different military governments managed to alleviate the tensions between the interests of the military-in-government and the military-as-institution that make military regimes prone to collapse (cf. Geddes 1999). Geddes argues that a military with an intact chain of command and institutional autonomy values the survival and unity of the military institution over the survival of the military regime. Because controlling the helms of government often create rivalries within the military, "military regimes carry the seed of their own destruction" (Geddes 1999, p. 131). Even though the *Tatmadaw* has also suffered from latent factional conflict, these were always defused before they could threaten military cohesion or regime survival (Hewison and Nyein 2009, p. 26). The junta included between 19 and 21 officers, including members of the army, navy, air force, and the Directorate of Defence Services Intelligence (DDSI) as well as most of the 12 regional commanders (Selth 2002, pp. 51, 59; Min 2008, p. 1024; Steinberg 2010, p. 82). DDSI became the most important government instrument for opposition surveillance and the internal affairs of the *Tatmadaw*. Finally, the army was modernized and military units were stationed in strategic locations all over the country (Myoe 2007). In addition, the military government tried to co-opt different rebel groups and strengthened direct military control over the most lucrative branches of the national economy (Bünte 2008) but allowed regional commanders and military units to pursue their own business interests (Myoe 2007; Hewison and Nyein 2009, p. 27; Jones 2013, p. 149).

Through all this, the junta managed to preserve the coherence of the military institution with the help of several counter-strategies. These included frequent personnel rotations, the appointment of loyal commanders for key positions, and the co-optation of potential military counter-elites (Kühn and Croissant 2011, p. 147). Moreover, the scholarship on the *Tatmadaw* has long emphasized the fact that, despite the dominance of Bamar senior officers at the highest levels of the Burmese army, racial background has been less of an issue in promotions than social and religious backgrounds. Rakhine, Mon, and Shan officers could indeed reach the ranks of colonel and above, as long as they could prove that they were Buddhist, well-educated, and wed to similarly educated spouses (Egreteau 2015c, p. 349). The military strengthened the authority of the commander-in-chief, enhanced the position of the Ministry of Defence, and placed elite combat units under the control of the Bureau for Special Operations (Callahan 2005, p. 211). Prior to 2004, the military junta also relied on DDSI to monitor military units (Fink 2009, pp. 168–170), but conflicts between military intelligence and other military services led to a purge of the clique around the chief of military intelligence, Khin Nyunt, and the installation of a new intelligence service, the Military Affairs Security (Min 2008, pp. 1028–1030). Ideological indoctrination was meant to increase the *esprit de corps* among officers and troops (Fink 2009, pp. 153–155). In addition, their families and retirees enjoyed access to a system of material incentives, including welfare, health, and education services as well as privileged access to foodstuff and rare goods. Overall, more than 2 million people, or about 4% of the population, enjoy these advantages and other benefits (Steinberg 2010, p. 101).

7.9   Political Culture, Civil Society, and Media System

So far, neither the World Values Survey nor the Asia Barometer Survey has published comprehensive data on the political beliefs, values, and motivations of the people of Myanmar (but see Welsh and Huang 2016 for preliminary ABS results). Indirect measures such as the frequency of demonstrations and public mass protests, political performance data, and election results in which opposition parties contested indicate that large parts of the population appear to not support the military's claim to political leadership. Rather, mass protests in 1988 ("8-8-88 Uprising") and 2007 ("Saffron Revolution") and the NLD's landslide victory in 1990 and 2015 support the view that the *Tatmadaw* has been rather unsuccessful in engendering and maintaining the popular belief that military-controlled political institutions are the most appropriate for Myanmar's society. Yet, weak support for the military government does not necessarily mean strong support for democracy.

As documented in the first nationwide survey of Myanmar conducted by the Asia Foundation among more than 3000 respondents across all 14 states and regions in 2014, public knowledge and awareness of government institutions and processes are poor. More than 80% of respondents are unable to name any branches of government, and most people have no knowledge about the selection or appointment processes for key government positions, including the parliament and the president of the Union and the chief minister of their state or regional government. While people appear to be cautiously optimistic about the direction in which the country is heading, the level of optimism is markedly higher in the Bamar majority regions than in the ethnic states (Asia Foundation 2014). As in most countries of Southeast Asia, people express a strong preference for abstract democracy, but possess a limited understanding of the principles and practices that underpin a democratic system. While 37% of Burmese stress equality as an essential element of democracy, less than a quarter name procedure, freedom, or good governance, and almost three quarters of respondents oppose the principle of horizontal accountability (Welsh and Huang 2016, pp. 30, 32). Finally, social trust is low and political disagreements are deeply polarizing (Asia Foundation 2014).

Civil society structures in Myanmar traditionally existed at the local level within religious groups, emerging from Buddhist and Christian-initiated social welfare activities that focused on social service delivery. Particularly in areas of armed conflict, such groups often filled the state's service-delivery role (ADB 2015). In precolonial times, Burma had numerous informal solidarity associations and self-help networks. Some of these exist until today or have evolved into contemporary forms of societal self-organization (Kramer 2011, p. 6). The origins of "modern" civil society—understood as an intermediary sphere of voluntary organizations that publicly articulate and organize societal interests, values, and demands autonomously from the state (Croissant 2000, p. 16)—emerged in colonial times (Hewison and Nyein 2009, p. 17). Since political associations were banned, Buddhist groups like the Young Men's Buddhist Association (YMBA) and student associations became pioneers of political civil society (Steinberg 1999, pp. 4–5; Hlaing 2004; Hewison and Nyein 2009). In addition, Christian organizations gained importance among ethnic minorities and contributed to the creation of formal organizations, such as the Karen National Association created in 1881 (Kramer 2011; Taylor 2009, p. 156). Inspired by examples in British India and resonating with the urban population, various "modern" associations emerged in the first half of the twentieth century, including charitable organizations, interest groups, worker unions, and cultural or civic associations (Steinberg 2001, p. 106; Kramer 2011, p. 7).

While Burma did have a relatively lively civil society compared to many other countries in Southeast Asia, the military junta in 1962 relied on several tools of repression and co-optation to suppress any form of political dissent or associational pluralism. In the following years, the military either disbanded existing organizations or forced them to join various front organizations of the BSPP. The military also barred the establishment of non-registered associations, whereas Buddhist monasteries and monks (*sangha*) were obliged to register with the Ministry of Religious Affairs. Monasteries were infiltrated with informants, but the military also hoped to win *sangha* acceptance through generous donations (Smith 1991; Matthews 1993; Hlaing 2004, p. 393; Kramer 2011, p. 8). Yet, the government never tried to enforce a complete monopoly on associational life. Community-based and Christian-led organizations were allowed to continue their apolitical social welfare activities (Seekins 2005; Lorch 2006). The existence of some groups from pre-authoritarian times, including the Union of Burma Chamber of Commerce and Industry (UBCCI) and the All-Burma Young Monks' Association, were condoned at least tacitly because the military did not perceive them as a threat (Hlaing 2004, p. 394; Kramer 2011, p. 11). In addition, students, teachers, and university lecturers organized clandestine discussion groups in monasteries or private apartments that helped spread opposition literature and alternative political thinking (Hlaing 2004, pp. 395–396).

In spite of repression, including a rigid command system that managed people's lives and systematic surveillance through networks of informers (Fink 2001), there were a number of demonstrations and protests against military rule over the years, with the biggest explosions of public frustration in 1988 and 2007 (Schock 2005; Chenoweth and Stephan 2013). Following the 1988 uprising, hard repression, including abductions, murder, and incarceration of civil society activists, made oppositional civil society activity all but impossible. At the same time, SLORC replaced BSPP with new mass organizations, including the Union Solidarity and Development Association. USDA forcibly organized up to 12% of the population and became the new source of paramilitary groups and repression against the opposition (ICG 2001, p. 10; Hlaing 2004, p. 406). The junta tried to limit the political clout of the *sangha* by creating new control mechanisms meant to monitor the admission, education, and conduct of the 300,000 Buddhist monks in Myanmar (Matthews 1993; Lorch 2006, p. 16). Local and international NGOs could engage in village-level social services delivery if local military commanders decided to tolerate them, but all NGO activity above the village-level had to acquire a license (Lidauer 2012, p. 94). Despite these pressures, there were more than 200,000 community-based service providers and almost 300 local NGOs in Myanmar at the beginning of the twenty-first century (South 2009; McCarthy 2012, pp. 4–5). After Cyclone Nargis in 2008, many new organizations emerged and operated in a legal gray area because they eschewed the difficulties of applying for registration with the state (Lidauer 2012, pp. 89, 95).

The transition from military rule towards a less repressive political order since 2008 triggered a resurrection of civil society activity in Myanmar, although this was a consequence probably unintended by the military (Lidauer 2012, p. 89). In addition, domestic civil society is increasingly networked into the international development and rights-based communities. The legalization of independent trade unions, better protections for the freedom of assembly and association, the abolishment of censorship, and the creation of a national human rights commission and a national press council are other tangible results of the recent reforms. A pluralist media is emerging and there is relatively broad space for critical reporting (Wagstaff 2010; Holliday 2013, p. 95). While internet and social media still play a relatively minor role in Myanmar, as only 22.4% of the population has access to the internet (Internet World Stats 2017), radio remains the most popular source of information. Radio stations and public television are monitored by the Information Ministry and the *Tatmadaw*, but foreign radio broadcast can be received easily in many parts of the country and enjoy a large audience (Wagstaff 2010, pp. 13–15). Myanmar's position in the World Press Freedom Index improved from rank 171 in 2009 to 131 in 2017, placing it ahead of Malaysia and Singapore (Reporters without Borders 2017). The Freedom House ranking Freedom of the Press also documents an improvement, moving Myanmar from 193rd place of the 195 countries in the sample to 161st place among 199 countries and territories (Freedom House 2015).

Yet, civil society organizations still face many legal and informal constraints, and the expansion of civil society is not without its own contradictions. On the one hand, hundreds of Burmese exiles have returned to the country over the last few years after the government invited dissidents to come home and removed more than 2000 names from its blacklist. This contributed to latent tensions and sometimes manifest conflicts between more "politically" oriented exiles and domestic activists over how to cooperate and to what extent to collaborate with the then still military-dominated government (Kramer 2011, p. 28). On the other hand, divisive groups have taken advantage of the new political and media freedoms to pursue a nationalist or xenophobic agenda that threatens the country's Muslim minority (Lee 2016). For example, since 2012, Buddhist groups have played a role in the creation of the "969 movement,"[3] an extremist group that is believed to have organized anti-Islamic protests in the country and to have escalated tensions between Buddhists and Muslim minorities in the northern Rakhine State (ICG 2013; Than 2014, p. 28). The movement was renamed the Patriotic Association of Myanmar after its original name was declared illegal and championed four controversial laws passed in 2015 in the name of "protection for race and religion." These included a law on population control, interfaith marriage, monogamy, and religious conversion (McCarthy 2016).

7.10 Outlook

The two key challenges of political development in postcolonial Burma have been center–periphery conflicts resulting from unsolved problems of state- and nation-building and the institutionalization of stable and effective civilian political structures. The failure to integrate ethnic minorities into the postcolonial nation-state has resulted in numerous and persistent intrastate conflicts between the state and ethnic rebel groups. Sixty years or so of intrastate conflict, in turn, have contributed to a notoriously weak state that not only lacks the monopoly on the use of force in some areas but whose administrative structures barely reach beyond central Myanmar and into the peripheral territories of the ethnic states (Dukalskis 2009; Englehart 2005; Yhome 2011; Nilsen 2013, p. 116). Failed nation-building

---

[3]The numbers symbolize the nine attributes of Buddha, the six elements of Buddhist teachings, and the nine attributes of the *sangha* (ICG 2013).

and center–periphery conflicts are closely related to the second problem: the relationship between the military, society, and politics. The failure of civilian institutions to integrate ethnic minorities and insurgencies at the periphery provided motive and opportunity for military intervention and the long-lasting rule of the *Tatmadaw*. At the same time, the military's strategy of coercive state-building has undermined civilian state institutions and further eroded interethnic trust and center–periphery relations.

Weak public infrastructure, widespread extreme poverty, and the exploitation of Myanmar's natural resources by a small group of regime beneficiaries will impede a comprehensive transition towards constitutional democracy. Nevertheless, the country's political system is much less repressive and provides more space for political parties, civil society, and the media as well as more autonomy for ethnic minorities than at any point in the last five decades. Still, Myanmar is far from completing its "first transition" (O'Donnell 1992) from an authoritarian government towards a democratically elected one and will not face the "second transition" towards a consolidated democratic regime in the near future. Considering the economic strength and autonomy of the *Tatmadaw*, the cohesive character of the military institution, its control over the most powerful ministries—Home Affairs, Border Affairs, and Military Affairs—and the fact that the constitution is designed to be impossible to change without the military's approval, it is unrealistic to expect the new NLD-led government to control its military. Yet, Myanmar's political liberalization also brings new uncertainties for political stability and the fragile interethnic peace. The first challenge is the subversive consequences of the new representative institutions. Even though the 2008 Constitution enshrines significant political prerogatives and autonomy for the military, it also limits the power of the generals. Overstepping these new boundaries in case of a conflict between civilian and military regime elites or between the government and the opposition would be costly and might destabilize the political transformation that is currently under way. Furthermore, military leaders will have to control centrifugal tendencies within the *Tatmadaw*. In the past, the regime managed to subdue regional commanders and preserve the institutional coherence of the armed forces. There are, however, latent tensions among different patronage networks as well as between senior officers and the ranks because the latter never partook in the appropriation of the country's economic resources (Englehart 2012, p. 675). The co-optation of most rebel groups has eliminated the common enemies that helped unify the military in the past (Williams 2011, p. 1206). In addition, the ceasefire agreements have triggered the emergence of distinct rentier economies in the border areas (Jones 2013, 2014) but have done little to solve tensions between the center and the periphery or the underlying grievances among the many ethnic minorities (Englehart 2005). Finally, political liberalization and the institutionalization of political contestation has not only resulted in a "resurrection of civil society" (O'Donnell and Schmitter 1986) but has also created ethno-nationalist, xenophobic, and violent groups and has contributed to sectarian violence, as reflected in mass violence against the country's Muslim minority.

References

ADB. (2015). *Civil society briefs Myanmar*. Nay Pyi Taw: Asian Development Bank.

Asia Foundation. (2014). *Myanmar 2014: Civic knowledge and values in a changing society*. San Francisco: Asia Foundation.

Bellwood, P. (1999). Southeast Asia before history. In N. Tarling (Ed.), *Cambridge history of Southeast Asia: Vol. I, Part 1* (pp. 55–136). Cambridge: Cambridge University Press.

Bigelow, L. S. (1960). The 1960 election in Burma. *Far Eastern Survey, 29*, 70–74. https://doi.org/10.2307/3024046

Brooker, P. (2009). *Non-democratic regimes* (2nd ed.). Houndmills, Basingstoke: Palgrave Macmillan.

Bünte, M. (2008). *Myanmar: Autoritarismus im Wandel*. GIGA Fokus Asien 07/2008. Hamburg: GIGA.

Butenschøn, N. A., Stiansen, Ø., & Vollan, K. (2015). *Power-sharing in conflict-ridden societies: Challenges for building peace and democratic stability*. New York: Routledge.

Callahan, M. P. (2001). Myanmar: Soldiers as state builders. In M. Alagappa (Ed.), *Coercion and governance: The declining political role of the military in Asia* (pp. 413–429). Stanford: Stanford University Press.

Callahan, M. P. (2005). *Making enemies: War and state building in Burma*. Ithaca, NY: Cornell University Press.

Callahan, M. P. (2012). The generals loosen their grip. *Journal of Democracy, 23*, 120–131. https://doi.org/10.1353/jod.2012.0072

Carr, A. (2017). *Psephos: Adam Carr's election archive*. Retrieved June 10, 2017, from http://psephos.adam-carr.net/

Charney, M. W. (2009). *A history of modern Burma*. Cambridge: Cambridge University Press.

Cheesman, N. (2009). Thin rule of law or un-rule of law in Myanmar? *Pacific Affairs, 82*, 597–613. https://doi.org/10.5509/2009824597

Cheesman, N. (2011). How an authoritarian regime in Burma used special courts to defeat judicial independence. *Law & Society Review, 45*, 801–830. https://doi.org/10.1111/j.1540-5893.2011.00457.x

Chenoweth, E., & Stephan, M. J. (2013). *Why civil resistance works: The strategic logic of nonviolent conflict*. New York: Columbia University Press.

CIA. (2017). *The world factbook*. Langley: Central Intelligence Agency.

Croissant, A. (2000). Zivilgesellschaft und transformation: Ein internationaler vergleich. In W. Merkel (Ed.), *Systemwechsel 5: Zivilgesellschaft und Transformation* (pp. 9–49). Opladen: Leske & Budrich.

Croissant, A. (2015). Southeast Asian militaries in the age of democratization: From ruler to servant? In W. Case (Ed.), *Routledge handbook of Southeast Asian democratization* (pp. 314–332). London: Routledge.

Croissant, A. (2016). *Electoral politics in Cambodia: Historical trajectories and current challenges*. Singapore: ISEAS.

Croissant, A., & Kamerling, J. (2013). Why do military regimes institutionalize?: Constitution-making and elections as political survival strategy in Myanmar. *Asian Journal of Political Science, 21*, 105–125. https://doi.org/10.1080/02185377.2013.823797

Crouch, M., & Lindsey, T. (2014). Introduction: Myanmar, law reform and Asian legal studies. In M. Crouch & T. Lindsey (Eds.), *Law, society and transition in Myanmar* (pp. 3–24). Oxford: Hart Publishing.

Dinmore, G., & Guyitt, W. (2015). Final results confirm scale of NLD election victory. Myanmar Times. Retrieved June 13, 2017, from http://www.mmtimes.com/index.php/national-news/17747-final-results-confirm-scale-of-nld-election-victory.html

Dressel, B., & Bünte, M. (2014). Constitutional politics in Southeast Asia: From contestation to constitutionalism? *Contemporary Southeast Asia, 36*(1), 1–22.

Dukalskis, A. (2009). Stateness problems or regime unification?: Explaining obstacles to democratization in Burma/Myanmar. *Democratization, 16*, 945–968. https://doi.org/10.1080/13510340903162119

Egreteau, R. (2015a). *Military delegates in Myanmar's legislature: What do they do? What will they (continue to) do? ISEAS perspectives 25/2015.* Singapore: ISEAS.

Egreteau, R. (2015b). Myanmar: Transition, praetorian politics, and the prospects for democratic change. In W. Case (Ed.), *Routledge handbook of Southeast Asian democratization* (pp. 410–426). London: Routledge.

Egreteau, R. (2015c). Who are the military delegates in Myanmar's 2010–2015 union legislature? *Sojourn: Journal of Social Issues in Southeast Asia, 30*(2), 338–370.

Englehart, N. A. (2005). Is regime change enough for Burma?: The problem of state capacity. *Asian Survey, 45*, 622–644. https://doi.org/10.1525/as.2005.45.4.622

Englehart, N. A. (2012). Two cheers for Burma's rigged elections. *Asian Survey, 52*, 666–686. https://doi.org/10.1525/as.2012.52.4.666

Ezrow, N. M., & Frantz, E. (2011). *Dictators and dictatorships: Understanding authoritarian regimes and their leaders.* New York: Continuum.

Ferrara, F. (2003). Why regimes create disorder: Hobbes's dilemma during a Rangoon summer. *Journal of Conflict Resolution, 47*, 302–325. https://doi.org/10.1177/0022002703252366

Fink, C. (2001). *Living silence in Burma: Surviving under military rule.* New York: Zed Books.

Fink, C. (2009). *Living silence: Burma under military rule* (2nd ed.). Bangkok: Silkworm Press.

Frasch, T. (2001). Myanmar (Burma). In D. Nohlen, F. Grotz, & C. Hartmann (Eds.), *Elections in Asia and the Pacific: A data handbook, Vol. II: South East Asia, East Asia, and the South Pacific* (pp. 596–620). Oxford: Oxford University Press.

Freedom House. (2015). *Freedom of the press index 2014: Harsh laws and violence drive global decline.* Retrieved June 2, 2017, from https://freedomhouse.org/report/freedom-press/freedom-press-2015

Furnival, J. S. (1960). *The governance of modern Burma.* New York: Institute of Pacific Relations.

Geddes, B. (1999). What do we know about democratization after twenty years? *Annual Review of Political Science, 2*, 115–144. https://doi.org/10.1146/annurev.polisci.2.1.115

Gravers, M. (1999). *Nationalism as political paranoia in Burma: An essay on the historical practice of power* (2nd ed.). Richmond: Curzon.

Guyot, J. F. (1989). Burma in 1988: "Perestroika" with a military face. *Southeast Asian Affairs, 16*, 107–133.

Hewison, K., & Nyein, S. P. (2009). Civil society and political opposition in Burma. In C. Li & W. Hofmeister (Eds.), *Myanmar: Prospect for change* (pp. 13–34). Singapore: Konrad Adenauer Foundation.

Hlaing, K. Y. (2004). Burma: Civil society krirting the regime. In M. Alagappa (Ed.), *Civil society and political change in Asia: Expanding and contracting democratic space* (pp. 389–418). Stanford: Stanford University Press.

Holliday, I. (2013). Myanmar in 2012. *Asian Survey, 53*, 93–100. https://doi.org/10.1525/as.2013.53.1.93

Huang, R. L. (2013). Re-thinking Myanmar's political regime: Military rule in Myanmar and implications for current reforms. *Contemporary Politics, 19*, 247–261. https://doi.org/10.1080/13569775.2013.804149

IBA. (2012). *The rule of law in Myanmar: Challenges and prospects.* London: International Bar Association.

ICG. (2001). *Myanmar: The role of civil society.* Asia Report No. 27. Bangkok: International Crisis Group.

ICG. (2012). *Myanmar: Storm clouds on the horizon.* Asia Report No. 238. Jakarta: International Crisis Group.

ICG. (2013). *Not a rubber stamp: Myanmar's legislature in a time of transition.* Asia Briefing No. 142. Jakarta: International Crisis Group.

IFES. (2017). *Election guide: Union of Myanmar.* Retrieved June 26, 2017, from http://www.electionguide.org/countries/id/148/

IISS. (2014). *The Military balance 2014: International institute for strategic studies.* London: Oxford University Press.

Internet World Stats. (2017). *Internet usage statistics: World internet users and 2017 population stats.* https://www.internetworldstats.com/stats.htm

Jones, L. (2013). The political economy of Myanmar's transition. *Journal of Contemporary Asia, 44,* 144–170. https://doi.org/10.1080/00472336.2013.764143

Jones, L. (2014). Explaining Myanmar's regime transition: The periphery is central. *Democratization, 21,* 780–802. https://doi.org/10.1080/13510347.2013.863878

Jory, P. (2013). *On Myanmar's plural society* http://www.newmandala.org/on-myanmars-plural-society/

Kean, T. (2014). Myanmar's parliament: From scorn to significance. In N. Cheesman, N. Farrelly, & T. Wilson (Eds.), *Debating democratization in Myanmar* (pp. 43–75). Singapore: ISEAS.

Kramer, T. (2011). *Civil society gaining ground: Opportunities for change and development in Burma.* Amsterdam: Transnational Institute.

Kratoska, P., & Batson, B. (1999). Nationalism and modernist reform. In N. Tarling (Ed.), *Cambridge history of Southeast Asia: Vol. II, Part 1: From c. 1800 to the 1930s* (pp. 253–320). Cambridge: Cambridge University Press.

Kudo, T. (2011). *Results of the 2010 elections in Myanmar: An analysis.* Tokyo: Institute of Developing Economics.

Kühn, D., & Croissant, A. (2011). *Militär und zivile Politik* (Politikwissenschaften). München: Oldenbourg Wissenschaftsverlag.

Lee, R. (2016). The dark side of liberalization: How Myanmar's political and media freedoms are being used to limit Muslim rights. *Islam and Christian-Muslim Relations, 27,* 195–211. https://doi.org/10.1080/09596410.2016.1159045

Lidauer, M. (2012). Democratic dawn?: Civil society and elections in Myanmar 2010–2012. *Journal of Current Southeast Asian Affairs, 31*(2), 87–114.

Lintner, B. (1999). *Burma in revolt: Opium and insurgency since 1948* (2nd ed.). Chiang Mai: Silkworm Press.

Linz, J. J., & Stepan, A. C. (Eds.). (1996). *Problems of democratic transition and consolidation: Southern Europe, South America, and post-communist Europe.* Baltimore: Johns Hopkins University Press.

Lorch, J. (2006). Zivilgesellschaft in autoritären Staat: Der Fall Myanmar. *Südostasien aktuell, 25* (2), 5–34.

Lwin, S. (2014). *President to test new Constitutional Tribunal with eight laws.* Retrieved June 13, 2017, from http://www.mmtimes.com/index.php/national-news/9400-president-to-test-new-constitutional-tribunal-with-eight-laws.html

Matthews, B. (1993). Buddhism under a military regime: The iron heel in Burma. *Asian Survey, 33,* 408–423. https://doi.org/10.2307/2645106

McCarthy, S. (2012). *Civil society in Burma: From military rule to 'disciplined democracy'.* Griffith Asia Institute Regional Outlook Paper 37. Brisbane: Griffith University.

McCarthy, S. (2016). Myanmar in 2015: An election year. *Asian Survey, 56,* 138–147. https://doi.org/10.1525/as.2016.56.1.138

Min, W. (2008). Looking inside the Burmese military. *Asian Survey, 48,* 1018–1037. https://doi.org/10.1525/as.2008.48.6.1018

Minahan, J. (2015). *Ethnic groups of South Asia and the Pacific: An encyclopedia.* Santa Barbara: ABC-CLIO.

Myoe, M. A. (2007). A historical overview of political transition in Myanmar since 1988. Asia Research Institute Working Paper Series No. 95. Singapore: NUS.

Nardi, D. J. (2014). Finding justice scalia in Burma: Constitutional interpretation and the impeachment of Myanmar's constitutional tribunal. *Pacific Rim Law & Policy Journal, 3*(3), 631–680.

Negretto, G. L. (2013). Authoritarian constitution making. In T. Ginsburg & A. Simpser (Eds.), *Constitutions in authoritarian regimes, comparative constitutional law and policy* (pp. 83–110). New York: Cambridge University Press.

Nilsen, M. (2013). Will democracy bring peace to Myanmar? *International Area Studies Review, 16*, 115–141. https://doi.org/10.1177/2233865913492961

Nixon, H., Joelene, C., Saw, K. P. C., Lynn, T. A., & Arnold, M. B. (2013). *State and region governments in Myanmar*. Washington: Asia Foundation.

Nyein, S. P. (2009). Expanding military, shrinking citizenry and the new constitution in Burma. *Journal of Contemporary Asia, 39*, 638–648. https://doi.org/10.1080/00472330903076966

O'Donnell, G. A. (1992). Transitions continuities, and paradoxes. In S. Mainwaring (Ed.), *Issues in democratic consolidation: The new South American democracies in comparative perspective* (pp. 17–56). Notre Dame, IN: University of Notre Dame Press.

O'Donnell, G. A., & Schmitter, P. C. (1986). *Tentative conclusions about uncertain democracies*. Baltimore: Johns Hopkins University Press.

OECD. (2014). *Multi-dimensional review of Myanmar: Vol. 2: In-depth analysis and recommendations*. Paris: OECD.

Oo, Z. (2014). Emerging political parties in Myanmar. In W. Sachsenröder (Ed.), *Party politics in Southeast Asia: Organization, money, influence* (pp. 171–213). Singapore: ISEAS.

Osborne, M. E. (1990). *Southeast Asia: An illustrated history*. Ithaca: Cornell University Press.

Owen, N. G. (Ed.). (2005). *The emergence of modern Southeast Asia: A new history*. Honolulu: University of Hawai'i Press.

Poling, G., Nguyen, P., & Weatherby, C. (2014). *Myanmar's constitutional review committee shies away from needed changes*. Washington: Center for Strategic & International Studies.

Reporters without Borders. (2017). World press freedom index. RSF. Retrieved June 22, 2017, from https://rsf.org/en/ranking

Ricklefs, M. C. (2010). *A new history of Southeast Asia*. Basingstoke: Palgrave Macmillan.

Sakhong, L. H. (2012). *The 2008 constitution and ethnic issues: To what extent did it satisfy the aspirations of verious ethnic groups?* Burma Center for Ethnic Studies, Peace and Reconciliation Analysis Paper No. 5.

Saw, K. P. C., & Arnold, M. B. (2014). *Administering the state in Myanmar: An overview of the general administration department*. Discussion Paper No. 6. Yangon: Asia Foundation.

Schock, K. (2005). *Unarmed insurrections: People power movements in nondemocracies*. Minneapolis: University of Minnesota Press.

Seekins, D. M. (2005). Burma and U.S. sanctions: Punishing an authoritarian regime. *Asian Survey, 45*, 437–452. https://doi.org/10.1525/as.2005.45.3.437

Seekins, D. M. (2009). Myanmar in 2008: Hardship, compounded. *Asian Survey, 49*, 166–173. https://doi.org/10.1525/as.2009.49.1.166

Selth, A. (2002). *Burma's armed forces: Power without glory*. Norwalk: EastBridge.

Shein, N., & Myint, H. H. (2001). *The poverty ration in Myanmar*. Paper presented at the UNSD workshop on development indicators. Retrieved May 21, 2017, from http://www.nscb.gov.ph/events/ASEAN/papers/country/Myanmar%20.pdf

Sidel, J. (2013). Nationalism in post-indendence Southeast Asia: A comparative analysis. In J. Breuilly (Ed.), *The Oxford handbook of the history of nationalism* (pp. 472–495). Oxford: Oxford University Press.

Smith, M. J. (1991). *Burma: Insurgency and the politics of ethnicity*. London: Zed Books.

Smith, M. (2007). *State of strife: The dynamics of ethnic conflict in Burma* (Policy studies, Vol. 36). Washington: East-West Center.

Soe, P. (2014). *Review committee supports overturning article 436*. Retrieved June 13, 2017, from http://www.dvb.no/news/review-committee-supports-overturning-article-436-burma-myanmar/40902

South, A. (2009). *Ethnic politics in Burma*. London: Routledge.

Steinberg, D. (1999). A void in Myanmar: Civil society in Burma. In Burma Center Netherlands & Transnational Institute (Ed.), *Strengthening civil society in Burma: Possibilities and dilemmas for international NGOs* (pp. 1–14). Bangkok: Silkworm Press.

Steinberg, D. I. (2001). *Burma, the state of Myanmar*. Washington: Georgetown University Press.

Steinberg, D. I. (2007). Legitimacy in Burma/Myanmar: Concepts and implications. In N. Ganesan & K. Y. Hlaing (Eds.), *Myanmar: State society and ethnicity* (pp. 109–142). Singapore: ISEAS.

Steinberg, D. I. (2010). *Burma/Myanmar: What everyone needs to know*. New York: Oxford University Press.

Taylor, R. H. (1996). Elections in Burma/Myanmar: For whom and why? In R. H. Taylor (Ed.), *The politics of elections in Southeast Asia* (pp. 164–183). Cambridge: Woodrow Wilson Center Press.

Taylor, R. H. (2005). Pathways to the present. In K. Y. Hlaing, R. H. Taylor, & T. M. M. Than (Eds.), *Myanmar: Beyond politics to societal imperatives* (pp. 1–29). Singapore: ISEAS.

Taylor, R. H. (2006). 'One day, one fathom, bagan won't move': On the Myanmar road to a constitution. In T. Wilson (Ed.), *Myanmar's long road to national reconciliation* (pp. 3–28). Singapore: ISEAS.

Taylor, R. H. (2009). *The state in Myanmar* (2nd ed.). Honolulu: University of Hawai'i Press.

Taylor, R. H. (2012). Myanmar: From army rule to constitutional rule? *Asian Affairs, 43*, 221–236. https://doi.org/10.1080/03068374.2012.682367

Than, T. M. M. (2006). Myanmar: Military in charge. In N. J. Funston (Ed.), *Government and politics in Southeast Asia* (2nd ed., pp. 203–251). Singapore: ISEAS.

Than, T. M. M. (2009). Myanmar in 2008: Weathering the storm. *Southeast Asian Affairs, 1*, 195–222.

Than, T. M. M. (2014). Myanmar in 2013. *Asian Survey, 54*, 22–29. https://doi.org/10.1525/as.2014.54.1.22

Thawngmung, A. M. (2012). *The 'Other' Karen in Myanmar: Ethnic minorities and the struggle without arms*. Lanham: Rowman & Littlefield.

The Burma Fund. (2011). *Burma's 2010 elections: A comprehensive report*. New York: The Burma Fund.

The Guardian. (2016). *Aung San Suu Kyi to hold ministry in Myanmar's government*. http://www.burmalibrary.org/docs11/BurmaFund-Election_Report-text.pdf

Thein, M. (2004). *Economic development of Myanmar*. Singapore: ISEAS.

Transparency International. (2015). *Corruption perception index*. Retrieved June 1, 2017, from https://www.transparency.org/news/feature/corruption_perceptions_index_2016

Trinn, C. (2015). *Konflikt und Komplexität: Die Intensität innerstaatlicher Gewaltkonflikte in systemtheoretischer Perspektive*. Wiesbaden: Springer VS.

Wagstaff, J. (2010). *Southeast Asian media: Patterns of production and consumption*. Retrieved June 6, 2017, from https://www.opensocietyfoundations.org/sites/default/files/production-consumption-20100212.pdf

Welsh, B., & Huang, K.-P. (2016). *Myanmar's political aspirations & perceptions: 2015 Asian barometer survey report*. Taipeh: Center for East Asia Democratic Studies.

Williams, D. C. (2009). Constitutionalism before constitutions: Burma's struggle to build a new order. *Texas Law Review, 87*, 1658–1693.

Williams, D. C. (2011). Cracks in the firmament of Burma's military government: From unity through coercion to buying support. *Third World Quarterly, 32*, 1199–1215. https://doi.org/10.1080/01436597.2011.596753

World Bank. (2017a). *World development indicators*. http://data.worldbank.org/products/wdi

World Bank. (2017b). *Worldwide governance indicators*. http://data.worldbank.org/data-catalog/worldwide-governance-indicators

Yhome, K. (2011). Myanmar's changing political landscape: Key players and recent trends. *Strategic Trends, 1*(1), 1–16.

Zhu, X. (2009). Constitution in the scope of parliamentarism and authoritarianism: A comparative study on the 1947 and 2008 constitution of Myanmar/Burma. In C. Li & W. Hofmeister (Eds.), *Myanmar: Prospect for change* (pp. 35–53). Singapore: Konrad Adenauer Foundation.

Zöllner, H.-B. (2000). *Birma zwischen 'Unabhängigkeit zuerst - Unabhängigkeit zuletzt': Die birmanischen Unabhängigkeitsbewegungen und ihre Sicht der zeitgenössischen Welt am Beispiel der birmanisch-deutschen Beziehungen zwischen 1920 und 1948*. Hamburg: LIT Verlag.

Zöllner, H.-B. (2012). *The beast and the beauty: The history of the conflict between the military and Aung San Suu Kyi in Myanmar, 1988–2011, set in a global context*. Berlin: Regiospectra.

Philippines: People Power and Defective Elite Democracy

© Springer International Publishing AG 2018
A. Croissant, P. Lorenz, *Comparative Politics of Southeast Asia*,
https://doi.org/10.1007/978-3-319-68182-5_8

8.1 Historical Background

The Philippine archipelago consists of more than 7000 islands, about 800 of which are inhabited (see Table 8.1 for the Country Profile). First visited by the Spanish in 1521, the Conquest of Cebu in 1565 and Maynilad (renamed Manila) in 1570 initiated the era of Spanish rule over what is today the Republic of the Philippines. Precolonial Philippines was a loose agglomeration of cultural groups forming political units called *barangays* led by a *datu* (chieftain). Nevertheless, extending Spanish rule through lowland Luzon and the Visayas took many decades of combined military and missionary action, converting the population to Christianity in the process (Abinales and Amoroso 2005, pp. 27–29; McKenna 1998). For over two and half centuries, Spain commissioned the government administration of this outpost to the Viceroyalty of New Spain (Mexico). The Mexican War of Independence brought the end of Spanish rule and the galleon trade between Mexico and Manila in 1815; the Philippines received a seat in the Spanish Cortes and was placed under direct control from Madrid in 1821.

Before Spanish rule, the islands of the archipelago were never politically united, so that the Spanish had to create their own administrative structures. In addition, the Philippines was not profitable as a colony, as there were few tradeable natural resources and no direct trade with Spain. Therefore, the Castilian court could only provide very limited resources for the administration, economic development, and military security of its far-flung outpost in the Pacific. For the first 100 years, the

Table 8.1 Country profile

Population (2017)	Year of full national sovereignty	Form of government
104,256,076	1946	Republic
Total area	**Current constitution enacted**	**Head of state**
300,000 km^2	1987	Rodrigo Duterte (since 2016)
GDP p.c. (PPP, 2015)	**Official language**	**Head of government**
2904	Filipino, English	Rodrigo Duterte (since 2016)
Ethnic groups	**Democracy score (BTI 2016)**	**System of government**
Tagalog 28.1%, Cebuano 13.1%, Ilocano 9%, Bisaya/Binisaya 7.6%, Hiligaynon Ilonggo 7.5%, Bikol 6%, Waray 3.4%, other 25.3%	6.8 (range from 1 to 10, higher scores indicate higher levels of democracy)	Presidential
Religious groups	**Regime type**	**Cabinet type**
Catholic 82.9%, Muslim 5%, Evangelical 2.8%, Iglesia ni Kristo 2.3%, other Christian 4.5%, other/non/unspecified 2.5%	Defective democracy	Multiparty coalition

Sources: CIA (2017), World Bank (2017a)

Spanish governor-general exercised his rule in most areas through a type of tax farming imported from the Americas, known as the *encomienda* (from *encomendar*, "to trust"). In addition, colonial rule heavily relied on the Catholic Church and religious orders—especially Dominican friars—who together with secular state officials administered the colony. The result was a "clerical-secular state," or "friarocracy," in which Church and state were inseparably linked and civil servants, Catholic priests, and local elites closely collaborated (Abinales and Amoroso 2005, p. 67). By the end of the seventeenth century, the *encomienda* system was replaced by a provincial system of government (*alcaldias*, mayors), headed by judicial governors. Once the colony had been divided into provinces with relatively strong local governors, the king of Spain established a unitary system of government by naming a governor-general. The transformation of common land into private property and its accumulation by these elites created a stratum of indigenous landholders (*caciques*), many of whose descendants dominate local power structures until today (Atienza 2006, p. 441; Quimpo 2015).

Economic opening and liberalization after the end of the transcontinental trade in 1815 and the opening of the Suez Canal in 1869 that shortened travel time to Europe helped to bring new ideas to the Philippines and prompted the rise of the so-called *ilustrados*, enlightened members of the Filipino upper class who had studied in Europe. Filipino priests and the *ilustrados* became the standard bearers of a national movement that originally clamored for political reforms and adequate representation within the political institutions of the Spanish Kingdom and later for independence (Abinales and Amoroso 2005; Caoili 2006a, p. 251). In 1892, Filipino nationalists founded the *Katipunan*, a secret society whose primary goal was to overthrow Spanish rule. The Philippine Revolution began in 1896, but the declaration of the first Philippine Republic in June 1898 coincided with the defeat of the Spanish in the Spanish-American War. The Treaty of Paris (1898) transferred control of the Philippines, including its still unoccupied southern region of Muslim Mindanao, to the United States. In 1902, the U.S. Congress passed the Philippine Act, which installed a civilian administration supervised by an American governor-general. The Americans allowed limited self-rule, modernized the bureaucracy and the judicial system, and invested heavily in education, infrastructure, and economic development. Already in 1919, the share of Americans in the colonial administration was reduced to 6% (Abinales and Amoroso 2005, p. 140). Moreover, the per capita GDP of the Philippines increased from 699 USD in 1902 to 1587 USD in 1940, and by the 1930s, about 50% of the population had become literate (Maddison 2001, pp. 558–560).

New political and administrative structures such as an elected legislature co-opted local elites into the colonial system but also consolidated the decentralized nature of political power in the Philippines (Atienza 2006, p. 421). The passage of the Tydings-McDuffie Act of 1934 and the inauguration of the Philippine Commonwealth under a democratic constitution patterned after the United States' bicameral system in 1935 laid the groundwork for the transition to full sovereignty. The roadmap to independence was interrupted by Japanese military occupation of the Philippines in 1942. Some Filipino elites collaborated with the Japanese under the puppet state of the Second

Philippine Republic, created in 1943, whereas the *Hukbalahap* (Huk), a guerrilla movement led by the *Partido Komunista ng Pilipinas* (PKP), fought against the Japanese (Kerkvliet 2002). After the war, the (Third) Republic of the Philippines was the first Western colony in Southeast Asia to become independent on July 4, 1946, even though the country remained closely associated with the U.S. militarily, economically, and politically.

The postcolonial political order was one where a handful of traditional political families effectively ruled a society driven by political and socioeconomic inequality. It was democratic in form, borrowing many American elements such as regular elections, a two-party system, a bicameral Congress, and a presidential system of government, but for the mass of Filipinos, democracy meant little more than elections every 4 years. Local politics remained the center of gravity in Philippine politics and here, traditional politicians (called *trapos*) dominated the political process through a mixture of collusion, clientelism, and coercion (Bello and Gershman 1990).

In 1965, Ferdinand Marcos became president. He became the first president to be reelected in 1969. Nearing the end of his second and last term as president, he declared martial law in 1972 and established a personalist authoritarian regime. Its ostensible goal of transforming the Philippines into a "New Society" through quick social reform turned out to be mere rhetoric. The constitution of 1973 never constrained Marcos's personalist rule, and the pro-Marcos *Kilusang Bagong Lipunan* (New Society Movement, KBL) did not develop into an organizationally mature institution and remained a façade party.

In the early 1980s, the Philippine economic situation deteriorated rapidly under the combined pressure from accelerating foreign debts, declining economic growth, and spiraling inflation, caused by a combination of external shocks, government policy failures, and crony capitalism driven by the self-enrichment of Marcos and his ruling coalition (Dohner and Intal 1989). A parallel increase in communist guerilla activities and the failure of the government's counterinsurgency operations further aggravated the political crisis of the Marcos regime (Kessler 1989). As a result, urban middle classes, national businesses, worker unions, many representatives of the Catholic Church, and reform-minded government technocrats and officers in the Armed Forces of the Philippines (AFP) lost faith in the ability of the government to effectively deal with these challenges (Thompson 1995). The political crisis was further exacerbated by the assassination of opposition leader Benigno Aquino Jr. in August 1983. Marcos erroneously hoped to save his rule by calling snap elections in January 1986. Yet the opposition united behind the candidacy of Corazon Aquino, Benigno's widow. Following the presidential election on February 7, 1986, both Marcos and Aquino claimed victory. Disloyal troops under the command of General Fidel V. Ramos and Defense Minister Juan Ponce Enrile with support from junior officers of the Reform the Armed Forces Movement (RAM) led by Colonel Gregorio Honasan tried to take advantage of the political turmoil and set into motion a coup attempt against Marcos on February 22. While the coup failed, it triggered the People Power Revolution on the Epifanio de los Santos Avenue (or EDSA, the main highway of Metro Manila).

Confronted by mass protests and military defections, Marcos fled to exile in Hawaii with the strong encouragement of the American government.

Immediately after assuming the presidency, President Corazon Aquino established a revolutionary government and issued an interim constitution. A newly installed constitutional convention drafted a new basic law that was ratified by referendum in February 1987. Elections to the Philippine Congress in May and July 1987 completed the transition to democracy. Despite the restoration of democratic institutions, the enactment of freedom of the press, and the abolition of repressive laws, the transition from authoritarian rule to democracy also paved the way for the restoration of elite democracy and the reemergence of entrenched political families. For example, of those members of the House of Representatives elected in 1987, more than 83% were members of the same families and political dynasties who had dominated politics since the American period and the premartial law era (Gutierrez et al. 1992, pp. 159–161). The newly elected Senate had a similar sociological profile (Abinales and Amoroso 2005, p. 236).

The People's Power Revolution of 1986 occurred without the kind of elite pacts argued to have been crucial for the successful democratization of Indonesia (cf. Chap. 5). Nevertheless, elite settlement between different elite groups was pivotal for the survival of the "imperfect democracy" (Putzel 1999) after 1986. Shared social backgrounds, political socialization under Marcos, and economic interests provided a measure of elite cohesion, as well as the common understanding that an electoral democracy would serve elite interests much better than another authoritarian regime with a much narrower winning coalition. Yet, the emphasis on institutional checks and balances, institutionalized veto points, and diffusion of power has also limited effective governance, whereas the dominance of elite politics limited the value of elections as a mechanism to secure democratic accountability and ensure substantive representation (Holmes 2017). The electoral process thus remained "anarchic" (McCoy 1994) and prone to irregularities and violence. Political and non-state violence, corruption, crime, and collusion are also regular features of the country's political routine. Moreover, popular discontent with the political elite repeatedly culminated in mass protests against elected governments and the rise of populist leaders like Presidents Joseph Estrada (1998–2001) and Rodrigo Duterte (since 2016; Thompson 2011, 2017). Divisive politics and ongoing insurgencies in various parts of the country reflect the chronic weakness of Philippine democracy in successfully tackling problems relating to social, economic, and political inequality, both between social classes and between ethnic groups. In fact, vast segments of the population remain barred from equal access to economic opportunities and life chances in general. The Philippines is much less successful at fighting absolute poverty than most other Southeast Asian countries (ADB 2010, p. 143), and the country has turned into one of the largest exporters of cheap labor worldwide: About 10% of the country's population resides outside its national territories, often as Overseas Filipino Workers (OFWs). According to World Bank data, the contribution of remittances to the national GDP increased from 1.7% in 1977 to 10.2% in 2015 (World Bank 2017a). Yet, labor export as government policy also indicates the failure of consecutive governments to provide sufficient employment, a situation likely to deteriorate considering the rapid growth of the Philippine population (Rother 2009).

8.2 Constitutional Development

The constitutional history of the Philippines bears the hallmarks of American constitutionalism (Desirto 2009). Since 1899, the country has had six constitutions (Rebullida 2006a). The Commonwealth Constitution of 1935 followed the Malolos Constitution of the ephemeral First Philippine Republic (1899–1901). While the dominating influence was American, the 1935 Constitution also bore traces of the Malolos Constitution, the German Weimar Constitution, the Constitution of the Republic of Spain, the constitutions of several Latin American countries, and the unwritten British Constitution—all of which were consulted during the 1934 Constitutional Convention (Stevens 1993, p. 15). In order to legitimize his coup against the 1935 Constitution, President Ferdinand Marcos ordered a constitutional convention to draft a new basic law that was ratified by a constitutional plebiscite and obscure citizens' assemblies in 1973.[1] The Marcos Constitution replaced the presidential system of government and bicameralism with a semi-presidential system of government and introduced the position of a prime minister and a unicameral legislature (the *Batang Pambansa*). However, through a series of transitional regulations and amendments, ratified in the 1975 referendum, Marcos held on to existing presidential prerogatives and in 1977 secured the right to serve as both president and prime minister (Rebullida 2006b; Tigno 2006a). In March 1986, President Corazon Aquino proclaimed a transitional "Freedom Constitution" while a permanent constitution was to be drafted between June and October 1986 in a constitutional convention whose members were appointed by the president. The new constitution was approved in a referendum with a 77% majority and a turnout of 89% in February 1987 (Villacorta 1988).

The 1987 Constitution is a much more detailed document compared to previous constitutions. The text comprises 18 articles and several hundred sections, including 100 new sections that concern primarily social justice, the national economy, education, human resources, family rights, the Commission on Human Rights, and the autonomous regions of the Cordilleras and Muslim Mindanao. It is a very rigid constitution and contains numerous provisions that in other constitutional systems are embodied in statutes enacted by parliament. It even considers the sciences, technology, the arts, culture, and sports.

Political power is decentralized and the constitutional text provides for the establishment of elected representative bodies at the local level as well as in the autonomous regions of Muslim Mindanao and the Cordilleras. As in other post-authoritarian countries, the constitution is a direct reaction to the excesses of the old regime. There are new restrictions on the president's declaration of martial law and

---

[1]Technically, the constitution of the pro-Japanese Second Republic suspended the 1935 Constitution between 1943 to 1945.

the deployment of the AFP for domestic law enforcement. The power of the executive to suspend the writ of habeas corpus is subject to greater legislative and judicial review. Article II Section 26 of the Constitution prohibits political dynasties—often understood as families whose members have held public offices for several generations and often rely on substantial landed or business wealth to sustain and advance their political interests.[2] As a reaction to Marcos's plundering of state coffers by contracting foreign loans on behalf of state-owned enterprises controlled by himself or his cronies, the executive must seek approval from the president of the Central Bank of the Philippines before contracting foreign loans, who in turn is accountable to Congress (Rebullida 2006b, p. 191). Finally, Article XVII provides for three different modes of amending the constitution: (1) approval by a three-fourth majority in both houses of Congress; (2) by a constitutional convention to be called by a vote of two-thirds of all members of Congress, or alternatively, by a majority in both the Senate and House of Representatives plus approval of such a call in a referendum; (3) amendments directly proposed by the people through an initiative ("people's initiative") upon a petition of at least 12% of the total number of registered voters, of which every legislative district must be represented by at least 3% of the registered voters therein. In addition, a majority of votes cast in a plebiscite must ratify any amendment or revision of the constitution by any of the three procedures.[3] These rigid provisions, the lack of political agreement about possible constitutional amendments, and resistance from the Supreme Court have so far precluded any attempt to change the charter.

8.3   System of Government

The Philippines is "a democratic and republican state" (Art. II, Section 1) with a presidential system of government and a bicameral Congress. Judicial power is vested in the judiciary. Other state organs include the Civil Service Commission, the Commission on Elections (COMELEC), the Commission on Audit, and the Commission on Human Rights (Fig. 8.1).

8.3.1   Head of State and Government

The president is head of state and government. President and vice president are popularly elected by plurality rule for a 6-year term. The vice president is limited to

---

[2]Despite this constitutional provision, political dynasties are not defined by law.

[3]Technically, there is a difference between amendment and revision. Revision broadly implies a change that alters a basic principle in the constitution, i.e., the system of checks-and-balances. Amendment broadly refers to a change that adds, reduces, or deletes without altering the basic principle involved. A revision under the people's initiative is not allowed.

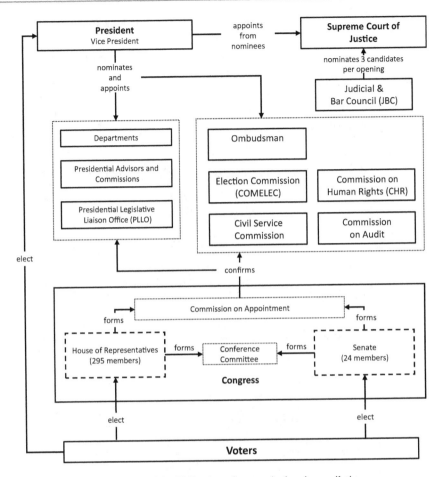

Fig. 8.1 Constitutional System of the Philippines. Source: Authors' compilation

two consecutive terms, whereas the president is barred from reelection unless (s)he succeeded to the office with less than 4 years remaining in the original term. In contrast to Indonesia, voters can choose a presidential candidate from one ticket and a vice president candidate from another ticket. In every election since 1992—except in 2004—candidates from competing tickets won (Table 8.2). The vice president succeeds the president if the latter can no longer fulfill his or her official duties for health reasons or is removed from office for the "culpable violation of the Constitution, treason, bribery, graft and corruption, other high crimes, or betrayal of public trust" (Art. XI, Section 2). Even though technically not member of the Cabinet, most presidents offer their vice presidents the chance to chair one or more government agencies or councils.

The following Table 8.3 compares the scores of presidential power in the two basic dimensions of presidential power (legislative/nonlegislative) identified by Shugart and Carey (1992, p. 150) under the constitutions of 1935, 1973, and

Table 8.2 Presidents, Vice Presidents and main electoral contenders in the Philippines, 1986–2016

Election	President	% Of popular vote	Vice President	% Of popular vote	Term of office
1986	Corazon Aquino[a]	–[b]	Salvador Laurel (UNIDO)	–[b]	25/02/1986–30/06/1992
	Ferdinand Marcos (KBL)	–[b]	Aturo Tolentino (KBL)	–[b]	
1992	Fidel V. Ramos (Lakas)	23.6	Joseph E. Estrada (PMP)	33.0	30/06/1992–30/06/1998
	Eduardo Cojuangco (NPC)	18.2	Emilio R. Osmeña (Lakas)	16.5	
1998	Joseph E Estrada (LAMMP)[c]	39.9	Gloria Macapagal Arroyo (Lakas)	49.6	30/06/1998–20/01/2001
	Jose Venecia (Lakas)	15.9	Edgardo J. Angara (LAMMP)	22.1	
…	Gloria Macapagal Arroyo (Lakas)[d]	–	–	–	20/01/2001–30/06/2004
2004	Gloria Macapagal Arroyo (K4)[e]	40.0	Noli de Castro	49.8	30/06/2004–30/06/2010
	Fernando Poe, Jr. (KNP)[g]	36.5	Loren Legarda (KNP)	46.9	
2010	Benigno C. Aquino (LP)	42.0	Jejomar Binay (PDP-Laban)[h]	41.6	30/06/2010–30/06/2016
	Joseph M Estrada (PMP)	26.2	Mar Roxas	39.5	
2016	Rodrigo Duterte, PDP–Lakas ng Bayan	39.0	Leni Robredo (LP)	35.1	30/06/2016–
	Mar Roxas (LP)	23.4	Bongbon Marcos (Indpendent)[i]	34.4	30/06/2016–

[a]Aquino ran on the ticket of the UNIDO opposition alliance and was supported by the LABAN (*Laban ng Bansa*) coalition in Congress
[b]No officially verified results available
[c]LAMMP (*Laban ng Makabayang Masang Pilipino*, Struggle of the Patriotic Filipino Masses) was an oppositional alliance of several political parties
[d]Inaugurated as president after Estrada's removal from office
[e]Coalition of Experience and Fidelity for the Future (K4) consisted of Lakas CMD, the Liberal Party, An NPC wing, and several smaller parties
[f]Independent candidate on Lakas ticket
[g]The Coalition for National Unity (KNP) consisted of LDP, PMP, KBL, and a NPC wing
[h]Simultaneously "guest candidate" of Estrada (PMP) for the vice presidency
[i]Member of Nationalist Party but ran as an independent
Source: Hartmann et al. (2001), Teehankee (2006), Kasuya (2008, pp. 157–158), Congress of the Philippines (2010), Carr (2017)

Table 8.3 Powers of the Philippine Presidency under the 1935, 1973, and 1987 constitutions

	1935	1973 (1981)[a]	1987
Legislative Powers (total)	8	13	7
Package Veto/Override	2	2	2
Line Item Veto/Override	3	3	3
Decree powers	1	2	0
Exclusive Introduction of Legislation	0	0	0
Budgetary powers	2	2	2
Proposal of referenda	0	4	0
Other Powers (total)	11	12	11
Cabinet Formation	3	4	3
Cabinet Dismissal	4	4	4
Censure	4	1	4
Dissolution of Legislature	0	3	0
Length of Term	4	6	6
Term Limit	2	None	1

Notes: see Chap. 4.31 for details on measurement
[a]Including amendments and transitional clauses passed in 1981. The president retained the prerogatives included in the 1935 constitution, could take over the office of prime minister, and was chosen in direct elections. Scores include the prerogatives of president and prime minister.
Source: Authors' compilation based on Chan Robles (2010)

1987. Shugart and Carey rate the relative authority of president and parliament according to 10 items. Any power is rated on a scale of 0–4 points. With a score of 7 in the first dimension, and 11 in the second, the president is less powerful under the 1987 Constitution than under previous constitutions.

The president has a suspensive veto against congressional bills and a line-item veto against individual items in the national budget and tax bills. Congress can overturn the veto by a two-thirds majority in both houses. The president can issue executive orders concerning the execution of existing laws (Republican Acts). The conduct of foreign policy is another presidential prerogative, even though international treaties need confirmation by a two-thirds majority of all members of the Senate. Finally, the president is the commander-in-chief of the AFP and can order the military to act against any rebel or criminal elements that pose an imminent danger to national security. Importantly, the president is de jure limited in initiating budgetary legislation. In all other policy areas, bills originating from the government have to be introduced by a member of Congress (Caoili 2006b, p. 320). Usually, the president announces future policy plans or endorses congressional legislative initiatives in the annual State of the Nation Address or through the Legislative-Executive Development Council (LEDAC).

Yet, it is also important to note that the powers listed in Table 8.3 do not fully capture the nature of presidential power in the Philippines. Although the 1987 Constitution limits the presidential power to suspend the writ of habeas corpus, the assumption of emergency powers, and the amendment of the constitution, the most important strengths of the presidency concern the national finance and budgetary appropriations, appointment authority, and the presidential veto (Teehankee 2006). The president submits the annual budget to Congress, which can only change the allocation but not the overall volume of government expenditure. Since the president drafts the budget and can veto any budget item, (s)he controls the disbursement of government resources and pork barrel funds to congressmen and local government officials. Moreover, based on Marcos's Presidential Decree 1177, the president can reserve parts of the budget for debt servicing (Kawanaka 2010, p. 11).

In addition, the president appoints all secretaries heading executive departments (cabinet ministers) and about 70,000 public servants, including ambassadors, justices, judges, and prosecutors as well as all military officers of the AFP from the ranks of colonels or naval captains and all police officers of comparable ranks (Quilop 2006, p. 9). The Commission of Appointments—a constitutional body under the 1987 Constitution consisting of the president of the Senate, 12 senators, and 12 members of the House of Representatives—can only turn down these appointments if they violate formal procedures (Art. VI Section 18). Judicial appointments involve the Judicial and Bar Council (see below). The president has complete and exclusive control and supervision over all executive departments, bureaus, and offices, and all agencies not under the judiciary or Congress.

8.3.2 Congress

The Philippine Congress comprises the House of Representatives and the Senate. The 17th Congress (2016–2019) had 295 members in the House of Representatives, elected for a 3-year term by a system of plurality rule in single-member constituencies and a parallel (non-compensatory) party-list system. Since the Republic of the Philippines is a unitary state, the Senate does not represent individual states or regions but the national electorate. The 24 senators are elected by plurality rule in a nationwide multi-member district for a 6-year term, with half of the seats contested every 3 years. Senators are limited to two and congressional representatives to three consecutive terms of office. Both chambers of parliament elect a speaker, who appoints the committee chairs and the members of the conference committee. The speakers also determine the plenary agenda and assign bills to committees. The number and responsibilities of congressional committees have varied over time: Standing committees usually mirror the portfolio of government ministries, other committees are formed to implement certain parliamentary functions, and special committees deal with complicated or crosscutting legislative bills. The Senate (2010–2013) had 37 standing committees as well as 30 special committees. The House of Representatives in 2013 had 59 standing and 11 special committees. The House Appropriations Committee, responsible for the budget, is of key importance and had 125 members in May 2013. This extremely diversified committee system has contributed to parliamentary efficiency problems, especially during legislative proceedings (Caoili 2006b, p. 305).

The Philippine Congress has several instruments to monitor the executive. In addition to its right of interpellation and congressional investigations, Congress can demand the suspension of martial law. Congressional members in the Commission of Appointments must confirm all presidential appointments, with the exception of Supreme Court justices (Caoili 2006b, p. 307). Impeachment proceedings against a sitting president, vice president, ombudsman, Supreme Court justice, or members of other constitutional organs are the most powerful instrument in the congressional toolkit. A complaint for impeachment may be filed by any member of the House of Representatives or by any citizen upon a resolution of endorsement by any member of the House and is referred to the judiciary committee of the House. The committee, by majority vote, will determine whether grounds for impeachment exist. The House debates the committee's resolution and in case a resolution of impeachment is filed by at least one-third of all members of the House, the Senate proceeds with a trial. The chief justice of the Supreme Court chairs the impeachment trial against the president. The Philippine Constitution requires a two-thirds majority for conviction.

The post-1986 Congress is often regarded a bastion of elite democracy and political dynasties (Gutierrez et al. 1992, pp. 159–161; Caoili 2006b; Quimpo 2015). In fact, a glance at the sociological profile of Congress demonstrates the continuities between pre- and post-Marcos legislative and party politics. An empirical analysis of the 15th Congress (2010–2013) found that political dynasties comprised 70% of legislators elected in congressional districts. These members of vested political families possessed higher net worth and won elections by larger margins compared to the minority of members of Congress who did not belong to political families. Furthermore, and pointing to crucial equality issues neglected by the elite-dominated Congress, districts dominated by political dynasties are characterized by higher poverty incidences and higher levels of deprivation and inequality as well as lower average incomes and living standards than those with non-dynastic representatives (Mendoza et al. 2012, p. 140). Other studies find even higher levels of dynastic prevalence in local politics and local government units. Moreover, introducing term limits and a party-list system under the 1987 Constitution does not appear to have had a significant impact on curbing the persistence of powerful political dynasties or made congressional demographics more diverse and representative of the wider society (Querubin 2012, 2016; Quimpo 2015).

Legislative proposals, bills, and resolutions can (only) be introduced by members of Congress from either house, but bills that concern taxes, government spending, or state loans and bills with only local application must originate in the House of Representatives. Draft legislation is assigned to a committee, where it can be rejected, consolidated with other drafts, or amended. Since there is no deadline on committee proceedings, these can last for years. Once a bill has successfully passed the committee, it is forwarded for a second reading, during which any congressional representative can request amendments that are then subject to a debate. Once the amendment process is complete, the bill is subjected to a third and final reading. If a majority of the votes cast support the bill, it undergoes the same process in the other chamber of Congress. In case Senate and House disagree, conflicts are resolved in closed meetings in the bicameral Conference Committee. During the bargaining over the annual government budget, the Conference Committee is the main arena for resolving conflicts over the allocation of political "pork" (Caoili 2006b, p. 323). Once both sides reach an agreement, final votes take place in each chamber. If both houses agree on the bill, the president has 30 days to sign it into law. If the president declines, Senate and House can override the veto by a two-thirds majority. So far, however, Congress has never overruled a presidential veto (Kasuya 2008, p. 88).

The amount of parliamentary time that is spent scrutinizing and debating legislation is often disproportionate to its importance, as many bills are of only local relevance, such as renaming public schools or redrafting the territorial boundaries of individual *barangays*, the smallest administrative district in the Philippines, which are all matters of congressional discretion. In addition, the many stages of the legislative process through which a bill must pass mean there are plenty of opportunities for obstruction and delays. Furthermore, there is little coordination or harmonization of committee work in both the House and the Senate. Many committees in the House are disproportionally large, whereas the small number of Senators (24) means that individual senators serve on too many committees at the same time.[4] It is no surprise that legislative delays are a permanent fixture of congressional routine and that legislative output is low and has further eroded over the years (see Table 8.4).

Even though the weak coherence of political parties, a lack of party discipline among representatives of the same caucus, and frequent changes of political party affiliation by elected representatives following a presidential election ("turncoatism") allow the executive to create supermajorities in the House, the volatile and often ad hoc nature of presidential coalitions increases credible commitment problems in policy-making. Mediating commitment problems occupies a central place in the president's engagement with Congress. However, the president also has institutional instruments at his disposal, such as the presidential prioritization of bills, thereby shortening the legislative process to two readings (Claudio 2004, pp. 86–87). In addition, the government of Corazon Aquino created a liaison office and the Legislative-Executive Development Council (LEDAC) as consultative bodies to support priority legislative processes (Caoili 2006b, pp. 323–324).

However, budgetary appropriations and "pork barrel politics" remain the executive's most important tools to resolve legislative blockades (Kasuya 2008, pp. 52–54). The origins of the current system of congressional pork barreling, under which elected officials try to win funds from the national budget for projects specifically targeting their districts, date back to the 1920s (Noda 2011, p. 3). After 1946, this system became highly elaborated until it was supplanted by Marcos's cronyism. However, re-democratization in 1986 also revived the tradition of pork barrel politics and in 1990, the Countrywide Development Fund (CDF),

---

[4]For example, in the 17th Congress, the appropriations committee of the House of Representatives had 125 members (42% of total members; Congress of the Philippines 2016).

Table 8.4 Legislative output in the Philippine Congress, 1987–2004

Congressional term	Bills filed			Bills passed				Success rate
	House	Senate	Total (A)	Signed into law		Veto	Total (B)	B/A (%)
				National	Local			
8th (1987–92)	35,420	2211	37,631	191	809	39	1039	2.6
9th (1992–95)	14,632	2079	16,711	189	345	37	571	3.1
10th (1995–98)	10,551	2518	13,069	149	424	17	590	4.3
11th (1998–01)	12,961	2283	15,244	67	348	20	435	2.7
12th (2001–04)	6697	2749	9446	45	31	0	76	0.8

Source: Caoili (2006b, p. 328)

renamed Priority Development Assistance Fund (PDAF) in 2000, was established
(Noda 2011, p. 3). It allocates an average of 200 million pesos (about USD4
million) to each senator and about 70 million pesos (about USD1.4 million) to
every member of the House. The funds can be used, upon their discretion, for both
"soft" and "hard" projects. "Soft" projects include, among others, scholarships for
students and livelihood assistance for poorer families, whereas "hard projects"
mean infrastructure (Noda 2011, p. 8; Kasuya 2008, pp. 74–76). Many observers
note that these funds are prone to wasteful spending and are often used to fuel
corruption and patronage politics (Parreño 1998, pp. 41–42; Kawanaka 2007). Pork
barrel allotment is the result of negotiations between president and Congress during
the annual budget process, and members of Congress who chair a committee or sit
on the appropriations committee are most successful during the allotment process
(Kawanaka 2007).

8.4   Legal and Judicial System

The Philippine legal system is an amalgamate of diverse influences, including
precolonial ("traditional") law; Spanish civil law traditions; American colonial law,
through which various elements of common law entered Philippine legal thought and
jurisprudential experience; and post-independence law (Desirto 2009, p. 407).

The 1987 Constitution establishes the basic principles and structure of the
judiciary (Art. VIII). Courts are independent and possess administrative and budgetary autonomy. The president upon proposal of the Judicial and Bar Council
(JBC) appoints all judges and justices, who have secure tenure until they reach the
mandatory retirement age of 70.

The JBC consists of the chief justice of the Supreme Court, the secretary of
justice, representatives of both houses of Congress, a former justice of the Supreme
Court, a university professor of law, a representative of the Philippine Bar Association, and an additional representative of the Philippine society. The latter four
members are nominated by the president and confirmed by Congress. For each
judicial vacancy, including Supreme Court justices, the JBC presents the president
with a list of three candidates from which the president appoints one without
congressional confirmation (Atienza and Baylon 2006, p. 356).

Local Trial Courts, consisting of Metropolitan Trial Courts in Metro Manila
(MeTCs), Municipal Trial Courts in Cities (MTCCs), Municipal Trial Courts
(MTCs), and Municipal Circuit Trial Courts (MCTCs), are the courts of first
instance in most matters of civil law. In provinces or regions with a large share of
Muslims, there are additional Sharia Circuit Courts (SCC) of first instance. The
second level of the court system consists of 13 Regional Trial Courts (RTCs) as
both appellate courts and courts of first instance for some matters as well as Sharia
District Courts (SDCs). The Court of Appeals (CoA), the Sharia Appellate Court
(SAC), the Court of Tax Appeals (CoTA), and the *Sandiganbayan* ("People's
Advocate") form the level layer. The *Sandiganbayan* court tries corruption cases

against members of Congress, higher officials, local officeholders, and members of the judiciary.

The Supreme Court, established in 1901, is the highest court of the land and exercises final jurisdiction over all cases decided by Philippine courts. It also reviews and interprets congressional legislation, presidential decrees and proclamations, and administrative acts and serves as the electoral tribunal for the election of the president of the Republic. Its decisions are final and binding on all state organs.

The Supreme Court is composed of 15 justices, including the chief justice, and has "administrative supervision over all courts and the personnel thereof" (Article VIII Section 6 Constitution). The court has constituted itself in three divisions with five members each and only rarely hears or decides cases in front of the whole court (*en banc*). Appointees must be natural-born citizens, 40 years or older, and have served as judge of a lower court for 15 years or more or engaged in the practice of law in the Philippines and have "proven competence, integrity, probity, and independence" (Art. VIII Section 7 Constitution). Justices can only be removed by congressional impeachment.

Throughout the American period and the post-1946 democratic era, the Supreme Court enjoyed the reputation as a highly professional and independent institution (Tate and Haynie 1993). Yet, under the 1973 Constitution, the process by which the chief justice and the associate justices were appointed was changed to grant President Marcos sole appointment authority. While individual justices took a firm anti-martial law stance and tried to resist attempts by the Marcos administration to alter the organization and independence of the judiciary, the Supreme Court was increasingly subordinated to presidential authority. To survive, it bent to the executive, and in the process, provided a semblance of legitimacy for the regime (Celoza 1997, p. 84).

Unsurprisingly, President Corazon Aquino, following her inauguration, ordered the Supreme Court justices to submit their letters of resignation. Despite this initial confrontation between government and Supreme Court, the 1987 Constitution restored the court's independence and authority. Nevertheless, the court has often been criticized for its activist stance, especially in the fields of economic, financial, and social policy, where according to critics, it tried to shape policy rather than review it (Atienza and Baylon 2006). In addition, the court is often criticized for acting as a veto player who takes a deliberate status quo position, slows down political, economic, and social reforms, and blocks more effective governance. Finally, the court has been accused of taking a partisan stance against the government—i.e., during the impeachment of President Estrada in January 2001 (Kasuya 2003)—and has been criticized because President Arroyo (2001–2010) had used her appointment authority to pack the court with loyalists (Abinales 2011, p. 165). The Arroyo-appointed Chief Justice Renato C. Corono was removed from office after being impeached and convicted of corruption in May 2012 (Zimmermann 2012), raising new concerns that the decision was actually politically motivated, would strengthen the hands of the executive and legislative, and would further erode the independence of the Supreme Court.

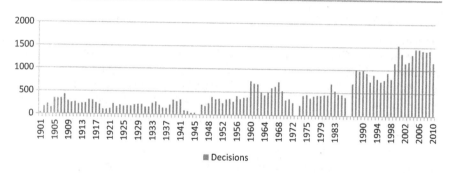

Fig. 8.2 Decisions and resolutions by the Supreme Court of the Philippines, 1901–2010. Source: Authors' compilation based on data from Chan Robles (2010)

Several factors contributed to the present crisis of the Supreme Court. First, the extension of the court's supervisory authority over all courts and judicial personnel dramatically increased the court's administrative workload and shifted some of the blame for the dismal state of the Philippine judiciary upwards (Haynie 1998).

Second, the court's activist stance on matters of judicial review and the abandonment of the "Political Question Doctrine" also contributed to the loss of its institutional reputation, as observers concluded that the court appeared to accept "virtually any opportunity to decide presented to it" (Haynie 1998, p. 464). Third, the court suffers from work overload due to the vast number of cases it has to decide (Fig. 8.2). Each of the three divisions rules on several hundred cases annually. To cope with the large and still rising case numbers, the court has begun to assign individual justices as rapporteurs (*ponente*) responsible for assessing the facts of the case and formulating the majority opinion, giving the *ponente* what some consider "omnipotent power" over the outcomes of cases (Vitug 2010).

Finally, the introduction of the JBC failed to end the practice of partisan appointment started under Marcos (Haynie 1998). Despite its name, the JBC is not purely a professional body but includes several politicians ex officio or through presidential nomination. This has weakened the procedural legitimacy of judicial recruitment, and the lack of congressional approval for nominees expanded presidential influence over judicial nominations after 1987. In recent years, justices have often been nominated close to the constitutionally mandated age limit, the average age at appointment being 63, putting their effective term of office only around 5 years, much shorter than the 9.7 years during pre-authoritarian years (Gatmaytan and Magno 2011, pp. 8–10). The quick turnover of justices has also contributed to more volatile legal positions of the Supreme Court over time and precedents are frequently overturned. Finally, after their retirement many justices enter positions in law firms and serve as intermediaries for claimants, plaintiffs, or defendants, confronting the court with conflict of interest charges (Haynie 1998).

More generally, the Philippine court system suffers from chronic funding shortages, insufficient facilities, inefficiency, and unequal access to the court system for the lower stratum of society (Santos et al. 1997, p. 78; Haynie 1998; Rogers 2004). The courts are seriously understaffed as 22.7% of judicial positions in 2009 remained vacant, resulting in a backlog of roughly 617,000 cases, some going back decades (Supreme Court of the Philippines 2009, pp. 57–58). Moreover, lower courts often ignore or violate procedural regulations in exchange for bribes, further lowering the public's trust in the judiciary (Atienza and Baylon 2006, p. 372).

The crisis of the Supreme Court and the overall judicial system is in line with a general crisis in the rule of law that favors powerful elites over the principle of equal protection of the law (Rogers 2004, p. 116). Corruption is structurally entrenched in politics, state, and the economy. In the late 1990s, the Office of the Philippine Ombudsman calculated that the Philippine state had lost more than USD48 billion due to corruption, i.e., more than the country's foreign debt (Quimpo 2009, p. 342). In comparative indicators of the rule of law, the Philippines has scored below average in recent years. According to the World Bank's Worldwide Governance Indicators, the Philippines ranks 7 out of 11 countries in regard to the quality of rule of law in 2015 (below Thailand and Vietnam) and sixth in the "Control of Corruption" Indicator (slightly above Vietnam). In both indicators, the scores over the past 10 years or so indicate stagnant development (World Bank 2017b).

8.5 Electoral System and Elections

The Philippines has a long tradition of competitive multiparty elections tracing back to the first election of provincial governors in 1902. Elections for a national legislature and local assemblies were introduced in 1907 and the president has been elected since 1935. Suffrage was restricted to literate non-Muslim men, but it was expanded to include women in 1937 and Muslims in 1946 (Tigno 2006b, pp. 29–31). Since 1973, the voting age has been 18, and compulsory voting was abolished in 1987. Only natural-born citizens of at least 25 (House), 35 (Senate), and 40 years (President) can register as candidates. The electoral legal framework allows persons to register and participate as candidates in presidential and congressional (except for party list) elections even if they are not nominated by a political party, and multiple political parties can agree to run the same candidate (Hartmann et al. 2001).

Since the downfall of Marcos, there have been six presidential elections (see Table 8.2) and ten congressional elections. In addition, there have been regular elections for provincial governors, mayors, barangay captains, and local assemblies. In 1989, Congress passed the "People's Initiative and Referendum Act," which was intended to cover initiatives to propose amendments to the constitution. However, the Supreme Court declared this law void (Rüland 2003). There is thus no law that effectively provides for the exercise of the people's initiative.

Elections in the Philippines are synchronized, which means elections for about 40,000 national and local offices are held on the same day. The Commission on Elections (COMELEC), founded in 1940, is responsible for voter registration and the organization of elections, vote counting and notification of the results, and the resolution of election complaints. To guarantee the integrity of the polls, COMELEC holds wide-ranging administrative and quasi-judicial powers and can even deputize police and military personnel to provide security to COMELEC staff, election candidates, and voters before and on voting day. The president appoints the seven commissioners with congressional approval for a nonrenewable term of 7 years (Art. IX). The election results for the House of Representatives presented in Table 8.5 suffer from several problems. Official statistics published by the Commission for Elections are notoriously incomplete and error-prone (Hartmann et al. 2001; Teehankee 2006), and copies of the official certificates of the district results contain only those three parties that received the most votes (Hellmann 2011, p. 151). Calculating political parties' share of the vote at the national level is also difficult because some candidates are nominated by multiple parties while others run as "guest candidates" for parties other than the one they are a registered member of. In addition, political parties may build coalitions in some districts but not in others or build different coalitions in different districts. Some candidates are included in more than one coalition, and some party members decide to officially run as independent candidates (Kasuya 2008, pp. 108–109). The election statistics for the Senate shown in Table 8.6 suffer from similar problems.

The 24 senators are elected under a plurality-at-large voting system in one national district; each voter has a number of votes corresponding to the number of seats to be filled. Senators serve terms of 6 years each; the terms are staggered so that one-half of the seats are up for election every 3 years. Elections for the House follow a system of parallel voting: 80% of the seats are filled by plurality vote in single-member districts, whereas the remaining 20% are elected by a closed party-list system. Voters have two votes, one for the district candidate and one for the party-list group (Table 8.7).

The party-list system introduced in 1987 is a unique feature of the Philippine electoral system. The aim is to improve the political representation of specific groups like workers, youths, indigenous groups, veterans, cultural communities, specific professional sectors, people with disabilities, and senior citizens (RA No. 7941, COMELEC 1996, 2000). Only religious associations and those parties that nominate district candidates are barred from the party-list system. The party-list system is, therefore, a de facto quota system (Co et al. 2005, p. 78). Despite its name, it is not a proportional system since party-list groups may obtain a maximum of only three seats; party-list groups that win at least 2% of the total number of party-list votes are awarded one seat. If there are still vacant seats, one additional seat is allocated to each party that obtained at least 2% of the party-list votes and, if there are still vacant seats, one additional seat is awarded to the highest ranking (in terms of percentage share) party-list group. Finally, if there are still vacant seats, then one seat each is awarded to the next ranking party-list groups until all the vacant seats are filled (cf. Muga 2014).

Philippine elections have always suffered from irregularities despite the country's long experience with elections, the existence of an independent election commission (since 1940), and the tradition of independent election monitoring by nongovernmental organizations (first conducted in 1957). Violations of the integrity of the election (Fig. 8.3) include substantial problems with vote-buying, bribery of polling officials, ballot stuffing, voting in multiple districts by so-called flying

Table 8.5 Elections for the Philippine house of representatives, 1987–2016

		1987	1992	1995	1998	2001	2004	2007	2010	2013	2016
Lakas ng Bansa	%	17.5	–	–	–	–	–	–	–	–	–
	M	24	–	–	–	–	–	–	–	–	–
PDP-Laban	%	17.3	33.7[b]	–	–	–	6.1[b]	1.9[b]	–	–	1.9
	M	43[a]	86[b]	–	–	–	15[b]	5[b]	–	–	3
Lakas-CMD	%	–	21.1	51.1[c]	49.0	35.6	37.2	33.1	38.2[d]	5.3	1.5
	M	–	40	125	111	73	93	89	106[d]	14	4
KAMPI	%	–	–	–	–	–	–	16.4	–[d]	–	–
	M	–	–	–	–	–	–	44	–[d]	–	–
Liberal Party	%	10.5	8.8[b]	1.9	7.3	9.2	11.8	8.6	19.6	39.2[f]	41.7
	M	16	11[b]	5	15	19	34	23	42	113	115
Nacionalista Party	%	7.2	3.9	–	–	–	–	4.1	10.8	8.5	9.4
	M	4	7	–	–	–	–	11	25	17	24
Nationalist People's Coalition (NPC)	%	–	18.7	12.2	4.1	19.5	21.5	10.4	15.2	17.4	17.0
	M	–	30	22	9	40	54	28	31	42	42
LAMMP	%	–	–	10.8	26.7[e]	10.2[e]	–	–	–	–	–
	M	–	–	17	55[e]	21[e]	–	–	–	–	–
UNIDO	%	12.8	–	–	–	–	–	–	–	–	–
	M	19	–	–	–	–	–	–	–	–	–
United Nationalist Alliance (UNA)	%	–	–	–	–	–	–	–	–	13.4[g]	6.6
	M	–	–	–	–	–	–	–	–	10	11
Nationalist Unity Party (NUP)	%	–	–	–	–	–	–	–	–	8.7	9.7
	M	–	–	–	–	–	–	–	–	24	23
Others & Independent	%	34.7	13.8	23.0	12.1	45.5	23.4	25.5	16.2	7.5	12.2
	M	94	32	35	16	52	13	20	25	14	17

(continued)

Table 8.5 (continued)

		1987	1992	1995	1998	2001	2004	2007	2010	2013	2016
Total (w/o party lists)	%	100	100	100	100	100	100	100	100	100	100
	M	200	199	204	206	205	209	220	229	234	238
Voter turnout	%	90.0	70.6	77.7	78.8	81.1	77.0	63.7	75.0	77.2	82.0

[a]Includes 21 seats of the PDP-Laban/Lakas ng Bansa alliance
[b]Coalition of PDP-Laban and Liberal Party
[c]Coalition of Lakas-CMD and LDP
[d]Merger of von Lakas and KAMPI (Lakas-KAMPI-CMD)
[e]LAMMP-LDP
[f]Liberal Party Alliance includes four smaller parties
[g]Alliance of PDB-Laban, PMP, and three smaller parties
Source: Authors' compilation based on data from Teehankee (2002, 2006), COMELEC (2000, 1996), IDEA (2017), Golder (2005), Kasuya (2008, pp. 19–20)

Table 8.6 Elections for the Philippine Senate, 1987–2016

Senate		1987	1992	1995	1998	2001	2004	2007	2010	2013	2016
Lakas ng Bansa	Votes	64.9	–	–	–	–	–	–	–	–	–
	Seats	22	–	–	–	–	–	–	–	–	–
GAD	Votes	26.6	–	–	–	–	–	–	–	–	–
	Seats	2	–	–	–	–	–	–	–	–	–
LDP	Votes	–	45.0	–	–	–	–	–	–	5.4	–
	Seats	–	16	–	–	–	–	–	–	1	–
NPC	Votes	–	17.7	15.8	–	–	–	18.3	4.7	10.1	–
	Seats	–	5	1	–	–	–	2	1	1	2
Liberal Party[a]	Votes	–	6.9	–	–	–	–	10.8	27.6	11.3	31.1
	Seats	–	1	–	–	–	–	2[d]	3[d]	1	5
PDP-Laban	Votes	–	–	–	–	–	–	8.7	–	4.9	–
	Seats	–	–	–	–	–	–	2	–	1	–
Nacionalista Party	Votes	–	5.2	–	–	–	–	10.2	17.6	15.3	10.1
	Seats	–	–	–	–	–	–	2	2	3	–
Lakas-CMD	Votes	–	17.6	68.6	45.5	–	–	–	12.4	–	–
	Seats	–	2	10	5	–	–	–	2	–	–
PRP	Votes	–	–	10.9	–	–	–	–	–	–	–
	Seats	–	–	2	–	–	–	–	–	–	–
LAMMP	Votes	–	–	–	44.3	–	–	–	–	–	–
	Seats	–	–	–	7	–	–	–	–	–	–
Reporma-LM	Votes	–	–	–	6.5	–	–	–	–	–	–
	Seats	–	–	–	–	–	–	–	–	–	–
PPC[b]	Votes	–	–	–	–	50.8	–	–	–	–	–
	Seats	–	–	–	–	8	–	–	–	–	–
PnM[c]	Votes	–	–	–	–	45.8	–	–	–	–	–
	Seats	–	–	–	–	5	–	–	–	–	–

(continued)

Table 8.6 (continued)

Senate		1987	1992	1995	1998	2001	2004	2007	2010	2013	2016
PMP	Votes	–	–	–	–	–	–	–	13.7	–	–
	Seats	–	–	–	–	–	–	–	2	–	–
K-4[f]	Votes	–	–	–	–	–	52.2	–	–	–	–
	Seats	–	–	–	–	–	8	–	–	–	–
KNP[g]	Votes	–	–	–	–	–	37.7	–	–	–	–
	Seats	–	–	–	–	–	4	–	–	–	–
UNA[h]	Votes	–	–	–	–	–	–	–	–	27.0	7.6
	Seats	–	–	–	–	–	–	–	–	3	1
Akbayan	Votes										5.0
	Seats										1
Others & Independents	Votes	8.5	7.6	5.3	3.7	3.4	10.1	52.2	24.0	25.8	42.3
	Seats	–	–	–	–	–	–	4	2	2	3
Total		24	24	13	12	13	12	12	12	12	12
Voter turnout		90.0	70.6	77.7	78.8	81.1	77.0	63.7	75.0	77.2	82.0

[a]Liberal Party–PDP-Laban coalition
[b]Ruling coalition of Lakas-NUCD-UMDP, LP, Reporma-Lam, Ksyon Demokratiko, PROMDI, and PDP-Laban
[c]Oppositional coalition of LDP, LAMMP, independence, and small parties
[d]13 seats since one seat became vacant during the Senate term
[e]Liberal Party
[f]Arroyo's presidential coalition of Lakas CMD, Liberal Party, one wing of NPC, and smaller parties
[g]Opposition coalition of LDP, PMP, KBL, and a wing of NPC
[h]13 mandates since one seat became vacant during the Senate term after Senator de Castro was elected vice president; alliance of PDP-Laban and PMP
Source: see Table 8.5

Table 8.7 Electoral system of the Philippines as of May 2016

	Senate	President	Vice President	House of representatives	
				Parallel voting	
Type	Plurality-at-large	Plurality	Plurality	District	Party list
# of seats	24	1	1	238	59
District magnitude	12	1	1	1	59
Candidacy	Individual	Individual	Individual	Individual	Closed list
Seat allocation formula	Plurality	Plurality	Plurality	Plurality	(see above)
Threshold	–	–	–	–	2% + 6% cap
Term length	6	6	6	3	3
Term limit	2	1	2	3	3

Source: Authors' compilation

voters, manipulation of voter registries, and election-related violence, especially in local elections (Teehankee 2006; Linantud 1998; Patiño and Velasco 2006).

Some problems are caused by the antiquated election system (Velasco 2006, p. 100). Before the introduction of automated elections in 2016, a system of write-in-ballots first introduced in 1907 was practiced, in which voters received a blank ballot and had to write-in the candidates—up to 36 in synchronized local and national elections—they wanted to cast their vote for. However, other problems result from confusing interpretation of the election law by COMELEC and a lack of administrative capacity, but also from problems of limited stateness in districts affected by insurgencies and high levels of violent crime. Moreover, the poor evaluation of campaign finance (Fig. 8.3) coincides with the widely shared view that elections in the Philippines are the playground of political dynasties and that regulations for transparency in campaign finance are not enforced (Teehankee 2006; Hellmann 2011, p. 168).

8.6   Parties and Party System

Political parties defined as political groups "identified by an official label that presents at elections, and is capable of placing through elections (free or nonfree), candidates for public office" (Sartori 1976: 63) appeared in the Philippines for the first time in the early 1900s. Early political parties formed along the cleavage national independence versus cooperation with the U.S. colonial government and included the Federal Party (1900), the *Partido Independista* (1906), and the *Nacionalista Party* (1907). This cleavage lost much of its salience after the passage of the Jones Law by the U.S. Congress in 1916, which declared the United States would recognize the independence of the Philippines when a stable government could be established, a liberal policy of including Filipinos in the colonial

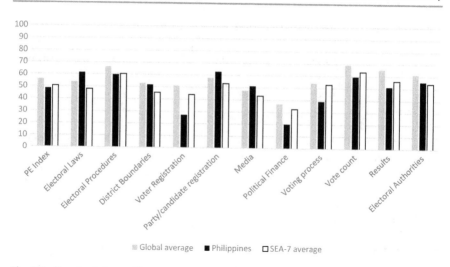

▨ Global average ■ Philippines ☐ SEA-7 average

Fig. 8.3 Perceived electoral integrity index Philippines, 2013. Notes: The PEI index evaluates the quality of elections based on 49 indicators. Assessments by more than 2000 domestic and international election experts are clustered into 11 stages occurring throughout the electoral cycle and are then summed to construct an overall 100-point PEI index. The index covers a total of 180 elections in 139 countries between July 1, 2012 and December 31, 2015. The average score for elections in seven Southeast Asian countries (Cambodia, Malaysia, Myanmar, Philippines, Thailand, Singapore, and Indonesia, SEA-7) is 50.59. *Source*: PEI (2016)

government ("Filipinization") was implemented, and the colonial legislature was transformed into a directly elected, Filipino-controlled body (Onorato 1970; Abinales 2002). With elections becoming the norm in the Philippines, Filipino lawmakers turned the pork barrel into a weapon to ensure their reelection, and "blood, friendship and regionalism" became the organizing principles of the emerging Filipino party system (Abinales 2002, p. 609; Tigno 2006b, p. 47). Elite families and political dynasties began constructing local political machines that dominated elections. This resulted in the emergence of political parties as national coalitions of local political clans (Coronel et al. 2004, p. 61; Tigno 2006b, pp. 35–37).

The post-1946 electoral democracy consolidated the power of political dynasties, local elites, and traditional politicians, especially since the repression of the peasant rebellion led by the *Hukbalahap* precluded the emergence of a legal political alternative left of the center (Manacsa and Tan 2005, p. 759). When in 1946 the Liberal Party split from the *Partido Nacionalista* (NP), which had emerged as a dominant party until 1947, a two-party system emerged. Under a system of "functional bifactionalism" (Landé 1965, p. 18), the two parties were mere organizational vehicles for local elites and candidates who sought office through elections, but they did not develop into effective organizations representative of mass politics. Within the two-party system, party switching or "turncoatism" became predominant (Banlaoi and Carlos 1996).

During the Martial Law period, the *Kilusang Bagong Lipunan*, or KBL, of Marcos dominated the hegemonic party system, though there were other minor parties, and a number of traditional politicians attempted to promote the United Nationalist Democratic Organization as a credible, noncommunist alternative to the regime. Left-wing groups, affiliated with the clandestine Communist Party of the Philippines, played an important role in anti-regime demonstrations after the assassination of Benigno Aquino Jr. in 1983, but the traditional political parties remained sidelined in the mass protests that led to the downfall of Marcos in early 1986 (Tigno 2006a, p. 85).

Instead of a revival of the traditional two-party system, the Philippines experienced the rise of multiparty politics in the post-Marcos era. Without Marcos, the KBL broke into smaller parties. After Marcos's downfall in 1986, both the *Nacionalista Party* and the Liberal Party never recovered their power and dynamism. For example, the two largest parties in the Philippines in 2016 (Liberals and NPC) together accounted for 59.4% of the votes and 65% of the seats at the district level. As Table 8.8 demonstrates, the effective number of political parties (ENEP) is now significantly higher than in the premartial law period, even not counting the dozens of party-list groups with one to three representatives in Congress.

Even after Marcos's downfall in 1986, the party system remained inchoate and only institutionalized to the extent that elites have bestowed legitimacy on open elections and have deemed parties as the key route for achieving power (Co et al. 2005; Hicken 2015). Parties remain the electoral vehicles for political clans or families and almost exclusively focus on their recruitment and electoral function (Hellmann 2011). Policy-oriented, ideological parties with mass memberships do not exist. For the most part, parties are political machines and electoral vehicles for office-seeking and lack the ideological appeal or party platforms that would link them with social groups and provide a voice to the populace. The "cadre-esque" and decentralized nature of political parties in the Philippines has allowed personalism, clientelism, and kinship ties to prevail among party members (Croissant and Völkel 2012).

Several factors account for the shift towards a multiparty system and the stubbornly under-institutionalized nature of political parties and the party system in the post-1986 Philippines. One is the impact of political institutions, such as the election system and party laws. Another is the sociological variable of social cleavages. While conventional wisdom would suggest a first-past-the-post-electoral system to produce a two-party format "in the long run" (Sartori 1994, pp. 40–41), this is only the case if a party system is "structurally consolidated" and the major parties' respective vote shares do not differ much between regions or geographical units. However, neither is the case in the Philippines (Croissant and Völkel 2012). Rather, the candidate-centered systems of plurality rule in single (House) or multi-member districts (Senate) provide strong incentives for personalized campaigning in the Philippines, rendering political parties more vulnerable to defections and splits. Moreover, the introduction of the party-list system has contributed to the chaotic state of party politics in the Philippines by creating a second, parallel party system. In 2016, 129 party lists contested the elections, and 46 won between one and three seats in the 17th Congress (Philippine Daily Inquirer 2016), but only a

Table 8.8 Effective number of political parties (seats) and presidential candidates (votes), 1946–2016

Year	Effective number of parties (House)[a]	Effective number of presidential candidates	Effective number of parties (Senate)[b]
1946	2.9	2.0	2.2
1949	2.1	2.4	1.4
1953	2.2	1.7	2.3
1957	1.4	3.3	1.5
1961	1.7	2.0	2.1
1965	2	2.2	2.1
1969	1.5	1.9	1.5
Average for 1946–1969	1.9	2.2	1.8
1987	6.9	–	–
1992	3.7	5.8	2.0
1995	3.6	–	4.0
1998	3.1	4.3	3.3
2001	5	–	5.8
2004	3.5	3.2	5.1
2007	4.4	–	7.5
2010	5.5	3.5	6.3
2013	3.6	–	6.0
2016	3.5	3.7	7.3
Average for 1987–2016	4.3	4.1	5.2

Notes: see Table 3.2 for details on calculation
[a]Without party-list groups
[b]Without Senate mid-term elections in 1947, 1951, 1955, 1959, 1963, 1967, and 1971
Source: see Table 8.5, Authors' calculation

handful of them have a recognizable identity as political organizations or present alternative policies. Many are lobby or interest groups or simply serve as another electoral vehicle for political families and *trapos* (Rimban 2005; Abinales 2011).

Furthermore, the organizational instability of the post-1986 party system is to some extent a consequence of the single-term limit for the presidency introduced under the 1987 Constitution (Choi 2001). Incumbents who are permitted only a single term have little incentive to invest in strengthening party organizations, whereas presidential term limits and the lack of an incumbency bonus facilitate intra-party competition, party splits, and increase the number of candidates competing for office (Kasuya 2006, p. 24). The effective number of presidential candidates that doubled from 2.2 (1946–1969) to 4.1 (1992–2016) demonstrates this. In addition, by lengthening the presidential term from four to six years and cutting the term of the House of Representatives from four to three, both elections only coincide every 6 years. This has weakened the bandwagon effect under which voters focus on parties that run the most promising presidential candidates during congressional elections (Kasuya 2008; Hicken 2009): Congressional mid-term elections produce a considerably higher effective number of parties than those that coincide with presidential races (Table 8.8).

Another important factor is the lack of relevance of social cleavages for the development of the party system. In the Philippines, ethnic, religious, regional, or socioeconomic cleavages do not seem to have a strong effect on the party system (Rüland et al. 2005, pp. 141–151): There are only rudimentary links between social cleavages and the national party system. Organizational instability, weak institutionalization, and prevailing personalism as well as clientelism have so far prevented a clustering of parties along cleavage lines (Manacsa and Tan 2005). With the exception of the outlawed Communist Party of the Philippines and a few smaller party groups, no political party represents the class cleavage between workers and owners or between the rich and poor (Quimpo 2005; Abinales 2006). It is not surprising that weak political parties leave an intermediary vacuum that, combined with low levels of political representativeness and democratic accountability, create the political space for populist entrepreneurs such as Presidents Estrada (1998–2001) and Duterte (2016–) who were swept into power on nationalist, populist, anticorruption, and law and order messages (Landé 2001; Gatmaytan 2006, p. 10; Holmes 2017).

8.7   State Administration

The Republic of the Philippines is a unitary state. Like other Southeast Asian countries, the independent republic adopted the administrative model of the colonial period as its own and until today, the state administration remains highly centralized. Strong administrative and fiscal centralization coexists with a considerable degree of political decentralization. The tradition of elected governors and local assemblies is also a colonial legacy, though it was de facto suspended under the martial law regime of President Ferdinand Marcos.

Despite significant efforts in administrative reform, often supported by international providers of development assistance, the Philippine state still lacks the capacity to push through policies in the interest of the public good. The state remains captured by oligarchs, who have dominated Philippine politics since U.S. colonial rule. Although some parts of the bureaucracy have functioned as "islands of competence," for the most part, social forces that have used its structures for electoral and personal interests have penetrated the Philippine state. In the most incisive analysis of the Philippine state, Paul Hutchcroft (1998) has categorized it as "patrimonial." The contrast with countries like Malaysia, Singapore, and Vietnam, in which the state has—despite the authoritarian nature of the regimes—been much more effective in the provision of public goods and of development writ large, is stark (Slater 2010; Croissant 2011).

As a response to the authoritarian centralism of the Martial Law regime and rising pro-decentralization sentiments among international donors and development agencies, the Local Government Code (LGC) of 1991 provided for the transfer of power and authority from central institutions to lower levels of the government system. Under the LGC, local government units (LGUs) consist of provinces, municipalities, and villages (*barangay*). Each of the 81 provinces, the National Capital Region (Metro Manila), the Autonomous Region of Muslim Mindanao (ARMM), and the yet to be implemented Cordilleras Autonomous Region are headed by a governor.[5] There are 145 independent cities and 1498 districts, and about 42,000 *barangays* (NSCB 2014). All governors and members of provincial boards, mayors for cities and municipalities, city and municipal councils, and the regional assembly of the AMMR are elected for a 3-year term and are allowed a maximum of three consecutive terms. The Department of Interior advises and monitors all LGUs and has its offices on all administrative levels; most other national ministries and agencies have regional offices to implement national programs. Although LGUs' share of public expenditure has risen from less than 6 to 26% in 2005, most have very limited abilities to generate revenues and depend on central government subsidies (Atienza 2006, p. 435). ARMM is particularly dependent on national subsidies (Casambre 2006).

In addition to weak administrative and fiscal capacity, the state's effective monopoly on the legitimate use of physical force is also limited. Local clans, and in some areas, particularly in Mindanao, warlords, are the real rulers in their territories. Very often, they employ private armies, which take the law into their own hands and have de facto privatized state structures and services.

Several factors account for the weak stateness of the Philippines. The first concerns (pre)colonial legacies. Under Spanish rule, claims of centralist administration focused around "imperial Manila" coexisted with the insufficient penetration of the country. Outside a few garrison towns, Spanish colonial authority was sporadic at best (Atienza 2006, p. 421). American reforms modernized the administration and deconcentrated the reach of national ministries down to the lowest administrative level. However, the program of Filipinization introduced informal power structures into the public sector (Hutchcroft 1998). Since 1946, all state agencies are subordinate to the office of the president. All presidents have used their appointment authority as a resource of both control and patronage, resulting in a system of state agencies with overlapping responsibilities that was neither politically autonomous nor efficient (Quilop 2006, p. 9).

Furthermore, organized crime, weak security governance, and political violence by non-state actors have further weakened the Philippine state. Local elites have not only accepted but have also embraced this situation, as strengthening the center would necessarily undermine their political and economic position in the periphery (Kreuzer 2007, II–III).

Moreover, several insurgent groups challenge the legitimacy of the Philippine nation-state. Even though the specific cycles of escalation and de-escalation in these conflicts differ just as much as their underlying causes and involved groups, the overall level of armed conflict and non-state violence in the Philippines is higher than in most other Southeast Asian nations (Trinn and Croissant 2012). Active

---

[5]The ARMM includes five provinces in Southern Mindanao.

insurgencies include, among others, the Communist Party of the Philippines (CPP) and the New People's Army (NPA), the Moro National Liberation Front (MNLF) and its spinoffs, the Moro Islamic Liberation Front (MILF), and the terrorist Abu Sayyaf Group. CPP/NPA have waged guerilla war against the government since the 1970s, reaching its apex in 1986 when Communist guerillas controlled a fifth of the state territory. Following democratization, their military and political position weakened considerably. At the beginning of the current decade, NPA had only about 4600 fighters (Croissant et al. 2013, p. 144; The Philippine Star 2001). The MILF claims to represent the Muslim minority in Mindanao, who sees itself more as Moro (the Spanish word for Moor, the Reconquista-period term used for Muslims) than Philippine people, and adheres to the idea of *Bangsamoro* (Moro nation). Negotiations between the government and MILF and the integration of the insurgents into the regional autonomy program for Muslim Mindanao have not yet resulted in a settlement of the conflict (Santos and Paz 2010). A presidential initiative for a separate Bangsamoro Basic Law (BBL) was voted down by Congress in 2015 amidst claims of its unconstitutionality (Hernandez 2016).

8.8 Civil–Military Relations

The relationship between soldiers, state, and society in the Philippines evolved in three phases. During the first phase, from the establishment of the Armed Forces of the Philippines in 1935 to 1973, the principle of civil supremacy over the military was the key aspect of Philippine civil–military relations. Since the Philippine elite were well integrated in the colonial system and national independence resulted from negotiations rather than armed struggle, the AFP played no role in the process of decolonization, depriving it of a strong source of legitimacy. On the other hand, a cohesive civilian elite accepted elections as the only legitimate route to political office, and therefore, military elites represented a formidable barrier for the military to become an arbitrator in civilian politics. On the contrary, military officers depended on the support of president, Congress, and local politicians since promotions are based on civilian patronage. This precluded the development of an officer corps with values distinct from the civilian population in terms of ruling ambitions but also the thorough professionalization of the AFP. Finally, the U.S. military had a large impact on the AFP and Philippine civil–military relations. The first generation of military officers was trained by the United States and fought the Japanese under U.S. leadership. Since the United States guaranteed Philippine defense under the terms of the 1947 Military Bases Agreement and the 1951 Mutual Defense Treaty, the Philippine military became a pure counterinsurgency military with a strong focus on internal security and socioeconomic development (Woo 2011, p. 40). From 1951 to 1954, the central government deployed the military to fight the *Partido Komunista ng Pilipinas* and its military arm, the Huk army, and expanded the nontraditional roles of the AFP, which included development projects, law enforcement, and local administration (Hernandez 2006, p. 393). After the defeat of the Huk army, the AFP fought the Communist Party of the

Philippines (CPP) and its military arm, the New People's Army, which started its rebellion against the government in 1968. From the early 1970s onwards, it fought a second war against Moro rebels in Mindanao.

Marcos's declaration of martial law in 1972 marks the beginning of the second phase of Philippine civil–military relations. The dictator replaced the existing system of joint presidential and congressional oversight with his patrimonial control over the AFP. Through a combination of favoritism, expansion of the military budget and personnel, and a centralized command and control system with Marcos at its top, the president managed to subjugate the military and bend its leadership to his will (Hernandez 1985, 2006, p. 394). Marcos's strategy of consolidating his personal control over the Philippine military had far-reaching implications, as it came at the expense of military professionalism and cohesion, and created factional competition within the AFP, while the attritional struggle against Communist rebels and Muslim insurgents alienated younger officers from the regime (Celoza 1997, p. 79; Wurfel 1988, pp. 237–240). In February 1986, a small group of military officers (publicly known as the Reform Armed Forces Movement, RAM) led by Marcos's civilian Defense Minister, Juan Ponce Enrile, and the AFP Vice Chief of Staff, General Fidel Ramos, attempted a coup against President Marcos. The attempt failed, but catalyzed the "People Power" mass protests that toppled the dictator (Thompson 1995).

The end of the Marcos presidency marks the beginning of the third phase of conditional submission of the armed forces under civilian control. The core of post-Marcos civil–military relations in the Philippines was a double challenge for civilian actors (Przeworski 2003, pp. 81–85). The first challenge concerned the inauguration of a democratic government without provoking military resistance. The second challenge was to establish functional institutions of civilian control over the military. Despite a wave of seven failed coup attempts and mutinies between 1986 and 1989, Philippine democracy survived the first challenge. However, it was less successful in dealing with the second challenge of institutionalizing civilian supremacy over the AFP. On the one hand, the 1987 Constitution provides institutional safeguards for effective civilian control, including the establishment of a Commission for Human Rights, the separation of police and military, the reestablishment of congressional oversight, and the incompatibility of active military service and holding political office (Hernandez 2007, pp. 86–87). On the other hand, all governments so far have failed to punish officers involved in mutinies or uprisings or soldiers who committed human rights violations (Hutchcroft 2008, p. 147). Furthermore, presidents such as Fidel Ramos (1992–1998) and Gloria Macapagal Arroyo (2001–2010) relied heavily on co-opting military officers into the civilian government apparatus, appointing several dozen (former) military officers to advisory, cabinet, and administrative posts. This ambivalent character of Filipino civil–military relations is aptly summarized by two Filipino political scientists, who conclude that the AFP "does not really seek to capture political power for itself (despite all the instances of attempted coups) and instead institutionally (through the upper ranks of the military leadership) aligns itself with certain political factions" (Hernandez and Kraft 2010, p. 130).

8.9 Political Culture and Civil Society

The basis for civil society in the Philippines was already formed during the Spanish and American colonial periods. Even though indigenous concepts such as mutual self-help and charity were common, voluntary assistance or charity associations in addition to Catholic welfare organizations spread throughout the Spanish period, in addition to various *cofradías* (brotherhoods; Bankoff 2004). Nationalist associations like the Cofradía de San Jose (1838) and civic associations and intellectual circles like the reformist propaganda movement of the Philippine national hero José Rizal (1872) or the revolutionary *Katipunan*, which emerged in the nineteenth century, provided inspiration for student activists in the 1960s and 1970s (Franco 2004, pp. 103–105). The American colonial government delineated the boundaries between the state provision of public goods, religious philanthropy, and private philanthropy, and the Philippine Corporation Law of 1906 recognized the right to create private nonprofit organizations, some of which received government subsidies. Government support for farmer credit cooperatives and widespread dissatisfaction among peasants fueled growth in such voluntary associations but also the membership of communist-affiliated labor organizations, such as the Congress of Labor Organizations. In addition to a rich tapestry of different "modern" civil society organizations, interest groups, and professional associations, the Catholic Church, the Protestant Church, and other non-Catholic churches expanded their services to directly engage with workers and peasants through rural development, cooperatives, and credit unions (Clarke 1998). While this dynamic continued after 1946, ties of family, neighborhood, region, and friendship remained the most important mechanism of social self-organization and mutual cooperation (Abad 2005, p. 50).

During the Martial Law regime, there was discernibly little space for civil society except in areas where the government could not deliver the necessary social services and NGOs had to step in. In order to avoid state repression, many civil society activists either joined the armed struggle of the CPP or went into "inner immigration" by affiliating with university or religious organizations. In the end, however, the regime failed to control or sideline civil society completely (Thompson 1995). Rather, the "resurrection of civil society" (O'Donnell and Schmitter 1986) was a key moment in the People Power Revolution. Owing to the favorable legal environment and the inflow of ODA funds to the country, the number of civil society organizations (CSOs) mushroomed after 1986 from 27,100 to 95,000 in 2000 (Clarke 1998, p. 70; Franco 2004, p. 109). Even though these numbers are somewhat misleading—since local politicians and administrators also formed their own associations to gain additional influence over Local Development Councils for which CSO participation is mandatory by law (Kawanaka 2010)—they nevertheless indicate a very vital civil society pluralism (CIVICUS 2011, p. 30). Successive governments have maintained some openness to CSOs, although the democratic space for civil society has fluctuated over the years depending on the inclinations of both elected politicians and appointed bureaucrats, and general political conditions (Abinales and Amoroso 2005, p. 15).

Yet, civil society in the Philippines also has its dark side, and mass mobilization by civil society actors and organizations, like the broad-based protest movements for and against the impeachment of President Estrada in January and May of 2001, demonstrates some of the more problematic aspects of contentious politics in the Philippines (Gatmaytan 2006; Arugay 2013). While such actions may be driven by the wish to defend the democratic order, these forms of political contention generated unintended consequences detrimental to democratization, making democracy in the Philippines "volatile, unstable, and unpredictable," and bringing it to "the edge of mob rule" [Amando Doronilla quoted by Abinales and Amoroso (2005, p. 278)].

The mass protests of 2000/01 reflect the ineffective democratic representation and lack of democratic accountability and responsibility as institutions and procedures provided by the democratic regime remain dominated by traditional political families and elites. This has contributed to the electoral rise of populists like Joseph Estrada and created a basis for populist mobilization and countermobilization. Together, these processes have eroded the public perception that political institutions or the political elite can help solve virulent social problems. For example, the Asia Barometer Survey indicates that institutional trust in state and government bodies in the Philippines is significantly lower than the regional average across the board and also below those for NGOs, television, and newspapers. For instance, only 50.2% of respondents in 2014 reported some or a great deal of trust in the chief executive and 42.7% in the national government, whereas 38.3% trusted the national parliament and 31.3% political parties. The averages for seven Southeast Asian countries were 76.7, 73.3, 69.6, and 58.6%, respectively (ABS 2017).

This is in line with survey findings that the Philippines ranks last in the region concerning respondents' satisfaction with the way democracy functions (Liu 2012, p. 31). At the same time, Philippine citizens seem to trust more in their individual capabilities to affect political decisions than citizens in other Asian countries and are more willing to engage in collective political action. This indicates that Philippine political institutions have failed to harness the strong participatory drive of their citizens and transform it into a relationship of trust (Guerrero and Tusalem 2008, p. 81).

8.10   Media System

Democratization in 1986 produced a significantly higher level of media freedom than had been the case during the Martial Law regime and witnessed the resurrection of political journalism in the Philippines (Coronel 2001). In contrast to many other Southeast Asian countries, print media outlets can publish without a government license, as Congress and the National Telecommunications Commission only allocate broadcasting licenses and frequencies. Still, critics admonish the current system for favoring ownership concentration that diminishes media pluralism (Santos 2003, p. 134), and indeed, many media corporations are controlled by politically well-connected families and business conglomerates (Tuazon 1998, p. 241; FRD 2006, p. 21). In the mid-2000s, there were seven national daily newspapers as well as several hundred local dailies and weeklies. Four in five newspapers are produced in part or completely in English (Maslog 2000, p. 383), although newspaper circulation is quite low with only 78.6 copies per 1000 inhabitants (UNESCO 2017).

In contrast, television is the dominant source of political information in urban areas, whereas radio broadcasting is predominant in rural areas (Vogel et al. 2008, p. 82). There are more than 200 TV and 950 radio stations. While public broadcasting like the People's Radio (*Radyo ng Bayan*) usually serves as government mouthpieces (Vogel et al. 2008, p. 84), private stations provide for a broad spectrum of different views and opinions. More than 90% of the population has access to TV and radio, and internet access has spread quickly in recent years and has reached 52% (Internet World Stats 2017).

Despite its limited readership, the Manila-based political press can have a very substantial impact on public opinion, and the print media fulfills an important "watchdog" function (Coronel 2001). The Filipino tradition of political journalism began in the late nineteenth century and survived the Marcos years by going underground. Today, it is represented by the National Union of Journalists of the Philippines and independent media agencies. These groups have uncovered numerous political scandals (Vogel et al. 2008, p. 83).

However, since the 2000s, the political environment for journalists has grown more difficult and freedom of the press has suffered. The country's position in the Press Freedom Index from Reporters without Borders declined from rank 89 in 2002 to rank 141 (of 180 countries) in 2015 (Reporters without Borders 2015). In the Freedom of the Press Index from Freedom House, the Philippines slid from 30 points, signifying a free press in 2002, to 44 in 2014, indicating an only partially free press (Freedom House 2015). This development is due to a conjunction of several conditions, such as new antiterrorism laws (i.e., the 2007 Human Security Act), the use of damaging libel suits against journalists who reported on corruption cases involving politicians, and—especially—violence against journalists (Vogel et al. 2008, pp. 87, 92). According to the National Union of Journalists of the Philippines (NUJP), 174 journalists were killed between the end of the dictatorship and early 2016, 122 of these since 2001. Only 10 suspects have been convicted (quoted in Espina-Varona 2016).

8.11   Outlook

On February 25, 2016, the Philippines celebrated the 30th anniversary of the "People Power Revolution." Government representatives, party politicians, and democracy activists of 1986 commemorated the victims of the dictatorship, conjured up traditions of the democracy movement, and stressed that the Philippines had been in the vanguard of countries with peaceful transitions initiated by mass protest. Critics used the anniversary to remind the public that EDSA I had merely restored the power of a few influential family clans and did little to ameliorate the Philippines's social and economic problems.

Despite 30 years of democratic politics, the political system of the Philippines remains a highly "defective democracy" (Merkel et al. 2003). There are regular and strongly contested elections, and parties are free to organize and campaign for votes. There is a vibrant civil society, a pluralist media, and decentralization reforms that have brought the government closer to the people. However, human rights violations are widespread and have further increased in recent years. Nevertheless, the relevant political elites and social actors seem to accept the democratic institutions as "the only game in town" (Przeworski 2003). Even the military, despite not being completely under civilian control, seems to have made its peace with democracy. Yet two caveats are in order: First, many of the major political players, including current President Duterte and many of his followers, have an electoralist rather than liberal understanding of what constitutes democracy (Thompson 2017). Secondly, elite support for democracy appears to be rooted, at least to some extent, in the fact that the post-Marcos democratic order has been essential for the preservation of elite control over the political process and its outcomes.

Despite regime changes in 1972 and 1986, many facets of the late colonial period and the first Filipino democracy from 1946 to 1972 have survived until today. This is true for the basic constitutional make-up and organization of the state, the electoral system, the judiciary, as well as the basis of the party system, the sociological profile of the political elite, and their relationship with the electorate and the broader society. The question is therefore how much of a revolution the People Power Revolution actually was. Yet, as the great French political scientist and historian Alexis de Tocqueville observed in his study of the French Revolution, there is often strong continuity of the old regime and the (post-)revolutionary regime (Tocqueville 1955). Institutions created at the onset of the Third Republic have shaped the political system until today. In their form and function, these institutions have adapted gradually to new political and social circumstances and survived times of crisis. In fact, incremental change is a much more frequent phenomenon than abrupt, fundamental collapse, and smaller changes can over time accumulate to much more fundamental changes (Mahoney and Thelen 2010). In the Philippines, this point has not yet been reached.

References

Abad, R. G. (2005). Social capital in the Philippines: Results from a national survey. *Philippine Sociological Review, 53*, 1–57.

Abinales, P. N. (2002). American rule and the formation of filipino 'Colonial Nationalism'. *Southeast Asian Studies, 39*(4), 604–621.

Abinales, P. N. (2006). Asia's last people's war: The communist insurgency in the post-Marcos Philippines. In A. Croissant, S. Kneip, & B. Martin (Eds.), *The politics of death: Political violence in Southeast Asia* (pp. 189–218). Münster: LIT Verlag.

Abinales, P. N. (2011). The Philippines in 2010. *Asian Survey, 51,* 163–172. https://doi.org/10.1525/as.2011.51.1.163

Abinales, P. N., & Amoroso, D. J. (2005). *State and society in the Philippines* (State and society in East Asia series). Lanham: Rowman & Littlefield.

ABS. (2017). *Asian barometer survey: Electronic data release for Wave 4, 2014–2016.* http://www.asianbarometer.org/data/data-release

ADB. (2010). *Key development indicators.* Mandahyong City: Asian Development Bank.

Arugay, A. A. (2013). Saviors or spoilers?: Explaining 'Civil Society Coups' in an age of democratization. *Thammasat Review, 16,* 167–187.

Atienza, M. E. L. (2006). Local governments and devolution in the Philippines. In T. S. E. Tadem & N. M. Morada (Eds.), *Philippine politics and governance: Challenges to democratization and development* (pp. 415–441). Diliman: University of the Philippines Press.

Atienza, M. E. L., & Baylon, F. C. (2006). The judiciary. In T. S. E. Tadem & N. M. Morada (Eds.), *Philippine politics and governance: Challenges to democratization and development* (pp. 333–391). Diliman: University of the Philippines Press.

Bankoff, G. (2004). Local associations and social services in the rural Philippines, 1565–1964. *IIAS Newsletter, 34*(July), 19.

Banlaoi, R. C., & Carlos, C. (1996). *Elections in the Philippines: From the pre-colonial period to the present.* Manila: Konrad Adenauer Foundation.

Bello, W., & Gershman, J. (1990). Democratization and stabilization in the Philippines. *Critical Sociology, 17,* 35–56. https://doi.org/10.1177/089692059001700102

Caoili, O. (2006a). The Philippine legislature: From pre-Spanish times to the eve of martial law. In T. S. E. Tadem & N. M. Morada (Eds.), *Philippine politics and governance: Challenges to democratization and development* (pp. 249–279). Diliman: University of the Philippines Press.

Caoili, O. (2006b). The restored Philippine congress. In T. S. E. Tadem & N. M. Morada (Eds.), *Philippine politics and governance: Challenges to democratization and development* (pp. 299–333). Diliman: University of the Philippines Press.

Carr, A. (2017). Psephos: Adam Carr's election archive. Accessed June 10, 2017, from http://psephos.adam-carr.net/

Casambre, A. L. (2006). Autonomous regions – The Cordillera autonomous region. In T. S. E. Tadem & N. M. Morada (Eds.), *Philippine politics and governance: Challenges to democratization and development* (pp. 441–459). Diliman: University of the Philippines Press.

Celoza, A. F. (1997). *Ferdinand Marcos and the Philippines: The political economy of authoritarianism.* New York: Praeger Publishers.

Chan Robles. (2010). Chan Robles Virtual Law Library: Philippine Political Law.

Choi, J. (2001). Philippine democracies old and new: Elections, term limits, and party systems. *Asian Survey, 41*(3), 488–501.

CIA. (2017). *The world factbook.* Langley: Central Intelligence Agency.

CIVICUS. (2011). *Civil society index: Philippines: An assessment of Philippine civil society.*

Clarke, G. (1998). *The politics of NGOs in South-East Asia: Participation and protest in the Philippines.* London: Routledge.

Claudio, G. (2004). Executive-legislative relations. In J. V. Abueva, V. A. Bautista, P. Domingo-Tapales, M. O. Z. Domingo, & E. E. Nicolas (Eds.), *The Macapagal-Arroyo presidency and administration: Record and legacy, 2001–2004: President Gloria Macapagal-Arroyo and her administration* (pp. 83–101). Diliman: University of the Philippines Press.

Co, E. E. A., Tigno, J. V., Lao, M. E. J., & Sayo, M. A. (2005). *Philippine democracy assessment: Free and fair elections and the democratic role of political parties.* Pasing City: Ateneo de Manila University Press.

COMELEC. (1996). Commission on Elections Resolution No. 2847 dated June 25, 1996 entitled, 'Rules and regulations governing the election of the party-list representatives through the party-list system'. Accessed June 10, 2017, from http://www.chanrobles.com/comelecresolutiono2847.htm

COMELEC. (2000). Commission on Election Resolution No. 3307-A dated November 9, 2000 entitled, 'Rules and regulations governing the filing of petition for registration, manifestation to participate, and submission of names of nominees under the party-list system of representation in connection with the May 14, 2001 National and Local Elections.' Accessed June 10, 2017, from http://www.chanrobles.com/comelecresolutiono3307a.htm

Congress of the Philippines. (2010). Resolution of Both Houses No. 1, approving the Report of the Joint Committee, declaring the results of the national elections held on May 10, 2010, for the Offices of President and Vice President, and proclaming the duly elected President and Vice President of the Republic of the Philippines. http://www.gov.ph/downloads/2010/06jun/20100609-laws-Joint-Resolution-1.pdf

Congress of the Philippines. (2016). House committees: Appropriations. Accessed 12.07 from http://www.congress.gov.ph/committees/search.php?id=0504

Coronel, S. S. (2001). The media, the market and democracy: The case of the Philippines. *Media and democracy in Asia, 8*(2), 109–126.

Coronel, S. S., Chua, Y. T., Rimban, L., & Cruz, B. B. (2004). *The rulemakers: How the wealthy and well-born dominate congress.* Quezon City: Philippine Center for Investigative Journalism.

Croissant, A. (2011). Staatlichkeit und Demokratie in Südostasien. In A. T. Paul, A. Pelfini, & B. Rehbein (Eds.), *Globalisierung Süd* (pp. 54–86, SpringerLink: Bücher). Wiesbaden: VS Verlag.

Croissant, A., & Völkel, P. (2012). Party system types and party system institutionalization: Comparing new democracies in East and Southeast Asia. *Party Politics, 18*, 235–265. https://doi.org/10.1177/1354068810380096

Croissant, A., Kuehn, D., Lorenz, P., & Chambers, P. W. (2013). *Democratization and civilian control in Asia.* Houndmills: Palgrave Macmillan.

Desirto, D. (2009). A universalist history of the 1987 constitution. *Historia Constitucional, 10*, 383–444.

Dohner, R. S., & Intal, P. I. (1989). Debt crisis and adjustment in the Philippines. In J. Sachs (Ed.), *Developing country debt and the world economy* (pp. 169–192). Chicago: University of Chicago Press.

Espina-Varona, I. (2016). Opinion: Lawyering for the killers of journalists. *ABS-CBN News.* Accessed June 12, 2017, from http://news.abs-cbn.com/blogs/opinions/05/31/16/opinion-lawyering-for-the-killers-of-journalists

Franco, J. C. (2004). The Philippines: Fractious civil society and competing visions of democracy. In M. Alagappa (Ed.), *Civil society and political change in Asia: Expanding and contracting democratic space* (pp. 79–137). Stanford: Stanford University Press.

FRD. (2006). *Country profile: Philippines. Library of congress, federal research division.* Accessed June 10, 2017, from http://lcweb2.loc.gov/frd/cs/profiles/Philippines.pdf

Freedom House. (2015). *Freedom of the Press Index 2014: Harsh laws and violence drive global decline.* Accessed June 2, 2017, from https://freedomhouse.org/report/freedom-press/freedom-press-2015

Gatmaytan, D. B. (2006). It's all the rage: Popular uprisings and Philippine democracy. *Pacific Rim Law & Policy Journal, 15*(1), 1–37.

Gatmaytan, D. B., & Magno, C. (2011). Averting diversity: A review of nominations and appointments to the Philippine Supreme Court (1988–2008). *Asian Journal of Comparative Law.* https://doi.org/10.2202/1932-0205.1259

Golder, M. (2005). Democratic electoral systems around the world, 1946–2000. *Electoral Studies, 24*, 103–121. https://doi.org/10.1016/j.electstud.2004.02.008

Guerrero, L. L., & Tusalem, R. F. (2008). Mass public perceptions of democratization in the Philippines: Consolidation in Progress? In Y.-h. Chu, L. J. Diamond, A. J. Nathan, & D. C. Shin (Eds.), *How East Asians view democracy.* New York: Columbia University Press.

Gutierrez, E. U., Torrente, I. C., & Narca, N. G. (1992). *All in the family: A study of elites and power relations in The Philippines.* Quezon City: Institute for Popular Democracy.

Hartmann, C., Hassall, G., & Santos, S. M., Jr. (2001). Philippines. In D. Nohlen, F. Grotz, & C. Hartmann (Eds.), *Elections in Asia and the Pacific: A data handbook, Vol. II: South East Asia, East Asia, and the South Pacific* (pp. 185–238). Oxford: Oxford University Press.

Haynie, S. L. (1998). Paradise lost: Politicisation of the Philippine supreme court in the post Marcos era. *Asian Studies Review, 22*, 459–473. https://doi.org/10.1080/10357829808713210

Hellmann, O. (2011). *Political parties and electoral strategy: The development of party organization in East Asia.* New York: Palgrave Macmillan.

Hernandez, C. G. (1985). The Philippine military and civilian control: Under Marcos and beyond. *Third World Quarterly, 7*, 907–923. https://doi.org/10.1080/01436598508419874

Hernandez, C. G. (2006). The military in Philippine politics: Democratization, governance, and security sector reform. In T. S. E. Tadem & N. M. Morada (Eds.), *Philippine politics and governance: Challenges to democratization and development* (pp. 391–408). Diliman: University of the Philippines Press.

Hernandez, C. G. (2007). The military in Philippine politics: Retrospect and prospects. In L. C. Salazar & R. Severino (Eds.), *Whither the Philippines in the 21st century?* (pp. 78–99). Singapore: ISEAS.

Hernandez, C. G. (2016). The Philippines in 2015: A house still not in order? *Asian Survey, 56*, 115–122. https://doi.org/10.1525/as.2016.56.1.115

Hernandez, K. M. G., & Kraft, H. J. S. (2010). Armed forces as veto power: Civil-military relations in the Philippines. In P. W. Chambers & A. Croissant (Eds.), *Democracy under stress: Civil-military relations in South and Southeast Asia* (pp. 126–148). Bangkok: ISIS.

Hicken, A. (2009). *Building party systems in developing democracies.* New York: Cambridge University Press.

Hicken, A. (2015). Party and party system institutionalization in the Philippines. In A. Hicken & E. M. Kuhonta (Eds.), *Party system institutionalization in Asia: Democracies autocracies and the shadows of the past* (pp. 307–327). New York: Cambridge University Press.

Holmes, R. D. (2017). The dark side of electoralism: Opinion polls and voting in the 2016 Philippine presidential election. *Journal of Current Southeast Asian Affairs, 35*(3), 15–38.

Hutchcroft, P. D. (1998). *Booty capitalism: The politics of banking in the Philippines.* Ithaca: Cornell University Press.

Hutchcroft, P. D. (2008). The Arroyo Imbroglio in the Philippines. *Journal of Democracy, 19*(1).

IDEA. (2017). *Voter turnout database.* Accessed June 10, 2017, from http://www.idea.int/data-tools/data/voter-turnout

Internet World Stats. (2017). *Internet usage statistics: World internet users and 2017 population stats.* https://www.internetworldstats.com/stats.htm

Kasuya, Y. (2003). Weak institutions and strong movements: The case of President Estrada's impeachment and removal in the Philippines. In J. C. Baumgartner & N. Kada (Eds.), *Checking executive power: Presidential impeachment in comparative perspective* (pp. 45–64). Westport: Praeger Publishers.

Kasuya, Y. (2006). *Presidential term limits and party system stability in new democracies.* Prepared for delivery at the 2006 Annual Meeting of the American Political Science. http://citation.allacademic.com/meta/p_mla_apa_research_citation/1/5/2/7/4/pages152743/p152743-1.php

Kasuya, Y. (2008). *Presidential bandwagon: Parties and party systems in the Philippines.* Manila: Anvil.

Kawanaka, T. (2007). *Who eats the most?: Quantitative analysis of pork barrel distributions in the Philippines.* IDE Discussion Paper 126. Chiba.

Kawanaka, T. (2010). *Checking executive power: Presidential impeachment in comparative perspective.* IDE Discussion Paper 233. Chiba: IDE.

Kerkvliet, B. J. (2002). *The Huk rebellion: A study of peasant revolt in the Philippines.* Lanham: Rowman & Littlefield.

Kessler, R. J. (1989). *Rebellion and repression in the Philippines.* New Haven: Yale University Press.

Kreuzer, P. (2007). *Formen und Dynamiken politischer Gewalt in den Philippinen*. HSFK-Report 8/2007. Frankfurt am Main: Hessische Stiftung für Friedens- und Konfliktforschung.

Landé, C. H. (1965). *Leaders, factions, and parties: The structure of Philippine politics*. New Haven: Yale University Press.

Landé, C. H. (2001). The return of "People Power" in the Philippines. *Journal of Democracy, 12*, 88–102. https://doi.org/10.1353/jod.2001.0029

Linantud, J. L. (1998). Whither guns, goons, and gold?: The decline of factional election violence in the Philippines. *Contemporary Southeast Asia, 20*(3), 298–318.

Liu, J. (2012). *Democratic conceptions in East Asian societies: A contextualized analysis*. Asian Barometer Working Paper Series No. 56.

Maddison, A. (2001). *The world economy: Vol. 1 & 2*. Paris: OECD.

Mahoney, J., & Thelen, K. (2010). A theory of gradual institutional change. In J. Mahoney & K. Thelen (Eds.), *Explaining institutional change: Ambiguity, agency, and power* (pp. 1–37). New York: Cambridge University Press.

Manacsa, R. C., & Tan, A. C. (2005). Manufacturing parties. *Party Politics, 11*, 748–765. https://doi.org/10.1177/1354068805057608

Maslog, C. C. (2000). Philippines. In S. A. Gunaratne (Ed.), *Handbook of the media in Asia* (pp. 372–402). New Delhi: SAGE Publications.

McCoy, A. W. (1994). *An anarchy of families: State and family in the Philippines*. Quezon City: Ateneo de Manila University Press.

McKenna, T. M. (1998). *Muslim rulers and rebels: Everyday politics and armed separatism in the southern Philippines*. Berkeley: University of California Press.

Mendoza, R. U., Beja, E. L., Jr., Venida, V. S., & Yap, D. B. (2012). Inequality in democracy: Insights from an empirical analysis of political dynasties in the 15th Philippine Congress. *Philippine Political Science Journal, 33*(2), 132–145.

Merkel, W., Puhle, H.-J., & Croissant, A. (2003). *Defekte Demokratien, Bd. 1: Theorie*. Opladen: Leske & Budrich.

Muga, F. P. (2014). *How to fill the 58 party-list seats*. http://www.rappler.com/nation/politics/elections-2013/29567-how-to-fill-the-58-party-list-seats

Noda, K. (2011). *Politicization of Philippine budget system: Institutional and economic analysis on 'Pork-Barrel'*. PRI Discussion Paper Series (No.11 A-04). Tokyo: Research Department Policy Research Institute.

NSCB. (2014). *Philippine statistical yearbook*. Manila: National Statistical Coordination Board.

O'Donnell, G. A., & Schmitter, P. C. (1986). *Tentative conclusions about uncertain democracies*. Baltimore: Johns Hopkins University Press.

Onorato, M. P. (1970). Governor General Francis Burton Harrison and his administration: A re-appraisal. *Philippine Studies, 18*(1), 178–186.

Parreño, E. (1998). Pork. In S. S. Coronel (Ed.), *Pork and other perks: Corruption & governance in the Philippines* (pp. 32–56). Quezon City: Philippine Center for Investigative Journalism.

Patiño, P., & Velasco, D. (2006). Violence and voting in post-1986 Philippines. In A. Croissant, S. Kneip, & B. Martin (Eds.), *The politics of death: Political violence in Southeast Asia* (pp. 219–250). Münster: LIT Verlag.

PEI. (2016). *The perceptions of electoral integrity dataset: Version 4.5*. Accessed June 22, 2017, from https://sites.google.com/site/electoralintegrityproject4/projects/expert-survey-2

Philippine Daily Inquirer. (2016). *Winners of 59 seats in party-list race announced*. http://newsinfo.inquirer.net/786644/winners-of-59-seats-in-party-list-race-announced#ixzz4Zasa87le

Przeworski, A. (2003). Democracy and the market: Poltical and economic reforms in Eastern Europe and Latin America. In R. A. Dahl, I. Shapiro, & J. A. Cheibub (Eds.), *The democracy sourcebook* (pp. 76–92). Cambridge: MIT Press.

Putzel, J. (1999). Survival of an imperfect democracy in the Philippines. *Democratization, 6*, 198–223. https://doi.org/10.1080/13510349908403603

Querubin, P. (2012). Political reform and elite persistence: Term limits and political dynasties in the Philippines. *APSA 2012 Annual Meeting Paper*.

Querubin, P. (2016). Family and politics: Dynastic persistence in the Philippines. *Quarterly Journal of Political Science, 11*, 151–181. https://doi.org/10.1561/100.00014182

Quilop, R. (2006). Nation-state formation in the Philippines. In T. S. E. Tadem & N. M. Morada (Eds.), *Philippine politics and governance: Challenges to democratization and development* (pp. 1–13). Diliman: University of the Philippines Press.

Quimpo, N. G. (2005). The Left, elections, and the political party system in the Philippines. *Critical Asian Studies, 37*, 3–28. https://doi.org/10.1080/1467271052000305241

Quimpo, N. G. (2009). The Philippines: Predatory regime, growing authoritarian features. *The Pacific Review, 22*, 335–353. https://doi.org/10.1080/09512740903068388

Quimpo, N. G. (2015). Can the Philippines' wild oligarchy be tamed? In W. Case (Ed.), *Routledge handbook of Southeast Asian democratization* (pp. 335–351). London: Routledge.

Rebullida, L. G. G. (2006a). The executive: Martial law, constitutional authoritarianism, and the marcos administration. In T. S. E. Tadem & N. M. Morada (Eds.), *Philippine politics and governance: Challenges to democratization and development* (pp. 153–179). Diliman: University of the Philippines Press.

Rebullida, L. G. G. (2006b). The Philippine executive and redemocratization. In T. S. E. Tadem & N. M. Morada (Eds.), *Philippine politics and governance: Challenges to democratization and development* (pp. 179–217). Diliman: University of the Philippines Press.

Reporters without Borders. (2015). *World press freedom index 2015*. Accessed June 2, 2017, from https://rsf.org/en/world-press-freedom-index-2015

Rimban, L. (2005). *Party list: Messing with the party list*. Philippine Center for Investigative Journalism Special Report. Accessed June 10, 2017, from http://pcij.org/stories/messing-with-the-party-list/

Rogers, S. (2004). Philippine politics and the rule of law. *Journal of Democracy, 15*, 111–125. https://doi.org/10.1353/jod.2004.0071

Rother, S. (2009). Changed in migration?: Philippine return migrants and (un)democratic remittances. *European Journal of East Asian Studies, 8*, 245–274. https://doi.org/10.1163/156805809X12553326569713

Rüland, J. (2003). Constitutional debates in the Philippines: From presidentialism to parliamentarianism? *Asian Survey, 43*, 461–484. https://doi.org/10.1525/as.2003.43.3.461

Rüland, J., Jürgenmeyer, C., Nelson, M. H., & Ziegenhain, P. (2005). *Parliaments and political change in Asia*. Singapore: ISEAS.

Santos, J. M. C. (2003). Out of reach: Television, the public sphere and civil society in the Philippines. In P. Kitley (Ed.), *Television, regulation, and civil society in Asia* (pp. 131–148). London, New York: RoutledgeCurzon.

Santos, S. M., Jr., & Paz, V. M. (2010). *Primed and purposeful: Armed groups and human security efforts in the Philippines*. Geneva: Graduate Institute of International and Development Studies.

Santos, S. M., Jr., Abad, F., Rocamora, J., & Chay, F.-H. (1997). *Shift*. Manila: Ateneo Center for Social Policy and Public Affairs.

Sartori, G. (1994). *Comparative constitutional engineering: An inquiry into structures incentives and outcomes*. Basingstoke: Macmillan.

Shugart, M. S., & Carey, J. M. (1992). *Presidents and assemblies: Constitutional design and electoral dynamics*. Cambridge: Cambridge University Press.

Slater, D. (2010). *Ordering power: Contentious politics and authoritarian leviathans in Southeast Asia*. Cambridge: Cambridge University Press.

Stevens, M. (1993). *Origins of the 1986 Constitution*. Washington: National Defense University National Research Project F 26.

Supreme Court of the Philippines. *Annual Report 2009*. Accessed June 12, 2017, from http://sc.judiciary.gov.ph/publications/reports/SC_Annual_09.pdf

Tate, C. N., & Haynie, S. L. (1993). Authoritarianism and the functions of courts: A time series analysis of the Philippine Supreme Court, 1961–1987. *Law & Society Review, 27*, 707–740. https://doi.org/10.2307/3053951

Teehankee, J. (2002). Electoral politics in the Philippines. In A. Croissant, G. Bruns, & M. John (Eds.), *Electoral politics in Southeast & East Asia* (pp. 149–202). Singapore: Friedrich Ebert Foundation.

Teehankee, J. (2006). Consolidation or crisis of clientelistic democracy?: The 2004 synchronized elections in the Philippines. In A. Croissant & B. Martin (Eds.), *Between consolidation and crisis: Elections and democracy in five nations in Southeast Asia* (pp. 215–277). Münster: LIT Verlag.

The Philippine Star. (2001). *NPA strength growing, MILF decreasing.* Accessed June 12, 2017, from http://www.philstar.com/headlines/128079/npa-strength-growing-milf-decreasing

Thompson, M. R. (1995). *The anti-Marcos struggle: Personalistic rule and democratic transition in the Philippines.* New Haven: Yale University Press.

Thompson, M. R. (2011). Moore meets Gramsci and Burke in Southeast Asia: New democracies and civil society. In A. Croissant & M. Bünte (Eds.), *The crisis of democratic governance in Southeast Asia* (pp. 57–74). Houndmills: Palgrave Macmillan.

Thompson, M. R. (2017). Bloodied democracy: Duterte and the death of liberal reformism in the Philippines. *Journal of Current Southeast Asian Affairs, 35*(3), 39–68.

Tigno, J. V. (2006a). Electoral and party politics during the martial law period. In T. S. E. Tadem & N. M. Morada (Eds.), *Philippine politics and governance: Challenges to democratization and development* (pp. 77–97). Diliman: University of the Philippines Press.

Tigno, J. V. (2006b). Electoral and party politics in prewar Philippines. In T. S. E. Tadem & N. M. Morada (Eds.), *Philippine politics and governance: Challenges to democratization and development* (pp. 29–53). Diliman: University of the Philippines Press.

Tocqueville, A. d. (1955). *The old régime and the French revolution.* New York: Anchor Books.

Trinn, C., & Croissant, A. (2012). Democratic and semi-democratic conflict management in Southeast Asia. In J. J. Schwarzmantel & H. J. Kraetzschmar (Eds.), *Democracy and violence: Global debates and local challenges* (pp. 188–217). London: Routledge.

Tuazon, R. R. (1998). Sociocultural factors as determinants of press freedom: The Philippine expierence. In A. Latif (Ed.), *Walking the tightrope: Press freedom and professional standards in Asia* (pp. 238–250). Singapore: Asian Media Information and Communication Centre.

UNESCO. (2017). *UNESCO Institute for Statistics Data Center.* Accessed June 12, 2017, from http://data.un.org/Browse.aspx?d=UNESCO

Velasco, R. S. (2006). Parties, elections, and democratization in post-martial law Philippines. In T. S. E. Tadem & N. M. Morada (Eds.), *Philippine politics and governance: Challenges to democratization and development.* Diliman: University of the Philippines Press.

Villacorta, W. V. (1988). The dynamics and processes of writing the 1987 constitution. *Philippine Journal of Public Administration, 32*(3&4), 299–309.

Vitug, M. D. (2010). *Shadow of doubt: Probing the Supreme Court.* Quezon City, Philippines: Public Trust Media Group.

Vogel, B., Grabow, K., & Rieck, C. E. (2008). *KAS-Demokratiereport 2008.* Bonn: Konrad Adenauer Foundation.

Woo, J. (2011). *Security challenges and military politics in East Asia: From state building to post-democratization.* New York: Continuum.

World Bank. (2017a). *World development indicators.* http://data.worldbank.org/products/wdi

World Bank. (2017b). *Worldwide governance indicators.* http://data.worldbank.org/data-catalog/worldwide-governance-indicators

Wurfel, D. (1988). *Filipino politics: Development and decay.* Ithaca: Cornell University Press.

Zimmermann, R. (2012). Alte Bande reißen nicht?: Richterliche (Un-)Abhängigkeit am philippinischen Supreme Court. *Internationales Asienforum, 43*(3–4), 325–350.

Singapore: Contradicting Conventional Wisdoms About Authoritarianism, State, and Development

9

© Springer International Publishing AG 2018
A. Croissant, P. Lorenz, *Comparative Politics of Southeast Asia*,
https://doi.org/10.1007/978-3-319-68182-5_9

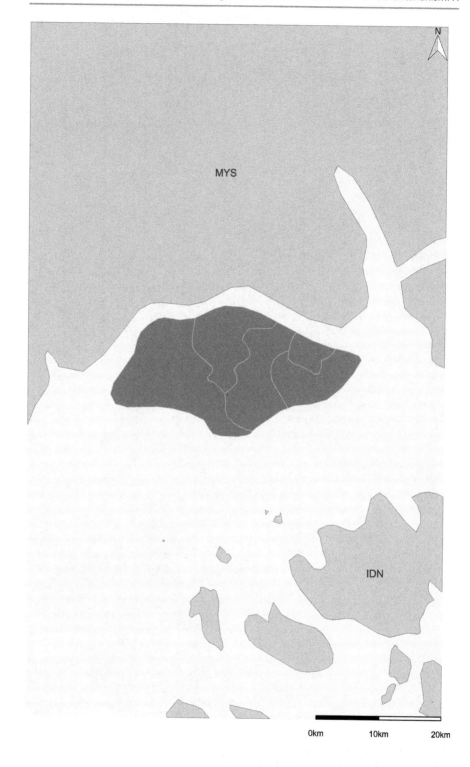

9.1 Historical Background

Singapore is an island city-state situated at the southern tip of the Malay Peninsula, surrounded by Malaysia and Indonesia and with a land area of slightly more than 700 km^2, and one of the 20 smallest states worldwide. As of 2012, only 61.8% of its 5.4 million inhabitants are Singaporean citizens, of which 74.3% are ethnic Chinese, 13.4% are Malayan, and 9.1% are of Indian descent (see Table 9.1). Despite the many different languages, religions, and regional groups that make up these communal groupings, they are usually perceived as three distinct ethnic groups (Hefner 2001; Mauzy and Milne 2002; Vasu 2012).

In 1819, the British established a trading post on the Temasek Island. In 1826, Singapore, Malacca, Penang, and Dinding became the "Strait Settlements," which were under direct British control as a Crown colony from 1867 until 1947. Singapore's position as the hub of the regional sea trade, its efficient colonial administration, well-developed infrastructure, and British legal system contributed to the continuous growth of the city's population from little more than 10,000 people in 1824 to almost 940,000 in 1947 (Saw 2012, p. 30). During its colonial period, Singapore's economy was dominated by *entrepôt*[1] trade. Already in 1913, Singapore had the highest GDP per capita in all of Southeast Asia, which further increased from USD1279 in 1913 to USD2129 in 1950, the highest among all economies in Asia-Pacific (Maddison 2001, p. 215).

From 1942 to 1945, Japanese troops occupied the city. Much like in other parts of Southeast Asia, Japanese rule and repression kindled nationalist sentiments and political mobilization in the postwar years. The Chinese-dominated Malayan Communist Party, trade unions, and student associations were at the forefront of the anti-colonial agitation, which accentuated the substantial ethnic tensions between Chinese and Malays (Wah 1973) and ultimately forced the British to introduce limited self-rule (Carnell 1955, p. 97). In 1955, the first elections for a predominantly elected legislative assembly were held (Hwee 2002, pp. 203–204). This triggered the formation of political parties like the People's Action Party (PAP) and the Labour Front, the latter providing Singapore's first chief minister after the election. In 1959, Singapore adopted a new constitution and attained self-government. The PAP under its leader Lee Kuan Yew decisively won the elections in May of the same year, and the party has remained in power until today.

Negotiations between Singapore and the Federation of Malaya led to the union of Singapore, Malaya, Sarawak, and Sabah—formerly British Northern Borneo—in September 1963. Singapore joined the Federation under a set of special conditions, including wide-ranging political autonomy and relatively minor contributions to the federal budget (Milne 1966, pp. 175–177). Moreover, Malays in Singapore did not enjoy the same prerogatives as in the rest of the country, threatening the fragile power-sharing arrangement among the Malay, Chinese, and Indian population (Cheong 1999, p. 123). Clashes between Chinese and Malays in the city further

---

[1]Exporting imported goods without processing or repackaging.

Table 9.1 Country profile

Population (2017)	Year of full national sovereignty	Form of government
5,888,926	1965	Republic
Total area	**Current constitution enacted**	**Head of state**
709 km²	1959	Halimah Yacob (since 2017)
GDP p.c. (PPP, 2012)	**Official language**	**Head of government**
53,266	Mandarin, English, Malay, Tamil	Lee Hsien Loong (since 2004)
Ethnic groups	**Democracy score (BTI 2016)**	**System of government**
Chinese 74.3%, Malays 13.4%, Indians 9.1%, others 3.2%	5.37 (range from 1 to 10, higher scores indicate higher levels of democracy)	Semi-presidential
Religious groups	**Regime type**	**Cabinet type**
Buddhists 33.9%, Muslims 14.3%, Taoists 11.3%, Christians 18.1% Hindus 5.2%, others/no religion 17.1%	Electoral authoritarian regime	One-party cabinet

Sources: CIA (2017), World Bank (2017a)

strained relations with the federal government in Kuala Lumpur (Leifer 1964, p. 1115). Ultimately, the governments in Singapore and Kuala Lumpur failed to conclude a mutual agreement about the distribution of tax revenues and for a common market. This resulted in the expulsion of Singapore from the Federation on August 9, 1965.

In the following five decades, Singapore became one of the most affluent and developed societies in Asia. Soon after independence, Singapore's per capita income exceeded—and continues to exceed—that of the United Kingdom, and from 1965 until 2012, the average annual growth in real per capita GDP has been 5.6%. In addition, the PAP government provided for continuously high investment and saving rates, secure property rights and political stability, a highly effective state bureaucracy, and low levels of corruption, resulting in the provision of public goods like education, housing, social security, and health. This development was due to a conjunction of several conditions, such as a dedicated and benevolent, yet authoritarian, government, as well as favorable historical legacies of British rule, including a professional civil service, a reliable legal system, and statutory boards such as the Housing and Development Board (HDB) and the Central Provident Fund (CPF). The CFP was created to secure pensions, housing development, and medical services, and is financed through a mandatory contribution paid by all Singaporean employees and self-employed citizens. All contributors can access their money at 55 years of age, but the government has used the capital stock to finance its economic policies (Haque 2004, p. 233). Most importantly, however, the government of Lee Kuan Yew (1959–1990) recognized that to remain in power, the PAP would need to improve overall living conditions instead of simply convincing citizens of the government's legitimacy through ideological appeals or repression (Rodan 2008, p. 236).

For political scientists, Singapore in many ways presents a fascinating puzzle (Verweij and Pelizzo 2009, p. 19). First, the city-state appears to contradict the assumptions of modernization theory, which states a causal link between economic development, social modernization, and democratization (Lipset 1960; Boix and Stokes 2003). While Singapore has become one of the most affluent non-oil exporting countries in the world (UNDP 2015) and possesses all the prerequisites modernization theory considers necessary for sustaining a political democracy, the country still has an authoritarian government. The scholarship on Singapore classifies it as a "party regime" (Geddes et al. 2014), "dominant party authoritarianism" (Hadenius and Teorell 2006), "semi-democracy" (Case 2002), "soft authoritarianism" (Means 1996), "electoral authoritarianism" (Case 2011), or "hegemonial electoral authoritarianism" (Schedler 2013). In fact, Singapore combines institutional trappings of democracy such as multiparty elections with authoritarian political practices. Elections are the only legitimate route to power, but the PAP government systematically abuses the advantages of incumbency to insulate its monopoly on political power against political challengers by imposing disadvantages on opposition parties, curtailing the development of civil society and the media, and suppressing political dissent. In contrast to Malaysia, where opposition parties are in a position to challenge the ruling *Barisan Nasional* (National Front) government (see Chap. 6), no opposition force in Singapore is able to threaten the hegemonic position of the People's Action Party.

Secondly, the description of Singapore as a "party regime" points to the fact that the government since 1959 has consistently been in the hands of the same party. However, in contrast to other party regimes in Southeast Asia such as Vietnam and Laos, there is a rigid separation between state and party institutions. As some observers have aptly noted: "The PAP is everywhere, but it is the PAP government, not the party apparatus" (Mauzy and Milne 2002, p. 49). Finally, the characterization of Singapore's political order as "soft authoritarianism" emphasizes the fact that repression is of secondary importance for the longevity of PAP rule. Even though repression is one part of the toolkit of authoritarian survival strategies in Singapore, it remains of low intensity (Levitsky and Way 2010) and takes mainly the form of more or less subtle techniques of social control. In fact, over the past six decades, the PAP government has created a highly effective system of "calibrated coercion" and the depoliticization of its society (George 2007).

9.2 Constitutional History

Singapore's constitution came into power in 1959. It granted Singapore full autonomy in internal affairs as part of the British Commonwealth of Nations. After expulsion from Malaysia, it became the new basic law of the Republic of Singapore on December 22, 1965. Singapore's first Chief Minister, David Marshall, once described the constitutional text as the "untidiest and most confusing constitution that any country has started life with" (quoted in Tan and Thio 2009, p. 8). This is due to two main factors. First, accession to and expulsion from Malaysia required several amendments, which are still part of the constitutional charter. Second, since the 1960s, parliament has constantly refined the constitution, amending the text some 38 times between 1965 and 2008 (Thio 2008, p. 256).

The constitution contains 14 parts and 204 articles as of July 2010. Parts I to IV include the declaration of national sovereignty, recognition of the constitution as the Supreme Law of the land (Art. 4), the amendment procedure, and a catalogue of basic rights (Art. 9–16). Parts V to VIII determine the organization and powers of state organs, including the presidency (Art. 17–22o); the Council of Presidential Advisors (CPA, Art. 37a-37m); the Presidential Council for Minority Rights; the government, consisting of cabinet and prime minister (Art. 23–37); the unicameral parliament (Art. 38–67); and the judiciary (Art. 93–101). Part IX provides regulations on administration and public service (Art. 102–119); Part X contains provisions on citizenship (Art. 128–141); and Part XI (Art. 142–148h) includes financial provisions. Part XII grants parliament and president special powers against subversion and emergency powers. The final two, Parts XIII (Art. 152–156) and XIV (Art. 157–163), include general regulations concerning—among other things—minority rights (Art. 152), the Muslim religion (Art. 153), as well as transitional and closing regulations (Art. 157–163).

Unlike most other Southeast Asian constitutions, the Singaporean basic law does not address social, economic, or cultural rights or collective human rights. Art. 152 recognizes the rights of ethnic and religious minorities and the special status of Malays as an indigenous group, but does not contain justiciable group entitlements. Rather, the rights of minority groups are realized by securing the individual rights of their members under the equal protection clause in Art. 12 (Thio 2008, p. 254) and the Presidential Council for Minority Rights that was formed in 1970.

Overall, the constitution is a peculiar conglomeration of constitutional principles (Thio 2008). On the one hand, Singapore's constitution is inextricably shaped by British influences. Following the tradition of "Queen in Parliament," the executive is part of the legislature (Art. 38); until 1994, the British Judicial Committee of the Privy Council remained the court of final appeal (Silverstein 2008). Furthermore, Singapore follows the Westminster model of parliamentarianism and concentrates political power in the cabinet and the office of the prime minister. On the other hand, Singapore's constitutional law breaks with the British tradition of parliamentary sovereignty: Singapore has a written constitution that is granted a privileged status as the Supreme Law and is more difficult to change than other legislation. There are two amendment procedures: First, two-thirds of the members of parliament can amend the constitution (Art. 5.2a). Second, the president can request a constitutional plebiscite if the amendment would affect fundamental liberties, individual regulations concerning the presidency, national sovereignty, or the process of dissolving parliament (Art. 5.3). Finally, fundamental liberties in Art. 9 through 16 are granted special protection, and the constitution grants the Supreme Court the right to the judicial review of legislation (Art. 93 and Supreme Court of

Judicature Act). Although the constitution has been formally rigid, this has not precluded the PAP-dominated parliament and government from adjusting the constitutional text to their political needs. The sheer number of constitutional amendments indicate de facto parliamentary sovereignty (Tan and Thio 2009). Furthermore, the fact that courts are precluded from denying the applicability of a law severely constrains judicial review. Judges are also bound by a strict constructionist interpretation of the constitution, i.e., they can only base their judgments of the text on the constitution and not its underlying goals, as is the case under teleological interpretations (Thio 2008; Rajah 2012). Finally, Art. 149 and Part XII of the constitution preclude any judicial review of legislation that limits the freedom of expression, association or assembly, the free exercise of religion, and the freedom of movement. In addition, parliamentary laws, including Paragraph 18 of the Maintenance of Religious Harmony Act and Paragraph 8B(2) of the Internal Security Act, also exclude other state actions from judicial review (Thio 2008, pp. 283–284).

9.3   System of Government

Before 1993, Singapore had a parliamentary system of government. Following constitutional amendments in 1991, the presidency became a popularly elected office, leading political scientists to disagree about how to classify the country's system of government. Classifications range from parliamentary (Blondel 2006) and semi-presidential (Wu 2011) to presidential (Elgie 2013). Based on the constitutional position as well as the role and powers of the presidency relative to that of the prime minister and the parliament, it seems appropriate to consider Singapore a case of semi-presidentialism. The president is head of state, while the prime minister is the head of government. Prime minister and cabinet are accountable to the president, who can dismiss the prime minister by "acting in his discretion" (Art. 26 1b) but also collectively accountable to parliament (Art. 24.2), which can dismiss the prime minister by majority vote for political reasons.[2] Considering the political reality of Singapore since 1959—a tradition of decisive PAP majorities in parliament, PAP's monopoly over government, and the unwillingness of presidents to make use of their constitutional powers—Articles 26(1b) and 24 (2) are dead letter provisions. Moreover, Singapore lacks all the institutional safeguards meant to limit the power of an otherwise omnipotent elected government, including a strong opposition, a nonpartisan bureaucracy, strong judicial review, powerful interest groups, and a pluralist media (cf. Sajó 1999; Lijphart 2012).

---

[2]The fact that the constitution mentions this power of parliament merely in passing in a clause detailing the authority of appointed members of parliament (Art. 39 2(d)) is emblematic of the text's confusing structure.

9.3.1   President

The president is head of state and a component of the legislative branch of government, but the prime minister is head of the cabinet, which determines the general direction of the government. Since 1991, the president is no longer appointed by parliament but is popularly elected for a single 6-year term. While members of political parties are barred from running for Singapore's highest political office, all persons elected to the office of president since 1993 have been approved by the ruling PAP.

The president can be impeached for criminal misconduct or violation of his or her constitutional duties (Art. 79 2). The prime minister or a quarter of the elected members of parliament (MPs) can file a complaint for impeachment. The Supreme Court proceeds with the trial if a majority of elected MPs supports the resolution (Art. 22L). The president is assisted by the Council of Presidential Advisors (CPA), whose six permanent members are appointed by the president (2) and the prime minister (2), the chief justice of the Supreme Court (1), and the chair of the Public Service Commission (1) (Art. 37b). The CPA has substantial authority since the president must consult the council in the exercise of several of his powers. Should the president act against its recommendation, parliament can overturn the president's decision. The 1991 amendments to the constitution empowered the president with new oversight and veto powers over the government and civil service. Following a series of disputes over the interpretation of these new powers between President Ong Teng Cheong (1993–1999) and the cabinet, the Supreme Court ruled in favor of the government's position that in most cases the president exercises powers in accordance with the advice of the prime minister acting under the cabinet's general authority (George 2002, p. 188). In the 2000s, a series of constitutional amendments again reduced presidential authority (Mauzy and Milne 2002, pp. 153–154; Thio 2008, p. 258).

The constitutional powers of the presidency fall into three substantive categories (Tan 1997; Thio 2008). First, the president has limited oversight authority over the national budget and fiscal policies: After consulting with the CPA, the president can veto the annual budget and other financial legislation, government loans against the CPF, as well as the budget plans for several Statutory Boards and state-owned enterprises (Art. 21, 22, 142 and 148B).

Second, the president has substantial appointment authority. He or she appoints and dismisses the prime minister and, upon proposal, the remaining cabinet (Art. 25). Yet, the president is obliged to respect parliamentary majorities. At the request of the prime minister or at his or her own discretion, the president can dissolve parliament if no member of parliament appears to be able to form a cabinet that has the support of the majority of MPs (Art. 21, Abs. 2[b]; Art 65, Abs. 1[f]). Furthermore, (s)he can block the appointment of several senior officials, justices of the Supreme Court, the attorney general, the chief of defence force, and the chief of police, but parliament can overturn the presidential veto by two-thirds majority if the head of state acted against CPA recommendation (Art. 21, 22, 25, 151).

The third category includes the right of pardon and the declaration of a state of emergency; (s)he can request constitutional interpretations by the Supreme Court and call for a constitutional referendum. Finally, the president has the authority to stop any measures implemented by the government based on the Internal Security Act (ISA) or the Maintenance of Religious Harmony Act (MRHA). It is also worth mentioning what powers the presidency lacks: The president can neither veto nor initiate any parliamentary bills, nor can he or she pass executive decrees. While the presidential Council for Minority Rights reviews all legislation and can send it back to parliament if it violates the principle of equal protection of ethnic or religious groups (Art. 78), this does not include financial or tax legislation as well as laws concerning internal security and public order or legislation prioritized by the prime minister. Moreover, the prime minister nominates the members of this council, for which the president cannot withhold approval.

9.3.2 Prime Minister and Cabinet

Prime minister and cabinet control the general direction of the government. The cabinet currently has 18 ministers, who are collectively accountable to parliament. The president appoints the prime minister and the other members of the cabinet from among the members of parliament. There is no formal parliamentary confirmation vote of the government. Together with the Central Executive Committee of the People's Action party and the National Armed Forces Council, the cabinet is Singapore's main policy-making body and there is substantial overlap in the membership of the three institutions.

The prime minister is the head of government, decides the portfolio of his or her ministers, can issue political directives to individual ministers, and chairs cabinet meetings. The different departments are closely coordinated, but the cabinet's actual function depends largely on the leadership style of the prime minister (Leong 2000, p. 96). While Lee Kuan Yew (1959–1990) preferred a more paternalistic style and directed government policy, his successors Goh Chok Tong (1990–2004) and Lee's Kuan Yew's eldest son, Lee Hsien Loong (since 2004), prefer a more coordinative style (Leong 2000). The prime minister is also the general secretary of the ruling PAP and commands a large staff in the Prime Minister's Office (PMO), which further strengthens the position. The PMO coordinates the work of ministries and policy-making within the cabinet. It also directs the implementation of those programs and policies that fall under the responsibility of government agencies like the Elections Department, the Public Service Division, the National Security Coordination Secretariat, or Statutory Boards like the Monetary Authority of Singapore and the Civil Service College. Finally, the office monitors the Corrupt Practices Bureau, an intragovernmental anticorruption unit (Hamilton-Hart 2000; Croissant et al. 2013).

9.3.3 Parliament

Singapore has a unicameral legislature elected for a 5-year term. The 89 members (MPs) are elected in a first-past-the-post-system in 13 single-member constituencies

(SMCs) and 16 multi-member districts, or the so-called Group Representation Constituencies (GRC). In every GRC, one of the four to six seats is reserved for a person of Singapore's Malay, Indian, or other ethnic minority. Furthermore, the selection committee of the parliament can nominate up to nine persons without party affiliation as Nominated Members of Parliament (NMP) by the president. Finally, to guarantee the minimum representation of political parties other than the PAP in parliament, opposition candidates who were defeated in a general or by-election can be appointed as Non-Constituency Members of Parliament (NCMPs). The actual number of NCMPs is determined by subtracting the number of elected seats won by the opposition from nine (Art. 39). For example, in the general elections of 2015, the Worker's Party won six mandates, and therefore, the parliament selected three NCMPs (see below). Nominated and Non-Constituency MPs only serve for half of the regular parliamentary term and are barred from voting on the budget, financial legislation, constitutional amendments, and motions of no-confidence or motions to impeach the president (Art. 39, 2). The PAP government justified the creation of NCMPs in 1984, GRCs in 1988, and NMPs in 1990 by pointing to the necessity of increasing the representativeness of the parliament and making it more inclusionary (Hwee 2002, p. 208). Yet, it also created convenient co-optation mechanisms for the ruling party: While GRCs provide a minimal degree of representation of ethnic minorities in the legislature, NMPs and NCMPs allow the government to co-opt potential societal opposition and to make limited policy concessions to obtain the cooperation needed.

The sociological profile of the Singaporean parliament has changed substantially since the 1980s. This also reflects important changes in the structure of the "power elite" (Chen 1975) in Singapore. While in the early years, the political elite as represented in the national parliament referred to party cadres, and also included many middle-class professionals, intellectuals, and trade union leaders, today the members of parliament—though still PAP members—are more often civil bureaucrats (i.e., permanent secretaries and chairmen of statutory boards), other top civil servants, and university professors. Likewise, the number of well-educated ex-military officers or "scholar-soldiers" who continue their career in state or government bodies after retiring from active service has been on the rise (Vennewald 1993, pp. 113–115; Mauzy and Milne 2002, p. 46).

The main functions of the parliament in Singapore are representing and deliberating government-initiated legislation but not overseeing the government, which, of course, is no surprise given the decades-long PAP hegemony over the political system. Legislative initiatives of individual MPs, the so-called Private Members Bills, are extremely rare (Croissant et al. 2013). Parliament also delegated significant legislative authority to the cabinet, allowing it to issue substantial legislation without parliamentary involvement. High levels of party discipline and the fact that the Central Executive Board of the PAP controls the process of candidate selection before elections have reduced the blackmail potential of parliamentary backbenchers who are not members of the cabinet. Following the creation of "Government Parliamentary Committees," charged with reviewing government initiatives in 1987, noncabinet members of parliament have been better involved in the legislative process (Rodan 2008, p. 242). Nevertheless, weak and ineffective opposition parties mean that parliamentary instruments of government oversight such as written or oral inquiries, question time, or the Public Accounts Committee are rarely used (Chee 1976, p. 425; Rodan 2008).

Since Singapore is a case of resilient electoral authoritarianism, a better understanding of the role of parliament requires shifting the focus from the standard functions of legislative assemblies in democratic political systems to the question of how nominally democratic institutions such as an elected legislature contribute to the survival and maintenance of PAP rule in Singapore. In fact, Singapore confirms the prevalent view in contemporary authoritarianism studies that parliaments can perform important functions for authoritarian regimes (cf. Gandhi 2008). First, having an elected assembly, even as a subordinate institution, provides the regime with some semblance of procedural legitimacy for the outcome of political decision-making. Second, it provides a handy tool for the ruling party to co-opt and control opposition political parties into the existing institutional framework. Third, citizens can have their voices heard, for example, by petitioning members of parliaments, which not only offers a legitimate opportunity to raise questions or concerns about government policies but also provides the government important feedback on its policy options and policy experimentations. For example, the LGBT movement has recently used this approach to initiate a debate about the decriminalization of homosexual practices (Weiss 2014). Fourth, reserved representation for ethnic minorities was instrumental in integrating economically underprivileged groups like Malays into the political system (Chee 1976, p. 438; Mutalib 2011). Fifth, PAP delegates provide linkages between the government and local constituencies in their districts. Sixth, PAP members of parliament provide cross-links with influential Statutory Boards, the National Trade Union Congress (NTUC), and trade union cooperatives (Chee 1976, pp. 433–434). Finally, elected members of parliament are empowered to lead so-called Town Councils, created in 1989. Town Councils are administrative units rather than representative bodies. Town Councils decide on local estate management matters and manage Housing and Development Board (HDB) estates in Singapore, which house more than 90% of the population (Croissant et al. 2013; Thio 2008, p. 252). Each of the 16 GRCs overlap with one of the Town Councils. Only the electoral district Potong Pasir, represented in parliament by the opposition from 1984 to 2011, had its own Town Council. Each of the councils is provided with a subsidy of three million SGD or 15% of HDB revenue (Croissant et al. 2013). These subsidies and the privileged position of districts represented by PAP members of parliament can be used by the ruling party to effectively distribute government resources to maximize their political payoff (Ooi 1998, pp. 367–368; Mauzy and Milne 2002; Mutalib 2002, p. 667).

9.4 Legal and Judicial System

Singapore's legal system is based on the British common law. The criminal justice system follows the rules for a fair trial, i.e., the right to be heard by an independent tribunal, public hearing, and right to counsel and freedom from torture. Unlike Malaysia, Singapore does not apply Malay *adat* customary law. The constitution

(Art. 153) and the Administration of Muslim Law Act allow for the creation of Islamic courts, whose jurisdiction is restricted to family, inheritance, and funeral law (Thio 2008, p. 266; Rajah 2012, p. 3). In all other cases, the Anglo-Singaporean legal system applies to all residents irrespective of race, religion, or place of origin. The State Courts—or Subordinate Courts prior to 2014—form the first tier of the court system. They consist of District Courts, Magistrates' Courts, Juvenile Courts, Coroners' Courts, Small Claims Tribunals, and a Family Court. Even though Singapore is often characterized as an administrative state in which power is concentrated in the hands of a bureaucratic elite and administrative law, that is, "the law relating to the control of government power...including the detailed rules which govern the exercise of administrative decision taking" (Thio 2008, p. 260) is of paramount importance in the Singaporean context, there is no system of administrative courts.

The Supreme Court is the highest court of the land. It is made up of the Court of Appeals and the High Court and hears both civil and criminal matters. Prior to 1994, the Judicial Committee of Her Britannic Majesty's Privy Council served as Singapore's court of appeal. Singapore lacks a specialized constitutional court, and judicial review rests with the Supreme Court. In some cases, the president can request an expert opinion on the effects of constitutional articles or constitutional amendments from an ad hoc constitutional tribunal situated in the Supreme Court.

The State Courts Act regulates the organization and jurisdiction of the State Courts and the selection of judges. Section VIII of the constitution and the Supreme Court of Judicature Act together provide the legal basis of the Supreme Court. There are currently 14 judges (including four judges of appeal and the chief justice), five senior judges on the Supreme Court Bench, and 11 judicial commissioners (Supreme Court of Singapore 2017). The president on recommendation by the prime minister appoints the judges. Their tenure ends once they turn 65, but they can continue on a contractual basis (Silverstein 2008, p. 85). They can be dismissed from office for misbehavior, inability, and infirmity of body or mind by an ad hoc tribunal of five current or former justices of the Supreme Court formed by the president (Art. 98, 3). The attorney general, who serves as the government's legal advisor, and all judges of the lower courts are administrative officials and thereby part of the executive. Judges at lower courts are appointed by the government and can be transferred to other administrative posts at any time (Worthington 2001, p. 494). The actual tenure of the judges in the State Court is usually 1–2 years (Thio 2008; Silverstein 2008).

One of the exceptional features of Singaporean authoritarianism is that a "regime that has systematically undercut 'rule of law' freedoms has managed to be acclaimed as [a] 'rule of law' state" (Rajah 2012, p. 3). For example, the World Bank's Worldwide Governance Indicators project, which reports aggregate and individual governance indicators for over 200 countries over the period 1996–2015 for six dimensions of governance, has continuously ranked Singapore highest in Southeast Asia for the rule of law and control of corruption. Furthermore, according to the World Bank data, Singapore is also among the top-ranked countries worldwide, with more than 95% of countries in its high-income countries group rating

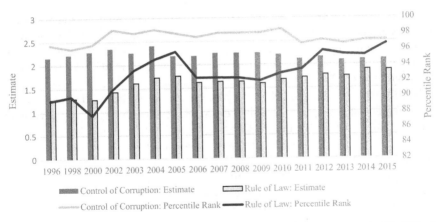

Fig. 9.1 Rule of Law and Control of Corruption in Singapore, 1996–2015. Note: The World Bank reports the aggregate indicators in two ways: (1) in their standard normal units, ranging from approximately −2.5 to 2.5, and (2) in percentile rank terms from 0 to 100, with higher values corresponding to better outcomes. Percentile indicates the percentage of countries worldwide that rate below the selected country. Source: World Bank (2017b)

below Singapore in terms of both rule of law and controlling corruption (see Fig. 9.1).

This result appears to contradict the conventional view among scholars that a lack of democratic competition necessarily leads to the spread of corruption and nepotism (Verweij and Pelizzo 2009, p. 19) and suggests a successful marriage of autocracy and rule of law in Singapore. However, this should be taken with a grain of salt. Singapore's score on the World Bank indicators reflects mainly the successful protection of (economic) property rights, the reliable enforcement of contracts, the quality of the police, the effective judicial system as a prerequisite for an investment and business friendly environment, the small risk of becoming a victim of a crime in Singapore, and the absence of political terror and torture. While these are important ingredients of the rule of law, they alone do not provide a comprehensive picture (Thiery et al. 2009). Singapore's "strategic management of law" (Rajah 2012, p. 3) gives the country all formal aspects of a rule of law state as all administrative and government action is based on law. At the same time, the government uses laws as the most convenient way to regulate society and to govern (Silverstein 2008; Moustafa and Ginsburg 2008, p. 4). This is the classic understanding of rule by law, where oppressive laws are used to limit citizen's rights and to inhibit political opposition, while the rule of law envisages that the law will limit the power and right of the state to impose restrictions on citizen's basic and fundamental human freedoms (Rajah 2012, p. 4). Such limitations and restrictions include the frequent appointment of career officials and PAP members as temporary judges at State Courts or the Supreme Court as well as legal constraints on the exercise of civil liberties, which penalize several forms of undesired political behavior (Worthington 2001; Rajah 2012, p. 42). A notable aspect of this system of using law as a tool for oppressing civil society and potential opposition is that its impact is mainly to preempt the open articulation of dissent or opposition. Common knowledge about its existence serves as an effective deterrent against contention, while coercion is only used selectively and as an effective warning against anyone wanting to get involved in oppositional behavior (Case 2002; George 2007; Ortmann 2010). The government's toolkit includes the Internal Security Act (ISA) of 1960 (amended in 1985), the Maintenance of Religious Harmony Act of 1991, the Societies Act (1967 [1988]), the Sedition Act (1964 [1985]), the Official Secret Act (1935 [2012]), the Public Order Act (2009), and the Defamation Act (1957 [2014]). The ISA allows for the preventive arrest of suspects without a warrant for up to 2 years; the Societies Act requires the official registration of all noncommercial associations of more than 10 members, and groups with a political agenda have to register as political organizations. The Public Order Act empowers authorities to banish individuals or order them to "move on" under suspicion that a location will be used to pursue a political agenda without a permit (Croissant et al. 2013). The MRHA grants the power to impose restraining orders against anyone threatening the peaceful coexistence of different racial and religious groups (Rajah 2012, pp. 236–237). Key concepts in these laws are underspecified, and it is impossible for targeted individuals to challenge the validity of the claims made against them since the government can act preemptively, i.e., before a punishable offense has been committed (Rajah 2012, p. 17). The same is true for the so-called out-of-bounds (OB) markers meant to delineate illegal from tolerated political criticism (Ortmann 2012, 165). Furthermore, the Defamation Act grants public officials a privileged status, and opposition figures can easily be sued for defamation upon criticizing members of the government or the parliament, facing draconic fines. In the past, litigation was pursued until opposition politicians such as Joshua Benjamin Jeyaretnam (Worker's Party) and Chee Soon Juan (Singapore Democratic Party) were declared bankrupt, whereupon they had to resign their seats in parliament (Tey 2008, p. 898; Rajah 2012, p. 18).

9.5   Electoral System and Elections

Multiparty elections have been the hallmark of electoral authoritarianism in Singapore since 1959. As in other authoritarian regimes where multiparty elections take place, they are used as a tool of the government rather than an instrument of choice. As Schedler (2002, p. 36) notes, "by organizing periodic elections" authoritarian regimes "try to obtain at least a semblance of democratic legitimacy, hoping to satisfy external as well as internal actors. At the same time, by placing those elections under tight authoritarian controls they try to cement their continued hold on power." Yet, in contrast to Malaysia's competitive authoritarianism, where opposition parties are forced to compete with the government on an uneven playing field but still have a chance to challenge the ruling parties in the electoral arena, in hegemonic electoral authoritarian regimes such as Singapore, the opposition is just too weak and ineffective to pose any threat to the regime. Elections serve the self-reproduction of power in three distinct ways. First, elections provide the PAP with procedural and input legitimacy for its rule. Second, multiparty elections serve an informational role as well. The results help the PAP government identify opposition strongholds and reveal information about the popularity of the opposition's demands, voter preferences, and the popularity of the PAP's own party candidates. With this information, the government can target opposition strongholds and by withholding government subsidies, intimidate local constituencies into switching allegiance before the next election (Gandhi and Lust-Okar 2009, p. 404). In a typical example, the government threatened to cut housing development in districts showing strong opposition support following the 1997 general election (Mauzy and Milne 2002, p. 151). Third, elections are a tool for the PAP and its government to co-opt the opposition through mechanisms like non-constituency MPs.

In 1955, Singapore adopted the British electoral system of plurality vote in single-member constituencies. Compulsory voting was introduced in 1959. Nonvoters have their names deleted from the voter list and have to file an application to be reregistered (Rieger 2001, pp. 244–246). Since 2001, Singaporean citizens with residence in other countries are allowed to vote in some of Singapore's embassies (Hwee 2002). The government is free to schedule new elections during the 5-year parliamentary term, but elections have to be held within 90 days after the dissolution of parliament (Rieger 2001, p. 243). There are no legal requirements to fill vacant seats in by-elections within a specific period. The Election Department under the domain of the Prime Minister's Office is responsible for organizing national parliamentary elections, which create the only popularly elected institution in the city-state.

Registered voters with a residency of at least 10 years are eligible for parliamentary office. Any person who has been sentenced to a minimum of 1 year in prison or a fine of at least 2000 SGD by a Singaporean or Malaysian court (Art. 45)—a relatively low fine by local standards—within 5 years of the election is barred from running as a candidate. Nonparty candidates ("independents") can contest single-member districts, while in GRCs all candidates running on the same ticket have to be members of the same party or be a group of independent candidates (Ooi 1998, p. 376). Teams of candidates for GRCs must meet a quota for Malay, Indian, or "other" minority community candidates (Rieger 2001, p. 247). All candidates are required to deposit a security of 16,000 SGD, and only candidates who win at least 12.5% of the vote in their district get reimbursed. While this is ostensibly meant to discourage insincere campaigns, it also impedes opposition parties and sincere independents (Croissant et al. 2013, p. 8). In addition, candidates for the presidency must not be a member of a political party and are required to have served as a cabinet minister or senior official in the government administration, such as chief justice of the Supreme Court or attorney general, or as chairman of the board of directors or chief executive officer of a company registered under the Companies Act with a paid-up capital of at least USD100 million. In 1999 and 2005, only one candidate in the respective elections fulfilled the strict requirements. The 2011 poll was the first election with three candidates, two of which were endorsed by the PAP, however (Tan 2012, p. 274).

Multiparty elections in Singapore are free but not fair. The playing field is heavily skewed in favor of the ruling PAP (Hwee 2002). While there was meaningful electoral competition between different political parties in the 1950s, as well as between 1968 and 1984, no opposition party managed to win a parliamentary seat, and it was not until 2011 that the opposition succeeded in winning a single Group Representation Constituency (Table 9.2).

One of the major instruments that the PAP uses to manipulate and control the electoral arena is the electoral system. The use of the British first-past-the-post system in SMCs and GRCs ensures a very strong disproportionality of the electoral system, which allows for a wide difference between the percentage of votes received and the percentage of seats allotted in the resulting legislature for each party (Gallagher 1991). The brutal treatment of smaller parties by the electoral system is reflected in the high values of the "Least Squares Index" (LSq) shown in Table 9.2. With an average disparity of 22.9% points, the electoral system produces substantially more disproportionate results than the plurality system in Malaysia (Croissant 2006, p. 368). The introduction of the GRCs in 1988 has further increased the disproportionality effects of the electoral system, despite the nominal increase in district size (M) from 1 to 3.1 (cf. Table 9.2). Generally, the scholarship on the political consequences of electoral systems assumes that an increase in district size improves the chances of smaller parties to win a seat because it reduces the number of votes a party needs to gain a seat and thereby lowers the effective electoral threshold (cf. Taagepera 1998). However, this is not true for Singapore, where seats allocation is *en bloc* and based on list plurality. In 2015, two GRCs had six members, eight had five, and six had four (ELD 2014). The remaining 11 out of 87 contested seats were allocated in SMCs.

However, this is not the only tool reinforcing PAP's electoral hegemony without the party resorting to outright electoral fraud or election-related violence. First, the PAP makes extensive use of gerrymandering, i.e., the redrawing of district boundaries to maximize the political advantage for PAP candidates or groups of candidates. Gerrymandering also includes announcing modifications to district boundaries on very short notice, which makes it very difficult for opposition parties to select the "right" candidates for particular constituencies and organize effective campaigns (Fetzer 2008). Second, all political parties are barred from canvassing for votes outside the official campaign period that only lasts 9 days, one of which is a "cooling off day" during which all campaign activities are forbidden. Since PAP is omnipresent through its members of parliament and the media presence of the government between elections, the restrictions mainly impede opposition campaigning. Third, rigid limits on campaign financing and limited opposition access to the media, especially since official media have a pro-PAP bias, also contribute to an uneven playing field. Yet, before the 2011 election, the government relaxed regulations on the use of SMS or the Internet and social media sites like Twitter or Facebook for publishing political news or opinions (Abbott 2012, p. 20). According to some observers, this benefited the opposition since it could more easily spread its message and mobilize voters (Ortmann 2011, p. 154; Chong 2012;

Table 9.2 Legislative elections in Singapore, 1959–2015

Party		1959	1963	1968	1972	1976	1980	1984	1988	1991	1997	2001	2006	2011	2015
Singapore Alliance (SA)	%	20.7	8.4	–	–	–	–	–	–	–	–	–	–	–	–
	Seats	4	1	–	–	–	–	–	–	–	–	–	–	–	–
People's Action Party (PAP)	%	54.1	46.9	86.7	70.4	74.1	77.7	64.8	63.2	61	65	75.3	66.7	60.1	69.9
	Seats	43	37	58	65	69	75	77	80	77	81	82	82	81	83
Singapore People's Party (SPP)	%	–	–	–	–	–	–	–	–	–	2.3	–[d]	–[d]	3.1	2.2
	Seats	–	–	–	–	–	–	–	–	–	1	–	–	–	–
Workers' Party	%	–	0.1	4	12.2	11.5	6.2	12.7	16.7	14.3	14.2	3	16.4	12.8	12.5
	Seats	–	–	–	–	–	–	1	–	1	1	1	1	6	6
Singapore Democratic Alliance (SDA)	%	–	–	–	–	–	–	–	–	–	–	12	13	2.8	2.1
	Seats	–	–	–	–	–	–	–	–	–	–	1	1	–	–
Barisan Sosialis (BS)	%	–	33.2	–	4.6	3.2	2.6	2.8	–	–	–	–	–	–	–
	Seats	–	13	–	–	–	–	–	–	–	–	–	–	–	–
Singapore Democratic Party (SDP)	%	–	–	–	–	–	1.8	3.7	11.8	12	10.6	8.1	4.9	4.8	3.8
	Seats	–	–	–	–	–	–	1	1	3	–	–	–	–	–
National Solidarity Party (NSP)	%	–	–	–	–	–	–	–	–	–	–	–[e]	–[e]	12	3.5
	Seats	–	–	–	–	–	–	–	–	–	–	–	–	–	–
Others and Independents	%	24.9	11.5	9.3	9.7	4.1	7.4	15.9	4.5	5.4	0.4	1.6	–	4.8	3.5
	Seats	4	–	–	–	–	–	–	–	–	–	–	–	–	–
Total[a]	%	100	100	100	100	100	100	99.9	100	100	99.2	100	100	100	100
	Seats	51	51	58	65	69	75	79	81	81	83	84	84	87	89
Voter Turnout	%	n/a	95.1	91.8	93.5	95.1	95.5	95.6	94.7	95	95.9	94.6	94	93.1	93.6
Effective Number of Parties (ENEP)[b]	%	2.7	2.9	1.3	1.9	1.7	1.6	2.2	2.2	2.2	2.1	1.7	2	2.5	2
	Seats	1.4	1.7	1	1.1	1	1	1	1	1.1	1.1	1.1	1.1	1.1	1.1
LSq-Index[c]		25	26.2	11.8	23.6	20.8	17.1	25.8	29.1	27	26	18.5	26.1	25.8	17.8
Total Number of Districts	#	51	51	58	65	69	75	79	55	36	24	23	23	27	29
Average District Size (M)	#	1	1	1	1	1	1	1	1.4	2.2	3.4	3.6	3.6	3.2	3.1

[a]Without NMPs and NCMPs

[b,c]See Table 3.2 for details on calculation

[d]Part of the SDA

Source: Authors' compilation with data from IPU (2016), ELD (2014), Rieger (2001)

Table 9.3 Contested seats in Singapore's legislative elections, 1963–2015

	Number of seats (with opposition candidates)	Number of parties (independents)[a]
1963	51 (31)	8 (16)
1968	58 (7)	2 (5)
1972	65 (57)	6 (2)
1976	69 (53)	7 (2)
1980	75 (38)	8
1984	79 (49)	9 (3)
1988	81 (70)	8 (4)
1991	81 (40)	6 (7)
1997	83 (36)	6 (1)
2001	84 (29)	5[b] (1)
2006	84 (47)	4[b]
2011	87 (82)	7
2015	89 (89)	9 (2)

[a]Includes PAP

[b]The four parties organized in the Singapore Democratic Alliance are counted as one party

Source: Hwee (2002, p. 210), Ortmann (2011), ELD (2014)

Tan 2012, p. 267). Yet, in the 2015 election campaign, the government's social media campaign caught up to the opposition's first mover advantage (Tan 2016).

In the past, opposition parties tried to overcome these obstacles with a by-election strategy under which opposition parties only competed in some districts, coordinated their strategies, and pooled their resources, as in joined platforms like the Singapore Democratic Alliance, a four-party coalition formed in 2001 (Table 9.3). Since the opposition ran candidates in only a handful of districts, the outcome of the elections was usually decided on nomination day (Mauzy and Milne 2002). Since 2011, the opposition has abandoned this strategy and runs candidates in almost all or all SMCs and GRCs (Tan 2016).

9.6   Political Parties and Party System

Political parties became a regular feature of Singaporean politics already before World War II, when the Communist Party of Malaya and the anti-communist Chinese Nationalist Party (*Kuomintang*, KMT) competed for political support among Singapore's Chinese population. In the postwar years, new parties emerged, among them the Progressive Party in 1947 as well as the Labour Front and the People's Action Party in 1954. The pro-British Progressive Party had dominated the Legislative Council under centennial suffrage that excluded many Chinese immigrants, but lost its relevance after the introduction of universal suffrage (Wah 1973). The Labour Front emerged from an alliance of two socialist parties and was affiliated with the Singapore Trade Union Congress (STUC), an umbrella organization of several public sector trade unions (Carnell 1955, p. 100). Following factional struggles, the Worker's Party split off from the Labour Front in 1957, making it the oldest opposition party still active today: In 2011, the party won six GRC seats and had two additional non-constituency members in parliament.

Similar to the Labour Front and the Worker's Party, the People's Action Party traces its origins back to the Chinese labor movement. The party was founded in 1954 as an alliance of left-wing groups and moderate nationalists from the Chinese middle class, led by Lee Kuan Yew, then a trade union lawyer (Vennewald 1993, p. 46). When the government arrested Communist Party members for illegal activities, the moderate wing of the party under Lee Kuan Yew took the opportunity to amend the party statutes in order to limit the influence of the more radical party base, and in the 1959 election, it became the city's ruling party. The pro-communist majority wing retaliated by founding the Socialist Front (*Barisan Socialis*) in 1961, taking with it most of the PAP's membership, party cadres, and local party branches (Vennewald 1993, p. 49). Before the 1963 elections, the PAP retaliated by arresting most *Barisan Socialis'* cadres ("Operation Coldstore," cf. Slater and Simmons 2012). *Barisan Socialis* won 13 seats but decided to boycott parliament, and in the 1968 election, PAP won all 58 seats. The leadership of the Socialist Front went into exile in Indonesia, where the party finally dissolved in 1988 (Mauzy and Milne 2002, p. 24).

The 1968 election completed the transformation of Singapore's competitive multiparty system into a hegemonic system (Cheung 2008, p. 130). Yet, there are still genuine opposition parties, of which eight contested the 2015 election. However, these small or tiny parties lack organizational strength, finances, and membership and have difficulties in attracting promising or qualified candidates (Ooi 1998; Ortmann 2010). Unlike opposition parties in Malaysia or Cambodia, the opposition political parties avoid outright conflict with the PAP. As "loyal," pro-system parties, they do not demand regime change, and criticism of the governments almost always stays within the confines of the PAP-dominated discourse (Ortmann 2010, p. 165). Nevertheless, opposition parties have managed to win 25–40% of the total votes in elections since the 1980s. Traditionally, opposition voters came from among the ranks of those disadvantaged by the national economic model, including the Malay population and lower-class Chinese-speaking workers, who worry about increasing income disparity and labor migration (Vennewald 1993, p. 228; Ooi 1998, p. 361). However, the 2011 election indicated that the opposition, with its call for more social justice and better political participation and civil liberties, has begun to attract younger middleclass voters as well (Ortmann 2011; Tan 2012).

The PAP is a cadre party that recruits its members and candidates based on strict criteria and after a careful screening process (Mauzy and Milne 2002; Fionna 2008). Since the 1960s, the party has co-opted a number of social organizations, most importantly the National Trade Union Congress (NTUC), which serve as transmission belts between the party and society, although they are organizationally independent from the PAP. Even though state institutions like district councils and "para-political" organizations formed in the 1980s like the People's Associations, Community Centres, and Citizens' Consultative Committees serve as de facto party structures and are led by PAP MPs (Rodan 2008, p. 235), PAP has no party cells inside the state.

The party organization has different tiers (Mauzy and Milne 2002, pp. 39–41). At the top is the Central Executive Committee. The CEC mostly consists of the members of the cabinet and is chaired by the PAP's general secretary, who also serves as prime minister. The PAP general secretary chairs the General Election Committee, which determines PAP's candidates for parliamentary elections and serves an important function for the party's ability to rejuvenate. The second tier consists of the roughly 1000 party cadres who are appointed by the CEC (Mauzy and Milne 2002, p. 41). Their main task is the election of the CEC, but eight of the 18 candidates are nominated by the incumbent CEC itself (Ooi 1998; Rodan 2008, p. 234). The party's MPs, who are not part of the cabinet, form another tier of the party organization, provide a linkage with regular party members, and serve as the public face of the party (Tan and Chew 2008). While the PAP does not issue membership reports, the number of regular party members is estimated to be between 10,000 and 15,000 (Mauzy and Milne 2002, p. 41; Leong 2000, p. 94).

Even though the formal party organization has not changed much since the 1950s, the PAP has experienced profound ideological and sociological transformations in the past six decades: It abandoned its left-of-the center roots and adopted a conservative government mentality (Lee 2010, p. 4; Mauzy and Milne 2002, pp. 38–40). Only the most recent election indicates that the party has again moved slightly to the left to retain its traditional voter base (Tan 2016). The party's membership organizations do not provide relevant linkages between the party's leadership and its voters. Rather, the aforementioned Town Councils and para-political organizations perform linkage functions. Most importantly, the party organization itself has lost much of its relevance in recruiting cabinet and senior party posts. Instead, CEC and cabinet are recruited from the ranks of co-opted military, economic, and administrative elites, that is, the "technocrats" (Vennewald 1993; Mauzy and Milne 2002, pp. 49–51; Cheung 2008, pp. 130–131; Barr 2014). This technocratic takeover of the party has shifted the locus of decision-making from formal party bodies to informal negotiation circles in the cabinet and other state institutions (Rodan 2008, p. 239).

9.7   State Administration

Singapore has a centralized, high capacity state run by a professional and efficient civil service. In addition to the unelected Town Councils, the government established five semigovernmental appointed Community Development Councils (CDCs) that provide government services on behalf of the national ministries. Their main task is to foster local integration and community bonding through integrative social services. The CDCs are led by elected MPs and are funded by a combination of private donations and government subsidies (Croissant et al. 2013).

Singapore's civil service and bureaucracy are highly efficient, almost corruption free, and remarkably effective at enforcing its notion of social order. The Singapore Public Service currently employs 139,000 people or about 7% of all Singaporean employees (PSD 2013). There are about 300 career civil servants in the "administrative service," an administrative elite that is also a key element of Singapore's ruling elite and which provided six out of 15 cabinet ministers in 2012 (Barr 2014, p. 83).

Since 1959, the state has been the driving force behind Singapore's economic development. Based on the guarantee of a stable political and economic environment, the government combined economic regulation with plan-rational industrial and technology policies implemented through pilot industries, but also invited foreign companies to invest in the national economy. Since the 1950s, the more than 80 so-called Statutory Boards (StBs) such as the Housing and Development Board and the Central Provident Fund, and profit-oriented Government-linked Companies (GLCs), were a distinctive feature of Singapore's government and played a major role in the post-independence development strategy of Singapore's "developmental state" (Huff 1995). The StBs are autonomous government agencies, separate from the formal government structure and not staffed by civil servants, but are overseen by a cabinet minister who has jurisdiction over the board of directors, whose members typically include senior civil servants, businessmen, professionals, and trade union officials. The StBs do not receive regular allocations of funds from the public treasury but have to generate their own funds from their activities (Vennewald 1993, pp. 73–74). Unlike the StBs, GLCs are companies in which the government, through Temasek, another government agency, or another GLC, is the controlling shareholder.[3] GLCs were intended to serve as pilot institutions to diversify Singapore's *entrepôt* economy. Their share of the overall economy is quite substantial, and in 2010 they contributed 13% to the Singaporean GDP (Temasek 2011). It is, therefore, a surprise that the Index of Economic Liberty (Heritage Foundation 2017) ranks Singapore as one of the freest market economies in the world despite its high degree of state intervention.

While the origins of Singapore's strong state capacity date back to the colonial period, the Singaporean government did its utmost to strengthen the autonomy and capacity of the state bureaucracy after independence. At the same time, the close-knit network of political, administrative, and economic elites allowed the "embedded" state apparatus to mobilize resources for national development and coordinate its intricate development program (cf. Evans 1995). The relative weakness of organized civil society and an already existing professional civil service provided the government with the necessary political space and institutional capacity. At the same time, the PAP leadership around Lee Kuan Yew was careful to avert the transformation of one-party rule and economic interventionism into a patrimonialization of the state. To prevent corruption and improve the quality of the bureaucracy, the government employs several instruments. Employees in the higher echelons of administration and government enjoy generous salaries (Huat 2008, p. 57) and are subject to a sophisticated system of institutionalized political and legal oversight. Unlike in many other Southeast Asian countries, a rigid and meritocratic recruitment and promotion system has placed a premium on talent, expertise, and performance and has prevented nepotism (Bellows 2009).

---

[3]Temasek Holding is a state-owned holding company that owns and manages a portfolio of SGD242 billion.

9.8   Civil–Military Relations

Since independence, the country has adopted the model of the citizen army. To promote a sense of national unity and patriotism and to bind the military to its society, the Singapore Armed Forces (SAF) became a conscription force (Da Cunha 1999). Conscription is mandatory for all male citizens and second-generation permanent residents between 18 and 40 years of age. In 2004, the duration of the conscription was reduced from 30 to 24 months (Tan 2011). Conscripts make up about half of Singapore's 72,000 active military personnel. With an overall strength of 312,000 troops, the majority of Singapore's armed forces is made up of the operative reserve, whose members are required to serve for a maximum of 14 days annually until the age of 40 in the army or navy or 50 in the air force. During the initial years after the separation from Malaysia, Singaporeans of Malay origin were de facto excluded from conscription (Walsh 2007). Even today, Malay conscripts serve mostly in the Coast Guard or as part of the Singapore Civil Defence Force (Huxley 2000; Mauzy and Milne 2002, p. 109).

Despite its small size and more than six decades of peace and political stability, the country employs one of the largest and most modern and professional militaries in Southeast Asia, and its military expenditure is the highest in the region. In addition, the SAF has increased cooperation with counterparts in other countries, especially Brunei, the United Kingdom, and the United States, and has also become involved in regional and international humanitarian, peacekeeping, and relief operations (Huxley 2000, p. 73; Tan and Chew 2008, p. 249). Between 1966 and 2001, defense expenditure accounted for an average of 24.8% of total government spending and 4.5% of GDP.[4] According to the Stockholm International Peace Research Institute (SIPRI) database, Singapore spent USD9841 million, or USD1798 per capita, on defense in 2014. Military expenditure thus accounted for 3.3% of GDP and 18.3% of total government spending (SIPRI 2014). The Global Militarization Index ranks Singapore the second-most militarized country in the world after Israel (BICC 2013). In addition, military and defense policy ranks high on the political agenda of the government. The extensive defense expenditure and the prevalent security discourse reflect a deep-seated feeling of external vulnerability and insecurity among the city-state's political elites (Huxley 2000; Tan 2001).

Similar to Brunei and Malaysia, civilian supremacy over the military has been fully achieved in Singapore (Beeson and Bellamy 2008). Yet, the emergence of professional civil–military relations in Singapore rather resembles the experiences of revolutionary regimes (Vietnam, Laos) than the former British or American colonies in Southeast Asia. The Singaporean Armed Forces (SAF) were created by the PAP after the country's expulsion from Malaysia and had no role in the country's decolonization process, which allowed civilians to maintain strict civilian control while keeping the military a politically neutral, professional force (Croissant and Kuehn 2017). PAP and the SAF are strictly separated: During active

---

[4]Authors' compilation based on Huxley (2000, p. 29), IISS (2014), World Bank (2017a).

service, SAF personnel are barred from joining a political party and cannot run for political office. Still, party–military relations in Singapore exhibit a high degree of elite dualism and a unique "fusion" of military, bureaucratic, and political roles that ensures strict civilian control (Huxley 2000, p. 242; Tan 2011, p. 164). In fact, similar to the administrative service, retired military officers are a key component of Singapore's ruling elite: In 2012, six of the then 15 members of the cabinet, including Prime Minister Lee Hsien Loong, were former SAF officers (Barr 2014, p. 82). The military education and promotion system encourages officers to acquire expertise on military and nonmilitary issues alike. Even during their active service, senior members of the SAF are assigned to serve on StBs, administrative bodies, or at universities to gather administrative experience or to continue their training. These measures are meant to transition officers ending their active service in their mid-forties into a career in public service (Huxley 2000, pp. 232–234). However, this development does not reflect the SAF's institutional influence on Singaporean politics, but is rather indicative of the continued attempts of the political leadership to tap new recruitment pools and co-opt those functional elites vital for the political survival of the government and—according to the PAP—the country (Tan 2011). Unlike in other Southeast Asian countries like Thailand, Indonesia, Vietnam, or Laos, the SAF lacks non-budgetary sources of income and there is no military business complex (Tan 2011, pp. 153–154).

The SAF are part of a civilian-led security sector with a unified chain of command under a civilian-led Ministry of Defence (MINDEF). Civilians—and only occasionally former military officers—also lead major departments, such as Security and Intelligence, the Defence Management Group, and the MINDEF/SAF Manpower Centres. Government authority in routine questions is exercised through the Armed Forces Council that consists of the minister of defence and other ministers, the Senior Minister of State, the chief of defence force (CDF), and the three service chiefs as well as up to four additional members appointed by the president. Important decisions are made in the Armed Forces Council, which is led by the prime minister and includes the ministers and state ministers of defense, home affairs, foreign affairs, and information and arts, the CDF as well as senior members of the intelligence services (Huxley 2000, p. 81). The National Security Coordination Secretariat that is part of the Prime Minister's Office coordinates the civilian and military elements of the security apparatus (Tan 2011, p. 150).

9.9 Political Culture and Civil Society

Political leaders of Singapore such as former Prime Ministers Lee Kuan Yew (1959–1990) and Goh Chok Tong (1990–2004) were at the forefront of the so-called Asian values debate (Zakaria 1994; Barr 2007). According to the "Asian Values" thesis, Asian societies are characterized by a pronounced orientation towards the community, a hard-working ethos, and the acceptance of authority (Dalton and Ong 2005). Moreover, the family is considered the cornerstone of society. Individual rights are less important than the rights and interests of the community, and the state should be the authority to define and represent those social goals. A paternalistic state is regarded as a central pillar for the concept of Asian values (Blondel and Inoguchi 2006). The cultural specificity of "Asian values" and the differences between "Asian" and "Western" values are said to require a substantially different form of state-society relations and political organization, often dubbed "Asian-style democracy" (Neher 1994). Due to a lack of space, the various strands of the debate, its relevance for the understanding of multiple modernities in Asia and the West, and the empirical findings regarding the validity of the basic assumptions of this debate will not be dealt with here.[5] Yet, glancing at some of the data from the Asian Barometer Survey (ABS) offers interesting insights into the congruence of political attitudes and opinions of citizens and the structures of political authority in Singapore. In fact, the ABS data indicate that institutional trust in government bodies in Singapore is significantly higher than the regional average across the board and exceeds those for NGOs, television, and newspapers. For instance, 88.8% of respondents in 2014 reported some or a great deal of trust in the chief executive and 87.7% in the national government, whereas 89.1% trusted the courts and 85.9% the parliament. The averages for seven Southeast Asian countries were 76.7, 73.3, 69.2, and 69.6%, respectively (ABS 2017). Another finding worth mentioning is the negative perception of the electoral process in Singapore: Only 10.2% of respondents reported some or a great deal of trust in the fairness of elections. Given the fact that multiparty elections in Singapore are free, but not fair, this finding is no surprise.

Other studies of political attitudes conclude that support for the PAP government and its political regime is based primarily on its very good economic and political performance (Carlson and Turner 2008; Wong et al. 2011; Chang et al. 2013). A closer look at the ABS data shows that compared to their regional neighbors, Singaporean citizens evaluate the performance of their government especially favorably when it comes to the economy, corruption prevention, human rights protection, and public services. At the same time, Singaporeans are particularly dissatisfied with the protection of civil rights such as freedom of speech, association, and assembly and the opportunities to criticize the government (Carlson and Turner 2008).

The pattern of citizens' satisfaction and dissatisfaction with the performance of the political authorities in Singapore converges to a remarkably strong extent with scholarly assessments, especially in regards to the lack of strong pressure for democratic change and the dynamics of interaction between civil society and the state (cf. Kadir 2004; Ortmann 2010). In fact, despite a relatively strong level of social self-organization in community or functional organizations and other forms of voluntary activity before 1965, civil society in Singapore is today much weaker, less confrontational, and more functional in helping to maintain the political status quo than those in other electoral authoritarian regimes in Southeast Asia. Much like in Malaysia, and in contrast to Cambodia or other authoritarian regimes in the

---

[5]For critical reviews, see Kim (1997), Hood (1998), Thompson (2004), Bell (2006), and Blondel and Inoguchi (2006).

region, the government rarely uses hard repression to control civil society. When the PAP came to power, it faced a politicized civil society, including a leftist trade union movement, numerous functional and cultural associations, and an active student movement. Since then, the government has relied on a mix of repression, co-optation, and containment to occupy much of the public space originally occupied by autonomous associations. Trade unions, student groups, and cultural associations affiliated with the *Barisan Socialis* were dissolved and replaced by PAP-affiliated organizations such as the National Trade Union Congress, which was formed in 1963 (Mauzy and Milne 2002, pp. 158–159; Case 2002, p. 91; Ortmann 2010, p. 77; Rajah 2012, p. 288; Rodan 2008, pp. 234–235). At the same time, the PAP government allowed the continued presence of other organizations such as the Chinese Chamber of Commerce, mosque and temple associations, the National Council of Churches, and groups embracing a public issue with little potential to challenge the party's monopoly of government, such as environmental protection and animal rights (Kadir 2004; Rodan 2011, p. 505). Furthermore, representatives or activists of such groups are co-opted into political structures and feedback mechanisms of the regime and their associations receive government subsidies (Lee 2005; Ortmann 2012, pp. 17–18). Containment is achieved through a combination of monitoring and regulation with the selective use of "hard" coercion, and a rigid distinction between political and nonpolitical organizations is meant to prevent any cooperation between NGOs and opposition parties (Rodan 2011, p. 507). Especially the forced incorporation of business and employer associations as well as trade unions is the institutional core of Singapore's state corporatist model of state-society relations. The legal foundation for this statist corporatism is found in the Employment Act and the Industrial Relations Act (Amendment) of 1969, the tripartite National Wages Council formed in 1972, and the Trade Dispute Act of 1981 (Vennewald 1993, p. 273; Mauzy and Milne 2002, pp. 31–33). Unlike South Korea or Japan, Singapore lacks an institutionalist link between state and major enterprises because the PAP government relied on a strategic alliance with multinational corporations instead of promoting domestic businesses (Mauzy and Milne 2002, pp. 33–35; Case 2002, pp. 84–85).[6] Today, trade union membership in Singapore is relatively high at 23.7%, as compared to 10.5% in Malaysia, but the labor movement is essentially depoliticized (Neureiter 2013, pp. 1073–1075).

9.10   Media System

Singapore is one of Asia's leading media marketplaces and a digital media hub. More than 82% of its inhabitants and probably an even higher number of its citizens have access to the internet, making it one of the best-connected countries in the

---

[6]In 1998, the GDP share of foreign companies in Singapore was 44% while Singaporean companies contributed only 33% (Temasek 2011).

world with the widest use of digital or "new" media (Internet World Stats 2017; Abbott 2012, p. 9). However, the plethora of different print, electronic (TV, radio), and digital media does not mean that the media landscape is pluralistic. Even though the government has recently relaxed regulations on online media, it still exerts strict control over traditional and new media. For example, the 2017 World Press Freedom Index ranked Singapore 151st of 180 countries, trailing countries like Myanmar or Malaysia (Reporters without Borders 2017). Similarly, the Freedom of Press 2017 report assigned Singapore a Press Freedom Score of 67 out of 100 (higher scores indicate less freedom of the press), slightly ahead of Malaysia (67) and Cambodia (70), indicating a "not free" press (Freedom House 2017).

The PAP's approach to limiting the freedom of expression and opinion in Singapore, however, differs from the strategies employed in other Southeast Asian non-democracies. Its "elaborate press control regime" (Tey 2008, p. 883) is not based primarily on censorship or hard repression by state or non-state actors but relies on institutionalized self-censorship or "auto-regulation" (Lee 2010, pp. 14–15). The Ministry of Communications and Information is in charge of monitoring the media landscape and is assisted by a number of StBs, including the Media Development Authority of Singapore and the Infocomm Development Authority of Singapore (Lee 2010, pp. 9–10). Repressive tools like the ISA, Sedition Act, Official Secrets Act, and some regulations in the criminal code function mostly as a deterrent and are rarely used (Tey 2008, p. 884). The government also influences the ownership structures of domestic media corporations and has established a dense network of regulations, limitations, and prohibitions. Large media corporations like MediaCorp or Singapore Press Holding are government property (George 2002, p. 179; Tey 2008, p. 890). All domestic press corporations have to be locally owned and listed on the stock exchange. Only citizens of Singapore or corporations with a special government permit can hold so-called management shares, weighed at 200 times the vote of a regular share. Moreover, naturalized persons can only hold 3% of any one corporation (Rajah 2012, p. 145). This indirect control of ownership grants the government influence over the composition of editorial boards and thereby—indirectly—newspaper content and personnel decisions. This effectively prevents the publication of critical reporting (George 2002, p. 177; Tey 2008, p. 888).

By law, no newspaper or periodical requires a government permit to be printed or distributed in Singapore, including offshore newspapers whose content is determined abroad. Yet the government determines circulation and demands that foreign press identify a local representative who is liable in case of a libel suit (Tey 2008, p. 893). Foreign providers of radio or television broadcasts with access to the cable network, like CNN, are barred from "interfering" in Singaporean politics (George 2002, p. 178).

It is unclear whether the expansion of new media has promoted the development of an alternative public discourse and eased government control of society. While "new media" do provide new and better access to information in Singapore, impactful activism requires mobilization beyond media conversation (Weiss 2014). On the one hand, the number of Singaporeans who rely on online news is much larger than in other Southeast Asian countries with a higher degree of press freedom (Abbott 2012, p. 14). Some observers argue that this has "dramatically" affected the ability of civil society activists to articulate their demands for political change (Ortmann 2012, p. 20). On the other hand, the government employs the same techniques in shaping cyberspace as it does for controlling traditional media: Internet content and service providers (ICPs and ISPs) have to undergo registration and the internet is regulated by the Internet Code of Conduct, issued in 1997 (Rodan 2011, p. 511), and regulations in the Societies Act have applied to ICPs and ISPs since 1996. Banned content includes any statement or the recounting of statements that could endanger public security or national defense, stir up disaffection with the government, undermine public trust in the judiciary, denigrate individual ethnic or religious groups, or promote unrestrained sexuality or promiscuity (George 2002, p. 189). An amendment to the electoral law also outlawed any form of political campaigning online, whether through social media, email, or SMS (Lee 2010, pp. 125, 135). Furthermore, only ICPs and ISPs registered as political associations are allowed to report on campaign events, policy platforms, or voter polls and surveys (Mauzy and Milne 2002, pp. 140–141).[7]

9.11 Outlook

The political system of Singapore appears to contradict conventional wisdom in political science. Despite a very high level of social and economic modernization, a small group of administrative and political elites governs the city-state autocratically. Despite its authoritarian regime type, it scores well on established measures for the rule of law, bureaucratic quality, and public goods provision. While PAP has been in power since 1959, the party as organization is almost invisible in daily life. Even though genuine opposition political parties regularly achieve between 20 and 40% of the total vote, they are barely represented in parliament. While Singapore is a highly militarized country and party–military relations exhibit a high degree of elite dualism and a unique "fusion" of military, bureaucratic, and political roles, civil–military relations are characterized by military acceptance of civilian supremacy and the strict separation of party and armed forces. Despite the very substantial and interventionist role of the state in economic development, Singapore ranks among the freest market economies worldwide. The city is an international media hub and home to one of the most connected digital infrastructures and digital societies, yet its media is unfree. Finally, the state tightly administrates and regulates political and social activities, and the government in Singapore, as all authoritarian governments do, relies on repression to guarantee regime survival; its

---

[7]These restrictions were relaxed prior to the election of 2011, and several websites have used these new liberties to provide a space for alternative opinions and information that would not be reported in traditional or pro-government outlets.

use is highly selective and of low intensity, stressing self-regulation with the mere threat of coercion (George 2007, p. 142; Ortmann 2012, p. 165).

Such contradictions can only be understood by taking the particularities of the political geography of the city-state into account: In a city-state like Singapore, the government as employer and provider of economic opportunities and most social services, especially housing, can exert considerable social influence (Vennewald 1993, p. 50; Case 2002, pp. 85, 92). Furthermore, the small size of the national territory reduces the cost of surveillance and deterrence of political opposition and civil society (Levitsky and Way 2010, p. 59). Yet, the resilience of Singapore's party regime and its ability to adapt to new challenges and rejuvenate rest mainly on two mechanisms. The first is the ability of the PAP government to solve the problem of legitimacy, which is central in politics. Following Max Weber, legitimacy can be defined empirically (excluding any recourse to normative criteria) as the belief ("*Legitimitätsglaube*") that a rule, institution, or leader has the right to govern (Weber 1964, p. 382). Weber distinguishes among three main sources of legitimacy in society. While tradition ("Asian values") and the trust people have in the legality of the political order—specifically the rationality of the rule of law—may be important in Singapore, the sheer quality of governance provides the basis of output legitimacy as an additional source (cf. Scharpf 2002; Schmidt 2016). It is a consequence of the remarkable political performance of the PAP, measured in terms of economic growth and broad access to public goods, such as health, education, housing, social security, and legal protection and security for most of its citizens. In addition, the regime has accepted some legal limitations on state autonomy to generate procedural legitimacy and holds regular elections to ensure a modicum of electoral legitimacy (Silverstein 2008; Rajah 2012). Mentalities like "Asian" or "shared values" provide some additional normative justification for the regime.

Second, the PAP government complements these legitimations by co-opting important elite groups. Since the 1980s, the government has introduced new institutional channels to co-opt important socioeconomic groups as well as active or potential opposition actors, like the appointed and non-constituency members of parliament. In the past, opposition representatives have rarely questioned the legitimacy of Singapore's political system (Ortmann 2010, pp. 182–183). The regime also created social organizations and allowed limited participation in policy-making and since the 1970s increasingly co-opted new political, bureaucratic, and professional elites. While this preserved the regime's ability to regenerate and renew its leadership (Bellows 2009; Barr 2014), it marginalized the ruling party as the locus of decision-making and the primary channel for political recruitment.

So far, the PAP has managed to defy prognoses of Singapore's impending democratization before 2015 (Inglehart and Welzel 2005) or within a generation (Zakaria 2007). Even though Singapore is undoubtedly one of the most persistent, stable, and effectively governed non-democracies in Asia, and in fact, worldwide, there is a number of challenges with the potential to undermine PAP dominance in the future.

First, social disparities and income inequality have grown significantly since the 1990s. While the average income of the upper income brackets has grown

Table 9.4 Economic inequality in Singapore, 1998–2012

	1998	2003	2008	2012
Real average monthly income, upper quintile	5834	6378	7501	n/a
Real average monthly income of employed residents	2025	2260	2465	3133
Real average monthly income of employed residents, lowest quintile	809	776	751	n/a
Relative income of highest to lowest quintile	7.2	8.2	10	n/a
Gini coefficient, OECD method[a]	n/a	39.9	40.4	41.3
Gini coefficient, household income[b]	42.5	45.8	47.4	47.8

[a]After transfer payments and taxes, including employer share of CPF payments
[b]Based on the working income of all private household members
Source: OECD (2014), Ministry of Manpower (2012), DSS (2007, p. 8, 2013a, p. 12)

markedly in real terms, middle incomes have stagnated. Measured in real terms, the lower income bracket has even suffered a decline in income, considering the steeply rising consumer prices. In 2012, only Mexico (48.2) had a higher level of income inequality than Singapore as measured by the Gini-Coefficient among the 34 developed economies of the Organization for Economic Cooperation and Development (OECD) (Table 9.4). This threatens social cohesion and citizen trust in the PAP's ability to level social inequalities, especially since the restriction of political liberties has eliminated independent intermediaries who could communicate such problems to the political center peacefully (Vennewald 1993, p. 313).

Second, because of the extensive recruitment of foreign oversees workers and an increase in the number of binational marriages, the share of noncitizens grew from 14 to 38.2% between 1990 and 2012. About a quarter of these foreigners are permanent residents, i.e., family members of Singaporean citizens born abroad or highly paid and skilled foreign employees and their families, mostly from Western countries, Japan, or South Korea. The remaining 73.8% are nonresidents (DSS 2013b, p. 23). About 80% of these are labor migrants from South and Southeast Asia employed in low-paying jobs. These workers have minimal personal rights and are excluded from public life (Piper 2006). The potential for conflict this development breeds became visible during a violent unrest in Little India in 2013, a quarter frequented by many migrants on their day off, which the government suppressed by draconic means (Wall Street Journal 2013).

Third, Singapore is undergoing a process of cultural change, triggered by socioeconomic development. The election results of 2011 demonstrated that the political opposition is no longer restricted to Chinese-speaking workers and lower-class Malays. Even members of the well-educated Chinese middle class are willing to vote for the opposition because it promises more freedom for individual expression and political participation (Fetzer 2008; Chong 2012; Tan 2012, p. 265). While the PAP managed to reassert its dominance in the 2015 election, it had to adjust its policy to address redistributive demands (Tan 2016). In view of these and other challenges, the PAP's monopoly on government should not be taken for granted in the future.

References

Abbott, J. P. (2012). Cacophony or empowerment?: Analysing the impact of new information communication technologies and new social media in Southeast Asia. *Journal of Current Southeast Asian Affairs, 30*(4), 3–31.

ABS. (2017). *Asian barometer survey: Electronic data release for Wave 4, 2014–2016.* http://www.asianbarometer.org/data/data-release

Barr, M. D. (2007). Lee Kuan Yew and the "Asian values" debate. *Asian Studies Review, 24,* 309–334. https://doi.org/10.1080/10357820008713278

Barr, M. D. (2014). *The ruling elite of Singapore: Networks of power and influence.* London: I.B. Tauris.

Beeson, M., & Bellamy, A. J. (2008). *Securing Southeast Asia: The politics of security sector reform.* London: Routledge.

Bell, D. A. (2006). *Beyond liberal democracy: Political thinking for an East Asian context.* Princeton: Princeton University Press.

Bellows, T. J. (2009). Meritocracy and the Singapore political system. *Asian Journal of Political Science, 17,* 24–44. https://doi.org/10.1080/02185370902767581

BICC. (2013). *Global militarization index 2012.* Bonn: Bonn International Center for Conversion.

Blondel, J. (2006). The national executives in East and Southeast Asia. In R. Higgott & I. Marsh (Eds.), *Democratisation, governance, and regionalism in east and southeast Asia: A comparative study* (pp. 89–123). New York: Routledge.

Blondel, J., & Inoguchi, T. (2006). *Political cultures in Asia and Europe: Citizens states and societal values.* London: Routledge.

Boix, C., & Stokes, S. C. (2003). Endogenous democratization. *World Politics, 55*(4), 517–549.

Carlson, M., & Turner, M. (2008). Public support for democratic governance in Southeast Asia. *Asian Journal of Political Science, 16,* 219–239. https://doi.org/10.1080/02185370802504076

Carnell, F. G. (1955). Political ferment in Singapore. *Far Eastern Survey, 24,* 97–102. https://doi.org/10.2307/3023758

Case, W. (2002). *Politics in Southeast Asia: Democracy or less.* Richmond: Curzon.

Case, W. (2011). Electoral authoritarianism and backlash: Hardening Malaysia, oscillating Thailand. *International Political Science Review, 32,* 438–457. https://doi.org/10.1177/0192512110385296

Chang, A., Chu, Y.-h., & Welsh, B. (2013). Southeast Asia: Sources of regime support. *Journal of Democracy, 24,* 150–164. https://doi.org/10.1353/jod.2013.0025

Chee, C. H. (1976). The role of parliamentary politicians in Singapore. *Legislative Studies Quarterly, 1,* 423–441. https://doi.org/10.2307/439506

Chen, P. S. J. (1975). The power elite in Singapore. In P. S. J. Chen & H.-D. Evers (Eds.), *Studies in ASEAN sociology: Urban society and social change.* Chopmen Enterprises: Singapore.

Cheong, Y. M. (1999). The political structures of the independent states. In N. Tarling (Ed.), *Cambridge history of Southeast Asia: Vol. II, Part 2: From World War II to the present* (pp. 387–466). New York: Cambridge University Press.

Cheung, A. B. L. (2008). The story of two administrative states: State capacity in Hong Kong and Singapore. *The Pacific Review, 21,* 121–145. https://doi.org/10.1080/09512740801990188

Chong, T. (2012). A return to normal politics: Singapore general elections 2011. *Southeast Asian Affairs, 2012*(1), 283–298.

CIA. (2017). *The world factbook.* Langley: Central Intelligence Agency.

Croissant, A. (2006). Conclusion: Electoral politics in Southeast Asia. In A. Croissant & B. Martin (Eds.), *Between consolidation and crisis: Elections and democracy in five nations in Southeast Asia* (pp. 329–385). Münster: LIT Verlag.

Croissant, A., & Kuehn, D. (Eds.). (2017). *Reforming civil-military relations in new democracies.* Heidelberg: Springer VS.

Croissant, A., Ortmann, S., & Quah, J. S. T. (2013). *Need for reform and governance capacities in Asia. Country Report Singapore.* Gütersloh: Bertelsmann Foundation.

Da Cunha, D. (1999). Sociological aspects of the Singapore armed forces. *Armed Forces & Society, 25,* 459–475. https://doi.org/10.1177/0095327X9902500306

Dalton, R. J., & Ong, N.-N. T. (2005). Authority orientations and democratic attitudes in East Asia: A test of the 'Asian values' hypothesis. *Japanese Journal of Political Science, 6*(2), 1–22.

DSS. (2007). *Key household economic trends 2006.* Singapore: Department of Statistics Singapore.

DSS. (2013a). *Key household economic trends 2013.* Singapore: Department of Statistics Singapore.

DSS. (2013b). *Yearbook of statistics 2013.* Singapore: Department of Statistics Singapore.

ELD. (2014). *Election results.* Singapore: Election Department Singapore.

Elgie, R. (2013). *The semi-presidential one.* Accessed June 7, 2017, from http://www.semipresidentialism.com/

Evans, P. B. (1995). *Embedded autonomy.* Princeton: Princeton University Press.

Fetzer, J. S. (2008). Election strategy and ethnic politics in Singapore. *Taiwan Journal of Democracy, 4*(1), 135–153.

Fionna, U. (2008). Political parties in Singapore, Malaysia, and the Philippines: Reflection of democratic tendencies. *Makara, Social Humaniora, 12*(2), 65–71.

Freedom House. (2017). *Freedom of the press index 2017: Press Freedom's Dark Horizon.* Accessed June 2, 2017, from https://freedomhouse.org/report/freedom-press/freedom-press-2017

Gallagher, M. (1991). Proportionality, disproportionality and electoral systems. *Electoral Studies, 10,* 33–51. https://doi.org/10.1016/0261-3794(91)90004-C

Gandhi, J. (2008). *Political institutions under dictatorship.* Cambridge: Cambridge University Press.

Gandhi, J., & Lust-Okar, E. (2009). Elections under authoritarianism. *Annual Review of Political Science, 12,* 403–422. https://doi.org/10.1146/annurev.polisci.11.060106.095434

Geddes, B., Wright, J., & Frantz, E. (2014). Autocratic breakdown and regime transitions: A new data set. *Perspectives on Politics, 12,* 313–331. https://doi.org/10.1017/S1537592714000851

George, C. (2002). *Contentious journalism and the internet: Towards democratic discourse in Malaysia and Singapore.* Singapore: Singapore University Press.

George, C. (2007). Consolidating authoritarian rule: Calibrated coercion in Singapore. *The Pacific Review, 20,* 127–145. https://doi.org/10.1080/09512740701306782

Hadenius, A., & Teorell, J. (2006). *Authoritarian regimes: Stability, change, and pathways to democracy, 1979–2003.* Kellog Institute Working Paper Nr. 331.

Hamilton-Hart, N. (2000). The Singapore state revisited. *Pacific Review, 13,* 195–216. https://doi.org/10.1080/095127400363550

Haque, M. S. (2004). Governance and bureaucracy in Singapore: Contemporary reforms and implications. *International Political Science Review, 25,* 227–240. https://doi.org/10.1177/0192512104042314

Hefner, R. W. (Ed.). (2001). *The politics of multiculturalism: Pluralism and citizenship in Malaysia, Singapore, and Indonesia.* Honolulu: University of Hawai'i Press.

Heritage Foundation. (2017). *2017 Index of economic freedom.* Accessed June 8, 2017, from http://www.heritage.org/index/

Hood, S. J. (1998). The myth of Asian-style democracy. *Asian Survey, 38,* 853–866. https://doi.org/10.2307/2645622

Huat, C. B. (2008). Singapore in 2007: High wage ministers and the management of gays and elderly. *Asian Survey, 48,* 55–61. https://doi.org/10.1525/as.2008.48.1.55

Huff, W. G. (1995). The developmental state, government, and Singapore's economic development since 1960. *World Development, 23,* 1421–1438. https://doi.org/10.1016/0305-750X(95)00043-C

Huxley, T. (2000). *Defending the Lion City: The Armed Forces of Singapore.* St Leonards: Allen & Unwin.

Hwee, Y. L. (2002). Electoral politics in Singapore. In A. Croissant, G. Bruns, & M. John (Eds.), *Electoral politics in Southeast & East Asia* (pp. 203–232). Singapore: Friedrich Ebert Foundation.

IISS. (2014). *The Military Balance 2014: International Institute for Strategic Studies*. London: Oxford University Press.

Inglehart, R. F., & Welzel, C. (2005). *Modernization, cultural change, and democracy: The human development sequence*. Cambridge: Cambridge University Press.

Internet World Stats. (2017). *Internet usage statistics: World internet users and 2017 population stats*. https://www.internetworldstats.com/stats.htm

IPU. (2016). *Inter-Parliamentary Union Parline Database Singapore*. Accessed June 9, 2017, from http://www.ipu.org/parline-e/reports/2283_A.htm

Kadir, S. (2004). Singapore: Engagement and autonomy within the political status quo. In M. Alagappa (Ed.), *Civil society and political change in Asia: Expanding and contracting democratic space* (pp. 324–355). Stanford: Stanford University Press.

Kim, Y.-M. (1997). 'Asian-Style Democracy': A critique from East Asia. *Asian Survey, 37*, 1119–1134. https://doi.org/10.2307/2645761

Lee, T. (2005). Gestural politics: Civil society in 'new' Singapore. *Sojourn: Journal of Social Issues in Southeast Asia, 20*(2), 132–154.

Lee, T. (2010). *The media, cultural control and government in Singapore*. London: Routledge.

Leifer, M. (1964). Communal violence in Singapore. *Asian Survey, 4*, 1115–1121. https://doi.org/10.2307/2642213

Leong, H. K. (2000). Prime ministerial leadership and policy-making style in Singapore: Lee Kuan Yew and Goh Chok Tong compared. *Asian Journal of Political Science, 8*, 91–123. https://doi.org/10.1080/02185370008434161

Levitsky, S., & Way, L. (2010). *Competitive authoritarianism: Hybrid regimes after the Cold War*. New York: Cambridge University Press.

Lijphart, A. (2012). *Patterns of democracy: Government forms and performance in thirty-six countries* (2nd ed.). New Haven: Yale University Press.

Lipset, S. M. (1960). *Political man: The social basis of politics*. Garden City: Anchor Books.

Maddison, A. (2001). *The World economy: Vol. 1 & 2*. Paris: OECD.

Mauzy, D. K., & Milne, R. S. (2002). *Singapore politics under the people's action party* (1st ed., Politics in Asia). New York: Routledge.

Means, G. P. (1996). Soft authoritarianism in Malaysia and Singapore. *Journal of Democracy, 7*, 103–117. https://doi.org/10.1353/jod.1996.0065

Milne, R. S. (1966). Singapore's exit from Malaysia; the consequences of ambiguity. *Asian Survey, 6*, 175–184. https://doi.org/10.2307/2642221

Ministry of Manpower. (2012). *Singapore yearbook of manpower statistics*. Singapore: Ministry of Manpower.

Moustafa, T., & Ginsburg, T. (2008). Introduction: The function of courts in authoritarian politics. In T. Ginsburg & T. Moustafa (Eds.), *Rule by law: The politics of courts in authoritarian regimes* (pp. 1–23). New York: Cambridge University Press.

Mutalib, H. (2002). Constitutional-electoral reforms and politics in Singapore. *Legislative Studies Quarterly, 27*, 659. https://doi.org/10.2307/3598663

Mutalib, H. (2011). The Singapore minority dilemma. *Asian Survey, 51*, 1156–1171. https://doi.org/10.1525/as.2011.51.6.1156

Neher, C. D. (1994). Asian style democracy. *Asian Survey, 34*, 949–961. https://doi.org/10.2307/2645346

Neureiter, M. (2013). Organized labor and democratization in Southeast Asia. *Asian Survey, 53*, 1063–1086. https://doi.org/10.1525/as.2013.53.6.1063

OECD. (2014). *Stat. Extracts. Income distribution and poverty*. Accessed June 9, 2017, from http://stats.oecd.org/Index.aspx?DataSetCode=IDD

Ooi, C.-S. (1998). Singapore. In W. Sachsenröder & U. E. Frings (Eds.), *Political party systems and democratic development in East and Southeast Asia: Vol. I: Southeast Asia* (pp. 343–402). Aldershot: Ashgate.

Ortmann, S. (2010). *Politics and change in Singapore and Hong Kong: Containing contention.* London: Routledge.

Ortmann, S. (2011). Singapore: Authoritarian but newly competitive. *Journal of Democracy, 22,* 153–164. https://doi.org/10.1353/jod.2011.0066

Ortmann, S. (2012). Policy advocacy in a competitive authoritarian regime. *Administration & Society, 44,* 13S–25S. https://doi.org/10.1177/0095399712460080

Piper, N. (2006). Migrant worker activism in Singapore and Malaysia: Freedom of association and the role of the state. *Asian and Pacific Migration Journal, 15,* 359–380. https://doi.org/10.1177/011719680601500304

PSD. (2013). *Overview of public service.* Singapore: Public Service Division.

Rajah, J. (2012). *Authoritarian rule of law: Legislation, discourse, and legitimacy in Singapore.* Cambridge: Cambridge University Press.

Reporters without Borders. (2017). *2017 World Press Freedom Index. RSF.* Accessed June 22, 2017, from https://rsf.org/en/ranking

Rieger, C. (2001). Singapore. In D. Nohlen, F. Grotz, & C. Hartmann (Eds.), *Elections in Asia and the Pacific: A data handbook, Vol. II: South East Asia, East Asia, and the South Pacific* (pp. 239–261). Oxford: Oxford University Press.

Rodan, G. (2008). Singapore 'Exceptionalism'?: Authoritarian rule and state transformation. In J. Wong & E. Friedman (Eds.), *Political transitions in dominant party systems: Learning to lose* (pp. 231–251). London: Routledge.

Rodan, G. (2011). Embracing electronic media but suppressing civil society: Authoritarian consolidation in Singapore. *The Pacific Review, 16,* 503–524. https://doi.org/10.1080/0951274032000132236

Sajó, A. (1999). *Limiting government: An introduction to constitutionalism.* Budapest: Central European University Press.

Saw, S.-H. (2012). *The population of Singapore* (3rd ed.). Singapore: ISEAS.

Scharpf, F. W. (2002). *Governing in Europe: Effective and democratic?* Oxford: Oxford University Press.

Schedler, A. (2002). The menu of manipulation. *Journal of Democracy, 13,* 36–50. https://doi.org/10.1353/jod.2002.0031

Schedler, A. (2013). *The politics of uncertainty: Sustaining and subverting electoral authoritarianism.* Oxford: Oxford University Press.

Schmidt, M. G. (2016). Legitimation through performance?: Output legitimacy in authoritarian regimes. In U. Backes & S. Kailitz (Eds.), *Ideocracies in comparison: Legitimation – co-optation – repression* (pp. 289–304). London: Routledge.

Silverstein, G. (2008). Singapore: The exception that proves rules matter. In T. Ginsburg & T. Moustafa (Eds.), *Rule by law: The politics of courts in authoritarian regimes* (pp. 73–101). New York: Cambridge University Press.

Slater, D., & Simmons, E. (2012). Coping by colluding: Political uncertainty and promiscuous powersharing in Indonesia and Bolivia. *Comparative Political Studies.* doi:https://doi.org/10.1177/0010414012453447

Supreme Court of Singapore. (2017). *Justices.* Accessed June 8, 2017, from http://www.supremecourt.gov.sg/about-us/the-supreme-court-bench/justices

Taagepera, R. (1998). Effective magnitude and effective threshold. *Electoral Studies, 17,* 393–404. https://doi.org/10.1016/S0261-3794(97)00053-X

Tan, K. (1997). The presidency in Singapore. In K. Tan & P. E. Lam (Eds.), *Managing political change in Singapore: The elected presidency* (pp. 9–51, Politics in Asia series). London: Routledge.

Tan, T. Y. (2001). Singapore: Civil-military fusion. In M. Alagappa (Ed.), *Coercion and governance: The declining political role of the military in Asia* (pp. 276–293). Stanford: Stanford University Press.

Tan, T. Y. (2011). The armed forces and politics in Singapore: The persistence of civil-military fusion. In M. Mietzner (Ed.), *The political resurgence of the military in Southeast Asia: Conflict and leadership* (pp. 148–167). New York: Routledge.

Tan, E. K. B. (2012). Singapore: Transitioning to a "New Normal" in a Post-Lee Kuan Yew Era. *Southeast Asian Affairs, 2012*(1), 265–282.

Tan, K. P. (2016). Singapore in 2015: Regaining hegemony. *Asian Survey, 56*, 108–114. https://doi.org/10.1525/as.2016.56.1.108

Tan, S. S., & Chew, A. (2008). Governing Singapore's security sector: Problems, prospects and paradox. *Contemporary Southeast Asia, 30*(2), 241–263.

Tan, K., & Thio, L.-a. (Eds.). (2009). *Evolution of a revolution: Forty years of the Singapore constitution*. London: RoutledgeCurzon.

Temasek. (2011). *Statement of clarification: Temasek's share of the economy possibly around 10%*. Accessed June 9, 2017, from http://www.temasek.com.sg/mediacentre/medialetters?detailid=8258

Tey, T. H. (2008). Confining the freedom of the press in Singapore: A 'Pragmatic' press for 'Nation-Building. *Human Rights Quarterly, 30*, 876–905. https://doi.org/10.1353/hrq.0.0034

Thiery, P., Sehring, J., & Muno, W. (2009). Die Messung von Rechtsstaatlichkeit. In J. Estermann (Ed.), *Interdisziplinäre Rechtsforschung zwischen Rechtswirklichkeit, Rechtsanalyse und Rechtsgestaltung: Beiträge zum Kongress 'Wie wirkt Recht?', Luzern 2008* (pp. 211–230, Gesellschaftswissenschaftliche Beiträge, Vol. 9). Bern: Stämpfli.

Thio, L.-a. (2008). Singapore: The indigenisation of a westminster import. In C. Hill & J. Menzel (Eds.), *Constitutionalism in Southeast Asia: Vol. 1: National constitutions/ASEAN charter* (pp. 249–299). Singapore: Konrad Adenauer Foundation.

Thompson, M. R. (2004). Pacific Asia after 'Asian Values': Authoritarianism, democracy, and 'Good Governance'. *Third World Quarterly, 25*(6), 1079–1095.

UNDP. (2015). *Human development report 2015: Work for human development*. Houndmills: Palgrave Macmillan.

Vasu, N. (2012). Governance through difference in Singapore. *Asian Survey, 52*, 734–753. https://doi.org/10.1525/as.2012.52.4.734

Vennewald, W. (1993). *Singapur: Herrschaft der Professionals und Technokraten – Ohnmacht der Demokratie?: Grenzen und Möglichkeiten der Demokratisierung in einem südostasiatischen Schwellenland*. Wiesbaden: VS Verlag.

Verweij, M., & Pelizzo, R. (2009). Singapore: Does authoritarianism pay? *Journal of Democracy, 20*, 18–32. https://doi.org/10.1353/jod.0.0076

Wah, Y. K. (1973). *Political development in Singapore, 1945–55*. Singapore: Singapore University Press.

Wall Street Journal. (2013). *Rare riot hits Singapore: Fatal road accident angers foreign workers*. Accessed June 9, 2017, from http://www.wsj.com/articles/SB10001424052702303330204579246540635617948

Walsh, S. P. (2007). The roar of the Lion City: Ethnicity, gender, and culture in the Singapore armed forces. *Armed Forces & Society, 33*, 265–285. https://doi.org/10.1177/0095327X06291854

Weber, M. (1964). *The theory of social and economic organization*. New York: Free Press.

Weiss, M. L. (2014). Of inequality and irritation: New agendas and activism in Malaysia and Singapore. *Democratization, 21*, 867–887. https://doi.org/10.1080/13510347.2014.910764

Wong, T. K.-y., Wan, P.-s., & Hsiao, H.-H. M. (2011). The bases of political trust in six Asian societies: Institutional and cultural explanations compared. *International Political Science Review, 32*, 263–281. https://doi.org/10.1177/0192512110378657.

World Bank. (2017a). *World development indicators*. http://data.worldbank.org/products/wdi

World Bank. (2017b). *Worldwide governance indicators*. http://data.worldbank.org/data-catalog/worldwide-governance-indicators

Worthington, R. (2001). Between hermes and themis: An empirical study of the contemporary judiciary in Singapore. *Journal of Law and Society, 28*, 490–519. https://doi.org/10.1111/1467-6478.00200

Wu, Y.-S. (2011). Clustering of semi-presidentialism: A first cut. In R. Elgie, S. Moestrup, & Y.-S. Wu (Eds.), *Semi-presidentialism and democracy* (pp. 21–42). Basingstoke: Palgrave Macmillan.

Zakaria, F. (1994). Culture is destiny: A conversation with Lee Kuan Yew. *Foreign Affairs, 73*(2), 109–126.

Zakaria, F. (2007). *The future of freedom: Illiberal democracy at home and abroad*. New York: W. W. Norton.

Thailand: The Vicious Cycle of Civilian Government and Military Rule

10.1 Historical Background

Even though the history of Thai kingdoms reaches back even further, the Kingdoms of Sukhothai (thirteenth to fifteenth century) and Ayutthaya (1351–1767) are traditionally considered the beginning of Siam (renamed Thailand in 1939, see Table 10.1 for the Country Profile). After Burmese troops sacked the city of Ayutthaya in 1767, Rama I (1782–1809), the founder of the current Chakri Dynasty, moved his capital to Bangkok. During the reign of King Mongkut (Rama IV, 1850–1868), Siam yielded to the pressure of Western powers, particularly to France and Great Britain, and granted sweeping economic and legal concessions. Facing imperialist threats to the survival of the monarchy and Siam as a sovereign power in the 1870s, King Chulalongkorn (Rama V, 1868–1910) initiated Thailand's revolution from above, relying on the old aristocratic elite to carry out fundamental reforms of the state, economy, and society (Englehart 2001, p. 108). Unlike the Japanese monarchy during the Meiji Restoration, Thailand's monarchy was not just an integrative symbol but remained the driving force behind the transformation of Siam (Wyatt 1984, p. 206). The creation of a centralized bureaucracy and a modern military consolidated monarchical power, but the palace's claim to absolute power and its reliance on traditional aristocratic elites clashed with the interests of new elites in the civil service and army (Mead 2004, p. 97). Rapid social change, conflicts between new and old elites, and the fallout of the Great Depression of 1929 weakened the power of the absolute monarchy and finally culminated in a coup d'état by a group of military officers and bureaucrats against King Prajadhipok (Rama VII) on June 24, 1932 (Wyatt 1984, pp. 239–241).

Following the overthrow of the absolute monarchy in 1932, a "bureaucratic polity" (Riggs 1966) emerged, in which the state bureaucracy became the primary

Table 10.1 Country profile

Population (2017)	Year of full national sovereignty	Form of government
68,414,135	Never colonized	Constitutional monarchy
Total area	**Current constitution proclaimed**	**Head of state**
513,120 km^2	2017	King Maha Vajiralongkorn (Rama X) (since 2016)
GDP p.c. (PPP, 2015)	**Official language**	**Head of government**
16,340	Thai	Prime Minister Gen. Prayut Chan-ocha (since 2014)
Ethnic groups	**Democracy score (BTI 2016)**	**System of government**
Thai 75%, Chinese 14%, others 11%	3.30 (range from 1 to 10, higher scores indicate higher levels of democracy)	Military government
Religious groups	**Regime type**	**Cabinet type**
Buddhists 94.6%, Muslims 4.6%, others 0.8%	Military regime	Military (no-party)

Sources: CIA (2017), World Bank (2017)

arena of political rivalry for parcels of state control between two major forces: civilian bureaucrats and military elites (Connors 2003, p. 11). In contrast, King Bhumibol Adulyadej (Rama IX, 1946–2016), symbolizing the historical continuity of Siam/Thailand since ancient times, lent legitimacy to the military-bureaucratic elites but had little real political power himself. However, long-term processes of economic and social change starting in the 1950s created new socioeconomic groups, such as provincial capitalists, urban educated middle classes, and industrial workers with new political demands and ideologies. At the same time, rural poverty and underdevelopment, increasing tenancy and debts among farmers, and communist agitation, especially in Thailand's north and northeast (Isan) regions, turned Thai peasants to political action. Student protests in Bangkok against the corrupt and repressive government of General Thanom Kittikachorn on October 14, 1973 led to three days of violence followed by the collapse of the military dictatorship (Morell and Chai-anan 1981). The following democratic regime survived until October 6, 1976, when far-right paramilitary groups and security forces launched a massacre among students at Bangkok's Thammasat University and military leaders used the chaos to justify their seizure of the government.

During the staunchly anti-communist and highly repressive government of Thanin Kraivichien (1976–1977), thousands of intellectuals, student protesters, and trade union activists fled to join the Communists in the jungle (Wongrangan 1984). Fear of rural communism and the shifting balance of power in favor of more moderate military elites, civilian bureaucrats, and the king, whose political authority increased as the legitimacy of the rightist government eroded (Phongpaichit and Baker 1997, pp. 314–321), led to the overthrow of Prime Minister Thanin in a military coup in October 1977. In the 1980s, a new electoral authoritarian regime emerged when Army Commander General Prem Tinsulanonda became the unelected prime minister. Meanwhile, the popularly elected House of Representatives had to share its powers with the appointed Senate, whose members came primarily from the ranks of the civil service and the armed forces (Chai-anan 1995). When the government reintroduced parliamentary elections and legalized political parties, provincial capitalists turned their economic fortunes into political capital by financing political parties and candidates and mobilizing rural voters, who built the vast majority of the national electorate (Ockey 2004, p. 170).

In 1988, gradual liberalization under Prem opened the door for a short-lived democratic interregnum with an elected prime minister. Growing military suspicion of civilian interference in its domain, however, eventually led to an army coup under Commander General Suchinda Kraprayoon in February 1991 (LoGerfo 1997). When Suchinda declined to step down in favor of an elected civilian prime minister, mass protests took place in Bangkok from May 17–20, 1992. During the military's attempt to repress the anti-Suchinda demonstrations, soldiers killed numerous protestors, leading the king to intervene to ease Suchinda out of office. The massacre—known as "Black May"—forced the military to withdraw and to be content with its behind-the-scenes influence (Chai-anan 1997). The political parties who had opposed the Suchinda government won a narrow victory in the September 1992 parliamentary elections and formed a coalition government under Prime Minister Chuan Leekpai of the Democrat Party (Murray 1996; LoGerfo 1997, pp. 318–323). A series of short-lived coalitions took turns at governing in the following years. At the height of the Asian Financial Crisis, a new constitution came into force in October 1997. It established a "democratic regime of government with the King as Head of the State" (Section 2, 1997 Constitution).

Yet, the well-intentioned conclusions that this so-called People's Constitution of 1997 would pave the way for the deepening and consolidation of Thailand's democracy turned out to be unfounded. On the contrary, Thailand has been passing through a period of political uncertainty and crisis since the turn of the century. From 2001 to 2016, the country saw five of eight serving prime minister deposed by court orders or military coups, two out of six Lower House elections annulled, and consecutive waves of mass mobilization. Furthermore, in January 2004, a century-old conflict in Thailand's three southernmost provinces broke out once again, in which nearly 7000 people were killed and 12,000 wounded until June 2016 (Abuza 2016).

Although scholars still debate the nature and causes of Thailand's seemingly irreconcilable conflicts, most observers agree that they are the result of the country's deep fault lines between old and new elites, the rich and the poor, urban and rural social forces, and different conceptions of Thailand's national identity. The economic fallout of the Asian Financial Crisis hit the urban poor and the rural population hardest. Thailand's current political crisis was not a social conflict at the outset. However, because of the way in which Thaksin Shinawatra—a wealthy telecommunication tycoon-turned politician—took advantage of the plight of the poor, especially in the impoverished Isan region, it quickly became one. Thaksin and his *Thai Rak Thai* (Thais Love Thais, or TRT) party won the 2001 general election by a landslide. As prime minister, Thaksin systematically weakened mechanisms of horizontal accountability and marginalized the parliamentary opposition. He placed loyalists in key positions in the police and the military as well as in important state organs, such as the Election Commission and the Constitutional Court (McCargo and Ukrist 2005). By doing so, he threatened the informal, monarchical network that had formed since the 1970s that connected royalist elites in politics, military, civil service, economy, and society, and which checked the power of elected governments and parliaments (McCargo and Ukrist 2005). Furthermore, Thaksin and the "network monarchy" were also competing for the hearts and minds of the rural people, and Thaksin, implementing new welfare schemes and running a tough law and order approach ("war against drugs"), won an even more spectacular victory in the 2005 general election (Chambers 2006). Ultimately, Thaksin's attempt to establish an elective dictatorship by rounding up political power based on the support of provincial voters triggered counterreactions and resistance from vested interests and the Bangkok middle class. In February 2006, a diverse extra-parliamentary movement, the "People's Alliance for Democracy" (PAD, or "Yellow Shirts"), emerged and demanded Thaksin's resignation, and on September 19, 2006, the military seized the moment for a coup d'état while Thaksin was traveling abroad.

The military-appointed interim government dissolved the TRT, barred Thaksin and many of the party's senior officials from politics, drafted a new constitution, and organized general elections in late 2007. Despite a sloped playing field that disadvantaged TRT's successor organization, the People's Power Party (PPP), it won 48% of the seats, demonstrating the unbroken popularity of Thaksin among provincial and lower class voters and enabling the pro-Thaksin camp to form a coalition government. The return to electoral democracy did little to calm political polarization and confrontation. After prolonged PAD protests, Thailand's Constitutional Court impeached two pro-Thaksin prime ministers and banned the PPP. In 2010, the pro-Thaksin United Front for Democracy against Dictatorship (UDD, also known as "Red Shirts") organized mass protests in Bangkok that the Thai military dispersed with brutal force, claiming the lives of at least 23 people and injuring hundreds more. Nevertheless, another Thaksin-affiliated political creature, the Puea Thai Party (PTP), managed to win the 2011 election and formed a government under the nominal leadership of Thaksin's sister, Yingluck Shinawatra. This rekindled the anti-Thaksin protest movement under the banner of the newly established People's Democratic Reform Committee (PDRC), which openly agitated for another military coup. Finally, Thailand's military stepped in again when Army Chief Gen. Prayuth Chan-ocha proclaimed a state of emergency on May 20, 2014. Two days later, the military established the National Council for Peace and Order (NCPO), a junta headed by General Prayuth. Since then, the country has been under military rule. Moreover, in October 2016, Thai King Bhumibol Adulyadej died after a 70-year reign, depriving the divided nation of a rare source of stability and social unity.

10.2 Constitutional Development

Thailand's constitutional history began with the provisional constitution of July 1932 and is characterized by a tension between an "almost mythical belief" among Thai elites that a modern Thailand could be created by proclaiming modern codes, statutes, and constitutions (Ginsburg 2008, p. 86) on the one hand and blatant disregard of constitutional principles on the other. In addition, the public discourse about constitutions and constitutionalism in Thailand since the early 1990s has tended to emphasize technical reform agendas and more technocratic or anti-participatory mechanisms of horizontal accountability. Yet this has been at the expensive of overlooking the deeply undemocratic elements that some constitutions contained and has resulted in the inability to see the social and political power dimensions of accountability mechanisms (Rodan and Hughes 2014).

Between 1932 and 2017, Thailand had 20 constitutions, including eight interim constitutions, of which nine were suspended by military coups and 19 were promulgated under authoritarian rule (Table 10.2). The 2017 Constitution was drafted under the auspice of the NCPO, approved in a constitutional referendum on August 7, 2016, and promulgated on April 5, 2017.

The short life span of written constitutions—on average less than 4.5 years—contrasts with the resilience of the informal and unwritten constitutional rules, which have emerged gradually since the 1930s and primarily relate to the status of the monarchy

Table 10.2 Thai constitutions, 1932–2017

	Constitution valid from	Days valid	# of articles	Replaced because
1.	27/06/1932–10/12/1932	166	39	Interim
2.	10/12/1932–05/09/1946	4898	68	Transition to democracy
3.	09/05/1946–08/11/1947	548	96	Military Coup
4.	09/11/1947–23/03/1949	501	98	Interim
5.	23/03/1949–29/11/1951	981	188	Military Coup
6.	08/03/1952–20/10/1958	2417	123	Military Coup
7.	28/01/1959–20/06/1968	3431	20	Interim
8.	20/06/1968–17/11/1971	1245	183	Military Coup
9.	15/12/1972–07/10/1974	661	23	Interim
10.	07/10/1974–06/10/1976	730	238	Military Coup
11.	22/10/1976–20/10/1977	363	29	Military Coup
12.	09/11/1977–22/12/1978	408	32	Interim
13.	22/12/1978–23/02/1991	4446	206	Military Coup
14.	01/03/1991–09/12/1991	283	33	Interim
15.	09/12/1991–11/10/1997	2133	233	Democratic Reforms
16.	11/10/1997–19/09/2006	3235	336	Military Coup
17.	01/10/2006–24/08/2007	327	39	Interim
18.	24/08/2007–22/05/2014	2463	309	Military Coup
19	22/05/2014–05/04/207	1048	48	Interim
20.	05/04/2017–		279	

Source: Traimas and Hoerth (2008), Croissant (2016)

and royal prerogatives (Traimas and Hoerth 2008). In this regard, it is telling that Section 2 of the 2007 Constitution, which regulates the prerogatives of his majesty, the king, was the only section not abolished by the military junta in May 2014 (Mérieau 2016a).

Thailand's more recent constitutional development evolved with the so-called People's Constitution of 1997. In 1996, the National Assembly allowed for the establishment of a Constitutional Drafting Assembly (CDA), whose members were selected by two different groups: The 76 provincial representatives were selected by the National Assembly from lists prepared by provincial assemblies and the 23 legal and academic experts were selected from nomination lists compiled by various government and private universities (Uwanno and Burns 1998). The exclusion of political parties from the CDA reflected the skeptical view of the constitutional reform movement that had emerged in the early 1990s, which included conservatives and liberals, academics, democracy activists, NGOs, and even military figures, who all distrusted the elected parliament, political parties, and Thailand's "political class" (Connors 2007, pp. 153–162). The CDA invited the participation of various sectors of society and public debates over an eight-month period (Connors 2007, pp. 153–182). As Harding and Leyland argue, the draft text that the CDA submitted to the National Assembly represented in many ways Thailand's "most imaginative, concerted and inclusive effort to settle its constitutional system" (Harding and Leyland 2009, p. 23). The parliament only had a yea or nay vote over the whole draft, and against the backdrop of strong public sentiment in favor of the charter, the National Assembly approved the "People's Constitution" in October 1997 (Harding 2007, p. 19).

The 1997 Constitution was the first document declaring the constitution to be the supreme law of the land, binding and constraining all state organs. The introduction of a popularly elected Senate provided new opportunities for popular participation, whereas the ban on political party candidates aimed at increasing the Senate's political autonomy vis-à-vis the political parties. The constitution also called for the reform of local governance and the implementation of decentralization and stipulated an independent state organization to allocate the frequencies for radio and other telecommunication broadcasting. The most important innovations, however, concerned the introduction of a complex system of constitutional watchdogs, like a constitutional court, the office of the ombudsman and an auditor general, a national human rights commission, and a national anti-corruption commission. At the same time, the constitution introduced regulations that aimed at strengthening government stability and the control of the prime minister over coalition parties, limiting party switching and providing institutional incentives for better party institutionalization (Chambers and Croissant 2010; Croissant and Chambers 2010b). Political reality, however, quickly exhibited the pitfalls of these well-intentioned attempts to design a "better" democratic system. Indeed, it was mainly the unintended consequences of reforms to political parties, electoral politics, and the system of government that allowed Thaksin to control the parliamentary process and undermine constitutional checks and balances (Kuhonta 2008).

Following the 2006 military coup, a military-nominated constitutional draft assembly produced a new text that was submitted to a popular referendum in August 2007 (Traimas and Hoerth 2008). While the charter was approved by 56.9% of Thai voters with 57.6% of the public participating, more than 60% of the population in the northeastern Isan region, Thaksin's electoral stronghold, voted against the draft. The constitution clearly was aimed at preventing the rise of another all-powerful elected political leader (Chambers 2008b). It strengthened the autonomy of other constitutional bodies from the elected parliament and the influence of unelected institutions over the Senate by stipulating that 73 out of the 150 senators were to be appointed instead of elected. Furthermore, the constitution provided the military with full control over national defense and security policy and authorized the armed forces to intervene in politics in times of national crisis.

It is no surprise that the lack of elite consensus undermined the 2007 Constitution from the start. Thaksin supporters inside and outside the national parliament never accepted it as legitimate, whereas anti-Thaksin social forces and elite groups perceived the constitution as a mere tool to prevent a return of "Thaksinokracy" (Suehiro 2014). Unsurprisingly, the NCPO quickly replaced the 2007 Constitution with an interim document, which allowed Prime Minister General Prayuth Chan-ocha to exercise full legislative, executive, and judicial power (Section 44, 2014 interim Constitution). Following the playbook of the military junta in 2007, the military appointed a constitutional committee tasked with the responsibility to draft a new charter. The resulting 279-article long document envisions far reaching prerogatives for the military that would institutionalize a quasi-civilian regime in which the "guardian" armed forces (cf. Nordlinger 1977) would have enough power to decisively influence policymaking and safeguard their interests. Among the most controversial provisions of the draft is Section 269. It gives the NCPO the right to appoint 244 of the 250 senators and would reserve the remaining six seats for the permanent secretary of the defence, the supreme commander in chief, the commander-in-chief of army, navy and air force, and the commissioner general of the police.

Technically, the constitutional referendum on August 7, 2016 posed two questions. First, voters were asked whether they accepted the draft constitution. Second, voters cast their ballots to answer the question of whether or not the Senate should be allowed to join the House of Representatives in the voting process to select a prime minister. According to the official figures, 59.4% of the electorate participated, of which 61.3% were in favor of the draft charter and 58.0% approved the suggested procedure for the selection of the prime minister (Bangkok Post 2016).

Yet, on January 10, 2017, only weeks before the charter was due to come into force, King Vajiralongkorn refused to put the new constitution into effect. In sharp contrast to his father's approach, who had preferred to maintain the fiction that the monarchy is "above politics" while at the same time energetically meddling behind the scenes (Handley 2006), the new king requested changes to the text "to ensure his royal powers" (Cochrane 2017). While no official explanation was given as to which sections of the draft constitution the king objected to, observers noted three specific areas of dissent, including the provisions on regency; the request to end the need for a countersignature on all royal acts, which would mean that the king alone would be able, in specific matters, to sign executive orders and decrees; and the transfer of royal crisis powers away from the king to the constitutional court (Mérieau 2017). King Vajiralongkorn signed the revised copy of the charter in early April 2017.

10.3 System of Government

Since the 2014 putsch, Thailand is governed by the National Council for Peace and Order, a military junta that represents the army, navy, air force, and national police led by General Prayut, who was army commander from October 2010 until October 2014. The junta appointed a military-dominated legislature in August 2014, which then selected General Prayut as prime minister. Despite its authoritarian nature, the 48-articles long interim constitution follows the tradition of the 1997 and 2007 Constitutions by stipulating that Thailand is "a democratic regime of government with the King as Head of State" (Section 2, 2014 Interim Constitution). It replaced the bicameral National Assembly with a unicameral National Legislative Assembly of not more than 250 members, who were appointed by the king upon the advice of the military junta (Section 6). While members of political parties were banned from the legislature (Section 8, 2104 Interim Constitution), roughly half of the assembly consists of former or serving military and police officers (Chambers and

Waitoolkiat 2016; Phongpaichit 2016). The NCPO abolished all elected national bodies institutionalized under the previous constitutions but spared the Constitutional Court, which has played a key role in Thai politics since the mid-2000s and has been described by some scholars as a primary tool for royalist elites to control the political system (Mérieau 2016a).

10.3.1 Head of State

Thailand is a constitutional monarchy. The rules of royal succession are laid down in the 1924 Palace Law of Succession. The king is free to appoint his own heir and has the prerogative to amend the succession law (Handley 2006). King Bhumibol Adulyadej ascended to the throne in 1946. During the seven decades of his reign, the monarchy achieved a "position of paramountcy over the institutions of modern democracy, parliament, constitution, and rule of law" (Handley 2006, p. 7; Hewison and Kengkij 2010). Following the death of King Bhumibol Adulyadej on October 13, 2016, Crown Prince Vajiralongkorn took the throne as Rama X on December 2nd of the same year.

Even though previous constitutions provided the monarch with important constitutional prerogatives, a formal description of the constitutional rules cannot convey the real importance of the institution and the political influence of the palace. The monarch is the symbol of the Thai nation, and the monarchy has always claimed the right to define which foreign ideas and concepts correspond with the state's conception of Thai culture and national identity—embodied in the concept of *kwampenthai* ("Thainess"; cf. Zackari 2016)—and which are not. During King Bhumibol's reign, the palace preferred to maintain the illusion that the monarchy held a symbolic role and was "above politics." Yet, observers have noted that the palace interfered actively behind the scenes on various occasions (Hewison 1997; Handley 2006). For example, royal intervention triggered the resignation of Prime Minister Thanom Kittikachorn in 1973 and Prime Minister Suchinda Kraprayoon in 1992, and following public intervention by the king in May 2006, the Constitutional Court annulled the snap elections called by Prime Minister Thaksin earlier that year (Nelson 2007, p. 3). In other respects, the king's political influence had been indirect, but no less important (Bünte 2006, p. 36). Since the early 1980s, King Bhumibol and royalists had "forged a modern form of monarchy as a para-political institution," which McCargo in a seminal study has called the "network monarchy" (McCargo 2005). Under the network monarchy, the king "intervened actively in political developments, largely by working through proxies such as privy councillors [sic] and trusted military figures" (McCargo 2005, p. 501). At its heart, the power of the network monarchy "relied on placing the right people (mainly, the right men) in the right jobs" (McCargo 2005, p. 501).The allocation of key posts in the military and the civil service was the primary role of the Privy Council and its president, Prem Tinsulanonda.

Yet, the political crisis that has haunted Thailand since the mid-2000s has also damaged the image and legitimacy of the monarchy. While the concrete role of

King Bhumibol during the events that led to the coup d'état against Prime Minister Thaksin in September 2006 remain somewhat contested, many observers have identified frictions within the palace and between competing factions of Thailand's "monarchized military" (Chambers and Waitoolkiat 2016). These may threaten the very fundament of royal authority and power in the future (Chambers 2010a; Streckfuss 2013). One indication of the simmering legitimacy crisis of Thailand's monarchy is the excessive application of the law on *lèse majesté* (insulting the monarchy).[1] On paper, the law protects the king from undue criticism, but in practice, it is a convenient weapon to exile, physically assault, and threaten critics of royal actions and to prevent any public debate about the proper role of the monarchy in Thailand's rapidly changing society. After the 2006 coup, *lèse majesté* cases—which carry heavy penalties of up to 15 years imprisonment—have skyrocketed from an annual average of five between 1992 and 2004 to a high of 478 in 2010 alone (Streckfuss 2013). As Human Rights Watch reports, following the 2014 putsch, the military government has charged at least another 68 persons with *lèse majesté*, with several more arrests and investigations since the death of King Bhumibol in October 2016 (HRW 2017). According to most observers, the new king lacks his predecessor's gravitas and reputation, and hence, it is uncertain if the monarchy will survive as the keystone of Thailand's identity and a major unifying force.

10.3.2 The Executive and Legislature

Since 1932, Thailand has a parliamentary system of government with a prime minister who heads the cabinet or Council of Ministers. From democratization in September 1992 until the rise of Thaksin Shinawatra to power in January 2001, Thai governments were characterized by volatile and incoherent multiparty coalitions. There was a change of prime minister about every 2 years. However, adopting strict coding rules for the termination of a government (change in the party composition of a government, a change of prime minister, or a legislative election as the end-date for that government, cf. Conrad and Golder 2010), the average cabinet durability was less than a year (see Table 10.3). Small parties and intra-party factions had a large influence on the formation and survival of cabinets, and because of the fragmented nature of the cabinets, power did not rest with the prime minister or the Cabinet as a collective, but with powerful government ministers (Funston 2006, p. 342; Chambers 2008a).

However, the 1997 Constitution in combination with the election of Thaksin Shinawatra in 2001 shifted power from the myriad of political parties in parliament to the prime minister and the executive. Even before the 2001 election, Thaksin's TRT party had systematically absorbed minor parties and enticed party factions

---

[1]The law was added to the Criminal Code in 1908 and extended in 1976 to make it illegal to defame, insult, or threaten the king, queen, heir-apparent, or regent (Streckfuss 2011).

Table 10.3 Thai governments, 1992–2014

Term in office	Prime Minister	Type of cabinet	Duration (days)
23/09/1992–15/09/1993	Chuan Leekpai	Coalition (DP, NAP, PDP, SAP, Ekhapap)	357
16/09/1993–19/05/1995	Chuan Leekpai	Coalition (DP, NAP, PDP, Ekhapap)	665
13/07/1995–14/06/1996	Banharn Silpa-archa	Coalition (CTP, NAP, SAP, PDP, Muanchon, Nam Thai	337
15/06/1996–03/07/1996	Banharn Silpa-archa	Coalition (CTP, NAP, SAP, PDP, Nam Thai, Muanchon)	18
03/07/1996–15/08/1996	Banharn Silpa-archa	Coalition (CTP, NAP, SAP, PDP, Nam Thai, Muanchon, Thai Citizen)	43
15/08/1996–25/11/1996	Banharn Silpa-archa	Coalition (CTP, NAP, SAP, Nam Thai, Muanchon, Thai Citizen)	102
25/11/1996–09/11/1997	Chavalit Yongchaiyut	Coalition (NAP, Chart Pattana, SAP, Thai Citizen, Muanchon, Seritham)	349
09/11/1996–02/10/1998	Chuan Leekpai	Coalition (DP, CTP, SAP, Seritham, Ehapap, Palang Dharma, Thai Party, Citizen Party)	692
02/10/1998–11/07/1999	Chuan Leekpai	Coalition (DP, CTP, SAP, Seritham, Ehapap, Palang Darma, Thai party, Citizen Party, CPP)	282
11/07/1999–17/02/2001	Chuan Leekpai	Coalition (DP, CTP, SAP, Seritham, Thai party, Citizen Party, CPP)	587
17/02/2001–11/03/2005	Thaksin Shinawatra	Coalition (TRT, NAP, SAP, Seritham, CTP)	1483
11/02/2005–19/09/2006	Thaksin Shinawatra	Single party (TRT)	557
08/10/2006–06/02/2008	Surayud Chulanont	Transitional	486
06/02/2008–08/09/2008	Samak Sundaravej	Coalition (PPP, Chart Thai, Pue Paendin; Matchima; RJCP)	215
24/09–2008–02/12/2008	Somchai Wongsawat	Coalition (PPP, Chart Thai, Pue Paendin, RJCP, Matchima)	69
20/12/2008–06/06/2010	Abhisit Vejjajiva	Coalition (DP, Pue Paendin, Bhumjai Thai, RJCP, CT (P), SAP)	533
06/06/2010–05/08/2011	Abhisit Vejjajiva	Coalition (DP, Pue Paendin, Bhumjai Thai, RJCP, CTP, SAP, Matubhum)	428

(continued)

Table 10.3 (continued)

Term in office	Prime Minister	Type of cabinet	Duration (days)
10/08/2011–07/05/2014	Yingluck Shinawatra	Coalition (Puea Thai, Chartthaipattana, CPPP, Phalang Chon)	1001
07/05/2014–22/05/2014	Niwatthamrong Boonsongpaisan	Interim (Puea Thai, Chartthaipattana, CPPP, Phalang Chon)	15
22/05/2014–	Prayuth Chan-ocha	NCPO	

Source: Authors' compilation based on Chambers (2003), Orathai (2002), Prasirtsuk (2009), Secretariat of the Cabinet (2011)

from other parties to defect. After taking office, Thaksin continued this practice (Orathai 2002). The February 2005 election confirmed Thaksin in office and made him the first head of a single party government in Thai history (Chambers 2006). After the 2006 military coup and the military-appointed interim government between 2006 and 2008, heterogeneous multiparty coalitions made a comeback, and with it, a lack of executive power as well as weak cabinet and party discipline. Cabinets again became unstable, a trend exacerbated by frequent interventions of the Constitutional Court, which banned two successor parties of Thaksin's TRT and ousted three prime ministers, all of whom were political proxies of the exiled former prime minister.

From 1968 until 2014, Thailand had a bicameral National Assembly consisting of the House of Representatives and the Senate. Despite its relatively recent history, bicameralism is deeply entrenched in Thailand's constitutional tradition, and the new constitution adopted by referendum in August 2016 also provides for a bicameral legislature. Thailand's bicameralism is the result of a gradual parliamentarization of Thai politics and the rise of political parties. With the institutionalization of a fully elected House of Representatives, the Senate became a chamber of officers, bureaucrats, and traditional elites and for some time held a preeminent position in the legislative process (Chambers 2009). The 1997 Constitution for the first time established direct elections for the non-partisan Senate. As a reaction to the co-optation of the elected Senate by Thaksin after 2001, the 2007 Constitution provided for a partly appointed and partly elected upper house, in which 76 senators would be elected in non-partisan elections and 74 senators nominated by a non-partisan selection committee. The framers of the 2007 Constitution intended the upper house to be a conservative counterweight to the party-dominated House of Representatives, mainly by participating in the creation of other state organs. In fact, most appointed senators had backgrounds as businessmen or members of the civil service, military, or police (Chambers 2009, p. 30).

Following the transition to democracy in 1992, the main legislative powers rested with the fully elected House of Representatives. Especially the 1997 Constitution strengthened its powers of legislation, control of finance, and ability to hold the executive accountable. According to the 1997 and 2007 Constitutions, the House selected the prime minister from among its ranks, had almost exclusive power to initiate legislation, and was the predominant power to push it through the legislative process. In addition, the House played a major role in enforcing cabinet accountability. At the same time, the 1997 Constitution provided the basis for a rich tapestry of different "watchdog" (Leyland 2007) institutions, tasked with the responsibility to provide better horizontal and vertical accountability of elected politicians and governments. Important electoral reforms included the establishment of the independent Election Commission as well as new Organic Laws on Political Parties and the Election of Members of the House of Representatives and Senators. As Western scholars point out, these new measures were meant to "engineer" a more stable and better organized democratic system based on "good governance" and the "rule of law" (McCargo 2002; Kuhonta 2008; Thompson 2007). In practice, however, the 1997 Constitution induced a number of unintended consequences, the most significant being Prime Minister Thaksin Shinawatra's rise to near-hegemonic power (Kuhonta 2008). Accordingly, the drafters of the 2007 Constitution weakened the authority of the prime minister over his or her cabinet and turned back those provisions that had aimed at engineering cohesive parliamentary parties and establishing a more centralized, coherent party government (Hicken 2007). Furthermore, as decisively counter-majoritarian devises, the 2007 Constitution for the first time recognized the official position of the opposition leader in the House of Representatives, introduced legal guarantees of the parliamentary rights of the opposition, and curtailed the influence of the elected House over the creation of other constitutional organs. The 2017 Constitution further weakens the position of the House vis-à-vis the Senate and other extra-parliamentary forces. While the Senate only has a delaying role in most legislation, its approval at a joint sitting is required for certain "organic" laws, like those on elections and the operation of the Constitutional Court. Most importantly, the 500-member House of Representatives lost its exclusive right to elect the prime minister. The military-appointed senators now join the elected members of the House in choosing the prime minister. Furthermore, Section 160 of the 2017 Constitution removes the requirement for the prime minister to be an elected member of the House, a hallmark achievement of the 1992 democracy movement.

10.3.3   Mechanisms of Horizontal Accountability and Watchdog Organizations

A key innovation of the 1997 Constitution concerned the creation of various independent "watchdog" organizations. These included the National Counter Corruption Commission (NCCC), Constitutional Court, Administrative Court, National Human Rights Commission, Office of the Ombudsman, State Audit Commission, and the Election Commission equipped with the potentially powerful instrument of oversight and sanction and charged with organizing and conducting elections (Leyland 2007). This network of mechanisms of horizontal accountability was meant to uphold the standards of "good governance," provide effective control of the abuse of public office by elected politicians, and defend basic rights. To eliminate party influence over the composition and inner workings of these new bodies, they were designed to be independent of the executive and legislature (Schaffar 2005). With the exception of the State Auditor, however, none of these bodies managed to fulfill the high hopes put into them: Either Thaksin succeeded in staffing the new bodies with loyalists and cronies (McCargo 2005; Leyland 2007) or they became the site of political battles.

In reaction, the military junta further strengthened anti-majoritarian elements in the 2007 Constitution. For example, the nine commissioners of the NCCC were to be selected by a joint committee comprised of the presidents of the Constitutional Court and the Supreme Court as well as the president and opposition leader of the House of Representatives (Art. 246, 2007 Constitution). Furthermore, the members of the Human Rights Commission, the State Auditor, and the Office of the Ombudsman were selected by the presidents of the highest courts of the land, another representative of both the Supreme Court and the Supreme Administrative Court, and the opposition leader and the speaker of the Lower House. The 2017 Constitution further strengthens their autonomy from and oversight over the elected House of Representatives, but increases military leverage over the recruitment of their members. Therefore, it certainly supports the view of Rodan and Hughes (2014), who caution against interpreting the growing number of accountability institutions in Thailand and in other Southeast Asian countries as a trend towards liberal democracy. Instead, the invention and implementation of these institutions (also) constitute an attempt by national elites to recalibrate their power.

10.4 Legal System and Judiciary

Thailand's modern legal system and its judiciary are the result of the introduction of Western law during the reforms of King Chulalongkorn in the late nineteenth century. The legal system is based on civil law combined with common law influence. Under the 1997 and 2007 Constitutions, the courts were independent and subject only to the law. Law also regulates the organization of the courts, including court self-administration and budget autonomy. The king upon the advice of specific selection committees appoints all judges (Thammanoon 2003). When the junta annulled the 2007 Constitution, this did not affect the National Counter Corruption Commission, the Constitutional Court, or the Election Commission.

Courts of the first instance, magistrates' courts, or juvenile courts exist in each of the provincial capitals and in Bangkok. There are nine regional courts of appeal as well as a national Court of Appeal in Bangkok. Specialized administrative, labor, and tax courts are subordinate to the Supreme Administrative Court. The Audit Commission oversees public expenditure, conducts legally mandatory audit procedures, and has legal oversight over budget implementation. The Supreme Court of Justice, consisting of at least three judges, is the highest court of the land. The court has final and executory authority, but decides only on points of law, meaning it refers the case back to the original court for a decision. It functions separately from the Constitutional Court, which reviews the constitutionality of particular laws, rules, or regulations, and the Administrative Court, which decides disputes between private individuals and a government entity or between government entities. Military courts deal primarily with military justice, but have broader jurisdiction when martial law is in force. Military court decisions cannot be appealed. Between May 2014 and September 2016, more than 1000 cases brought against civilians were tried in military courts before Prime Minister Gen. Prayut revoked the respective NCPO orders that had empowered military courts to try civilians for national security offenses, including *lèse majesté* and sedition (HRW 2016). Finally, Islamic courts hear civil cases concerning Muslims.

Given the growing politicization of anti-corruption agencies, the judiciary, and accountability organizations in Thailand, it is no surprise that the state of rule of law and the relationship between politics and the judiciary has experienced an ongoing crisis; especially corruption prosecution has become a political weapon in Thailand. While the military junta claims to follow a hard-handed approach in holding former officeholders responsible for corruption, anti-corruption efforts are strongly biased against the political camp of ex-PM Thaksin. In particular, the Constitutional Court, established in 1998, has been accused of being a tool for royalist elites who oppose Thaksin and his political parties. Under the constitutions of 1997 and 2007, the court's main functions were policing other independent bodies and political parties, determining the (un)constitutionality of parliamentary acts and laws, resolving jurisdictional disputes among state institutions, removing officials who violated the law from office, and deciding whether political parties were violating the constitution (Harding and Leyland 2009). Yet, from the early years of its operation until the collapse of the constitutional order in 2014, the Court was embroiled in political controversies that weakened the Court's independence vis-à-vis other political powers, which contributed to its failure in effectively acting as the guardian of democracy based on the rule of law (Ginsburg 2008). Moreover, since 2006, the Court—willingly or not—has became a key player in the struggle between anti-Thaksin forces and several pro-Thaksin governments, disbanding not only the *Thai Rak Thai* party and its successor, the *Palang Prachachon Party* (PPP), but also removing three pro-Thaksin prime ministers. Additional rulings, including the annulment of the April 2006 and February 2014 elections, have further tarnished the integrity of the court and the idea of independent judicial control (Mérieau 2016a, b).

10.5 Electoral System and Elections

Between the introduction of universal suffrage in 1932, indirect elections for a legislative assembly in 1933, and the derailed snap election of February 2, 2014, there have been 29 parliamentary elections, including nine elections for the House of Representatives and four elections for the Senate since 1992. Elections at provincial, municipal, and subdistrict (*tambon*) levels and for the governor of Bangkok (but not for other provincial governors) are held every 4 years. As in previous constitutions, the 2017 Constitution grants suffrage to all citizens aged 18 or older, excluding Buddhist monks, novices, and nuns. Table 10.4 lists all election results for the House of Representatives since 1992 except for the snap elections of April 2006 and February 2014, which the Constitutional Court annulled.

The requirements for candidacy for the bicameral National Assembly have changed several times since 1992. Until 2014, candidates for the House of Representatives and the Senate had to be at least 25 and 40 years of age, respectively. Those who held political office during the 5 years prior to their candidacy, members of political parties, or persons who did not hold at least a Bachelor's Degree or an equivalent level of education were ineligible for the non-partisan Senate (Sec. 115, 2007 Constitution). For the House of Representatives, party-affiliated candidacy is required since 1974 (Orathai 2002). Yet, Section 98 of the 2017 Constitution lists 13 paragraphs of prohibitions for running for the House, including "being the owner or a shareholder in newspaper business or any mass media" (such as Thaksin Shinawatra before 2006). Section 108 enumerates qualifications and prohibitions for members of the Senate, which aim to increase its autonomy vis-à-vis political parties and the elected House.

Even though the kingdom was among the first Southeast Asian countries to adopt representative national elections for the legislature, elections remain deeply controversial in Thailand. Nevertheless, the return to electoral politics in 2007 and the announcement of the NCPO to hold elections for the House of Representatives in 2017 or 2018 indicate that elections have become so entrenched in Thai politics that even the "monarchized military" (Chambers and Waitoolkiat 2016) cannot suspend them indefinitely.

The results of the Perceptions of Election Integrity (PEI) survey suggest that elections in Thailand are by and large well administered in terms of technical aspects (PEI 2016). Following the introduction of a permanent and specialized election management body in 1997, election fraud and other forms of manipulation such as flawed voter registries and the irregular compilation of election results have become less of a problem. Yet, vote buying, corruption, and political party financing are still considered key problems in Thai elections (Callahan 2000; Hicken 2007; Bowie 2008). Furthermore, polarization between the different political camps and the politicization of the election commission have entrenched or created other problems, such as the intimidation of candidates and voters and a general lack of trust in the impartiality of election authorities. A non-negligible and politically powerful segment of elites and citizens even rejects elections outright (Groemping 2015).

From 1983 to 1996, Thailand had a multiple nontransferable vote system (also known as block vote) with constituencies of one to three seats and an average district magnitude (M) of 2.4 (1983) to 2.5 (1996). Seats were allocated by province (*changwat*) and the seats per province were commensurate with population size. Voters were allowed to cast as many votes as there were available seats and the candidates with the most votes won, even if they did not manage to secure a majority of the votes (Hicken 2009, p. 101). The block vote gave electoral

Table 10.4 Elections for the house of representatives in Thailand, 1992–2011[a]

		1992	1995	1996	2001[b]	2005[b]	2007[b]	2011[b]
Democrat Party	Votes (%)	21.0	22.3	31.8	26.4	23.2	40.4	35.1
	Seats	79	86	123	128	96	164	159
New Aspiration Party (NAP)	%	14.2	12.3	29.1	7	–	–	–
	Seats	51	57	125	36	–	–	–
Chart Pattana	%	15.9	12	12.4	6.2	–	–	–
	Seats	60	53	52	29	–	–	–
Chart Thai	%	15.8	22.8	9.9	5.3	6.6	4	–
	Seats	77	92	39	41	25	34	–
Palang Dharma	%	18	7.7	2.7	–	–	–	–
	Seats	47	23	1		–	–	–
Social Action Party	%	4	4	5.2	0.2	–	–	–
	Seats	22	22	20	1	–	–	–
Seritham	%	3.6	3.1	1.2	5.3	–	–	–
	Seats	8	11	4	14	–	–	–
Thai Chart Party	%	3.1	4.5	4.1	–	–	–	–
	Seats	3	18	18	–	–	–	–
Nam Thai	%	–	6.3	–	–	–	–	–
	Seats	–	18	–	–	–	–	–
Thai Rak Thai (TRT)	%	–	–	–	40.7	61.1	–	–
	Seats	–	–	–	248	377	–	–
Mahachon	%	–	–	–	–	4.3	–	–
	Seats	–	–	–	–	2	–	–
Palang Prachachon Party	%	–	–	–	–	–	41.0	–
	Seats	–	–	–	–	–	233	–
Matchima Thippathai	%	–	–	–	–	–	1.4	–
	Seats	–	–	–	–	–	11	–
Puea Pandin	%	–	–	–	–	–	5.3	–
	Seats	–	–	–	–	–	24	–
Ruam Jai Thai Chat Pattana (RJTCP)	%	–	–	–	–	–	2.4	–
	Seats	–	–	–	–	–	9	–
Pracharaj	%	–	–	–	–	–	0.4	–
	Seats	–	–	–	–	–	5	–
Puea Thai Party	%	–	–	–	–	–	–	48.2
	Seats	–	–	–	–	–	–	265
Bhumjaithai Party (BJT)	%	–	–	–	–	–	–	3.9
	Seats	–	–	–	–	–	–	34
Chart Thai Pattana Party	%	–	–	–	–	–	–	2.8
	Seats	–	–	–	–	–	–	19
Chart Pattana Puea Pandin	%	–	–	–	–	–	–	1.5
	Seats	–	–	–	–	–	–	7
Rak Patthai Party	%	–	–	–	–	–	–	3.1
	Seats	–	–	–	–	–	–	4

(continued)

Table 10.4 (continued)

		1992	1995	1996	2001[b]	2005[b]	2007[b]	2011[b]
Others	%	4.2	5	3.6	8.9	4.8	5.1	5.3
	Seats	13	11	11	3	–	–	12
Total	%	100	100	100	100	100	100	100
	Seats	360	391	393	500	500	480	500
Voter turnout	%	61.6	62	62.4	69.9	75.1	85.3	75
Effective number of political parties[c]	%	6.6	6.9	4.6	4	2.4	4	2.8
	Seats	6.1	6.2	4.4	3	1.6	2.8	2.5

[a]Except for the 2011 election, only parties with at least 3% of votes or seats are listed
[b]Sum of seats and votes from both direct and party lists
[c]See Table 3.2 for details on calculation
Source: Nelson (2001, 2012), Orathai (2002), Croissant and Chambers (2010a)

premiums to smaller parties and undermined the party cohesion and the value of party organizations, as voters were free to vote for as many candidates as they had votes (Hicken 2009). In the 1990s, the voting system therefore became a primary target for electoral reforms aimed at strengthening the institutionalization of political parties and combating party factionalism and fractionalization.

Since 1997, Thailand has seen several important changes to its electoral system (Table 10.5), including the introduction of a permanent Election Commission with wide-ranging powers to organize and ensure the integrity of the elections, a shift from block vote to a mixed member majoritarian system, and the establishment rigid party bylaws and election laws.

The 1997 Constitution introduced a system of parallel voting where voters participated in two separate elections using different systems: 400 seats were allocated in single-member constituencies by plurality rule, whereas the remaining 100 were allocated based on closed party lists. The results of the single-member districts did not affect the results of the party-list election, as voters would cast two votes, one for the candidate in the district and one for the nationwide party list.[2] This system, which gave an electoral premium to larger parties with nationwide support and strengthened the role of party leaders, was widely considered one of the main institutional factors that contributed to the rise of Thaksin's TRT party to electoral dominance in the 2001 and 2005 elections (Kuhonta 2008; Hicken 2009).

The 2007 Constitution amended the parallel system in some important ways. The number of members of parliament was reduced to 480, with 400 seats to be allocated in single- and multi-member constituencies of up to three seats, while the remaining 125 were elected through party-list proportional representation in eight multi-member regional constituencies. For the 2011 election, the total number of seats was 500: 375 elected in single-member constituencies, 125 by proportional representation in a single nationwide constituency as before. Furthermore, the new

---

[2]For the Senate elections of 2000, 2006, 2008, and 2014, a system of plurality rule in multi-member constituencies was applied.

Table 10.5 Electoral systems in Thailand, 1992–2016

	1992	1995	1996	2001–2006	2007	2011	2016[a]
Type	Block vote	Block vote	Block vote	Parallel voting	Parallel voting	Parallel voting	Parallel voting
# of seats	360	391	393	400/100	400/80	375/125	350/150
# of districts	142	155	156	400/1	157/8	375/1	350/1
District magnitude (M)	2.5	2.5	2.5	1/100	2.5/10	1/125	1/150
Ballot structure	Nominal	Nominal	Nominal	Dividual	Dividual	Dividual	Nominal
# of votes cast	1–3	1–3	1–3	2	2–4	2	1
Type of party list	–	–	–	Closed	Closed	Closed	Closed
Level of seat allocation	District	District	District	District/national	District/regional	District/regional	District/national
Seat allocation method	Plurality	Plurality	Plurality	Plurality/LR[b]	Plurality/LR[b]	Plurality/LR[b]	Plurality/LR[b]
Election threshold	–	–	–	5%	5%	–	–

[a] According to the 2017 Constitution
[b] Largest Reminder (Hare-Niemeyer)
Source: (Hicken 2009, p. 101; IPU (2017), 2017 Constitution

system did away with the requirement that a party needs to receive 5% of the total party-list votes in order to obtain seats from this system.

As several scholars have noted, the new electoral system aimed at breaking the electoral dominance of Thaksin-affiliated political parties, weakening party cohesion, and strengthening intra-party factions, with the result of increasing the fractionalization of the political party system and the need to form multiparty coalitions (Chambers 2008b; Hicken 2009, p. 142). Despite institutional engineering, Thaksin's TRT surrogate parties, the *Palang Prachachon Party* (PPP) and the *Puea Thai Party*, won a substantial plurality in the 2007 and 2011 elections.

Under the 2017 Constitution, the 500 members of the House will be elected using mixed-member proportional representation.[3] The primary difference between the new and the 2011 election system is that 350 seats are allocated within single-member constituencies while the remaining 150 members are determined by a system of closed party lists in which seats are awarded in proportion to the number of votes from the election on a constituency basis throughout the country as obtained by each political party. Voters will receive one ballot, which is used to cast a vote for the candidate (Section 91). While this system will deliver a higher degree of overall proportionality for the allocation of seats, its impact on Thai politics is unclear. On the one hand, it will make it harder for larger parties to win a majority and likely result in broader coalitions. This, in turn, might reduce confrontation in Thai politics and diminish the use of extra-constitutional political means. On the other hand, it could lead to a fragmented House and weak, unstable coalition governments, like those that existed before 1997.

10.6 Political Parties and Party System

The history of political parties in Thailand is relatively short. While the People's Party was founded in 1927 as an anti-absolutist proto party, it had few commonalities with "modern" political parties (Darling 1971). Indeed, parties did not become a common element of Thai politics until the constitution of 1946, which explicitly permitted the free organization of parties. Under this constitution, several parties emerged, of which only the Democrat Party has survived until today.

Effective control over state apparatuses, frequent coup d'états, the forced dissolution of existing parties, and legislative enactments by the ruling powers of the "bureaucratic polity" hindered the emergence of well-organized and politically powerful parties in Thailand before the mid-1970s (Anusorn 1998, pp. 403–436). Unaffected by competing ideologies, the formation of Thai parties was influenced by three political and institutional factors: (1) the vertical centralization of political power and access to state resources within the unitary organized state; (2) the horizontal decentralization of decision-making authority between state agencies and cabinet ministries; and (3) the dispersion of political power within oversized

---

[3] At the time of writing in summer of 2017, elections were expected to be held in 2018.

multiparty cabinets and factionalized political parties (Hicken 2006; Siripan 2006a). The block vote system and ubiquitous money politics further fostered the impact of these three factors on the party system.

Since the 1980s, scholars have noted five related features of Thailand's political parties and party system that are still relevant today to various extent. The first is high party system fractionalization. From the reintroduction of regular parliamentary elections in 1979 to 2001, as many as 16 parties won seats in an election, and the average for the effective number of parties in parliament was around six. After 1997, the effective number of political parties (seats) dropped from 4.4 (1996) to 1.6 in the 2005 election, only to climb again to 2.8 in 2007 (Table 10.4). Another key feature of the Thai party system is its regionalization (Hicken 2009). Most political parties do not draw their MPs from all regions. Even the TRT, which won a three-quarter majority of seats in 2005, was not able to gain seats in the southern region—a traditional Democrat stronghold. Despite the transformation from "candidate" to "party-centered" campaigns in recent years (Siripan 2006a, p. 121), the electoral success of many candidates in the various constituencies still depends primarily upon local issues. That said, it is important to note that most political parties, except the Democrat Party in the south, do not actually represent the interests of particular regions: "As representation in Thailand is more local than national, this role belongs largely to MPs not parties" (Anusorn 1998, p. 419). However, in regionalized party systems such as Thailand's, public policies are directed far more towards the satisfaction of particularized local interests, often to the detriment of the national common good. Furthermore, as parties concentrate on certain groupings of provinces, political polarization between regional constituencies tends to deepen. Considering electoral results in the regions, the TRT and its successors enjoy particularly steady support in the Isan, the less affluent northeast of the country. The Democrats, on the other hand, enjoy a quasi-monopoly in the south (Table 10.6).

The outcomes of the 2007 and 2016 constitutional referendums confirmed this pattern of regionalization of voters' political allegiances: In both referendums, the draft was most strongly rejected in the 20 pro-Thaksin provinces of the Isan.

Table 10.6 Regional strongholds of the Democrat Party and Pro-Thaksin political parties, 2001–2011

	Pro-Thaksin parties				Democrat Party			
	2001 (TRT)	2005 (TRT)	2007 (PPP)	2011 (Puea Thai)	2001	2005	2007	2011
National	49.6	75.4	48.5	53.0	25.6	19.2	34.3	31.8
Bangkok	75.6	59.4	25.0	30.3	24.3	10.8	75	69.6
Central	35.0	82.4	39.7	42.7	20.6	7.2	35.7	26
Northeast	61.7	92.4	75.5	82.5	3.6	1.4	3.7	3.1
North	68.4	92.1	62.6	73.1	20.7	6.5	21.3	19.4
South	1.8	1.8	3.5	0.0	88.8	96.2	87.5	94.3

Source: Nelson (2001, 2012), Hicken (2009), Orathai (2002, p. 278), Croissant and Chambers (2010a)

A third key feature of political parties in Thailand concerns their weak institutionalization and the inchoate nature of the party system. McCargo (1997, p. 118) refers to the political parties as being characterized by "the dominance of personalities and the influence of money and personalism, clientelism, and kinship ties prevail among party members." In fact, Thai parties have only been institutionalized to the extent that elites have bestowed legitimacy on open elections and parties as the key route for achieving power, but most parties do not possess any organizational identity (Croissant and Völkel 2012).

Fourth, intra-party factions (*phak puak*) are essential actors in Thai party politics (Ockey 1994). Factions are often temporary groupings of politicians, and their support groups both within and outside of the overarching party structure. Factions come together to achieve common material or political interests. Power relationships within factions are based on a central personality or financier, who maintains his or her power through dependency relationships with faction-based politicians. Factions are differentiated by personality but also by geography. In this latter regard, factions are often provincial groupings of politicians and sitting members of parliament (Chambers and Croissant 2010). Provincial and regional factions control *rabob hua kanaen* (vote-canvassing networks), on which national parties depend to collect votes and to act as intermediaries between central party offices and voters on the ground (Chambers 2008b). Intra-party factions often leave parties *en bloc* when they feel they are not being heard. Others leave because they feel their leader is not awarded a suitable position (e.g., minister; cf. Chambers 2008b). While the 1997 Constitution did succeed in hemming factions in by strengthening party hierarchy, the 2007 Constitution emancipated factions from the 1997 restrictions. Factions thus remain important actors in the making and breaking of both parties and cabinets.

Fifth, Thai political parties generally follow two models: the leader-dominated party and the cadre party (Siripan 2006b). Mass-bureaucratic political parties with large memberships and elaborated party platforms do not exist in Thailand. For the most part, political parties preoccupy themselves with achieving material gains for their leaders and are office-seeking instead of policy seeking. This is combined with a lack of ideological appeal and party platforms that would link political parties with social groups and provide a voice to rank-and-file members (Chambers and Croissant 2010; Siripan 2006b, p. 166). In this regard, political parties were also hindered in developing better linkages to society, because until 1997, social organizations were explicitly banned from supporting parties or candidates financially (Siripan 2006b, pp. 88–89).

The rise of the TRT in the late 1990s was a watershed event for Thai politics and also represented the emergence of a new type of political party. Like previous parties, it emerged as a conglomerate of factions, but its founder, Thaksin Shinawatra, quickly consolidated his power over the party and established a centralized and vertical leadership structure. In addition, the TRT was the first party to tailor its political message to lower class voters, whose grievances had been aggravated by feelings of relative deprivation during the Asian Financial Crisis (Phongpaichit and Baker 2004, 2008). Several observers have described Thaksin's political style; his strategy of gaining, maintaining, and exerting power; and some of his policies, which targeted low-income groups and rural constituencies, as

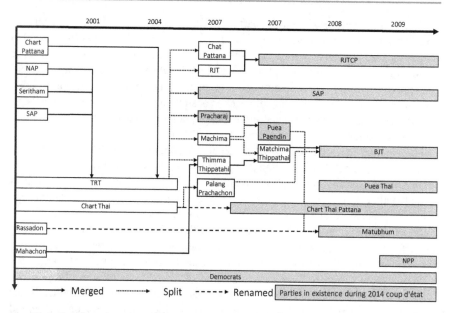

Fig. 10.1 Development of political parties in Thailand, 2001–2014. Source: Chambers (2008a), Chambers and Croissant (2010), Croissant and Chambers (2010b)

"populist" (Phongpaichit and Baker 2004, 2008; Funston 2009). Even though Thaksin's populism resulted in the regression of Thailand's electoral democracy into an "elective dictatorship," it functioned as a political corrective insofar as Thaksin's politics drew attention to the democracy's manifest deficits concerning political representation and political performance.

As already mentioned, between 2001 and 2005, the party system went through a process of transformation, including a sharp drop in the number of political parties. Since the 2006 military coup, Thailand's party system has again fractionalized. In 2007, a total of 66 parties registered with the Election Commission, and 40 parties contested the 2011 election. Most of them were micro-parties, unable to win representation at the national level (Fig. 10.1).

Of the seven parties that managed to win seats in the 2007 general election (2011: 11), five were political groupings founded after the 2006 military coup against Thaksin. Most of these parties were fractionally derived from Thaksin's TRT party, whereas the Democrats (and the smaller Chart Thai) had been around for more than three decades. The *Palang Prachachon Party* (PPP) was the largest of the TRT remnants. It won a substantial plurality in the 2007 election and afterwards formed a coalition government with four minor parties. In December 2008, Thailand's Constitutional Court ruled to dissolve the PPP for its complicity in the election irregularities caused by one of its party executives. As a result, the vast majority of the party's members of parliament rushed to join the newly created *Puea Thai* ("For Thais") party (Croissant and Chambers 2010a). Following the 2011 election, the *Puea Thai* formed a coalition government with several smaller parties under the nominal leadership of Thaksin's sister, Prime Minister Yingluck Shinawatra.

At the opposite end of the political spectrum is the Democrat Party, which spearheaded the opposition during the era of Prime Minister Thaksin. The Democrat Party is Thailand's oldest still-functioning political party. Formed in 1946 as a royalist force, by the late 1950s, the party had effectively become the parliamentary opposition to the military dictatorship (Chaloemtiarana 2007, p. 87; Connors 2003, p. 61). The 1976 military coup against a Democrat-led government cemented this party's identification with pro-democratic elements (Askew 2008).

Many of the Democrat Party's founders were Sino-Thais from Bangkok or were from Thailand's south. Since the 1970s, southerners have increasingly placed their trust in the Democrat Party, turning the party into a vehicle for southern political identity. Today, the Democrat Party still has its southern stronghold, but also receives a sizeable share of votes from Bangkok (Askew 2008; Croissant and Chambers 2010b). The party's relative longevity compared to other Thai parties has contributed to its institutionalization, and its factions are not as visible as in other parties. Personalities are important in the Democrat Party, but region seems to best differentiate one 'stream' from another (Anusorn 1998, p. 424; Askew 2008). From September 1992 to July 1995, October 1997 to January 2001, and December 2008 to August 2011, Democrat leaders and Prime Ministers Chuan Leekpai and Abhisit Vejjajiva directed volatile multiparty cabinets. Especially among Western democracy promotion organizations, the party has enjoyed the reputation as Thailand's main democratic reform party. However, the failure of the Abhisit government to prevent the military crackdown on peaceful pro-Thaksin protestors in Bangkok in May 2010 tarnished the party's reputation internationally as well as inside Thailand.

10.7 State Administration

From King Chulalongkorn's reforms in the late nineteenth century until the 1990s, Thailand was a centralized unitary state. Administratively, the country was divided into 75 provinces (*changwat*) plus the Bangkok Metropolitan Area (BMA), which can be grouped into six main regions: the north, northeast (Isan), east, south, west, and central regions. Each province is divided into districts (*amphoe*), subdistricts (*tambons*, not to be confused with *king amphoe*), and villages (*muban*). As of 2010, there were 877 districts, 7255 subdistricts, and 74,944 villages (Mohib 2010; Tanchai 2010). Generally, municipalities are organized as city (*thesaba nakhon*), town (*thesaban mueang*), and subdistrict (*thesaban tambon*), but the Bangkok Metropolitan Area and Pattaya have their own administrative structures. Province governments are headed by governors appointed by the Ministry of Interior. Only the governor of Bangkok and the mayor of Pattaya City as well as the BMA assembly and the Pattaya assembly, the Provincial Administrative Organizations (PAO), and the PAO chairmen as well as Tambon Administrative Organizations (TAO) are directly elected (Table 10.7).

Table 10.7 Elected subnational bodies in Thailand

Subnational level	Executive branch	Legislative branch
PAO	Directly elected PAO-chair plus 2–4 councilors	PAO assembly, 24–48 elected members
Thesaban	Directly elected mayors	Assembly of 12 (*tambon*), 18 (*mueang*), and 24 (*nakhon*) elected members
TAO	TAO-Chair elected by TAO council	Elected assembly of 6–36 members
BMA	Directly elected governor with 4 deputies, 38 district chiefs	Elected city council of 38 members and elected district assemblies of 7 members
Pattaya City	Directly elected mayor	Elected assembly of 24 members

Source: Haque (2010, p. 680)

Thailand has a dual structure of public administration. The central government's administration reaches down to the local level but remains distinct from the parallel structures of local self-administration (Nelson 1998; Nagai et al. 2007, p. 17). The control of the Ministry of Interior Affairs over local administrations provided the basis for population control and the most important power resource of the bureaucracy until the mid-1990s. The rise of political parties, a simultaneous decline of military-bureaucratic power, and increased policy competition in elections created the conditions for a pro-decentralization drive in the early 1990s (Wongpreedee and Mahakanjana 2011, p. 79). The Tambon Council and the Tambon Administrative Organization Act of 1994 (TAO), the 1997 Constitution, and the revision of the Local Government Act in 1999 laid the legal groundwork for the transfer of responsibilities, authority, and resources to local administrations and elected local representative bodies (Nelson 1998; Haque 2010).

While the 2007 Constitution upheld the principle of decentralization, it granted provincial administrations budget and planning authority, weakening the fiscal independence of the elected PAO assemblies (Haque 2010, p. 683). In recent years, decentralization has lost most of its steam, first under the Thaksin government and then under the military government. To some extent, development, education, welfare, and health planning have shifted to the local level. However, there has been very little transfer of political decision-making or resources. Even though political decentralization formally expanded political participation, elected representative bodies at the subnational levels possess little authority over local administrative units, which are deconcentrated units of the Ministry of the Interior supervised by provincial administrations (Mohib 2010). Decentralization has so far failed to break up local power structures. Established political elites have often even managed to expand their influence by winning new local offices for themselves or their close relatives (Wongpreedee 2007, p. 455).

Thailand's current revenue structure is typical for centralized unitary states. Between 1996 and 2010, the revenue of lower administrative units rose from 9.8 to 25.3% (Tanchai 2010; Jansen and Khannadbha 2009, p. 349) but did not achieve the official target of 35%. Thailand also retains a largely centralized tax regime, of which the central government's revenue share is 94% (Mohib 2010). On average, local and community taxation contributes to less than 40% of the overall revenue of local units (Jansen and Khannadbha 2009, p. 349). The remainder consists of other central government transfers that are beyond the discretion of local authorities (Mohib 2010). While the capital of Bangkok can cover about 70% of its expenditure from own its revenues, many districts depend almost exclusively on central government transfers (Haque 2010, p. 683).

10.8 Civil–Military Relations

The Royal Thai Armed Forces (RTAF) have been at the forefront of Thai politics since 1932. From 1932 until 1991, Thailand experienced 19 coups and coup attempts (Thanet 2001). Many observers initially believed that the "Black May" massacre of 1992 had permanently tarnished the image of the armed forces, forcing them to the political sidelines (Bunbongkarn 1996, pp. 63–66). Nevertheless, after a period of apparent military decline in the 1990s, political unrest since the early 2000s has once again placed the military into a pivotal role. The visible manifestation of this development were the military coup d'états of 2006 and 2014.

Four key developments have shaped Thai civil–military relations in the twentieth century (Croissant et al. 2013, Chap. 8). First, Thailand's modern military was created in the 1870s as an internal security force to consolidate the absolute monarch's claim to power (Chambers 2013). However, it was military officers in collaboration with civil servants, who organized the 1932 coup d'état against King Prajadhipok that provided the basis for the emergence of a triarchy of military, bureaucratic, and monarchical interests (Croissant et al. 2013, p. 157) that would dominate the political landscape for most of the twentieth century.

Second, under the bureaucratic polity, competition over political influence led to factional struggles within the military between informal yet close-knit and homogenous cliques (Bunbongkarn 1988). Grouped around influential, high-ranking officers, their members were linked by shared socialization at the military academy, close personal contacts, lifelong relationships of mutual loyalty, and common interests. The balance of power between different groups shifted considerably over time, which resulted in frequent changes in the military leadership and numerous military coups in the pre-democratic era. In the late 1940s and early 1950s, military factionalism intensified as a result of interservice rivalries among the army, navy, air force, and police (Wyatt 1984). As the army became the dominant service, membership in a class at the Chulachomklao Royal Military Academy or the Armed Forces Academies Preparatory School became the main distinguishing feature (Chambers 2010a, b).

Third, since the 1930s, the military has been a socially and politically autonomous actor and has claimed the role of guardian over the state, nation, and monarchy for itself, coupled with significant influence over political decision-making (Ockey 2001). The military's activities were focused on the broadly defined internal mission of furthering "national development" and safeguarding internal security. Over the course of military-directed national development programs, the military expanded its mission beyond counterinsurgency operations against separatists and communists to infrastructure improvements, disaster relief, and economic activities. All of this was legitimized as a means of increasing the people's love for the king and nation (Croissant et al. 2013, p. 158). At the same time, the military became increasingly involved in Thailand's economy, and an impenetrable complex of military-run businesses inside and outside of the state soon emerged (Thomas 1988).

Fourth, the monarchy was politically weak during the first decades after the 1932 coup (Nattapoll 2010). By the end of the 1950s, however, the military leadership was convinced that an expanded and more active role for the monarchy could increase the legitimacy of the authoritarian order (Chaloemtiarana 2007). National development projects initiated in the name of the king strengthened the crown's prestige among the rural population, and more and more aspects of social life were given reference to the royal family (Phongpaichit and Baker 1997, pp. 315–316; Handley 2006, pp. 156–195; Streckfuss 2011). This shifted the power differential within the ruling triarchy towards the monarchy, as the political and economic power of the bureaucracy and the military increasingly depended on royal legitimacy (Morell and Chai-anan 1981, p. 68). The symbiotic relationship between the monarchy, the civilian bureaucracy, and the military and the armed forces' loyalty to the crown was particularly strengthened in the 1980s, when General Prem Tinsulanonda served as prime minister and, after his resignation, as president of the Privy Council (Chai-anan 1997). This enabled Prem—and through him the king—to create a system of loyalty between the palace, the military and the state apparatus, political parties, the media, and the economy, or the so-called network monarchy (McCargo 2005).

While the armed forces "seemed prepared to maintain a low-key political presence" (Funston 2006, p. 348) after May 1992, it still had full authority over annual military promotions as well as in matters of training, troop structures, and defense procurement. Even though the number of serving and former military officers in the cabinet and Senate declined and military budgets went down, indicating changing priorities in public spending and government expenditures (Ockey 2001; Croissant et al. 2013), civilians had little capacity and political will to challenge the remaining reserved domains of military influence and autonomy (Croissant 2015). Thaksin Shinawatra shattered this equilibrium of civil–military cooperation in the early 2000s when he attempted to expand his personal sway over the RTAF by co-opting former military officers into his party and cabinet, offering material spoils and substantial increases in the defense budget, promoting loyal officers to the top brass, and distributing the profits from privatized military firms among his military cronies (McCargo and Ukrist 2005, pp. 121–165). However, Thaksin's attempt to turn the "monarchized military" (Chambers and Waitoolkiat 2016) into a tool of personal rule ultimately brought the confrontation between the military leadership and Thaksin to a head and culminated in the 2006 coup (Ukrist 2008).

Civil–military relations remained tumultuous after the 2007 elections. Under the façade of an elected civilian government, the military continued to intervene in cabinet formation and policy decisions whenever it deemed necessary for its own benefit or to defend the nation and monarchy. For example, military leaders helped bring down a pro-Thaksin government in 2008, cobbled together another multiparty coalition under Democrat Party leader Abhisit (2008–2011; see Chambers 2010b, pp. 58–59), and acted with deadly force against anti-government protesters of the pro-Thaksin "Red Shirts" in 2010. While the military was unable (or unwilling) to block the ascendancy of another pro-Thaksin government in June 2011, the military again seized power in 2014. Officially, the coup d'état of May 2014 was justified as a means to safeguard the monarchy and to seek a way out of the country's ongoing crisis. Even though political conflicts and extra-parliamentary forces knocking at the barracks' doors pulled the military back into the political fray, additional factors likely strengthened the military's disposition for political intervention. These include ensuring an orderly royal succession and the survival of the network monarchy as well as consolidating the domination of the junta leaders' military faction over the RTAF (Chambers and Waitoolkiat 2016). A glance at the words and deeds of the NCPO since 2014 suggests that the powerful army aims to keep a tight grip on power and wants to preserve its role as the guardian of the monarchy, state, and nation after the return to elections and (quasi-)civilian cabinets.

10.9 Political Culture and Civil Society

It is no surprise that comparative studies of mass political culture based on surveys such as the Asian Barometer Survey (ABS) suggest a profound impact of the escalating political crisis on citizens' support for democracy and its alternatives as well as on their trust in political institutions. In the early 2000s, ABS findings seemed to indicate that a vast majority of Thai citizens supported the idea of democracy. For example, in 2001, almost 90% of respondents were either "very" or "somewhat satisfied" with the state of democracy in Thailand (Albritton and Bureekul 2008, p. 123). In the second wave of the ABS (2005–2008), the Kingdom of Thailand was the only country in the region where more than 80% of the population preferred democracy to any other form of government (82.6%). Almost as many respondents explicitly opposed the idea of military rule (81.2%; Chu et al. 2008, p. 25). However, in the third wave of the ABS (2010–2012), the percentage of respondents who preferred democracy over its alternatives declined to 68, but 89% still accepted democracy as the best form of government (Park and Chang 2013, p. 51). Yet, the most recent data from the first to the fourth wave (2014) shows that the percentage of respondents who agreed with the statement "We should get rid of parliament and elections and have strong leaders decide things" increased from 23% in 2001 to 37% in 2014. Likewise, the percentage of respondents who agreed with the statement "The army should get in to govern the country" rose from 18 to 54% between 2001 and 2014 (ABS 2012). Concomitantly, trust in major political

Table 10.8 Institutional trust in Thailand, 2001–2014

Trust in	Thailand				SEA7 average	
	ABS I 2001	ABS II 2006	ABS III 2011	ABS IV 2014	ABS II 2005–2008	ABS III 2010–2012
Political parties	50	50	35	43	56	53
Parliament	60	59	49	62	65	64
Executive	n.a.	64	62	76	73	67
Military	80	74	69	90	77	78
Court	72	70	63	77	65	66
National government	69	60	55	66	69	69

Notes: Aggregated share of respondents who indicated "a great deal" or "quite a lot of trust"
Source: ABS (2012, 2017), Albritton and Bureekul (2008), Wang (2013)

institutions appears to have eroded over time. Interestingly, the 2014 ABS registers a significant increase in trust across all institutions. It is unclear why and how the military coup d'état would have increased citizen trust in institutions, such as political parties and the parliament (Table 10.8).

There is little doubt that eroding support for democracy and declining trust scores reflect the impact of failing democratic governance and increasing political instability on mass political culture since the mid-2000s. In this regard, Yun-han Chu and his co-authors (2008, pp. 24–25) suggest that Thai democracy did not fail because it lacked manifest citizen support, but because political elites did not favor it. Yet, it is important to note that some studies find that the majority of people in Thailand exhibit "authoritarian notions of democracy" (Welzel and Kirsch 2017), that is, their understanding of what democracy means is twisted into an authoritarian direction (Shin and Cho 2011, p. 21, 35; Chu et al. 2008, p. 34). Accordingly, Chang et al. conclude that Thailand, like some other Asian countries, appears to "have a large number of equivocal and confused citizens whose inconsistent political orientations burden their democracies with a fragile foundation of legitimacy" (Chang et al. 2007, p. 73).

Furthermore, notions of and support for democracy vary widely between respondents with different levels of income and education and between urban and rural populations. Contrary to conventional wisdom, poorer, less-educated, and rural Thais are more supportive of democracy than their wealthier, better-educated, and urban compatriots (Albritton and Bureekul 2008, p. 129). Moreover, urbanites from Bangkok are significantly more likely to accept party bans and are less willing to participate in politics than their rural compatriots (Albritton and Bureekul 2008, p. 134; Chu et al. 2008, p. 14). These findings can provide insight for understanding public opinion, political participation, and political struggles in Thailand, as they lend support to the controversial thesis of Thailand's "two democracies" first formulated by Laothamatas as early as 1996: While urban middle and upper classes hold notions of democracy that emphasize good governance, the rule of law, and political accountability, rural and lower class voters hold a competing conception of democracy that emphasizes elections and the socioeconomic results of politics. Educated urbanites are skeptical about the political qualifications of rural voters, who, on the other hand, feel marginalized and wish for better political participation and a larger share of the national wealth (Laothamatas 1996).

Different notions of democracy also provide a key to understanding the ambivalent role of social movements and civil society in the rise and regression of Thai democracy. While the beginnings of Thai civil society can be traced back to the early twentieth century, the first manifestations of modern civic associations emerged from traditional forms of social self-organization in the first half of the twentieth century. When civil society expanded in the 1960s, the ruling elite eyed the new groups with suspicion and often subjected them to disdain or repression. Intellectuals, workers, and university students carried a protest movement that contributed to the fall of the authoritarian regime. In the 1980s, former student activists, who had been driven into the communist underground in 1976, returned in great numbers to public life and played an important role in the foundation of many new nongovernmental organizations (Clarke 1998, pp. 29–30). However, the May 1992 protests were not spearheaded by students and workers' associations but by civil rights groups, political NGOs, and a loosely organized mass of urbanites and members of Bangkok's middle class (LoGerfo 1997). Since then, the character of social movements and civic associations in Thailand has changed drastically. Structural changes in the countryside, an expansion of spatial and horizontal inequality, and an increase in economic opportunities have motivated the rural population to articulate new political demands (Walker 2012). Overall, the rural population now seems more eager for political participation, a trend reinforced by the spread of new techniques of political communication and mobilization (Missingham 2003; Walker 2012).

Even though the number of civic associations and NGOs has rapidly increased in recent decades (Thabchumpon 2002), their contribution to the establishment and consolidation of democratic values in society remains unclear. As in other Southeast Asian countries, social movements provide citizens with alternative channels for political participation, allow them to learn new means of political organization, and can catalyze the realization of new interests and demands. They do not, however, serve as the "schools of democracy" Alexis de Tocqueville made them out to be (Park 2011, p. 53), especially since there seems to be a lack of "students." More than three-quarters of the population reported no associational membership whatsoever, ranking Thailand last in Southeast Asia when it comes to the level of associational membership (ABS 2012, 2017). Moreover, the lion's share of memberships is in neighborhood or farmer's associations, whereas "modern" NGOs like human rights groups and other public interest groups or even trade unions have very few members (Park 2011, p. 43). The widespread use of violent tactics during the protests of "Red" and "Yellow Shirt" activists illustrate the "dark side" (Armony 2004, p. 80) of a polarized "civil" society activism that picks up on social cleavages to aggravate existing tensions and further undermine weak democratic institutions (Croissant and Bünte 2011; Thompson 2011).

10.10 Media System

Thailand has numerous print and other media outlets, including more than 500 commercial and 8000 community radios as well as several terrestrial, satellite, and cable TV programs. This includes the Thai Public Broadcasting Service (TPBS), Thailand's first public television station,—formed from iTV and owned by ITV Public Company Limited, a unit of Thaksin Shinawatra's Shin Corporation—which was nationalized in 2007. There are more than 80 newspapers and magazines in circulation, including 25 national and two English-language dailies, as well as 28 internet service providers and eight mobile network providers (IFES 2010, p. 6).

The establishment of local community radios was one of the most important demands of the media reform movement in the 1990s and became possible with the Frequencies Act of 2000 (Siriyuvasak 2005). Community radio reaches about 40% of the population. Its rapid spread in the last decade made it an important source of entertainment and information, but it rarely covers political news except shortly before an election (Vogel et al. 2008). With an internet penetration rate of 60.0%, Thailand is ahead of the Philippines and Vietnam but trails Malaysia, Singapore, and Brunei (Internet World Stats 2017).

All media outlets have to be officially registered, and broadcast media require a license from the National Broadcasting Commission. While the 1997 Constitution provided for the transfer of all broadcasting frequencies to an independent agency, the plan was dropped after 2006. The 2007 Broadcasting Law guarantees the military and other state agencies the right to own TV and radio stations. Together, both control a substantial share of broadcasting frequencies: The armed forces alone run 211 of the 525 radio stations and two of the six free TV stations. Considering this degree of influence or even control over the media by state actors, the degree of structural entanglement of state and electronic media is considerable. Thaksin was, however, the first politician to exploit this for political gain (Siriyuvasak 2007).

Television is by far the most important source of information, followed by radio and the internet, while newspapers rank last. The domestic reach of English-language newspapers like the *Bangkok Post* and *The Nation* is limited to middle and upper classes in Bangkok and a handful of other cities. Still, they have a disproportionate impact on public opinion, as broadcast media often pick up the print topics (McCargo 2000). Political parties lack news media of their own, even though some individual politicians own shares in media companies. In this regard, Thaksin, who had bought iTV, the only widely available private television network and turned it into a government mouthpiece (McCargo and Ukrist 2005), was an exception.

The political and legal environment for a pluralist media has dramatically eroded over the past 15 years. This trend was initiated by the Thaksin government but gained momentum after 2006 as legal restrictions and harassment of critical voices in the media increased. Legal restrictions are derived from the Internal Security Act and Computer Crime Act, both passed in 2007, as well as individual regulations in the criminal code, like Art. 112, which imposes heavy penalties for the defamation of the monarchy (*lèse-majesté*), and Art. 326, which concerns libel. The Press Registration Act and the Printing and Advertisement Act authorize the police to confiscate publications and issues believed to endanger public order and safety or public morals (FES 2011, p. 34; Siriyuvasak 2007). The Ministry for Information and Communication now monitors websites and occasionally shuts them down (FES 2011, p. 25). *Lèse-majesté* has been used as a political weapon against dissidents, members of the opposition, internet activists, and the media in general much more frequently in recent years. Due to these developments, freedom of the press has deteriorated considerably in recent years. Thailand plummeted from rank 59 on the Press Freedom Index of Reporters without Borders in 2004 to rank 142 in 2017 (Reporters without Borders 2017). Freedom House's Freedom of the Press Index mirrors this development, as Thailand today trails even Myanmar and ranks well behind the Philippines and Indonesia (Freedom House 2017).

10.11 Outlook

Despite some initial progress in the 1990s, Thailand's process of democratization regressed in the 2000s, a process that twice cumulated in the collapse of civilian government and democratic rule after military political intervention. Yet, the political developments of the past 15 years or so appear to reflect a deeper crisis of legitimacy and identity in Thai politics and society rather than one merely among political elites. Among observers, four different interpretations of the underlying causes and processes of this crisis prevail. The first views the crisis as a struggle between different notions of political order—one that understands democracy in plebiscitary terms or as rule of the majority and a second that equates democracy with "mob rule" and favors notions such as "meritocratic rule," "good governance," and "rule of law" (Chachavalpongpun 2010, p. 339; Ferrara 2015).

A second perspective identifies structurally ingrained socioeconomic conflicts as the root cause of current conflicts. Thailand's deep political crisis is a conflict between the "haves" (elites, establishment, capitalists, etc.) on one side and the "have-nots" (masses, poor, workers, etc.) on the other. The monarchy, capitalists, military, and bureaucrats feel threatened by demands for redistribution and social justice as articulated by urban and rural lower classes and instrumentalized by Thaksin and have managed to convince the urban middle class that giving in to such demands would also go against their interests (Hewison 2014).

A third perspective focuses on intra-elite conflict. The old elite identified above has come into competition with a new business elite, represented by Thaksin. Whereas the old elite has benefited from the established state interventionist economic model, the latter are in favor of the neoliberal opening of the Thai economy following the Asian Financial Crisis. Both groups have mobilized supporters in social movements who now fight a proxy conflict that distracts from the actual interests underlying the conflict. Elite networks rather than red or yellow shirts are at the heart of the conflict.

Finally, a fourth position takes cues from modernization theory. The political conflicts of recent years are an outgrowth of a process of socioeconomic and cultural change in Thailand. The country's industrialization and economic transformation created new social strata and affected the distribution of cognitive power resources in society. A parallel process of cultural change has increased the emancipatory drive of formerly passive groups by changing their self-image as well as their expectations of the political system. At first, the urban middle class carried these demands, most visibly during democratic protests in 1992. Now that the provinces have emerged as a political actor, urbanites feel increasingly threatened by the procedures of parliamentary democracy. This has resulted in superficially antidemocratic middle-class radicalism that is in fact mostly an anti-majoritarian attitude. As the structural minority, the middle class rejects unchecked majority rule rather than democracy per se (Pongsudhirak 2008, 2013).

All four perspectives lead to an equally gloomy conclusion: The current crisis is more than a transient struggle for governmental power and the May 2014 coup more than the result of actions by power-hungry officers. At its core, the crisis challenges the legitimacy of Thailand's current political and social model. Under the pressure of a shifting social grid, renegotiating a new political compact to settle the crisis is in fact much more complicated than the current debate about constitutional revisions and the military's return to the barracks suggest. Even after power is returned to a civilian government, difficult waters are ahead for Thailand's democratic transformation.

References

ABS. (2012). *Asian barometer survey: Electronic data release for Wave 3, 2010–2012*. http://www. asianbarometer.org/data/data-release

ABS. (2017). *Asian barometer survey: Electronic data release for Wave 4, 2014–2016*. http://www. asianbarometer.org/data/data-release

Abuza, Z. (2016). *Violence in Thailand's Deep South. The New Mandala*. http://www.newmandala. org/violence-thailands-deep-south/

Albritton, R., & Bureekul, T. (2008). Developing democracy under a new constitution in Thailand. In Y.-h. Chu, L. J. Diamond, A. J. Nathan, & D. C. Shin (Eds.), *How East Asians view democracy* (pp. 114–139). New York: Columbia University Press.

Anusorn, L. (1998). Thailand. In W. Sachsenröder & U. E. Frings (Eds.), *Political party systems and democratic development in East and Southeast Asia: Vol. I: Southeast Asia* (pp. 403–449). Aldershot: Ashgate.

Armony, A. C. (2004). *The dubious link: Civic engagement and democratization*. Stanford: Stanford University Press.

Askew, M. (2008). *Performing political identity: The Democrat Party in Southern Thailand*. Chiang Mai: Silkworm Press.

Bangkok Post. (2016). *Official charter referendum figures posted*. http://www.siam247.com/5/ bangkok-post-news/32227-official-charter-referendum-figures-posted

Bowie, K. A. (2008). Vote buying and village outrage in an election in Northern Thailand: Recent legal reforms in historical context. *Journal of Asian Studies, 67*, 8. https://doi.org/10.1017/ S0021911808000673

Bunbongkarn, S. (1988). The Thai military's effort to institutionalise its political role. *The Pacific Review, 1*, 400–411. https://doi.org/10.1080/09512748808718789

Bunbongkarn, S. (1996). *State of the nation Thailand*. Singapore: ISEAS.

Bünte, M. (2006). Das thailändische Königtum: Stabilitätsanker und Legitimitätsreserve des politischen Systems. *Südostasien aktuell, 3*, 29–40.

Callahan, W. A. (2000). *Pollwatching, elections and civil society in Southeast Asia*. Aldershot: Ashgate.

Chachavalpongpun, P. (2010). "Unity" as a discourse in Thailand's polarized politics. *Southeast Asian Affairs*, 332–342.

Chai-anan, S. (1995). Thailand: A stable semidemocracy. In L. J. Diamond, J. J. Linz, & S. M. Lipset (Eds.), *Politics in developing countries: Comparing experiences with democracy* (pp. 323–368). Boulder: Lynne Rienner.

Chai-anan, S. (1997). Old Soldiers Never Die. They are just bypassed: The military, bureaucracy and globalization. In K. Hewison (Ed.), *Political change in Thailand: Democracy and participation*. London: Routledge.

Chaloemtiarana, T. (2007). *Thailand: The politics of despotic paternalism*. Ithaca, NY: Cornell University Press.

Chambers, P. W. (2003). *Factions, parties, coalition change, and cabinet durability in Thailand, 1979–2001: Unpublished dissertation*. DeKalb: Northern Illinois State University.

Chambers, P. W. (2006). Consolidation of Thaksinocracy and crisis of democracy: Thailand's 2005 election. In A. Croissant & B. Martin (Eds.), *Between consolidation and crisis: Elections and democracy in five nations in Southeast Asia* (pp. 277–329). Münster: LIT Verlag.

Chambers, P. (2008a). Factions, parties and the durability of parliaments, coalitions and cabinets. *Party Politics, 14*, 299–323. https://doi.org/10.1177/1354068807088124

Chambers, P. W. (2008b). *The resurrection of faction politics in Thailand: How the 2006 coup institutionally destabilized Thai political parties*. Paper presented at the 10th International Thai Studies Conference, January 9–11, Bangkok.

Chambers, P. W. (2009). Superfluous, mieschievous or emancipating?: Thailand's evolving Senate today. *Journal of Current Southeast Asian Affairs, 28*(3), 3–80.

Chambers, P. (2010a). Thailand on the brink: Resurgent military, eroded democracy. Asian Survey, 50, 835–858. https://doi.org/10.1525/as.2010.50.5.835

Chambers, P. W. (2010b). U-turn to the past? The resurgence of the military in contemporary Thai politics. In P. W. Chambers & A. Croissant (Eds.), *Democracy under stress: Civil-military relations in South and Southeast Asia* (pp. 63–101). Bangkok: ISIS.

Chambers, P. W. (2013). *Knights of the realm: Thailand's military and policy then and now*. Bangkok: White Lotus Press.

Chambers, P. W., & Croissant, A. (2010). Monopolizing, mutualizing, or muddling through: Factions and party management in contemporary Thailand. *Journal of Current Southeast Asian Affairs, 29*(3), 3–33.

Chambers, P. W., & Waitoolkiat, N. (2016). The resilience of monarchised military in Thailand. *Journal of Contemporary Asia, 46*, 425–444. https://doi.org/10.1080/00472336.2016.1161060

Chang, Y.-t., Zhu, Y., & Pak, C.-m. (2007). Authoritarian nostalgia in Asia. *Journal of Democracy, 18*, 66–80. doi:https://doi.org/10.1353/jod.2007.0043

Chu, Y.-h., Diamond, L. J., Nathan, A. J., & Shin, D. C. (2008). Introduction: Comparative perspectives on democratic legitimacy in East Asia. In Y.-h. Chu, L. J. Diamond, A. J. Nathan, & D. C. Shin (Eds.), *How East Asians view democracy* (pp. 1–39). New York: Columbia University Press.

CIA. (2017). *The world factbook*. Langley: Central Intelligence Agency.

Clarke, G. (1998). *The politics of NGOs in South-East Asia: Participation and protest in the Philippines*. London: Routledge.

Cochrane, L. (2017). New Thai King requests constitutional changes to 'ensure his royal powers': Prime Minister. *ABC News*. http://www.abc.net.au/news/2017-01-10/thai-king-requests-constitutional-changes-to-ensure-powers/8174062

Connors, M. K. (2003). *Democracy and national identity in Thailand*. New York: Routledge.

Connors, M. K. (2007). *Democracy and national identity in Thailand* (Vol. 7, 2nd ed.). Copenhagen: NIAS Press.

Conrad, C. R., & Golder, S. N. (2010). Measuring government duration and stability in Central Eastern European democracies. *European Journal of Political Research, 49*, 119–150. doi: https://doi.org/10.1111/j.1475-6765.2009.01888.x

Croissant, A. (2015). Southeast Asian militaries in the age of democratization: From ruler to servant? In W. Case (Ed.), *Routledge handbook of Southeast Asian democratization* (pp. 314–332). London: Routledge.

Croissant, A. (2016). Ways of constitution-making in Southeast Asia: Actors, interests, dynamics. In M. Bünte & B. Dressel (Eds.), *Politics and constitutions in Southeast Asia* (pp. 25–47). London: Routledge.

Croissant, A., & Bünte, M. (2011). Conclusion: The challenges and prospects of democratic governance in Southeast Asia. In A. Croissant & M. Bünte (Eds.), *The crisis of democratic governance in Southeast Asia* (pp. 251–271). Houndmills: Palgrave Macmillan.

Croissant, A., & Chambers, P. W. (2010a). Intra-party democracy in Thailand. *Asian Journal of Political Science, 18*(2), 195–223.

Croissant, A., & Chambers, P. W. (2010b). Unravelling intra-party democracy in Thailand. *Asian Journal of Political Science, 18*, 195–223. https://doi.org/10.1080/02185377.2010.492990

Croissant, A., & Völkel, P. (2012). Party system types and party system institutionalization: Comparing new democracies in East and Southeast Asia. *Party Politics, 18*, 235–265. https://doi.org/10.1177/1354068810380096

Croissant, A., Kuehn, D., Lorenz, P., & Chambers, P. W. (2013). *Democratization and civilian control in Asia*. Houndmills: Palgrave Macmillan.

Darling, F. C. (1971). Political Parties in Thailand. *Pacific Affairs, 44*, 228–241. https://doi.org/10.2307/2755379

Englehart, N. A. (2001). *Culture and power in traditional Siamese government*. Ithaca: Cornell University Press.

Ferrara, F. (2015). Democracy in Thailand: Theory and practice. In W. Case (Ed.), *Routledge handbook of Southeast Asian democratization* (pp. 351–370). London: Routledge.

FES. (2011). *Asian media barometer: A locally based analysis of the media landscape in Asia: Thailand 2010*. Bangkok: Friedrich Ebert Foundation.

Freedom House. (2017). *Freedom of the press index 2017: Press freedom's dark horizon*. Accessed June 2, 2017, from https://freedomhouse.org/report/freedom-press/freedom-press-2017

Funston, N. J. (2006). Thailand: Reform politics. In N. J. Funston (Ed.), *Government and politics in Southeast Asia* (2nd ed., pp. 328–371). Singapore: ISEAS.

Funston, N. J. (2009). *Divided over Thaksin: Thailand's coup and problematic transition*. Singapore: ISEAS.

Ginsburg, T. (2008). Constitutional afterlife: The continuing impact of Thailand's postpolitical constitution. *International Journal of Constitutional Law, 7*, 83–105. https://doi.org/10.1093/icon/mon031

Groemping, M. (2015). *Southeast Asian elections worst in the world*. Accessed June 22, 2015, from http://www.newmandala.org/southeast-asian-elections-worst-in-the-world/

Handley, P. (2006). *The King never smiles*. New Haven: Yale University Press.

Haque, M. S. (2010). Decentralizing local governance in Thailand: Contemporary trends and challenges. *International Journal of Public Administration, 33*, 673–688. https://doi.org/10.1080/01900692.2010.514443

Harding, A. J. (2007). *A turbulent innovation: The Constitutional Court of Thailand, 1998–2006*. Paper presented at the Workship New Courts in the Asia-Pacific region, July 13–15, 2007. Melbourne.

Harding, A. J., & Leyland, P. (2009). *Constitutional courts: A comparative study*. London: Wildy Simmonds & Hill.

Hewison, K. (1997). The Monarchy and democratisation. In K. Hewison (Ed.), *Political change in Thailand: Democracy and participation* (pp. 58–74). London: Routledge.

Hewison, K. (2014). Considerations on inequality and politics in Thailand. *Democratization, 21*, 846–866. https://doi.org/10.1080/13510347.2014.882910

Hewison, K., & Kengkij, K. (2010). Thai-style democracy: The royalist struggle for Thailand's politics. In S. Ivarsson & L. Isager (Eds.), *Saying the unsayable: Monarchy and democracy in Thailand* (pp. 179–203). Copenhagen: NIAS Press.

Hicken, A. (2006). Stuck in the mud: Parties and party systems in democratic Southeast Asia. *Taiwanese Journal of Democracy, 2*(2), 23–46.

Hicken, A. (2007). How do rules and institutions encourage vote buying? In F. C. Schaffer (Ed.), *Elections for sale: The causes and consequences of vote buying* (pp. 47–60). Boulder: Lynne Rienner.

Hicken, A. (2009). *Building party systems in developing democracies*. New York: Cambridge University Press.

HRW. (2016). *Thailand: No new military trials of civilians*. New York: Human Rights Watch.

HRW. (2017). *Country report Thailand*. New York: Human Rights Watch.

IFES. (2010). *Electoral survey 2010*. Washington, DC: International Federation for Electoral Systems.

Internet World Stats. (2017). *Internet usage statistics: World internet users and 2017 population stats*. https://www.internetworldstats.com/stats.htm

IPU. (2017). *Interparliamentary Union Parline Database Thailand*. Accessed June 20, 2017, from http://www.ipu.org/parline-e/reports/2387_A.htm

Jansen, K., & Khannadbha, C. (2009). The fiscal space of Thailand: A historical analysis. In R. Roy & A. Heuty (Eds.), *Fiscal space: Policy options for financing human development* (pp. 325–398). London: Earthscan.

Kuhonta, E. M. (2008). The paradox of Thailand's 1997 "People's Constitution": Be careful what you wish for. *Asian Survey, 48*(3), 373–392.

Laothamatas, A. (1996). A tale of two democracies: Conflicting perceptions of elections and democracy in Thailand. In R. H. Taylor (Ed.), *The politics of elections in Southeast Asia* (pp. 201–223). Cambridge: Woodrow Wilson Center Press.

Leyland, P. (2007). Thailand's constitutional watchdogs: Dobermans, bloodhounds or lapdogs? *Journal of Comparative Law, 2*(2), 151–177.

LoGerfo, J. P. (1997). Civil society and democratization in Thailand, 1973–1997: Unpublished PhD theses. New York: Columbia University.

McCargo, D. (1997). Thailand's political parties: Real, authentic and actual. In K. Hewison (Ed.), *Political change in Thailand: Democracy and participation* (pp. 114–131). London: Routledge.

McCargo, D. (2000). *Politics and the press in Thailand: Media machinations*. London: Routledge.

McCargo, D. (2002). Introduction: Understanding political reform in Thailand. In D. McCargo (Ed.), *Reforming Thai politics* (pp. 1–21). Copenhagen: NIAS.

McCargo, D. (2005). Network monarchy and legitimacy crises in Thailand. *Pacific Review, 18*, 499–519. https://doi.org/10.1080/09512740500338937

McCargo, D., & Ukrist, P. (2005). *The Thaksinization of Thailand*. Copenhagen: NIAS.

Mead, K. K. (2004). *The rise and decline of Thai absolutism*. New York: Routledge.

Mérieau, E. (2016a). Thailand's Deep State, Royal Power and the Constitutional Court (1997–2015). *Journal of Contemporary Asia, 46*, 445–466. https://doi.org/10.1080/00472336.2016.1151917

Mérieau, E. (2016b). The legal-military alliance for illiberal constitutionalism in Thailand. In M. Bünte & B. Dressel (Eds.), *Politics and constitutions in Southeast Asia* (pp. 140–161). London: Routledge.

Mérieau, E. (2017). *Thailand's new king is moving the country away from being a constitutional monarchy: King Rama X is transforming the nominal powers granted by the constitution into real powers to be exercised at his own discretion*. Accessed July 17, 2017, from https://scroll.in/article/828462/thailands-new-king-is-moving-the-country-away-from-being-a-constitutional-monarchy

Missingham, B. D. (2003). *The assembly of the poor in Thailand: From local struggles to national protest movement*. Chiang Mai: Silkworm Press.

Mohib, S. A. (2010). *Fiscal decentralization in Thailand: Reflections on a decade of reforms*. Proceedings of the First International Conference on Local Government, November 18–19, Khon Kaen College of Local Administration.

Morell, D., & Chai-anan, S. (1981). *Political conflict in Thailand: Reform reaction revolution*. Cambridge, MA: Cambridge University Press.

Murray, D. (1996). *Angels and devils: Thai politics from February 1991 to September 1992, a struggle for democracy?* Bangkok: White Orchid Press.

Nagai, F., Ozaki, K., & Kimata, Y. (2007). *JICA Program on capacity building of Thai local authorites*. Tokyo: Japan international Cooperation Agency.

Nattapoll, C. (2010). The monarchy and the royalist movement in modern Thai politics, 1932–1957. In S. Ivarsson & L. Isager (Eds.), *Saying the unsayable: Monarchy and democracy in Thailand* (pp. 165–186). Copenhagen: NIAS.

Nelson, M. H. (1998). *Central authority and democratization in Thailand: A case study from Chachoengsao Province*. Bangkok: White Lotus Press.

Nelson, M. H. (2001). Thailand. In D. Nohlen, F. Grotz, & C. Hartmann (Eds.), *Elections in Asia and the Pacific: A data handbook, Vol. II: South East Asia, East Asia, and the South Pacific* (pp. 261–320). Oxford: Oxford University Press.

Nelson, M. H. (2007). Thaksin Overthrown: Thailand's 'Well-Intentioned' Coup of September 19, 2006. *Journal of Contemporary Eastern Asia, 6*, 1–16. 10.17477/jcea.2007.6.1.001

Nelson, M. H. (2012). Thailand's election of July 3, 2011: An overview. Research report submitted to the King Prajadhipok's Institute. Nakhorn Si Thammarat: Walailak University.

Nordlinger, E. A. (1977). *Soldiers in politics: Military coups and governments*. Englewood Cliffs, NJ: Prentice-Hall.

Ockey, J. (1994). Political parties, factions, and corruption in Thailand. *Modern Asian Studies, 28*, 251. https://doi.org/10.1017/S0026749X00012403

Ockey, J. (2001). Thailand: The struggle to redefine civil-military relations. In M. Alagappa (Ed.), *Coercion and governance: The declining political role of the military in Asia* (pp. 187–209). Stanford: Stanford University Press.

Ockey, J. (2004). *Making democracy: Leadership, class, gender, and political participation in Thailand*. Honolulu: University of Hawai'i Press.

Orathai, K. (2002). Electoral politics in Thailand. In A. Croissant, G. Bruns, & M. John (Eds.), *Electoral politics in Southeast & East Asia* (pp. 277–320). Singapore: Friedrich Ebert Foundation.

Park, C.-m. (2011). Associations and social networks in Southeast Asia: Schools of democracy? In A. Croissant & M. Bünte (Eds.), *The crisis of democratic governance in Southeast Asia* (pp. 39–56). Houndmills: Palgrave Macmillan.

Park, C.-m., & Chang, Y.-t. (2013). Regime performance and democratic legitimacy. In L. J. Diamond, M. F. Plattner, & Y.-h. Chu (Eds.), *Democracy in East Asia: A new century* (pp. 48–75, A journal of democracy book). Baltimore, MD: Johns Hopkins University Press.

PEI. (2016). *The Perceptions of electoral integrity dataset: Version 4.5*. Accessed June 22, 2017, from https://sites.google.com/site/electoralintegrityproject4/projects/expert-survey-2

Phongpaichit, P. (2016). Inequality, wealth and Thailand's politics. *Journal of Contemporary Asia, 46*, 405–424. https://doi.org/10.1080/00472336.2016.1153701

Phongpaichit, P., & Baker, C. (1997). *Thailand: Economy and politics*. Kuala Lumpur, Oxford: Oxford University Press.

Phongpaichit, P., & Baker, C. (2004). *Thaksin: The business of politics in Thailand*. Copenhagen: NIAS.

Phongpaichit, P., & Baker, C. (2008). Thaksin's populism. *Journal of Contemporary Asia, 38*, 62–83. https://doi.org/10.1080/00472330701651960

Pongsudhirak, T. (2008). Thailand since the Coup. *Journal of Democracy, 19*, 140–153. https://doi.org/10.1353/jod.0.0030

Pongsudhirak, T. (2013). Thailand's uneasy passage. In L. J. Diamond, M. F. Plattner, & Y.-h. Chu (Eds.), *Democracy in East Asia: A new century* (pp. 148–163, A Journal of democracy book). Baltimore, MD: Johns Hopkins University Press.

Prasirtsuk, K. (2009). Thailand in 2008: Crises continued. *Asian Survey, 49*, 174–184. https://doi.org/10.1525/as.2009.49.1.174

Reporters without Borders. (2017). *2017 World Press Freedom Index. RSF.* Accessed June 22, 2017, from https://rsf.org/en/ranking

Riggs, F. W. (1966). *Thailand: The modernization of a bureaucratic polity.* Honolulu: University of Hawai'i Press.

Rodan, G., & Hughes, C. (2014). *The politics of accountability in Southeast Asia: The dominance of moral ideologies.* Oxford: Oxford University Press.

Schaffar, W. (2005). *Verfassung in der Krise: Die thailändische ,Verfassung des Volkes' von 1997.* Southeast Asian Studies Working Paper No. 23. Bonn: Institut für Orient- und Asienwissenschaften.

Secretariat of the Cabinet. (2011). *Historical sequence of Thai cabinet.* Accessed February 4, 2011, from http://www.cabinet.thaigov.go.th/eng/bb_main11.htm

Shin, D. C., & Cho, Y. (2011). Contours and barriers to democratization in Southeast Asia: A comparative analysis of how Southeast Asians view democracy. In A. Croissant & M. Bünte (Eds.), *The crisis of democratic governance in Southeast Asia* (pp. 16–39). Houndmills: Palgrave Macmillan.

Siripan, N. S. (2006a). Party elites in the business conglomerate model of Thai political parties. In R. Niyom (Ed.), *Eyes on Thai democracy: National and local issues* (pp. 103–137). Bangkok: KPI.

Siripan, N. S. (2006b). *Thai political parties in the age of reform.* Bangkok: Institute of Public Policy Studies.

Siriyuvasak, U. (2005). A genealogy of media reform in Thailand and its discourses. In S. Wangvivatana (Ed.), *Media reform going backward?* (pp. 50–74). Bangkok: Thai Broadcast Journalists Association.

Siriyuvasak, U. (2007). New media for civil society and political censorship in Thailand. *Asia Rights Journal, 8,* 1–12.

Streckfuss, D. (2011). *Truth on trial in Thailand: Defamation treason and lèse-majesté.* London: Routledge.

Streckfuss, D. (2013). *The future of the monarchy in Thailand.* Accessed June 7, 2017, from https://kyotoreview.org/issue-13/the-future-of-the-monarchy-in-thailand

Suehiro, A. (2014). Technocracy and Thaksinocracy in Thailand: Reforms of the Public Sector and the Budget System under the Thaksin Government. *Southeast Asian Studies, 3*(2), 299–344.

Tanchai, W. (2010). *Decentralization and local governance: Revisit and revitalization for local governments in Thailand.* A presentation by Assoc. Prof. Woothisarn Tanchai for DELGOSEA Capacity Development Workshop for Local Coaches in Pattaya, Thailand, November 18, 2010. http://www.delgosea.eu/cms/Downloads/Conference-Presentations/misc

Thabchumpon, N. (2002). NGOs and grassroots participation in the political reform process. In D. McCargo (Ed.), *Reforming Thai politics* (pp. 183–203). Copenhagen: NIAS.

Thammanoon, P. (2003). *Strengthening the independence and efficiency of the judiciary in Thailand.* Paper presented at the 8th ASEAN Law Association General Assembly, November 29–December 2, 2003, Singapore. Accessed June 8, 2017, from http://elib.coj.go.th/Article/Strengthening.pdf

Thanet, A. (2001). *The search for order: Constitutions and human rights in Thai political history.* Accessed June 8, 2017, from https://openresearch-repository.anu.edu.au/bitstream/1885/42075/2/Thanet.pdf

Thomas, M. L. (1988). Limited disengagement of the military from Thai politics. In C. P. Danopoulos (Ed.), *Military disengagement from politics.* London: Routledge.

Thompson, M. R. (2007). The dialectic of "Good Governance" and democracy in Southeast Asia: Globalized discourses and local responses. *Globality Studies Journal,* (10), 1–19.

Thompson, M. R. (2011). Moore meets Gramsci and Burke in Southeast Asia: New democracies and civil society. In A. Croissant & M. Bünte (Eds.), *The crisis of democratic governance in Southeast Asia* (pp. 57–74). Houndmills: Palgrave Macmillan.

Traimas, C., & Hoerth, J. (2008). Thailand: Another constitution as a way out of the vicious cycle? In C. Hill & J. Menzel (Eds.), *Constitutionalism in Southeast Asia: Vol. 1: National Constitutions/ASEAN Charter* (pp. 299–326). Singapore: Konrad Adenauer Foundation.

Ukrist, P. (2008). A different coup d'état? *Journal of Contemporary Asia, 38*, 139. https://doi.org/10.1080/00472330701651994

Uwanno, B., & Burns, W. D. (1998). The Thai constitution of 1997: Sources and process. *The University of British Columbia Law Review, 32*(2), 227–249.

Vogel, B., Grabow, K., & Rieck, C. E. (2008). *KAS-Demokratiereport 2008*. Bonn: Konrad Adenauer Foundation.

Walker, A. (2012). *Thailand's political peasants: Power in the modern rural economy*. Madison, Wisconsin: University of Wisconsin Press.

Wang, Z.-X. (2013). Institutional trust in East Asia: Asian Barometer Working Paper Series No. 92. http://www.asianbarometer.org/publications/abs-working-paper-series

Welzel, C., & Kirsch, H. (2017). Democracy misunderstood: Authoritarian notions of democracy around the globe. *World Values Research, 9*(1), 1–29.

Wongpreedee, A. (2007). Decentralization and its effect on provincial political power in Thailand. *Asian and African Area Studies, 6*(2), 454–470.

Wongpreedee, A., & Mahakanjana, C. (2011). Decentralization and local governance in Thailand. In E. M. Berman (Ed.), *Public administration in Southeast Asia: Thailand, Philippines, Malaysia, Hong Kong and Macau* (pp. 79–94). Boca Raton: Springer VS.

Wongrangan, K. (1984). The revolutionary strategy of the communist party of Thailand: Change and persistence. In J.-J. Lim & S. Vani (Eds.), *Armed Communist movements in Southeast Asia* (pp. 131–185, Issues in Southeast Asian security). Singapore: ISEAS.

World Bank. (2017). World development indicators. http://data.worldbank.org/products/wdi

Wyatt, D. K. (1984). *Thailand*. New Haven/London: Yale University Press.

Zackari, K. (2016). Violence on the periphery of the Thai state and nationhood. In B. Koch (Ed.), *State terror, state violence: Global perspectives* (pp. 71–92). Wiesbaden: Springer VS.

Timor-Leste: Challenges of Creating a Democratic and Effective State

11

© Springer International Publishing AG 2018
A. Croissant, P. Lorenz, *Comparative Politics of Southeast Asia*,
https://doi.org/10.1007/978-3-319-68182-5_11

11.1 Historical Background

The Democratic Republic of Timor-Leste is the newest state in Southeast Asia.[1] It comprises the eastern part of the island of Timor and the enclave Oecusse, which is surrounded by Indonesian West Timor on three sides. It is one of the least developed countries in the region and one of the world's smallest countries with an extremely young population of 1.2 million people in 2015—according to the latest census figure (see Table 11.1).

The first Europeans to arrive on the island of Timor were the Portuguese in the early sixteenth century. Upon their arrival, the east of Timor was divided into a "loose collection of independent kingdoms with languages and cultures vastly different from those of its neighbours to the west" (Taudevin 1999, p. 15). Although Dominican friars and merchants from Portugal established trading posts and mission stations in the 1550s, it was not until the 1700s that a governor was installed in Dili and claimed authority over the eastern half of the island.[2] Even then, the Portuguese exercised little territorial control, and due to the tenuous nature of its rule, the colonial authorities heavily cooperated with local rulers (*liurai*). Only when Portuguese Timor became an autonomous colony in 1896 was a unified territorial administration with a particularly repressive form of direct rule established (Taylor 1999).

After 1945 Timor was granted greater fiscal and administrative autonomy, and the "Timorization" of the colonial state beginning in the 1960s gave locals access to posts in the civil and military administration (Hughes 2009, p. 35; Guterres 2006, 101–103). Yet this policy primarily benefited the Lusophone elite (Gunn 2001), while the majority of the population retained traditional Timorese customs, beliefs, and languages (Guterres 2006). Moreover, the colonial power did little to improve Timor-Leste's rudimentary infrastructure, weak state capacity, and economic underdevelopment, resulting in poor living conditions that hardly improved over the course of colonization (Guterres 2006).

The "Carnation Revolution" in Portugal in April 1974 triggered a wave of political mobilization in Portuguese-Timor. Several political parties were founded, including the left-wing nationalist *Frente Revolucionária do Timor-Leste Independente* (FRETILIN), the conservative, pro-Portuguese Timorese Democratic Union (UDT), and the pro-Indonesian Timorese Popular Democratic Association (APODETI). In August 1975, conflict between these parties culminated in a brief civil war. FRETILIN emerged as the victorious party and subsequently declared independence (Lawless 1976). This served the Indonesian government as a pretext for invasion in December 1975. Following the adoption of a petition for annexation by a handpicked Timorese assembly, Timor-Leste was integrated into Indonesia as its 27th province (Taylor 1999).

---

[1] While both East Timor and Timor-Leste are internationally accepted names for the country, we opted for Timor-Leste as it is the country's chosen name.

[2] The western half was the dominion of the Dutch East India Company and has belonged to Indonesia since 1949.

Table 11.1 Country profile Timor-Leste

Population	Year of full national sovereignty	Form of government
1,291,358	2002	Republic
Total area	**Current constitution enacted**	**Head of state**
14,874 km²	2002	Francisco Guterres (since 2017)
GDP p.c. (2005 PPP, 2012)	**Official language**	**Head of government**
4271	Tetum (official), Portuguese (official), Indonesian, English (working languages within civil service)	Mari Alkatiri (since 2017)
Ethnic groups	**Democracy score (BTI 2016)**	**System of government**
More than 30 languages and dialects, at least 14 different ethnic groups	–	Semi-presidential
Religions	**Regime type**	**Cabinet type**
96.9% Catholics, 0.3% Muslims, 2.2% Protestants, 0.5% Others	Democracy	Minority coalition

Sources: CIA (2017), World Bank (2017a)

The Indonesian occupation employed a "two-pronged strategy" and flanked accelerated economic and social development with brutal repression of the Timorese (Moxham and Carapic 2013). On the one hand, Jakarta built up government services, improved infrastructure, and invested in agriculture, health, and education. While poverty remained widespread, Indonesian rule resulted in high annual average growth of the local economy with 7.8% between 1983 and 1990 and an average of 10% during the 1990s. Moreover, the introduction of a comprehensive and widespread education system marked the first time a large section of the population gained access to formal education. On the other hand, lacking local support and met with fierce resistance from FRETILIN and its military wing Falintil (*Forças Armadas da Libertação Nacional de Timor-Leste*), the occupation took on a distinctly coercive character. Although the exact figure is disputed, it is estimated that between 120,000 and 200,000 Timorese—effectively a quarter to a third of the population—died from violence, hunger, and disease at the hands of the Indonesians (Cotton 2000; Traub 2000).

Yet the Indonesian occupation also helped propagate a common history and group identity among the local population, furthering Timorese nationalism (Hughes 2009). In the course of the occupation, the Catholic Church turned from a religious institution of colonial oppression into a symbol of cultural identity and faith-based resistance to Indonesian assimilation (Borgerhoff 2006).[3] Moreover, the Church advocated for the use of the native Tetum language, unifying and enabling a nationalist discourse. The Indonesian occupation thus created the basis for

---

[3]The share of Catholics rose from 27.8% (1973) to 81.4% of the population 1989, Simonsen (2006, p. 577).

Timorese nation-building, as mutual suffering proved to be an important aspect in overcoming vast ethnic and linguistic differences. Disagreements between the Timorese diaspora and members of the independence movement on the ground remained, yet the organizational separation of Falintil and FRETILIN in the 1980s and the creation of a National Resistance Council (CNRT),[4] which included various political parties as well as religious and social groups, enabled the formation of a broad national movement (Guterres 2006).

The United Nations (UN) never recognized the annexation of Timor-Leste, and FRETILIN cadres-in-exile actively lobbied for Timorese independence. After the collapse of the Suharto regime in Indonesia (see Chap. 4), Interim President B.J. Habibie agreed to hold a popular referendum over the future of the province. The referendum was organized under auspices of the UN on August 30, 1999, during which 78.5% of voters rejected the Indonesian offer of autonomy, effectively voting for independence (Robinson 2010, p. 154). Yet even before the results were officially announced, pro-Indonesian militias began "Operation Clean Sweep" (Cotton 2000; Croissant 2008). Targeted killings of political activists and voters throughout the island left between 1500 and 3000 Timorese dead and the majority of the population either displaced or forcibly removed to West Timor. Moreover, an estimated 70–80% of Timor-Leste's stock buildings and public and social infrastructure were destroyed (Beauvais 2001; Huang and Gunn 2004). The humanitarian crisis only subsided when an International Force in East Timor (INTERFET) with a UN mandate to restore peace (Huang and Gunn 2004) began arriving on September 20, 1999, after which the Indonesian military and civil personnel as well as pro-Indonesian militias retreated to West Timor (Beauvais 2001). In October 1999, the UN Transitional Administration for East Timor (UNTAET) was inaugurated. Initially, UNTAET completely took over the government and quickly transitioned from a peace enforcement operation to becoming the basic state structure and restoring the country's economic and social infrastructure as well as reintegrating refugees (Croissant 2008). In August 2001, a constitutional assembly was elected and subsequently passed a constitution in April 2002. After the head of CNRT and former commander of Falintil, José Alexandre "Xanana" Gusmão, was elected president, Timor-Leste gained independence on May 20, 2002.

As part of the successor mission UNMISET(see Table 11.6 for full names of UN Missions), an international police and security force remained in the country for a transition period (see also Table 11.6). When conflicts inside the army and among the police and military led to severe unrest in the capital of Dili in August 2006, President Gusmão petitioned the UN to send in an International Stabilization Force (ISF) and to create a UN mission (UNMIT) to reestablish political stability. Despite two assassination attempts against President Horta and Prime Minister Gusmão by mutinous soldiers in February 2008 and sporadic social violence, the internal security situation is again under control, and both the UNMIT and ISF missions have ended (ICG 2013).

---

[4]Initially known as *Conselho Nacional da Resistência Maubere* (CNRM, 1986) and since 1998 as *Conselho Nacional da Resistência Timorense* (CNRT).

Nonetheless, Timor-Leste's defective democracy is still frail and threatened by a number of structural problems. First among these are unresolved problems of state- and nation-building, a common phenomenon among post-conflict societies. Despite FRETILIN's attempt to base Timorese national identity on the myth of "common blood, soil and shared suffering" (Arnold 2009, p. 444), competing interpretations of the liberation struggle and the foreign occupation still remain. Furthermore, Timor-Leste lacks state capacity and effective state institutions, and the government struggles with reintegrating former guerilla fighters, so-called veterans, creating a nationwide judicial system, and reforming the military and police (ICG 2008).

Second, Timor-Leste is destabilized by elite conflicts exacerbated through a semi-presidential system of government that fosters institutional tensions between the president, prime minister, and parliament. While the origins of elite tensions date back to the 1975 civil war and the occupation period (Guterres 2006, p. 173; Shoesmith 2012), political conflict has been aggravated by the instrumentalization of regional identities and historical grievances (Guterres 2006, p. 251).

Third, the living conditions of most Timorese remain precarious. Problems such as a lack of decent housing, widespread unemployment, and poverty are likely to remain as the country has one of the highest global birthrates and a very young population with a median age of only 18.5 years (UNDP 2016, p. 222). Furthermore, young males aged 15–24 made up 30.6% of the overall male population above the age of 14 in 2010, making Timor-Leste the third-largest "youth-bulge" country worldwide after Swaziland and Zimbabwe (see Fig. 11.1). The country lacks the ability to provide such a large youth cohort with adequate employment opportunities, raising the potential of social conflict and since 2002 contributing to social unrest and youth violence (Curtain 2006; Neupert and Lopes 2006).

In this context, the boom in the petroleum sector appears a welcomed develop-ment at first glance. However, the increased oil revenues between 2005 and 2013 has turned Timor-Leste into one of the most oil-dependent nations in the world: Currently, about 90% of state revenue is produced by the petroleum sector, which also made up to about 80% of the country's GDP in recent years (GDP, see

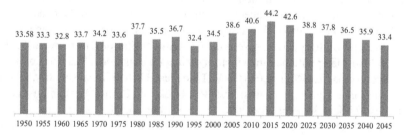

Fig. 11.1 Male Youth-Bulge in Timor-Leste, 1950–2045. Notes: Figure shows share of men in the age cohort 15–24 of total male population above the age of 14 (intermediate variant). Source: UNDES (2013)

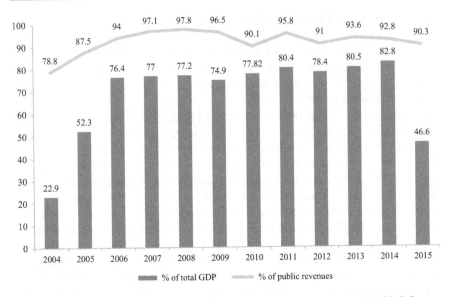

Fig. 11.2 Petroleum sector share of public revenue and GDP in Timor-Leste, 1991–2015. Source: IMF (2009, 2013)

Fig. 11.2). The recent decline in the petroleum sector's share in the GDP does not indicate economic diversification but reflects the slump in crude oil prices: from USD105 per barrel in 2012 to USD51 in 2015 (IMF 2016). Mainly on account of this devaluation of global oil prices, petroleum revenue fell by 40% in 2015.

In contrast to Brunei (see Chap. 2), the government's use of petroleum revenue is transparent and subject to political accountability. The income is administered by an independent oil fund under the central bank and can be budgeted only with parliamentary consent (Sýkora 2013). Still, the socioeconomic and political impact of oil has been ambivalent so far. On the one hand, the government has used oil revenue to pay for inclusive welfare policies that have targeted especially those constituencies associated with the political unrest of the mid-2000s. This includes generous severance payments for mutinous soldiers and thousands of "veterans," an expansion of the public sector, and government contracts to businesses tied to potential entrepreneurs of violence (Sahin 2010, p. 356; ICG 2013, pp. 3, 13; Leach 2013, p. 160). On the other hand, the state budget approximately doubled from 2010 to 2015 (Scheiner 2015). The growth effect of government spending financed through fluctuating revenues seems weak. Furthermore, increased spending has not been accompanied by improved long-term planning, but has instead created new opportunities for rent-seeking, government inefficiency, and waste. Finally, Timor-Leste's oil and gas reserves are limited and revenues are dropping rapidly, mainly because extant fields are being used up and new fields are not in production yet (Scheiner 2014; Sýkora 2013, pp. 71–73).

11.2 Constitutional Development

The constitution of Timor-Leste was drafted by an elected Constitutional Assembly and enacted without a referendum on May 20, 2002. It consists of a preamble and seven parts with 170 sections overall and has not been amended since its promulgation. The preamble invokes the historical struggle of the Timorese people for independence and affirms the contribution of FRETILIN, CNRT, and the Catholic Church. Part I concerns fundamental state organization and important regulations on citizenship (Section 3), the relationship between state and religious communities (Section 12), as well as the status of Portuguese and Tetum as the official languages (Section 13).[5] The constitution defines Timor-Leste as a republican, "democratic, sovereign, independent and unitary state, based on the rule of law, popular will and respect for the dignity of the human person" (Section 1 I). Political power is to be decentralized (Section 5) and the exercise of universal suffrage and the existence of a multiparty system are to be respected and advanced (Section 7). The programmatic character of the document is obvious in its listing of essential state functions, such as: the protection of national sovereignty, civil rights, and liberties; the defense of democracy; the protection of the environment, natural resources, and cultural heritage; and the advancement of harmonious coexistence of different sectors and regions, social justice, general welfare, and gender equality (Section 6).

Part II enumerates a catalogue of basic rights, civil liberties, as well as economic, social, and cultural rights. Part III (Section 62–136) determines the structure and operating principles of constitutional bodies, including the president (Section 74–89), Council of State (Section 90–91), National Parliament (Section 92–102), Government (Section 103–117), and the courts (Section 118–136). This part also covers elections and referenda (Section 65–66), the role of political parties (Section 70), and the general principles of public administration (Section 137).

Part IV comprises constitutional rules governing the economic system, public finances, and the tax system, whereas Part V deals with national defense, the armed forces, and the national police (Section 146–148). The provisions in Part VI concern judicial review as well as constitutional amendments. The constitutionality of laws and any other statute is overseen by the Supreme Court of Justice. Amendments to the constitution require a two-thirds majority in the National Assembly and must respect the separation of power; judicial independence; national independence and the unity of the state; the rights, freedoms, and guarantees of citizens; the multiparty system and the right to democratic opposition; the basis of democratic suffrage; the electoral system of proportional representation; and the principle of deconcentration and decentralization (Section 155). The final Part VII contains transitional and closing regulations, including an important section on national reconciliation (Section 160–162), the organization of the court

---

[5] Yet the constitution also requires that "Indonesian and English shall be working languages within civil service side by side with official languages as long as deemed necessary" (Sect. 159).

system (Section 163–164), the continuation of the laws established under the Indonesian occupation and UNTAET mandate (Section 165), and finally, for the transformation of the Constitutional Assembly into the National Parliament (Section 167).

The elections to the Constitutional Assembly in April 2001 marked the beginning of the constitutional drafting process. FRETILIN, together with its ally, the Social Democratic Association of Timor (ASDT), controlled two-thirds of the seats in the Constitutional Assembly. There were talks between FRETILIN and UNTAET, but UNTAET chose to take a "hands off" approach during the constitution-making process (Brandt 2005, p. 24) and FRETILIN ignored any efforts to render the process more participatory. Instead, the party pushed its own draft through the Constitutional Assembly (Brandt 2005, p. 15; Samuels 2006, p. 19). After only ten days of debate and against a backdrop of objections by the opposition parties, who felt sidelined, the assembly adopted FRETILIN's draft (Brandt 2005, p. 20). The lack of consensus among the different political parties meant that the constitution was regarded by many as a "FRETILIN Constitution," and only 65 of 88 delegates voted for the draft, the remaining 23 abstained (Aucoin and Brandt 2010; Shoesmith 2007, p. 224).

Two key factors shaped the outcome of constitutional deliberations. First, the delegates took inspiration from the Portuguese constitution, including the choice of a semi-presidential system of governance and the division of legislative power among government and parliament (see below). FRETILIN cadre returning from Portugal or other Lusophone states like Mozambique dominated the assembly, and Portuguese constitutional experts counseled the committees during the drafting process (Guterres 2006; Goldstone 2013; Neto and Costa Lobo 2012). Second, against the backdrop of widespread criticism from opposition parties, UNTAET, and civil society activists, and anticipating the possibility of a non-FRETILIN candidate winning the upcoming presidential election, FRETILIN pushed for a strong position of government and parliament vis-à-vis the president, opposed popular approval of the draft by referendum, and favored the transformation of the incumbent constitutional assembly into a regular parliament.

11.3 System of Government

Timor-Leste has a semi-presidential constitution with a popularly elected fixed term president and a prime minister and cabinet (Council of Ministers) who are politically accountable to parliament.[6] Legislative power rests with the National Parliament, and the government, president, and prime minister share executive power

---

[6]The concept of semi-presidentialism was first introduced by the French political scientist Maurice Duverger (1980) and developed further by Robert Elgie (1999).

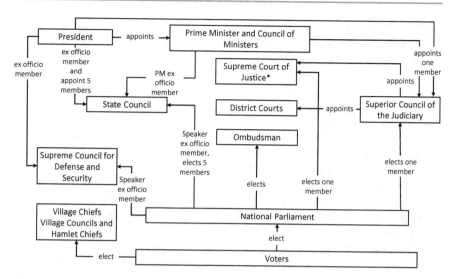

Fig. 11.3 Timorese system of government. Source: Authors' compilation. Notes: * Currently, the Dili Court of Appeal serves as Timor-Leste's Supreme Court

(see Fig. 11.3). The judicial branch of government is headed by the Supreme Court. Other constitutional bodies include the Council of State (Section 90–91), the Ombudsman (Section 27), the Superior Council for Defence and Security (Section 148), the Superior Council for the Judiciary (Section 133, 134), and the Central Bank (Section 143).

11.3.1 President

The president is head of state, guardian of national independence and unity, as well as supreme commander of the National Defence Force (Section 74). He or she is popularly elected in a two-round system with absolute majority for a fixed 5-year term that is renewable once (Section 75). The president can be impeached by the Supreme Court of Justice for crimes committed in office or for "clear and serious violations of his or her constitutional obligations" (Section 79 II). The motion to impeach can be initiated by a fifth of the members of parliament and sustained by a two-thirds majority (Section 79).

The president is not part of the cabinet but wields considerable executive and governmental powers. He or she appoints the prime minister upon a proposal of the majority party or a majority coalition in the National Parliament (Art. 85d, Art. 106). The president can only dismiss the prime minister and the Council of Ministers after the government has lost the support of parliament, or if it is necessary to "ensure the regular functioning of democratic institutions" (Section 112). In addition, the president appoints and dismisses the cabinet ministers and the chief of staff of the Defence Force upon proposal of the prime minister. The president can advise government and National Parliament and is the guarantor of the functioning of the democratic system, which gives him or her the authority to mediate between other constitutional bodies (Section 74). The president has exclusive authority to initiate the preventive or abstract judicial review of legislation, possesses legislative veto powers, and can initiate popular referenda (Section 85). The president can veto parliamentary legislation as well as decree-laws passed by the government (*Decreto-Lei do Governo*). The National Parliament can overturn a presidential veto by either an absolute majority of its members (Section 88 IV) or by a majority of two-thirds concerning statutes on matters provided for in Section 95 of the constitution, which comprises many different policy areas and constitutional matters. The president also presides over meetings of the Council of State, an inter-institutional deliberative body, and the Superior Council for Defence and Security, which advises the president in matters of national defense. The president appoints the president of the Supreme Court of Justice and all administrative, tax, and audit courts; the prosecutor general; and ambassadors. He holds the right of pardon and can impose a state of emergency when authorized by parliament. Finally, the president has to dissolve parliament after consultation with the parliamentary groups and the Council of State if parliament fails to elect a government after more than 60 days or turns down the national budget (Section 86f).

11.3.2 Prime Minister and Council of Ministers

The prime minister and the Council of Ministers also possess executive power. The prime minister is head of government, directs the actions of the Council of Ministers, sets out the essential political guidelines, and ensures the coordination of government actions and the public administration. The government has the power to initiate bills, and the National Parliament can authorize the government to make laws on a wide range of different topics, including, inter alia, the organization of courts and state administration, public service, finances, environmental protection, media and military legislation, the nationalization of private property, as well as the privatization of public property (Section 96). Statutes other than those approved under the exclusive legislative powers of the government may be submitted to the National Parliament for appraisal, whereas bills and draft resolutions approved by parliament need approval by the Council of Ministers (Section 116d).

The prime minister and the Council of Ministers are collectively accountable to the president and to the National Assembly (Section 107), and can only be dismissed after the National Parliament has rejected the government's program for two consecutive times, a vote of confidence is not passed by parliament, or a vote of no confidence is passed by an absolute majority of the members of the legislature (Sections 86g, Section 112). According to the constitution, the prime minister can determine the number, responsibilities, and organization of government ministries. For example, Prime Minister Gusmão (2007–2015) significantly increased the size of the Council of Ministers and centralized decision-making and the budgetary authority in his office. Compared to the Alkatiri government (2002–2006), the Council of Ministers' size increased from 12 to 17 (since 2015: 16), and the number of state secretaries and vice ministers went from 17 to 39 in 2012 (Jornal da República 2017). Moreover, Prime Minister Gusmão took direct control of the Ministry of Defence, the National Development Agency, the Economic Planning and Investment Unit, the State Audit Agency, the National Procurement Commission, the Domestic Intelligence Service, and the State Infrastructure Fund. Altogether, the prime minister personally controlled half of the national budget (ICG 2013, p. 13).

11.3.3 Parliament

Timor-Leste has a unicameral legislature (*Parlamento Nacional de Timor-Leste, Parlamentu Nasionál*). The 65 members of the National Parliament are elected through a proportional representation system for a 5-year term. Parliament can petition and interpellate members of the Council of Ministers and can appoint a commission of inquiry at the request of at least 10 members. In addition, parliament has affirmed its authority to deny the president legislation necessary to fulfill his and her constitutional role, like the initiation of popular referenda, and can veto presidential appointments of judges and preclude him or her from leaving the country on state visits (Section 95 III). Parliamentary affairs are coordinated by parliament's executive committee under the leadership of the speaker of the National Parliament. Legislative work is conducted in seven standing committees, which are usually chaired by members of the majority party or the political parties that form the majority coalition (Parlamento Nacional 2014). Responsibility for law-making is shared between government and parliament: Both can propose laws, but certain political matters are reserved for parliament (Section 95), and government sponsored laws as well as laws sponsored by parliament need to be approved by parliament. In contrast, parliament can authorize the government to make decree-laws, which do not require the approval of parliament. Constitutional amendments and the national budget can only be passed by parliament with a two-thirds or absolute majority, respectively. In practice, however, parliament has not been terribly active in the legislative domain. The frequent authorizations of the government to make laws that do not require the approval of parliament indicates a de facto shift of the law-making process from the legislature to the government. The National Parliament is therefore often considered a "sleepy parliament" (ICG 2013, pp. 13–14), an assessment supported by the statistics on the number of parliamentary laws (*Leis do Parlamento Nacional*) relative to decree-laws and government decrees (*Decretos do Governo*, cf. Fig. 11.4). Nevertheless, the National Parliament is still an important consultative and reviewing body and a forum for public debate, as opposition parties have made frequent use of parliamentary debates to criticize the government, and past presidents have used their power to address parliament in order to shape political debates and hold both government and parliament accountable (Beuman 2016).

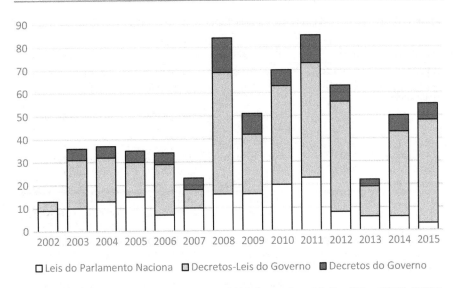

Fig. 11.4 Material laws in Timor-Leste, 2002–2015. Source Jornal da República (2017), DGSU-UNMIT (2008–2012)

11.3.4 Interactions Between Presidency, Cabinet, and Legislature

Interactions between the presidency, the cabinet, and the legislature occupy the center of the political scene in semi-presidential regimes (Protsyk 2006). There are two types of conflicts that are empirically recurrent in Timor-Leste: (1) intra-executive conflict characterized by intense confrontation between the president and the prime minister, who is supported by parliament, and (2) conflict between a united executive and parliament, which takes place when the president and prime minister form an alliance vis-à-vis the legislature (Beuman 2016). While no president has formally been a member of a political party while holding office before 2017, all were supported by certain political parties or coalitions of political parties (Table 11.2).

The cohabitation of President Gusmão and Prime Minister Mari Alkatiri (FRETILIN) between 2002 and 2006 was particularly conflict-ridden (Shoesmith 2003, 2007; Beuman 2016). The president imposed his veto power over four parliamentary bills only to see it overturned by the government's parliamentary majority every time (Beuman 2016). The president also tried to stop legislation by appealing for judicial review in five cases (Beuman 2015). Furthermore, Gusmão imposed a state of emergency without parliamentary authorization in both 2006 and 2007 and frequently pressured Alkatiri to step down (Beuman 2015, pp. 125–128, 135, 141). Section 112 provided President Gusmão (2002–2007) the opportunity to push through the dismissal of eight ministers and finally that of Prime Minister Mari Alkatiri, naming the independent José Ramos-Horta prime minister (Beuman 2015; Feijó 2014).

Table 11.2 Presidents and prime ministers in Timor-Leste since 2002

President	Term of office	Prime Minister	Term of office	Type of government
Xanana Gusmão (independent)[a]	20/05/2002– 20/05/2007	Mari Alkatiri (FRETILIN)	20/05/2002– 26/06/2006	One-party government (FRETILIN)
		José Ramos-Horta (independent)	26/06//2006– 19/05/2007	Minority government
José Ramos-Horta (independent)[b]	20/05/2007– 20/05/2012[d]	Estanislau da Silva (FRETILIN)	20/05/2007– 07/08/2007	Interim government (FRETILIN)
		Xanana Gusmão (CNRT)	08/08/2007– 07/08/2012	APM Coalition government (CNRT, PSD, ADST, PD)
Taur Matan Ruak (independent)[c]	20/05/2012– 20/05/2017	Xanana Gusmão (CNRT)	08/08/2012– 16/02/2015	BGK Coalition government (CNRT, PD)
		Rui Maria de Araújo (FRETILIN)	16/02/2015– 20/05/2017	All-party coalition
Francisco Guterres (FRETILIN)	20/05/2017–	Rui Maria de Araújo (FRETILIN)	20/05/2017– 15/09/2017	Coalition Government (FRETILIN, CNRT)
		Mari Alkatiri (FRETILIN)	Since 15/09/ 2017	Minority Coalition (FRETILIN, PD)

[a]Gusmão was accepted as the unofficial leader by the opposition parties
[b]Supported by CNRT
[c]Supported by APM
[d]From February 11, 2008 to April 17, 2008, Vicente da Silva Guterres and Fernando de Araújo ("Lasama") served as acting presidents
Source: Guterres (2008, p. 367), Leach (2013), Beuman (2016), Feijó (2012, 2014), Freedom House (2017)

The second phase of divided government between June 2006 and May 2007 was more cooperative. The conflict shifted to parliament, where the FRETILIN, now excluded from the government, still held the majority. During this time the president vetoed legislation twice and initiated one preventive judicial review (Beuman 2016). The third phase of a united majority government followed the 2007 election, when President Horta rejected a request from FRETILIN, which had won the most votes but only a minority of seats in parliament, to form a government in favor of a four party coalition, the so-called *Alliança da Maioria Parlamentar* (APM) of Prime Minister Gusmão. The APM and the following BGK coalition under CNRT leadership supported the candidacy of both Presidents Ramos-Horta (2007–2012) and Taur Matan Ruak (since 2012). Both presidents applied a more restrained approach than President Gusmão, in part because they lacked Gusmão's gravitas as an icon of resistance against the Indonesian occupation (Shoesmith 2003, 2012). Altogether, Ramos-Horta initiated five judicial reviews of legislation and vetoed four pieces of legislation, three of them only days before he failed to win a second term (La'o Hamutuk 2012; Beuman 2016). President Taur, in office from 2012 to 2017, acted with even more restraint. In late 2015, however, he vetoed the new budget law out of political concern, marking a deterioration in the relationship between the president on the one hand and the government and parliament on the other. When parliament unanimously approved an identical budget, the president decided not to issue a constitutional veto and not to send the budget law to court for judicial review.

11.4 Legal and Judicial System

Timor-Leste's legal system is based not only on the Roman civil law tradition but also includes traditional law (*adat* and *lisan*). Sources of formal law include Indonesian occupation law, UNTAET regulations, the constitution, as well as legislation and regulations enacted since 2002. Customary law dispensed by local officials, village elders (*lian nain*), and other notables is prevalent in rural areas (Roschmann 2008; Asia Foundation 2009; Grenfell 2009; Marriott 2012).

According to the constitution, all courts are independent and bound only by law (Section 119). The Superior Council for the Judiciary holds the power of appointment, administrative oversight, and disciplinary authority. It is led ex officio by the president of the Supreme Court (Section 128). District courts are the court of first instance for civil, social, and criminal cases, while members of the armed forces are tried in military courts for criminal offenses (Section 130) and a designated appellate court provides the next instance. In addition, the constitution stipulates the creation of administrative and tax courts led by a High Administrative, Tax and Audit Court that also serves as a general accounting office (Section 129).

However, military, administrative, tax, and audit courts as well as the Supreme Court of Justice have not been established yet and the Court of Appeal serves as the country's highest court with the authority of constitutional review. Two of the three justices are elected by the Superior Council for the Judiciary and one by the National Parliament for a renewable 4-year term. In its function as a constitutional court, the appellate court can be petitioned by only the president, who can file for preventive and abstract review of legislation (Section 85e). In addition, lower courts of instance are able to question the constitutionality of any legal norm, which is then decided by the Court of Appeal (Section 126 Ic). Furthermore, the constitutional court can ban political parties and sits in judgement over the president during an impeachment trial (Section 79 IV).

Different presidents have used their "constitutional veto" to block parliamentary legislation, but the National Assembly has sometimes ignored the court's verdict: In 2003, the Court of Appeal declared two clauses in the Immigration and Asylum Bill unconstitutional, but parliament nevertheless passed the law in identical form. In 2008, the Court found parts of the national budget law to be unconstitutional. While the speaker of parliament demanded a revision of this decision and disciplinary action against the judges, Prime Minister Gusmão simply ignored the court's ruling (Grenfell 2009, p. 135; Wigglesworth 2010, p. 233).

Yet the key problems and challenges for a working judicial system in Timor-Leste concern a lack of capacity and marginal accessibility to the formal judicial system. For example, the construction of a functioning justice system—a prerequisite for the establishment of the rule of law—is hampered by poor staffing. Until 1999, all prosecutors and judges originated from the other provinces of Indonesia. The lack of qualified local legal experts after the Indonesian withdrawal could not be compensated, and numerous senior positions are now occupied by lawyers from other Portuguese-speaking countries. This is also why Portuguese has been established as the de facto court language (Marriott 2012). However, this impairs the population's access to the formal legal system: A 2009 study found that less than 10% of respondents understand Portuguese; in contrast, Tetum is understood by more than 80% (Asia Foundation 2009). Moreover, the formal judicial system hardly extends beyond urban areas. Currently, there are courts in only four of the 13 districts. Due to this lack of capacity and functional weaknesses, citizens are increasingly turning to informal dispute resolution mechanism. Yet such mechanisms are insufficient in guaranteeing human rights, especially those of women and other vulnerable groups (Asia Foundation 2009; Marriott 2012). Moreover, the low prosecution rate, a large number of cases awaiting resolution, and political influence in "sensitive" issues, such as dealing with mutinous soldiers, have engendered a culture of impunity and has damaged confidence in the system. The Anti-Corruption Commission formed by the Ombudsman in 2010 has failed to remedy this (ICG 2013, p. 36; Grenfell 2009, p. 136).

Weak rule of law and endemic corruption are reflected in a low rule of law score in the World Bank's Worldwide Governance Indicators (WGI) and Transparency International's Corruption Perception Index (CPI). The governance score for the Rule of Law Indicator declined from −0.81 in 2004 (on a scale from −2.5 to 2.5, with higher values indicating better rule of law) to −1.17 in 2014. This score is significantly lower than the mean scores of other countries in the low income group, and it is the second-lowest in Southeast Asia (World Bank 2017b). Similarly, Transparency International ranks Timor-Leste ahead of only Laos, Cambodia, and Myanmar in the perceived level of corruption in its public institutions (Transparency International 2015; World Bank 2017b).

11.5   Electoral System and Elections

Portuguese Timor's only—local—elections were held in March 1975, and these remained the most democratic elections until 2001. The civil war and Indonesian intervention that followed precluded the general elections planned for later that year (Gunn 2011, pp. 81–82). Under the occupation, the Indonesian government kept a tight rein over elections, and only President Suharto's Golkar party and two "official" opposition parties, PPP and PDI (see Chap. 4), were allowed to campaign. The 2001 election for a constitutional assembly was a watershed for Timor-Leste. Since then, parliamentary elections were held in 2007, 2012, and 2017, presidential elections in 2002, 2007, 2012, and 2017, and local elections in 2004/5, 2009, and 2016 (see Table 11.3). All elections were widely considered to be free and fair, and there was broad participation of the population despite sporadic violence, some vote-buying, and threats by losing political parties to not to accept the election

Table 11.3 Parliamentary elections in Timor-Leste, 2001–2017

Party name		2001 (list)[b]	2001 (districts)	2007	2012	2017
Frente Revolucionária do Timor-Leste Independente (FRETILIN)	%	57.7	66	29.0	29.9	29.7
	Seats	43	12	21	25	23
Partido Democrático (PD)	%	8.7	5.8	11.3	10.3	9.8
	Seats	7	–	8	8	7
Partido Social Democrata (PSD)	%	8.1	4.7	b	2.1	
	Seats	6	–	–	–	–
Associaçao Social-Democrata de Timor (ASDT)	%	7.8	10.7	b	1.8	
	Seats	6	–	–	–	–
União Democrática Timorense (UDT)	%	2.3	n/a	0.9	1.1	
	Seats	2	–	–	–	–
Partido Socialista de Timor (PST)	%	2.2	n/a	0.9	0.5	
	Seats	2	–	–	–	–
Partido Democrata Cristão (PDC)	%	1.9	n/a	1.0	0.2	
	Seats	2	–	–	–	–
Klibur Oan Timor Asuwain (KOTA)	%	2.1	n/a	c	–	
	Seats	2	–	–	–	–
Partido do Povo de Timor (PPT)	%	1.7	n/a	c	–	
	Seats	2	–	–	–	–
(Congresso Nacional da Reconstrução Timorense) CNRT	%	–	–	24.1	36.7	29.5
	Seats	–	–	18	30	22
PSD-ASDT	%	–	–	15.7[b]	–	–
	Seats	–	–	11[b]	–	–
Partido Unidade Nacional(PUN)	%	–	–	4.6	0.7	–
	Seats	–	–	3	–	–
Aliança Democratica (AD) (Kota-PPT)	%	–	–	3.2[c]	0.5	–
	Seats	–	–	2[c]	–	–
União Nacional Democrática de Resistência Timorense (UNDERTIM)	%	–	–	3.2	1.5	–
	Seats	–	–	2	–	–
Frente-Mudança	%	–	–	–	3.1	–
	Seats	–	–	–	2	–
Kmanek Haburas Unidade Nasional Timor Oan (KHUNTO)	%	–	–	–	–	6.4
	Seats	–	–	–	–	5
Partidu Libertasaun Popular (PLP)	%	–	–	–	–	10.6
	Seats	–	–	–	–	
Others	%	7.5	n/a	6.2	11.5	11.3
	Seats	3	1	–	–	–
Total	%	100	87.2	100	100	100
	Seats	75	13	65	65	65
Turnout	%	93.0	93.0	80.5	74.8	76.7
Effective number of parties[a]	%	2.8	n/a	5.4	4.1	5.0
	Seats	2.4	1.1	4.4	2.6	3.7

(continued)

Table 11.3 (continued)

Party name		2001 (list)[b]	2001 (districts)	2007	2012	2017
LSq-Index[a]		2.23		4.48	10.53	5.3

[a]See Table 3.2 for details on calculation
[b]PSD and ASDT with a common list in 2007
[c]KOTA and PPT with a common list (Democratic Alliance) in 2007
Notes: Only relevant parties with at least 3% of the vote or seat share are listed
Source: Authors' compilation based on Guterres (2006, p. 199), Guterres (2008, p. 363), Feijó (2012, p. 49), Carr (2017)

results. The presence of international election observers, democracy assistance, and foreign aid conditionality has helped stabilize Timor-Leste's electoral regime (Guterres 2006; Shoesmith 2012, p. 38).

All Timorese citizens aged 17 or older hold suffrage. Candidates for the presidency can be no younger than 35 years of age and need the signatures of at least 5000 eligible voters with no less than 100 from each of the 13 districts. In principle, Timorese living abroad can cast their vote in national elections as well, but this regulation has not yet been implemented (Feijó 2012, p. 37). Automatic voter registration is carried out by the National Election Commission (CNE). In contrast to parliamentary elections, nonparty candidates can run in presidential elections.

In 2001, parliamentary seats were allocated under a mixed system in which 13 MPs were elected by plurality from single-member districts and 75 were elected from closed party lists under proportional representation (PR) in a single, nationwide district. Since 2007, all 65 MPs elected are under a PR system in one national district. Seats are allocated according to the D'Hondt highest average method among parties and coalitions of parties obtaining at least 3% of the total votes. Party lists can be submitted to the CNE by parties or party alliances, and at least one-third of candidates on each party list must be women.

The president is popularly elected for a 5-year term that is renewable once. Both nonparty and party candidates are allowed. Should no candidate gain over half of the total valid votes after the first ballot, a runoff between the two candidates with the highest number of votes in the first round is held. Before 2017, all of the eventually elected candidates have run as independents, but in 2007 and 2012, respectively, the CNRT and its coalition partners supported Ramos-Horta and General Ruak against the FRETILIN candidate.

Popular elections and referenda are organized by the CNE and the Technical Secretariat for Electoral Administration (STAE). The CNE is an independent and financially, administratively, and organizationally autonomous agency and monitors the election process. STAE, on the other hand, is a government agency that oversees the administrative and organizational implementation of CNE's directions. The Commission allocates a campaign subsidy of USD35,000 for every party list; joint lists receive USD45,000. Presidential candidates receive USD10,000 and this amount is doubled when a runoff election is held (Feijó 2012, p. 41).

While state funding of political parties follows the constitutional mandate to foster the development of a multiparty system, it has also contributed to a proliferation of party lists (Feijó 2012, p. 47; Shoesmith 2012, pp. 42–43). Yet, the relatively

Table 11.4 Presidential elections in Timor-Leste, 2002–2017

Candidate	2002	2007 (1)	2007 (2)	2012 (1)	2012 (2)	2017
José Alexandre ("Xanana") Gusmão (I)	82.6	–	–	–	–	
Francisco Xavier do Amaral (ASDT)	17.3	14.4	–	–	–	
José Ramos-Horta (I)	–	21.8	69.2	17.4	–	
Francisco Guterres ("Lu Olo") (FRETILIN)	–	27.9	30.8	28.7	38.4	57.1
Ferndando Lasama de Araújo (PD)	–	19.2	–	17.3	–	–
Lucio Lobato (PSD)	–	8.8	–	–	–	–
Manuel Tilman (I)	–	4.1	–	–	–	–
Taur Matan Ruak (I)	–	–	–	25.7	59.6	–
Rogério Lobato (I)	–	–	–	3.5	–	–
Anonio da Cenceicao (PD)	–	–	–	–	–	32.5
Others	–	3.8	–	7.4	–	10.4
Turnout	86.0	81.8	81.0	78.2	73.1	71.2
Effective number of candidates	1.4	5.8	1.7	4.7	1.9	2.3

Source: Authors' compilation based on Guterres (2006), Beuman (2016), Feijó (2012), IDEA (2014), Carr (2017)

high disproportionality of the PR system (see Table 11.4) has prevented the over-fractionalization of parliament: The number of parties and party lists in parliament declined from 11 in 2001 to 4 in 2012. While there is no systematic data on voter migration patterns, anecdotal evidence suggests that voters have begun migrating towards CNRT and FRETILIN as well as smaller parties with clearly stated coalition preferences prior to elections. Winners of this development during the polarized campaign of 2012 were CNRT, but also the *Partido Democrático* (PD) and *Frente-Mudança*, a FRETILIN breakaway faction. Losers included the Social Democratic Party (PSD) as well as the *Associaçao Social-Democrata de Timor* (ASDT), the latter of which had formed a successful joint list in 2007 but went their separate ways in 2012 without clear statements as to their preferred coalition partners (Feijó 2012, 2014).

11.6 Political Parties and Party System

Under the authoritarian Estado Novo, the National Union was the only legal political party in Portugal and all Portuguese overseas territories. However, the 1974 "Carnation Revolution" triggered the formation of a Timorese party system. New parties that were organized included the conservative UDT, the pro-Indonesian ("integrationist") APODETI, the Social Democratic Association of Timor (ASDT)—to be merged with the left nationalist FRETILIN later—, the

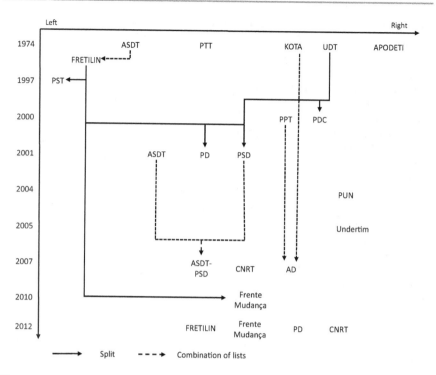

Fig. 11.5 Development of the Timorese party system 1974–2012. Notes: After 2001, only parties represented in parliament are included. No information for PPT (est. 2000). Source: Saldanha (2007), Shoesmith (2012); authors' categorization

monarchist KOTA, and the Timorese Worker Party (PTT). During the occupation, legalized Indonesian parties never gained a foothold among the Timorese population, but some of the Timorese parties such as FRETILIN survived as clandestine organizations or were reestablished in exile (Lawless 1976, p. 955; Saldanha 2007, p. 70; Beuman 2016, p. 65).

The post-1999 development of the party system exhibits both continuity and change compared to 1974/75 and the occupation period. While the ideological conflict about integration versus independence has been overcome, Indonesian parties and the Timorese parties who favored autonomy in 1999 have disappeared from party politics (Shoesmith 2012). The same is true for the cleavage separating anti-communist and Marxist parties, as FRETILIN abolished its Marxist views and accepted the principles of democratic pluralism in the 1990s, although most political parties can still be located along the left–right continuum (Fig. 11.5; Shoesmith 2012, p. 37).

However, since 1999, a number of new conflicts have reemerged or gained relevancy, among them the antagonism between the eastern and western parts of the country and the confrontation between FRETILIN and the coalition of parties around CNRT. While ideological conflicts have vanished, the new parameters of electoral competition and party politics mainly revolve around contested memories and views of the role of political parties, political elites, and regional groups during

Table 11.5 Regional FRETILIN and CNRT strongholds, 2001–2012

West (Loro Munu)	FRETILIN			CNRT	
	2001	2007	2012	2007	2012
Aileu	21.1	8.3	14.9	20.4	52.5
Ainora	27.6	9.9	13.2	11.8	37.1
Liquiçá	72.4	12.0	23.7	38.9	41.9
Manufahi	54.6	25.4	31.8	13.8	31.3
Ermera	31.9	13.9	19.9	13.6	40.6
Bobonaro	57.4	16.8	17.7	20.5	37.6
Cova Lima	61.4	28.5	26.4	15.4	31.8
Oecusse	38.6	27.5	18.6	34.6	38.9
East (Loro Sae)					
Baucau	82.0	62.4	51.3	13.4	23.0
Lautém	62.8	45.5	43.8	14.6	20.2
Viqueque	74.9	59.8	59.5	12.6	16.2
Dili	66.0	22.3	28.4	45.2	49.5
Manatuto	47.6	17.5	20.5	33.1	45.3
National	57.7	29.0	29.9	24.1	36.6

Source: Authors' compilation based on UNMIT and UNDP (2012, pp. 148–149), Leach (2012), Carr (2017)

the Indonesian occupation and the struggle for national liberation. Nevertheless, Lusophone elites dominate the leadership of all major political parties (Guterres 2006, pp. 212–218; Myrttinen 2008; Shoesmith 2007, 2012). Still, FRETILIN's electoral strongholds are mostly in the eastern districts (Loro Sae), where the population—since Portuguese rule referred to as *Firaku* ("easterners")—claim to have suffered more under the occupation than the *Kaladi* ("westerners") in the western districts (Loro Munu). About half of the population lives in the western part of the country, roughly a quarter in the eastern.[7] In contrast, electoral support for CNRT is strongest in the west, and the party strives to reintegrate those sections of the population who collaborated with Indonesians or were in favor of Indonesia's 1999 autonomy plan (Table 11.5).

While the conflict between the western Loro Muno districts and the eastern Loro Sae has a historical dimension (King 2003, pp. 753–755; Trinidade and Castro 2007), its political salience is considered a new phenomenon (Sahin 2007; Leach 2013). It is mainly caused by the failure to deal with the political and sociocultural legacies of the occupation as well as the politicization and instrumentalization of regional resentments by political parties and party leaders (Rich 2007, pp. 14–15; Guterres 2006; Saldanha 2007; Yamada 2010; Shoesmith 2012).

In contrast to some other party systems in Southeast Asia, political parties in Timor-Leste are not just organizational shells for the political ambitions of

---

[7]The assignment of the districts to the regions is not uniform. Sometimes Manatuto is assigned to Loro Sae, while Oecusse, Dili, and, at times, Manatuto, are not ordered to one of the two regions at all.

individual politicians, and their role in politics is not limited to the recruitment of political personnel. Most political parties—with the exception of FRETILIN—remain weakly institutionalized and lack a strong organizational base (Shoesmith 2011, pp. 325–326; Feijó 2014, p. 88), but FRETILIN and CNRT have developed a recognizable political program and campaign on policy issues (Shoesmith 2012).[8] In regard to the type of political party system that has emerged since 2001, Timor-Leste has transitioned from a party system with one dominant party (FRETILIN) in 2001 to a moderate multiparty system in 2007 and, since 2012, to a moderately polarized, bipolar two-and-a-half party system with a more balanced relative strength of the two major political parties, CNRT and FRETILIN. While the structure of the system is still volatile, the "effective number of political parties" fell from 4.4 to 2.6 (Table 11.4). In the 2012 election, the two largest parties, FRETILIN and CNRT, won a combined 84% of the total vote. Yet, despite the sometimes harsh confrontations between FRETILIN on the one hand and the CNRT and its coalition partners on the other, the emerging two-block confrontation turned out to be less polarized than some observers had feared. In contrast to the dire predictions that a polarized party system would make it difficult to create a stable government and strain parliamentary institutions, in 2015, all four parties in parliament agreed to build an all-party coalition government under Prime Minister Rui Maria de Araújo (FRETILIN). This development indicates a shift to centripetal party competition and inclusive and flexible coalition politics at the governmental level. Even though the election of 2017 saw an end of this inclusive coalition and the installation of a minority FRETILIN government, the oppositional CNRT indicated its willingness to cooperate with the government on key policy issues (Leach 2017).

11.7 State Administration and Stateness

The Democratic Republic of Timor-Leste is a unitary and decentralized state. Except for the western enclave of Oecusse and the island Atauro, state administration is uniformly organized across the country. Currently, Timor-Leste has 13 districts, 67 subdistricts, 442 townships (*suco*), and 2225 villages or neighborhoods (*aldeia* or *barrio*, cf. NSD and UNPF 2011). The heads of the district and subdistrict administrations are appointed by the national government and act under instructions from the government and are responsible to the Ministry for State Administration. Political decentralization, as constitutionally mandated, is limited to local councils (*Konsellu Suco*) and their heads (*Chefes de Suco*) as well as the village heads (*Chefes de Aldeia*). Local (*suco*) elections were held in 2004/05, 2009, and 2016. Local councils have nine to 19 members and include the *Chefes de Aldeia*, two elected representatives for women and youths, a village elder, and a nonelected local dignitary (*Lian nain*) as well as council chiefs. Members of the local councils are not public servants but receive allowances. Although their

---

[8]Most parties report impressive membership statistics (Ryan 2007), but these are impossible to verify.

Table 11.6   UN missions in Timor-Leste

	Date	Military force	Military observers	UN Police	International civilian personnel
UN Mission in East Timor (UNAMET)	11/06/1999–30/09/1999	0	50	271	667
International Force in East Timor (INTERFET)	20/09/1999–28/02/2000[a]	N/A	N/A	0	0
UN Transitional Administration for East Timor (UNTAET)	25/10/1999–20/05/2002	6281	118	1288	1745
UN Mission of Support in East Timor (UNMISET)	20/05/2002–20/05/2005	4656	120	771	465
UN Office in East Timor (UNOTIL)	20/05/2005–25/08/2006	0	15	56	171
UN Integrated Mission in Timor-Leste (UNMIT)	25/08/2006–31/12/2012	0	33	1546	464
International Stabilization Force (ISF)	25/05/2006–27/03/2013	ca. 920	0	0	0

[a]After 2000 part of UNTAET peace force
Source: Myrttinen (2009, pp. 231–232) and authors' additions

decisions are nonbinding for the administration, they perform important functions as local mediators and interfaces for the upper administrative level. The subnational units receive their budget directly from the central government and are not authorized to raise their own revenue (Sýkora 2013, p. 80). The 2009 decentralization law leaves little room or creative leeway for the local administrations to take the specific situation of the districts into account. Furthermore, since 2009, there has been a pronounced recentralization (Farram 2010), as the national government put several decentralization measures on hold, strengthened its oversight authority, and postponed local elections indefinitely.

Since 1999, Timor-Leste has faced considerable challenges in establishing its stateness.[9] The biggest challenge lies in the reorganization and enforcement of the state's monopoly on violence. Aware of the difficulties of securing peace in a fragile post-conflict and post-occupation environment, the expiration of the UNTAET mandate was followed by the United Nations Mission of Support in East Timor (UNMISET; cf. Table 11.6) in 2002. Initially, UNMISET confronted a

---

[9]Without fully entering the theoretical debate, we can identify three key components or dimensions of stateness: (1) political order and the monopoly on violence; (2) basic administration and administrative effectiveness; and (3) the dimension of citizenship agreement—that is, whether a body politic is recognized by its members as legitimate. For more details, see Andersen et al. (2014), Carbone and Memoli (2015).

number of potential security threats. Pro-Indonesian militias, which had retreated to West Timor, had not been disarmed by Indonesian authorities there and posed a potential danger. This risk waned quickly, however, as the government in Jakarta lost interest in the conflict and withdrew its support for the militia. Deprived of financial means, the militia disbanded. Members either remained in Indonesia or returned to Timor-Leste seeking political means to secure financial support by the government; others simply disappeared into the criminal milieu (Myrttinen 2012).

Yet within Timor-Leste itself, armed groups such as the *Sagrada Família*, *Colimau 2000*, the Committee for the Popular Defence of the Republic of Democratic Timor-Leste (CDP-RDTL), self-declared veterans, as well as so-called martial arts groups and youth gangs caused security concern (Croissant 2008; Myrttinen 2012). Threats advanced by these groups were particularly acute due to the difficulty the UN and Timorese authorities faced in the disarmament, demobilization, and reintegration (DDR) of a large number of Falintil veterans as well as the rebuilding of the security sector (see below). In recent years, and following the failed assassination attempts by mutinous soldiers (so-called petitioners) on the then President Horta and Prime Minister Gusmão in February 2008, as well as recurring outbreaks of social violence on behalf of youth gangs, the security situation has stabilized (Butler 2012; Kingsbury 2014).

Timor-Leste has also faced significant challenges in building up an effective administration, in large part due to a dearth of educated and qualified personnel (Goldfinch and DeRouen 2014). The state budget approximately doubled from 2010 to 2015 (Scheiner 2015) and spending on public administration increased by 90% from 2007–2013. However, infrastructure, governance, and benefits (mostly for veterans), respectively, make up 35, 18, and 16% of the state budget, and only 14% of the budget is invested into education and health, compared to 30% in other developing countries (Scheiner 2015).[10] Lastly, only 2% is invested into agriculture, even though a large portion of Timorese engage in subsistence farming (Scheiner 2015).

The shortcomings in the first two dimensions of stateness contrast with the strength of the Timorese citizenship agreement and state identity. As Goldfinch and Derouen (2014) write, this is to a large extent an outgrowth of the Timorese independence struggle. Nonetheless, while the Timorese state is recognized by its people as legitimate—reflected in the absence of secessionist movements or conflicts over citizenship—this should not be confused with the existence of a universally accepted conception of national identity. As aforementioned, Timorese national identity emerged from anticolonial nationalism and common suffering, yet as Arnold notes, "While this form of nationalism may have been useful during the resistance era as a consolidating dynamic, interpreting that resistance history since independence has proven to be a divisive exercise" (Arnold 2009; see also

---

[10]Almost 200,000 so-called veterans of the war of independence, i.e., almost a sixth of the population, receive pensions or are registered for government programs (Yamada 2010; Sahin 2010, p. 356; ICG 2013, p. 3).

Table 11.7 Demographic, languages and quality of life in Timor-Leste by district, 2007–2010

Province	% of total population	Male youth-bulge (%)	Most wide-spread native language (%)	Poverty rate[a]	Infant mortality[b]	Literacy rate[c]
West (Loro Munu)						
Aileu	4.1	36.9	Tetum (49.3)	68.6	94	55.4
Ainora	5.5	30.4	Mambei (61.5)	79.7	111	44.0
Liquiçá	5.9	34.8	Tokodede (61.7)	44.9	81	50.8
Manufahi	4.5	31.4	Tetum (56.9)	85.2	85	57.2
Ermera	10.9	35.0	Tetum (48.1)	54.6	98	38.7
Bobonaro	8.6	30.6	Kemak (43.7)	54.5	109	44.7
Cova Lima	5.5	32.6	Bunak (48.6)	49.1	97	55.0
Oecusse	6.0	27.1	Baikenu (96.1)	61.0	106	37.8
East (Loro Sae)						
Baucau	10.5	31.1	Makasai (56.6)	22.3	99	55.1
Lautém	5.6	31.2	Fataluku (61.4)	21.3	83	57.3
Viqueque	6.5	26.1	Makasai (39.5)	43.4	103	51.1
Dili	21.9	39.4	Tetum (88.1)	43.3	60	85.5
Manatuto	4.0	32.7	Galoli (31.0)	73.7	79	52.0

[a]District population below the poverty line
[b]Average number of children dying before age 1 per 1000 life births
[c]Percentage of literate population above the age of 15
Source: NSD and UNPF (2011), NSD and World Bank (2008)

Myrttinen 2013). Tensions between the various resistance factions, former collaborators, and self-declared veterans as well as conflicts between older and younger cohorts have emerged. Struggles over inequalities relating to resources, power, and land disputes have likewise sprung up. These struggles have, as mentioned, slowly taken on a regional character, revealing animosities between the western and the eastern districts of the country (Hohe 2004). Measured by the proportion of those living under the national poverty line and the infant mortality rate—indicators often used to measure socioeconomic status and access to health care—the east of the country with the exception of Viqueque performs better than the west, although there appears to be no systematic economic, social, or political discrimination of a particular ethnic or regional group (cf. Table 11.7).

11.8 Civil–Military Relations and Security Governance

In the 2000s, Timor-Leste's security sector has suffered particularly from the conflicts between the east and the west of the country. The security sector comprises three services: the military (*Falintil-Forças de Defesa de Timor-Leste*, F-FDTL), the national police (*Polícia Nacional de Timor-Leste*, PNTL), and the national intelligence service (*Serviço Nacional de Inteligência*, SNI). While the military, particularly the officer ranks, are staffed mostly by Falintil veterans, many of the early PNTL members were former Indonesian POLRI personnel (Kammen 2013, p. 111). The SNI was established in 2009. Together with the military intelligence services and the reconnaissance section of PNTL, it forms the Timorese intelligence sector.

The principles of civilian control over and the political neutrality of the military are enshrined in the constitution (Section 146). The president serves as supreme commander of the defence force, but the minister of defence holds actual command authority. Since 2005, the Superior Council for Defence and Security advises the president in all matters of defense and security as well as the appointment of the armed forces chief of staff. It consists of the president; the prime minister; the ministers for defense, justice, interior, and foreign affairs; the incumbent F-FDTL chief of staff; the commanding PNTL officer; and three representatives of parliament (ICG 2013). Parliamentary oversight over the security sector is exercised by the Committee for Defence and Security, and government activities in internal security are coordinated by the prime minister (ISA 2010, Art 11), who is assisted by an interdepartmental security committee. A council to monitor the intelligence services was established together with the domestic intelligence service. While the president and parliament appoint its members, the council reports to the government.

Both during UNTAET and its successor mission UNMISET, the focus of UN efforts in security sector reform was on the police (see Myrttinen 2012). In contrast, the newly established F-FDTL was largely controlled by the Timorese elite, and after 2002, almost entirely. As such, the officer corps of the F-FDTL was mainly recruited from Falintil veterans, whereas the PNTL is mostly comprised of former Timorese members of the Indonesian Police (POLRI) and only a small number of former guerrilla fighters.

The haphazard process of DDR under UNTAET and the political interference in the establishment of the F-DTL are two major reasons for the continuing problems of the Timorese security sector, which include a lack of civilian oversight over the military, a poorly disciplined police, regional cleavages, and conflict between a politicized military and police force (Croissant 2008; ICG 2008, 2013; Kammen 2013). The most significant setback so far was the near collapse of the Timorese state in April 2006: Fighting between the army and police, as well as civil unrest in the capital of Dili, resulted in more than 30 deaths and the internal displacement of 150,000 people. The breakdown of public order could only be averted through the deployment of an approximately 3000 troop strong International Stabilization Force (ISF; Cotton 2007; Moxham and Carapic 2013). The disorder eventually led to the creation of the United Nations Mission in Timor-Leste (UNMIT). Moreover, since 2011, military and police forces have been responsible for policing throughout the territory, and 2012 saw the end of ISF and the UNMIT missions.

The Timorese Defence Force is responsible for defending the country against external threats (Section 146). Internal security is provided by the police, SNI, the immigration agency, and those civilian agencies responsible for disaster management. According to the Internal Security Law of 2010, the armed forces can take on a supporting role in anti-terrorism, disaster management, and in maintaining public order. In addition, the president can involve the military to quell riots and unrest. Since 2002, the military has also taken on some additional police tasks, while the police has increasingly become a paramilitary force with the creation of several heavily armed special units (Rees 2004, p. 24; ICG 2008, p. 5; Sahin 2012, p. 343). The resulting institutional conflicts over resource allocation and relative authority contributed to the rivalry between military and police.

A series of institutional reforms—including the establishment of the Ministry for Defence and Security, new laws on national and internal security, and a defense law—integrated both the military and the police under a common ministry to reduce friction after 2008. However, the new ministry lacks the capacity to exert leadership and oversight over the military, and divisions between both services persist (ICG 2013, p. 19). In addition, "poor accountability, weak investigations, over-reliance on large-scale special operations (generally featuring military back-up), and weak crowd and riot control capacity" remain (IPAC 2014). Furthermore, the government policy of buying the loyalty of potential conflict spoilers has affected the security apparatus. The size of F-FDTL has more than doubled since 2008, as has the budget for defense and security. The mutineers of 2006 received generous severance packages or were readmitted into the armed forces, and those responsible for the 2008 assassination attempts on President Horta and Prime Minister Gusmão were convicted that same year only to be pardoned in 2010, contributing to widespread perceptions of impunity and the politicization of justice.

11.9 Civil Society

Despite its small size, Timor-Leste is an ethnically and culturally heterogeneous society. The existence of numerous ethnic and linguistic groups with different traumatic historical experiences has resulted in widely different perceptions, conceptions, and ideas about political legitimacy. When considering political culture and mass perceptions in Timor-Leste, it is also important to note that there is very little empirical data on political attitudes and values available. Timor-Leste is one of only four countries in Southeast Asia not included in either the World Values Survey or the Asian Barometer Survey. Available data comes from qualitative studies in cultural anthropology and political ethnology or is the result of a handful of social surveys conducted by international agencies.

Nevertheless, the available studies reveal that traumatic experiences of civil war, occupation, collaboration, and resistance remain influential in shaping political culture and political identities in Timor-Leste. These experiences have shaped not only political cleavages, but the fault lines running deep into village communities and even individual families (Wigglesworth 2010, 2013). The independence movement managed to unify large segments of society under the banner of resistance to occupation (Taylor 1991, p. 157), and adherence to the Catholic faith also had a unifying effect (Anderson 2001, p. 138), although its integrative power has weakened after independence. Today, Timorese society is characterized by particularistic identities (Simonsen 2006; Leach 2008; Scambary 2009). Qualitative studies indicate that indigenous forms of social organization remain influential and that traditional conceptions of political power, authority, and legitimacy remain prevalent (Myrttinen 2009, p. 223; Molnar 2012). Society is based largely on social networks, the extended family, and regional linguistic communities. These structures are complemented by more recent phenomena like religious organizations and formal or informal associations including veterans' associations, gangs, militias, or martial arts groups but also civil society and grassroots organizations. Local organizations are often the basis for political patronage, and many smaller political parties form around the social networks and prestige of their individual leaders. Even the larger parties show pronounced regional differences in support based on their connection to existing social networks (Myrttinen 2009, p. 223; Molnar 2012).

Due to a lack of valid and reliable data, the actual level of political awareness and the distribution of norms that might support democratic institutions among the general population are difficult to gauge, but the available data suggest widespread interest in political participation and strong belief in the efficacy of individual political action (IRI 2008). For example, elections in Timor-Leste produce robust voter turnout, but beyond that, more conventional political participation in political organizations or civic associations is largely restricted to certain segments of society, such as the young and better-educated (Myrttinen 2009, p. 222; Wigglesworth 2010).

As mentioned earlier, nonviolent opposition during the Indonesian occupation came mainly from students and youth organizations, the Catholic Church, and exiled Timorese. Both student and youth organizations as well as religious communities can be considered the historical core of today's civil society in Timor-Leste. In addition, some Indonesian nongovernmental organizations (NGOs) and the Timor-Leste NGO-Forum (FONGTIL), an umbrella organization of a few human rights and advocacy groups, could legally operate in the province. As a consequence of colonial repression, geographical remoteness, economic backwardness before 1975, and Indonesian authoritarianism after 1975, however, Timor-Leste did not have a strong civil society tradition at independence (Yamada 2010). Moreover, the repressive policy of the occupation authorities and Timorese reactions to it contributed to the emergence of a broad "gray zone" between "civic" forms of resistance and "uncivil" or violent forms.

There is no reliable data on the number of currently active organizations, but observers agree that the number of civil society groups has grown very fast since 1999. Two types are particularly relevant: NGOs that work on several issues such as the environment, development, human rights, women, etc., and community-based organizations (CBOs; UNDP 2002; Yamada 2010, pp. 23–24). Moreover, the Catholic Church still plays a major role in Timor-Leste's public life. Latest census data suggest that 96.9% of the population is Catholic (NSD and UNPF 2011, xxi). Religious networks and organizations provide charitable services, and the Roman Catholic Church remains the best-organized social institution in the country. The Church has demonstrated eminent political influence on policy issues such as the introduction of religious education in public schools or resistance against providing broad access to birth control (Yamada 2010; McGregor et al. 2012).

The Law No. 1/2006 on the Freedom of Assembly and Demonstration and the 2003 Internal Security Act (repealed in 2010) employed provisions that would have allowed the government to restrict political rights and civil liberties (Guterres 2006, pp. 257–259; Molnar 2012). Immediately following independence in 2002, the relationship between civil society and the government was tense, as FRETILIN tended to equate civil society with political opposition. However, the actual degree of conflict varied widely by NGO, district administration, or ministry, and also largely depended on the personal relationship between involved persons (Wigglesworth 2010, pp. 216–217). Although the relationship between civil society and political actors or the state has since improved, and the political and legal environment is more supportive compared to most other Southeast Asian nations, civil society still faces some obstacles and challenges. For example, CBOs are often neglected in the political decision-making process, whereas national NGOs are highly reliant on donors and international NGOs (INGOs) for support. Moreover, the actual extent to which the organizations contribute to the socialization of democratic values and norms is unknown for a lack of empirical data (Engel 2003, pp. 173–174). To facilitate better coordination between international development agencies, INGOs, the Timorese government, and NGOs, the last are encouraged to register with the Ministry of Justice. Moreover, development actors have called for a national consultation mechanism to expand the participation of civil society in state administration and planning (Wigglesworth 2010).

Furthermore, path dependencies from the occupation era, contested memories of struggle and survival before and in 1999, and the politicization of local identities have created different forms of an ambivalent or outright "uncivil society" in Timor-Leste. This can especially be seen in the number of veterans' organizations that have been set up since 1999. These include the *Associação dos Veteranos da Resistência*, *the Fundação dos Veteranos das FALINTIL*, the Women of Resistance Organization (OPMT e OMT), Youth's Organizations (OPJT, OPJTIL), and ASSEPOL, the Ex-Political Prisoners Association. However, many of these associations are reported to be politicized, and some are said to have been involved in the 2006 crisis (cf. Rees 2004; Simonsen 2006, p. 592). Furthermore, there are other groups who claim to represent former combatants of the national liberation movement, but who are actually militias or armed gangs. Examples include the *Sagrada Família, Colimau 2000*, or the Popular Council for the Defence of the Democratic Republic of Timor-Leste (CPD-RDTL; Simonsen 2006, p. 593; ICG 2011). These groups are involved in criminal activities and have more or less openly threatened the use of violence to push for political participation and economic support. At best, these groups represent the "dark side" of civil society (Armony 2004, p. 80).

11.10 Media System

Timor-Leste is one of the least literate societies in the Asia-Pacific. According to World Bank data, only 58.3% of the population above the age of 15 are able to read and write. There are, however, significant geographical and generational differences. While literacy rates range from 38.5% in Oecusse to 85.5% in Dili, among the population aged between 15 and 24, 79.5% are literate. About 56.1% of the adult population can read and write Tetum, followed by Bahasa Indonesia with 45.4%, and Portuguese with 25.2% (NSD and UNPF 2011, xxii). Consequently, newspapers play a minor role as a medium for mass communication.

In 2009, there were more than 15 local radio stations, three commercial stations, and several international broadcasts in Tetum, Bahasa Indonesia, English, or Portuguese. In remote and mountainous areas, however, radio and television reception is sometimes poor, and about 37% of the population has no access at all (UNMIT 2011, p. 4). Access to new social media is still low but has risen in recent years: 27.5% of the population has access to the internet (Internet World Stats 2017). Consequently, radio is the main source of political information, followed by personal communication and television (Soares and Mytton 2007; UNMIT 2011). Many Timorese still receive their political information through personal communication: 13% rely on friends, family, or neighbors and 9% rely on local authorities (Soares and Mytton 2007).

The constitution guarantees freedom of the press, communication, information, and expression. Media regulations were issued by UNTAET, followed by national laws in 2003, 2009, and 2015. Most media only report the news and provide little political commentary or critical journalism, but watchdog functions are performed by NGOs like La'o Hamutuk. While state radio and television are generally considered government-friendly, electronic and print media can report freely. The government established the Secretary of State for Social Communication (*Secretario Estadu Komunikasaun Sosial* or SECOM) in 2012, parliament passed a new media law in 2014, and in 2015, the Council of Ministers established a Press Council as an independent body for media self-regulation. The Press Council is composed of two representatives from the community of journalists, one representative of media owners, and two representatives from the public, who are selected by the National Parliament. However, several actors voiced concerns over some regulations that might threaten freedom of the press. These included international observers such as the International Federation of Journalists and the Association of Journalists in Timor-Leste (AJTL) but also the Court of Appeals to whom President Taur Matan Ruak had submitted the 2014 Press Law with a request for a review of its constitutionality (La'o Hamutuk 2016). While the court declared parts of the new law unconstitutional, the National Parliament changed only some clauses and passed the law unanimously in October 2014 (La'o Hamutuk 2016). While no journalists have been jailed or even killed for their work, press freedom in Timor-Leste has declined in recent years. Reporters Without Borders ranked Timor-Leste 98th in the world in 2017, the highest rank in Southeast Asia (Reporters without Borders 2017). However, compared to rank 30 in 2003, this is a significant decline.

The Freedom of the Press Index 2017 also rates press freedom in Timor-Leste more favorably than in other Southeast Asian countries with a score of 35 (Freedom House 2017).

11.11 Outlook

Since it gained independence in 2002, the Democratic Republic of Timor-Leste has strived to create a democratic and effective state out of the ashes of colonial rule, armed conflict, and foreign occupation. With the assistance of the UN and other international actors, the new nation has undergone enormous state- and democracy-building efforts since the turn of the century. As unique as this development has been, Timor-Leste still faces challenges that plague many postcolonial states, post-conflict societies, and least developed countries. Foremost among these is the emergence of a commodity oil-based rentier economy, weak state capacity, a vulnerable security situation, organized crime and gang violence, as well as challenging demographics. Despite these challenges, democracy has been surprisingly resilient. So far, the Timorese political system has not become overly fragmented and polarized, and the state—with international assistance—has avoided near collapse despite polarization between the east and west. Timor-Leste's relatively long tradition of a centralized—albeit weak—state and the lack of communal violence, tribalism, and secessionist movements have provided the country with relatively favorable conditions for successful nation-building (Arnold 2009, p. 446). However, its conclusion would require an elite consensus to stop exploiting the existing fault lines. Most of the political crises during the last decade resulted from elite conflict, and as such, the fact that all four parties in parliament formed a coalition government in 2015 can be considered a sign of successful political learning. Be this as it may, for the foreseeable future, East Timor's stateness will likely remain diminished and its democracy unconsolidated as the international community and the Timorese continue in their state- and democracy-building efforts. Considering the country's challenges and tribulations, and the fact that Timor-Leste is Asia's youngest state, however, this is still a laudable achievement.

References

Andersen, D., Moller, J., & Skaaning, S.-E. (2014). The state-democracy nexus: Conceptual distinctions, theoretical perspectives, and comparative approaches. *Democratization, 21*, 1203–1220. https://doi.org/10.1080/13510347.2014.960206

Anderson, B. (2001). *Imagining East Timor*. Accessed May 14, 2017, from http://lusotopie. sciencespobordeaux.fr/anderson.pdf

Armony, A. C. (2004). *The dubious link: Civic engagement and democratization*. Stanford: Stanford University Press.

Arnold, M. B. (2009). Challenges too strong for the nascent state of Timor-Leste: Petitioners and mutineers. *Asian Survey, 49*, 429–449. https://doi.org/10.1525/as.2009.49.3.429

Asia Foundation. (2009). *A survey of citizen awareness and attitudes regarding law and justice.* Accessed May 14, 2017, from https://asiafoundation.org/resources/pdfs/2008LawJusticeSurvey.pdf

Aucoin, L., & Brandt, M. (2010). East Timor's constituttional passage to independence. In L. E. Miller & L. Aucoin (Eds.), *Framing the state in times of transition: Case studies in constitution making* (pp. 245–274). Washington: United States Institute of Peace Press.

Beauvais, J. C. (2001). Benevolent despotism: A critique of U.N. state-buidling in East Timor. *New York University Journal of International Law and Politics, 33*(4), 1101–1178.

Beuman, L. M. (2015). Cohabitation in new post-conflict democracies: The case of Timor-Leste. *Parliamentary Affairs, 68,* 453–475. https://doi.org/10.1093/pa/gst016

Beuman, L. M. (2016). *Political institutions in East Timor: Semi-presidentialism and democratisation.* Abingdon: Routledge.

Borgerhoff, A. (2006). The double task: Nation- and state-building in Timor-Leste. *European Journal of East Asian Studies, 5,* 101–130. https://doi.org/10.1163/157006106777998098

Brandt, M. (2005). Constitutional assistance in post-conflict countries: The UN experience. Cambodia, East Timor & Afghanistan. New York: United Nations Development Program.

Butler, M. J. (2012). Ten years after: (Re)-assessing neo-trusteeship and UN state-building in Timor-Leste. *International Studies Perspectives, 13,* 85–104. https://doi.org/10.1111/j.1528-3585.2011.00443.x

Carbone, G., & Memoli, V. (2015). Does democratization foster state consolidation?: Democratic rule, political order, and administrative capacity. *Governance, 28,* 5–24. https://doi.org/10.1111/gove.12056

Carr, A. (2017). Psephos: Adam Carr's election archive. Accessed June 10, 2017, from http://psephos.adam-carr.net/

CIA. (2017). *The world factbook.* Langley: Central Intelligence Agency.

Cotton, J. (2000). The emergence of an independent East Timor: National and regional challenges. *Contemporary Southeast Asia, 22,* 1–22. https://doi.org/10.1355/CS22-1A

Cotton, J. (2007). Timor-Leste and the discourse of state failure. *Australian Journal of International Affairs, 61,* 455–470. https://doi.org/10.1080/10357710701684914

Croissant, A. (2008). The perils and promises of democratization through United Nations transitional authority: Lessons from Cambodia and East Timor. *Democratization, 15,* 649–668. https://doi.org/10.1080/13510340801972403

Curtain, R. (2006). *Crisis in Timor Leste: Looking beyond the surface reality for causes and solutions.* Canberra: SSGM.

DGSU-UNMIT. (2008–2012). *Monthly governance report: The state of democratic governance in Timor-Leste.* Dili: UNMIT Democratic Governance Support Unit.

Engel, R. E. (2003). Reaching for stability: Strengthening civil society-donor partnerships in East Timor. *Journal of International Affairs, 57*(1), 169–181.

Farram, S. (Ed.). (2010). *Locating democracy: Representation, elections and governance in Timor-Leste.* Darwin: Charles Darwin University Press.

Feijó, R. (2012). Elections, independence, democracy: The 2012 Timorese electoral cycle in context. *Journal of Current Southeast Asian Affairs, 3,* 29–59.

Feijó, R. (2014). Timor-Leste in 2013: Marching on its own feet. *Asian Survey, 54*(1), 83–88.

Freedom House. (2017). *Freedom of the press index 2017: Press freedom's dark horizon.* Accessed June 2, 2017, from https://freedomhouse.org/report/freedom-press/freedom-press-2017

Goldfinch, S., & DeRouen, K. (2014). In it for the long haul?: Post-conflict statebuilding, peacebuilding and the good governance agenda in Timor-Leste. *Public Administration and Development, 34,* 96–108. https://doi.org/10.1002/pad.1679

Goldstone, A. (2013). Building a state and state-building: East Timor and the UN. 1999–2012. In M. Berdal & D. Zaum (Eds.), *Political economy of statebuilding: Power after peace* (pp. 209–230). Hoboken: Taylor and Francis.

Grenfell, L. (2009). Promoting the rule of law in Timor-Leste: Security, development, and nation-building in Timor-Leste. A cross-sectional assessment. *Conflict, Security & Development, 9*, 125–148. https://doi.org/10.1080/14678800902925143

Gunn, G. C. (2001). The five-hundred-year Timorese Funu. In R. Tanter, M. Selden, & S. R. Shalom (Eds.), *Bitter flowers, sweet flowers: East Timor, Indonesia, and the world community* (pp. 3–14). Sydney: Rowman & Littlefield.

Gunn, G. C. (2011). *Historical dictionary of East Timor*. Lanham: Scarecrow Press.

Guterres, F. (2006). *Elites and prospects of democracy in East Timor*: PhD Dissertation. Brisbane: Griffith University.

Guterres, J. (2008). Timor-Leste: A year of democratic elections. *Southeast Asian Affairs*, 359–372.

Hohe, T. (2004). Local governance after conflict: Community empowerment in East Timor. *Journal of Peacebuilding & Development, 1*, 45–56. https://doi.org/10.1080/15423166.2004.681592442113

Huang, R., & Gunn, G. C. (2004). *Reconciliation as state-building in East Timor*. Accessed June 22, 2017, from http://lusotopie.sciencespobordeaux.fr/gunn-huang2004.pdf

Hughes, C. (2009). *Dependent communities: Aid and politics in Cambodia and East Timor*. Ithaca: Cornell University Press.

ICG. (2008). *Timor-Leste: Security sector reform*. Asia Report No. 143. Brüssel: International Crisis Group.

ICG. (2011). *Timor-Leste: Reconciliation and return from Indonesia*. Asia Briefing No. 122. Brüssel: International Crisis Group.

ICG. (2013). *Timor-Leste: Stability at what cost?* Asia Report No. 249. Brüssel: International Crisis Group.

IDEA. (2014). *Voter turnout data for East Timor*. http://www.idea.int/data-tools/country-view/286/40

IMF. (2009). *Democratic Republic of Timor-Leste: 2009 Art IV consultation*. Staff Report, Public Information Notice on the Executive Board Discussion, and Statement by the Executive Director for the Democratic Republic of Timor-Leste. New York.

IMF. (2013). *Democratic Republic of Timor-Leste: 2013 Art IV consultation*. Staff Report, Public Information Notice on the Executive Board Discussion, and Statement by the Executive Director for the Democratic Republic of Timor-Leste. New York.

IMF. (2016). *Democratic Republic of Timor-Leste: 2016 Art IV consultation*. Staff Report, Public Information Notice on the Executive Board Discussion, and Statement by the Executive Director for the Democratic Republic of Timor-Leste. New York.

Internet World Stats. (2017). *Internet usage statistics: World internet users and 2017 population stats*. https://www.internetworldstats.com/stats.htm

IPAC. (2014). *Timor-Leste after Xanana Gusmao*. Jakarta: Institute for Policy Analysis of Conflict.

IRI. (2008). *Timor-Leste: National survey results*. Washington, DC: International Republican Institute.

ISA. (2010). *Law on Internal Security, 4/2010*. Accessed July 19, 2017, from http://www.jornal.gov.tl/lawsTL/RDTL-Law/RDTL-Laws/Law%204-2010.pdf

Jornal da República. (2017). *Decretos do Governo*. Accessed June 26, 2017, from http://www.mj.gov.tl/jornal/?q=node/18

Kammen, D. (2013). The armed forces in Timor-Leste: Politicization through elite conflict. In M. Mietzner (Ed.), *The political resurgence of the military in Southeast Asia: Conflict and leadership* (pp. 107–126). New York: Routledge.

King, D. Y. (2003). East Timor's founding elections and emerging party system. *Asian Survey, 43*, 745–757. https://doi.org/10.1525/as.2003.43.5.745.

Kingsbury, D. (2014). Democratic consolidation in Timor-Leste: Achievements, problems and prospects. *Asian Journal of Political Science, 22*, 181–205. https://doi.org/10.1080/02185377.2014.899507.

La'o Hamutuk. (2012). *President vetoes three land laws*. Accessed June 25, 2017, from http:// www.laohamutuk.org/Agri/land/2012/12PNpassPRveto.htm

La'o Hamutuk. (2016). *Proposed law on media*. Accessed June 22, 2017, from http://laohamutuk. org/misc/MediaLaw/14MediaLaw.htm

Lawless, R. (1976). The Indonesian takeover of East Timor. *Asian Survey, 16*, 948–964. https:// doi.org/10.2307/2643535.

Leach, M. (2008). Surveying East Timorese tertiary student attitudes to national identity: 2002–2007. *South East Asia Research, 16*, 405–431. https://doi.org/10.5367/ 000000008787133472.

Leach, M. (2012). *A preliminary district analysis of Timor-Leste's parliamentary election, 2012*. Accessed June 25, 2017, from http://proxanana.blogspot.de/2012/07/preliminary-district-anal ysis-of-timor.html

Leach, M. (2013). Timor-Leste in 2012. *Asian Survey, 53*, 156–161. https://doi.org/10.1525/as. 2013.53.1.156.

Leach, M. (2017). *Timor-Leste heads for minority government*. Accessed November 24, 2017, from https://www.lowyinstitute.org/the-interpreter/timor-leste-minority-government

Marriott, A. (2012). Justice sector dynamics in Timor-Leste: Institutions and individuals. *Asian Politics & Policy, 4*, 53–71. https://doi.org/10.1111/j.1943-0787.2011.01319.x.

McGregor, A., Skeaff, L., & Bevan, M. (2012). Overcoming Secularism?: Catholic development geographies in Timor-Leste. *Third World Quarterly, 33*, 1129–1146. https://doi.org/10.1080/ 01436597.2012.681497.

Molnar, A. K. (2012). *Timor Leste: Politics, history, and culture*. London: Routledge.

Moxham, B., & Carapic, J. (2013). Unravelling Dili: The crisis of city and state in Timor-Leste. *Urban Studies, 50*, 3116–3133. https://doi.org/10.1177/0042098013487774.

Myrttinen, H. (2008). Notizen zur Gewalt in Osttimor. In A. Borgerhoff & M. Schmitz (Eds.), *Osttimor am Scheideweg: Chaos oder Neuanfang?* (pp. 27–31). Essen: Asienhaus.

Myrttinen, H. (2009). Timor-Leste: A Relapsing 'Success' Story. *Taiwan Journal of Democracy, 5*(1), 219–239.

Myrttinen, H. (2012). Guerillas, gangsters, and contractors: Reintegrating former combatants and its impact on SSR and development in post-conflict societies. In A. Schnabel & V. Farr (Eds.), *Back to the roots: Security sector reform and development* (pp. 225–247, Geneva Centre for the Democratic Control of Armed Forces (DCAF)). Münster: LIT Verlag.

Myrttinen, H. (2013). Resistance, symbolism and the language of stateness in Timor-Leste. *Oceania, 83*, 208–220. https://doi.org/10.1002/ocea.5021.

Neto, O., & Costa Lobo, M. (2012). Semi-presidentialism in lusophone countries: Diffusion and operation. *Democratization, 21*, 434–457. https://doi.org/10.1080/13510347.2012.738327.

Neupert, R., & Lopes, S. (2006). The demographic component of the crisis in Timor-Leste: Political demography: Ethnic, national and religious dimensions, associations for the study of ethnicity and nationalism. LSE. Accessed June 25, 2017, from http://www.sneps.net/RD/uploads/THE% 20DEMOGRAPHIC%20COMPONENT%20OF%20THE%20EAST%20TIMORESE%20CRI SIS%20-%20first%20complete%20draft.pdf

NSD, & UNPF. (2011). *2010 Timor-Leste population and housing census: Analytical report on education*. Dili: National Statistics Directorate; United Nations Population Fund.

NSD, & World Bank. (2008). *Timor-Leste: Poverty in a young nation*. Dili: National Statistics Directorate; World Bank.

Parlamento Nacional. (2014). Comissões Especializadas Permanentes, Competencia e Composição. Accessed June 25, 2017, from http://www.parlamento.tl/comisaun/pt/III_ legislatura.php

Protsyk, O. (2006). Intra-executive competition between President and Prime Minister: Patterns of institutional conflict and cooperation under semi-presidentialism. *Political Studies, 54*, 219–244. https://doi.org/10.1111/j.1467-9248.2006.00604.x.

Rees, E. (2004). Under pressure: Falintil – Forças de Defesa de Timor Leste. Three decades of defence force development in Timor Leste, 1975–2004. DCAF Working Paper No. 139.

Reporters without Borders. (2017). *2017 World Press Freedom Index. RSF*. Accessed June 22, 2017, from https://rsf.org/en/ranking

Rich, R. (2007). Introduction: Analysing and categorising political parties in the Pacific Islands. In R. Rich, L. Hambly, & M. G. Morgan (Eds.), *Political parties in the Pacific Islands* (pp. 1–27). Canberra: ANU Press.

Robinson, G. (2010). *If you leave us here, we will die: How genocide was stopped in East Timor*. Princeton: Princeton University Press.

Roschmann, C. (2008). East Timor (Timor-Leste): Constitutional framework for a country in the making. In C. Hill & J. Menzel (Eds.), *Constitutionalism in Southeast Asia 2: Reports on National Constitutions*. Konrad Adenauer Foundation: Singapore.

Ryan, G. (2007). Political parties and groupings of Timor Leste: Australian Labor Party International Projects report (2nd ed). Accessed June 25, 2017, from https://de.scribd.com/document/95121619/Timor-Leste-Political-Parties-ALP-Int-Projects

Sahin, S. B. (2007). Building the state in Timor-Leste. *Asian Survey, 47*, 250–267. https://doi.org/10.1525/as.2007.47.2.250.

Sahin, S. B. (2010). Timor-Leste in 2009: Marking ten years of independence or dependence on international "assistance"? *Southeast Asian Affairs*, 345–364.

Sahin, S. B. (2012). Timor-Leste: A more confident or overconfident foreign policy actor? *Southeast Asian Affairs*, 341–358.

Saldanha, J. M. (2007). Anatomy of political parties in Timor-Leste. In R. Rich, L. Hambly, & M. G. Morgan (Eds.), *Political parties in the Pacific Islands* (pp. 69–83). Canberra: ANU Press.

Samuels, K. (2006). *Constitution Building Processes and Democratization: A Discussion of Twelve Case Studies*. Geneva: IDEA.

Scambary, J. (2009). Anatomy of a conflict: The 2006–2007 communal violence in East Timor. *Conflict, Security & Development, 9*, 265–288. https://doi.org/10.1080/14678800902925184.

Scheiner, C. (2014). *How long will the Petroleum Fund carry?* Accessed June 25, 2017, from http://www.laohamutuk.org/econ/model/ScheinerPetrolFund17Feb2014en.pdf

Scheiner, C. (2015). Can the petroleum fund exorcise the resource curse from Timor-Leste. La'o Hamutuk. Accessed June 22, 2016, from http://www.laohamutuk.org/econ/exor/ScheinerFundExorciseCursePrePubEn.pdf

Shoesmith, D. (2003). Timor-Leste: Divided leadership in a semi-presidential system. *Asian Survey, 43*, 231–252. https://doi.org/10.1525/as.2003.43.2.231.

Shoesmith, D. (2007). Timor-Leste: Semi-presidentialism and the democratic transition in a new, small state. In R. Elgie & S. Moestrup (Eds.), *Semi-presidentialism outside Europe: A comparative study*. London/New York: Routledge.

Shoesmith, D. (2011). Timor-Leste: On the road to peace and prosperity. *Southeast Asian Affairs*, 323–335.

Shoesmith, D. (2012). Is small beautiful?: Multiparty politics and democratic consolidation in Timor-Leste. *Asian Politics & Policy, 4*, 33–51. https://doi.org/10.1111/j.1943-0787.2011.01318.x.

Simonsen, S. G. (2006). The authoritarian temptation in East Timor: Nationbuilding and the need for inclusive governance. *Asian Survey, 46*, 575–596. https://doi.org/10.1525/as.2006.46.4.575.

Soares, E., & Mytton, G. (2007). *Timor-Leste National Media Survey Final Report*. Accessed June 25, 2017, from http://pdf.usaid.gov/pdf_docs/Pnadl058.pdf

Sýkora, J. (2013). Oil in Timor-Leste: A ticket to prosperity? *Acta Oeconomica Pragensia, 21*(3), 68–85.

Taudevin, L. (1999). *East Timor: Too little too late*. Sydney: Duffy & Snellgrove.

Taylor, J. G. (1991). *Indonesia's forgotten war: The hidden history of East Timor*. London: Zed Books.

Taylor, J. G. (1999). *East Timor: The price of freedom* (2nd ed.). London: Zed Books.

Transparency International. (2015). *Corruption perception index*. Accessed June 1, 2017, from https://www.transparency.org/news/feature/corruption_perceptions_index_2016

Traub, J. (2000). Inventing East Timor. *Foreign Affairs, 79*, 74. https://doi.org/10.2307/20049810.

Trinidade, J., & Castro, B. (2007). Technical assistance to the rethinking Timorese identity as a peace-building strategy: The Lorosa'e-Loromonu conflict from a traditional perspective. Final

Report for GTZ-IS. Accessed June 25, 2017, from http://www.indopubs.com/Trindade_Castro_Rethinking_Timorese_Identity.pdf

UNDES. (2013). *World population prospects: The 2012 revision.* Accessed June 25, 2017, from https://esa.un.org/unpd/wpp/

UNDP. (2002). *Situation analysis of civil society organisation in East Timor.* Accessed June 25, 2017, from http://undp.east-timor.org/documentsreports/governance_capacitydevelopment/Civil%20Society%20Organisations.pdf

UNDP. (2016). *Human Development Report 2016: Human Development for everyone.* Houndmills: Palgrave Macmillan.

UNMIT. (2011). *Timor Leste communication and media survey.* Dili: UNMIT.

UNMIT, & UNDP. (2012). *Compendium of the 2012 Elections in Timor Leste as of June 12, 2012.* Dili: UNMIT; United Nations Development Program.

Wigglesworth, A. (2010). *Becoming citizens: Civil society activism and social change in Timor Leste.* PhD thesis. Victoria Unversity, Melbourne.

Wigglesworth, A. (2013). The growth of civil society in Timor-Leste: Three moments of activism. *Journal of Contemporary Asia, 43*, 51–74. https://doi.org/10.1080/00472336.2012.735545.

World Bank. (2017a). *World development indicators.* http://data.worldbank.org/products/wdi

World Bank. (2017b). *Worldwide governance indicators.* http://data.worldbank.org/data-catalog/worldwide-governance-indicators

Yamada, M. (2010). Peace building and state building of East Timor: What is the role of civil society? *Waseda Studies in Social Sciences, 11*(1), 17–36.

Vietnam: The Socialist Party State

12

© Springer International Publishing AG 2018
A. Croissant, P. Lorenz, *Comparative Politics of Southeast Asia*,
https://doi.org/10.1007/978-3-319-68182-5_12

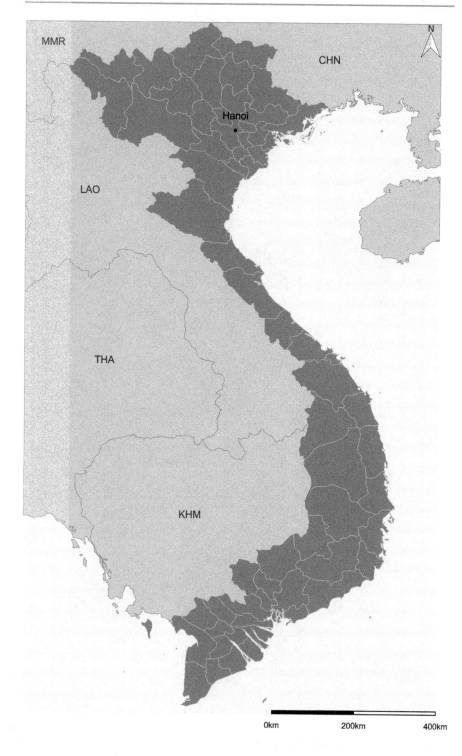

12.1 Historical Background

The Socialist Republic of Vietnam, Vietnam's official name since 1976, is one of five "communist dictatorships" in the world (Dimitrov 2013) that survived the collapse of the Soviet Union. The Communist Party has ruled North Vietnam since 1954 and all of Vietnam since 1975, making it one of the longest ruling parties in the world (see Table 12.1 for the Country Profile).

The origins of Vietnamese ancient statehood are traditionally traced back to the Kingdoms of Aun Lac and Nam Viet, established in the third century BC. Under the Han Dynasty, Nam Viet became a prefecture of China in 111 BC. From the tenth century CE on, a succession of changing dynasties managed to overcome Chinese rule, although Chinese traditions and neo-Confucian state orthodoxy remained prevalent and the bureaucracy of the Kingdom of Dai Viet during the Lê Dynasty (1428–1788) followed the Chinese model (Schirokauer and Clark 2004).

Dai Viet's power was initially limited to northern Vietnam (Tonkin) and parts of central Vietnam (Annam), but expansion at the expense of Cambodia and Champa remained a recurring theme. The southwestern Champa Empire was fully incorporated in 1698, and Sai Gon (then Cambodian) in the Mekong river delta was absorbed in the eighteenth century. Recurrent wars and the decline of the power of the Lê Dynasty meant that competing noble families were the de facto rulers of the northern and southern parts of the country, fragmenting state power (Schirokauer and Clark 2004, pp. 104–106). In the eighteenth century, the Nguyen dynasty took control of the south and—with French aid—expanded its reach to the royal seat of Thang Long (Hanoi) in the north. Under the adopted name Gia Long,

Table 12.1 Country profile Vietnam

Population (2016)	Year of full national sovereignty	Form of government
96,160,163	1954	Republic
Total area	**Current constitution enacted**	**Head of state**
331,210 km^2	1992 (latest amendment 2016)	Tran Dai Quang (since 2016)
GDP p.c. (PPP, 2015)	**Official language**	**Head of government**
6034.3	Vietnamese	Nguyen Xuan Phuc (since 2016)
Ethnic groups	**Democracy score (BTI 2016)**	**System of government**
Kinh (Viet) 85.7%, Tay 1.9%, Thai 1.8%, Muong 1.5%, Khmer 1.5%, Mong 1.2%, Nung 1.1%, others 5.3%	3.52 (range from 1 to 10, higher scores indicate higher levels of democracy)	Semi-presidential government
Religious groups	**Regime type**	**Cabinet type**
Buddhist 7.9%, Catholic 6.6%, Hoa Hao 1.7%, Others 1.9%, none 81.8%	Party regime	Single party

Sources: CIA (2017), World Bank (2017a)

Nguyen Anh proclaimed the Empire of Viet Nam in 1802 and founded the new capital in Hue in central Vietnam.

Vietnamese unification under Nguyen collided with French expansion into Indochina. French troops occupied Da Nang, then Saigon (today Ho Chi Minh City, HCMC) and neighboring provinces in 1858 and 1862, and forced the Nguyen Emperor to relinquish sovereignty over all of South Vietnam to France in 1874. Furthermore, Annam and Tonkin became French protectorates in 1882. Unlike in the south, now called Cochin China, where the French established direct rule, these protectorates remained under the nominal sovereignty of the Vietnamese court. However, the emperor and his Confucian mandarins were subject to oversight by a French governor-general in Hanoi, who also oversaw Cambodia and Laos (Schirokauer and Clark 2004, p. 111).

As in other parts of the French colonial dominion, economic relations between France and the colonies in Indochina were based on the exploitation of local resources under a repressive labor regime, the opening of domestic markets for French products, and the excessive taxation of local peasants (Brocheux and Hémery 2011, pp. 116–118). Colonial misgovernment, corruption in the old but powerless Vietnamese bureaucracy, excessive taxation, and poverty and misery among the peasantry resulted in social unrest and localized protest. Even though several reformist movements emerged at the turn of the twentieth century, France failed to cooperate with Vietnamese constitutionalists who sought political and social reforms. French repression of conservative anticolonial movements and bourgeois political organizations unintentionally strengthened the communist movement, which gained strong support from workers and the urban intelligentsia. The French suppressed the Yên Bái mutiny of 1930, but it indicated a failure of the policy of forcible depoliticization (Brocheux and Hémery 2011, pp. 292–294).

In February 1930, the Communist Party of Indochina united with the Communist Party of Annam and the Communist League of Indochina to establish the Communist Party of Vietnam. Under the leadership of Nguyen Tat Thanh, later known as Ho Chi Minh, the party transformed itself into the Indochinese Communist Party in October 1930 in order to reach out to the whole of French Indochina, including Cambodia and Laos. Even though the French government sought to suppress communist agitation, the party was able to resume clandestine operations, first from China and finally from a base within Vietnam itself (Blanc 2004). Japanese occupation in July 1941 and the collaboration of the Vichy government gave the Communists the chance to become the dominant force in the anticolonial movement. The party founded the League for Vietnamese Independence (Viet Minh), which started a revolutionary insurgency in March 1945 and quickly gained full control over all of Vietnam. Shortly after the Japanese surrender, Ho Chi Minh proclaimed the Democratic Republic of Vietnam (DRV) in Hanoi on September 2, 1945. Unwilling to give up on its colonial empire, French troops took control over the south, but the Provisional Government of the French Republic had to recognize the DRV as a sovereign state within the French Union.

In December 1946, fighting broke out between French and communist troops. The French-Vietnamese or First Indochina War lasted until French troops were decisively defeated by the Viet Minh in the battle of Dien Bien Phu in 1954 (Tucker 1999, pp. 48–50). Negotiations between France and the DRV government without participants from South Vietnam resulted in the Geneva Accords. Under the Accords, Vietnam was to remain separated at the 17th parallel, the troops of both sides were to be withdrawn, and a supervisory commission would be put in place to oversee countrywide elections (Stockwell 1999, p. 43). Yet the elections never took place because the government of South Vietnam (officially the Republic of Vietnam) under President Ngo Dinh Diem refused to participate. North and South Vietnam remained separated, and while the north followed the political and economic lead of the Soviet Union and China, the south came under American influence.

The Communist Party (renamed the Workers Party of Vietnam in 1951) quickly established single-party rule in the north, whereas the anti-communist Diem government in the south was overthrown by its own military in 1963. The Second Indochina or Vietnam War began the following year. After the United States, North Vietnam, and South Vietnam agreed on a complete withdrawal of American troops in the Paris Peace Accords of 1973, the fall of the southern military regime was only a matter of time. When communist troops crossed the demarcation line in March 1975, the Republic of Vietnam collapsed within weeks and the unconditional surrender of the Saigon government on May 1, 1975, paved the way for the unification of North and South Vietnam into the Socialist Republic of Vietnam (SRV) in July 1976.

Overall, communist rule in Vietnam developed in three stages (cf. Dimitrov 2013). During the initial stage of formation and enforcement between 1954 and 1975, the Workers' Party of Vietnam implemented an orthodox socialist program in the north, including the nationalization of banking and industries, the collectivization of agriculture, and the introduction of a centrally planned economy. The party promulgated a socialist constitution in 1959 (Hill 2008, p. 333). With Chinese support and accompanying national mass campaigns, purges within the party, and the establishment of local party organizations in all parts of the country, the institutionalization of a communist party state was completed by the mid-1960s (Vuving 2013). The socialist system embodied five key principles: (1) the party's monopoly on power; (2) striving to become a sovereign and strong nation based on rapid socioeconomic development and establishing a rudimentary but universal system of healthcare and education; (3) state control of the means of production; (4) centralized economic planning; and (5) political mobilization of the masses by the party and its front organizations. However, the party's claim to legitimacy did not only rest on its communist ideology. Rather, anti-colonialism, nationalism, and patriotism were important co-determinants of regime legitimacy (Vasavakul 1995, p. 288). At the same time, a system of collective leadership and power-sharing among different groups within the Workers' Party averted the development of a personalist dictatorship similar to Stalin's in the Soviet Union or Chairman Mao's in China (Vasavakul 1995, pp. 263–264).

The second stage of regime consolidation from 1975 until 1986 saw the implementation of North Vietnam's communist system in South Vietnam. Land was collectivized and private enterprises and market activity nearly eliminated. The communist institutions of governance were extended to the south, and the Workers' Party of North Vietnam was merged with the People's Revolutionary Party of South Vietnam and renamed the Communist Party of Vietnam (CPV). Furthermore, levels of repression were high and real or supposed political opponents and representatives of the old regime sent to reeducation camps. Following the armed conflict with China after the Vietnamese invasion of Cambodia in 1978, the regime's foreign policy leaned exclusively on the Soviet Union. The revolutionary transformation of South Vietnam's economy ended in fiasco and was met by fierce local resistance: Until 1985, only a quarter of agricultural land was collectivized (Schirokauer and Clark 2004, p. 420). Furthermore, more than 1.6 million southerners, including many of the educated, economic, and bureaucratic elites, fled the country. This and the reduction of foreign aid from other communist countries further deepened the economic crisis in Vietnam.

The identity crisis of the Communist Party that followed national unification and the failure of its orthodox policies in the south as well as the worsening economic supply crisis threatened to expand into a crisis of the whole regime. Party elites therefore began to rethink their economic policy in the late 1970s (Vasavakul 2006, p. 377). As a result, the Sixth Party Congress in 1986 announced the *doi moi* or renovation policy, which signaled the shift from revolutionary to bureaucratic rule, the adoption of market mechanisms, and the transition from a centrally planned economy to a multi-sectoral economy based on different types of ownership, private property rights, and open-door policies towards foreign direct investment (Vuving 2013). Under this mixed economic system, private, state-owned, and joint venture companies with foreign investment coexist today (Mensel 2012, pp. 286, 453).

Under the new "socialist-oriented market economy," as Article 51 (1) of the 2014 Constitution describes it, Vietnam's economy grew an average of 6.9% annually, and per capita GDP quadrupled between 1986 and 2012 (Fig. 12.1). Despite rising horizontal, territorial, and vertical inequalities, economic growth quickly improved the livelihood of vast segments of the populace. On indicators like life expectancy, infant mortality, education level, and reduction of absolute poverty, Vietnam scores significantly better than most other countries at similar income levels (London 2004, p. 132; Besley and Kudamatsu 2007). So far, the party has successfully adapted to economic changes and resulting social pressures, co-opted new societal and economic elites, and introduced new mechanisms of elite coordination without giving up on the fundamental "three noes": no political pluralism, no political opposition outside of the party, and no multiparty system (London 2014; Vu 2014).

Nevertheless, rapid economic modernization and social change constitute challenges to which Vietnam's authoritarian regime must adapt. The first challenge concerns deepening problems of social and economic inequality—horizontally between different ethnic groups, geographically between prospering and economically less successful provinces, and vertically between upper and lower income groups (London 2004; Dixon 2004; Jandl 2013). Another challenge concerns the

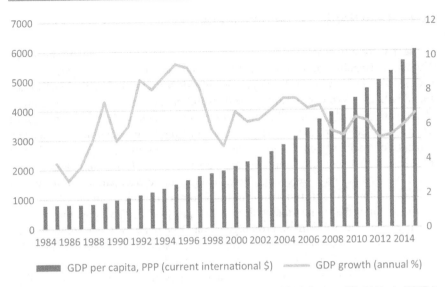

Fig. 12.1 Economic growth and income in Vietnam, 1984–2015. Source: World Bank (2017a)

impact of economic diversification between public sector, private sector, and domestic–foreign partnership companies that have corrosive effects on elite cohesion and the ability of the Workers' Party's sociopolitical and socio-professional organizations and mass associations to organize, control, and integrate different social communities into the political system in accordance with the party's principles (Elliott 2012; Vu 2014, p. 36). As a result, new cleavages based on different economic or provincial backgrounds have emerged inside the Workers' Party, which are increasingly difficult to reconcile. Fragmentation of center–periphery relations, centrifugal tendencies in the more successful provinces, and the rise of rent-seeking elites inside the state and mixed economy pose problems for the central government to control and coordinate subordinate units (Vuving 2013). Some experts believe these are signs of "institutional decay" (Vu 2014) or represent a systemic political crisis (Fforde 2013). The third challenge concerns the party's search for new or additional ways to legitimize its monopoly on government. Until the 1980s, the party based its claim to legitimacy on its struggle against imperialism and foreign domination as well as communist ideology. By the 1990s, collective leadership, rule of law, and continuous economic growth while maintaining social equality became the new rationale for regime legitimacy. After more than three decades of economic reforms, widening economic disparities, and the loss of ideological appeal, the party leadership has sought to find new sources of political legitimacy. This includes emphasizing the patriotic services of the party, the proclamation of "Ho Chi Minh Thought"—a blend of Marxism–Leninism and nationalism—as the official state ideology, and more pragmatic notions of good governance and social stability and cohesion, all of which have become important pillars of the communist regime (Thayer 2010, p. 427; Le Hiep 2012, p. 145).

12.2   Constitutional Development

Vietnam's constitutional development began with the 1946 Constitution of the Democratic Republic of Vietnam (1946 Constitution) and can be divided into two phases.[1] The first phase of development towards a socialist constitutional model started with the 1946 Constitution. The constitutional text reflected Ho Chi Minh's attempts to create a national liberation front, which would include non-communist groups (Sidel 2008, pp. 27–28). Most importantly, the 1946 Constitution lacked key elements of socialist constitutions, such as references to Marxism–Leninism, a socialist-planned economy, and the vanguard role of the Communist Party. Only the 1959 Constitution gave constitutional expression to Vietnam's turn towards a planned economy, the institutionalization of communist rule in the north, and the abandonment of the front strategy (Sidel 2008, pp. 45–46). The Constitution of the Socialist Republic of Vietnam, promulgated on December 18, 1980, completed the institutionalization of the socialist constitutional model. It followed the 1977 Constitution of the Soviet Union and was the first document to declare the Communist Party "the force leading the State and society" (Art. 4; Hill 2008, p. 337).

In the late 1980s, the second phase of reforms began, namely the switch from an orthodox socialist constitution to a hybrid or socialist reform constitution. The 1992 Constitution first appeared as an amendment of the 1980 Constitution but was later adopted as a new constitution. It reflects the shift from an orthodox socialist state and the reform spirit of the *doi moi* reforms. Amendments in 2001 and 2013 brought the constitutional system in line with the ongoing economic and social changes without fully abandoning the notion of a socialist constitution. Most importantly, the constitution refers to a "socialist-oriented market economy" (Art. 15.1) and discusses the ideas of Ho Chi Minh in its preamble. Furthermore, it states that the Communist Party is one of the leading forces, but not the leading force. The constitution also reformed the relationship between state and party and adopted a parliamentary system of government with an indirectly elected president as head of state and a prime minister elected by parliament as head of government. The constitution also introduced property right guarantees, a bill of rights, and the idea of "socialist rule of law" (Art. 2; Dixon 2004, p. 21; Nguyen 2012, p. 3).

A series of constitutional reforms in the 2000s empowered the National Assembly and other state organs of horizontal accountability—such as the procurator general—by reorganizing relations between central and provincial governments and introducing new regulations concerning the national economic order and the enforcement of constitutionalism and rule of law in Vietnam (Sidel 2008, pp. 24–26). Additional constitutional amendments followed in August 2011. In November 2013, the National Assembly passed amendments for 101 of the 115 articles of the 1992 Constitution, added 12 new articles, and left only seven articles unchanged. Even though the constitutional reform process lacked democratic legitimacy as the ruling party remained in control from beginning to end, it

---

[1]South Vietnam also had three constitutions, proclaimed in 1956, 1964, and 1967, respectively.

contained some participatory elements. The draft was published online to subject it to public discussion, and citizens were invited to comment on the constitution. This provoked many submissions, including a petition from 72 public intellectuals for fundamental democratic reforms, commonly referred to as "Petition 72," which was supported by 15,000 signatories (Nicholson 2016, p. 201; Thayer 2014b, p. 362).

The new constitution came into effect on January 1, 2014. It has 11 chapters and 120 articles. The preamble proclaims the Communist Party's role in the national liberation struggle under the leadership of Ho Chi Minh, whereas Chap. 1 (Art. 1–13) establishes the core principles of Vietnam's political and socioeconomic order. The following three chapters concern human rights and the fundamental rights and duties of citizens (Art. 14–49), the economic system, social life, culture, education, science and technology, and the environment (Art. 50–63) as well as defense and national security (Art. 64–68). Chapters 5 through 9 address the National Assembly (Art. 69–85), the presidency (Art. 86–93), the government (Art. 94–101), the judiciary (Art. 102–109), and local administration (Art. 110–116). The last two chapters establish the National Election Council and the State Audit Office (Art. 117–118) as well as the constitutional amendment process (Art. 119–120).

Overall, the constitution is a peculiar mixture of liberal constitutionalism with its focus on limiting state power and protecting rights and liberties, and socialist constitutional principles (Nguyen 2012, p. 9). The liberal innovations include a stronger emphasis on the rule of law and constitutionalism (Art. 2, 4, 9, 119), whereas the commitment to Marxism–Leninism as the ideological basis of the sociopolitical order and state ownership of land (Art. 53) constitute important remnants of the socialist system. A large number of declaratory regulations with uncertain normative content and diffuse implementation resonate with the forward-looking character of other socialist constitutions (Brunner 1978; Grimm 2013, pp. 128–129). The CPV is still considered the "vanguard of the working class" and the Vietnamese nation and is said to "faithfully" represent their interests (Art. 4). For the first time, the constitution explicitly declares that the loyalty of the People's Army and the revolutionary People's Public Security Force is to the Communist Party (Art. 65). Article 9 grants the Vietnam Fatherland Front (VFF) and the five major mass organizations of the Communist Party a monopoly on representation and a privileged position in the sociopolitical system. Finally, "democratic centralism" remains the core organizational principle of the party, the state, and all communist mass organizations (Art. 8).

12.3 System of Government and the Socialist Party State

Vietnam is a one-party regime. Following unification in 1975, the Soviet-style dual structure of party and state (Brooker 1995) that North Vietnam adopted after 1945 was applied to the whole country. Similar to Laos and other socialist countries, the party state is still the institutional blueprint for today's political system. Through its network of party organizations in all administrative units and the dual function of party cadres as party representatives and state officials, the CPV has complete

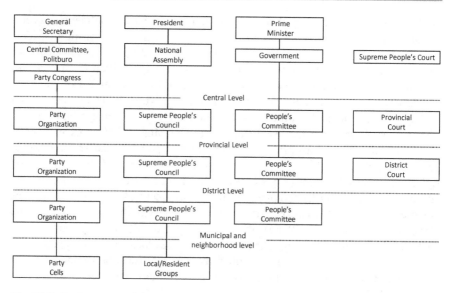

Fig. 12.2 Dual structure of the party state in Vietnam. Source: Authors' compilation

control and authority over politics. In addition, the Central Committee of the Communist Party and the CPV's Politburo are the supreme decision-making bodies (Fig. 12.2).

Nominally, the National Assembly is the highest state body. Its 500 members are elected every 5 years by a majority two-round system. President and prime minister wield executive authority and the Council of Ministers serves as the cabinet. The president is head of state; the prime minister leads the government. Judicial power rests with the courts and the supreme people's prosecutor of Vietnam.

Under the constitution, the National Assembly is the sole state organ that has constitutional and legislative rights. It elects the president and prime minister and confirms other members of the cabinet, the chief justice of the Supreme People's Court, and the procurator general. More than 90% of National Assembly members are CPV members. Only about a quarter of MPs are full-time legislators, and the Assembly meets only twice a year. Since parliament is only in session in the spring and fall of each year, the Standing Committee of the National Assembly is a powerful organ, though its powers and prestige have varied throughout the years. It consists of the speaker, four deputies, and the chairpersons of the ten expert committees as well as the leaders of the parliamentary volunteer service, the office for legislative affairs, and the secretariat of the National Assembly. The committee can propose members for other committees and the State Audit Office and interprets the constitution, while the speaker of parliament conducts the constitutional amendment procedure. The chair of the Standing Committee acts as the primary conduit for party guidance and shepherds a legislative body whose members are almost exclusively CPV members but who demand an increasingly independent role in legislative drafting, oversight, and constituent service.

From 1980 until 1992, the members of the Council of State, as the Standing Committee was formerly known, served as a collective presidency. The 1992 Constitution returned Vietnam to the system of a dual executive consisting of president and prime minister that had been abandoned in 1980 (Vasavakul 2006, p. 382). The president of the republic is the head of state and is elected from among the members of the National Assembly for a 5-year term. While there is no constitutional term limit, the president de facto serves a maximum of two consecutive terms. The state president can introduce legislation, is commander-in-chief of the People's Armed Forces, and chairs the National Defense and Security Council, the equivalent of China's Central Military Commission. She or he promulgates laws and ordinances, has the power of amnesty, and nominates candidates for other important state offices, including the offices of the vice president and the prime minister. Like the president, the prime minister is necessarily a member of the National Assembly, which elects him or her and to which he or she is accountable. The prime minister directs the work of the cabinet, nominates government ministers, and appoints the chairs of People's Committees of provinces and cities under the authority of the central government (Art. 114). The prime minister also controls the Department of Organization and Personnel, allowing him or her to fill positions in the state administration without consulting party bodies (Malesky et al. 2011, p. 352). Administrative reforms that followed the initiation of the renovation policy in 1986 strengthened the positions of the prime minister, cabinet ministers, and ministries of the central government vis-à-vis other party units. For example, since 2006 the prime minister no longer requires the permission of the party to ask parliament to dismiss the chairs of People's Committees (Abrami et al. 2013, p. 257). While party units are responsible for ideological indoctrination and oversight at all state levels, they have no authority over personnel decisions and cannot overrule decisions by the government or administrative agency in charge.

While Vietnam's party state shares basic similarities with other socialist states like Laos or the People's Republic of China, there are two important differences. The first is the existence of a "power troika," consisting of the general secretary of the Central Committee of the CPV, the prime minister, and the state president. The balance of power between these three different offices—which are never occupied by a single person alone (Table 12.2)—provides for a system of collective leadership and responsibility, but also creates a cumbersome, consensus-driven decision-making process that is constantly criticized by Vietnam's political and business elite as frustratingly slow.

The second unique feature of Vietnam's party state concerns the growing stature of the National Assembly. From 1962 to 1981, the National Assembly was officially suspended, allowing the Ministry of Justice, the president, and the government to issue laws by decree. Overall, 8914 documents with the force of law were released between 1945 and 1986. Of these, only 62 were formal acts of parliament; the rest consisted of "sub-law documents" like presidential instructions or government and ministerial decrees (Abuza 2001, p. 96). In the past two decades or so, the National Assembly and its members have increasingly demanded a more independent role in legislative drafting, oversight, and constituent service. While the

Table 12.2 Presidents, Prime Ministers, and CPV General Secretaries in Vietnam since 1960

CPV General Secretary	President	Prime Minister/Chairmen of the Council of Ministers
Le Duan (1960–1986)	Ton Duc Thang (1976–1980)	Pham Van Dong (1976–1987)
Truong Chinh (1986)	Truong Chinh[a] (1981–1987)	Pham Hung (1987–1988)
Nguyen Van Linh (1986–1991)	Vo Chi Cong[a] (1987–1992)	Vo Van Kiet (1988)
Do Muoi (1991–1997)	Lee Duc Anh (1992–1997)	Do Muoi (1988–1991)
Le Kha Phieu (1997–2001)	Tran Duc Luong (1997–2006)	Vo Van Kiet (1991–1997)
Nong Due Manh (2001–2011)	Nguyen Minh Triet (2006–2011)	Phan Van Khai (1997–2006)
Nguyen Phu Trong (2011–)	Truong Tan Sang (2011–2016) Tran Dai Quang (2016–)	Nguyen Tan Dung (2006–2016) Nguyen Xuan Phuc (2016–)

[a]Chairman of the Council of State
Source: Authors' compilation

government and party are still dominant in the political process, the National Assembly has asserted its authority in vetoing some decisions by the CPV Politburo (Abrami et al. 2013, p. 247). Much unlike the parliaments in Laos or Singapore, the assembly even turned down major government projects like the construction of a high-speed train connection between Ho Chi Minh City and Hanoi for USD56 billion in 2006 or the passage of the so-called Capital Law in 2011 (Malesky et al. 2011, p. 344; Bergstermann and Geiger 2011). Parliamentary committees have also helped the government gauge the feasibility of specific policy projects (Schuler and Malesky 2014, p. 681). In addition, a number of new parliamentary tools to scrutinize executive orders and projects have been introduced since 2001, including live televised Q&A sessions between members of parliament and members of the Cabinet and votes of no confidence against the state president, the prime minister, and 45 other senior government officials (Thayer 2014b, p. 355). If an official fails to gain a confidence vote by the majority of members of parliament for two consecutive votes, he or she must step down. The secret ballots thus give MPs an opportunity to express discontent with government policy or the official conduct of individual ministers (Malesky 2014).

However, it is important to note that the National Assembly's evolution is not a move away from one-party rule or a party-dominated system. Just as state bureaucracies are assuming an increasing degree of autonomy in the day-to-day management of government, so too is the National Assembly taking on a greater oversight role. Yet ultimately, both the executive and the legislative branches are dominated by the CPV. Discussions of important policies are not public, even though in most cases they are simply rubber-stamp decisions already made by the Politburo. Still, these mechanisms are relevant for the political system, just like the authoritarian legislature is an important channel for co-optation (Schuler and Malesky 2014).[2] At times, the Politburo uses the parliamentary plenum as a forum to test policy proposals on which it cannot reach consensus within itself. Delegates can make statements or direct petitions to committees or government agencies, and they can also draw material gain from their status if they establish connections with corporations or investors (cf. TRUEX 2014). In addition, the National Assembly provides the government with important feedback about the feasibility of their political plans. The relatively high degree of political competition among electoral candidates in contested districts is an important incentive for them to distinguish themselves as advocates of local interests. This has greatly improved the position of regional interests and, among other things, resulted in a relatively well-developed system of vertical redistribution (Malesky et al. 2011).

12.4 Parties and Party System

Modern political parties began to emerge in Vietnam in the early twentieth century, but the French colonial authorities vehemently tried to suppress any form of organized nationalist movement, including left-wing and conservative political parties (Brocheux and Hémery 2011, pp. 281–282). In the regime of South Vietnam, political organizations unified under the communist-led *Front National de Libération* (FNL) became subject to heavy-handed repression. Non-communist groups not yet destroyed by the military junta in Saigon were forced to dissolve when the Communists took power in 1975. Originally, the SRV government tolerated a few satellite parties (Le Hiep 2014, p. 351), but since 1988 the CPV is the only legal political party in Vietnam.

The Communist Party of Vietnam traces its lineage back to the Revolutionary Youth League, founded in 1925 by representatives of the Soviet-dominated Communist International (Comintern) and Vietnamese nationalists led by Ho Chi Minh in southern China. The actual Communist Party of Vietnam was founded in Hong Kong in 1930 and was immediately renamed the Indochinese Communist Party. Officially disbanded in 1945, it survived French repression in the post-World War II years as the clandestine Association of Marxist Study Groups and was again renamed the Workers' Party of Vietnam in 1951. In 1976 after the end of the Vietnam War, the Workers' Party and the Communist People's Revolutionary Party of South Vietnam merged into the CPV (Thayer 1998, pp. 455–456).

The CPV nominally exists alongside the Vietnamese Fatherland Front, an umbrella group of pro-government mass movements founded in 1955 as a

---

[2]This effect is, of course, weaker in a parliament with no opposition than in multiparty legislatures (Gandhi 2008). Moreover, the mass organizations of the party, the structural amalgamation of party and state, and the alignment of cadre and economic interests provide a more effective way to allocate economic rents than the National Assembly (Schuler and Malesky 2014).

replacement for the North Vietnamese National Popular Front (Abuza 2001, p. 20). The CPV is a Leninist cadre party modeled after the Communist Party of the Soviet Union (CPSU). Even though the party has amended its charter several times, its three core organizational principles have remained unchanged: (1) democratic centralism as the key decision-making practice and disciplinary policy; (2) monolithic unity of the party with strict party discipline and a ban on factions; and (3) collective leadership. Previously a party of workers and peasants, since 2006 party members can become entrepreneurs, and business owners can apply for membership in line with the adoption of a "multi-sectoral economy" into the charter that same year (Koh 2012, pp. 366–367). In fact, private entrepreneurs have increasingly applied for party membership, and the CPV enjoys a steady supply of new members since party affiliation is still required of all state employees and is necessary for a career in state-owned enterprises. With about 3.6 million current members in 54,000 basic units (sometimes referred to as primary cells), basic party organizations (also known as primary party organizations), party chapters, and party organizations, membership has increased by almost 70% since 1996 (Thayer 1998; Koh 2012). The socio-demographic diversification of party membership and its leadership—regarding provincial, sectoral, and occupational backgrounds—is one indicator that the CPV is no longer the unified organization it once was. The most serious cleavages in its leadership concern the ideological goal of socialism and communism, differences in strategies to cope with China ("anti-China" and "China-friendly" factions), and economic issues ("conservative" and "reform" factions), whereas there appears to be little if any support among party leaders for political liberalization or democratization.

The formal party organization is similar to most other communist parties. Primary cells of three to ten members form the base organizations at the local level. They exist in every sector of the state, including the state administration, state-owned enterprises, and the military. District-level and provincial-level party committees form the second level. The National Party Congress is the supreme party organ (Abuza 2001, p. 18). Due to the ongoing wars against French troops and South Vietnamese-US troops, the first four Party Congresses did not follow a common time schedule. Since 1976, a Party Congress has been held every 5 years. The delegates consist of lower party units and members of the party's Central Committee as ex officio members. Provincial party committees, mass organizations, and party chapters of different sectors such as the military, state administration, government apparatus, and state-owned enterprises nominate the delegates (Abrami et al. 2013). The National Party Congress determines the party line and thereby the domestic and foreign policy of the regime. It accepts the accountability report of the Central Committee and the report of the party's Central Control Commission, can change the charter of the party, and elects the Central Committee, whose Politburo is the highest decision-making body of the CPV outside of the National Congress (Thayer 1998; Vasavakul 2006). In practice, however, delegates have very limited actual political influence because the party's executive committees prepare all political decisions ahead of time (Gainsborough 2010, pp. 138–140). Consequently, the National Congress serves mostly as an instrument of legitimation for the party leadership, to integrate sectoral, regional, and ideological interests and party wings, and to provide delegates with access to patronage and political protection.

As in other communist party states, the Central Committee and the Politburo of the Central Committee are the core power centers of the CPV. However, in contrast to other ruling socialist parties such as the communist parties of the former Soviet Union, China, and Cuba, the Central Committee is relatively strong vis-à-vis the Politburo (Abrami et al. 2013). The Central Committee of the CPV holds at least one plenary session every six months, and there were 61 plenary sessions between 1982 and 2010, compared to only 36 in China (Abrami et al. 2013, p. 251), indicating a much larger institutional significance. In the plenums, the Politburo and the general secretary of the Central Committee determine the party's policy. In the aftermath of a Party Congress, the Central Committee elects the members of the new Politburo and its general secretary. It maintains several sections in charge of different party affairs and political departments, of which the Commission of Internal Affairs is the most important body as it supervises party discipline and party cadres' adherence to the party line (Thayer 1998; Abuza 2001).

The Central Committee selected at the Twelfth Party Congress in 2016 has 180 full members and 20 alternate members (Table 12.3). The alternate members (also known as candidates) participate in plenary sessions in an advisory function. Until 2011, the Politburo nominated and the National Congress confirmed full members and candidates for the incoming Central Committee. Starting in 2011, party members could nominate themselves (Koh 2012, p. 362). As a result, the number of applicants during the Eleventh Congress exceeded the number of seats by almost 25% for the full and 44% for alternate members. While most of those ultimately selected had been nominated in the traditional way, delegates withheld confirmation for six serving ministers and one member of the Politburo (Koh 2012, p. 363). The 2016 Congress returned to the old system of predetermined nominations, under which candidates succeed if they are supported by at least two-thirds of the delegates (Case 2016).

The general secretary of the Central Committee is the highest party office and is also the secretary of the Party's Central Military Commission, and while he or she issues party directives, the position holds no autonomous decision-making authority (Mensel 2012, p. 141). Unlike the Chinese Communist Party under Mao Zedong (1943–1976) and the CPSU under Stalin, Ho Chi Minh only served as general secretary between 1956 and 1960. Consequentially, this position holds less power in Vietnam than in other communist states. When Ho Chi Minh transferred the office of the general secretary to Le Duan (1960–1986), the 1960 Party Congress reaffirmed the collective leadership of the party by the Central Committee and Politburo. This precluded a crisis of leadership after Ho Chi Minh's death in 1969 and kept the party from degenerating into an instrument of personalist rule. Rather, the office of the general secretary is limited to two terms (Vasavakul 2006, p. 403; Gainsborough 2010, p. 141). In addition, since the Sixth Party Congress in 1986, all provinces are represented in the Central Committee and provincial cadres today make up about 60% of the whole body (Abrami et al. 2013).

The Politburo selected by the Twelfth Central Committee at the 2016 Party Congress has 19 members. While the Standing Committee of the Politburo has

Table 12.3 Central committee and Politburo of the CPV, 1930–2016 (full members)

	Term of office	Politburo	Central committee
I. Party Congress	1930–1951	5	13
II. Party Congress	1951–1960	12	19
III. Party Congress	1960–1976	10	47
IV. Party Congress	1976–1982	14	101
V. Party Congress	1982–1986	14	116
VI. Party Congress	1986–1991	13	124
VII. Party Congress	1991–1996	13	146
VIII. Party Congress	1996–2001	19	170
IX. Party Congress	2001–2006	15	150
X. Party Congress	2006–2011	14	160
XI. Party Congress	2011–2016	16	175
XII. Party Congress	2016-	19	180

Source: Thayer (1988, p. 187, 2013, p. 66, 2014a, p. 137, 2015)

become the actual power center of the Communist Party in China, in Vietnam, it only existed between 1996 and 2001 before it was abolished again (Abrami et al. 2013, p. 249). Finally, the Central Committee can overrule the Politburo. Although this is rare, it does occur. For example, in June 2001, the Central Committee refused to approve a second term in office for the unpopular General Secretary Le Kha Phieu after months of ideological struggles between conservatives and reformers and instead nominated the reformer Nong Duc Manh (Abuza 2001; Malesky et al. 2011, p. 348; Thayer 2014b, p. 357).

12.5 Judicial and Legal System

Vietnam's precolonial legal system was strongly influenced by China and is a mix of traditional and indigenous elements (Nguyen and Ta 1987). The Lê-Codex, a legal canon introduced by the Lê Dynasty in the fifteenth century, followed Chinese legal conceptions of the Tang and Ming Dynasty. Under the Nguyen emperors, the codex was reformed following the example of the Qing Dynasty (1644–1912; Gillespie 2017, pp. 39–41). Under French rule, two legal systems coexisted. French law applied in Cochinchina, urban centers like Hanoi, and for all French citizens. Vietnamese citizens were subject to the precolonial legal regime unless it conflicted with French law. Moreover, "natives" in Cochin China and Tonkin but not Annam could voluntarily submit to French law (Gillespie 2017, pp. 49–50). The Communists replaced this hybrid system with a socialist legal order. Following the principles of Marxist–Leninist legal theory, the judiciary was meant to execute the will of the ruling class (Sidel 2008).

Since 1986, the legal system is in a state of transition. The shift from a socialist to a post-socialist legal order is accompanied by a broad constitutional dialogue that found expression in the constitutional concept of a "socialist state ruled by law"

(Art. 2, 1992 Constitution). To support economic reforms, Vietnam adopted international legal standards regarding contract, tax, and corporate law, improved property right protections, and introduced a civil law code. Criminal, administrative, procedural, and environmental law also saw improvements. Vietnam's accession to the World Trade Organization in 2007 also promoted the process of economic juridification (Gillespie 2006; Hill 2008; Nguyen 2013). Already in the 1990s, the party began an internal debate about the need to establish an independent judiciary as an effective tool against corruption and to strengthen the regime's legitimacy (Gillespie 2006; Sidel 2008). However, a truly independent judiciary is irreconcilable with both the subordination of law under the Marxist–Leninist state ideology and the CPV's status as the vanguard of society. In fact, the constitution affirms the party's control over the courts, contradicting the notion of judicial independence (Art. 70, 88, 105). Consequently, the "socialist state ruled by law" remains an oxymoron that tries to integrate two mutually exclusive concepts (Sidel 2008; Nguyen 2012; see also Grimm 2013, p. 129). Even though the constitution requires the state to respect the law, recognize freedom of expression and other basic rights, and guarantees a fair trial (Art. 16, 24, 25, 31, 102, and 103), the exercise of these rights may not infringe upon the national interest (Art. 15). Furthermore, these rights can be limited for reasons of "national defense, national security, social order and safety, social morality and community well-being" (Art. 14).

The judiciary consists of three tiers: district, province, and national (Supreme People's Court). There are also three appeals courts located in three regions of Vietnam. A separate procuratorate is organized in parallel to the court system, following the Soviet model. Finally, there is a separate system of military courts. The establishment of a constitutional court or council was debated in 2013 but was ultimately rejected (Nicholson 2016). On paper, the National Assembly is charged with the judicial review of laws, but it is in fact exercised by the procurator general. The Ministry of Justice and its local branches are charged with overseeing legal education, but do not have the power to appoint judges or to administer the justice system. The chief justice of the Supreme People's Court and the procurator general are selected by and report to the National Assembly. Judges at the remaining levels of government are appointed for a fixed term of 5 years by the party committee of the same level with the approval of the party committee of the higher level and are all held accountable to party committees at their respective levels (Sidel 2008).

Even though there have been no systematic studies, the judiciary is considered to suffer from corruption, low levels of professional qualifications for court personnel, and a serious shortage of qualified judges (Gillespie 2017; Sidel 2008; Nguyen 2012). It is, therefore, no surprise that conventional indicators of rule of law such as the World Bank's Worldwide Governance Indicators show a weak rule of law and high levels of corruption (World Bank 2017b). The high incidence of corrupt behavior is one of the consequences of Vietnam's poor rule of law record. In recent years, several high-profile corruption cases involved various ministries and state-owned enterprises. The resulting perception that corrupt elites and networks have captured the state and economy presents a particularly urgent problem for the party, as it endangers its "revolutionary morality" (Gillespie 2006, p. 487). It is, therefore, no surprise that the party leadership has repeatedly launched anti-corruption campaigns (Thayer 2014b, p. 357). Furthermore, the National Assembly passed anti-corruption legislation in 2005, and the government established the Anti-Corruption Authority in 2006. The Central Committee of the CPV has also passed several anti-corruption resolutions and guidelines (Koh 2012, p. 370). In contrast to Laos, party cadres have become the target of corruption investigations: The Central Committee's Steering Committee on Prevention and Control of Corruption reported more than 11,500 violations of the party's anti-corruption resolutions in the period 2007–2012, and the Central Committee launched investigations against four of its members and 17 local party secretaries (BTI 2014). At the same time, party inspections were often abused as a means to discredit internal opponents, and collusion between party and state organs impedes the fight against office abuse and patronage practices (Malesky et al. 2011, p. 351). For example, seven of the 16 members of the Anti-Corruption Authority as well as its chairman are also Politburo members. The loyalty of party cadres depends on their access to private goods (i.e., tax breaks, tolerance for corrupt official and business conduct, and immunity from criminal prosecution). Therefore, any serious anti-corruption strategy would threaten the party's ability to co-opt vested and new elites as well as the patronage networks operating at all levels of the political system that hold the party together (Fritzen 2009).

12.6   Electoral System and Elections

Vietnam's first elections to the legislature were held in 1946 in the communist-controlled northern part of the country. The newly elected National Assembly remained in office until 1960. Since then, national representative elections to the legislature were held every 5 years.[3] There is universal suffrage, but elections in the Democratic Republic of Vietnam before 1976 and the Socialist Republic of Vietnam since 1977 have been neither free nor fair and only candidates approved by the Vietnam Fatherland Front are allowed to run for office. In the 2016 elections, 870 candidates stood for election, including 97 nonparty members (down from 118 in 2011) and 11 candidates who were not nominated by state or party agencies (known as self-nominated candidates, down from 15 in 2011). Compared to the 2011 election, the number of nonparty candidates among the elected members of parliament declined from 42 to 21 and the number of self-nominated candidates from four to two (IPU 2016). Overall, the ratio of candidates per seats increased slightly from 1.66 in 2011 to 1.74 in 2016 (cf. Fig. 12.3).

---

[3]There were 13 parliamentary and presidential elections in South Vietnam, all of which were held under irregular conditions and can be considered semi-competitive at best (Wurfel 1967; Hartmann 2001).

Voting is de facto mandatory because on election day, local party cadres and state officials knock on everyone's doors to remind voters to go cast their votes. If someone does not vote, he or she might be denied future services by the local government. However, many voters make use of the right to have others vote for them, which is usually the head of the family (Malesky et al. 2011). This has resulted in almost perfect turnout, for example, 99.35% in 2016 (IPU 2016). In addition to the National Assembly, voters elect the People's Councils at the provincial, district, and local level. Since 2011, national and local elections take place on the same day shortly after the Party Congress. This permits the CPV to select its nominees based on the results of the Party Congress and increases the national party leadership's leverage over provincial party elites (Bergstermann and Geiger 2011).

The not more than 500 members of the National Assembly are elected by a majority two-round system in 184 constituencies. Each of the 63 provinces and cities is divided into two and ten constituencies with one to three seats depending on its population size (Koh 2012). Within each constituency, candidates obtaining more than half of the votes cast are declared elected. If seats are not filled in the first round, a simple majority second round vote takes place among the original candidates. Technically, electors do not vote for candidates per se but cross out the names of the candidates they disapprove of on the ballot (Hartmann 2001).

An interesting contrast between single-party elections in Vietnam and other one-party regimes in Asia such as Laos, North Korea, and China is that in Vietnam, since 1987, there have to be at least two more candidates on the ballot than there are seats to allocate in a district (Porter 2009, pp. 155–156). While it would be naïve to assume that this has led to meaningful political contestation between substantial political alternatives, within the limits of the one-party system, the competitiveness of elections has indeed increased (cf. Fig. 12.3).

Since more than 90% of the candidates are CPV members, and all candidates are screened by the VFF, this means the process of intra-party selection and the nomination of candidates is more important than the actual election (Gainsborough 2005, p. 68). During National Assembly elections, about a quarter of the seats are reserved for candidates nominated by the Politburo, whereas the remainder is filled by provincial party organizations (Gainsborough 2005; Koh 2012, p. 369). The VFF plays a key role in a complex selection process that aims to reconcile the interests of the center and the provinces and to make sure that various sectors and state organs are represented adequately. Local selection committees have to take into account mandatory quotas concerning educational and ethnic backgrounds, gender, place of origin and residence, profession, membership in functional groups, mass organizations, or economic sectors, and so on (Abrami et al. 2013, pp. 270–271). Within these limits, local party leadership is relatively free to propose candidates and express their preferences. The lists of candidates prepared by the VFF are then submitted to the Politburo for approval (Gainsborough 2005, p. 62; Malesky and Schuler 2013, p. 45; Koh 2012, p. 367). Finally, the Election Commission allocates candidates to individual constituencies. Candidates nominated by the Politburo are usually assigned constituencies with a small number of candidates per seat or with little known alternative candidates or constituencies that have a proven record of

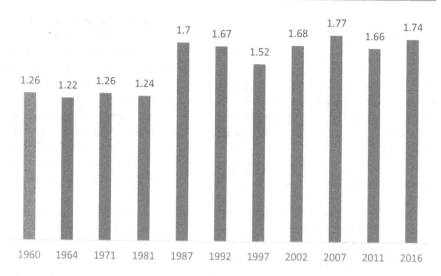

Fig. 12.3 Average number of candidates per seat in Vietnam, 1960–2016. Notes: Data for 1975 and 1976 is missing; Source: Malesky et al. (2011), Gainsborough (2005, p. 69), Koh (2012, p. 368), IPU (2016)

voting for Politburo nominees. Consequently, these positions are considered safe (Gainsborough 2005, pp. 67–69; Malesky et al. 2011; Malesky and Schuler 2013). Nevertheless, 15 candidates nominated by the Politburo failed to win in 2011, by far the highest number to date (Koh 2012, p. 369). In the past, voters also used their ballots to express discontent with government policies. For example, constituencies in provinces that are net contributors to the interprovincial fiscal transfer system have turned down candidates nominated by the Politburo at a much higher rate than provincial constituencies that are net beneficiaries of national transfer payments. According to some observers, this indicates that the degree of fiscal independence from the center has influenced the willingness of provinces to defy national party leadership (Malesky and Paul 2011, p. 520; Malesky et al. 2011).

Obviously, elections play only a minor role for the selection of political leaders as a mechanism of political participation for the citizens and their ability to hold the government accountable for its conduct. Nevertheless, elections can help the ruling party to overcome a universal problem of autocratic rule, described by Wintrobe as the "dictator's dilemma."[4] Turnout rates and the electoral successes or failures of

---

[4]Wintrobe (2009, p. 366) explains the dilemma as follows: "The use of repression of course breeds fear on the part of a dictator's subjects, and this fear breeds reluctance on the part of the citizenry to signal displeasure with the dictator's policies. This fear on their part in turn breeds fear on the part of the dictator, since, not knowing what the population thinks of his policies, he has no way of knowing what they are thinking and planning, and of course he suspects that what they are thinking and planning is his assassination. The problem is magnified the more the dictator rules by repression, i.e., through fear. The more his repressive apparatus stifles dissent and criticism, the less he knows how much support he really has among the population."

prominent candidates provide party leaders with potentially valuable information about the loyalty of local party cadres, their ability to mobilize voters, voter preferences, and the popularity of party candidates and policies. In addition, elections help to identify potential pockets of dissidence, opposition, or even resistance and allow the CPV to spread benefits more effectively, build popular support for the government, and punish disobedient subalterns and disloyal voters (Malesky and Paul 2011, p. 495; Gainsborough 2005, p. 63).

12.7   State Administration and Decentralization

Vietnam is an ethnically diverse society with a decentralized unitary state organization. Ethnic Vietnamese (also known as Kinh) constitute the majority of the population with 85.7% (87% if ethnic Chinese or Hoa are included). The remaining 15% or so are made up of 54 officially recognized ethnic groups (Mensel 2012, p. 193). Administratively, the country is divided into 58 provinces and the cities (also known as municipalities) of Hanoi, Haiphong, Ho Chi Minh City, Da Nang, and Can Tho, which are under the authority of the central government. Provinces consist of provincial cities, districts, and district-level towns, which are subdivided into communes and commune-level towns. Provinces and cities are routinely grouped together into regions for planning purposes.

Similar to Laos, the Vietnamese system of public administration is a case of decentralized authoritarianism. Provincial governments can have significant autonomy because provincial party chiefs are also members of the Central Committee. Top central party leaders are not their superiors, but only *primus inter pares*. The provinces enjoy relatively broad decision-making authority in matters of economic development and, especially, the promotion of (foreign) investment, which is a key source of horizontal competition among the provinces (Jandl 2013). Financially, the central government has great control over provincial budgets through the centralized tax and budget regime. This has helped increase central authority over the provinces but has not been sufficient to reign in the high levels of wasteful spending in many provinces or socioeconomic disparities between affluent and remote provinces (Malesky et al. 2011).

Local People's Councils are selected for 5-year terms and can make decisions in policy areas delegated by the national government, but they have no autonomous legislative authority (CECODES et al. 2014). The Councils appoint People's Committees, which serve as the executive arm of the provincial government and which have the responsibility to formulate and implement policies at the subnational level (Abrami et al. 2013, p. 246). Vietnam's degree of fiscal decentralization is lower than in Laos (cf. Chap. 5) but is still substantial: In 2009, subnational units accounted for 35% of total government revenues and 45% of total government expenditure (Martinez-Vazquez 2011).

According to the International Labor Organisation, Vietnam's public sector accounted for 10.3% of total employment in 2004. Of the 5.5 million public employees, about 200,000 worked for the civilian central government and almost

1.1 million in the subnational government. Furthermore, education and health employees accounted for another 900,000 persons. The police made up 951,000 and the armed forces 484,000. Finally, state-owned enterprises (SOEs) employed 1.9 million workers (UNDP 2004, p. 3).

Provinces differ greatly in their dependence on the nationwide system of vertical financial equalization. Fifteen provinces are net payers. They have to cede about 70% of their revenue to the central government and receive disproportionally less national transfer payments. Most other provinces run a deficit and would be unable to provide basic services without transfer payments (Vo 2005; Malesky et al. 2011). Consequently, considerable discrepancies in terms of income, living conditions, and access to government services remain between provinces and regions. Poverty and underdevelopment disproportionately affect rural and highland regions, the latter of which are home to many minority ethnic groups. The industrial and agricultural zones in the Red River Delta and in the southeast fare much better (Table 12.4).

The Vietnam Provincial Governance and Public Administration Performance Index (PAPI), which measures citizen experiences with central to local governments in terms of governance, public administration, and public service delivery functions calculated along six dimensions, demonstrates that there are substantial differences between provinces and regions in Vietnam (CECODES et al. 2016). Provinces in the Red River Delta and along the central coast achieve the best results; provinces in the poorer regions of the northeast and central highlands score worst. In general, state administration and infrastructure are reasonably well developed, but state penetration of remote regions is incomplete, and corruption and low bureaucratic quality hamper the operation of administrative structures. Furthermore, comparing the PAPI mean scores by dimension from 2011 to 2014 reveals that the overall score has dropped in four of the six dimensions, indicating weaker performance and less citizen satisfaction. The dimensional scores for citizens' participation at local levels and control of corruption showed the steepest decline, whereas public service delivery has improved (CECODES et al. 2016). Other notable findings are that more well-off provinces do not always perform better than poorer provinces and that the relatively affluent cities of Da Nang, HCMC, and Can Tho only achieve mediocre ratings. As the survey indicates, citizens regard corruption in the public administration as a major problem, particularly in the metropolitan areas in the north and south (Tran 2014, p. 44).

12.8   Civil–Military Relations

Civil–military relations in Vietnam, like all the fundamental dynamics of its political system, derive from the structural relationship between the CPV and the other institutions of the polity. Although the Communist Party directs and supervises all other institutions, there is no clear division between civilian party elites and military elites. Furthermore, as in all communist systems, neither civilian party elites nor military elites in Vietnam subscribe to the norm that the military ought to be

Table 12.4 Regional development disparities in Vietnam, 2004–2013[a]

Region	Infant mortality rate		Average life expectancy		Population share	Average monthly p.c. income (1000 Dong)		% of population below national poverty line		FDI (in Mio USD)	Share of national industrial production (in %)
	2005	2013	2005	2013	2013	2004	2012	2004	2013	2013	2013
National	17.8	15.3	72.2	73.1	100	484	2000	18.1	9.8	22,352	100
Red River Delta[a]	11.5	12.2	74.6	74.3	22.7	498	2351	12.7	4.9	6731	20.39
Northwest[b]	26.4	23.2	69.4	70.4	12.8	327	1258	29.4	21.9	3712	2.69
Northeast & central coast[c]	22.4	17	70.7	72.5	21.5	361	1505	25.3	14	6465	10.41
Central Highlands[d]	28.8	26.1	68.7	69.5	6.0	390	1643	29.2	16.2	6.3	0.67
Southeast[e]	10.6	9.1	75.0	75.7	17.2	893	3173	4.6	1.1	4713	44.32
Mekong Delta[f]	14.4	12	73.4	74.4	19.4	471	1797	15.3	9.2	708	9.28

[a]9 provinces, Hanoi and Haiphong
[b]14 provinces
[c]13 provinces plus Da Nang
[d]5 provinces
[e]5 provinces and HCMC
[f]12 provinces and Can Tho
Source: GSOV (2014)

apolitical. In Vietnam, the military's subordination to the political leadership is ensured not by making the military a politically neutral tool, but by politicizing the military and fusing the political and military spheres (Perlmutter and LeoGrande 1982). The Communist Party came to power by waging guerrilla war, first against French colonial rule and, after 1954, against the anti-communist, pro-American government of South Vietnam. This had two important consequences for Vietnam's civil–military relations. First, the Communist Party created the People's Liberation Armed Forces in 1944 (renamed the Vietnamese People's Army in 1950) as a tool for enforcing its claim to power and realizing its ideological and nationalist goals, and not the other way around as in Myanmar and Indonesia, where military leaders established political parties as vehicles for their political hold on power. Second, guerilla war as a form of politico-military combat inevitably led to the fusion of political and military elites and assigned an important role in the construction of a socialist society to the VPA (Vasavakul 2001; Thayer 2013). Whereas communist troops fought the French army as a classic guerilla army, the VPA transformed itself into a conventional force during the Vietnam War with a total strength of up to 1.5 million troops (Thayer 1994). After 1975, the VPA fought two other military campaigns: the intervention in Cambodia from 1978 to 1989 and the Sino-Vietnamese Border War in early 1979. In contrast to most armies in Southeast Asia, the VPA therefore has significant battle experience.

Like in all socialist countries, military service is compulsory in Vietnam. Service obligation for men between 18 and 25 years old is 18 months for the army and air defense and 24 months for the navy and air force. However, military service is de facto selective, as many young men do not enter the military because of tertiary education. Mandatory military service for women was abandoned in 1975, but the requirement that women register for military service was reinstated in 2001. Pre-service military education is mandatory for high school and university students (Thayer 2013, p. 77). Since the 1950s, paramilitary units—called the People's Militia Force in rural and the People's Self-Defense Force in urban areas—exist in all mass organizations, public administrations, and SOEs. Paramilitary units have about five million members and are under the authority of the Ministry of Public Security but are in practice under the control of local party organizations and the People's Councils (IISS 2014, 2017; Thayer 2014a, p. 137).

Vietnam's defense budget is a state secret. According to expert assessments, actual defense spending is much higher than officially announced figures and is estimated to have reached USD3.84 billion in 2015. This represents 7.0% of nominal government spending (IISS 2017). Estimated military expenditure data often do not include civil defense, reserves and auxiliary forces, paramilitary forces, dual-purpose forces such as military and civilian police, military research and development, or income generated by military-owned or managed enterprises (MOEs).

Nevertheless, experts agree that Vietnam has experienced defense retrenchment since the late 1980s, reflecting a mix of different influences: the end of the Cambodia intervention, the drop in foreign military aid by the Soviet Union and other communist countries of Eastern Europe, and a shrinking economy in the late

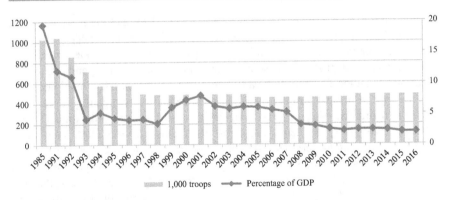

Fig. 12.4 Defense spending and VPA personnel, 1985–2016. Source: IISS (2017), Thayer (2013, p. 70)

1980s. As Fig. 12.4 shows, there was a decline in defense spending from 19.4% of GDP in 1989 to 2.01% in 2016. In comparison to 1985, military personnel strength was reduced by more than half by the year 2016.

Yet, the drop in estimated Vietnamese defense spending as a fraction of GDP from 6.1 in 2005 to 2.0% in 2016 is also the result of a growing economy. In USD, Vietnam's military spending increased by 314% in the decade between 2005 and 2014 (IISS 2017). In order to compensate the VPA for its shrinking budget and to free up resources for military modernization, VPA units gained permission to engage in commercial activities, and MOEs were put on the same legal footing as SOEs (Thayer 2000; Vasavakul 2001, p. 354). Even though the VPA had been continuously engaged in economic affairs since it was founded, the adoption of *doi moi* changed the nature of its economic activities radically, as the People's Army became a commercial actor with distinct commercial interests. MOEs are active in banking, construction, commodity trade, import and export, telecommunications, and real estate. VPA units and MOEs conduct business in neighboring countries like Cambodia and Laos as well as oversees, for example, in Haiti (Thayer 2013, p. 75). Inside Vietnam, the VPA controls economic security zones in geographically remote but strategically important areas where soldiers and their families are settled (Thayer 2013, pp. 73, 82). Official statistics put the business volume of all military corporations at USD11.4 billion and its net profit at USD1.86 billion (Vietnam Business Forum 2014). While the government has increased its efforts to reform MOEs and to regulate military-owned or controlled businesses, the military business complex has further expanded in recent years (Thayer 2013, p. 75). For example, the Military Electronics Telecommunications Corporation (Viettel) is Vietnam's largest mobile network operator and internet service provider and operates telecom services in countries such as Tanzania, Cameroon, and Mozambique (Vietnam Breaking News 2017).

As in all communist political systems, the VPA is the "party in uniform" (Perlmutter and LeoGrande 1982) and accepts the supremacy of the CPV. In fact, the constitution legally binds the VPA to defend socialism and the party (Art. 65). In the 1940s, the party adopted the Soviet model of a dual leadership of military officers and political commissars. In fact, first generation military leaders were party cadres rather than professional soldiers, and until today, party membership is a necessary condition for a military career (Vasavakul 2001, p. 341). In addition, the existing system of dual military oversight by state and party organs forms another effective instrument to ensure the military's loyalty and subordination (Thayer 2013, p. 68). The president is commander-in-chief of the VPA and—since 1997—oversees the General Department of Military Intelligence, which is responsible for both internal and external intelligence and is an official department of the Ministry of National Defence although it reports directly to the CPV and the state president. While a full general leads the ministry, the Central Military Commission, chaired by the general secretary and monitored by the Politburo, is the highest party organ for military policy and the key decision-making forum for all matters of defense policy, national security, and military affairs. Furthermore, the People's Army, like other functional groups, enjoys representation in the National Assembly, in People's Councils, and at the Party Congress. Senior military officers also sit in the Central Committee and the Politburo of the VPC. However, the number of military members in both party organs has dropped in recent decades (Fig. 12.5). In the 12th Party Congress in 2016, the police for the first time gained greater representation in the Politburo at the expense of the military—there are currently four former or current police generals compared to only one military general.

As in most authoritarian regimes, the military is the ultimate guardian of regime survival in Vietnam. The government's Vietnam Defence White Paper 2004 states that defense against counterrevolutionary attempts to exact a "peaceful evolution" (the party euphemism for attempts to end one-party rule in Vietnam) of the political

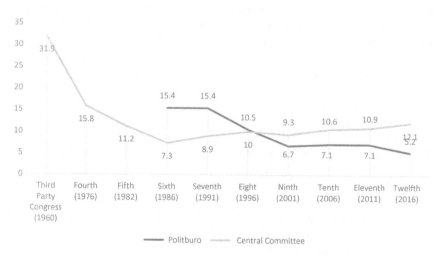

Fig. 12.5 Share of active military officers in Politburo and CPV Central Committee, 1960–2016. Source: Thayer (1988, p. 187), Thayer (2013, p. 66, 2014a, p. 137), Abuza and Nguyen Nhat Anh (2016)

system is a key responsibility of the People's Army (Thayer 2013, p. 72). However, for day-to-day repression, the Communist Party relies on internal security agencies such as the 900,000 strong People's Police, the paramilitary border police with about 40,000 troops, and the People's Security Force (PSF; IISS 2014), which performs regular policing functions and serves as an auxiliary force for the repression of "counterrevolutionary activities." The People's Police is part of the portfolio of the Ministry of Public Security, which also oversees the General Department of Strategic Intelligence (GDSI). The GDSI monitors national communication systems and oversees anti-terrorism and other police tasks. It also serves as the state prosecutor for political crimes. The Ministry for Culture and Information controls other intelligence services (Thayer 2014a, pp. 135–136). Taken together, this multitude of military, paramilitary, police, and intelligence services forms an efficient machinery of repression that, in part, explains the absence of organized opposition against party rule in Vietnam since the late 1970s (Vu 2014; Kerkvliet 2014).

12.9 Political Culture, Media System, and Civil Society

In Vietnam's "mono-organizational socialism" (Thayer 2010, p. 424), the party's mass organizations and the Vietnam Fatherland Front (VFF) are granted the monopoly on the representation of societal interests. The five mass organizations (or sociopolitical organizations) mentioned in the constitution include the Vietnam Trade Union (also known as Vietnam General Confederation of Labor, VGCL), the Vietnam Peasant Society, the Ho Chi Minh Communist Youth Union, the Vietnam Women Society, and the Vietnam Veteran Society (Art. 9, 2013 Constitution). Together with the Communist Party and the People's Army, they form the VFF. Legally and formally, each mass organization is autonomous, but their top functionaries are selected by the Central Committee of the CPV (Thayer 2010). The mass organizations' main function is ultimately to implement the party's directions and policies and to convey the ideas and intentions of the party to target sectors of society corresponding to the sphere of each organization (i.e., workers, youth, women, ethnic minorities, etc.). The CPV oversees the way the sociopolitical organizations implement the Party's directions and policies. As Lenin puts it, they are "transmission belts" between the party and the masses. In addition, they serve as a recruitment pool for new party members and a training ground for new cadres (Menge 2011, p. 141). The official membership statistics for these organizations cannot be verified and do not differentiate between functionaries and activists on the one hand and nominal or inactive members on the other. Nevertheless, experts agree that the Women Society with at least 12 million registered members and more than 12,000 branches is the largest of these organizations, followed by the Peasant Society with roughly 8 million, the VGCL with 7.3 million, the Youth Union at 4 million, and the Veteran Society with about 2 million members (Abuza 2001, p. 13; Menge 2011, p. 138).

The VFF is organized and led according to the principle of democratic centralism, and its chairman is also a member of the Politburo (Thayer 2010; Wischermann 2013, p. 340). As a consequence of *doi moi* and the privatization of state-owned enterprises (called "socialization" in communist rhetoric), the VGCL has suffered a crisis of representation (Thayer 2010). While its more than 100,000 workplace unions are used to represent about half of all employees in industry and construction sectors in the mid-1990s (Abuza 2001, p. 13), special regulations for private enterprises and enterprises with foreign shareholders ("FDI enterprises," see Table 12.5) have weakened the VTU considerably. This, in turn, contributed to a spike in unauthorized strikes and reduced trust in official unions (Collins et al. 2013).[5]

As Nørlund (2007, p. 68) notes, "[t]he concept of civil society is not familiar in the Vietnamese context … However, the term is increasingly being employed by scholars and practitioners, and even the state is beginning to open up to its use. The reasons for the change in the way the concept is perceived are partly due to international debates, the increasing role played by nonprofit organizations and the change in Party policy, accepting the necessity of social work and education by organizations outside the state administration." Since 2000, about 1700 so-called government-oriented non-governmental organizations have emerged (Kerkvliet 2015, p. 433), which aim to fill service delivery gaps in education, health, and welfare sectors that emerged as a consequence of the privatization of social services (Thayer 2010; Wischermann 2013, p. 336). An increasing number of international NGOs setting up offices in Vietnam—monitored by the People's Aid Coordination Committee, itself a subsidiary of the Vietnam Union of Friendship Associations (a minion of the VFF)—now collaborate with the similarly multiplying number of smaller local NGOs and public sector counterparts. The diverse and increasing spectrum of social organizations, associations, and interest groups, or what can be considered the equivalent of a Vietnamese "proto-civil society," comprises several categories of actors and groups (Wischermann 2013; Menge 2011, pp. 138–140). Other than traditional mass organizations, these include professional organizations; trade associations such as the Chamber of Commerce; issue-oriented NGOs; research institutions with an NGO status; nonprofit companies and charity funds; community-based organizations and informal groups (i.e., peasant and village associations or cooperatives); and faith-based organizations like the Vietnam Association for Buddhism, the Committee for Catholic Solidarity, or the Vietnam Protestant Association. There are more than 100,000 informal, unregistered community-based organizations of this "Third Sector" that offer various kinds of social services (Thayer 2010; Kerkvliet 2015, p. 433; Blanc 2004, p. 162). Party and state officials tolerate or even support the proliferation of such groups as long as they remain in a pre-political space (Thayer 2010, p. 427; Sidel 2008, pp. 143–145;

---

[5]The VGCL is organized into territorial and sectoral unions. There are about 100,000 workplace unions with 5.7 million members in the 63 provinces and cities; in addition, the 20 sector unions have a membership of about 1.58 million, organized into 6400 workplace unions.

Table 12.5 GDP and employment share of different economic sectors in Vietnam, 1990–2010

	1990	1995	2000	2005	2010
Share of total gross domestic product (in %)					
Agriculture & Forestry & Aquaculture Sector	38.7	27.2	24.5	21	20.6
Industry & Construction Sector	22.7	28.8	36.7	41	41.1
Services sector	38.6	44.1	38.7	38	38.3
State sector (public agencies & SOEs)		40.2	38.5	38.4	33.7
None-state sector (nonpublic agencies & domestic enterprises)		53.5	48.2	45.6	47.5
FDI sector		6.3	13.3	16	18.7
Share of total employment (in %)					
Agriculture & Forestry & Aquaculture Sector	72.1	71.3	64.4	57.2	48.7
Industry & Construction Sector	8.8	8.6	13.3	18.2	21.7
Services sector	19.1	20.1	22.3	24.6	29.6
State sector			11.7	11.6	10.4
Non-state sector			87.3	85.8	86.1
FDI Sector			1.0	2.6	3.5

Source: Mensel (2012, pp. 286, 453), GSOV (2014)

Wischermann 2013). In contrast, activists of the alternative "political civil society" (Pollack 2004) like the Bloc 8406 dissident network, the exiled Democratic Party, the United Workers'/Farmers' Association independent trade union, or underground churches like the United Buddhist Church of Vietnam obviously stand outside of the VFF (Abuza 2001; Thayer 2010, p. 437). Their critical distance or open resistance to the single-party state subject them to hard repression by security forces, which has so far precluded them from becoming a serious threat to CPV rule.

Criticism of the government or party and political debates outside of the CPV and its official organizations are not tolerated in Vietnam. In spite of restrictions on freedom of association and speech, a wide variety of rural, environmental, and labor protests have proliferated over the past 10 years. Often involving workers, fishermen, or farmers and their families, and sometimes led by Catholic priests, these protests stem from grievances like bad working conditions, unpaid wages, bureaucratic neglect, or forced land requisitions, whereby government authorities and local-level party officials—often in collusion with private developers—seize land from villagers with little to no compensation. Even this increase in grassroots protest does not pose an existential threat to CPV rule because they are uncoordinated, unconnected, and unconcerned about questions of systemic change, and Vietnamese authorities frequently use coercive measures and hard repression to quell them.

According to the Press Law of 2016, only an organization or agency of the government or authorized by the government can engage in a media business, and all print media require a license issued by the Ministry for Culture and Information, which has also served as the government's internet censorship agency since 1999.

Media outlets must provide information "to serve the interests of the people and the country," and various pieces of legislation provide state agencies with ample authority to stop any form of critical news coverage. In both the Press Freedom Index of Reporters without Borders and Freedom House's Freedom of the Press Index, Vietnam is on par with other communist autocracies like Laos and China, ranking 175th among 180 countries (Reporters without Borders 2017) and 186th among 199 countries, respectively (Freedom House 2015). Yet, despite legal restrictions and threats of crackdown by the police, the frequency of critical reports has increased in recent years, thanks in part to the growth of social media. Even within traditional media, however, editors and journalists are increasingly searching for ways to reveal the abuse of public office, criticize the misconduct of local bureaucrats, and report on corruption scandals or intra-party conflicts (Wagstaff 2010, pp. 107–109).

The CPV leadership is particularly concerned about the rise of a semi-pluralist "second public" or underground press and, especially, the exposure of corruption scandals involving party and state officials because it fears a loss of legitimacy in the eyes of its own members or the public. Ever since the economic crisis of the 1980s, the implementation of *doi moi* in 1986, and the ensuing transformation of Vietnam's society and economic model, the party has struggled to find a more durable basis of authority, utilizing different resources to legitimize its rule. Performance-based regime support is important, but the larger picture is more complex and encompasses different rationales. First, there is ideological legitimation based on the utopian ideology of Marxism–Leninism, reinterpreted to some extent by emphasizing the so-called Ho Chi Minh thought, which has appeared coequally with Marxism–Leninism as part of the official party ideology since the early 1990s (Vu 2014). Second, the party increasingly invokes reinvented Confucian notions of "good rule," traditional (or reinvented) conceptions of personal morality and authority, and the revolutionary morality of Vietnamese socialism (Abuza 2001, p. 21; Sidel 2008). Third, and most importantly, is the reliance on output or performance-based political legitimacy. The notion of performance is not limited to the provision of public goods but includes the party's past successes in the anti-imperialist struggle and in reunifying the country after bitter wars as well as its preservation of social stability and harmony (Dixon 2004, p. 17; Le Hiep 2012, p. 145; Vasavakul 1995, 2014; Thayer 2010).

It is in this context that systematic examinations of levels of regime support and its underlying factors can explain regime legitimacy in Vietnam. Data collected in the second to fourth wave of the ABS (2005–2014) appears to show the relative success of the party's legitimation attempts. Among the seven Southeast Asian countries—Cambodia, Indonesia, Malaysia, the Philippines, Singapore, Thailand, and Vietnam—the country exhibits the strongest support for regime institutions among respondents (Chang et al. 2013). While 95.3% of respondents in 2014 reported some or a great deal of trust in the national government, 93.4% trusted the national parliament and 86.63% the political parties (i.e., the CPV); the averages for the seven Southeast Asian countries were 73.3, 69.6, and 58.6%, respectively (ABS 2017). Moreover, quantitative studies suggest that good social and economic performance, the improvement of government services, as well as the prevalence of traditional political values and nationalism are the main determinants for the positive evaluations of political institutions and regime support among Vietnamese (Chang et al. 2013, p. 160).

12.10 Outlook

Similar to Laos, Vietnam is a communist one-party regime in transition. With the implementation of *doi moi*, the CPV replaced a centrally planned economy with a "socialist-oriented market economy." The transition from a fully planned economy to a mixed economy generated dynamic economic growth and socioeconomic modernization that puts the Communist Party in a potentially vulnerable position. In addition, the CPV is no longer a revolutionary party striving for a utopian socialist ideal, but a bureaucratic party seeking to preserve the political status quo.

After 1986, relatively strong elite cohesion, collective leadership, and the invention of new instruments of intra-party consultation and consensus-oriented decision-making have helped the CPV to contain centrifugal tendencies and factional conflicts, which would threaten the survival of its rule from within the party itself. At the same time, the party has reacted resolutely against any demands for political liberalization or a more open political process. Overall, it appears that the communist rulers have successfully adapted the pillars of regime stability to changing international and domestic contexts. The strategy of economic transformation and institutional innovation has enabled the CPV to keep its regime coalition together and to reconcile increasingly diverse sectoral and regional interests (Abrami et al. 2013). In addition, the available data seem to suggest that the CPV has succeeded in maintaining the popular belief that the existing political institutions are the most appropriate ones for Vietnamese society. The main reason could be that the party and government do not only base their efforts for the legitimacy of their rule solely on ideology, tradition, or economic performance, but also on a multitude of different sources and rationales. However, this does not mean they do not have to fear what Samuel Huntington (1991, pp. 50–52) has termed the "performance dilemma": If a government is not (economically) performing well, its people will be dissatisfied, the regime will be deemed incapable of governing appropriately, and both the rulers and the political system will lose legitimacy. Yet the legitimacy of an autocratic regime is also undermined if it delivers on its promises, as good economic performance actually weakens the "authoritarian bargain" (Desai et al. 2009) by which citizens relinquish political rights for economic security. In fact, findings from cross-national, cross-regional empirical research suggest that economic and social development increases the capacity of citizens to place demands on their governments. This is because citizens will develop stronger self-expression values, rendering individuals more willing to and capable of desiring participation in politics and producing greater expectations for their government and its institutional framework (Welzel and Inglehart 2009; Welzel 2013). This is not to suggest that communist leaders would necessarily be immune to horizontal threats emerging from within the party or against "anti-incumbent mass-protests" (Hale 2013, p. 336) demanding regime change, as occurred in communist Eastern Europe in the late 1980s and in the Arab world around 2010/11. There are signs that 30 years of *doi moi* have generated conflict between the government and society in general, within the party, and within different social groups in various forms, as indicated by the steadily growing number of protests since the late 1990s. But even with the challenges cited above, Communist Party rule in Vietnam appears resilient and adaptive.

References

Abrami, R., Malesky, E., & Yu, Z. (2013). Vietnam through Chinese eyes: Divergent accountability in single-party regimes. In M. K. Dimitrov (Ed.), *Why communism did not collapse: Understanding authoritarian regime resilience in Asia and Europe* (pp. 237–275). New York: Cambridge University Press.

ABS. (2017). *Asian barometer survey: Electronic data release for Wave 4, 2014–2016.* http://www.asianbarometer.org/data/data-release

Abuza, Z. (2001). *Renovating politics in contemporary Vietnam.* London: Lynne Rienner.

Abuza, Z., & Anh, N. N. (2016). Little fallout: Vietnam's security policy after the 12th congress of the Vietnam communist party. Center for International Maritime Security. Accessed June 2, 2017, from http://cimsec.org/21720-2/21720

Bergstermann, J., & Geiger, A. (2011). *Vietnam im Superwahljahr: Das Durchsteuern wird schwieriger.* Berlin: Friedrich Ebert Foundation.

Besley, T., & Kudamatsu, M. (2007). *Making autocracy work* (Development Economics Discussion Paper Series). London: London School of Economics and Political Science.

Blanc, M.-E. (2004). An emerging civil society? Local associations working on HIV/AIDS. In D. McCargo (Ed.), *Rethinking Vietnam* (pp. 153–165). London: RoutledgeCurzon.

Brocheux, P., & Hémery, D. (2011). *Indochina: An ambiguous colonization 1858–1954.* Berkeley: University of California Press.

Brooker, P. (1995). *Twentieth century dictatorships: The ideological one-party states.* Basingstoke: Macmillan.

Brunner, G. (1978). Die Funktion der Verfassung in den sozialistischen Staaten im Spiegel der neueren Verfassungsgebung. In F.-C. Schroeder & B. Meissner (Eds.), *Verfassungs- und Verwaltungsreformen in den sozialistischen Staaten* (pp. 11–43). Berlin: Duncker & Humblot.

BTI. (2014). *Bertelsmann transformation index 2014.* Gütersloh: Bertelsmann Foundation.

Case, W. (2016). Vietnam in 2015: Factional battles, economic tailwinds, and neighborhood jitters. *Asian Survey, 56,* 93–100. https://doi.org/10.1525/as.2016.56.1.93.

CECODES, VFF-CRT, & UNDP. (2014). The Viet Nam governance and Public Administration Performance Index (PAPI) 2013: Measuring citizens' experiences. A Joint Policy Research Paper. Hanoi: Center for Community Support and Development Studies; Centre for Research and Training of the Viet Nam Fatherland Front; United Nations Development Program.

CECODES, VFF-CRT, & UNDP. (2016). The Viet Nam provincial governance and Public Administration Performance Index (PAPI) 2015: Measuring citizens's experiences. A Joint Policy Research Paper. Hanoi: Center for Community Support and Development Studies; Centre for Research and Training of the Viet Nam Fatherland Front; United Nations Development ment Program.

Chang, A., Chu, Y.-h., & Welsh, B. (2013). Southeast Asia: Sources of regime support. *Journal of Democracy, 24,* 150–164. https://doi.org/10.1353/jod.2013.0025.

CIA. (2017). *The World Factbook.* Langley: Central Intelligence Agency.

Collins, N., Sitalaksmi, S., & Lansbury, R. (2013). Transforming employment relations in Vietnam and Indonesia: Case studies of state-owned enterprises. *Asia Pacific Journal of Human Resources, 51*, 131–151. https://doi.org/10.1111/j.1744-7941.2012.00056.x.

Desai, R. M., Olofsgard, A., & Yousef, T. M. (2009). The logic of authoritarian bargains. *Economics and Politics, 21*, 93–125. https://doi.org/10.1111/j.1468-0343.2008.00337.x.

Dimitrov, M. K. (2013). Understanding communist collapse and resilience. In M. K. Dimitrov (Ed.), *Why communism did not collapse: Understanding authoritarian regime resilience in Asia and Europe* (pp. 3–39). New York: Cambridge University Press.

Dixon, C. (2004). State, party and political change in Vietnam. In D. McCargo (Ed.), *Rethinking Vietnam* (pp. 15–26). London: RoutledgeCurzon.

Elliott, D. W. P. (2012). *Changing worlds: Vietnam's transition from the Cold War to globalization*. Oxford: Oxford University Press.

Fforde, A. (2013). Vietnam in 2012. *Asian Survey, 53*, 101–108. https://doi.org/10.1525/as.2013.53.1.101.

Freedom House. (2015). *Freedom of the Press Index 2014: Harsh laws and violence drive global decline*. Accessed June 2, 2017, from https://freedomhouse.org/report/freedom-press/freedom-press-2015

Fritzen, S. (2009). The 'Misery' of implementation: Governance, institutions, and anti-corruption in Vietnam. In N. Tarling (Ed.), *Corruption and good governance in Asia* (pp. 98–120). London: Routledge.

Gainsborough, M. (2005). Party control: Electoral campaigning in Vietnam in the Run-up to the May 2002 National Assembly Elections. *Pacific Affairs, 78*(1), 57–75.

Gainsborough, M. (2010). *Vietnam: Rethinking the state*. London: Zed Books.

Gandhi, J. (2008). *Political institutions under dictatorship*. Cambridge: Cambridge University Press.

Gillespie, J. (2006). Evolving concepts of human rights in Vietnam. In R. P. Peerenboom, C. J. Petersen, & A. H. Y. Chen (Eds.), *Human rights in Asia: A comparative legal study of twelve Asian jurisdictions, France and the USA* (pp. 487–517). London: Routledge.

Gillespie, J. (2017). *Transplanting commercial law reform: Developing a 'rule of law' in Vietnam*. London: Routledge.

Grimm, D. (2013). Types of constitutions. In M. Rosenfeld & A. Sajó (Eds.), *The Oxford handbook of comparative constitutional law* (pp. 98–133). Oxford: Oxford University Press.

GSOV. (2014). *Statistical yearbook of Vietnam 2013*. Hanoi: General Statistics Office of Viet Nam.

Hale, H. E. (2013). Regime change cascades: What we have learned from the 1848 revolutions to the 2011 Arab uprisings. *Annual Review of Political Science, 16*, 331–353. https://doi.org/10.1146/annurev-polisci-032211-212204.

Hartmann, C. (2001). Vietnam: A data handbook. In D. Nohlen, F. Grotz, & C. Hartmann (Eds.), *Elections in Asia and the Pacific: A data handbook, Vol. II: South East Asia, East Asia, and the South Pacific* (pp. 321–343). Oxford: Oxford University Press.

Hill, C. (2008). Vietnam: Constitutional development in a re-united country. In C. Hill & J. Menzel (Eds.), *Constitutionalism in Southeast Asia: Vol. 1: National constitutions/ASEAN charter* (pp. 327–355). Singapore: Konrad Adenauer Foundation.

Huntington, S. P. (1991). *The third wave: Democratization in the late twentieth century*. Norman: University of Oklahoma Press.

IISS. (2014). *The military balance 2014: International institute for strategic studies*. London: Oxford University Press.

IISS. (2017). *The military balance 2017: International institute for strategic studies*. London: Oxford University Press.

IPU. (2016). *Inter-parliamentary Union parline database Vietnam*. Accessed June 2, 2017, from http://www.ipu.org/parline-e/reports/2349_E.htm

Jandl, T. (2013). *Vietnam in the global economy: The dynamics of integration, decentralization, and contested politics*. Lanham: Lexington Books.

Kerkvliet, B. J. (2014). Government repression and toleration of dissidents in contemporary Vietnam. In J. D. London (Ed.), *Politics in contemporary Vietnam: Party, state and authority relations* (pp. 100–134). Basingstoke: Palgrave Macmillan.

Kerkvliet, B. J. (2015). Democracy and Vietnam. In W. Case (Ed.), *Routledge handbook of Southeast Asian democratization* (pp. 426–441). London: Routledge.

Koh, D. (2012). Vietnam: A glass half full or half empty? *Southeast Asian Affairs*, 361–378.

Le Hiep, H. (2012). Performance-based Legitimacy: The case of the communist party of Vietnam and Doi Moi. *Contemporary Southeast Asia: A journal of international and strategic affairs, 34*(2), 145–172.

Le Hiep, H. (2014). The communist party of Vietnam: A party in transition. In W. Sachsenröder (Ed.), *Party politics in Southeast Asia: Organization, money, influence* (pp. 346–409). Singapore: ISEAS.

London, J. D. (2004). Rethinking Vietnam's mass education and health systems. In D. McCargo (Ed.), *Rethinking Vietnam* (pp. 127–143). London: RoutledgeCurzon.

London, J. D. (2014). Politics in contemporary Viet Nam. In J. D. London (Ed.), *Politics in contemporary Vietnam: Party, state and authority relations* (pp. 1–20). Basingstoke: Palgrave Macmillan.

Malesky, E. (2014). Understanding the confidence vote in Vietnam: An update on 'Adverse Effects of Sunshine'. In J. D. London (Ed.), *Politics in contemporary Vietnam: Party, state and authority relations* (pp. 84–100). Basingstoke: Palgrave Macmillan.

Malesky, E., & Paul, S. (2011). The single-party dictator's dilemma: Information in elections without opposition. *Legislative Studies Quarterly, 36*, 491–530. https://doi.org/10.1111/j.1939-9162.2011.00025.x.

Malesky, E., & Schuler, P. (2013). Star search: Do elections help nondemocratic regimes identify new leaders? *Journal of East Asian Studies, 13*, 35–69.

Malesky, E., Schuler, P., & Tran, A. (2011). Vietnam: Familiar patterns and new developments ahead of the 11th party congress. *Southeast Asian Affairs*, 337–363.

Martinez-Vazquez, J. (2011). *Fiscal decentralization in Asia: Challenges and opportunities*. Manila: Asian Development Bank.

Menge, J. (2011). *Zivilgesellschaft in Vietnam: Ein westlich-demokratisches Konzept auf dem Prüfstand*. Berlin: Regiospectra.

Mensel, N. (2012). *Der Entwicklungsprozess der Sozialistischen Republik Vietnam: Erfolge und Herausforderungen durch staatlich gelenkte Entwicklung*. Wiesbaden: Springer VS.

Nguyen, T. H. (2012). Pursuing constitutional dialogue within socialist Vietnam: The 2010 debate. *Australian Journal of Asian Law, 13*(1), 1–18.

Nguyen, T. T. (2013). The World Trade Organization's (WTO) impact on the policy and the law of Vietnam from 2007 onwards. *ASLI Working Paper Series*(WPS029).

Nguyen, N. H., & Ta, V. T. (1987). *The Lê code law in traditional Vietnam: A comparative Sino-Vietnamese legal study with historical-juridical analysis and annotations*. Athens: Ohio University Press.

Nicholson, P. (2016). Vietnamese constitutionalism: The reform possibilities. *Asian Journal of Comparative Law, 11*, 199–207. https://doi.org/10.1017/asjcl.2016.18.

Nørlund, I. (2007, October). Civil society in Vietnam: Social organizations and approaches to new concepts. *Asien, 105*, 68–90.

Perlmutter, A., & LeoGrande, W. M. (1982). The party in uniform: Toward a theory of civil-military relations in communist political systems. *American Political Science Review, 76*, 778–789. https://doi.org/10.1017/S0003055400189609.

Pollack, D. (2004). Zivilgesellschaft und Staat in der Demokratie. In K. Kern & B. Geißel (Eds.), *Zivilgesellschaft und Sozialkapital: Herausforderungen politischer und sozialer Integration* (Bürgergesellschaft und Demokratie, Vol. 14).

Porter, G. (2009). *Vietnam: The politics of bureaucratic socialism* (2nd ed.). Ithaca: Cornell University Press.

Reporters without Borders. (2017). *2017 World Press Freedom Index. RSF.* Accessed June 22, 2017, from https://rsf.org/en/ranking

Schirokauer, C., & Clark, D. N. (2004). *Modern East Asia: A brief history.* South Melbourne: Thomson.

Schuler, P., & Malesky, E. (2014). Authoritarian legislatures. In S. Martin (Ed.), *The Oxford handbook of legislative studies* (pp. 676–695). Oxford: Oxford University Press.

Sidel, M. (2008). *Law and society in Vietnam: The transition from socialism in comparative perspective.* New York: Cambridge University Press.

Stockwell, A. J. (1999). Southeast Asia in war and peace: The end of European colonial empiries. In N. Tarling (Ed.), *Cambridge history of Southeast Asia: Vol. II Part 2: From World War II to the present* (pp. 1–58). New York: Cambridge University Press.

Thayer, C. A. (1988). The regularization of politics: Continuity and change in the party's central committee, 1951–1986. In D. G. Marr (Ed.), *Postwar Vietnam: Dilemmas in socialist development* (pp. 177–193). Ithaca: Cornell University Press.

Thayer, C. A. (1994). *The Vietnam people's army under Doi Moi.* Singapore: ISEAS.

Thayer, C. A. (1998). Vietnam. In W. Sachsenröder & U. E. Frings (Eds.), *Political party systems and democratic development in East and Southeast Asia: Vol. I: Southeast Asia* (pp. 449–509). Aldershot: Ashgate.

Thayer, C. A. (2000). The economic and commercial roles of the Vietnam people's army. *Asian Perspective, 24*(2), 87–120.

Thayer, C. A. (2010). Political legitimacy in Vietnam: Challenge and response. *Politics & Policy, 38,* 423–444. https://doi.org/10.1111/j.1747-1346.2010.00242.x.

Thayer, C. A. (2013). Military politics in contemporary Vietnam: Political engagement, corporate interests, and professionalism. In M. Mietzner (Ed.), *The political resurgence of the military in Southeast Asia: Conflict and leadership* (pp. 63–84). New York: Routledge.

Thayer, C. A. (2014a). The apparatus of authoritarian rule in Vietnam. In J. D. London (Ed.), *Politics in contemporary Vietnam: Party, state and authority relations* (pp. 135–162). Basingstoke: Palgrave Macmillan.

Thayer, C. A. (2014b). Vietnam in 2013: Domestic contestation and foreign policy success. *Southeast Asian Affairs, 2014*(1), 355–372.

Thayer, C. A. (2015). *Vietnam: An analysis of politburo and secretariat voet of confidence.* Thayer Consultancy Background Briefing. https://www.scribd.com/document/253021090/Thayer-Vietnam-Results-of-Politburo-Vote-of-Confidence

Tran, T. B. (2014). The cycle of transparency, accountability, corruption, and administrative performance: Evidence from Vietnam. *Journal of Economics and Development, 16*(3), 32–48.

Truex, R. (2014). The returns to office in a "Rubber Stamp" parliament. *American Political Science Review, 108,* 235–251. https://doi.org/10.1017/S0003055414000112.

Tucker, S. (1999). *Vietnam.* London: UCL Press.

UNDP. (2004). *The socialist Republic of Viet Nam public administration country profile.* Accessed June 6, 2017, from http://unpan1.un.org/intradoc/groups/public/documents/un/unpan023247.pdf

Vasavakul, T. (1995). Vietnam: The changing models of legitimation. In M. Alagappa (Ed.), *Political legitimacy in Southeast Asia: The quest for moral authority* (pp. 257–291). Stanford: Stanford University Press.

Vasavakul, T. (2001). From revolutionary heroes to red entrepreneurs. In M. Alagappa (Ed.), *Coercion and governance: The declining political role of the military in Asia* (pp. 336–356). Stanford: Stanford University Press.

Vasavakul, T. (2006). Vietnam: Doi Moi difficulties. In N. J. Funston (Ed.), *Government and politics in Southeast Asia* (2nd ed., pp. 372–410). Singapore: ISEAS.

Vasavakul, T. (2014). Authoritarianism reconfigured: Evolving accountability relations within Vietnam's one-party rule. In J. D. London (Ed.), *Politics in contemporary Vietnam: Party, state and authority relations* (pp. 42–64). Basingstoke: Palgrave Macmillan.

Vietnam Breaking News. (2017). *Vietnam's top telecom firm Viettel to expand to Indonesia.* Accessed June 2, 2017, from https://www.vietnambreakingnews.com/tag/vietnam-military-telecom-group-viettel/

Vietnam Business Forum. (2014). *Military enterprises: Defending and developing Vietnam's economy.* Accessed June 6, 2017, from http://vccinews.com/news_detail.asp?news_id=29950

Vo, D. H. (2005). *Fiscal decentralisation in Vietnam: A preliminary investigation.* https://www.researchgate.net/publication/23697435_Fiscal_Decentralisation_in_Vietnam_a_Preliminary_Investigation

Vu, T. (2014). Persistence amid decay: The communist party of Vietnam at 83. In J. D. London (Ed.), *Politics in contemporary Vietnam: Party, state and authority relations* (pp. 21–40). Basingstoke: Palgrave Macmillan.

Vuving, A. L. (2013). Vietnam in 2012: A rent-seeking state on the verge of a crisis. *Southeast Asian Affairs*, 325–347.

Wagstaff, J. (2010). *Southeast Asian media: Patterns of production and consumption.* Accessed June 6, 2017, from https://www.opensocietyfoundations.org/sites/default/files/production-consumption-20100212.pdf

Welzel, C. (2013). *Freedom rising: Human empowerment and the quest for emancipation.* New York: Cambridge University Press.

Welzel, C., & Inglehart, R. F. (2009). Mass beliefs and democratic institutions. In C. Boix & S. C. Stokes (Eds.), *The Oxford handbook of comparative politics* (pp. 297–316). Oxford: Oxford University Press.

Wintrobe, R. (2009). Dictatorship: Analytical approaches. In C. Boix & S. C. Stokes (Eds.), *The Oxford handbook of comparative politics* (pp. 363–397). Oxford: Oxford University Press.

Wischermann, J. (2013). Zivilgesellschaften als Stütze autoritärer Regime: Das Fallbeispiel Vietnam. In S. Kailitz & P. Köllner (Eds.), *Autokratien im Vergleich* (Vol. 47, Politische Vierteljahresschrift: Sonderheft ed., pp. 324–354). Baden-Baden: Nomos.

World Bank. (2017a). *World development indicators.* http://data.worldbank.org/products/wdi

World Bank. (2017b). *Worldwide governance indicators.* http://data.worldbank.org/data-catalog/worldwide-governance-indicators

Wurfel, D. (1967). Preliminary report of Vietnam election observer for methodist peace division, SANE, friends committee on National Legislation, and Unitarian Universalist Association. Washington.

Conclusions: Comparing Governments and Political Institutions in Southeast Asia 13

13.1 Introduction

The aim of this textbook was to discuss the structures, processes, and actors of the political systems as well as the current political situation of 11 Southeast Asian countries. The purpose of this final chapter is to connect the insights derived from the previous chapters and provide a comparative perspective. The deep and numerous political, economic, cultural, historical, and social differences among the countries in the region defy any straightforward generalization, even more so than in other world regions. Still, a comparative approach can yield important insights not only for understanding regional politics but also for interregional research. The structure of this final chapter follows that of the country chapters and selectively emphasizes those aspects most relevant for understanding political systems in the region.

13.2 Constitutions

Following the end of World War II, "formal written constitutions have become ubiquitous features of modern nation-states" (Ginsburg and Simpser 2014, p. 1; Go 2003; Brown 2003). Southeast Asia is no exception to this development. While some countries experimented with written constitutions prior to independence, constitutions became an essential symbol of national sovereignty in the 1940s and 1950s. A second wave of constitution making occurred in the 1970s, when the original constitutions were replaced in many countries. Finally, the downfall of the Marcos dictatorship in the Philippines and the passing of the provisional "Freedom Constitution" in 1986 ignited another wave of constitutional reforms in the region, which resulted in the drafting of new constitutions or a "total revision" (Indonesia; Indrayana 2008, p. 101) of the constitutional texts in eight countries (Table 13.1).

© Springer International Publishing AG 2018
A. Croissant, P. Lorenz, *Comparative Politics of Southeast Asia*,
https://doi.org/10.1007/978-3-319-68182-5_13

Table 13.1 Southeast Asian constitutions by decade

	1890s	1900s	1910s	1920s	1930s	1940s	1950s	1960s	1970s	1980s	1990s	2000s	Total
Brunei							1959[a]						1
Cambodia						1947			1972 1976	1981[b]	1993		5
Indonesia						1945 1949	1950(I) 1959[d]					(2002)[j]	4
Laos						1947[c]					1991		2
Malaysia							1957[e]						1
Myanmar						1947			1974			2008	3
Philippines	1898				1935	1943 1945[f]			1973	1986(I) **1987**			7
Singapore							1959[g]						1
Thailand					1932(I) 1932	1946 1947(I) 1949	1952[h] 1959 (I)	1968	1972 (I) 1974 1976 1977 (I) 1978		1991 (I) 1991 **1997**	2006 (I) 2007 2014 (I) 2017	20
Timor-Leste												**2002**	1
South Vietnam							1956	1964(I) 1967					3
North Vietnam						1946	1959			1980	1992[i]		4
Total	1				3	11	9	3	9	4	6	4	50

Notes: I: interim constitution; [a]amended 2004–2006; [b]amended in 1989; [c] excluding the 1945 provisional constitution ("Lao Issara" constitution ("Lao Issara" constitution); [d]reinstated the 1945 Constitution; [e]with several amendments; [f]reinstated the 1935 Constitution; [g]Constitution of Singapore with various amendments in 1965; [h]reinforced the 1932 Constitution; [i]amended in 2001–2002 and 2013; [j]amended the 1945 Constitution. **Bold**: constitution promulgated under a democratic regime
Sources: Croissant 2014 and chapters in this book

Differing constitutional designs are highly correlated with a country's political and historical background. The Philippine constitution was shaped by American influences while Brunei, Malaysia, and Singapore are more strongly influenced by British constitutional law. Likewise, its colonial past explains why Timor-Leste follows the constitutional model of other Lusophone countries. The constitutions of Laos, Vietnam, Burma (1974), and pre-UNTAC Cambodia are examples of socialist constitutions. The historical experience of liberation struggles (Indonesia, Vietnam, and Laos), lessons drawn from past authoritarian abuses of existing constitutions (Philippines), and the international diffusion of norms and legal doctrines are other important factors that have shaped basic laws in the region. The last factor is evident in the widespread adoption of human rights of the so-called second and third generation—economic, social, cultural, and collective rights—as well as in the proliferation of articles decentralizing authority from the national government. Fewer countries have chosen to adopt independent constitutional courts, and elements of direct democracy are even rarer—even though both are considered part of the repertoire of the New Constitutionalism. These developments have made constitutions increasingly eclectic while they converged on similar models (Tan 2002; Dressel and Bünte 2014).

From a constitutionalist perspective, constitutions can be viewed as a framework (*Rahmenordnung*) or as a legal foundation (*Grundordnung*) for society as a whole (Böckenförde 1994). Constitutions provide the basic rules for the political process and consequently need an element of stability. At the same time, constitutions need to be flexible enough to adapt to changing social conditions without losing their regulatory function (Elkins et al. 2009). Overly rigid constitutions that are unable to do so run the risk of losing or never gaining the acceptance of elites and the wider citizenry. Constitutions that are regularly changed and subordinated to the whim of political majorities will over time lose their binding force.

As Table 13.1 suggests, Southeast Asian constitutions differ markedly in this regard. While Brunei, Malaysia, and Singapore have had only a single constitution each, Thailand can claim the dubious honor of providing two-fifths of the region's distinct constitutional texts. This statistic, however, somewhat obscures actual constitutional changes as well as constitutional practices over time. The seemingly stable constitutions of Brunei, Malaysia, and Singapore were adapted to the needs of power holders quite frequently, while Thailand retained a large degree of constitutional stability through a core of unwritten quasi-constitutional conventions developed since the 1930s.

Constitution-making procedures and rules for constitutional amendments differ widely. Myanmar and the Philippines have the most rigid amendment requirements (Table 13.2). In Myanmar, constitutional rigidity protects the constitutional prerogatives of the *Tatmadaw*. In the Philippines, it has stalled any attempt to adapt the constitution to the social and political changes that have taken place since the mid-1980s, fueling judicial activism at the Supreme Court. In contrast, the constitution in Brunei can be amended at the whim of the sultan. Super-majoritarian requirements do exist in other countries, but with the exception of Timor-Leste and Indonesia, the predominance of ruling parties render them largely meaningless.

Table 13.2 Constitutional amendment procedures in Southeast Asia

	Established in	Approving body	Required majority	Entrenched clause
Brunei	1959	Sultan	–	–
Cambodia	1993	National Assembly	Two thirds[a]	Art. 153
Indonesia	2002	MPR (joined session of DPR and DPD)	Two thirds	Art. 37
Laos	1991	National Assembly	Two thirds	–
Malaysia	1957	Both houses of parliament	Two thirds in both chambers[b]	–
Myanmar	2011	Both houses of parliament	Three quarters in both chambers, simple majority in referendum	–
Philippines	1987	Senate and house of representatives	Three quarters in both chambers, simple majority in referendum[b]	
Singapore	1959	Parliament	Two thirds majority plus two thirds majority of valid votes in facultative referendum[b]	
Thailand	2017	National Assembly (joint session of house of representatives and senate)	More than half of the total number of the existing members of the NA; simple majority in referendum[b]	Art. 2, 256
Timor-Leste	2002	Parliament	Two thirds	Art. 155
Vietnam	1992	Parliament	Two thirds	–

[a]Since 2005, the newly constituted assembly can pass constitutional amendments by majority vote
[b]See discussion in country chapter for details and exceptions to the basic procedure
Source: Authors' compilation

Thailand's 2017 Constitution is a particularly interesting case: Any amendment to the constitution must be approved by an absolute majority in the National Assembly, as well as the joint session of House of Representatives and Senate, providing the military, which nominates the members of the Senate, a de facto veto over constitutional amendments.

Since most constitutions in Southeast Asia were promulgated by authoritarian governments, most nations' constitutional histories are shaped by a long tradition of what Okoth-Ogendo describes as "constitutions without constitutionalism" (Okoth-Ogendo 1993): With few exceptions, constitutional documents were designed as political tools for the rulers, usually drafted in secret, ratified by a handpicked assembly, and sometimes subjected to "ritualistic plebiscites" (Brown 2003, p. 38). Where constitutional referenda were organized, they were not meant to involve the broader public in the process but to legitimate the imposition of constitutions by autocratic rulers. Particular infamous examples include the 1974 referendum in Burma and the 1973 Constitution of the Philippines that was drafted under martial law, adopted by a Constitutional Convention under duress, and "ratified" by voice vote in village assemblies where soldiers and policemen were in prominent attendance (Croissant 2014, p. 32). Even among the region's democracies, the constitution-making procedures often produced little "upstream legitimacy," "process legitimacy," or "downstream legitimacy" (Elster 1993; Croissant 2014).

Nevertheless, autocratic constitutions in the region are more than mere window dressing. Often, authoritarian constitutions are commitment signals to citizens, regime elites, and external actors. They can provide a measure of legal certainty, provide a solution to problems of coordination within a regime coalition, and improve the regime's legitimacy vis-à-vis international partners (Law and Versteeg 2014, p. 187). In some instances, the process of authoritarian "constitutionalization" can gain unintended momentum towards further liberalization, as recent developments in Myanmar suggest.

13.3 Legal Systems and Constitutional Review

Countries in Southeast Asia differ in their legal tradition, the structures of the judicial system, and the extent to which they realize the rule of law. Even though it fails to capture the hybrid character of legal systems and the widespread combination of formal as well as informal mechanisms of conflict regulation in the region, the distinction of common law (Brunei, Malaysia, Myanmar, Singapore, and the Philippines) and civil law countries (Thailand, Indonesia, Timor-Leste, Cambodia, Laos, and Vietnam) is a useful heuristic.

The establishment of centralized constitutional review in most countries demonstrates the convergence of constitutional design in the region in recent years. While the "expansion of judicial power" (Tate and Vallinder 1995) is less pronounced in Southeast Asia than, for example, in Latin America or Eastern Europe, political reforms in Cambodia, Indonesia, Thailand, Timor-Leste, and Myanmar saw the creation of specialized constitutional courts. Singapore, Malaysia, and the Philippines, the latter since 1901, all have supreme courts with the authority for judicial review. In general, common law systems tend towards the American model of a Supreme Court, whereas civil law systems favor specialized constitutional courts. Laos, Vietnam, and Brunei lack a constitutional court, and in Brunei, any constitutional review of executive or legislative decisions is prohibited *expressis verbis*.

Some courts grant plaintiffs no procedure for individual constitutional complaints or lower court judges lack the ability to petition the constitutional court for the review of a law under concrete judicial review. Few courts play a role in election disputes, the removal of elected officials from office, or decisions about party bans (see Table 13.3). Singapore, Malaysia, and the Philippines lack procedures for an abstract constitutional review of parliamentary acts. In addition, the constitutional courts in these countries are only accessible after plaintiffs exhaust other remedies available through the regular court system.

Recruitment procedures range from pure appointments to a combination of election and appointment. There is no constitutional court in the region with a

Table 13.3 Constitutional court powers in Southeast Asia, 2017

	Constitutional complaint	Judicial review		Jurisdictional disputes	Party ban[b]	Election disputes	Impeachment[a]
		Abstract	Concrete				
Cambodia	No	Yes	Yes	Yes	(Yes)[b]	Yes	No
Indonesia	Yes	Yes	No	Yes	Yes	Yes	Yes
Malaysia	No	No	Yes	Yes	No	No	No
Myanmar	No	Yes	Yes	Yes	No	No	No
Philippines	No	No	Yes	No	No	No	No
Singapore	No	No	Yes	No	No	No	No
Thailand[d]	Yes	Yes	Yes	Yes	Yes	No	Yes
Timor-Leste[c]	Yes	Yes	Yes	Yes	Yes	No	Yes

[a] Presidential impeachment, removal from office of members of parliament or other elected officials
[b] Review of non-admission of party by election commission on appeal
[c] Tasks of Constitutional Court are carried out by the Dili court of appeals
[d] 2017 Constitution, Section 210
Source: Authors' compilation

fully elected constitutional judiciary (see Table 13.4). Under the representative model of judicial recruitment practiced in Indonesia and Cambodia, the head of state, parliament, and judiciary each select three judges autonomously. In Myanmar, constitutional court justices are appointed by the two houses of parliament and the president. In Timor-Leste, the president plays no role, but parliament and the judiciary must cooperate in the selection process. In Singapore and the Philippines, the de facto right of appointment rests with the head of government, leaving the other branches with only a formal role—the state president in Singapore cannot reject nominations for political reasons—or a role in the selection of suitable candidates, as in the Philippines. In Malaysia, a selection commission assists the prime minister, but since most of its members are appointed by the prime minister, the process is de facto exclusive. The appointment procedure for constitutional judges in Thailand is particularly elaborate: Sections 203 through 205 of the 2017 Constitution stipulate that justices are selected by a commission consisting of members of the Supreme Court, the Administrative Court, other constitutional organizations, the House of Representatives, and the official opposition leader in the House. Those candidates selected need majority approval from the members of the military-appointed Senate—providing the military with a veto—and are appointed by the king.

On paper, legislatures and executives in the region lack the authority to turn down constitutional court decisions, and judges can only be removed from office for personal misconduct or professional negligence. However, the legal meaning of these concepts is open to interpretation. This restricts the independence of judges, unless the court itself, but not political actors, such as the parliament in Myanmar or the Thai Senate, decides on the impeachment, or if the government establishes the composition of the responsible jurist committee (Malaysia).

A court's institutional design is an important predictor of its position in the wider political system. However, the country chapters in this volume demonstrate that formal regulations and constitutional reality are rarely the same. The Cambodian Constitutional Council has so far hardly played a meaningful role as the guardian of the constitution. In Malaysia, throughout the 1990s, the government curtailed the authority and autonomy of the Federal Court, as the government removed several justices from office for political reasons. A series of partisan judicial appointments by President Arroyo damaged the public image of the Supreme Court of the Philippines in the 2000s (Deinla 2014; Pangalangan 2015). In Thailand, a series of party bans and the court's impeachment of three pro-Thaksin prime ministers tainted its role as a non-partisan arbiter and yielded allegations of it acting as a proxy for the conservative elite (Dressel 2010; McCargo 2015).

The extent to which the rule of law has been realized differs widely across the region (Table 13.5). Only Singapore, Malaysia, and Brunei achieve positive scores in the Rule of Law Index of the World Bank's Worldwide Governance Indicators, the latter two with a downward trend in recent years. Yet, it is important to note that the World Bank's Rule of Law Indicators primarily measure formal aspects of the rule of law, not "material" or substantive aspects. Hence, it measures a formal or "thin" conception of the rule of law that covers the more technical aspects related to legal state actions, which comprise the obligation to formal statute law, structures

Table 13.4 Composition and independence of Southeast Asian Constitutional Courts, 2017

	Terms of office			Recruitment		Mode of selection
	# of judges	Length	Renewable	Removal from office[a]	Type	Participating bodies	

	# of judges	Length	Renewable	Removal from office[a]	Type	Participating bodies	Mode of selection
Cambodia	9	9 years	No	No	Mixed	Lower House, SCM, King	Representative
Indonesia	9	5 years	Once	No	Mixed	Supreme Court, President, DPR	Representative
Malaysia	15	Until age 65	–	Yes[b]	Appointment	Premier	Exclusive
Myanmar	9	5 years	No	Yes	Mixed	President, Upper and Lower House	Representative
Philippines	15	Until age 70	–	–	Appointment	President, Selection Committee	Exclusive
Singapore	18	Until age 65	–	No	Appointment	Premier	Exclusive
Thailand[c]	9	7 years	No	No	Mixed	Interorganizational Selection Committee, Senate, King	Cooperative
Timor-Leste	3	4 years	Yes	No	Mixed	Parliament, Committee of Judges	Cooperative

[a]Judicial impeachment by executive or legislature for enumerated reasons
[b]By committee of judges appointed by Prime Minister
[c]2017 Constitution

Source: Authors' compilation

Table 13.5 Rule of law and corruption control, 1996–2015

	Rule of law: estimate			Control of corruption: estimate		
	1996	2006	2015	1996	2006	2015
Brunei	0.748	0.206	0.443	0.538	0.229	0.640
Cambodia	−1140	−1191	−0.920	−0.964	−1229	−1044
Indonesia	−0.366	−0.729	−0.412	−0.560	−0.812	−0.453
Lao PDR	−0.978	−0.975	−0.750	−0.472	−1356	−0.839
Malaysia	0.606	0.531	0.574	0.512	0.288	0.284
Myanmar	−1483	−1468	−1220	−1405	−1698	−0.893
Philippines	0.258	−0.149	−0.036	−0.176	−0.818	−0.430
Singapore	1275	1627	1881	2169	2197	2129
Thailand	0.541	−0.026	−0.106	−0.205	−0.355	−0.400
Timor-Leste	–	−1153	−1176	–	−0.846	−0.690
Vietnam	−0.403	−0.439	−0.268	−0.431	−0.763	−0.447

Notes: The composite measures of governance generated in the WGI are in units of a standard normal distribution, with mean zero, standard deviation of one, and running from approximately −2.5 to 2.5, with higher values corresponding to better governance; Source: World Bank (2017)

of state organization and judicial review, and the liability of public authorities to pay compensation. Based on a more substantive or "thick" conception of the rule of law, which does not separate formal and material elements, but, instead, emphasizes their interdependence and also includes the guarantee of individual human rights claims, even Singapore, Malaysia, and Brunei are cases of limited rule of law. While the rule of law in Cambodia, Laos, and Myanmar has improved in recent years, it remains very weak. The region's electoral democracies, including Indonesia, the Philippines, and most significantly Thailand, today score worse than 10 or 20 years ago. Informal institutions can somewhat alleviate the problem of legal uncertainty but have further weakened formal state institutions. Overall, the World Bank indicators show that the rule of law declined in seven of the region's 11 countries between 1996 and 2013.

Moreover, the cozy relationship between economic and political elites allowed business, family, or party networks to capture state structures and has led to endemic corruption. Again, World Bank indicators suggest a decline in the control of corruption in the majority of the countries considered, and democracies score worse than autocracies on average. These measures are in line with the results of quantitative comparative research (Montinola and Jackmann 2002; Pellegata 2013), indicating that corruption is more common in weak democracies than in successful authoritarian regimes.

13.4 Systems of Government

In seven countries, presidents serve as the heads of state. Two countries possess a hereditary line of succession for their heads of state (Thailand, Brunei), while two are elective monarchies (Cambodia, Malaysia). In the latter cases, the monarch serves mostly a ceremonial and integrative function, even though the Malaysian king also symbolizes the privileged status of the Malay or Bumiputera population since he is elected from among the ranks of the traditional Malay rulers. The sultan in Brunei and the king in Thailand are actual centers of domestic political power. Despite its traditional role as a source of legitimation and an anchor of political and social stability, the Thai monarchy has suffered a crisis of legitimacy in recent years. It remains unclear whether the new king will carve out a different political role for the monarchy and what effects this would have on the wider political system. However, his exceptionally public attempts to influence the text of the new constitution and purges among the members of the Privy Council seem to indicate that King Vajiralongkorn is favoring a more confrontational and proactive role in politics than his father before him.

Political systems in the region do not all fit existing typologies neatly: In authoritarian Brunei, the sultan also serves as prime minister, and Thailand's nominally parliamentary system of government is actually led by a military junta whose chair serves as prime minister. Myanmar has a system of government with an elected but unimpeachable president who directs the government. However, the creation of the post of state counsellor of Myanmar for Aung San Suu Kyi in April 2016—with the authority of a prime minister in all but name—seems to suggest a return to a largely ceremonial role for the president, as under the 1947 Constitution of the Union of Burma.

Of the remaining eight systems, Indonesia and the Philippines have a presidential system, while Singapore and Timor-Leste are semi-presidential systems with a popularly elected president and a prime minister who directs a cabinet, which is collectively responsible solely to the legislature. Finally, Malaysia, Cambodia, Laos, and Vietnam all have cabinet or parliamentary systems.

So far, considerations of shifting from a presidential to a cabinet system in the Philippines have not resulted in concrete political action (Santos et al. 1997; Rüland 2003). Yet, both in the Philippines and Indonesia, constitutional reforms as part of the transition from authoritarianism to democracy resulted in significant restrictions on presidential powers. In both countries, the introduction of presidential term limits has proven to be the most important limitation on presidential authority, although presidents in these two countries still marshal significantly more powers than the popularly elected presidents of Timor-Leste and Singapore (Table 13.6).

A lack of reliable data makes any systematic analysis of the process of cabinet formation and cabinet composition difficult. What can be gleaned from the available information is that coalition governments are the norm in Indonesia's presidential system, Thailand's parliamentary system, and Timor-Leste's semi-presidential system, at least since 2007. Malaysia and—until 2013—Cambodia had nominal government coalitions. With the exception of Thailand, there is relatively high cabinet stability in these countries.

Six countries have bicameral legislatures. Second chambers differ in their mode of creation (election, appointment, or hybrid) and their relative authority in the political process (asymmetrical or symmetrical). In Malaysia, the second chamber is meant to represent the federal states, but 44 of the 70 members of the upper house are appointed by the king on the prime minister's proposal. In Cambodia, 57 of the

Table 13.6 Powers of popularly elected presidents

	Timor-Leste	Singapore	Indonesia	Philippines
	2002	1991	2002	1987
Legislative powers (total)	4.5	2	8	7
Package Veto/Override	1.5	0 (2)[a]	4	2
Line Item Veto/Override	0	0	0	3
Decree powers	0	0	2	0
Exclusive introduction of legislation	0	0	1	0
Budgetary powers	0	0	1	2
Proposal of referenda	(2)[b]	2	0	0
Other powers (total)	4	5	11	11
Cabinet formation	1	0	3	3
Cabinet dismissal	2	2	4	4
Censure	0	2	4	4
Dissolution of assembly	1	1	0	0

Notes: Scores based on index proposed by Shugart and Carey (1992, p. 150), expanded by legal standing to appeal for judicial review
[a]Only concerning laws enacted under Art. 21, 22, 142, and 148. An amendment to ease overturning a veto was passed in 1996
[b]No enacting legislation. Source: Authors' compilation

61 senators are elected in eight regional bodies by deputies of district assemblies and members of the lower house of parliament. The Indonesian regional representative council consists of directly elected regional representatives. Three quarters of the members in Myanmar's upper house represent provinces and states and are directly elected; the remaining quarter is appointed by the military (see Table 13.7). Members of the Philippine Senate are popularly elected and represent the nation instead of regions or subnational communities. The Thai Senate stands out among Southeast Asian second parliamentary chambers as an historical anachronism. From 1947 to 2000, senators were appointed by the king upon nomination by the government. From 2000 and 2006, they were popularly elected in nonparty elections, and from 2007 to 2014, the Senate was partly elected and partly appointed by a nongovernmental selection committee from among candidates put forward by associations and other social organizations. The latter procedure was aimed at guaranteeing the traditional elite a measure of influence on the composition of the second chamber and cemented the Senate's conservative character (Chambers 2009). The 2017 Constitution returned to a fully appointed chamber and grants military and royal palace elites free reign over the selection process.

Both the Philippine Senate and the Upper House in Myanmar have powers symmetrical to their respective first chambers. In both countries, the second chamber is directly elected, providing strong democratic legitimacy to the upper house, equal to the lower house. In the remaining four bicameral parliaments, the second chamber has significantly less authority than the first and so far failed to influence national legislation or become a chamber of reflection and consultation. These are examples of rather weak bicameralism. The Indonesian regional chamber can only influence legislation concerning regional matters. The Thai Senate, a chamber of

Table 13.7 Mode of creation and composition of second chamber of parliament

	Indonesia	Cambodia	Philippines	Thailand	Malaysia	Myanmar
Creation by	Popular election	Committee, Parliament, King	Popular election	Military Council/King	Parliament, Prime Minister	Popular election, military commander
Election system	Single non-transferable vote (SNTV)	PR in multi-member districts	Block vote	–	Plurality in two-member districts	Plurality rule in single-member districts
# of seats	132	61	24	250	70	224
# of appointed	–	2	–	250	44	56
# of districts	33	8	1	–	13	168[a]
District magnitude	4	6–10	12[1]	–	2	14
Level of seat allocation	District	District	District	–	Electoral district	Electoral district
Term length	5	6	6	5	3	5
Term limit	2	No term limit	2 (consecutive)	1	2	No term limit

[a]Staggered elections for half of the seats are held every 3 years

Source: Authors' compilation based Croissant (2006), Hicken and Kasuya (2003) and information from the country chapters

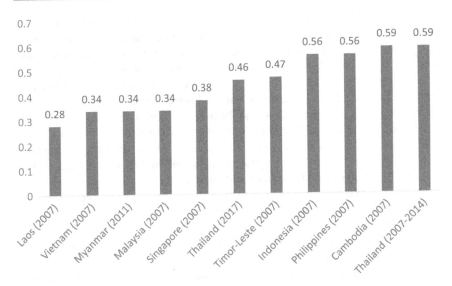

Fig. 13.1 Parliamentary powers in Southeast Asia (first or only chamber). Notes: The PPI ranges from zero (least powerful) to one (most powerful). The PPI score is calculated by summing the scores for 32 potential powers that the national legislature possesses and dividing this by 32; Source: Fish and Kroenig (2009); authors' calculations for Myanmar (2011), Thailand (2017)

generals and bureaucrats, used to be the most influential upper house in the region but lost much of its power after 1992 (Chambers 2009). In Malaysia and Cambodia, political majorities in both chambers converge, further reducing the relevance of the upper house.

One of the most consistent findings for Southeast Asia, the fact that executive–legislative relations are dominated by the executive (Marsh et al. 1999; Case 2011), is borne out by the country chapters. Compared to legislatures in other world regions, Southeast Asian parliaments have relatively weak formal powers as measured by the Parliamentary Power Index (PPI, see Fig. 13.1). However, there are differences in the actual degree of parliamentary influence on legislation and the extent of parliamentary oversight that are not reflected in the PPI scores. The Philippine Congress and the Indonesian People's Representative Council are relatively powerful legislatures even though they are not terribly efficient in terms of legislative output. While the Philippine president can play an active role in the legislative process through "pork barrel politics" and by building policy coalitions in Congress and prioritizing issues, the result is a time-consuming and resource-intensive bargaining system, which makes it more difficult to find a reasonable balance of interests and appropriate solutions for the country's problems concerning the provision of public goods.

Overall, parliaments serve somewhat different functions in authoritarian regimes compared to democracies. But there are also differences among authoritarian regimes, depending on constitutional rules but also—and more importantly—the fact of whether genuine opposition parties are represented in parliament (Cambodia, Malaysia, Myanmar since 2011, and, although much less so, in Singapore) or if it is a single-party parliament (Laos, Vietnam). In electoral autocracies where opposition parties are allowed in the national parliament, the regime leadership is most likely to use parliament as a forum for making political concessions, dispense economic rents to co-opt oppositional elites, provide a forum to balance competing regime elites, and recruit elites (Schuler and Malesky 2014). This is true for Cambodia and Malaysia and to a lesser extent for Singapore, where the People's Action Party has developed other channels for elite recruitment and the political opposition is only very weakly represented in parliament. It is doubtful whether parliaments in single-party states like Laos or Vietnam can develop a similar relevance. Those parliamentary functions most relevant in democracies—representing the electorate, drafting and passing legislation, and overseeing the government—are of much less importance in authoritarian regimes. Our case studies could not confirm that authoritarian regimes are less stable across the board if they do not tolerate opposition parties or lack parliaments (see also Pepinsky 2014).

In contrast, in Vietnam, the higher degree of competition among candidates on the single-party list seems to have improved regime stability by including local party elites (Schuler and Malesky 2014). Simultaneously, allowing a larger extent of parliamentary criticism of the government provided it with valuable information about the feasibility of political projects and the loyalty of party cadres. In Myanmar, on the other hand, the introduction of an elected parliament had a detrimental effect on the stability of the authoritarian regime in the absence of a well-institutionalized regime party: Existing splits in the regime coalition formed the basis for cooperation between the opposition and regime softliners before the 2015 election and following the November 2015 poll. In doing so, the National League for Democracy was able to transform its majority in both chambers of parliament into control over the government, at least within the military-guaranteed constitutional boundaries.

13.5 Elections and Electoral Systems

With the exception of Brunei, all Southeast Asian countries hold popular elections for parliament, and in four of these, the upper house of parliament is also chosen in direct elections. Another four countries hold direct elections for their head of state. Universal suffrage was introduced between 1933 (Thailand) and 1957 (Laos). In certain cases, specific social or professional groups were excluded, most importantly, Buddhist monks in Myanmar, Laos, Cambodia, and Thailand; active soldiers in Indonesia and the Philippines; and religious minorities like Muslims in the Philippines prior to 1946. Today, most countries grant voting rights to those who are at least 18 years old. Indonesians can vote from the age of 17 on and Malaysians from 21. In many cases, candidates have to be older to stand for election. In some cases, there are additional requirements as well. These include a minimal level of education or other personal qualifications, at least for certain offices. Restrictions tend to discriminate against smaller parties (as in Indonesia) or members of the political opposition (Singapore, Myanmar). Singapore and Thailand (before 2014) have made voting in national elections compulsory. The long tradition of elections for representative bodies—reaching back as far as 1907 in the Philippines—contrasts with the lack of meaningful elements of direct democracy. Moreover, authoritarian leaders often exploited referenda for plebiscitary legitimation for their authoritarian rule, for example in Cambodia, Thailand, and the Philippines (Kobori 2014). Only the Philippine constitution of 1987 currently allows for popular initiatives as a path to constitutional amendments. As in Myanmar, all constitutional amendments also have to be confirmed by popular referendum. In Timor-Leste and Singapore, the president has the authority to initiate a facultative referendum on constitutional amendments or draft legislation. From 1997 to 2014, Thai constitutions allowed a quorum of citizens to demand the recall of certain officeholders. None of the countries in Southeast Asia allow for popular legislation in which the right to initiative and passage of a bill are in the hands of the electorate.

Presidential elections follow different election modes. In Indonesia, only those parties or party coalitions with at least 20% of parliamentary seats or 25% of the vote in the previous parliamentary election are allowed to field their own candidates for presidential office. In Timor-Leste and the Philippines, party-based as well as independent candidates are allowed; Singapore only allows "independent" candidacies. To be elected, presidential candidates in Indonesia, Singapore, and Timor-Leste require an absolute majority of the total valid votes. A run-off election is called if no candidate achieves a majority during the first round. The Philippine president is elected by plurality vote. In Myanmar, Vietnam, and Laos, parliament selects the head of state (Table 13.8).

The electoral systems for lower house elections in the region follow no clear trend. Indonesia, Cambodia, and Timor-Leste adopted proportional representation (PR) systems. Four countries employ single-member plurality (SMP; Malaysia, Myanmar), multi-member plurality systems (MMP; Laos), or a plurality system with SMP and group constituencies (Singapore). A two-round system with multi-member districts is practiced in Vietnam. The Philippines (since 1998) and Thailand (since 2001) use mixed parallel systems: Most seats are allocated at the district level, and a small number is allocated based on proportional representation in national (Philippines) or regional multi-member districts (Thailand 2007–2014). Both components are completely separated ("parallel"). The 2017 Constitution of Thailand envisions a parallel voting system with a nominal ballot structure. That is, voters have only one ballot for the party candidate in their district, and party-list seats are allocated according to the parties' accumulated national vote shares (Table 13.9).

Interestingly, there is a strong element of path dependency in election institutions: Most countries stuck to their path once their political leaders had made a choice about the basic electoral formula following independence (plurality, proportional representation, or absolute majority; Nohlen et al. 2001). For example, Indonesia maintained the PR formula adopted in the 1950s throughout the authoritarian rule of President Suharto (1966–1998) as well as the post-Suharto period since 1999. However, there have also been seemingly minor institutional changes with broad political consequences. For example, an electoral threshold was

Table 13.8 Presidential election systems in Southeast Asia

	Selection by	Required majority	Term length	Term limit
Indonesia				
1950–1959	Acclamation	–	–	–
1959–1998	MPR	Absolute majority	5 years	No
1999	MPR	Absolute majority	5	2 terms
2004–	Popular election	Absolute majority	5	2
Timor-Leste, 2002	Popular election	Absolute majority	5	2
Philippines				
1935–1972	Popular election	Plurality	4	2
1981–1986	Popular election	Plurality	6	No
1987–	Popular election	Plurality	6	1
Singapore				
1959–1990	Parliament	Absolute majority	4	No
1991	Popular election	Plurality	6	No
Myanmar				
1947–1962	Parliament	Two-thirds majority	5	No
1974–1988	Council of State	Informal	5	No
2011–	Both houses of parliament	Absolute majority	5	2
Laos (1991–)	Parliament	Two-thirds majority	5	No
Vietnam (1980–)	Parliament	Informal	5	2

Source: Authors' compilation Hicken and Kasuya (2003) and information from the country chapters

introduced in 2009, and the number of votes necessary for a parliamentary seat was increased by successively shrinking the average size of electoral districts. With the adoption of single-member plurality, Myanmar, too, returned to its own British-inspired electoral tradition in 2008. In Timor-Leste, the mixed system adopted as a compromise between the United Nations (UN) administration and FRETILIN was abandoned in favor of proportional representation in a single national district with a 3% threshold in 2007. A combination of UN influence and power interests of the larger domestic parties resulted in the choice of proportional representation in small districts with a resulting majoritarian effect in Cambodia (1993). The shift towards parallel voting in the Philippines and Thailand reflects a variety of political considerations and motivations. In the Philippines, the de facto quota system is supposed to give marginalized groups access to parliamentary representation. In Thailand, the electoral rules first applied in 2001 were to reduce the number of parliamentary parties, favor the creation of stable majorities, and improve citizen participation. In 2007, the adoption of a list system with regional multi-member districts was meant to reverse this effect and weaken the political camp of former

Table 13.9 Electoral systems in Southeast Asia (first or only chamber, most recent election)

	PR system			Mixed parallel system		Plurality				Vietnam
	Indonesia	Cambodia	Timor-Leste	Philippines	Thailand[a]	Malaysia	Singapore	Myanmar	Laos	Vietnam
Total # of seats	560	123	65	234 + 58	350 +150	222	99	440	132	500
# appointed seats	0	0	0	0	0	0	12	110	0	0
Ballot structure	Categorial	Categorial	Categorial	Dividual	Nominal	Categorial	Categorial	Categorial	Categorial	Categorial
# of districts	33	24	1	235	351	222	27	330	17	188
Average district magnitude	16.96	5.12	65	1.27	1.42	1	3.22	1	7.75	2.65
Choice of candiature	Open list	Closed list	Closed list	SMC/ closed list	Closed list	SMC	SMC/ GRC	SMC	Closed list	Open list
# of votes	1	1	1	2	1	1	1	1	n/a	n/a
Tier	1	1	1	1	2	1	1	1	1	1
Seat allocation formulae	LR-Hare	D'Hondt	D'Hondt	Plurality/ LR-Hare	Plurality/ LR-Hare	Plurality	Plurality	Plurality	Plurality	Majority two round
Formal electoral threshold	3.5% (national)	No	3% (national)	2% + 6% cap	No	No	No	No	No	No
Length of term	5	5	5	3	4	5	5	5	5	5

[a] According to the 2017 Constitution

Source: Authors' compilation based on country chapters

Prime Minister Thaksin Shinawatra. The most recent election rules as described in the current constitution even more clearly serve this political purpose.[1]

Although elections are defining features of democracy, most authoritarian regimes in Southeast Asia also hold elections. In democracies, elections are seen as the means by which citizens choose government leaders or the set of policies that the government will follow and can hold their politicians accountable for the quality of governance (Geddes 2006). Yet elections can only perform these functions in the presence of freedom of speech and information, accountability requirements, and a free press. The democracies in the region have realized these requirements to a sufficient degree and administer functional voting processes. However, especially in the Philippines, political violence, organizational shortcomings, and vote buying negatively affect the procedural integrity of elections. In Thailand (1992–2006, 2007–2014), vote buying and a partisan electoral commission had similar consequences. Voters in both countries have lost faith in the electoral process: The 2014 World Values Survey reports that only 51.4% of respondents in the Philippines and 62.8% in Thailand believe that the election commission in their countries was neutral. A majority—58.8% in the Philippines and 52.1% in Thailand—believe votes are bought, and 77.6% of respondents in the Philippines and 55.5% in Thailand believe that rich politicians are able to simply buy the election (WVS 2014). In contrast, elections and election processes in Timor-Leste and Indonesia are of relatively high integrity.

In authoritarian regimes, citizens rarely have the ability to choose government leaders or sets of policies or to hold representatives accountable through elections since changes in leadership and policy choices are decided by elite actors such as military officers or high-level party officials, not citizens. Nevertheless, elections in authoritarian regimes also perform certain functions. In Laos and Vietnam, elections are under the exclusive control of the ruling party. They are an expression of its dominance, serve to mobilize voters, and are a means to reinforce the unity of people and party. In Singapore, Malaysia, and Cambodia, electoral competition is real but unfair. As in the communist countries, elections are not meant to jeopardize the status quo. Instead, they provide the political leadership with information about the loyalty and policy preferences of the electorate, help mitigate conflict by channeling dissent through official regime channels, and co-opt elite actors with access to crucial resources. Especially in countries like Cambodia and Myanmar, which depend on international assistance, elections also help legitimize the regime to the outside world.

The country studies have demonstrated that authoritarian regimes in Southeast Asia employ a range of instruments to prevent multiparty elections from developing unintended consequences. Their "menu of manipulation" (Schedler 2002) favors measures intended to skew the electoral playing field in their favor and to reduce the level of uncertainty elections entail. This includes manipulating the composition of the election commission, unfair regulations regarding campaigning and party

---

[1]At the time of writing this chapter in May 2017, the election bylaw has not yet been published.

financing, as well as the more technical details of the electoral system, including district size, malapportionment, and seat allocation formulae, are all tailored to discriminate against opposition parties. Political violence, vote buying, and blatant electoral fraud are only relevant in Cambodia (Croissant 2016). Most countries avoid them as these are difficult to hide from national or international election observers. If the outcome of an election is close, such open forms of manipulation are more likely to result in postelection protests organized by the opposition.

In all electoral authoritarian regimes studied in this volume, the regime employs self-serving rules of representation (Schedler 2002, p. 44) that favor parties aligned with the regime and prevent opposition parties from achieving a seat share that corresponds with their vote share. The resulting disproportionality of the electoral system can be gauged by Gallagher's Least Squares (LSq) Index. Even though electoral geography, including the territorial homogeneity of electoral support for certain parties throughout a country's regions, and party system fragmentation can also influence the index, the design of the electoral system has a strong effect.

Indeed, the electoral systems of authoritarian regimes in the region create a significantly higher degree of disproportionality that favors the largest party, i.e., the ruling party (Table 13.10). In Malaysia in 2013, the *Barisan Nasional* managed

Table 13.10 Electoral disproportionality in Southeast Asia (first or only chamber of parliament)

	LSq-Index[a]	Vote share of largest party (%)	Seat share of largest party (%)	Difference vote and seat share
Electoral autocracies				
Cambodia (1993–2013)	10.1	48.2	57.6	9.4
Malaysia (1959–2013)	17.4	55.9	75.6	19.6
Singapore (1959–2011)	23.3	66.5	94.9	28.3
Myanmar (2015)[b]	21.3	57.1	80.6	23.5
Electoral democracies				
Indonesia (1999–2014)	4.3	24.7	25.5	0.8
Timor-Leste (2001–2012)	5.5	41.1	41.9	0.7
Philippines (1987–2013)[c]	6.8	37.1	43.8	6.6
Thailand (1992–1996)	3.4	24.3	25.7	1.4
Thailand (2001–2011)[c]	7.4	47.8	56.6	8.8

[a]See Table 3.2 for details on calculation
[b]No data for 2010; only contested seats without military representatives and vacant seats
[c]Without party-list seats/votes
Source: Authors' compilation with data from country chapters

to win 59.9% of all seats in the lower house even though it only won 47.4% of the vote. In Singapore, electoral disproprortionality is even more pronounced and for many years completely excluded the political opposition from parliamentary representation. In Cambodia, the majoritarian system with its small and mostly uneven number of seats per district also favors the ruling party. Yet, disproportionality can also help defeat authoritarian incumbents: In Myanmar in 2015, the NLD managed to win 80% of all seats in the lower house even though the party only won 57% of the vote.

13.6   Political Parties and Party Systems

Differences in political regimes correspond with variation in party systems and party development in Southeast Asia. In most countries of the region, the historical origins of political parties date back to the interwar period and the years immediately following the end of World War II. The Philippines with its very early onset of party system development—the Federalist Party was founded in 1900—and Brunei and Timor-Leste as latecomers with their first parties founded in 1956 and 1974, respectively, are the exceptions. Like elsewhere, political parties emerged as organizational manifestations of social conflicts and interests resulting from socio-economic change at the beginning of the twentieth century.

With the exception of Thailand, early party development was characterized by national movements striving for political mobilization and participation. Some of these early political parties were willing to cooperate with colonial authorities while others opted for a more conflictual stance. The first category was mainly comprised of conservative bourgeois political parties, but also some socialist parties as well as ethnic minority parties. The second category included communist parties, nationalist bloc movements, and political groups rooted in the religious milieu.

Often, however, political circumstances prevented continuous party development. In Cambodia, Laos, and Vietnam, the Indochina Wars and communist rule left no room for the development of a pluralist party system. Indonesia, Malaysia, and Singapore developed party systems aligned with social milieus and cleavages. During the New Order, President Suharto "simplified" the party system and forced all political streams outside of the Golkar regime party into just two officially sanctioned opposition parties. In Singapore, the PAP overwhelmed all other political parties and pushed them into oblivion. Only in Malaysia did a relatively pluralistic party system persist. In Thailand, political parties have been legal since 1957, but changing regulatory regimes and regime discontinuities prevented them from developing stable linkages with society. In the Philippines, where a two-party system with power alternation arose early on, the martial law regime under President Marcos marginalized and weakened political parties after 1972.

The differentiation between clientelist elite parties and cleavage-based milieu parties by Ufen (2012a, p. 100) is a helpful distinction as it shows the empirical diversity of historical party developments in the different countries. Yet, one needs to add a third political party type, namely the hierarchically organized cadre parties following an authoritarian leadership principle, usually of socialist orientation. The clientelist elite party type dominates the party systems of the Philippines, Thailand, and East Malaysia, whereas cleavage-based or milieu parties can be found mainly in Indonesia and West Malaysia (Ufen 2012a, p. 100). The (socialist) cadre parties can be found in Vietnam and Laos today, but it is important to keep in mind that parties like the People's Action Party, the Cambodian People's Party, and the FRETILIN in Singapore, Cambodia, and Timor Leste, respectively, also have a history as socialist cadre parties. This distinction of different types of political parties also points to the different degrees of institutionalization of parties and party systems in Southeast Asia. In comparative party research, institutionalization is defined as a process through which organizations and procedures achieve stability and gain enough significance to surpass their function (cf. Huntington 1968, p. 12). The process of institutionalization describes "the consolidation of the organization, the passage from an initial, structurally fluid, phase when a new-born organization is still forming, to a phase in which the organization stabilizes" (Panebianco 1988, p. 18). Party systems are thus institutionalized "when actors develop expectations and behavior based on the premise that the fundamental contours and rules of party competition and behavior will prevail into the foreseeable future. In an institutionalized party system, there is stability in who the main parties are and how they behave" (Mainwaring and Torcal 2006, p. 207).

Thailand and the Philippines lack well-institutionalized party systems: Party competition is highly volatile, and party identification among voters is low, just like individual trust in parties and elections. In most cases, parties are built around individuals and serve as electoral machines without broad membership bases or elaborate organizational apparatuses. With few exceptions, like the Democrat Party, founded in 1946; the *Partido Nacionalista*, founded in 1907; or the Liberal Party, founded in 1946, party organizations have a short lifespan. In contrast, party systems in Indonesia and (West) Malaysia are relatively well-institutionalized (Ufen 2012b; Mietzner 2013). Timor-Leste, Singapore, and Cambodia occupy an intermediate position: each of these party systems has one very well-institutionalized party (FRETILIN, PAP, and CPP, respectively), whereas other the political parties are much more volatile and usually centered around an influential individual.

The relevance of political cleavages also varies between countries.[2] The party systems of Indonesia and (West) Malaysia are formed along relatively stable cleavage lines (Ufen 2012b), whereas ethnic, religious, regional, or economic conflicts in society have not had a significant impact on the party system of the

---

[2]What constitutes a cleavage is contested in party research. Bartolini and Mair distinguish *political conflict* from *cleavage* by arguing that the latter must fulfill three necessary criteria (Bartolini and Mair 1990, pp. 215–216). First, a cleavage must be grounded in a closed social relationship of some form (socio-structural criterion). Second, there must be a group of shared ideas that produce a consciously shared identity within the given social group (normative criterion). Third, there must be a network of interactions resulting in a political representation of the relevant cleavage, ideally in the form of a political party (organizational criterion).

Philippines (Rüland et al. 2005, pp. 141–143). In Thailand, the *Thai Rak Thai*, founded in the late 1990s, was the first party to politicize the latent conflict between urban and rural areas as well as that between peasants and urban lower-class voters on the one hand and urban middleclass voters on the other. In Timor-Leste, the struggle for national independence and the role political parties played in the creation of the Timorese state still echo through the party system. During the Indonesian occupation, these conflicts manifest themselves along the frontlines separating insurgents and collaborators. At least for a time, this conflict was somewhat overshadowed by a parallel regional conflict between the eastern and western parts of the country. However, it remains to be seen whether political conflicts actually constitute political cleavages.

The differences in regime types across the region, ranging from (defective) democracies to electoral autocracies and single party states, further impedes straightforward comparisons. Following Mainwaring's (2015) differentiation between competitive and noncompetitive party systems, the latter can be further differentiated into hegemonic and party-state systems. With their single parties, Laos and Vietnam are examples of the latter, while Singapore, Malaysia, and Cambodia are examples of hegemonic party systems: party competition is skewed in favor of the ruling party hegemon. In recent years, there was a trend towards increased competition among the region's hegemonial party systems. Opposition parties have increasingly managed to merge, form coalitions, or agree to tactical agreements to compete only in certain election districts. In doing so, they managed to unify against the government as a common enemy and thereby mobilize more voters. In Myanmar, it remains unclear whether the NLD will manage to remain the dominant party in the nascent party system.

Competitive party systems in the region fall into two categories. Indonesia and the Philippines both have moderately polarized multiparty systems with a low degree of structural asymmetry, a regionally varying degree of centripetal party competition, and variable coalition formation. Thailand and Timor-Leste have moderately fragmented multiparty systems with bipolar patterns of competition, regionalization, and—at least in the Thai case—structural asymmetry in favor of one of the major parties. Compared to Western party systems, the Philippines, Thailand, and Timor-Leste have an uncommon combination of structural characteristics and policy positions. Moreover, constant structural changes and high electoral and organizational volatility seem to indicate that all three countries have yet to stabilize the basic structures of their party system.

Overall, the case studies reiterate the significance of political parties and party systems for the persistence of autocratic regimes as well as for the consolidation or crisis of post-authoritarian democracies. In Indonesia, polarization in the party system is relatively low, and political parties tend to be rooted in social milieus. This created flexible and open patterns of coalition-building, helping to stabilize democratic institutions (Mietzner 2013). In contrast, the Philippine and Thai party systems were unable to integrate wide sections of their societies into the political system and failed to mediate social conflict. As a result, distributional conflicts between traditional political elites and their supporters on the one side and newly emerging actors who had managed to mobilize formerly unpolitical supporters on the other side escalated. Relatively well-institutionalized regime parties in Cambodia, Malaysia, and Singapore are an important factor for the survival of their autocratic regimes. Well-institutionalized parties can help rulers overcome the information dilemma, dampen intra-elite conflict, and help control parliament and fragmented opposition parties (Magaloni 2006; Morse 2012). Indeed, party-based authoritarian regimes in Southeast Asia have demonstrated a greater degree of resilience against social challenges or the defection of partial elites from the ruling coalition. At the same time, more personalistic autocracies like Suharto's New Order regime in Indonesia or Marcos's New Society in the Philippines were susceptible to elite defections or—like Myanmar—had to compensate for their institutional liabilities with increased repression.

13.7 State and Administration

Malaysia is the only federation in Southeast Asia, whereas the rest of the region houses unitary and centralized states. However, decentralization reforms have taken place in many countries in recent decades. As in other regions, decentralization measures often came in the wake of political democratization or were promoted by international donors and Western development agencies as tools of improving "good governance." Therefore, decentralization programs have been implemented in both democracies and autocracies.

The regional wave of decentralization since the late 1980s has been affecting the distribution of fiscal and administrative competences between national and subnational units as well as subnational political authority by introducing elections for representative assemblies or executive offices at the lower levels of the political system. In several countries, autonomous regions, administrative zones, or special economic zones with expanded budgetary or administrative authority were formed (Shair-Rosenfield et al. 2014). Unsurprisingly, considering their relatively small territorial size, Brunei, Singapore, and Timor-Leste have abstained from the decentralization trend so far, although there are local elections in Brunei and Timor-Leste. Against the overall trend, the representation of the federal states in Malaysia was curtailed, fiscal authority was centralized, and the territories Kuala Lumpur, Labuan, and Putrajaya were subjected to central government control between 1974 and 2001.

Indonesia and the Philippines have implemented the farthest reaching decentralization reforms in the region (Table 13.11). These states have elected assemblies and executives at all levels of the political system. In Malaysia, state parliaments are popularly elected and in turn select the governments of all 13 states. Local elections, however, have been suspended since 1964. Myanmar, Cambodia, and Thailand all have dual governing structures (Shair-Rosenfield et al. 2014): Provincial governors are appointed by the central government while regional parliaments (Myanmar), commune councils (Cambodia), and Tambon-level and provincial administrations (Thailand) are elected. Political decentralization is least developed

Table 13.11 Political and fiscal decentralization in Southeast Asia

	Elected bodies			Subnational share of government...	
	Provinces/Regions	Districts/ Counties	Municipalities	Expenditure (%)	Revenue (%)
Indonesia (2011)	Parliaments, Governors	Yes	Yes	39	7.2
Cambodia (2007)	None	No	Yes	8.4	6.2
Laos (2006)	None	No	No	45	55
Malaysia (2001)	Parliaments, Governments[a]	No	No	10.8	11.4
Myanmar (2012)	Parliaments only	No	No	6.7	4.5
Philippines (2009)	Parliaments, Governors	Yes	Yes	25	10
Thailand (2010)	Provincial Administrative Organization (PAO)[b]	Yes	Yes	25.2	9
Vietnam (2009)	People's Councils	(Yes)	(Yes)	45	35

[a]Except Kuala Lumpur, Labuan, and Putrajaya
[b]Governor of Bangkok is elected
Source: Authors' compilation and OECD (2014)

in Vietnam and Laos, where the central government appoints provincial governments and People's Councils are elected, albeit following the model of the national single-party elections.

The situation is more complex with regard to the degree of fiscal decentralization. The share of subnational revenues and expenditures as the percentage of total government revenue and expenditures, respectively, is largest in Laos and Vietnam, followed by Indonesia, the Philippines, and Thailand. It is lowest in Malaysia, Cambodia, and Myanmar. Concerning administrative decentralization, Indonesia and the Philippines have transferred a large number of responsibilities to the subnational level. Provinces in Vietnam and Laos have become relatively autonomous in their economic policies and receive a large share of national tax revenue. In all other decentralized countries, subnational governments mainly serve as implementation agencies for the central government. Moreover, local administrations often lack personnel, and coordination between different administrative levels introduces an element of friction into state governance.

State capacity differs particularly widely among Southeast Asian nations (Marsh 2006), as evident from a recent measure of state capacity developed by Hanson and Sigman (2013). Singapore has a high capacity state with an efficient and lean bureaucracy (Fig. 13.2). Public administration, planning, and implementation capacities are weaker in Brunei and parts of Malaysia. In none of the remaining countries has the development of state institutions kept up with recent economic

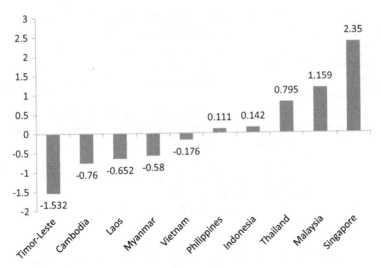

Fig. 13.2 State capacity in Southeast Asia, 2002–2010. Notes: The figure shows data for capacity1, a general-purpose measure of state capacity that draws from a variety of indicators (24) representing the three dimensions of extractive, administrative, and coercive capacity. Taken from version 0.95 of the data set. Data for Brunei not available. Source: Hanson and Sigman (2013)

growth and, with the exception of Singapore, Malaysia, and Brunei, no state has secured the monopoly of violence throughout its territory. Functional deficits in state administration, an inability to implement administrative decisions, center–periphery conflicts with minorities, or organized crime and corruption have created areas of limited statehood (Brozus and Risse 2009) where the state fails or struggles to provide order for its society. Cambodia, Laos, Myanmar, and especially Timor-Leste are low capacity states, although the specific deficits in terms of coercive, extractive, and administrative capacity vary.

13.8 Civil–Military Relations

The formation of sovereign nation states in Southeast Asia also resulted in the creation of national armed forces. Again, there is no such thing as either a typical Southeast Asian military or a characteristic model of civil–military relations. In Indonesia, Myanmar, and North Vietnam, guerilla units who had fought in anti-colonial wars of liberation formed the core of the new militaries. In Malaysia and the Philippines, they were created from colonial militaries and retained close connections with the former colonial power. The same was true for Singapore and remains true for Brunei to this day. The United States helped shape militaries and civil–military relations in the anti-communist countries of Southeast Asia. North Vietnam took inspiration from the Soviet Union and China. Again, Thailand is a special case, as it already developed a hierarchical military modeled after European examples at the beginning of the twentieth century.

External defense is the quintessential task and organizational standard only for the Singaporean and Malaysian militaries. Everywhere else in the region, securing internal security and upholding state sovereignty against internal challengers is the dominant military mission. As such, the armed forces in many countries often took over genuinely civilian tasks in the bureaucracy, supplied public services, and became economic actors.

A typology first proposed by Amos Perlmutter (1974, 1977, 1986), to which Croissant and Kuehn (2017) added the fourth type of a neo-patrimonial military, is a useful heuristic to describe civil–military relations in the region. Under *professional* civil–military relations, civilian and military spheres of autonomy and responsibility are clearly separated. The army (though it has legitimate political interests) does not intervene in the decision-making activities of the executive or legislative branches of government. That is, governments in such regimes exercise political control over their militaries.

Under *revolutionary* civil–military relations, the military is political by definition, and the structures of the ruling political organization interpenetrate the armed forces, which serve as an instrument of mobilization and regime security for the revolutionary political party (Perlmutter 1977, pp. 13–14). Although the relationship between soldier and party can change over time, revolutionary political–military relations are generally characterized by a "symbiosis" of military and party elites. To ensure the convergence of interests between party and military elites, military leaders are co-opted into the party apparatus (Perlmutter and LeoGrande 1982).

Praetorian civil–military relations emerge in countries with low levels of political institutionalization, fragmented political parties, and a lack of sustained mass support for civilian political structures. The mismatch between weak civilian institutions and a strong military contributes to the rise of a "praetorian state," in which the army intervenes in the government frequently, acting either as arbitrator, controlling affairs behind the scenes through a chosen civilian agent, or as actual ruler (Perlmutter 1974, pp. 8–11).

Neo-patrimonial political–military relations are characterized by a single leader's domination of both the political regime structures and the military. As Geddes (2003, p. 51) explains, "(t)he leader may be an officer and has created a party to support himself but neither the military nor the party exercises independent decision-making power insulated from the whims of the ruler." Here, the military serves as another element in the leader's toolbox of personal authoritarian control instruments to protect him from both popular revolt and internal coups. Simultaneously, the military is a franchise system for the ruler, in which officers seeking career opportunities and financial benefits must seek access to the dictator's patronage system.

However, it should be noted that these are not mutually exclusive categories: There can be borderline cases that are not easily assignable to one of the types or hybrid cases that contain characteristics of two or more types. For instance, party–military relations in Singapore exhibit a high degree of elite dualism and a unique "fusion" of military, bureaucratic, and political roles, although the Singaporean Armed Forces are considered highly professional and remain under the effective control of a civilian

Table 13.12 Types of political–military relations in Asia, 1950 to 2016

	1950	1970	1980	2016
Brunei	–	–	–	Professional/ Neo-patrimonial
Cambodia	–	Neopatrimonial	Revolutionary	Neo-patrimonial
Indonesia	Praetorian	Praetorian	Praetorian	Professional
Laos	–	Praetorian	Revolutionary	Revolutionary
Malaysia	–	Professional	Professional	Professional
Myanmar	Praetorian	Praetorian	Praetorian	Praetorian
Philippines	Professional	Professional	Neo-patrimonial	Praetorian/ Professional
Singapore	–	Professional	Professional	Professional
Thailand	Praetorian	Praetorian	Praetorian	Praetorian
Timor-Leste	–	–	–	Neo-patrimonial
(North) Vietnam	Revolutionary	Revolutionary	Revolutionary	Revolutionary/ Professional
South Vietnam	–	Praetorian	–	–

Source: Croissant and Kuehn (2017)

government (Tan 2013). Moreover, political–military relations are not static, but evolve in tandem with and in response to different political and social dynamics.

To an extent, regime changes and continuities correlate with developments in the relationship between the soldier and the state (Table 13.12). Yet despite the general declining salience of military involvement in Southeast Asian politics, the direction of change has not always been towards professional civil–military relations. Taking a historical perspective, the overview reveals four cross-national patterns.

First, for much of the post-World War II period, most civil–military relations in Asia can be summarized by two patterns. The first is civil–military fusion within revolutionary party regimes. Here, control over the political system rests securely with party leaders, and political–military relations, though not free of frictions, remained stable. This pattern prevails in Cambodia (1975–1991), Vietnam, and Laos (since 1975). A second major pattern is military dominance over the political system, exemplified in a high frequency of military coups and/or extended periods of direct military rule ("praetorianism"). This was prevalent in countries such as Thailand, Indonesia, and Myanmar as well Laos and South Vietnam before 1975 (Hoadley 2012). However, the number of open military intervention into politics in Asia dwindled significantly in the 1990s and 2000s (Table 13.13).

Second, while the praetorian and revolutionary scenarios aptly characterize civil–military relations in many Southeast Asian polities, civilian supremacy is the hallmark of political–military relations in party-led autocracies such as Malaysia and Singapore (Beeson and Bellamy 2008) but also in monarchical autocracies like Brunei. Despite high-profile efforts of the United Nations to reform the security sector, civil–military relations in Cambodia and Timor-Leste have developed strong neo-patrimonial features. While in Cambodia the military serves as another instrument in Hun Sen's personal authoritarian toolset to protect him

Table 13.13 List of military coup attempts in Southeast Asia (1950–2016)

	Indonesia	Laos	Myanmar	Philippines	Thailand	S Vietnam
1950s			**1958**		**1951,** 1951, **1957, 1958**	
1960s	1965, **1966**	**1960, 1960, 1964,** 1965, 1965, 1965, 1967	**1962**			1960, **1963, 1964,** 1964, **1965,** 1965, **1965**
1970s		1973	1976		**1976, 1977,** 1977	
1980s			**1988**	1986, 1987, 1987, 1989	1981, 1985	
1990s				1990	**1991**	
2000s					**2006, 2014**	

Notes: No military coups d'état attempts in Brunei, Cambodia, Timor-Leste, Malaysia, Singapore, and (North) Vietnam, excluding civilian-led coups, military mutinies, and coup d'état attempts before 1950. **Bold**: successful military coup. Source: Croissant and Herre (2013), based on Powell and Thyne (2015)

from both popular revolt and internal coups (Morgenbesser 2017), party elites in Timor-Leste instrumentalize existing fissures and cleavages within the army and police for political purposes.

Third, in most countries that experienced democratic changes since the late 1980s, the new political environment necessitated drastic reforms of civil–military relations, as the old modes of civil–military interaction were no longer sustainable or acceptable under the changed circumstances. Although political liberalization correlates with "a reduction in the political power, influence and role of the military" (Alagappa 2001, p. 433) in the region, democratization has not always depoliticized the armed forces. Rather, there is evidence to suggest that the military has often remained a significant political force after the transition to democratic governance (Mietzner 2012; Croissant 2015). Furthermore, mutinies in the Philippines in the 2000s (Lorch 2017) and the 2006 and 2014 military takeovers in Thailand indicate that coups d'état remain a threat even for electoral democracies that have persisted for over a decade (Croissant et al. 2013).

Fourth, and related, there are various hybrid cases that are not easily pigeon-holed into one of the four categories but exhibit characteristics of multiple types. In Brunei, this hybridity is a reflection of the particular regime structure, where a small but modern and professional military force is both under the strict control of the monarchy and deeply integrated into its oil and natural gas-based rentier state. In the Philippines, in turn, the democratic transitions have gone hand in hand with greater professionalization and political control, without having succeeded in fully overcoming deeply ingrained patterns of decades of military meddling in politics. Long-term transformations of a military's political role are not limited to instances of regime change. However, in Vietnam, for example, the VPA is undergoing processes of professionalization and modernization, although the economic roles of the military (similar to Laos) and the military-business complex build an important deviation from the professionalism type.

13.9 Political Legitimacy and Civil Society

The country chapters have demonstrated considerable differences between democracies and autocracies of the region, both in terms of the specific system structures and regime institutions, relevant political actors, internal structures, power resources and relations, as well as the political performance of the political systems. Furthermore, democracies and autocracies in the region differ in their political stability and resilience. Overall, democracies seem much more vulnerable to systemic crises than autocracies. Two of the region's five "emerging" democracies, Cambodia and Thailand, did not survive, and two more, the Philippines and Timor-Leste, experienced recurring crises that threatened the survival of their defective democracies. In contrast, Singapore, Laos, Brunei, Malaysia, and Vietnam did not suffer similar upheavals or at least managed to defuse these crises within their existing supporting or ruling coalitions. Despite differences, autocracies in the region all had to rely on a combination of repression and co-optation directed against the political opposition. Their ability to do so, however, is not the whole story of why autocracies have managed to survive at a much higher rate. Rather, democratic regimes in the region do not seem to have an advantage when it comes to legitimizing their rule, and some autocracies have managed to generate more political support and legitimacy than the democracies in the region.

The reasons for this are complex and still uncertain. Overall, authoritarian regimes seem to have tapped into different sources of legitimacy, explaining in part why even modernization successes in Singapore, Malaysia, Brunei, and Vietnam have not been trapped in the so-called performance dilemma (Huntington 1991, p. 51), whereas the developmentalist "authoritarian bargain" (Desai et al. 2009), by which citizens relinquish political rights for economic security, seems to hold.[3]

---

[3]The "performance dilemma" thesis essentially argues that if a regime that bases its efforts to legitimize its power on (economic) performance is *not* performing, its people will be dissatisfied, the regime will be deemed incapable of governing appropriately, and both the rulers and the political system will lose legitimacy. But the legitimacy of an autocratic regime is undermined not only if it fails to deliver on its promises, but also if it succeeds in achieving its purpose (Huntington 1991, p. 51): Economic development presumably increases the capacity of a society to place demands upon a government. Individuals are more likely to desire participation in government and have greater expectations for their government and its institutional framework. Accordingly, good economic performance actually weakens the developmentalist "authoritarian bargain" (Desai et al. 2009), by which citizens relinquish political rights for economic security.

In the past, reliable data for the empirical analysis of legitimation and regime legitimacy in Southeast Asia was hard to come by, especially for the nondemocratic regimes. Researchers had to rely on proxy indicators, including the frequency of political unrest and protests, the prevalence of insurgencies, but also data on economic growth and other performance indicators (Gilley 2006, p. 49). This approach was not without its problems: The absence of peaceful or violent anti-regime campaigns could mean either political support for the regime, be a sign of political apathy among the subjects, or reflect the regime's ability to act preemptively. Socioeconomic performance indicators suggest that relying on "output legitimacy" (Schmidt 2016) can be a successful strategy, but growth can also lead to increased social pressure for reforms—creating the "performance dilemma." The expansion of international survey projects like the World Values Survey and regional endeavors like the Asian Barometer Survey (ABS) have made more data available, even though conducting survey research in autocratic regimes comes with its own reliability and validity problems, especially when respondents are asked about their political support for the regime. Consequently, the results must be taken with a grain of salt. Nevertheless, they also provide new opportunities for research on political legitimacy and regime legitimation. The ABS has conducted up to four waves of surveys in all countries of the region with the exception of Laos, Brunei, and Timor-Leste. Myanmar was included in the most recent wave, but the full data has not yet been made accessible for researchers. Utilizing the ABS data, there are some indications that autocratic regimes are indeed able to legitimize their rule more effectively, as Shin Doh Chul reports (Shin 2013). Shin developed a measure that includes four survey items, each for the breadth and stability of diffuse support for the political system as a whole as well as several core institutions. Figure 13.3 presents the results for seven Southeast Asian countries.

With the exception of Cambodia, there seems to be an inverse relationship between the democratic character of the regime and the extent of systemic and institutional support. Regime support in the region is highest in Vietnam, followed by Singapore and Thailand. However, due to intense political conflicts in recent years that repeatedly culminated in mass protests among the opposing camps, institutional trust has recently suffered. Across the board, respondents seem to have a more favorable opinion of the overall political system than its actual political institutions, but there are significant differences between the countries as well as among the respective institutions (Table 13.14).

Of course, systematic differences between democratic and autocratic regimes also influence these results. By design, democracies are more likely to tolerate public criticism of the political system. Moreover, existing survey and attitude research suggests that democratic citizens have higher expectations for their political system and make more extensive demands than citizens in autocratic regimes (Norris 1999, 2012). Also, with limited freedom of expression, a lack of independent media outlets, and without real political alternatives, citizens are less likely to have a realistic picture of the relative merit of their regime or government (Chu et al. 2012; Chang et al. 2013). While recent studies (Chu et al. 2012; Chang et al. 2013) seem to indicate that

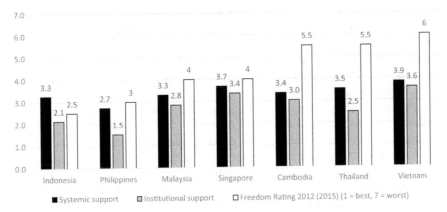

Fig. 13.3 Levels of systemic and institutional support in Southeast Asia. Notes: Systemic support is calculated as the summed up share of aggregated positive responses ("strongly agree"/"agree somewhat") to four questions regarding government problem-solving capability (q80 ABS3, q83ABS4), pride in the system (q81 ABS3, q84 ABS4), support in times of crisis (q82 ABS3, q85 ABS4), and preference to live under this rather than other systems of government (q83 ABS3, q86 ABS4). Institutional trust is calculated as the summed up share of aggregated positive responses ("a great deal of trust"/"quite a lot of trust") to items inquiring about the level of trust for courts (q8), the national government (q9), political parties (q10), and parliament (q11). The resulting index ranges from 0 to 4; higher values indicate greater levels of support. Source: Authors' calculation based on the measurement proposed by Shin (2013) with data from ABS (2012, 2017), Wave 4 (2014, Philippines and Thailand), Wave 3 (2010–12, remaining countries), and Freedom House (Freedom House 2015; data from 2015 for Thailand and Philippines, 2012 for the remaining countries)

Table 13.14   Institutional trust in Southeast Asia

	CA	IN	MA	PH	SG	TH	VN	Average
Executive	84.7	73.7	82.2	55.2	88.8	75.5		76.7
Courts	63.1	55.1	75.0	41.2	89.1	76.9	84.4	69.2
National gov.	81.9	61.1	78.3	42.7	87.7	66.2	95.3	73.3
Political parties	73.9	46.0	57.4	31.3	71.7	42.6	86.6	58.5
Parliament	82.6	52.9	72.3	38.3	85.9	61.6	93.4	69.6
Civil service	81.3	74.5	81.8	54.6	79.8	64.1	84.6	74.4
Military	88.9	89.1	87.8	62.6	77.8	89.7	97.7	84.8
Local gov.	81.8	73.7	76.7	61.2		65.4	83.9	73.8
Newspapers	72.0	64.4	62.5	65.4	61.1	59.5	80.0	66.4
Election Commission	83.1	70.4	71.6	54.7	59.2	66.0	90.2	70.7
NGOs	88.9	71.9	67.6	54.0	47.5	57.8	66.5	64.90

Notes: Aggregated share of respondents professing "a great deal of trust" or "quite a lot of trust";
Source: ABS (2012, 2017), Wave 4 (Philippines, Thailand), Wave 3 (others)

autocracies in Southeast Asia manage to yield a "legitimacy premium" (Gilley 2014, p. 40), the country chapters indicate a process of erosion. Public criticism of corruption, nepotism, red tape, and increasing social inequality are on the rise in most authoritarian regimes. There are more and more protests against manipulated elections, arbitrary coercive practices, and office abuse by state officials or members of local party boards. Especially in Singapore and Malaysia, a growing and vocal minority among the citizenry strives for political emancipation and demands more democratic freedoms than in the past.

Another somewhat surprising result of the World Values Survey data concerns the extent of citizen support for democracy in Southeast Asia, an aspect that received special attention during the "Asian Values" debate of the 1990s that, back then, remained largely bereft of empirical support. The WVS data suggest that democracy is desirable for a large majority of respondents across all countries. However, on its own, this is not a particularly meaningful result, as Christian Welzel (2013, p. 277) explains:

> At this point in history, democracy is almost ubiquitously preferred, so what matters today is not whether democracy is preferred but whether it is preferred for the proper reason. The proper reason, from the emancipatory perspective, is that people prefer democracy because they value the freedoms through which democracy emancipates them.

Liberal values and attitudes are less prevalent in Southeast Asia than in other world regions, and democracy in the region is often understood as "effective governance" with an emphasis on the provision of public goods and services (Shin 2012a, b). Authentic supporters for democracy as a liberal and participatory system remain a minority across Southeast Asia. In the Philippines and Thailand, they are particularly rare (Shin and Cho 2011, p. 34).

A comparative analysis of civil society in Southeast Asia meets the same challenges as comparative party system analysis: Societies and political systems are extremely diverse in their historical experiences and sociocultural and political structures. By their nature, authoritarian regimes limit freedom of expression and organizational pluralism, but there are significant differences among this group, and even the most democratic regimes seem inclined to curtail an all-too vivid expression of civil society.

The civil society concept has been called diffuse or fuzzy (Carothers and Barndt 1999). The country chapters have conceptualized civil society as the full spectrum of collective actors outside the sphere of the individual, economic, or political society with an orientation towards public affairs who articulate and organize social interests, values, and demands, do not pursue a position in government, and accept tolerance as a guiding principle (Croissant et al. 2000). The persistence of autocratic regimes in Malaysia (Giersdorf and Croissant 2011) and Vietnam (Wischermann 2013), the erosion and crises of democracies in the Philippines and Thailand (Thompson 2011), and the upsurge of ethnically and religiously motivated violence in Indonesia (Beittinger-Lee 2009) and Myanmar (South 2009) indicate that an "un-civil society" can play a much more ambivalent role (Kuhonta and Sinpeng 2014). Especially in relatively closed regimes, like in Laos,

Vietnam, or Myanmar, it makes sense to further differentiate a political and a pre-political civil society (Pollack 2004): The latter can be an important precursor to more political organizations and provides spaces for social self-regulation even under an authoritarian setting.

Five overall trends for civil society in the region emerge from the country studies. First, democracies provide more opportunities for civil society organizations to develop, thrive, and participate in public affairs. While this in itself is trivial, there is significant variation within regime types as well, especially between Malaysia and Singapore or Indonesia and Thailand prior to 2014 (Thompson 2011). Second, some societies, including Indonesia and the Philippines, have developed broad, pluralistic, and decidedly political civil societies, whereas civil societies in other countries are either weak (Singapore, Timor-Leste) or remain in the pre-political realm (Vietnam). Third, the destabilization of democracy in Thailand and the Philippines demonstrates the risks of antidemocratic elements entering or remaining part of civil society and also reflects their deeply polarized societies. Calls to defend democracy against a supposedly antidemocratic opponent or competing claims of "direct" legitimacy of the popular will have manifested in street protests and were often contrasted with the merely formal legitimacy of democratic officials. This can become a lethal danger for young democracies, especially if supported by military intervention. In these cases, the "dark side" of civil society and its emancipatory and participatory drive to limit the extent of state authority threatens to overwhelm the capacity of the political system. Fourth, the co-optation of organizations in the pre-political space is an essential element of state-society relations in authoritarian regimes as varied as Singapore and Vietnam. Research on Singapore paints the picture of a regulatory state, guaranteeing stability through "rule by law" in the context of an ethnically divided society. At the same time, electoral-authoritarian regimes like Malaysia, Cambodia, and Myanmar tolerate self-regulation attempts beyond the reach of the state by individuals and organizations working on topics including—but not limited to—environmental protection or women's or minority rights. It is unclear whether these groups can serve as "schools of democracy" in the sense imagined by Alexis de Tocqueville (Hoffmann 2001; Croissant et al. 2000), but based on the handful of existing empirical results, this seems doubtful (Park 2011).

Fifth, and finally, civil societies in Southeast Asia struggle with limits imposed on the freedom of the press and electronic media (see Table 13.15). Despite methodological problems associated with comparing the data of Reporters without Borders or Freedom House, a survey of their press freedom indices suggests a rather worrisome state for the overall region. As in most other world regions, freedom of the press is on the wane or has stagnated at a low level. The situation has declined particularly in Thailand, the Philippines, and Timor-Leste. Only in Myanmar did it improve significantly, albeit starting from a particularly low entry level. Moreover, liberalization has not unequivocally been a force of good for democracy. In Myanmar, "divisive groups have taken advantage of Myanmar's new political and media freedoms to pursue an agenda that will limit the civil and political rights of the country's Muslim population" (Lee 2016, p. 195).

Table 13.15 Press in Southeast Asia, 2002–2016

	World Press Freedom Index[a]		Freedom of the Press Score[b]	
	2002	2016	2002	2014
Brunei	38.00 (Rank 111)	53.85 (155)	78 (not free)	76 (not free)
Cambodia	24.25 (71)	40.70 (128)	68 (not free)	69 (not free)
Indonesia	20.00 (57)	41.72 (130)	53 (partly free)	49 (partly free)
Laos	89.00 (133)	71.58 (173)	82 (not free)	84 (not free)
Malaysia	37.83 (110)	46.57 (146)	71 (not free)	67 (not free)
Myanmar	96.83 (137)	45.48 (143)	96 (not free)	73 (not free)
Philippines	29.00 (89)	44.66 (138)	30 (free)	44 (partly free)
Singapore	47.33 (144)[c]	52.96 (154)	68 (not free)	67 (not free)
Thailand	22.75 (65)	44.53 (136)	30 (free)	77 (not free)
Timor-Leste	5.50 (30)[c]	33.02 (99)	21 (free)	35 (partly free)
Vietnam	81.25 (131)	74.27 (175)	92 (not free)	85 (not free)

[a]Lower scores indicate better press freedom
[b]0 = Best, 100 = Worst
[c]2003
Sources: Reporters without borders (2017), Freedom House (2017)

Of course, problems and particularities are country specific. However, even in the more democratic or liberalized political systems of the region, freedom of the press has its bounds. States like Vietnam, Myanmar, Laos, Malaysia, Singapore, and Cambodia tolerate only minimal criticism from their press or none at all. The extent to which "new" media, i.e., web-based or social (see Ebersbach et al. 2011 for a conceptual discussion), can serve as a substitute for traditional media cannot be detailed here. However, neither the praise chorus of new media as a "liberation technology" (Diamond 2010) nor the pessimistic counterpoint of "networked autocracies" (Kneuer and Demmelhuber 2012) that employ new media as surveillance technology seems to resonate with the majority of states in the region. Moreover, access to the internet is too limited in states like Laos, Myanmar, Cambodia, or Timor-Leste to have an effect in either direction. Only Singapore comes close to the model of a networked autocracy.

13.10 Outlook

Contrary to the optimistic expectations of the 1990s, democracy has yet to prevail in Southeast Asia. While there were several democratic transitions in the region between 1986 (Philippines) and 2002 (Timor-Leste), none of them resulted in institutionally coherent, liberal democracies. All Southeast Asian democracies remain "defective" and are subject to legitimacy crises, deficiencies in the rule of law, or problems with their sociopolitical structures of representation and integration. With the partial exception of Indonesia, they have either struggled to consolidate their democracies or seen them collapse. Even in Indonesia, democracy has not yet moved beyond possible setbacks, and a deconsolidation still seems possible

(Mietzner 2015). Deeply entwined with the authoritarian Suharto regime and personally responsible for a number of human rights violations during the 1990s, Prabowo Subianto ran for president and managed to win 46.8% of the vote in 2014 with a platform that promoted revoking the constitutional changes passed after the transition and a return to a semi-authoritarian order (Mietzner 2015).

The democratic momentum that dominated regime development in the region during the late twentieth century seems to have run out. At the same time, autocracies in the region also struggle with numerous social, economic, and political challenges. While their stability and persistence is far from guaranteed, on average, authoritarian regimes have been more successful in establishing and safeguarding their monopoly on violence, the development of state capacity, and the provision of political stability than democracies. Of course, there are exceptions, including Myanmar and its recent transition or the endemic weakness of state institutions in Laos. Authoritarian regime crises or even the defeat of authoritarian regime parties in multiparty elections, however, are no guarantee for a democratic transition. Transitions can, just as likely, result in liberalized autocracies or even more repressive regimes, like by Cambodia between 1993 and 1997 or Myanmar between 1988 and 1990. The differences among autocracies are more pronounced than among the defective democracies in the region. Malaysia and Singapore remain stable with the help of illiberal political structures resulting in a high degree of stateness and government capacity and are the world's most persistent electoral autocracies (Croissant and Hellmann 2017). Laos and Vietnam sustain closed single-party regimes. Brunei is governed by a dynastic authoritarian regime while the military remains more or less openly in charge of the political process in Myanmar and Thailand (since May 2014).

The majority of autocracies have been more successful in establishing internal stability than their democratic counterparts. Democracies have failed to channel the distributional conflicts resulting from their transitions into institutional channels and often failed to reconcile the opposing parties. The resulting lack of political legitimacy has created intermittent waves of mass mobilization and politically motivated and often violent street protests as well as fueled the rise of populist political entrepreneurs.

The persistence of nondemocratic rule in the region is not merely the result of successful repression but a combination of different forms of co-optation, repression, and legitimation available to autocratic rulers. The actual tools employed by different regimes vary from country to country and over time. Which instruments are applied and how effective they are depends on the nature of the threat to the regime leadership, i.e., whether it comes from within the regime coalition or from society "below." Co-optation is universally applied, but hard repression is most typical for closed autocracies, whereas electoral autocracies rely on soft, more calibrated repression to secure their rule. The country studies suggest that autocrats in the region remain in power if they manage to grant their "winning coalition" and members of the moderate opposition access to private goods but maintain their ability to counter opponents or dissidents by coercive force. Especially the well-institutionalized regime parties in Malaysia, Singapore, and Vietnam have maintained social stability by balancing elite interests. Successful management of interethnic conflict in Singapore and Malaysia or winning independence in Vietnam, Laos, or Myanmar provide an important additional source of regime legitimacy. In Myanmar, the failure to provide effective governance has weakened the rule of the generals repeatedly. In Brunei, the legitimacy of the sultanate rests on similar pillars as in the gulf monarchies of the Arabian Peninsula: Neo-traditionalist elements and rentier payments fueled by oil and natural gas reserves allow the monarchy to sustain an authoritarian welfare state that provides its citizens with social benefits in exchange for political loyalty. Across both communist single-party regimes as in Vietnam and Laos as well as state-socialist systems in Myanmar and Cambodia, ideological sources of legitimacy are declining in importance. Whether this "structural legitimacy deficit" (Schmidt 2016) will result in eventual collapse or whether regimes in the region will manage to tap into new sources of legitimacy or refine their systems of co-optation and repression remains speculative. It would not be the first sudden mood swing, should democratic pessimism, so prevalent in the current research on democracy and autocracy, again make way for a new wave of democratic optimism.

References

ABS. (2012). *Asian barometer survey: Electronic data release for Wave 3, 2010–2012*. http://www.asianbarometer.org/data/data-release

ABS. (2017). *Asian barometer survey: Electronic data release for Wave 4, 2014–2016*. http://www.asianbarometer.org/data/data-release

Alagappa, M. (2001). Conclusion. In M. Alagappa (Ed.), *Coercion and governance: The declining political role of the military in Asia* (pp. 433–498). Stanford: Stanford University Press.

Bartolini, S., & Mair, P. (1990). *Identity, competition and electoral availability: The stabilisation of European electorates, 1885–1985*. New York: Cambridge University Press.

Beeson, M., & Bellamy, A. J. (2008). *Securing Southeast Asia: The politics of security sector reform*. London: Routledge.

Beittinger-Lee, V. (2009). *(Un)civil society and political change in Indonesia: A contested arena*. London: Routledge.

Böckenförde, E.-W. (1994). Die verfassungsgebende Gewalt des Volkes. In U. K. Preuß (Ed.), *Zum Begriff der Verfassung* (pp. 58–82). Frankfurt am Main: Fischer.

Brown, N. J. (2003). Regimes reinventing themselves. *International Sociology, 18*, 33–52. https://doi.org/10.1177/0268580903018001003

Brozus, L., & Risse, T. (2009). Staatlichkeit und Governance: Regieren mit begrenzten Konzepten in Räumen begrenzter Staatlichkeit. In H.-J. Burchardt (Ed.), *Nord-Süd-Beziehungen im Umbruch: Neue Perspektiven auf Staat und Demokratie in der Weltpolitik* (pp. 43–69). Frankfurt am Main: Campus.

Carothers, T., & Barndt, W. (1999). Civil society. *Foreign Policy, 18*. https://doi.org/10.2307/1149558

Case, W. (2011). Executive accountability in Southeast Asia: The role of legislatures in new democracies and under electoral authoritarianism. In *East West Center Policy Studies 57*. Honolulu: East-West Center.

Chambers, P. W. (2009). Superfluous, mieschievous or emancipating?: Thailand's evolving Senate today. *Journal of Current Southeast Asian Affairs, 28*(3), 3–80.

Chang, A., Chu, Y.-h., & Welsh, B. (2013). Southeast Asia: Sources of regime support. *Journal of Democracy, 24*(2013), 150–164. https://doi.org/10.1353/jod.2013.0025

Chu, Y.-H., Welsh, B., & Chang, A. (2012). *Congruence and variation in sources of regime support in Asia.* Asian Barometer Working Paper Series No. 64. http://www.asianbarometer.org/publications/abs-working-paper-series

Croissant, A. (2006). Conclusion: Electoral politics in Southeast Asia. In A. Croissant & B. Martin (Eds.), *Between consolidation and crisis: Elections and democracy in five nations in Southeast Asia* (pp. 329–385). Münster: LIT Verlag.

Croissant, A. (2014). Ways of constitution-making in Southeast Asia: Actors, interests, dynamics. *Contemporary Southeast Asia, 36,* 23–51. https://doi.org/10.1355/cs36-1b

Croissant, A. (2015). Southeast Asian militaries in the age of democratization: From ruler to servant? In W. Case (Ed.), *Routledge handbook of Southeast Asian democratization* (pp. 314–332). London: Routledge.

Croissant, A. (2016). *Electoral politics in Cambodia: Historical trajectories and current challenges.* Singapore: ISEAS.

Croissant, A., & Hellmann, O. (2017). Introduction: State capacity and elections in the study of authoritarian regimes. *International Political Science Review.* https://doi.org/10.1177/0192512117700066

Croissant, A., & Herre, B. (2013). *Coup Leader Data Set 1.0.* Heidelberg.

Croissant, A., & Kuehn, D. (Eds.). (2017). *Reforming civil-military relations in new democracies.* Heidelberg: Springer VS.

Croissant, A., Lauth, H.-J., & Merkel, W. (2000). Zivilgesellschaft und transformation: Ein internationaler Vergleich. In W. Merkel (Ed.), *Systemwechsel 5: Zivilgesellschaft und transformation* (pp. 9–50). Opladen: Leske & Budrich.

Croissant, A., Kuehn, D., Lorenz, P., & Chambers, P. W. (2013). *Democratization and civilian control in Asia.* Houndmills: Palgrave Macmillan.

Deinla, I. (2014). Public support and judicial empowerment of the Philippine supreme court. *Contemporary Southeast Asia, 36,* 128–158. https://doi.org/10.1355/cs36-1f

Desai, R. M., Olofsgard, A., & Yousef, T. M. (2009). The logic of authoritarian bargains. *Economics and Politics, 21,* 93–125. https://doi.org/10.1111/j.1468-0343.2008.00337.x

Diamond, L. J. (2010). Liberation technology. *Journal of Democracy, 21,* 69–83. https://doi.org/10.1353/jod.0.0190

Dressel, B. (2010). Judicialization of politics or politicization of the judiciary? Considerations from recent events in Thailand. *Pacific Review, 23,* 671–691. https://doi.org/10.1080/09512748.2010.521253

Dressel, B., & Bünte, M. (2014). Constitutional politics in Southeast Asia: From contestation to constitutionalism? *Contemporary Southeast Asia, 36*(1), 1–22.

Ebersbach, A., Glaser, M., & Heigl, R. (2011). *Social web* (2nd ed., UTB ed.). Stuttgart: utb.

Elkins, Z., Melton, J., & Ginsburg, T. (2009). *The endurance of national constitutions.* Cambridge: Cambridge University Press.

Elster, J. (1993). Constitution-making in Eastern Europe: Rebuilding the boat in the open sea. *Public Administration, 71,* 169–217. https://doi.org/10.1111/j.1467-9299.1993.tb00972.x

Fish, M. S., & Kroenig, M. (2009). *The handbook of national legislatures: A global survey.* Cambridge: Cambridge University Press.

Freedom House. (2015). *Freedom of the Press Index 2014: Harsh laws and violence drive global decline.* Accessed June 2, 2017, from https://freedomhouse.org/report/freedom-press/freedom-press-2015

Geddes, B. (2003). *Paradigms and sand castles: Theory building and research design in comparative politics.* Ann Arbor: University of Michigan Press.

Geddes, B. (2006). *Why parties and elections in authortarian regimes?* Revised version of a paper prepared for presentation at the annual meeting of the American Political Science Association, Washington DC, 2005. Accessed June 20, 2017, from https://www.scribd.com/document/133702645/Barbara-Geddes-Why-Parties-and-Elections-in-Authoritarian-Regimes-2006

Giersdorf, S., & Croissant, A. (2011). Civil society and competitive authoritarianism in Malaysia. *Journal of Civil Society, 7*, 1–21. https://doi.org/10.1080/17448689.2011.553401

Gilley, B. (2006). The determinants of state legitimacy: Results for 72 countries. *International Political Science Review, 27*, 47–71. https://doi.org/10.1177/0192512106058634

Gilley, B. (2014). *The nature of Asian politics*. New York: Cambridge University Press.

Ginsburg, T., & Simpser, A. (2014). Introduction: Constitution in authoritarian regimes. In T. Ginsburg & A. Simpser (Eds.), *Constitutions in authoritarian regimes, Comparative constitutional law and policy* (1st ed., pp. 1–21). New York: Cambridge University Press.

Go, J. (2003). A globalizing constitutionalism?: Views from the Postcolony, 1945–2000. *International Sociology, 18*, 71–95. https://doi.org/10.1177/0268580903018001005

Hanson, J. K., & Sigman, R. (2013). *Leviathan's latent dimensions: Measuring state capacity for comparative political research*. Unpublished manuscript. Accessed June 20, 2017, from http://faculty.maxwell.syr.edu/johanson/papers/hanson_sigman13.pdf

Hicken, A., & Kasuya, Y. (2003). A guide to the constitutional structures and electoral systems of east, south and southeast Asia. *Electoral Studies, 22*, 121–151. https://doi.org/10.1016/S0261-3794(01)00053-1

Hoadley, J. S. (2012). *Soldiers and politics in Souteast Asia: Civil-military relations in coparative perspective, 1933–1975*. New Brunswick: Transaction Books.

Hoffmann, S.-L. (2001). Tocquevilles, Demokratie in Amerika' und die gesellige Gesellschaft seiner Zeit. In H. Münkler (Ed.), *Gemeinwohl und Gemeinsinn: Historische Semantiken politischer Leitbegriffe* (pp. 303–326). Berlin: Akademie.

Huntington, S. P. (1968). *Political order in changing societies*. New Haven: Yale University Press.

Huntington, S. P. (1991). *The third wave: Democratization in the late twentieth century*. Norman: University of Oklahoma Press.

Indrayana, D. (2008). Indonesia: In search for a democratic constitution (1945–2008). In C. Hill & J. Menzel (Eds.), *Constitutionalism in Southeast Asia 2: Reports on national constitutions* (pp. 95–121). Singapore: Konrad Adenauer Foundation.

Kneuer, M., & Demmelhuber, T. (2012). Die Bedeutung Neuer Medien für die Demokratieentwicklung. *Informationen zur Politischen Bildung, 35*, 31–38.

Kobori, M. (2014). Referendums in Asia. In M. Qvortrup (Ed.), *Referendums around the world: The continued growth of direct democracy* (pp. 207–217). Basingstoke: Palgrave Macmillan.

Kuhonta, E. M., & Sinpeng, A. (2014). Democratic regression in Thailand: The ambivalent role of civil society and political institutions. *Contemporary Southeast Asia, 36*(3), 333–355.

Law, D. S., & Versteeg, M. (2014). Constitutional variation among strains of authoritarianism. In T. Ginsburg & A. Simpser (Eds.), *Constitutions in authoritarian regimes, Comparative constitutional law and policy* (1st ed., pp. 165–196). New York: Cambridge University Press.

Lee, R. (2016). The dark side of liberalization: How Myanmar's political and media freedoms are being used to limit muslim rights. *Islam and Christian-Muslim Relations, 27*, 195–211. https://doi.org/10.1080/09596410.2016.1159045

Lorch, J. (2017). Civil society support for military coups: Bangladesh and the Philippines. *Journal of Civil Society, 13*, 184–201. https://doi.org/10.1080/17448689.2017.1312790

Magaloni, B. (2006). *Voting for autocracy: Hegemonic party survival and its demise in Mexico*. Cambridge: Cambridge University Press.

Mainwaring, S. (2015). Party system institutionalization: Reflections based on the Asian cases. In A. Hicken & E. M. Kuhonta (Eds.), *Party system institutionalization in Asia: Democracies autocracies and the shadows of the past* (pp. 204–227). New York: Cambridge University Press.

Mainwaring, S., & Torcal, M. (2006). Party system institutionalization and party system theory after the third wave of democratization. In R. S. Katz & W. Crotty (Eds.), *Handbook of party politics* (pp. 204–227). London: SAGE.

Marsh, I. (2006). Democratization and state capacity in East and Southeast Asia. *Taiwan Journal of Democracy, 2*(2), 69–92.

Marsh, I., Blondel, J., & Inoguchi, T. (Eds.). (1999). *Democracy, governance, and economic performance: East and Southeast Asia*. New York: United Nations University Press.

McCargo, D. (2015). Competing notions of judicialization in Thailand. *Contemporary Southeast Asia, 36*, 417–442. https://doi.org/10.1355/cs36-3d

Mietzner, M. (2012). Indonesia's democratic stagnation: Anti-reformist elites and resilient civil society. *Democratization, 19*, 209–229. https://doi.org/10.1080/13510347.2011.572620

Mietzner, M. (2013). *Money, power and ideology: Political parties in post-authoritarian Indonesia*. Honolulu: University of Hawai'i Press.

Mietzner, M. (2015). Indonesia: Democratic consolidation and stagnation under Yudhoyono, 2004–2014. In W. Case (Ed.), *Routledge handbook of Southeast Asian democratization* (pp. 370–384). London: Routledge.

Montinola, G. R., & Jackmann, R. W. (2002). Sources of corruption: A cross-country study. *British Journal of Political Science*. https://doi.org/10.1017/S0007123402000066

Morgenbesser, L. (2017). Misclassification on the Mekong: The origins of Hun Sen's personalist dictatorship. *Democratization, 29*, 1–18. https://doi.org/10.1080/13510347.2017.1289178

Morse, Y. L. (2012). The era of electoral authoritarianism. *World Politics, 64*, 161–198. https://doi.org/10.1017/S0043887111000281

Nohlen, D., Grotz, F., & Hartmann, C. (Eds.). (2001). *Elections in Asia and the Pacific: A data handbook, Vol. II: South East Asia, East Asia, and the South Pacific*. Oxford: Oxford University Press.

Norris, P. (1999). Introduction: The grwoth of critical citizens? In P. Norris (Ed.), *Critical citizens: Global support for democratic government* (pp. 1–30). Oxford: Oxford University Press.

Norris, P. (2012). *Democratic deficit: Critical citizens revisited*. Cambridge: Cambridge University Press.

OECD. (2014). *Multi-dimensional review of Myanmar: Vol. 2: In-depth analysis and recommendations*. Paris: OECD.

Okoth-Ogendo, H. W. O. (1993). Constitutions without constitutionalism: Reflections on an African political paradox. In D. Greenberg, S. N. Katz, M. B. Oliviero, & S. C. Wheatley (Eds.), *Constitutionalism and democracy: Transitions in the contemporary world* (pp. 65–84).

Panebianco, A. (1988). *Political parties: Organization and power*. Cambridge: Cambridge University Press.

Pangalangan, R. C. (2015). The Philippines' post-Marcos judiciary: The institutional turn and the populist backlash. In J. Yeh & W.-C. Chang (Eds.), *Asian courts in context* (pp. 356–374). Cambridge: Cambridge University Press.

Park, C.-M. (2011). Associations and social networks in Southeast Asia: Schools of democracy? In A. Croissant & M. Bünte (Eds.), *The crisis of democratic governance in Southeast Asia* (pp. 39–56). Houndmills: Palgrave Macmillan.

Pellegata, A. (2013). Constraining political corruption: An empirical analysis of the impact of democracy. *Democratization, 20*, 1195–1218. https://doi.org/10.1080/13510347.2012.688031

Pepinsky, T. B. (2014). The institutional turn in comparative authoritarianism. *British Journal of Political Science, 44*, 631–653. https://doi.org/10.1017/S0007123413000021

Perlmutter, A. (1974). *Egypt: The Praetorian state*. New Brunswick: Transaction Books.

Perlmutter, A. (1977). *The military and politics in modern times: On professionals, praetorians, and revolutionary soldiers*. New Haven: Yale University Press.

Perlmutter, A. (1986). The military and politics in modern times: A decade later. *Journal of Strategic Studies, 9*, 5–15. https://doi.org/10.1080/01402398608437245

Perlmutter, A., & LeoGrande, W. M. (1982). The party in uniform: Toward a theory of civil-military relations in communist political systems. *American Political Science Review, 76*, 778–789. https://doi.org/10.1017/S0003055400189609

Pollack, D. (2004). Zivilgesellschaft und Staat in der Demokratie. In K. Kern & B. Geißel (Eds.), *Zivilgesellschaft und Sozialkapital: Herausforderungen politischer und sozialer Integration* (pp. 23–40). Wiesbaden: VS Verlag für Sozialwissenschaften.

Powell, J. M., & Thyne, C. L. (2015). *Global instances of coups from 1950 to the present*. Accessed June 20, 2017, from http://www.uky.edu/~clthyn2/coup_data/powell_thyne_coups_final.txt

Rüland, J. (2003). Constitutional debates in the Philippines: From presidentialism to parliamentarianism? *Asian Survey, 43*, 461–484. https://doi.org/10.1525/as.2003.43.3.461

Rüland, J., Jürgenmeyer, C., Nelson, M. H., & Ziegenhain, P. (2005). *Parliaments and political change in Asia*. Singapore: ISEAS.

Santos, S.M. Jr, Abad, F., Rocamora, J., & Chay, F.-H. (1997). *Shift*. Manila: Ateneo Center for Social Policy and Public Affairs.

Schedler, A. (2002). The menu of manipulation. *Journal of Democracy, 13*, 36–50. https://doi.org/10.1353/jod.2002.0031

Schmidt, M. G. (2016). Legitimation through performance?: Output legitimacy in authoritarian regimes. In U. Backes & S. Kailitz (Eds.), *Ideocracies in comparison: Legitimation – co-optation – repression* (pp. 289–304). London: Routledge.

Schuler, P., & Malesky, E. (2014). Authoritarian legislatures. In S. Martin (Ed.), *The Oxford handbook of legislative studies* (pp. 676–695). Oxford: Oxford University Press.

Shair-Rosenfield, S., Marks, G., & Hooghe, L. (2014). A comparative measure of decentralization for Southeast Asia. *Journal of East Asian Studies, 14*, 85–108. https://doi.org/10.1017/S1598240800009590

Shin, D. C. (2012a). *Confucianism and democratization in East Asia*. Cambridge: Cambridge University Press.

Shin, D. C. (2012b). *Is democracy emerging as a universal value?: A contrarian perspective*. Asian Barometer Working Paper Series No. 68.

Shin, D. C. (2013). Cultural origins of diffuse regime support among East Asians: Exploring an alternative to the theory of critical citizens. *Taiwan Journal of Democracy, 9*(2), 1–32.

Shin, D. C., & Cho, Y. (2011). Contours and barriers to democratization in Southeast Asia: A comparative analysis of how Southeast Asians view democracy. In A. Croissant & M. Bünte (Eds.), *The crisis of democratic governance in Southeast Asia* (pp. 16–39). Houndmills: Palgrave Macmillan.

Shugart, M. S., & Carey, J. M. (1992). *Presidents and assemblies: Constitutional design and electoral dynamics*. Cambridge: Cambridge University Press.

South, A. (2009). *Ethnic politics in Burma*. London: Routledge.

Tan, K. Y. L. (2002). The making and remaking of constitutions in Southeast Asia: An overview. *Singapore Journal of International & Comparative Law, 6*, 1–41.

Tan, T. Y. (2013). The armed forces and politics in Singapore: The persistence of civil-military fusion. In M. Mietzner (Ed.), *The political resurgence of the military in Southeast Asia: Conflict and leadership* (pp. 148–167). New York: Routledge.

Tate, C. N., & Vallinder, T. (Eds.). (1995). *The global expansion of judicial power*. New York: New York University Press.

Thompson, M. R. (2011). Moore meets Gramsci and Burke in Southeast Asia: New democracies and civil society. In A. Croissant & M. Bünte (Eds.), *The crisis of democratic governance in Southeast Asia* (pp. 57–74). Houndmills: Palgrave Macmillan.

Ufen, A. (2012a). *Ethnizität, Islam, Reformasi: Die Evolution der Konfliktlinien im Parteiensystem Malaysias*. Wiesbaden: Springer VS.

Ufen, A. (2012b). Party systems, critical junctures, and cleavages in Southeast Asia. *Asian Survey, 52*, 441–464. https://doi.org/10.1525/as.2012.52.3.441

Welzel, C. (2013). *Freedom rising: Human empowerment and the quest for emancipation*. New York: Cambridge University Press.

Wischermann, J. (2013). Zivilgesellschaften als Stütze autoritärer Regime: Das Fallbeispiel Vietnam. In S. Kailitz & P. Köllner (Eds.), *Autokratien im Vergleich, Politische Vierteljahresschrift: Sonderheft* (Vol. 47, pp. 324–354). Baden-Baden: Nomos.

World Bank. (2017). *Worldwide governance indicators*. http://data.worldbank.org/data-catalog/worldwide-governance-indicators

WVS. (2014). *World values survey online data analysis*. Accessed June 20, 2017, from http://www.worldvaluessurvey.org/WVSOnline.jsp

CPSIA information can be obtained
at www.ICGtesting.com
Printed in the USA
LVHW082001031221
705202LV00002B/71